From: James F. Maness

Y0-CLF-881

CHRISTIAN THEOLOGY

Volume II

by

H. Orton Wiley, S.T.D.

BEACON HILL PRESS OF KANSAS CITY
Kansas City, Mo.

COPYRIGHT, 1952
BEACON HILL PRESS

PRINTED IN THE UNITED STATES OF AMERICA

CONTENTS

Part II. The Doctrine of the Father (Continued)

CHAPTER	PAGE
XVII. Anthropology	7
XVIII. Hamartiology	51
XIX. Original Sin or Inherited Depravity	96

Part III. The Doctrine of the Son

XX. Christology	143
XXI. The Person of Christ	169
XXII. The Estates and Offices of Christ	187
XXIII. The Atonement: Its Biblical Basis and History	217
XXIV. The Atonement: Its Nature and Extent	270

Part IV. The Doctrine of the Holy Spirit

XXV. The Person and Work of the Holy Spirit	303
XXVI. The Preliminary States of Grace	334
XXVII. Christian Righteousness	379
XXVIII. Christian Sonship	402
XXIX. Christian Perfection or Entire Sanctification	440

PART II. THE DOCTRINE OF THE FATHER
(Continued)

CHRISTIAN THEOLOGY

CHAPTER XVII

ANTHROPOLOGY

The term Anthropology, as its composition indicates, is the science of man—from *anthropos,* man and *logos,* science. It is used in both a scientific and a theological sense. As a science, anthropology deals with the problems of primitive man, the distinction of races, their geographical distribution and the factors which enter into man's development and progress. In a theological sense the term is limited to the study of man in his moral and religious aspects. It may be said, however, that the two viewpoints are not mutually exclusive. The creation of man must of necessity be the subject, both of scientific study and religious meditation; and such theological subjects as the fall and original sin cannot be understood without a careful and scientific study of man's original state. Anthropology, then, in the truest sense, should be regarded as a study of man in the widest sense possible; and its theological usage should form the foundation for the several doctrines dependent upon it.

Apart from revelation, man has had only vague, mythological theories as to his origin. These have taken the form of poetry or religious mythology, and have generally been related to the materialistic or pantheistic conceptions of ancient philosophy. Men frequently regarded themselves as *terrigenæ* or earth-born, springing from the earth, the rocks, the trees, or from wild animals. Comparatively few of the ancient nations supposed that the human race sprang from the gods. Modern scientific and philosophical theories concerning the origin of man are in some sense merely a repetition of the ancient teachings couched in scientific terminology. Naturalistic evolution is but a revamping of the ancient materialism.

Theistic evolution, whatever faults it may have, makes a place at least for divine intervention in the inception of the living orders, and frequently recognizes the divine power in a continuous creative agency.

The Preparation of the World for Man. Before considering the final step in the creation of man, we must take into account the providence of God which marked the preparatory stages. Man is the crowning work of creation. *The heaven, even the heavens, are the Lord's: but the earth hath he given to the children of men* (Psalms 115:16). The geological ages represent long periods in the preparation of the world as the habitation of man. "There has been," says Agassiz, "a manifest progress in the succession of beings on the surface of the globe. This progress consists in an increasing similarity to the living fauna, and among the vertebrates especially in the increasing resemblance to man. But this connection is not the consequence of a direct lineage between the faunas of different ages. The fishes of the Paleozoic era are in no respect the ancestors of the reptiles of the Secondary Age, nor does man descend from mammals of the Tertiary Age. The link by which they are connected is of an immaterial nature, and their connection is to be sought in the thought of the Creator himself, whose aim in forming the earth, in allowing it to pass through the successive changes which geology has pointed out, and in creating successively all the different types of animals which have passed away, was to introduce man upon the face of the globe. Man is the end toward which all the animal creation has tended." Not only has the providence of God laid up in the strata of the earth vast resources of granite and marble, coal, salt and petroleum, but also the useful and precious metals so necessary to man's highest existence. Dr. Cocker points out that physical geography indicates, "not only a state of preparation for man, but also a special adaptation of the fixed forms of the earth's existence for securing the perfect development of man according to the divine ideal. And as the land which man inhabits, the food he eats, the air he breathes, the mountains and the rivers and seas which are his neighbors, the skies that overshadow him, the diversities of climate to which he is subject, and indeed all physical conditions, exert a powerful influence upon his tastes, pursuits, habits and character, we may presume that not only are all these conditions predetermined by God, but continually under His control and supervision" (cf. COCKER, *Theistic Conception of the World*, p. 257). St. Paul declares that God *hath made of one blood all nations of men for to dwell on all the face of the earth, and hath determined the times before appointed, and the bounds of their habitation; that they should seek the Lord, if haply they might feel after him, and find him, though he be not far from every one of us* (Acts 17:26, 27).

Anthropology, as we shall further consider it, involves a study of (I) The Origin of Man; (II) The Constituent Elements of Human Nature; (III) The Unity of the Race; (IV) The Image of God in Man; and (V) The Nature of Primitive Holiness.

The Origin of Man

The divine revelation as found in the Holy Scriptures must ever be our authority concerning the origin of mankind. Two accounts are recorded in Genesis. The first is brief, and is found in connection with the account of the animal creation on the sixth day (Gen. 1:26-30); the second is more extended and stands by itself (Gen. 2:4-35). There is no discrepancy in the accounts. Brief as they may be, we have here the only authoritative account of man's origin. The new order of being involved, and its pre-eminence over the animal creation are indicated by a change in the form of the creative fiat. No longer do we have the words, "Let there be," which involve the immediacy of the creative fiat in conjunction with secondary causes; but "Let us make man in our image, after our likeness"—an expression which asserts the power of the creative word in conjunction with deliberative counsel. This counsel, involving as it does the doctrine of the holy Trinity, becomes explicit only as read in the light of added revelation. Man, therefore, is the culmination of all former creative acts, at once linked to them as the crown of creation, and distinct from them as a new order of being. In him the physical and the spiritual meet. He is at once a creature and a son. It is evident, therefore, that in the first account the author introduces man as the crowning act of the creative process; while the second is intended to be the starting point for the specific consideration of man's personal history.

The Origin of Man as an Individual. The twofold creative act, or if one prefers, the two stages of the one creative act by which man came into being as a new and distinctive order, is expressed thus, *And the Lord God formed man of the dust of the ground, and breathed into his nostrils the breath of life,* [plural, *lives*]*; and man became a living soul* (Gen. 2:7). This statement apparently returns to the creative fiat of the first chapter in order to show that the body of man was connected with the earth; while the origin of his being as Man was due to the divine inbreathing which constituted him a living soul. The first step, then, in the origin of man was the formation of his body from the dust of the earth, and the chemical elements which compose it. The word "formed," as here used, carries with it the idea of creation out of pre-existent material. Nor are we to infer that this formation was indirect, through the gradual or instantaneous transformation of another previously formed body into that of the body of man. We are to understand that when the dust ceased to be such it existed in the flesh and bone constituting the human body. It is true that the lower animal creation was also formed from the earth and the same ingredients entered into its composition as in the body of man, but there is no place in the Genesis account for the naturalistic evolution of man from the lower animal kingdom. The Scripture account also precludes the idea of man as *autochthonic,* or springing from the soil, as the Greeks, especially the Athenians maintained. The Scriptures do teach us, however, that man in one aspect of his being is linked to nature; and that on his lower side he is the culmination of the animal kingdom, and represents its perfection in both structure and form.

But the distinctive feature in the creation of man is to be found in the concluding statement—He *breathed into his nostrils the breath of life; and man became a living soul.* Here there is creation *de novo,* and not mere formation. In the creation of man, God communicated to him a life which did not enter into that of the lower animals. He made him a spirit—a self-conscious and self-determining being, a *person.* While it was by the divine inbreathing that man was made a spiritual being, we are not to believe that the human spirit was a part of God by pantheistic emanation. God's spirit is unique, and so is man's—the one infinite, the other finite. We may use the term "impartation of life" but only in the sense of a higher creation. The son is of like essence with his father from whom he receives life, but he is not thereby identical with him. Of Christ alone, the "only begotten Son," may it be affirmed that He is of the same essence with the Father. Dr. Pope thinks that "the same divine act produced both body and soul, without any interval." Even if this be granted, it is evidently the purpose of the writer to mark off distinctly the difference between the formation of the body out of the earth and the inbreathing of the divine life which made man a living soul. Dr. Knapp, on the other hand, maintains that the body was created lifeless, and that "God vivified the previously lifeless body of man" by the divine inbreathing, or the breath of lives. If so, we may suppose that one of these lives was the natural life in common with the brute creation, and the other, the distinctive characteristic of man—an immortal spirit. This brings before us immediately, the question of the *dichotomous* or *trichotomous* nature of man, which must form the subject matter of a later discussion. If, on the other hand, Adam was created with that form of somatic or soul life which characterized the animal creation, then the first of these lives must have constituted man a living and immortal spirit; while the second would represent a spiritual endowment of divine grace, either *concreated* as the Protestants maintain, or a *donum superadditum*, as held by the Roman Catholic Church. This subject, also, will be given further consideration in our discussion of the nature of primitive holiness.

The Generic or Racial Aspect of Man's Origin. Man was created not only as an individual, but also as a racial being. The Hebrew word translated man, is not a proper noun, and is not so used until the second chapter. Had we only the account given us in the first chapter of Genesis, we may well have supposed that the male and the female of the species were created simultaneously. The second account is more specific. *And the Lord God caused a deep sleep to fall upon Adam, and he slept: and he took one of his ribs, and closed up the flesh instead thereof; and the rib, which the Lord God had taken from man, made he a woman, and brought her unto the man. And Adam said, This is now bone of my bones, and flesh of my flesh: she shall be called Woman, because she was taken out of Man* (Gen. 2:21-23). This statement has been a source of perplexity to commentators, and the theories suggested in its interpretation have been many and varied. It is evident, however, to the unprejudiced reader that the first account is intended to teach that the creative act referred to man generically; while the second deals not so much with the original creative act, as with the formative process by which generic man was elaborated into the two sexes. The word used does not signify creation *de novo*, but merely the formative act. Hence the Apostle Paul declares that *Adam was first formed, then Eve* (I Tim. 2:13). By this he appears to mean that the male was first brought to perfection, and from him the Lord God took that, out of which He made

"Enos signifies man, not as Adam does, which also signifies man, but is used in Hebrew indifferently for man and woman; as it is written, 'male and female created he them; and blessed them, and called their name Adam,' (Gen. 5:2), leaving no room for doubt that though the woman was distinctively called Eve, yet the name Adam, meaning man, was common to both. But Enos means man in so restricted a sense, that Hebrew linguists tell us it cannot be applied to woman."—AUGUSTINE, *City of God*, xv, 17.

St. Paul declares that "the man is not made out of (ἐκ) the woman, but the woman out of (ἐξ) the man" (I Cor: 11:8).

Woman. This fact was recognized by Adam when he said, *This is now bone of my bones, and flesh of my flesh: she shall be called Woman, because she was taken out of Man.*

The translation of the Hebrew word here rendered "rib" is unfortunate. The original word is found forty-two times in the Old Testament, and in no other instance except this, is it translated "rib." In the majority of cases it is translated "side" or "sides," and in some instances "corners" or "chambers." President Harper translated the verse as follows: "He took from his sides, and closed the flesh of it"; while Canon Payne-Smith says that woman comes from the flank of man, "so curiously from ancient times rendered 'rib'." In the Septuagint Version, the word "pleura" is used, which by the Greek writers, Homer, Hesiod, and Herodotus is invariably rendered "side," as it is also in the Greek of the New Testament. Thus the Genesis account teaches that every individual member of the race, including the first mother, has its antitypal representative in the first Man; and that in this way only could the Scriptures declare that God *hath made of one blood all nations of men* (Acts 17:26).

The generic aspect of the creation of man is presented not only from the physical viewpoint, but as forming also, the basis of the social structure. The occasion of the formation of woman is said to have grown out of Adam's necessity. *It is not good that the man should be alone; I will make him an help meet for him* (Gen. 2:18). Here it is evident that the formation of Eve and her separation from Adam contemplates the social virtues as a factor in the development of the race. This is not only recognized by Adam, but reinforced by an injunction later quoted by our Lord, *Therefore shall a man leave his father and his mother, and shall cleave unto his wife: and they shall be one flesh* (Gen. 2:24; cf. Matt. 19:4, 5). Hence St. Paul argues that *the man is not of the woman; but the woman of the man. Neither was the man created for the woman; but the woman for the man.* At the same time he grants that the man *is the image and glory of God: but the woman is the glory of the man* (I Cor. 11: 7-9); that is, man as a generic being was created by God, and is therefore, the image and glory of God; but woman was formed from man by a subsequent act, and hence is regarded as the glory, or outshining of the race. Viewing the relation of man and woman from the standpoint of ethics, the apostle argues further, that woman's duty to man is that of reverence on the ground of existence; man's duty to woman, that of devoted love as the foundation of the social structure.

St. Paul likewise builds upon this Genesis account, the symbolism of Christ and His Church. *Therefore as the church is subject unto Christ, so let the wives be to their own husbands in everything* (Eph. 5: 24); and for this he assigns the reason that *we are members of his body, of his flesh, and of his bones* (Eph. 5: 30). That this relationship should not be abused, as frequently it has been through too narrow an interpretation of the scripture, the apostle follows immediately with the injunction, *Husbands, love your wives, even as Christ also loved the church, and gave himself for it;* that is, the love of the husband for the wife must be of an abiding and vicarious nature—a love that will sacrifice every selfish purpose, and devote every human power to the furtherance of her best interests, whether physical, social or religious. *So ought men,* he says, *to love their wives as their own bodies;* and for this he gives the reason that *He that loveth his wife loveth himself. For no man ever yet hated his own flesh; but nourisheth and cherisheth it, even as the Lord the church: for we are members of his body, of his flesh, and of his bones* (Eph. 5: 28-30). This mystery of Christ and the Church He sums up in these words, ending in an ethical injunction, *For this cause shall a man leave his father and mother, and shall be joined unto his wife, and they two shall be one flesh. This is a great mystery: but I speak concerning Christ and the church. Nevertheless let every one of you in particular so love his wife even as himself; and the wife see that she reverence her husband* (Eph. 5: 31-33).

The Constituent Elements of Human Nature

The twofold position of man, at once a part of nature, and a free spirit transcending nature, gives rise to perplexing questions concerning the constituent elements of his personality. Chief among these may be mentioned the theories of Dichotomy and Trichotomy which regard man under a twofold or threefold aspect, and which lay the foundation for widely divergent opinions in later theological study.

The Theory of Dichotomy. Dichotomy holds that man is composed of two kinds of essence—a material portion (the body), and an immaterial portion (the spirit or soul). The body is material as formed from the earth. The spirit or soul, as a consequence of the divine inbreathing, constitutes the immaterial portion of man. The dichotomist, therefore, holds that man consists of two, and only two, distinct elements or substances—matter and mind, or the material and the spiritual. There is no *tertium quid,* or third substance which is neither matter nor mind. However, a distinction is frequently made between substance and powers—the one immaterial substance being considered as spirit under one aspect, and soul under another. Thus Godet says, "Spirit is the breath of God considered independent of the body;

> God formed man's body of the dust of the earth, and breathed into him the breath of life, and he became a living soul. This has been understood to teach that there are two, and only two, elements in the human constitution—one material and the other spiritual—the one matter and the other mind. These two are substances, entities, actually existing things, united in a manner to human thought, inscrutable, mysterious, incomprehensible, yet really united, and so united as to constitute one nature—a nature individualized, one, and yet both material and spiritual. It is only by the actuality of such union that certain facts of consciousness can be conceivably possible, such as pain from a fleshly wound. A spirit cannot be punctured by a pin, and though a dead body be punctured, pain is not produced. Matter is indispensable to the phenomenon, and mind to the consciousness produced by it. Man is not materialized mind, nor spiritualized matter, nor is he somewhat that is neither—or a somewhat between the two; but he is both, material as to his body, spiritual as to his mind, mysteriously united during his earthly existence in one individual person,—Raymond, *Syst. Th.,* II, p. 24.

soul, that same breath, in so far as it gives life to the body" (GODET, *Bib. Studies of the O. T.*, p. 32). Dr. Pope takes the same position. "The high distinction of human nature," he says, "is, that it is a union of the two worlds of spirit and matter, a reflection of spiritual intelligences in the material creation. The immaterial principle is the soul or ψυχή as connected with matter through the body, and the spirit or πνεῦμα as connected with the higher world. There is in the original record a clear statement as to the two elements of human nature" (POPE, *Comp. Chr. Th.*, I, p. 422). Perhaps the simplest definition of soul is to regard it merely as spirit in relation to body. Thus Hovey says that soul is spirit as modified by union with the body; while A. A. Hodge says that "by soul we mean only one thing, that is, an incarnate spirit, a spirit with a body. Thus we never speak of the souls of angels. They are pure spirits having no bodies (A. A. HODGE, *Pop. Lect.*, p. 227). This simpler position seems to be

The spirit of man, in addition to its higher endowments, may also possess the lower powers which vitalize dead matter into a human body. That the soul begins to exist as a vital force, does not require that it should always exist as such a force or in connection with a material body.—PORTER, *Human Intellect*, p. 39.

Brutes may have organic life and sensitivity, and yet remain submerged in nature. It is not life and sensitivity that lift men above nature, but it is the distinctive characteristic of personality.—HARRIS, *Philos. Basis of Theism*, p. 547.

The importance of these questions to theology is thus pointed out by Dr. Charles Hodge. "The scriptural doctrine of the nature of man as a created spirit in vital union with an organized body, consisting, therefore, of two and only two, distinct elements or substances, matter and mind, is one of great importance. It is intimately connected with some of the most important doctrines of the Bible; with the constitution of the person of Christ, and consequently with the nature of His redeeming work and of His relation to the children of man; with the doctrine of the fall, original sin and regeneration; and with the doctrines of the future state and of the resurrection. It is because of this connection, and not because of its interest as a question of psychology, that the true idea of man demands the careful investigation of the theologian.—HODGE, *Syst. Th.*, II, p. 48.

The scriptures used in support of the dichotomous position are the following: (1) Gen. 2:7 where the body is stated to be formed of the earth, and the soul by the inbreathing of the divine Spirit, that is, vitalized by a single principle. (2) Gen. 41:8 cf. Psalms 42:6; John 12:27 cf. 13:21. These scriptures and many others use the terms soul and spirit interchangeably. Matt. 10:28 cf. I Cor. 5:3; 6:20 where soul and body are mentioned together as composing the entire man.

Dr. Miley states that the dichotomic view is clearly given in the Scriptures, but since it is not the manner of the sacred writers to be always analytic, such subjects should be considered only on broad lines and the more prominent distinction made. Cf. MILEY, *Syst. Th.*, I, p. 400.

more in harmony with the scriptural representations of the constituent elements of man than the more elaborately worked out hypotheses.

The Theory of Trichotomy. There is another class of scriptures, found more especially in the New Testament Epistles, which seem to indicate that man is of a threefold or trichotomous nature. This usage grew out of the Platonic philosophy which the church inherited, and which regarded man as of a threefold essence. Pythagoras, and following him Plato, taught that man consists of three constituent elements, the rational spirit ($νοῦς$ or $πνεῦμα$, Latin *mens*), the animal soul ($ψυχή$, Latin *anima*), and the body ($σῶμα$, Latin *corpus*). This classification was so generally accepted by the later Greek and Roman philosophers that its usage came to be stamped upon popular speech as expressive of the entire nature of man. When, therefore, St. Paul would stress man in the totality of his being, he prays that the *whole spirit and soul and body be preserved blameless* (I Thess. 5:23). In emphasizing the penetrative power of the word of God, he speaks of it as *piercing even to the dividing asunder of the soul and spirit, and of the joints and marrow* (Heb. 4:12). "The use made of these terms by apostles," says Dr. A. A. Hodge, "proves nothing more than that they used words in their current popular sense to express divine ideas. The word $πνεῦμα$ designates the one soul emphasizing its quality as rational. The word $ψυχή$ designates the same soul emphasizing its quality as the vital and animating principle of the body. The two are used together to express popularly the entire man" (HODGE, *Outlines*, pp. 299, 300). This is the generally accepted position, especially in Western theology.

The Eastern church in general, held to the theory of trichotomy, the Western church to dichotomy. But trichotomy in the East led the church into a number of grievous errors, and this served to strengthen the West

---

The scriptures used in support of the trichotomous theory are I Thess. 5:23 and Hebrews 4:12. In addition the argument is drawn from those scriptures which refer to spirit and soul separately, and to the characteristic manner in which they appear.

in its dichotomous position. We may summarize these errors as follows: (1) The Gnostics regarded the spirit of man as an emanation from God and, therefore, a part of the divine essence. Hence they maintained that the spirit of man was incapable of sin. (2) The Apollinarians applied their tripartite conception of man to Christ, maintaining that in assuming human nature, He partook only of the body ($\sigma\hat{\omega}\mu\alpha$) and soul ($\psi\upsilon\chi\acute{\eta}$); but that the spirit in man was in Christ replaced by the divine Logos. Thus according to this theory Christ had only a deficient human nature. (3) The Semi-Pelagians greatly embarrassed the controversy concerning original sin, by maintaining that it was transmitted through the soul. (4) Placæus, whose name is generally associated with the theory of mediate imputation, taught that the $\pi\nu\epsilon\hat{\upsilon}\mu\alpha$ only, was directly created by God. He regarded the soul as mere animal life, created with the body, and therefore perishing with it. (5) Julius Mueller taught that the $\psi\upsilon\chi\acute{\eta}$ is derived from Adam, but he regarded the $\pi\nu\epsilon\hat{\upsilon}\mu\alpha$ as being pre-existent. He explains the doctrine of depravity by supposing that these pre-existent spirits which are embodied at birth had previously been corrupted. (6) There is the doctrine of the later annihilationists who hold that the divine element, breathed into man at his creation, was lost in the fall. Death is interpreted to mean annihilation of the soul, which can be restored to being only by regeneration. Immortality, therefore, is conditional and is the possession of the regenerate only.

We must conclude, then, that the Scriptures bear out the theory of dichotomy, in so far as the essential elements of man are concerned, that is, he is body and

In the early history of the church trichotomy flourished mostly in the school of Alexandria, and was introduced into Christian Theology through the Platonic philosophy. For awhile it seemed fairly on the way to a common acceptance, when adverse influences checked its progress and brought it into disrepute. Tertullian strongly opposed it, and his influence was very great. Even the seeming indifference of Augustus was indirectly against it; for his influence was so great on all doctrinal questions that nothing without his open support could hold a position of much favor in the more orthodox thought of the church.— MILEY, *Syst. Th.*, I, p. 399, spirit, a material and an immaterial essence conjoined to form one person. But we may admit, also, a practical trichotomy in both ordinary speech and in scriptural terminology. "It will be obvious, however, to those who weigh well the utterances of Scripture, that, provided the original constituent elements of human nature are only two, the whole religious history of man requires a certain distinction between soul and spirit; his one personality being connected by soul with the world of sense, and by his spirit with the world of faith. Yet soul and spirit make up one person" (POPE, *Compend. Chr. Th.*, I. p. 435). While man is composed of a material and an immaterial portion, the latter in exact Scripture terminology is viewed in a twofold manner. When viewed as the power of animating a physical organism it is called ψυχή or soul; when viewed as a rational and moral agent, this same immaterial portion is known as πνεῦμα or spirit. In the usage of St. Paul, the πνεῦμα is man's higher part in relation to spiritual things; the ψυχή is that same higher part in relation to bodily things. Hence the spirit or πνεῦμα is man's higher part looking Godward. It is therefore capable of receiving and manifesting the Holy Spirit (πνεῦμα ἅγιον) and of becoming a "spiritual" man. The soul or ψυχή is man's higher part descending to lower things, and hence absorbed in worldly interests. Such a person is called "soulish" in contradistinction to the "spiritual" man. Dr. Strong compares the immaterial portion of man to the upper story of a house, but having windows looking in two directions, toward earth and toward heaven. The element of truth in trichotomy then appears to be this, that the soul has a triplicity of endowment, bearing a threefold relation to matter, to self and to God.

The first part, the spirit, is the highest, deepest, noblest part of man. By it he is fitted to comprehend eternal things, and it is, in short, the house in which dwell faith and the word of God. The other, the soul, is this same spirit according to nature, but yet in another sort of activity, namely, in this, that it animates the body and works through it; and it is its method not to grasp things incomprehensible, but only what reason can search out, know and measure.—LUTHER.

THE UNITY OF THE RACE

There are two points involved in any proper consideration of the unity of the race: (I) The Community of Origin, and (II) The Unity of Species. Both are essential to a right understanding of the subject. When plants or animals are derived from a common stock they are regarded as being of the same species. But if, as the Scriptures seem to declare, God by a single fiat created at one time the vegetation of the whole earth, and at another the myriads of animals, these, too, would be regarded as belonging to the vegetable or animal realms, though not of a common parentage. The first subject, therefore, must be considered from the historical standpoint, the second is more philosophical in nature.

I

The Scriptures affirm both the unity of the human race and its community of origin. We have previously pointed out that the creation of man carried with it both the individualistic and generic aspect. The word "Adam" was at once the name of an individual and of a family— the personal name of the first man and the generic name of mankind. The divine record declares that man is one, and that he sprang from a common origin (Gen. 1:27). This is further confirmed by the Pauline statement that God *hath made of one blood all nations of men for to dwell on all the face of the earth* (Acts 17:26). This, as we have shown, the Genesis account teaches to the extent that Eve herself was taken from Adam to become the "mother of all living." The race, therefore, did not start originally from a single pair, but from generic Adam. With the establishment of the first pair we are to believe that all the races of mankind have descended from this common parentage (Gen. 3:20).

Arguments for the Community of Origin. For a time science disputed the claims of the Scriptures concerning the unity of the race, especially its community of origin. However, with the further advances in scientific discovery, the evidences in favor of the biblical position have steadily increased. The Genesis account has the following considerations in its favor. (1) The unity of the race is confirmed by the similarity of physical characteristics found in all peoples, such as the identity of vertebrate formation, the temperature of the body, length of pregnancy, the fertility of the races and the average number of years of life. (2) There are similar mental characteristics, tendencies and capacities in the various races as shown by a common body of tradition. (3) Closely allied to the above argument is that drawn from a common language origin. Philologists are generally agreed that the principles underlying the different languages are the same. Sanskrit seems to be the connecting link between the various Indo-Germanic languages. In the old Egyptian some parts of the vocabulary are Semitic and at the same time Aryan in grammar. (4) There is a common basic religious life. Man is universally religious, and the traditions found among the most widely separated people indicate a common dwelling place and a unity of religious life. There are traditional accounts in many nations, of a common origin, of a primeval garden and a golden age of innocence, of the serpent, the fall of man and the flood. Zockler thinks that these myths of the nations have been handed down from the time when the families of the earth had not separated, and that the changes are due to corruption of the accounts in transmission. It may also be argued at this point that the gospel makes an appeal to all peoples and finds a response among all nations.

The Primitive State of Man. The Scriptures teach that the primitive state of man was not one of barbarism, from which, by a gradual process of social evolution, he was brought to a state of civilization; but that man was originally created in a state of maturity and perfection.

The doctrine of the original unity of the human race is by no means a matter of indifference for religious and moral life. By it the high nobility of mankind is proved (Acts 17:28), by it the original equality and duty of brotherly love is shown (Matt. 7:12, Luke 10:30-37), by it the origin and complete universality of sin is declared (Rom. 5:12), by it the harmony between the domain of Creation and Redemption is announced (I Cor. 15:21, 22), and by it is secured the truth that the kingdom of God will come to all, since the gospel without distinction must be brought to every human being (Eph. 1:10, Matt. 28:19).—VAN OOSTERZEE, *Chr. Dogm.*, I, p. 364.

This perfection, however, must not be so interpreted as to preclude any further progress or development, but should be understood in the sense of a proper adaptation to the end for which he was created. As to the question of maturity, the Scriptures are opposed to the teaching of naturalistic evolution which regards early man as of crude physical constitution and low mentality, slowly developing for himself a language, and awakening only by gradual stages to moral and religious concepts. The oldest records furnish us with evidences of a high degree of civilization, even in the earliest periods of human history. Barbarism, as we have previously pointed out, is rather a degenerate civilization than a primitive state. The Scriptures are clear in their teaching on this subject, and for Christians this is decisive.

The Antiquity of the Race. The conflict of science with the scriptural account of man's origin, could but involve, also, the question of the antiquity of the race. Ussher's chronology makes the origin of man to precede the advent of our Lord by 4,004 years, reckoned on the basis of the Hebrew Scriptures; while Hales, on the ground of the Septuagint, reckons the number of years as 5,411. It is well known that the received chronology

Dr. Miley thinks that the intellectual grade of primitive man must be judged by a rational interpretation of relative facts. He regards the extreme views of man's intellectual state as being patterned after the extravagances of Milton, rather than after the moderation of Moses. He quotes Robert South as declaring that "an Aristotle was but the rubbish of a man," judged by the exalted position of man in his state of integrity. He points out also, that Mr. Wesley supposed that Adam in his unfallen state reasoned with unerring accuracy, if he found it necessary to reason at all (MILEY, *Syst. Th.*, I, p. 403). Dr. Charles Hodge also takes the position that "it is altogether probable that our nature, in virtue of its union with the divine nature in the person of Christ, and in virtue of the union of the redeemed with their exalted Redeemer, shall hereafter be elevated to a dignity and glory far greater than that in which Adam was created or to which he ever could have attained."—HODGE, *Syst. Th.*, II, p. 92.

We do not say that the faculties of man are in the same state now that they were before the fall, or the same that they would have been in if he had never fallen. Without doubt they are deteriorated, under the blighting and stupefying influence of sin. The understanding is enfeebled and darkened; the sensibilities are weakened and deranged; conscience has, in a measure, lost its power. Our faculties may have been all of them more or less impaired. Still it does not appear that any of them have been lost. In number and kind they remain the same that they were in Paradise.—POND, *Chr. Th.*, p. 354.

of the Bible has never been regarded as wholly accurate; and estimates such as that of Hales, which have been considered perfectly orthodox, increase the number of centuries sufficiently to allow for all racial and linguistic developments. The uncertainty of biblical chronology is due to the various methods of reckoning genealogies. The line is not always traced to the immediate ancestors. Thus the sons of Zilpah were two, Gad and Asher (Gen. 35: 26); while later (Gen. 46: 18) after recording the sons, grandsons and great-grandsons, the statement is made that the sons she bare unto Jacob were sixteen souls. Other instances of a similar nature are recorded in the same chapter. In the genealogy recorded in St. Matthew's Gospel, Josias is said to have begotten his grandson Jechonias, and Joram his great-grandson Ozias (Matt. 1: 8, 11). It is evident, therefore, that the genealogies are not always traced immediately from father to son; and consequently it is impossible to reach an exact chronology from the genealogical tables.

The unduly long periods of time which many scientists have affirmed as necessary for the development of the races, and for linguistical changes, are not supported by the facts. The known laws of population would account for the present number of the world's inhabitants, it is estimated, in six or seven thousand years. Furthermore, it is well known that linguistic changes occur very rapidly where there is no substantial body of literature. There is, therefore, no valid reason for supposing that the race is older than is commonly acknowledged by the received chronologies of the Bible.

II

But the unity of the race involves more than the community of origin; it involves also the unity of species, and leads immediately to the question as to the nature of genus and species. This is both a scientific and a philosophical problem. Agassiz maintained that the species does not depend merely upon outward characteristics as to color, form or size, but to what he calls the "immaterial principle." It is upon this that the constancy of the species depends. "All animals," he says, "may be traced back in the embryo to a mere point upon the yolk of an egg, bearing no resemblance whatever to the future animal. But even here an immaterial principle which no external influence can prevent or modify, is present and determines its future form; so that the egg of a hen can produce only a chicken, and the egg of a codfish only a cod" (AGASSIZ, *Prin. of Zoology*, p. 43). Dana takes the same position. "When individuals multiply from generation to generation," he says, "it is but a repetition of the primordial type-idea; and the true notion of the species is not in the resulting group, but in the idea or potential element which is at the basis of every individual of the group." Later scientific discoveries with a knowledge of genes and chromosomes, have confirmed the position of the earlier scientists; and now it is well understood that the parents are but the transmitters of a divided life-stream which when united gives rise to a new individual of the species.

Philosophically, the problem is much older than that represented by science. Christianity inherited Platonic realism which was the dominant philosophy during the period of the early church. The church of the middle ages was greatly influenced by the philosophy of Aristotle. Both philosophical systems were forms of realism. The formula of the first was *Universalia ante rem,* or the universal before the species; the latter *Universalia in re,* or the universal in the species. According to the first, genera and species are real substances, created prior to individuals and independent of them; while individuals are such only by virtue of their partaking of the original

In the ancient discussion between the realists and nominalists the question arose whether there is not in the divine mind, and in human thought reflecting the divine mind, a reality of human nature, of which every living man is an expression and representative. As there is an abstract θειότης, of which the Three Persons are representatives, so there is a human nature which the Second Person represented in the Incarnation, rather than as becoming a personal, individual man. Granting the truth of this mysterious principle—not the less true because we cannot fathom it—every man descended of Adam presents his own personal individualization of a generic character impressed by its Creator on mankind; and receives into himself the generic evil of original sin, which is the sin of the race in Adam.—POPE, *Compend. Chr. Th.,* I, p. 436.

essence. According to the latter, the universal while real, exists only in the individual. In modern theology, Dr. Shedd represents the position of Platonic realism, while Dr. Charles Hodge opposes it. The realism of Dr. Shedd, however, is not of an extreme type. He holds that whether or not the universal is prior to the individuals depends upon what individuals are meant. If the first two individuals of a species are in mind, then the universal is not prior to the species but simultaneous with it. The instant God created the first pair He created the human nature or species in and with them. But following this, he maintains that in the order of nature mankind exists before the generation of mankind; the nature is prior to the individual produced out of it. God created human nature in Adam and Eve and the millions of their descendants who now inhabit the earth are but individualizations of that original human nature. Dr. Shedd, however, is careful to make a clear distinction between "nature" and "person." As in the Trinity there are three Persons, the Father, the Son, and the Holy Spirit in one nature; and as in Christ there is one Person in two natures—divine and human; so also in man there is one person in two natures—spiritual and material. The distinction between "person" and "nature" so vital in Trinitarianism and Christology, is equally important in Anthropology. Men as "persons" are separate and distinct from each other, and must ever be; but each is possessed of a common human nature and together they form a living organism which as such, constitutes the human race. But regardless of the philosophical explanations offered, whether realism, nominalism, or conceptualism, the fact remains that man is both an individual and a racial being. He is like the fruit which must have a tree upon which to grow, and to which it is organically related. So also the race must be regarded not merely as an aggregation of individuals, but as an organism of vitally related and interacting parts, which are reciprocally means and ends in the attainment of that which is the good of the whole. The race is under the law of solidarity; it is bound up in a common life. Here is the basis of Paul's great metaphor. As the body is composed of many members, which by a common life are bound together into a living organism, so the Church, as the body of Christ, is composed of many members, all of whom have been baptized into one body by the one Spirit. They are thereby constituted a spiritual organism under the direction of their living Head. This solidarity of the human race forms the basis of the Pauline doctrine of redemption. Nor can the teaching of Jesus concerning the kingdom of God which forms the very core of the gospel be understood unless we view the human race as a unity of species. This unity regards each person, not only as a self-conscious, self-determining individual, but as an individual who is also a member of an organic race to which he is related both metaphysically and ethically. The relation of the individual to the race, then, becomes at once a theological as well as a philosophical problem. The body is admittedly propagated by the race through parentage, but what shall be said as to the origin of souls. Three theories have dominated the thought of the church —Pre-existence, Creationism and Traducianism.

Pre-existence. The doctrine of the pre-existence of the soul was inherited from Platonism, and was productive of a number of heretical opinions in the early church. Plato held to an ideal or intelligible world which existed previous to the present universe and furnished the archetypal forms for it. The universe, therefore, was simply these ideas in the mind of God clothed with material bodies and developed in history. Some of the more philosophically minded theologians of the early church identified this realm of ideas in the mind of God with the *genera* or species, which they therefore regarded as existing previous to the individual. It was in this manner that they explained the possession of ideas by the soul, which could not be derived from the sense world. Priscillianus was accused by Augustine of taking over the entire system of the Platonists, including the belief that the soul was a part of the divine nature, and that the material body was essentially evil. Origen, who is the best representative of this theory, derives his doctrine only indirectly from Platonism. He was apparently concerned with the disparity of conditions under which men enter the world, and attempted to account for it by the character of their sin in a previous state. It will readily be seen that this doctrine is closely connected with his idea of eternal creation. It was immediately rejected by both Eastern and Western churches, and therefore has been said to begin and end with Origen. It has reappeared a few times in modern philosophy and theology. Kant advocated it, as did also Julius Mueller and Edward Beecher—the ground of their argument being the supposition that inborn depravity can be explained only by a self-determined act in a previous state of being.

Creationism. The theory of creationism maintains that God immediately creates each human soul, the body being propagated by the parents. The origin of this theory is generally attributed to Aristotle; and with the rise of Aristotelianism in the middle ages, the schoolmen generally adopted it. Earlier than this both Jerome and Pelagius advocated the theory, as did also Cyril of Alexandria and Theodoret in the Eastern church, and Ambrose, Hilarius and Hieronymus in the Western church. Creationism as a theory seems to be closely connected with the attempts to emphasize the importance of the individual as over against an emphasis upon racial continuity and solidarity. Thus the Roman Catholic Church, which makes little of native depravity and much of individual freedom in spiritual things, has generally adopted the position of the schoolmen and accepted the theory of creationism. The Reformed Church, likewise, with its emphasis upon the individual, has favored creationism, and for the past two centuries it has been the prevailing theory. Pelagius and the Pelagians used this theory to justify their position concerning the original state of man. They maintained that if God created the souls of men He must have created them either pure and holy, or impure and sinful. Since the latter supposition is inconsistent with the holiness of God, the doctrine of native depravity must be rejected.

Creationism is sometimes associated with trichotomy and sometimes with dichotomy. In the former instance the spirit ($\pi\nu\epsilon\hat{\upsilon}\mu\alpha$) only is regarded as the direct creation of God; the soul (or $\psi\upsilon\chi\acute{\eta}$) being but the natural animal life, was held to be propagated with the body. When connected with dichotomy, the body alone was held to be propagated from the race, the spirit or soul being immediately created by God. Goeschel maintained that dichotomy leads necessarily to traducianism and trichotomy to creationism. Thus the family or racial name corresponds to the $\psi\upsilon\chi\acute{\eta}$; while the $\pi\nu\epsilon\hat{\upsilon}\mu\alpha$ is the Christian name. The best representatives of creationism in modern times are Martensen, Turretin and Hodge. Both Dr. Shedd and Dr. Strong oppose the position. Among the Arminian theologians no great importance is attached to the question concerning the origin of souls.

Traducianism. Traducianism holds that the souls of men as well as their bodies are derived from their parents. The word is derived from the Latin *traducere* which means to bring over as a layer of a vine for purposes of propagation. It is therefore an analogy with living things and supposes that new souls develop from Adam's soul like the shoots (*traduces*) of a vine or a tree. The theory appears to have been first propounded by Tertullian and is discussed by him in his *De anima*, where the word *tradux* is used frequently. It has been held widely in the Protestant church, Dr. Strong and Dr.

Dr. Minor Raymond states that "by far the larger portion of Christian thinkers have either entertained no opinion as to the origin of souls, not finding to their minds anything decisive in revelation, and not seeking to be wise above what is written, or have been divided between creationists and traducianists. It is conceded on the one hand, that if one can hold the doctrine of immediate creation, without affirming that God creates sinful souls, without denying inherited depravity, and without supposing that God in any way or degree sanctions every act of procreation with which His creative power is connected, his theory, though an error, will probably do him no harm. And on the other hand, it is conceded that if one can hold to the doctrine of traduction without affirming the numerical unity of the substance of all human souls, without affirming also the abscission and division of the essence of the human soul (that is, by asserting that the human person is only a part of the common humanity—an individualized portion of humanity), and without affirming the guilt and sinfulness of the humanity of Jesus Christ, then probably, though traduction be an error, it will as to him be harmless.— RAYMOND, *Syst. Th.*, II, pp. 35, 36.

Shedd being its most able representatives among theologians. The theory implies that the race was immediately created in Adam, both in respect to body and soul, and both are propagated by natural generation. The scriptural basis for this is usually found in the assertion that "Adam begat a son in his own likeness," which is interpreted to mean that it is the whole man who begets and is begotten. The theory receives strong support theologically, in that it seems to furnish an explanation for the transmission of original sin or depravity. Dr. Smith thinks that on the whole traducianism has been the most widely spread theory.

THE IMAGE OF GOD IN MAN

The distinctive note in the scriptural account of man's origin, is to be found in this—that he is created in the image of God. It is this likeness to his Creator that distinguishes him at once from the lower orders of creation, and at the same time relates him immediately to the spiritual world. Since there was a declaration of the divine purpose for man before even the creative fiat was executed, this image must belong to his inmost creaturely constitution. "As such it was essential and indestructible; the self-conscious and self-determining personality of man, as a spirit bearing the stamp of likeness to God—a reflection in the creature of the divine nature" (POPE, *Comp. Chr. Th.*, I, p. 423). Ewald states that the Genesis narrative at this point is particularly strong in its

---

Turretin in his "Institutes," states that "Some are of the opinion that the difficulties pertaining to the propagation of original sin are best resolved by the doctrine of the propagation of the soul; a view held by not a few of the fathers, and to which Augustine frequently seems to incline. And there is no doubt that by this theory all the difficulty seems to be removed; but since it does not accord with Scripture or sound reason, and is exposed to great difficulties, we do not think that recourse should be had to it." This represents a strong creationist view, with the admission that it best explains the doctrine of original depravity.

Tertullian's position as given by Neander is as follows: "It was his opinion that our first parent bore within him the undeveloped germ of all mankind; that the soul of the first man was the fountain head of all human souls, and that all varieties of individual human nature are but different modifications of that one spiritual substance. Hence the whole nature became corrupted in the original father of the race, and sinfulness is propagated at the same time with souls. Although this mode of apprehending the matter, in Tertullian, is connected with his sensuous habits of conception, yet this is by no means a necessary connection."

joyful exultation, as if the thought of man's peculiar excellence as a rational and moral being could not be expressed with sufficient vivacity.

Historical Development. While it is universally accepted that the image of God is intended to express man's general likeness to his Creator, the opinions of theologians have greatly differed as to the particular points of resemblance implied in the expression. In the earlier days of the Church there was a tendency to distinguish between the image (*imago*) and the likeness (*similitude*) of God, the former referring to the original constitution, or the innate powers of the human soul; the latter to the moral resemblance of the soul to God as manifested in the free exercise of these original powers. Some of the earlier fathers were inclined to regard the image as referring to the bodily form, and the likeness to the human spirit; but in general the "image" was understood to mean the rational basis of man's nature, and the "likeness" its free development. Thus Augustine relates the image to the intellectual faculties (*cognitio veritatis*), and the likeness to the moral faculties (*amor virtutis*). Tertullian places the image of God in the innate powers of the soul, especially in the freedom of choice between good and evil. Origen, Gregory of Nyssa and Leo the Great were of the same general opinion as Tertullian, and held that the image of God consisted chiefly in the freedom and rectitude of the will. In general, the Eastern theologians stressed the rationalistic basis as the ground of the divine image, while the Western theologians gave greater emphasis to the moral aspects of this image.

Later writers have usually followed one of three positions. *First,* they find the image of God in the rational soul, apart from moral conformity. Thus the schoolmen, following Augustine, distinguished between image and likeness, referring to the former, the powers of reason and freedom—or the natural attributes; and to the latter, original righteousness—or the moral attributes. But in this separation they held that the image only, was a part of the original constitution of man, and that moral conformity or original righteousness was a *donum super-*

additum, or superadded grace which alone was lost in the fall. *Second,* another type of rationalists, represented chiefly by the Pelagians and the Socinians, held that the image of God was to be found in man's dominion over the creatures of the earth, since this is mentioned in its immediate connection (Gen. 1:26). In modern times support is given this position by the advocates of rationalistic evolution, who view the primitive state of man as one of barbarism and savagery; and who regard the moral nature, not as an original endowment, but as the consequence of struggle and attainment. *Third,* and at the other extreme, are those who hold that the image of God is to be found in man's original constitution alone, and therefore was totally lost in the fall. Lutheranism, in its reactionary position, had a tendency to emphasize moral conformity to the disparagement of the rational basis, but extreme positions were the exception rather than the rule.

Protestantism generally rejects any distinction between the image and the likeness of God, regarding the one term as merely explanatory of the other. Thus Dr. Charles Hodge says that "image and likeness means an image which is like." The simple declaration of the Scripture is that man at his creation was like God (HODGE, *Syst. Th.,* II, p. 96). Calvin in his comments on Col. 3:10 and Eph. 4:24 makes the statement that "in the beginning the image of God was conspicuous in the light of the mind, in the rectitude of the heart, and in the soundness of all the parts of our nature (CALVIN, *Institutes* 1:15). Wakefield says that "It is vain to say that this image consisted in some one essential quality of human nature which could not be lost; for we shall find that it comprehended more qualities than one; and that while revelation places it, in part in what was essential to human nature, it included also what was not essential, and what might be lost and regained" (WAKEFIELD, *Chr. Th.,* p. 278). Almost all the Protestant confessions of faith hold that holiness was concreated in man, and that original righteousness was therefore included in the divine image. Protestantism is opposed to the rationalistic position, whether in the Pelagian form which admits only the possibility of holiness in the original creation of man; or the Roman Catholic position of original righteousness as a superadded gift. It is likewise opposed to the contrary view, which makes it amissible, and therefore lost in the fall. We are thus led to the more scriptural position which includes both the rational and moral elements, the former being commonly known as the Natural or Essential image of God; the latter as the Moral or Incidental image.

The Natural or Essential Image. By the Natural or Essential image of God in man, is meant his original constitution—that which makes him man, and thereby distinguishes him from the lower animal creation; while by the Moral or Incidental image is meant the use which he makes of the powers with which he was endowed at creation. The first may be summed up under the term *personality;* the second under moral likeness to God or *holiness.* By virtue of his personality, man possesses certain faculties, such as intellect, feeling or affection, and will; by virtue of his moral quality, he had certain right tendencies, or dispositions. Created in the image of God we may say then, that man was endowed with certain powers known as the natural image; and a certain direction was given these powers, which is known as the moral image of God. The natural image is uneffaced and ineffaceable, and exists in every human being; the moral image is accidental and amissible. The free spirit of man reflected the holiness of God in perfect conformity of mind, feeling and will, but this was lost in the fall and can be restored only through divine grace. There are three outstanding characteristics of the natural image of God which demand our attention—spirituality, knowledge and immortality.

1. *Spirituality.* Spirituality is the deepest fact in the likeness of man to God. This is evident from the scriptural statement that God is "the Father of spirits" (Heb. 12:9). It appears also from another statement found in St. Paul's address on Mars' Hill. *Forasmuch then as we are the offspring of God, we ought not to*

think that the Godhead is like unto gold, or silver, or stone, graven by art and man's device (Acts 17: 29). Here the apostle argues that if man possesses a spiritual nature as the offspring of God, then God himself must be spiritual and consequently cannot be represented by material substances such as gold, or silver, or stone. St. James speaks of *men which are made after the similitude of God* (James 3: 9), thereby implying the indestructibility of the natural image of God in man. Spirit in man is like Spirit in God, the one finite, the other infinite. The spiritual nature, therefore, is the deepest fact in the image of God and the ground of all other forms of likeness. Witsius points out that it is not to be considered in the light of a canvas upon which the image of God may be drawn, but that the spiritual nature is itself the likeness of God. Personality in man with its rational, affectional and volitional nature, is like personality in God; and this resemblance still obtains, although in the latter the attributes are infinite, and the essence altogether transcends the limitation of man's finite powers.

2. *Knowledge.* Man's cognitive powers belong also to the original image in which he was created. This is evident, not only from the fact that consciousness is an inherent property of spirit as well as self-determination, but also by a direct statement of the Scriptures. In his letter to the Colossians, St. Paul asserts that they *have put on the new man, which is renewed in knowledge after the image of him that created him* (Col. 3: 10). Here it is obvious that the original image in which man was created included knowledge, in both its intellectual and moral aspects; and having lost the moral image of God in the fall, this is to be restored by divine grace—a renewing in knowledge, after the image of God. The moral quality of the knowledge referred to here is found in the expression εἰς ἐπίγνωσιν which means literally "unto knowledge." The renewal therefore is not merely *in* knowledge, as a cognitive power; nor *by* knowledge, as a means to an end; but *unto* knowledge—a restoration to moral likeness and spiritual fellowship. It is evident, then, that knowledge in its intellectual or cognitive aspect

belongs to the natural image; while knowledge as an ethical and spiritual quality belongs to the moral image in which man was created. Thus as *wisdom* marked the transition from the relative to the moral attributes of God; so *knowledge* marks the transition from the natural to the moral image of God in man.

3. *Immortality.* The church with few exceptions, has constantly maintained that man was created immortal, and that death entered solely as a consequence of sin. When, however, we refer to man's immortality as forming a part of the image of God in which he was created, we are concerned more specifically with the soul, although it is frequently asserted as applicable to the whole nature of man. Exceptions to man's immortality have been advanced by the rationalists of every age. The Pelagians and Socinians urged their objections on the ground, (1) that Adam's body as a corporeal organization was not designed for immortality; and (2) that the animal creation as well as mankind, were created male and female in order to propagate the species, and therefore the design of the Creator was the continuation of a succession of individuals, rather than preservation of the same individuals. Two factors, then, are involved in the question of man's immortality as it relates to the image of God, *first,* the immortality of the body; and *second,* the immortality of the soul.

The first question concerns the immortality of the body, or man's exemption from bodily death. Wakefield

That God made man conditionally immortal cannot, I think, be reasonably doubted. Though formed out of the dust of the earth, his Maker breathed into his nostrils the breath of life, and he became a living soul; and as there was then nothing violent, nothing out of its place, no agent too weak or too slow on the one hand; or too powerful or too active, on the other; so all the operations of nature were performed only in time, in quantity, and in power, according to the exigencies of the ends to be accomplished. So that in number, weight and measure, everything existed and acted according to the unerring wisdom and skill of the Omnipotent Creator. There could therefore be no corruption or decay; no disorderly induration nor preternatural solution or solubility of any portions of matter; no disorders in earth; nothing noxious or unhealthy in the atmosphere. The vast mass was all perfect: the parts of which it was composed equally so. As He created, so He upheld all things by the Word of His power: and as He created all things, so by Him did all things consist; and among these man.—CLARKE, *Chr. Th.*, p. 87.

and Ralston understand immortality as applying to man's compound nature, the body as well as the soul. In this they follow Watson who states that "The Pelagian and Socinian notion, that Adam would have died had he not sinned, requires no further refutation than the words of the Apostle Paul, who declares expressly that death entered the world by sin; and so it inevitably follows that, as to man at least, but for sin there would have been no death. The opinion of those divines who include in the penalty attached to the first offense the very 'fullness of death' as it has been justly termed, death bodily, spiritual and eternal, is not to be puffed away by sarcasm, but stands firm on inspired testimony" (WATSON, *Institutes*, II, p. 386). In general two positions have been taken, (1) that the body is naturally mortal, and that the divine plan included counteracting agencies which effectually offset these death-working influences. This was the position of Martin Luther, who taught that the tree of life was intended to preserve the bodies of our foreparents in eternal youth. (2) The second position is, that man as such was immortal, but that provision was made in his original constitution for the gradual or sudden spiritualization of his bodily frame. Many of the earlier fathers taught that Adam was to pass a period of probation in the earthly garden, and if obedient would be translated to the heavenly Paradise of which the Garden of Eden was the earthly type. Among later writers, Dr. Sheldon thinks that the "tree of life" may stand for the divine efficiency which would have mediated the human spirit, in its continued communion with God, and through the human spirit thus vitalized would have raised man's sensuous nature, without the experience of any painful disruption, to the state of the glorified life (SHELDON, *Syst. Chr. Doct.*, p. 278). Dr. Charles Hodge and Dr. Pope take essentially the same position. Dr. Strong regards the body of man as itself mortal, and cites I Cor. 15:45 as his proof from Scripture. He holds, however, that if Adam had maintained his integrity the body might have been developed and transfigured without the intervention of death. These positions seem to be based upon the statement of the Apostle Paul that *We shall not all sleep, but we shall all be changed, in a moment, in the twinkling of an eye, at the last trump: for the trumpet shall sound, and the dead shall be raised incorruptible, and we shall be changed. For this corruptible must put on incorruption, and this mortal must put on immortality. So when this corruptible shall have put on incorruption, and this mortal shall have put on immortality, then shall be brought to pass the saying that is written, Death is swallowed up in victory* (I Cor. 15: 51-54). Dr. Charles Hodge argues that if St. Paul's statement to the effect that those who have borne the image of the earthy shall also bear the image of the heavenly, is meant to infer that our bodies are like the body of Adam as originally constituted, then his body no less than ours, required to be changed to fit it for immortality (HODGE, *Syst. Th.*, II, p. 116). Dr. Pope, emphasizing more especially the fact that man was made a "living soul," while the Second Man is a "quickening spirit" (POPE, *Compend. Chr. Th.*, I, p. 430) declares that "the comparison of Genesis with St. Paul's comment shows that there was a development of being, as it were, purposed and suspended in Adam: that he was to have enjoyed immortality through the gradual or sudden spiritualization of his bodily frame; but that it required the Last Adam to come to accomplish the design of creation. Through the fall the first Adam became the father of a dying nature: he bereft himself and us of the quickening Spirit who would have rendered the resurrection needless."

The second question is concerned with the immortality of the soul in its relation to the divine image. It resolves itself into this—is everlasting life in its literal sense, the exclusive privilege of those who are saved in Christ; or, is the soul by its natural constitution immortal in all men? Tertullian (c. 220) and Origen (c. 254) while differing widely on many questions, agreed in this, that immortality belongs to the very essence of the soul. The spirit is itself the person, and human personality is undying. This has ever been the faith of the Church. Nemesis (c. 400) appears to have been the first to advance the notion of conditional immortality in the early history of the Church. The opinion was short-lived, but was revived again by Nicholas of Methone in 1089 A.D. In 1513 the Lateran Council pronounced the proper immortality of the soul to be an article of faith, and since that time this position has been held so firmly that contrary opinions have been regarded as heretical. The confusion of those who maintain the doctrine of conditional immortality is due largely to a lack of discrimination in terms. To identify life with existence and death with annihilation is both irrational and unscriptural. It arose primarily as a means of meeting objections to the doctrine of eternal punishment. Protestantism has uniformly maintained that eternal life as a gift of Christ, does not apply to existence as such, but to the quality of that existence. The soul of man may exist in a state of life, or in a state of death. Hence our Lord says, *Fear not them which kill the body, but are not able to kill the soul* (Matt. 10: 28); and St. Paul declares that *even when we were dead in sins* God by His great love, *hath quickened us together with Christ* (Eph. 2: 1, 4, 5). Thus the soul has existence regardless of the state or quality of that existence which we call life or death. It may exist in a state of sin and death, or a state of life and righteousness, whether in this world or in the next. The Protestant churches have generally embodied this doctrine in their confessions, either directly or indirectly.

The Moral or Incidental Image. We have already mentioned some of the distinctions between the natural and the moral image of God, and these need not be repeated. It is sufficient to say, that in addition to the powers of personality with which man was endowed at creation, he was given also, a certain responsibility for the right use of these natural abilities. Having the power of self-determination, he is responsible for the use of his freedom; having affections reaching out to the objects of his choice, he is responsible for the quality of those affections; having intellectual powers, he is responsible for the direction of his thoughts and the nature of the adjustments which intelligence demands. We may further summarize the two positions as follows: the natural image of God in man has reference to personality, by which he is distinguished from the lower animal creation; while the moral image refers to the character or quality of this personality. The first has to do with the constitution of man as possessing self-consciousness and self-determination; the second has to do with the rightness or wrongness of the use of these powers. The natural image gives man his natural ability and moral responsibility; the moral image gives him his moral ability and makes possible a holy character. The moral image of God in man is therefore closely connected with the idea of primitive holiness, which furnishes us with our next subject for investigation. The older theologians were accustomed, in this connection to discuss at length the question of the freedom of the will, but the changed attitude toward the whole question of personality now makes this unnecessary. This subject, however, will be given some consideration in connection with our discussion of the Atonement and Prevenient Grace.

Christ as the Perfect Image of God. The doctrine of the divine image finds its perfect expression in the eternal Son as the second Person of the Trinity. He is the "express image of God," the outshining or effulgence of the divine glory. It was in the image of that image that man was created. In both his first and in his second creation, the Son was the archetype and pattern. It was this specific relation of the Son to man, and man to the Son, that made it possible for the Word to become flesh. Christ, therefore, preserved the full and exact image of

Man was created a personal being, and was by this personality distinguished from the brute. By personality we mean the twofold power to know self as related to the world and to God, and to determine self in view of moral ends. By virtue of this personality, man could at his creation choose which of the objects of his knowledge—self, the world, or God—should be the norm and center of his development. This natural likeness to God is inalienable, and as constituting a capacity for redemption gives value to the life even of the unregenerate (Gen. 9:6, I Cor. 11:7, James 3:9). This first element of the divine image man can never lose until he ceases to be man. St. Bernard well said that it could not be burned out, even in hell. Human nature, therefore is to be reverenced.—Strong, *Syst. Th.*, II, p. 515.

God in man, and thereby became the Redeemer of a fallen race, restoring man to the moral likeness of God in righteousness and true holiness.

THE NATURE OF PRIMITIVE HOLINESS

The different positions concerning the image of God in man which we have just indicated led to widely divergent opinions as to the nature of primitive holiness. The two extremes were represented by Pelagianism on the one hand, and Augustinianism on the other. To review briefly, both Pelagius and Augustine distinguished between the "image" of God, which they limited to man's natural constitution; and the "likeness" which they referred to his moral nature. But concerning the nature of this likeness they differed widely. Pelagius held that man was created with only the possibility of holiness; while Augustine maintained that holiness was a quality of man's original nature. The Roman Catholic fathers held with Augustine, that man was possessed of primitive holiness; but since this was amissible or capable of being lost, they early came to the conclusion, that it could not, therefore, have been an essential element of man's original constitution. Hence they regarded it as a *donum superadditum*, or a supernatural gift subsequent to his creation. The Roman Catholic Church in some measure, therefore, agreed with both Augustine and Pelagius—with the former it held that primitive man was holy; with the latter it agreed that this holiness was not a part of man's natural constitution. We may say, then, that the contrast between Pelagianism and Augustianism in the

Hence this image must belong to his inmost creaturely constitution. As such it was essential and indestructible: the self-conscious and self-determining personality of man, as a spirit bearing the stamp of likeness to God and capable of immortality, was the reflection in the creature of words, the question as to the existence and right of a natural knowledge the divine nature. While all creatures up to man reflect the perfections of their Creator, it is man's distinction, made emphatic in the act of his creation, that he alone should bear His image. This, therefore, is the ground of his dignity, and while that dignity belongs to his nature as a whole, it necessarily is found in that part which is imperishable. From beginning to end the holy record regards this image as uneffaced and ineffaceable, and still existing in every human being.—POPE, *Compend. Chr. Th.*, II, pp. 423, 424.

Roman Catholic Church lay in this—that the former regarded holiness as a mere possibility; the latter as a supernatural gift.

At the time of the Reformation Protestantism reacted sharply against the Roman Catholic idea of holiness as a supernatural gift. Its theologians returned to the original teaching of Augustine, that holiness was

> To the superficial observer the whole of this question may seem of subordinate importance; but when more closely examined it is of preponderating theological and anthropological value. For it is in other words, the question as to the existence and right of a natural knowledge of God; or even if this be put aside, it is at once apparent that, from the standpoint of the Romish Church, the fall becomes only more enigmatical, and in no case can be regarded as a properly so-called declension of human nature itself. Besides, the whole conception of such a *donum superadditum* is foreign to Holy Scripture, and originates in the unbiblical conception that the first man alone bore the image of God and lost it through sin.—VAN OOSTERZEE, *Chr. Dogm.*, I, pp. 376, 377.
>
> The Tridentine anthropology is a mixture of Pelagianism and Augustinianism. God created man *in puris naturalibus*, without either holiness or sin. This creative act, which left man characterless, God followed with another act by which he endowed man with holiness. Holiness is something supernatural, and not contained in the first creative act. Creation is thus imperfect, and is improved by an afterthought.—SHEDD, *Dogm. Th.*, II, p. 96.
>
> Concreated holiness is one of the distinguishing tenets of Augustinianism. Pelagianism denies that holiness is concreated. It asserts that the will of man by creation, and in its first condition, is characterless. Its first act is to originate either holiness or sin . . . . Adam's posterity are born, as he was created, without holiness and without sin. . . . . Semi-Pelagianism holds the same opinion; excepting that it concedes a transmission of a vitiated physical nature, which Pelagianism denies. So far as the rational and voluntary nature of man is concerned, the semi-Pelagian asserts that holiness, like sin, must be self-originated by each individual.—SHEDD, *Dogm. Th.*, II, p. 96.
>
> In order to point out the importance of the doctrinal differences, we may in a brief preview say, that Pelagianism held to the indeterminism of the will, as over against the Augustinians who held to determinism; that is, the former regarded the will merely as the power of choice, while the latter regarded it as having a character which determined the choices. Pelagianism held that original sin was not transmitted by Adam to his posterity; while Augustinianism held that the descendants of Adam were not only born depraved, but that guilt attached to this depravity. Pelagianism held that souls are born pure, and that sin originates in the environment; Augustinianism held that man's depravity is such, that he cannot either think or act right apart from divine grace. Grace, as Pelagius viewed it, was merely external instruction; while with Augustine it was closely allied with inward or effectual calling. Hence salvation with Pelagius was synergistic, or by means of co-operative grace; while with Augustine salvation was monergistic, that is, grace operated through predestination and election. Consequently Pelagius held to the idea of a universal atonement; Augustine to a limited atonement. Thus there arose two widely different systems of theology, solely as a consequence of certain fundamental doctrines being carried to extreme and unwarranted lengths. Arminianism arose as a mediating system of theology, and attempts to conserve the truth in each of the former systems.

concreated, and therefore an original quality of man's being. But in attempting to guard against the error of Pelagianism, they frequently fell into the opposite error of regarding this subjective state as one of fully established ethical holiness. This is a distinction of great importance. Hence the contrast between Pelagianism and Augustinianism in the Protestant church took on a new form. No longer was it a contrast between the possibility of holiness and a superadded gift; but between the possibility of holiness and an ethical state having merit. Thus there arose in Protestantism two systems of anthropology, with widely different and sometimes contradictory doctrinal implications.

Fundamental Distinctions of Primitive Holiness. There are two fundamental distinctions which must be observed in our discussion of primitive holiness. *First,* there is the distinction between a mere possibility of holiness, and holiness itself. The former is a negative state; the latter is marked by a positive attitude of soul—a spontaneous tendency to obey the right and reject the wrong. *Second,* there is the distinction between created holiness and ethical holiness. The former is a subjective state and tendency without personal responsibility; the latter springs from moral choices, and depends upon the action of a free personal being. Both of these aspects must be given due consideration. While differing from each other, the latter does not make void the former, but confirms it and builds upon it. By the exercise of right choices in

Thus we distinguish two aspects of holiness in Adam. First, there is that holiness which is the result of the creative act. The creative choice, the creative process and the creative product were holy with a holiness guaranteed by the absolute holiness of God. The creative product in the case of Adam was a holy being, sinless, in the image of God, a creature separate in kind from God but dependent upon Him and immortal in his duration. This was holiness as a result of creation. Second, there is the aspect of holiness resulting from Adamic moral choice. With the first right exercise of moral choice, ethical holiness begins. This does not void created holiness but as the major duty of human personality, it confirms created holiness and builds upon it. By the exercise of moral choice in harmony with that holiness as a consequence of the divine choice and process, the created person strengthens himself in it and by that choice testifies that he is possessed of an understanding of moral values, and acknowledges the value of fright. Thus the human development of holy character begins. Through its continuance holy character is enlarged and confirmed in righteousness.—Rev. Paul Hill, *The Man in the Garden,* p. 18ff.

harmony with the tendencies of created holiness, man acknowledges the value of right and thereby testifies that he is possessed of an understanding of moral values. Thus the development of holy character begins; and if continued through right choices is strengthened and confirmed in righteousness.

We are prepared now to point out the errors resulting from the extreme views of Pelagianism and Augustinianism. Both Pelagius and Augustine overlooked the distinction between holiness as a subjective state and holiness as a consequence of free moral choices, and therefore held only to the latter. Hence Pelagius maintained that the created subjective state could not be one of holiness, but only the possibility of holiness; while Augustine, insisting upon the created state as ethically holy, held that merit attached to it. Augustine therefore maintained that original sin meant native guilt and depravity; while Pelagius, holding to the impossibility of demerit apart from personal choices, denied native depravity altogether. Dr. Miley points out that "With the proper analysis the former might have maintained the whole truth of native depravity without the element of sinful demerit; while the latter might have held the same truth of native depravity, and yet have maintained his fundamental principle that free personal conduct absolutely conditions all sinful demerit" (MILEY, *Syst. Th.*, I, pp. 416, 417). We are prepared, further, to note the distinction between the holiness of a nature, and the holiness of personal agency. In all human life, there is an inner realm of thought, desire and aspiration which tends to come to expression in outward activity. But this inner life is not passive—it, too, is in the realm of free personal choices and therefore supremely ethical. However, below this inner realm there is a nature, and it is in this

---

Pelagianism is not so much the teaching of a single individual as a complete moral and religious system which took its name from Pelagius, a British monk, who came to Rome during the early part of the fifth century. By Augustinianism is meant that form of doctrine developed by the Reformers, and held mainly in the Calvinistic churches. Both the Roman Catholic Church and the Reformers assertedly built upon the teachings of Augustine, but developed vastly different systems of theology.

nature that we find the determining law of life. It is to this that our Lord referred when He said, *Either make the tree good and his fruit good; or else make the tree corrupt, and his fruit corrupt: for the tree is known by his fruit* (Matt. 12:33). Thus the tree has a quality in itself distinct from the fruit. So also man was created with a subjective nature which underlies and gives character to both the inner realm of personal choices and the outward realm of personal activity.

Mr. Wesley was strongly opposed to both Pelagianism and Socinianism. Dr. John Taylor of Norwich, a Unitarian of the first half of the eighteenth century, was one of the most learned and powerful defenders of Socinianism with which Mr. Wesley had to contend. The thoroughness of his position is seen in the following statement: "Adam could not be originally created in righteousness and true holiness; because habits of holiness cannot be created without our knowledge, concurrence, or consent; for holiness in its nature implies the choice and consent of a moral agent, without which it cannot be holiness" (WATSON, *Institutes*, II, p. 16). In order to make clear the distinction between the Socinian position and that of the later Arminians, we give Mr. Wesley's reply to Dr. Taylor. He says, "A man may be righteous before he does what is right, holy in heart before he is holy in life. The confounding of these two

The statement of Dr. Taylor appears to have been influenced by the philosophy of John Locke, which held that the soul of a child is a *tabula rasa* or white sheet of paper, upon which must be written by personal choice that which makes it good or bad. This, it will be seen, is the basic assumption of much of the religious education of the present time—an assumption which overlooks the fundamental distinction between personal activity and that quality of nature which underlies it.

From the first book of Pelagius on free will Augustine quotes the following: "All good and evil, by which we are praise or blameworthy, do not originate together with us, but are done by us. We are born capable of each, but not filled with either. And as we are produced without virtue, so are we also without vice; and before the action of his own will there is in man only what God made." This, says Dr. Miley, denies all change in the moral state of the race as consequent to the Adamic fall. In his moral nature man is the same in his original constitution. Adam was endowed with freedom and placed under a law of duty, but was morally indifferent as between good and evil. This denial of primitive holiness is not merely a speculative error. The principle of this denial carries with it a denial of the Adamic fall and depravity of the race, and therefore leaves no place for evangelical theology.—MILEY, *Syst. Th.*, I, p. 417.

all along seems the ground of your strange imagination, that Adam 'must choose to be righteous, must exercise thought and reflection before he could be righteous.' Why so? 'Because righteousness is the right use and application of our powers?' Here is your captial mistake. No, it is not; it is the right state of our powers. It is the right disposition of our soul, the right temper of our mind. Take this with you, and you will no more dream, that 'God could not create man in righteousness and true holiness'" (WESLEY, *Sermon on Original Sin*). The reason for Mr. Wesley's strong opposition is not far to seek. When Pelagius taught that the "good and evil, by which we are praise or blameworthy, do not originate together with us, but are done by us," he thereby denied any moral change in the race consequent upon the fall of Adam. Adam, being created characterless, his posterity would likewise be born without holiness or sin. Hence Pelagianism denied original sin as a corruption of man's nature through the fall, and held that saving grace was merely external instruction appealing to a nature wrong only through accident and bad example. Mr. Wesley, therefore, opposed these positions as destructive of the entire system of evangelical theology.

The Nature of Holiness in Adam. If we observe the distinction mentioned above, it becomes evident that there may be created holiness as a subjective state, which is something more than a mere possibility on the one hand, and something previous to free moral action on the other. This created holiness consists in a spontaneous inclination or tendency toward the good—a subjective disposition which always answers to the right. It is more than innocence. Man was created not only negatively innocent but positively holy, with an enlightened understanding of God and spiritual things, and a will wholly inclined to them. When, therefore, we speak of Adamic

The Pelagian position is expressed in the following statement: "At birth, each man's voluntary faculty, like Adam's, is undetermined either to sin or holiness. Being thus characterless, with a will undecided for either good or evil, and not in the least affected by Adam's apostasy, each individual man, after birth commences his voluntariness, originates his own character. and decides his own destiny by the choice of either right or wrong."

holiness, we mean thereby simply the spontaneous inclination, or positive disposition which belonged to him by virtue of his creation. If it be argued that this position differs but little from that held by the Pelagians, and later by the Socinians, we answer, there is a vast difference between the soul being produced with a nature free from either virtue or sin, and that soul being created with a positive direction toward the right. Then, too, the doctrinal implications are such as lead to widely different systems of theology. Pelagianism of necessity denied inherited depravity in the descendants of Adam; while Augustinianism with equal necessity, maintained that the descendants of Adam were not only depraved but guilty.

Arminianism is not only opposed to the error of Pelagianism, but also to the opposite error of Augustinianism. While it holds that the newly created state of Adam was one of holiness, it nevertheless denies that this state, however excellent, had any true ethical quality. It could not, therefore, be accounted either meritorious or rewardable. Augustinianism as developed by the Reformers, held that holiness was concreated, as we have previously indicated, and was therefore, not something superadded, but a quality of man's original nature. Their error lay in this, that they regarded the original state of man as one of ethical righteousness as well as inward holiness. It was therefore an ethical holiness, or an obligation under moral law; and as a quality of man's original nature even before any personal action, it is regarded as having the moral worth of ethical righteousness. Thus Van Oosterzee states that we should not

It may be well at this point to distinguish between innocence and holiness, though both of these were Adamic possessions at the beginning, and both the result of the divine act of creation. Innocence refers to blamelessness of wrongdoing; holiness refers to a positive attitude of soul favorable toward right and antagonistic toward wrong. Innocence does not require strenuous exercise of will; holiness presupposes the positive inclination of the will toward good and against evil. A newborn babe is innocent, but since the fall none are born holy. Childhood innocency remains until by act of disobedience the child definitely allies itself with sin, at which time innocence is forfeited. Adamic innocence was coupled with holiness. At creation it was connected first with created holiness, and later by the exercise of free choice became ethical.—REV. PAUL HILL, *The Man in the Garden*, p. 19.

"with the Romish Church, assume that the image of God in the first man was something merely additional (*accidens*) bestowed upon him in consequence of a supernatural communication; but not belonging to the essence of his nature. The Reformers most justly assert, in opposition to this mechanical view, that *justitia originalis* was an original and actual element of our nature, as it came forth from the hand of the Creator." Luther was especially insistent that original righteousness was a quality of man's proper nature, and necessary to its perfection and completeness. Jonathan Edwards at a somewhat later period, took the same position. "Adam was brought into existence capable of acting immediately, as a moral agent, and therefore he was immediately under a rule of right action; he was obliged as soon as he existed to act right. And if he was obliged to act right as soon as he existed, he was obliged even then to be inclined to act right. . . . . And as he was obliged to act right from the first moment of his existence, and did do so till he sinned in the affair of the forbidden fruit, he must have had an inclination or disposition of heart to do right the first moment of his existence, with an inclination, or, which is the same thing, a virtuous and holy disposition of heart" (EDWARDS, *Works*. Vol. II. p. 385). Dr. Miley in his comment upon this statement points out that "Not only is there here an overlooking of all distinction between purely spontaneous tendency and proper ethical action, but it is attempted to prove an original ethical holiness of Adam from its necessity to moral obligation which was instant upon his existence. The assumption of such instant obligation is a pure gratuity. . . . . We agree with the prevalent Augustinian anthropology respecting the reality of primitive holiness, but dissent respecting any proper ethical character of

We may suppose a being, like Adam, created with soul perfectly right. His preferential feelings anterior to action accord with the divine law. His sensibilities are so under easy volitional control, his mind is so clear and pure, that all in its primitive undisturbed state is right. His will is able to hold his whole being in subordination to the moral imperative. He is, in his grade of being, perfectly excellent; and his excellence is not mechanical merely or esthetical, but ethical. It is moral excellence, and perfect in its kind, yet wholly unmeritorious.—WHEDON, *Freedom of the Will*, p. 391.

that holiness, and also respecting its limitation to a mere quality of the Adamic nature. In that anthropology Adam often appears in the very beginning, and before any personal action, with the moral worth of ethical righteousness, with the activities of holy affection in the fear and love of God. We omit all this from the content of primitive holiness. The activities of holy affection may be spontaneous to the moral nature, but must be subsequent to its own constitution" (MILEY, *Syst. Th.*, I, pp. 411, 421).

Essential Elements of Primitive Holiness. In a brief summary, we may say that there are two essential elements in any true doctrine of primitive holiness. *First,* the moral rectitude of Adam's nature as a subjective state. We have shown that a thorough analysis distinguishes between the creation of a moral nature as a subjective state, and the activities of that moral nature in personal life. A true Arminianism thus distinguishes between the error of Pelagianism on the one hand, and that of Augustinianism on the other. These positions have already been given ample treatment. *Second,* the presence and agency of the Holy Spirit. This is necessary to a full understanding of the truth, and furnishes a basis, also, for discrimination against other forms of error. We have already pointed out the extreme position of the Roman Catholic Church in maintaining that holiness was a superadded gift, and therefore not a part of man's original constitution. We have noted also the extreme position of the Reformers in opposition to this, maintaining that holiness was concreated, and therefore limited to a quality of man's primal nature. The truth lies midway between these extreme positions. Arminianism has always objected to the papal doctrine that holiness is a supernatural gift, in that it involves a false

A primitive Adamic holiness is not an impossibility because Adam could not, simply as created, be holy in any strictly ethical or meritorious sense. In the fundamental distinctions of holiness we found a sense which is applicable to a nature in distinction from a personal agent. It lies in a spontaneous tendency to the good. The subjective disposition answers to the good on its presentation. It answers as a spontaneous inclination or impulse toward holy action. This is all that we mean by the nature of Adamic or primitive holiness.—MILEY, *Syst. Th.*, I, p. 412.

position as to the nature of the fall and original sin. It has equally objected to limiting holiness to a mere quality of the Adamic nature. The truth involved is this, that to the holiness of man's nature by creation, must be added the immediate presence and power of the Holy Spirit. Even Augustine admitted that "God had given man an assistance without which he could not have persevered in good if he would. He could persevere if he would, because that aid (*adjutorium*) did not fail by which he could. Without this he could not retain the good which he might will." Arminian theologians have always stressed this important aspect of primitive holiness, sometimes regarding the Holy Spirit as in close affiliation with man's estate and sometimes as acting more independently, but always present and operative. Thus Dr. Pope says, "This doctrine is incomplete without the addition of the supernatural gift of the Holy Ghost, if that may be called supernatural which belonged to the union of God with His elect creature .... He did not add the moral image, but He guided the principles of action of man's soul created in that image. This solves the difficulty sometimes expressed as to the creation of a char-

But this doctrine is incomplete without the addition of the supernatural gift of the Holy Ghost, if that may be called supernatural which belonged to the union of God with His elect creature. The Holy Trinity must be connected with every stage of the history of mankind. As the Protoplast was formed in the image of eternal Image—a son of God after the likeness of the only begotten Son, so he was under the spiritual and natural government of the Holy Spirit proceeding from the Father and the Son. He who brooded over the chaos, presided over all the successive dispensations of life in its advancing stages toward perfection, and was the supreme life inbreathed into the highest creature, took full possession of that new creature. He did not add the moral image, but He guided the principles of action of man's soul created in that image. This solves the difficulty sometimes expressed as to the creation of a character which, it is said, must of necessity be formed by him who bears it. Man was led of the Spirit, who was the power of love in his soul, already in his first estate, as now in his last estate. How long this holy discipline lasted we are not given to know; but we do know that the fall was its departure as a free and perfect education. This explains also the wonderful endowments of Adam, who reasoned and formed his language, and understood and gave names to his fellow creatures below him. The Lord God of the garden was the Holy Ghost in the human soul. The Spirit in man's spirit must not, however, be confounded with the image of God as such: the gift was distinct, but the true complement and perfection of every other gift. This is, as will be afterward seen, the secret of the trichotomy of body, soul and spirit in human nature.—POPE, *Compend. Chr. Th.*, I, p. 427.

acter which, it is said, must of necessity be formed by him that bears it. Man was led of the Spirit, who was the power of love in his soul, already in his first estate, as now in his last estate" (POPE, *Compend. Chr. Th.*, I, p. 427). Dr. Raymond states the same truth but from a somewhat different aspect. He says, "Others use the term original righteousness to signify the influences and agencies of the Holy Spirit which man enjoyed in his primeval state. That man enjoyed communion with his Maker; that the divine Spirit revealed to man a knowledge of God, and was with man a power of moral suasion to holy affections and holy volitions cannot be doubted. But to call this the righteousness of the man is plainly a misnomer. The term, to be of any valuable service, to represent any actually existing trait in man's original character, or any characteristic of his primal nature, should be used to express the perfection, the completeness of the whole nature and character. Man was originally righteous, constitutionally right, considered as to the whole and the parts of his being. He was a perfect man by creation" (RAYMOND, *Syst. Th.*, II, pp. 42, 43). Dr. Miley states the mediating position of Arminianism as follows: "We have previously dissented from the Augustinian limitation of that holiness to a mere quality of the Adamic nature. We have also dissented from the papal doctrine of its purely supernatural character; but the weighty objection, that it implies serious defects in the nature of man as originally constituted, is valid only against so extreme a view. The presence of the Holy Spirit as a constituent element of primitive holiness has no such implication. The Adamic nature could be holy in its own quality and tendency, and yet need the help of the Spirit for the requirements of a moral probation. . . . . Hence the divine plan might include the presence of the Spirit as an original and abiding element in the holiness of man. We need this truth for the proper interpretation of human depravity. The fall of man was not only the loss of holiness, but also the corruption of his nature. This corruption we may not ascribe to any immediate agency of God, but may interpret it as the consequence of the withdrawment of the presence and influence of the Holy Spirit. This is the doctrinal meaning of 'deprivation'" (MILEY, *Syst. Th.*, I, pp. 421, 422).

We close this discussion with a reference to the Scripture account of creation which declares that *God saw everything that he had made, and, behold, it was very good* (Gen. 1:31). By no possible interpretation can this refer to creation apart from man and, therefore, must express the divine approbation of man's goodness. Another text frequently quoted in this connection is from the Preacher, *Lo, this only have I found, that God hath made man upright; but they have sought out many inventions.* This cannot refer to man's conduct subsequent to his creation, and thus must refer to the rectitude of man's moral nature by creation. There are two texts in the New Testament, frequently quoted also, which have implications as to the original nature of man. *And that ye put on the new man, which after God is created in righteousness and true holiness* (Eph. 4:24); *And have put on the new man, which is renewed in knowledge after the image of him that created him* (Col. 3:10). These texts will be discussed more at length in connection with holiness as a state of grace, consequently it is sufficient here to point out, (1) that the transformation of grace here declared is something deeper than the life of personal action, and must therefore include the renovation of the moral nature; (2) this transformation is said to take place by the operation of the Holy Spirit—a purification of the moral nature; (3) this renewal is said to be a restoration to the original image in which man was created; hence (4) man must of necessity have been created holy —this holiness being a part of the original image of God in which he was created. We shall consider in the following chapters, some of the implications of this teaching, for which we have so carefully laid the foundation in this chapter.

CHAPTER XVIII
HAMARTIOLOGY

Hamartiology, or the Doctrine of Sin, is frequently treated as a branch of Anthropology. In such cases the doctrine of man is usually considered under two main heads—the *status integritas,* or man before the fall; and the *status corruptionis,* or man after the fall. Because of the importance of this doctrine, we prefer to treat it under a separate head. The word *Hamartiology* is derived from one of the several terms used to express the idea of sin—that of *hamartia* (ἁμαρτία), which signifies a deviation from the way or end appointed by God. The term is applicable to sin, both as an act and as a state or condition. As a doctrine it is closely interwoven with all the subsequent stages of theology, and therefore of fundamental importance to the whole system of Christian truth. "In every religion," said the saintly Fletcher, there is "a principle truth or error which, like the first link of a chain, necessarily draws after it all the parts with which it is essentially connected." In Christian theology this first link is the fact of sin. Since Christianity is a religion of redemption, it is greatly influenced by the various views concerning the nature of sin. Any tendency to minimize sin has its consequences in a less exalted view of the person and work of the Redeemer. The

In every religion there is a principal truth or error which, like the first link of a chain, necessarily draws after it all the parts with which it is essentially connected. This leading principle, in Christianity, distinguished from deism, is the doctrine of our corrupt and lost estate; for if man is not at variance with his Creator, what need of a Mediator between God and him? If he is not a depraved, undone creature, what necessity of so wonderful a Restorer and Saviour as the Son of God? If he be not enslaved to sin, why is he redeemed by Jesus Christ? If he is not polluted, why must he be washed in the blood of the immaculate Lamb? If his soul is not disordered, what occasion is there for such a divine Physician? If he is not helpless and miserable, why is he perpetually invited to secure the assistance and consolations of the Holy Spirit? And, in a word, if he is not born in sin, why is the new birth so absolutely necessary that Christ declares with the most solemn asseverations, without it no man can see the kingdom of God?—FLETCHER OF MADELEY.

three great central themes—God, sin and redemption are so interrelated that the views held concerning any one of them profoundly affect the other two.

In this chapter we shall consider the following subjects: (I) The Temptation and Fall of Man; (II) The Origin of Sin; (III) The Doctrine of Satan; and (IV) The Nature and Penalty of Sin.

The Temptation and Fall of Man

The Historical Character of the Genesis Account. We regard the account of the probation and fall of man found in Genesis 3:1-24, as an inspired record of historical facts, bound up with a deep and rich symbolism. All attempts to prove the account a collection of myths without divine authority; or to consider it an allegory in the sense of a divinely given illustration of truth apart from historical fact, must fail before the evidence which insists that the account is an integral portion of a continuous historical narrative. To lift this portion from the entire account and treat it as allegory, when the balance of the narrative is admittedly historical, is a procedure contrary to all accepted rules of interpretation. Furthermore the account is assumed as historical throughout both the Old and New Testaments. It is true that our Lord did

A large proportion of the church fathers, (for example, Justin, Irenæus, Theophilus, Tertullian, Augustine and Theodoret) and also most of the older theologians even in the Protestant church, were united in the opinion that this passage should not be explained as an allegory, although they differed among themselves in the interpretation of particular expressions. They agreed, however, for the most part, in considering the serpent as something else than a mere natural serpent, as it was regarded by Josephus and other Jewish interpreters. Some affirmed that the serpent was simply the devil—an opinion justly controverted by Vitringa, on account of the great difficulties by which it is encompassed. Others, and the greater part of the older Jewish interpreters, supposed that the serpent here spoken of was the instrument which was employed by the evil spirit to seduce mankind. So it is explained by Augustine, who was followed in this by Luther and Calvin; and this, from their time, was the prevailing opinion of Protestant theologians until the middle of the eighteenth century.—Knapp, *Chr. Th.*, p. 267.

We would not insist so strongly upon a literal exegesis as to say it is impossible that the account should be figurative, but on the other hand, we do insist that there is no necessity that we should consider it, and no advantage in doing so if we did. The Book of Genesis is historical in all its characteristics; it does not claim to be, nor does it appear to be, anything else than a literal record of actually occurring events.—Raymond, *Syst. Th.*, II, pp. 52, 53).

not directly refer to it; but if His words on divorce be weighed well, it will be seen that in sanctioning the Genesis account as historical, He must have indirectly included also, the account of the fall (cf. Matt. 19:4, 5; John 8:44). St. Paul in his epistles frequently refers to the Genesis account as historical (cf. II Cor. 11:3; I Tim. 2:13, 14). There are also undeniable allusions to the fall in the Old Testament (cf. Job 31:33; Hosea 6:7).

The Spiritual Meaning of the Paradisaical History. Both Bishop Martensen and Dr. Pope call attention to one of the aspects of the Paradisaical history which is overlooked by theologians in general, that is, "That the scene of Paradise though introduced into human history, belongs to an order of events very different from anything that human experience knows or can rightly appreciate. While the narrative is true, and every circumstance in it real, there is not a feature of the Paradisaical history of man that is purely natural, as we now understand the term. The process of human probation, whether longer or shorter, was supernaturally conducted by symbols, the deep meaning of which we know now only in part, though our first parents perhaps understood them by express teaching. The garden enclosed; the sacramental Tree of Life, the nourishment of conditional immortality; the mystical Tree of Knowledge, the fruit of which would reveal the profound secret of freedom; the one positive precept, representing the whole law;

It is precisely because Paradise lies outside the conditions of our present experience, that it is so easy a task for criticism to prove the impossibility of our forming for ourselves a picture of the first Adam. There is a certain analogy between the representation of Paradise, of the first conditions of human life; and the representation of the last conditions of human life, that is to say, of a future life. Both lie alike beyond the conditions of present experience; which is the reason why there are so many persons who esteem them as mere pictures of the fancy. But because we are not able to have any empirical intuition of the Paradise of our past or of our future, we are not on that account the less obliged to think of it, as we also see it in faith, as in a glass darkly. Although, therefore, the first Adam stands like a figure in the background of the human race, shrouded in a cloud, and with an undefined outline, a dim memory, as distinct as the recollection of the first awakening to self-consciousness in each individual; yet does the consciousness of the species, when directed upon itself, necessarily return to this dim memory; because without it the consciousness of the species would be entirely wanting in unity and connection.—MARTENSEN, *Chr. Dogm.*, pp. 153, 154.

the symbolical serpent form of the Tempter; the character of the threatenings and their fulfillment on all the parties; the exclusion from the garden and the flaming defenses of the forfeited Eden; all were emblems as well as facts, which almost without exception recur at the close of revelation in their new and higher meaning. Both in Genesis and in Revelation they are symbols or signs with a deep spiritual significance." Thus "the purely historical character of the narrative may be maintained in perfect consistency with a full acknowledgment of the large element of symbolism in it" (POPE, *Compend. Chr. Th.*, II, pp. 10, 11).

Some of the more orthodox theologians of the last century in their efforts to defend the historical character of the Mosaic account, failed to do justice to its rich symbolism. This not only narrowed the range of spiritual truth presented, but the method itself was out of harmony with the general trend of the Scriptures. Thus St. Paul did not deny the historical character of Sarah and Hagar when he said, *Which things are an allegory* (Gal. 4:24); neither did the author of Hebrews deny the historical facts concerning the giving of the law when he drew the parallel between Mount Sinai and Mount Sion (Heb. 12:18-24). The earlier Arminian and Wesleyan theologians were not under the necessity of combating destructive criticism, and hence took a truer and more scriptural position. Wakefield says that "though the literal sense of the history is thus established, yet that it has in its several parts, but in perfect accordance with the literal interpretation; a mystical sense, is equally to be proved by the Scriptures." Earlier than this Rich-

Dr. Pope says concerning the two trees in the garden, that they are symbols or signs with a deep spiritual significance. "The remembrance of this serves two purposes. It suggests our first parents were bound to their Creator by a religion which made all things around them sacramental, and some things more especially such. And it protects the simple details of the garden from the contempt of unbelievers, who see in them nothing but what appears on the surface of the narrative. The water of baptism and the eucharistic bread and wine are slight and common things in relation to the amazing realities they signify. But the infidel spirit finds nothing in these symbols to object against as such. Then why should it be thought a thing incredible that the two trees of Paradise should have borne sacramental fruit?"—POPE *Comp. Chr. Th.*, II, p. 11.

ard Watson reckons himself among those, "Who, while they contend earnestly for the literal interpretation of every part of the history, consider some of the terms used, and some of the persons introduced, as conveying a meaning more extensive than the letter, and as constituting several symbols of spiritual things and spiritual beings" (WATSON, *Dictionary, Art. The Fall of Man*). Only as the historical account is given its spiritual interpretation are we able to approach the depth of meaning which it holds for mankind.

Before taking up the study of the various events in the Paradisaical history, it may be well to mention the fact that the interpretation of these events has been the source of much controversy in the church. It is impossible, therefore, to give any thorough review of the literature on this subject. We shall note only the following: (1) *The Garden in Eden.* We are told that *the Lord God planted a garden eastward in Eden; and there he put the man whom he had formed* (Gen. 2:8). It is evident from this that God provided a special environment for the first pair, as a proper setting for their probationary trial. Dr. Shedd says that "the first sin was unique, in respect to the statute broken by it. The Eden commandment was confined to Eden. It was never given before or since. Hence the first Adamic transgression cannot be repeated. It remains a single, solitary transgression; the 'one' sin spoken of in Romans 5:12, 15-19" (SHEDD, *Dogm. Th.*, II, p. 154). (2) *The Tree of Life.* This not only represents the communication of divine life to man, but symbolizes, also, man's constant dependence upon God. If man but eat of the Tree of Life which is in the midst of the garden, then he is free also to eat of the other trees; for this act in itself, is a recognition of the divine sovereignty. It bears, therefore, a relation to the other trees in the garden, much as the bread of communion bears to bread as the staff of life. It is sacramental in that it gives meaning to the whole of life. Dr. Adam Clarke with others, held that the tree of life was intended as an emblem of that life which man should ever live, provided he continued in obedience to his Maker. And probably the use of this tree was intended as a means of preserving the body of man in a state of continual vital energy, and an antidote against death." (3) *The Tree of the Knowledge of Good and Evil.* Here a distinction must be made between a knowledge about evil, and a knowledge of evil as a reality in personal experience. "Man therefore ought to know evil," says Martensen, "only as a possibility that he has overcome; he ought only to see the forbidden fruit; but if he eats it, his death is in the act. If he attains the knowledge of evil as a reality in his own life, he has fallen away from his vocation, and frustrates the very object of his creation" (MARTENSEN, *Chr. Dogm.,* p. 156). (4) *The Serpent.* This mystical figure has been the occasion of much speculation in theology, and the views have varied from the strictest literalism to the purest symbolism. Perhaps the most widely accepted view is that which holds that the serpent was one of the higher created animals which Satan used as his instrument for securing the attention and making possible the conversation with Eve. Whatever else this figure may teach, two things are clearly evident—*first,* man was tempted by a spiritual being external to him-

Different opinions are held as to the agency of the temptation. Wakefield says, "The visible agent in man's seduction was the serpent, but the real tempter was that evil spirit called the devil and Satan. It is evident from the attributes and properties ascribed to the serpent, that some superior being was identified with it in the transaction. . . . . Here, then, without giving up the literal sense of the history, we must look beyond the letter, and regard the serpent as only the instrument of a superhuman tempter. In like manner and sentence pronounced upon the serpent, while it is to be understood literally as to that animal, must be considered as teaching more than is expressed by the letter, and the terms of it are therefore regarded as symbolical. The cursing of the serpent was a symbol of the malediction which fell upon the devil—the real agent in the temptation; while the prediction respecting the bruising of the serpent's head by the seed of the woman was indicative of man's redemption from the malice and power of Satan by our Lord Jesus Christ. The symbolical interpretation of the passage is confirmed by two considerations: (1) If the serpent was only a mere instrument employed by Satan, as was obviously the case, justice required that the curse should fall with its greatest weight upon the real seducer. But to interpret the history in a merely literal sense would confine the punishment entirely to the serpent, and leave the prime mover of the offense without any share in the malediction. (2) It would be ridiculous to suppose, under the circumstances, that the prediction respecting the bruising of the serpent's head was to be understood in no other than a literal sense."—WAKEFIELD, *Chr. Th.,* pp. 285, 286.

self; and *second,* this mystical figure furnished the instrumentality through which the Tempter gained access to our foreparents.

The extreme literalness of the account of the temptation by the serpent is best seen in the position of Dr. Knapp of Halle. He says, "The propriety and consistency of the account of the temptation by means of the serpent may be illustrated by the following remarks. The serpent was used by almost all the ancient nations as the symbol of prudence, adroitness, and cunning. Eve sees a serpent upon this forbidden tree, and probably eating of its fruits, which to a serpent might not be harmful. And it is very natural that this should be first observed by the woman. . . . . As to what follows, we very naturally understand that Eve reflected upon what she had seen, and expressed her thoughts in words. 'The serpent is a very lively and knowing animal, and yet it eats of the fruit which is forbidden us. This fruit cannot, therefore, be so hurtful, and the prohibition may not have been meant in earnest.' The same fallacies with which men still deceive themselves when the objects of sense entice and draw them away. The fact which she observed, that the serpent ate the fruit of the forbidden tree without harm, excited the thought which in verses 4 and 5 are represented as the words of the serpent, that it was worth while to eat this fruit. It did not seem to occasion death; and on the other hand, appeared rather to impart health, vigor and intelligence, as was proved from the example of the serpent, which remained after eating it, well and wise." "Consider me," the serpent might have seemed to say to her, "how brisk, sound and cunning I am." Now as she knows of no being who surpasses man in wisdom, excepting God only, she supposes in her simplicity, that if she became wiser than she then was, she would be like God. Meanwhile, the desire after that which was forbidden became continually more irresistible. She took of the fruit and ate. The man, who, as is common, was weak and pliable enough to yield to the solicitation of his wife, received the fruit from her and ate with her.—KNAPP, *Christian Theology,* p. 269.

Dr. Adam Clarke says, "We have here one of the most difficult as well as the most important narratives in the whole book of God." He calls attention to the word *nachash* which following the Septuagint is translated serpent. Through a labored argument he advances the theory that instead of the word *nachash* being translated serpent, it should have been translated ape. He comes to this conclusion on the ground that the Arabic word *chanas* or *khanasa* signifies, "he departed, drew off, lay hid, seduced, slunk away"; while the same root word *akhnas, khanasa* or *khanoos* all signify an ape, or satyrus, or any creature of the simia or ape genus. "Is it not strange," he asks, "that the devil and the ape should have the same name, derived from the same root, and that root so very similar to the word in the text?" Hence he argues that the *nachash* whatever it was had the following characteristics: (1) It was the head of all the inferior animals; (2) it walked erect; (3) it was endued with the gift of speech; (4) it was also endued with the gift of reason; and (5) these things were common to the creature, so that Eve evinced no surprise.

Richard Watson also argues along the same line. He says, "We have no reason to suppose, as is strangely done almost uniformly by commentators, that this animal had the serpentine form in any mode or degree at all, before his transformation."

Dr. Miley, and most Arminian theologians take the position that the serpent as an animal was merely the instrument in the temptation, and that the fact of intelligence connected with it evinces the presence of a higher agency.

The Probation of Man Necessary. If God was to be glorified by free creaturely service, man must be placed on probation, subjected to temptation, and this at the inevitable cost of the possibility of sin. Temptation, therefore, was permitted, because in no other way could human obedience be tested and perfected. The question immediately arises, How could a holy being sin? We must view this question as growing out of a misapprehension concerning the original nature of man. It implies that either man's will was not created free, or that it was created free in the Edwardean sense of being under the control of dominant motives. This latter, however, is after all only a necessitarian theory under the guise of freedom. Adam was indeed created holy, but not indefectibly so; that is, his will though conformed to the moral law was mutable because it was not omnipotent. Thus in God, as an infinite Being, voluntary self-determination could not be so reversed as to be considered a fall; while in finite beings such as men or angels, such a fall is possible. We may say with Dr. Shedd, that "A will determined to good with an omnipotent energy is not subject to change; but a will determined to good with a finite and limited force is so subject. By reason of the restricted power of his created will, Adam might lose the righteousness with which he was created, though he was under no necessity of losing it. His will had sufficient power to continue in holiness, but not so much additional power as to make a lapse into sin impossible" (cf. SHEDD, *Dogm. Th.*, II, p. 149). The Protestant position is ably stated in the Westminster Confession as follows: "God created man male and female, with righteousness and true holiness, having the law of God written in their hearts, and power to fulfill it: and yet under a possibility of transgressing, being left to the liberty of their own will, which was subject to change."

The schoolmen arranged the possible views concerning the will of Adam in its relation to sin as follows: *First*, if Adam's will was to move at all, it must of necessity result in sin. This is the *non posse non pecare* (not possible not to sin) view of the fall, and is held by those who find sin in the metaphysical imperfection of man, as did Leibnitz; or those who hold that sin is necessarily connected with the law of progress. Thus Kant and Schiller interpret the first transgression as a necessary transition of the reason from a state of nature to a state of culture; while Schleiermacher, Ritter and others, make sin the consequence of the superiority which the sensuous life had acquired over the spiritual. *Second,* Adam's will was neither holy nor unholy. It had no bias toward either the right or the wrong, and hence being in a state of equilibrium was free to move in either direction according to its own determination. This is the *posse pecare* (possible to sin) view which was held by the Pelagians, and which must be given much attention later. *Third,* Adam's will was holy, and therefore created with a tendency in the right direction, but not indefectibly so; that is, it had the power of reversing its course and moving in the opposite direction, and this solely through its own self-determination. This is the *posse non pecare* (possible not to sin) view and is generally accepted as the orthodox position. *Fourth,* it is conceivable that man might have been created holy, and free to forever advance in holiness, but not free to determine to the contrary. This is the *non posse pecare* (not possible to sin) view of the will but has never been held as an accepted doctrine in Christian theology.

We may now examine the account of the temptation in the light of the above statements, and in doing so, attempt to answer the question, "How can a holy being sin?"

1. Man by his very constitution is a self-conscious, self-determining being. He is a free moral agent, and hence has a capacity for performing moral action. Moral action in turn demands a law by which character is determined—a law which may be either obeyed or disobeyed by the subject. Otherwise there would be no moral quality, for neither praise nor blame could be attached to either obedience or disobedience. This would destroy the character of the moral agent. It is evident, therefore, that the power to obey or disobey is an essen-

tial element in a moral agent, and hence God could have prevented the fall only by the destruction of man's free agency.

2. Man was created holy, with spontaneous tendencies toward the right. But he was not created indefectibly so—that is, his holiness was not a fixed state. His will was not omnipotent, and therefore liable to change; his knowledge was not omniscient, and therefore deception was possible. We may say, then, that while man was created holy, nevertheless there existed in him certain susceptibilities to sin.

3. These susceptibilities lay in two directions—a lower and a higher. Man as composed of soul and body, becomes susceptible to the gratification of physical desires, which though lawful in themselves become the occasion of sin. From the higher or spiritual side of his being man may become impatient with the slow process of divine Providence, and become susceptible to suggestions which would seem to hasten the accomplishment of God's purpose. The use of false means in the attempt to attain good ends is a part of the deceptiveness of sin.

The probationary statute was a positive precept and not a moral command. The difference between the two lies chiefly in this, that in a positive command, the reason for it is hidden, while the very nature of a moral command embraces something of its propriety. Dr. Shedd in a reference to Anselm calls attention to this fact and points out that the Eden statute was thus a better test of implicit faith and obedience than a moral statute would have been, because it required obedience for no reason but the sovereign will of God. At the same time, this disobedience also involved a violation of the moral law, in that it was a contempt of authority, a disbelief of God and a belief of Satan, discontent with the existing state, impatient curiosity to know; pride and ambition. —cf. SHEDD, *Dogm. Th.*, II, pp. 153, 154.

The one absolute law had a negative and a positive form, as connected with the two symbolical trees of the garden: the Tree of Life and the Tree of Knowledge. The eating of the one was a positive condition of continued life and every benefit of creation; abstinence from the other was the negative condition.—POPE, *Compend. Chr. Th.*, II, p. 14.

Concerning the prohibition against eating the fruit from the tree of the knowledge of good and evil, Dr. Adam Clarke says, "The prohibition was intended to exercise this faculty in man, that it should constantly teach him this moral lesson, that there were some things fit and others unfit to be done; and that, in reference to this point, the tree itself should be a constant teacher and monitor. The eating of this would not have increased this moral faculty, but the prohibition was intended to exercise the faculty already possessed. There is certainly nothing unreasonable in this explanation: and, viewed in this light, the passage loses much of its obscurity. Vitringa strongly contends for this interpretation."—ADAM CLARKE, *Comm.*, Gen. 1:9.

HAMARTIOLOGY

4. The occasion of the temptation was the tree of the knowledge of good and evil, which the Lord God placed in the midst of the garden. The fruit of this tree was prohibited, doubtless as a positive instead of a moral commandment. However, if the opinion of Vitringa be allowed, the tree was intended to serve as a constant reminder that some things were fit and others unfit to be done, and that man is under the necessity of constantly exercising wise choices.

5. The agent in the temptation was the serpent, who as a deceptive spirit, presented God's good gifts in a false and illusory light. This was possible as an overemphasis, an underemphasis, or an otherwise perverting of the truth so as to place it in a setting of unrighteousness. Satan has nothing of his own to offer, and hence must tempt man solely through a deceptive use of God's gifts. It is for this reason that Bishop Martensen says that "The two momenta here described occur in every act of sin. No sin is committed without the presence of both fruit and serpent, an alluring phenomenon which attracts the sense, and an invisible tempter who holds up before man an illusory image of his freedom."

6. The deceitfulness of sin immediately appears. Presented in an illusive coloring, the temptation appeared good for food, pleasant to the eyes and a tree to be desired to make one wise. Led by the desire to think of its possible gratification, the good appeared to be that which God would wish to bestow; and since wisdom was desirable in intelligent beings, its increase would make man more like God. Hence a susceptibility was created for a false conclusion, into which Satan immedi-

---

It must not be supposed that the trees had any inherent virtue: the one to sustain life forever; the other to poison and corrupt the nature of man. The solemn eating of the fruit of the tree of life was only a sacrament of immortality; it was to the eating of every tree of the garden what the Christian Supper is to all other food. The fatal eating of the tree of knowledge was only the outward and visible sign of a sin which, by the divine law inwrought in human nature, would have been followed by shame and guilt and fear had no such tree existed. Through eating its fruit man came to the actual knowledge of good and evil, to the knowledge of his misery: a knowledge which made him acquainted with his own power over his destiny—as if he were his own god—and at the same time taught him that this power, independent of God, was his ruin.— POPE, *Compend. Chr. Th.*, II, p. 14.

ately injected the doubt, "Yea, hath God said." In the false glamor of the glittering fruit the truth was obscured—did God really mean to forbid its use; would He fulfill His threats, or could He even have intended them to be effective in prohibiting its use? The consequence is told in one brief sentence, *She took of the fruit thereof, and did eat, and gave also unto her husband with her; and he did eat* (Gen. 3:6).

The Fall of the Race. The external stages in the temptation we have endeavored to outline, but the internal reactions of the human spirit must forever remain a secret. There are two questions upon which Revelation gives us no special light—the mysterious point where temptation finds, because it creates, something to lay hold on, and thereby passes over into actual sin; and the manner in which the pure desire for knowledge passes into a desire for evil knowledge, or the sensibilities of the soul merge into evil concupiscence. Any knowledge of these matters must be gained indirectly from the scriptural account. However, there is considerable unanimity of opinion concerning the following points: (1) Sin began in the self-separation of the will of man from the will of God. Consequently the first formal sin is to be found in the entertainment of the question, "Yea, hath God said?" (2) Up to this point, the appetencies awakened were purely spontaneous, and the sensibilities innocent and entirely consistent with primitive holiness. (3) The only subjective susceptibility which Satan could address was the natural and innocent desire for the fruit of the tree of knowledge considered as good for food and pleasant to the eyes. (4) With the injection of the doubt, the desire for legitimate knowledge passed into a desire for illegitimate knowledge—of being wise like the gods. Such forbidden desire is sin (Rom. 7:7). This desire was originated by Adam himself, as something not previously existing in his submissive heart and obedient will. (5) With the severance of the self from God, the outward act was the look of concupiscence toward the tree, which had in itself it was the loss of divine grace by which man became subject to physical and moral corruption. If now we examine the fall in its external relations, we shall find that man no longer bears the glory of his moral likeness to God. The natural image in the sense of his personality he retained, but the glory was gone. From his high destination in communion with God, he fell into the depths of deprivation and sin. Having lost the Holy Spirit, he began a life of external discord and internal misery. In his domestic relations there was a deprivation of their intended perfection. No longer in the truer and best sense was the woman the glory of the man. In his relations with the external world of nature he found the earth cursed for his sake. No longer was he graciously provided with the abundance of the garden, but compelled to earn his bread by the sweat of his face. If we examine the fall from its internal aspect, we discover the birth of an evil conscience and a sense of shame and degradation. Having lost the Holy Spirit as the organizing principle of his being, there could be no harmonious ordering of his faculties, and hence the powers of his being became disordered. From this disordered state there followed as a consequence, blindness of heart, or a loss of spiritual discernment; evil concupiscence, or unregulated carnal craving; and moral inability, or weakness in the presence of sin. But even the heinousness of his sin and the shame of his fall did not result in the utter destruction of his being. The unseen hand of the promised Redeemer prevented it. Thus the mystery of sin and the mystery of grace met at the gate of Eden.

Having considered the origin of sin in the human race, we must now pursue the subject still further in a brief review of the philosophical theories concerning the origin of sin in the universe.

The effect of the sin or lapse of Adam was to bring him under the wrath of God; to render him liable to pain, disease and death; to deprive him of primeval holiness; to separate him from communion with God, and that spiritual life which was before imparted by God, and on which his holiness alone depended, from the loss of which a total moral disorder and depravation of his soul resulted; and finally to render him liable to everlasting misery.—WATSON, *Dictionary, Art. The Fall.*

The Origin of Sin

Christian Theology, as rooted in the Scriptures and the dominant thought of the Church, maintains that neither in a positive nor a negative sense is God the author of evil. The historical commencement of sin in our race was not due to an evil state, but to a sinful act, which in turn became inherent as both an evil and a sinful state. Evil existed previous to the fall of man, and in the person of Satan tempted man to sin. Thus in Protestantism the *Confessio Augustana* declares that "The cause of evil is to be found in the will of the devil and the godless who, immediately they were abandoned by God, turn from God to the Wicked One." So also the *Formula Concordiæ* and the *Variata* further confirm this position in the statement that "sin comes from the devil and the evil will of man." Philosophy, however, cannot rest content short of an attempt to explain the universality of sin by seeking for a common cause of its ultimate existence. These theories are commonly classified under two main heads—*first*, the Necessitarian Theories which either deny sin, or regard it as in some sense involved in the progress of the race; and *second*, the Libertarian Theories which find the origin of sin in the abuse of human freedom. To these there is sometimes added a *third*, or the Mediating Theories, which attempt a reconciliation of the above principles. These, however, are not of sufficient importance to demand attention. Since the question of the origin of sin is vitally connected with the next subject, that of Original Sin or Inherited Depravity, we shall give only a brief review

The Confessio Augustana mentioned above has sometimes been interpreted to mean that God is negatively the author of sin by the withdrawal of His hand, or the withholding of the *donum perseverantiæ*. This as will be readily seen, is closely related to the *donum superadditum* previously discussed. If righteousness is a supernatural gift, then it is dependent upon the continuance or perseverance of that gift. If God withdraws it, then man falls into sin. But this is not a true interpretation as is shown by the later creeds mentioned above. The withdrawal of God's presence must be regarded, not as a cause but an effect of sin.

Melanchthon's first edition of the Augsburg Confession is known as the *Invariata* and his three subsequent editions of 1531, 1535-1540, and 1540-42 are called the *Variata*.

of the philosophical explanations here, and reserve our theological treatment for the later discussion.

The Necessitarian Theories. The necessitarian theories either deny sin by obliterating the distinction between good and evil, as in the various forms of pantheism; by some form of finite limitation which admits the fact of sin but denies its reality; by maintaining an antagonism between the lower sensuous nature of man and his higher spiritual being, as in the evolutionary theories; or by a dualism which insists upon a necessary antagonism between the principles of good and evil, either temporary as in some of the dualistic forms of philosophy; or eternal, as in the case of ancient Persian dualism.

1. The pantheistic theories with their various modifications must either deny sin altogether, or make God its author. God is the absolute, and what seems to be the finite creature is only the Infinite in phenomenal exhibition. In the process of development there is either less or more of the element of Being. If less, then there is what men call evil; if more, it is correspondingly nearer perfection. Thus the transitory appearance is subject to metaphysical limitation, and this is considered sin. This, it will be readily seen, is simply the denial of sin as a reality.

2. The theories of Finite Limitation are closely related to the foregoing. (1) There is the theory that the finite or limited is as such, evil. Hence sin springs from the limitation of knowledge and power. The finite can approach the good only by passing into the infinite. This it will be seen is closely related to pantheism. (2) Another theory holds that sin is a mere negation. It is the simple absence of good, a deficiency rather than a matter of positive content. This theory is commonly attributed to Augustine, who held that if sin be regarded as a nonentity, theology would be under no necessity of seeking an efficient cause for it. Dr. Dickie points out that although this theory was in a measure accepted by Augustine, it was "the Neo-Platonist in him, and not the Christian that did so." It was this error which formed the philosophy underlying the theodicy of Leibnitz, in

the early modern period. In more modern times it was advocated by Dr. C. C. Everett of Harvard, in his *Essays Theological and Literary*. In every case, however, it may be said to be merely an expedient adopted by philosophy, in an attempt to defend the divine character for permitting evil in the world. (3) Still another theory, of even a more superficial character is held by those who view sin as appearing to be such, only because of our limited intelligences. We see only the fragments of the universe, it is said, never the whole. Seen at too close a range, it is like the daubs of paint on a canvas, which with proper perspective becomes a beautiful landscape. While this theory has been advanced with no little attractiveness in poetic disguise, it nevertheless fails to do justice to the fact of sin.

In reply to the above theories of sin we may say, (1) that sin cannot be defined as ignorance, because, it involves by its very nature the conscious choice of evil instead of good. It is further evident to all, that growth in knowledge is not necessarily a cure for sin. (2) Sin cannot be regarded as mere negation. Sin is a fact in the world and has phenomenal reality. Furthermore, sin must be regarded as a positive force which is both malignant and aggressive. For this reason the Scriptures use leaven as an emblem of its permeating power. (3) These facts also answer the theory that sin is merely a lack of perspective, due to limited finite intelligence. The philosophical answer, however, to all the above theories, is that they are forms of idealistic pantheism, which, traced to their logical conclusion, would find all finite forms of experience swallowed up in the experience of an Absolute. This philosophical Absolute is self-contradictory because it becomes at once holy and sinful,

---

Dr. Everett in the work mentioned above, says that "the most profound theologians have insisted that sin is a lack rather than a presence. Nothing is sinful in itself. The sinful act is such because it fills the place of a higher and better act. No tendency is wrong; it becomes so only when it is left alone by the failure of other tendencies which should complement it, and on occasion overpower it. Sin, then, is negative and not positive." It is evident that this fails to do justice to the scriptural ideas of sin. Sin, as Dr. James Orr views it, is "a power a tyranny, which defies all man's efforts in his natural strength to get rid of it."

omniscient and ignorant. The answer to these theories, therefore, is to be found in the answer to all pantheism.

3. The evolutionary theories, or those which find the origin of sin in the sensuous nature of man, depend upon the error that there is an essential antagonism between spirit and matter. In its earliest forms evil was regarded as an essential property of matter; in the modern evolutionary theories this antagonism is regarded as merely a stage in the genetic development of man. We may note the following positions: (1) In the earlier forms of Gnosticism evil was regarded as an essential property of matter, but later came to be regarded as merely accidental. Sin, therefore, was due to man's possession of a material body. The theory is untenable, for the Scriptures nowhere attach a moral quality to matter. Besides, some of the worst sins are not of the flesh but of the spirit—*idolatry, witchcraft, hatred, variance, emulations, wrath, strife, seditions, heresies, and envyings* (Gal. 6: 20). This error persists to the present in the belief held by many, that man cannot be delivered from sin while he dwells in a mortal body. (2) During the mediæval period, this sensuous theory took shape in the form of the Tridentine Decrees of the Roman Catholic Church. Here the lower nature was regarded as being under the restraint of the supernatural gift of grace. With the fall of man this restraint was withdrawn, and hence there was set in motion what came to be known as concupiscence. (3) At the beginning of the modern period Schleiermacher presented a most elaborate exposition of this theory, in which he made the antagonism to consist in the opposition between the God-consciousness in man, and his self-consciousness as related to the world. This conflict was explained by asserting that the higher powers of spiritual apprehension develop more rapidly than the powers of the will, and therefore we see the ideal before we are capable of realizing it. There is, he says, an even richer and fuller communication coming to man, and the antagonism consists in a refusal to receive it. In Christ, however, there is given to the world a revelation of what human nature did not and could not reach apart

from Him, in whom the God-consciousness was always perfectly ascendant and through whom it may become so to us. (4) The modern evolutionary theory is merely another application of the principle of antagonism between spirit and matter. It holds that the higher spiritual elements are developed out of the lower or sensuous part of man: but this sensuous part having been created first, the higher or spiritual part of man can never quite overtake it. As it concerns the origin of sin, the theory holds that moral evil is to be explained by a survival of those propensities which man's human ancestors, whatever they were, shared with the rest of the brute creation. Since the good is presented to man as a whole, and this can be only gradually realized in actual life; there is a disparity between the consciousness of his attainments and his goal. To this disparity guilt attaches. Since there can be no growth without the consciousness of imperfection, the weakness of this system lies in the fact that a consciousness of imperfection becomes a consciousness of sin. This subject is vitally related to the question of original sin and will be given further consideration under that head.

Dr. N. P. Williams in his Bampton Lectures for 1929 entitled, "The Ideas of the Fall and Original Sin," attempts an explanation of the fall constructed on the basis of modern evolutionary philosophy. He finds three complexes in human personality, the "herd complex," the "ego complex" and the "sex complex." In ideal personality, he holds that the herd complex would form an adequate counterweight to the other two, so that the soul would enjoy a condition of perfect equilibrium or poise on which conscious free will could play, reinforcing now one and now the other, of the dominant psychical structures and controlling, modifying, or inhibiting the flow of vital energy into them. The weakness of human nature, or what is essentially original sin, lies in this, that owing to the weakness of the herd instinct which feeds it, the herd complex does not possess anything like the vital energy necessary to place it on equal terms with the other two primary complexes, so as to preserve the equilibrium of the empirical self, or "me," which the transcendental self, or "I," needs in order to function with freedom (cf. pp. 491, 492). This appears to be a statement in psychological terms, and in so far as it contains truth, might be more simply expressed in the theological statement of prevenient grace, given to all men by virtue of the universal atonement in Christ. But the evolutionary phase of the above statement appears in the idea of a "herd instinct" or "herd complex" carried over from an animal ancestry of man. All such theories fail before the fact that sin consists in a self-severance of man's will from the will of God. This position only makes an adequate place for sin and the guilt which should attach to it.

4. The dualistic theories are perhaps the most ancient of all the attempts to explain the origin of sin. They hold that evil is a necessary and eternal principle in the universe. (1) The earliest expression of this is found in the religion of Parseeism (c. 1500 B.C.) and commonly known as Persian dualism. Zoroaster who is regarded as the real or imaginary founder of Parseeism, represented Ormuzd as the author of all good, and Ahriman as the author of all evil. The former dwelt in perfect light and the latter in the densest of darkness. These persons, later regarded as principles, were necessary and eternal. Each was independent of the other and ruled absolutely in his own dominion. Upon these fundamental principles, it was held, the whole visible world depended as to its origin, history and ultimate end. But the Persians could not rest ultimately in this dualism, hence there was a struggle upward to a belief in an eternal essence in which both would find their unity, and in the process of the ages their reconciliation. (2) Persian dualism reappeared in the Gnostic systems of the early church, which have been previously mentioned. (3) Manes (or Mani, 215-276 A.D.), a Persian, revived the ancient dualistic error, in what came to be known as Manichæism. However, he softened the antagonism by making it consist in the opposition of principles rather than persons. (4) Still later the Paulician heresy appeared in the seventh century and was revived again in the twelfth, but little is known of their teachings except that they held to a dualism in which evil appeared as the god of this world, and good as the god of the world to come. The error of all these systems lies in the belief that evil is an essential property of matter. (5) In modern philosophy Schopenhauer (1788-1860) and Hartmann (1842-1906) advocated a form of dualism based upon a distinction between the will and presentation, or the volitional and the

<small>The manner in which the rationalistic systems of philosophy account for sin, is scarcely less Christian than the theories of the ancient pagan religions. Thus Hegel regards sin as representing merely another stage in human development; Schleiermacher, Ritter, Lipsius and others represent it as a consequence of man's weakness of spirit and will; Ritschl regards sin as ignorance; while the modern evolutionary theory looks upon it as merely a stage of biological or moral development.</small>

logical, which they regarded as two mutually opposing powers in the Absolute. An equally futile theory is that of Schelling (1775-1854), who following Jacob Boehme (1575-1624), assumed that there was in God a dark, fiery principle, side by side with a light principle. By means of struggle and effort, the light principle breaks like lightning through the fire spirit, which although constantly overcome, yet remains as basic in the inner divine life. The self-working of this dark principle is the source of evil in the world. This theory is mentioned only because it has a tendency to reappear in the guise of a finite element in God. The heart of the dualistic theories lies in the fact that life does not exist without opposites; and the only solution of the problem is to be found in Christ—in whom all the contradictions of life are met and fully solved.

The Libertarian Theories. This class of theories is based upon the fact of freedom and its abuse. The erroneous theories need only brief mention. (1) Pelagianism holds that all sin originates in the abuse of freedom; that man is born without any bias to evil, and therefore character is due wholly to the nature of his choices. The only medium by which the sin of one person may be passed on to another is through the harm done by perverse influences. The philosophy of John Locke maintained a similar position as to the origin and transmission of sin. This theory fails to take into consideration all the facts of sin, especially that of original sin or human depravity. (2) The premoral theory holds that this abuse of freedom takes place in each individual, at the very beginning of personal life and antecedent to the memory. (3) The pre-existence theory of Origen was drawn from his Platonism. He held that each individual soul fell into sin in a pre-existent state. This theory was revived in modern times by Julius Mueller of Halle, one of the meditating theologians who followed Schleiermacher. To him this was the only solution of a dilemma which he stated as follows: "If it is impossible to escape sin, what place is there for freedom, the necessary presupposition of the sense of guilt? If freedom is a reality, how is it that there is no escape from sin?" Dr. Dickie points out, that aside from other defects, it falls into the serious error of too closely identifying sin and guilt; and that failure here leads to the denial of the guilty character of all sin. "This position," he says, "like every other which makes sin in any way necessary, is fundamentally unchristian" (cf. DICKIE, *Organism of Chr. Truth*, p. 146).

It is under this head, also, that we find what is known as the orthodox or ecclesiastical theory of sin, which in a more scriptural manner than the above, likewise finds the source of all evil in the abuse of freedom. To this we must now give attention.

The Biblical Teaching Concerning the Origin of Sin. The ultimate origin of evil can never be known by philosophy, nor can its purpose be discovered. We are here shut up to the disclosures which God has given us in His holy Word. We have a ray of light in the words of our Lord Jesus concerning the man born blind. His reply to the Jews was, *Neither hath this man sinned, nor his parents: but that the works of God should be made manifest in him* (John 9:3). Sin is called "the mystery of iniquity" (II Thess. 2:7; Rev. 17:5), and has excited the interest of speculative minds in every age, only to baffle them. But the Scriptures do give us a clue to the ultimate origin of sin, and this, even from the philosophical viewpoint is the most satisfactory answer which has ever been given to this perplexing question. The Bible connects the origin of sin with the abuse of freedom in free and intelligent creatures. We have already considered the account of man's temptation and fall, and found that the origin of sin in the human race was due to the voluntary self-separation of man from God. We took into account, also, that man was influenced by some superhuman power, and consequently are led to believe that sin existed in the universe before its origin in man. We may well suppose, also, that sin in the universe originated in the same manner as it did in the human race, the free choice of an intelligent being. This leads us immediately to a consideration of the doctrine of Satan or superhuman evil.

74   CHRISTIAN THEOLOGY

The Doctrine of Satan

Man was tempted by a superhuman being, called in the Scriptures, the devil or Satan. Evil then must have had an existence previous to the origin of the human race and external to it. The conflict between good and evil is in the Scriptures represented as essentially a conflict between superhuman powers, into which man is drawn by way of temptation. Hence we read that the church is called upon to wrestle against *principalities, against powers, against the rulers of darkness of this world, against spiritual wickedness in high places* (Eph. 6:12). Satan is usually regarded as one of the fallen angels and consequently treated under this head. This it seems to us, does not do justice to the importance of the subject. Satan is not merely one among the many representatives of evil. He is evil *in persona*. He is not merely evil in this or that relation, but evil in and for itself. In order to present the scriptural teaching on this subject, we shall present it under four heads as follows: (1) Satan in Relation to Creation; (2) Satan in Opposition to Christ; (3) Satan and the Redemptive Work of Christ; and (4) The Kingdom of Satan.

Attempts have been made to show that the doctrine of Satan in the Old Testament cannot be traced prior to the time of the Babylonian Captivity. If this be understood to mean that the Jews did not know of evil angels previous to that time, the position can be easily refuted from the Scriptures. Aside from the one reference in Zech. 3:1, 2, there is perhaps no reference to Satan in the post-Babylonian Scriptures, while there are numerous passages in the earlier books. (Cf. Job 1:6; I Chron. 21:1; Psalms 109:6 and 106:37.) There are also numerous references to evil angels under the name of "evil spirits" as in Judges 9:23; I Sam. 16:14 and others. The doctrine is more fully developed in the New Testament. Including the singular and plural forms of the word *diabolus* it is used forty times in the New Testament, the word Satan twenty-three times, evil spirit eight times, dumb spirit three times, and spirit of divination once.

Bishop Martensen in his Christian Dogmatics, pp. 186-203, gives us an attractive and interesting presentation of this subject. He has been accused of holding to a merely impersonal view of Satan as the "cosmical principle" limited to a creation and having no existence otherwise. This it seems to us is not a true statement of his position. Some of his statements, however, do not seem to be carefully guarded, and if lifted out of the whole discussion and interpreted by themselves, would seem to indicate that Satan is nothing more than this impersonal principle, which in this case would become the ultimate evil. Bishop Martensen's tendency is toward the cosmological, rather than the soteriological view of theology.

Satan in Relation to Creation. We have seen in our study of creation, that the Christian position maintains that there is an essential difference between God and the world. Both have reality or substantial existence—the one Absolute and Infinite, the other dependent and finite. In this way Christian thought preserves itself from the error of dualism on the one hand, and pantheism on the other. But because created things have reality in themselves, even though this be finite and dependent, there is the possibility of this created substance being set up in opposition to the Infinite, the creature against the Creator. This Bishop Martensen called the "cosmic principle" of the universe. In the realm of material things, this cosmic principle exists solely as a possibility. Hence the First and Second Commandments of the Mosaic law prohibited idolatry and the making of graven images as objects of worship. In man as a finite being endowed with self-consciousness and self-determination, there not only exists the possibility, but also the power of setting himself up in opposition to his Creator. This power of self-separation we have seen, marks the origin of sin in man. The account of the fall also reveals the presence of a superhuman power as the tempter of mankind. As to the nature of this power, the Scriptures teach us that in the purely spiritual realm there were angels which kept not their beginning, or first estate; and hence there appears to have been a fall in the spiritual realm previous to that of the human race. Nor are we to suppose that the angels simultaneously and volun-

Temptation from without was more than symbolized by the instrument—fallen now like the real tempter himself from his first estate—of that old serpent, called the devil, and Satan, which deceiveth the whole world. The distinctness of this record is of great importance. It establishes a difference between the original sin of earth and the original sin of the universe. We need not, indeed, assume that the angels who fell were only tempted from within: there is every reason to think that, as through envy of the devil came death into the world, so through the same envy, excited by another Object in heaven, death entered among the angels. It cannot be that sin should have its origin within the spirit of a creature of God independently of solicitation from without. But, in the case of man, the agency of Satan is made prominent from the beginning of Scripture to the end: not as reducing the guilt of the first transgression but as mitigating its punishment, and suggesting at least a difference put between sinful angels and the human race.—POPE, *Compend. Chr. Th.*, II, p. 14.

tarily fell, merely by temptation from within. There must have been among them a tempter who led them astray. Thus the Christian view of evil, in so far as it is set forth in the Scriptures, terminates in the idea of Satan, who as a superhuman, yet created spirit, originally good, fell from his high estate and became the enemy of God. Evil is personal in its origin. Beyond this reason cannot go and revelation is silent.

Satan in Opposition to Christ. St. John makes it clear that Satan is *that spirit of antichrist* which should come, and even now is in the world. The essential antagonism of this spirit to Christ finds its expression in the fact that he does not confess that Jesus Christ is come in the flesh (I John 4: 1-3). Furthermore sin, in the New Testament use of the term, is to be interpreted by the attitude which men take toward Christ. Thus the Holy Spirit convinces men of sin, because they believe not on Him; of righteousness because He goes to the Father; and of judgment, because the prince of this world is judged (John 16: 8-11). But if we would understand it rightly, we must trace this opposition back to its source. Referring again to our discussion of Creation and the Logos, we are now in a position to comprehend more clearly the deep significance of this truth. God created the world through the Logos or Word as the intermediary between Himself and the created universe. This Logos or Word was the Eternal Son, the second person of the Trinity. In Him as the express image of the Father were comprehended all the principles of truth, order, beauty, goodness and perfection. Hence as long as the relation between the finite

Dr. A. H. Strong points out some of the contrasts between the Holy Spirit and the spirit of evil as follows: (1) The dove and the serpent; (2) the father of lies and the Spirit of truth; (3) men possessed by dumb spirits and men given wonderful utterance in diverse tongues; (4) the murderer from the beginning and the life-giving Spirit, who regenerates the soul and quickens our mortal bodies; (5) the adversary and the Helper; (6) the slanderer and the Advocate; (7) Satan's sifting and the Master's winnowing; (8) the organizing intelligence and malignity of the Evil One and the Holy Spirit's combination of all the forces of matter and mind to build up the kingdom of God; (9) the strong man fully armed and a stronger than he; (10) the Evil One who works only evil and the Holy One who is the author of holiness in the hearts of men. The opposition of evil angels, at first and ever since their fall, may be a reason why they are incapable of redemption.—STRONG, *Syst. Th.,* II, p. 454.

and the Infinite was mediated through the Logos, it retained its true relationship to God. But as we have indicated in the previous paragraph, finite reality has in it the possibility of being set up in false relation of independency; or in the case of creatures endowed with self-consciousness and self-determination, the power of setting themselves up in this false relation through a voluntary self-separation from God. It is evident, therefore, that between God and the created universe two forms of mediation are possible, the one of truth and righteousness, the other of falsehood and sin.

We begin now to see something of the magnitude of Satan and sin. If we place over against the Logos a created being of such glory and power as would be worthy of God's created spirit—a true "son of the morning"; and if with the mystics we hold that this being contemplated his own beauty as self-contained, and becoming envious of the Son, sought to sit upon His throne, then we may begin to understand the Scripture which indicates that being lifted up with pride, he fell into condemnation. To this doubtless Jesus referred when He said, *I beheld Satan as lightning fall from heaven* (Luke 10:18). Its magnitude will be seen in this, that both Christ and Satan appear as mediators between God and the world, the one a true mediatorship of righteousness and holiness; the other a false mediatorship of unrighteousness and sin. Hence St. Paul speaks of Satan as "the god of this world" (II Cor. 4:4), and again as "the prince of the power of the air"—the spirit that now worketh in the children of disobedience (Eph. 2:2). St. John writes with discrimination when he says, "the whole world lieth in wickedness," or in the wicked one; not that the world is inherently evil, but lying in the wicked one, is perverted from the true purpose of its existence. The evil spirit as Satan (Σατανᾶς) is the "adversary," the "accuser" and the "deceiver"; as the devil (διάβολος) he is the "slanderer," the "calumniator" and the "destroyer of peace"; as Belial (Βελίαλ) he is the "low," the "unworthy" and the "abject"; while as Apollyon (Ἀπολλύων) he is the "destroyer." We may contemplate the fact of sin, also, in a new light, as the perversion of God's good gifts to false uses; the holding of the truth in unrighteousness; the false glamor of the things of God presented in a deceitful manner, the works of the flesh and the hollowness of insincerity. Sin is like leaven, in that it must feed upon another substance than itself, and in so doing corrupts and sours the whole.

Satan and the Redemptive Work of Christ. For the sake of clarity, we may now be permitted to place this whole subject over against the redemptive work of Christ, and thus set forth with greater clearness the nature of Satan and sin. We have seen that in creation, there is the possibility of the creature exalting itself against the Creator, and by a voluntary self-separation from God setting itself up in a false independency. Thus Satan in opposition to Christ as the true Logos, set himself up as a mediator of the "cosmical principle" of independency or self-sufficiency. Working in creation as the principle of perversion and sin, he thus hypostasizes evil in and for itself. Not having the power of creation himself, he is limited in his scope of activity to the per-

St. Peter tells us that the apostate angels were cast down to hell. Here the word "Tartarus" is used, the only place in the New Testament where it occurs. "By Tartarus," says Dr. Dick, "they understood the lowest of the infernal regions, the place of darkness and of punishment, in which those who had been guilty of impiety toward the gods, and of great crimes against men, were confined and tormented. The word as adopted by the apostle conveys the same general idea."

Here the question may be proposed, "Why was not provision made for the recovery of fallen angels, as well as for that of man?" but to this no decisive answer can be returned. Still there are some circumstances connected with their history, as also with the history of our race, which may reflect some light upon this mysterious subject, and which are therefore worthy of our consideration. (1) They were doubtless superior to man in intellectual endowments, and therefore less liable to be deceived. (2) As man was partly material and subject to the influence of the senses, his attention might have been diverted and his judgment biased by allurements addressed to them. But angels were purely spiritual beings and therefore could not have been liable to any such temptation. (3) The progenitor of the human race sustained a federal relation to all his posterity. In him they either stood or fell. But among the angels no such relation existed as they were individually responsible. (4) Man sinned in the earthly paradise through the subtilty of a tempter; but angels sinned in the heavenly paradise without a tempter. For though we do not possess a history of their apostasy yet we know that they were not solicited, as man was, by some being of superior artifice, because they were the sole inhabitants of heaven.—WAKEFIELD, *Chr. Th.*, p. 260. While not tempted by one outside their number, it seems clear from the preceding that they nevertheless fell through one of their own number.

version of those things which have the substantiality of God's creation. Hence he becomes *diabolos* (διάβολος) the deceiver and calumniator of whom Jesus said, *He was a murderer from the beginning, and abode not in the truth, because there is no truth in him. When he speaketh a lie, he speaketh of his own: for he is a liar, and the father of it* (John 8:44). We may believe that his first sphere of operation was in his own realm of the angels. Thus St. Peter says that *God spared not the angels that sinned, but cast them down to hell, and delivered them into chains of darkness, to be reserved unto judgment* (II Peter 2:4).

God then in His wisdom extended creation beyond the purely spiritual realm and created man as a being in whom were conjoined both spiritual and material substances. Furthermore He created man, not as an aggregate of individuals, but as a race of beings interrelated and dependent, and with the power of propagating their own kind. In creation man was so constituted that subjectively he was a creature dependent upon his Creator, and consequently a servant of God. In the physical realm man was the highest of all the creatures and therefore, in a true sense, the lord of creation. When man in this intermediary position looked up to God he saw himself as a servant; when he looked out upon creation he saw himself as its lord. In the temptation Satan made the lordship to appear more attractive than the servantship. He said, *Ye shall be as gods* (Gen. 3:5). But what Satan did not tell him was that this lordship was a delegated power, and that he held it by virtue of a faithful stewardship. When man fell, therefore, he ceased to be the servant of God and became the servant of Satan. Hence our Lord said of the unbelieving Jews, *Ye are of your father the devil, and the lusts of your father ye will do* (John 8:44). God is the Father of all men, because He always acts as a Father, but men are not always the sons of God because they do not act as sons. Losing his servantship, man lost his true lordship, and now makes all things minister to himself. He views the world from a false slant. He sees everything from a biased standpoint.

The things of God committed to his care he holds as his own. Like his father, Satan, he has become a usurper of the throne, untrue to his trust, a servant of sin and a child of Satan.

But God will forever triumph. He will make even the wrath of man to praise Him. He projects creation still farther, if we may thus guardedly use the term. He creates a new man—not merely a living soul, but a quickening spirit. As in the first man the spiritual rested in the material; so in this new man, the divine rests in the human. This new creation is an incarnation. The Son of God, who was made in the likeness of sinful flesh, took upon Him the form of a servant and became obedient unto death, even the death of the cross (Phil. 2: 6-8). By virtue of this true servantship, Christ brought man in His own Person back into his original relationship with God. He re-established spiritual fellowship and communion. As the Captain of our salvation He met the cross currents of the world and suffered at every step. But He never faltered and consequently overcame even the last enemy which is death. As a servant, He came not to be ministered unto, but to minister and to give His life a ransom for many. And having met the demands of a perfect servantship, He became the Lord of His people—not this time by creation, for that He never lost, but as their Redeemer, their Saviour and Lord. Having thus triumphed, He received the promise of the Holy Spirit, which now as the Lord of the Church, He gives freely to all who believe. Thus we may say with all the

To the argument frequently advanced that Jesus and the apostles merely accommodated themselves to the language and beliefs that were current in their day, Dr. Whately says, "Nor can it be said that Jesus and His apostles merely left man in their belief, not thinking it worth while to undeceive them, and trusting that in time they of themselves would discover their mistakes. On the contrary, our Lord and His followers very decidedly and strongly confirm the doctrine by numerous express declarations. For instance, our Lord in His explanation of the Parable of the Tares and Wheat, says expressly that the enemy who sows the tares is the devil. And again, in explaining that portion of the Parable of the Sower in which it is said that the birds devoured the seed that fell on the trodden wayside, he says, 'Then cometh the evil one, and snatcheth away that which hath been sown in his heart.' If, therefore, the belief in evil spirits is altogether a vulgar error, it certainly is not an error which Jesus and His apostles merely neglected to correct, or which they merely connived at, but which they decidedly inculcated."

redeemed, *Blessing, and honour, and glory, and power, be unto him that sitteth upon the throne, and unto the Lamb forever and ever* (Rev. 5:13).

The Kingdom of Satan. Since the work of Satan is to pervert the things of God, this perversion must extend also to the conception of the kingdom. As there is a kingdom of God and of heaven, so also there is a kingdom of Satan and of evil. Hence we have a reference to principalities, powers and rulers of darkness, which can indicate no other than an organization of evil forces. These are under the leadership of "the prince of this world" which Jesus mentions as being "cast out" (John 12:31), as having nothing in Him (John 14:30) and as being judged (John 16:11). St. Paul speaks of Satan as "the prince of the power of the air" (Eph. 2:2) and of "the spiritual hosts of wickedness" (Eph. 6:12, R.V.). That there are a great number of evil spirits under the leadership of Satan is indicated by a number of scriptures, as "My name is Legion" (Mark 5:9), and the lake of fire prepared for "the devil and his angels" (Matt. 25:41). This kingdom shall not stand, for *the accuser of our brethren is cast down, which accused them before our God day and night. And they overcame him by the blood of the Lamb, and by the word of their testimony* (Rev. 12:10, 11).

"The Scriptures clearly and emphatically teach the separate, distinct and personal existence of a devil, and of an innumerable host of evil spirits commonly called devils. While, in the strict propriety of scripture language, there is but one devil—the prince of the power of the air—one Belial—one adversary—he is joined by a host of evil spirits, partaking of the same nature and engaged in the same work with the father of lies. . . . Those who deny the personal existence of a devil have strangely different methods of interpreting the Scriptures. One says the devil personifies some evil principle; another says it is the evil propensity of the heart; while others say the devil means disease, madness, or insanity. A few plain passages of scripture will show the absurdity of this method of interpreting God's Holy Word. The sacred writers were not so careless as to use language vaguely. If there is no personal devil, how are we to understand the case of the man that dwelt among the tombs, as recorded in Mark 5:2-16 and Luke 8:27-38? This man was possessed of many devils. These devils 'besought him.' They 'came out from the man.' They 'entered into the swine.' These devils had a personal existence separate and apart from the man out of whom they were cast. They entered into the man and went out of him. They existed before they entered into him and they existed after they went out. The actions ascribed to these devils are such as belong only to real personal beings."—BISHOP WEAVER, *Christian Theology,* pp. 106, 107.

The Nature and Penalty of Sin

Having considered the philosophical theories as to the origin of sin, we may now turn our attention to the historical aspects of the subject. Here we shall consider the nature and development of sin as an actual experience in the history of the race. Our best approach will be by means of a brief survey of the terms used in the Scriptures to express the idea of sin. These words are *hamartia* (ἁμαρτία), *parabasis* (παράβασις), *adikia* (ἀδικία), *anomia* (ἀνομία), and *asebeia* (ἀσέβεια), with their many derivatives.

1. The word *hamartia* (ἁμαρτία) signifies a falling away from, a missing of the right way, or a missing of the mark. The word for sin is sometimes connected with the word iniquity, both of which signify a deflection from the right. In this sense the word for sin indicates a missing of the mark, while the word for iniquity signifies a wrong aim. In the Old Testament there are a number of words used to express the idea of sin, such as "falling away," "going astray," "vanity" and "guilt." This indicates that the subject was more fully developed among the Hebrews than among the Greeks, due, doubtless, to the emphasis placed upon the holiness of God. None of these designations of sin, however, in either Hebrew or Greek, limit the idea to a mere act. In fact they more naturally suggest the thought of sin as a disposition or a state. Thus *hamartia* conveys the idea that a man does not find in sin what he seeks therein; hence as Julius Mueller points out, he finds it a state of delusion and deception.

2. The second word is *parabasis* (παράβασις) which signifies sin as an act of transgression. This indicates that the idea of sin is limited by the idea of law, *For where no law is, there is no transgression* (Rom. 4:15). In the broadest sense, this law must be interpreted as the existence of an eternal moral order, with its distinctions of good and evil. This finds its earliest manifestation in the claims made by the conscience. In a more specific sense law is not advice or exhortation, but a positive demand. Consequently the relation to it must be either subjection

or transgression. But sin as thus indicated, is possible only to moral and rational beings. Hence brutes and infants may do wrong, but in this sense of the term they cannot sin. Man knows himself unconditionally under law by both reason and conscience. When that claim is disowned, in that instant sin is born.

3. But law cannot be regarded as impersonal. It is of necessity immediately connected with the Law-giver. Hence to transgress the law is positive disobedience regarded as a personal affront. Thus St. Paul says, *the law worketh wrath* (Rom. 4:15). Here the word is *parabasis* as previously indicated, but the point of emphasis now is, that voluntary disobedience subjects the offender to the wrath of the personal Law-giver. Virtue is therefore of the nature of obedience, and sin is disobedience to God, even when the wrong committed is against one's neighbor. In the Christian system morality is always included in the law of God. The sinner, therefore, who violates the law of God becomes a rebel in the moral realm. For this reason sin is frequently regarded as a breaking of a covenant through unfaithfulness as the word *parapiptein* (παραπίπτειν) denotes.

4. The next step in the progress of our thought is, that the character of the law and the character of the

Dr. Bruce says, "To understand Paulinism, we must carefully note the distinction between ἁμαρτία and παράβασις. 'Αμαρτία is objective and common; παράβασις is subjective and personal. 'Αμαρτία entails some evil effects, but παράβασις is necessary to guilt and condemnation" (cf. MACPHERSON, *Chr. Dogm.*, p. 247).

Dr. Olive M. Winchester calls attention to the fact that the above words for sin having the abstract ending ια denote "state" or "quality." Thus ἁμαρτία in the singular denotes sin as a state or quality, and in the plural "sins." There is also another noun from this verb ἁμάρτημα, a concrete noun instead of an abstract, and therefore denoting a thing or an act.

"Sin and lawlessness are convertible terms. Sin is not an arbitrary conception. It is the assertion of the selfish will against a paramount authority. He who sins breaks not only by accident or in an isolated detail, but essentially the 'law' which he was created to fulfill. This 'law' which expresses the divine ideal of man's constitution and growth has three chief applications. There is the 'law' of each man's personal being: there is the 'law' of his relation to things without him: there is the 'law' of his relation to God. To violate any part of this threefold law is sin, for all parts are divine" (James 2:10).—WESTCOTT, *Comm.* I John 3:4.

Dr. Westcott also points out that St. James regards sin as selfishness (1:14ff), and also the neglect of duty, or the violation of the law of growth (Jas. 4:17). St. John holds that "unrighteousness," or the failure to fulfill our obligations to others is also sin (I John 3:4).

Law-giver are indissolubly one. Hence the substance of the commandment is comprehended in the one word *"love."* This we have on the authority of our Lord, who when asked which is the great Commandment of the law replied, *Thou shalt love the Lord thy God with all thy heart, and with all thy soul, and with all thy mind. This is the first and great commandment. And the second is like unto it, Thou shalt love thy neighbour as thyself. On these two commandments hang all the law and the prophets* (Matt. 22:37-40). Here it will be seen that sin, flowing from a lack of love, is both an act and a quality of being. It is for this reason that St. John uses the word *adikia* in connection with *hamartia*. He says, *If we confess our sins,* [ἁμαρτίας], *he is faithful and just to forgive us our sins* [ἁμαρτίας], *and to cleanse us from all unrighteousness* [ἀδικίας] (I John 1:9). Following this he gives us the first of his profound and far-reaching definitions of sin. *All unrighteousness* [ἀδικία] *is sin* [ἁμαρτία] (I John 5:17). The word *adikia* signifies the absence of righteousness and consequently is generally translated as unrighteousness, injustice and sometimes as iniquity, although the latter is generally derived from another Greek word. The term means "crookedness" or a bending or perverting of what is right. Hence like the words *hamartia* and *anomia*, it signifies not only perverted actions, but also a state of unrighteousness or disorder, arising from such perversion. Sin, then, is self-separation from God in the sense of decentralization, the place which should be occupied by God being assumed by the self. The love of self which characterizes this state must not be thought to possess the true quality of love. As disobedience to the law of God is not a mark of strength but of weakness, so the love of self is not merely misplaced or exaggerated love, but manifests the very opposite character. Everything either flows from the self or is directed to it. The perfection of love as manifested in Christ, was found in the fact that He did not seek to please Himself (Matt. 22:37-40); and that He did not seek His own (I Cor. 13:5). On the other hand, St. Paul declares that the acme of sin in the last days would

HAMARTIOLOGY

be found in this, that "they were lovers of themselves" (II Tim. 3:1, 2). Thus *adikia* signifies a state or condition, wherein the center around which his thoughts, affections and volitions should revolve is displaced, and hence has become one of unrighteousness. For this reason St. John speaks of sins being forgiven, but unrighteousness as being cleansed.

5. The next word is *anomia* (ἀνομία) and is found in St. John's second definition of sin, although the text appears earlier in the epistle. It is placed second because it involves the use of a stronger term. The definition is found in the following text, *Whosoever committeth sin [ἁμαρτίαν] transgresseth also the law [ἀνομίαν]: for sin [ἁμαρτία] is the transgression of the law [ἀνομία]* (I John 3:4). Here the word *anomia* does not signify transgression in the sense of an overt act, but as "a lack of conformity to law," or "lawlessness." It is a stronger term than *adikia*, in that it does not signify merely a disordered state, but as added to this, the thought of hostility or rebellion. Thus Jesus said, *If I had not done among them the works which none other man did, they had not had sin: but now have they both seen and hated both me and my Father* (John 15:24). In this connection Van Oosterzee says, "Even the tenderest love is not free from a hidden selfishness, and love changes into hate, where the self-denial which it demands is rejected by flesh and blood. It even rises sometimes to the desire that there were neither law nor law-giver and, where a man can withdraw himself from the supremacy of the former at any cost, to powerless rage and spite, as seen in the Cain of Lord Byron .... and where a man dethrones God in order to deify self, he becomes at last destitute of natural

St. John's definition is important, as showing the difference between the act of transgression and the state of transgression. The words mean that the act is the result of the state, and the state also the result of the act. Sin is only the act of a primitive transgressing will, but that will forms the character behind the future will and shapes its ends. This final statement of St. John may be divided into its two branches, each of which will shed light upon the general terminology of Scripture. Sin is the voluntary separation of the soul from God: this implies the setting up of the law of self activity, and passively the surrender to internal confusion.—POPE, *Comp. Chr. Th.*, II, p. 30.

affection" (Rom. 1:31) (cf. Van Oosterzee, *Chr. Dogm.*, II, p. 395).

6. The last word which we shall mention is *asebeia* (ἀσέβεια), or ungodliness. This not only marks the separation of the soul from God, but carries with it the thought of a character unlike God and a state or condition characterized by the absence of God. It is a strong term. St. Paul uses it in his condemnation of sin in connection with *adikia*. *For the wrath of God is revealed from heaven against all ungodliness* [ἀσέβειαν] *and unrighteousness* [ἀδικίαν] *of men, who hold the truth in unrighteousness* [ἀδικία] (Rom. 1:18; cf. Eph. 2:12). The term also carries with it the thought of a verging toward doom. Thus St. Jude says, *Behold, the Lord cometh with ten thousands of his saints, to execute judgment upon all, and to convince all that are ungodly* [ἀσεβεῖς] *among them of all their ungodly* [ἀσεβείας] *deeds which they have ungodly* [ἠσέβησαν] *committed, and of all their hard speeches which ungodly* [ἀσεβεῖς] *sinners have spoken against him* (Jude 14, 15).

Definitions of Sin. Theologians have defined sin in different ways, but rarely is the fact overlooked that sin exists both as an act and as a state or condition. This is important in any system of theology where the evangelical principle of salvation by faith is given prominence. We have already cited Dr. Pope's definition that "Sin is the voluntary separation of the soul from God." This we have seen implies, *first,* a setting up of the law of self-activity, or actual sin; and *second,* the surrender, to internal confusion, or original sin. James Arminius defines sin as "something thought, spoken, or done against the law of God, or the omission of something which has been commanded by that law to be thought, spoken or done." Mr. Wesley's definition of sin as "a voluntary transgression of a known law" is familiar in Arminian theology. According to Dr. Miley, "Sin is disobedience to a law of God, conditional on free moral agency and opportunity for knowing the law." Dr. Raymond emphasizes the twofold nature of sin. He says, "The primary idea designated by the term sin in the

Scriptures is want of conformity to law, a transgression of law, a doing of that which is forbidden or a neglecting to do that which is required. In a secondary sense the term applies to character; not to what one does, but to what he is" (RAYMOND, *Syst. Th.*, II, pp. 54, 55). Van Oosterzee defines sin as "a positive negation of God and His will, in so far as it puts something entirely different in the place of that will. In the sinner there is not only a want (*defectus*) of that which must be found in him; but also an inclination, a tendency, a striving (*affectus*) which ought not to be in him" (VAN OOSTERZEE, *Chr. Dogm.*, II, p. 395). Dr. William Newton Clarke thinks that theology can give no *a priori* definition of sin, but must derive its definition from experience in the light of the Christian revelation. He presents the subject under five aspects which may be summed up as follows: (1) Sin may be viewed in the light of its own character—then it is badness; (2) it may be viewed in relation to the nature of man—then it is the abnormal; (3) it may be viewed in relation to the standard of duty—then it is a departure from duty; (4) it may be viewed in reference to its motive and inner quality—then it is the placing of self-will or selfishness above the claims of love and duty; and (5) it may be viewed in relation to the moral government of God—then it is opposition to the spirit and working of God's moral government (CLARKE, *Outline of Chr. Th.*, pp. 231-237). One of the clearest and most comprehensive definitions of sin is from Dr. A. H. Strong. He says, "Sin is lack of conformity to the moral law of God, either in act, disposition, or state" (STRONG, *Syst. Th.*, II, p. 549). The definition of sin as given in the Westminster Shorter Catechism is one of the most condensed and yet comprehensive definitions found in theology. According to this Confession, "Sin is any want of conformity to, or transgression of, the law of God."

The Consequences of Sin. It may be expedient at this time to call attention to the fact that the terms applied to sin and redemption are drawn from three universes of discourse—the home, the law court and the temple service. Stated in other words, there are three aspects of sin and redemption, the natural, the legal and the religious. Much confusion has arisen from a failure to distinguish these uses and to apply to sin or redemption a term which is properly applicable only in another universe of discourse. This will be brought out more clearly later. It is sufficient here to note the natural consequences of sin as an estrangement between the creature and the Creator; the legal consequences as guilt and penalty; and the religious as depravity and defilement. Since man is at once an individual and a social being, the consequences of sin apply to both the person and the race. Sin, whether actual or original, assumes two forms, guilt and corruption. Guilt in turn has a twofold aspect, first, it is personal blameworthiness as regards the commission of sin, commonly known as *reatus culpæ;* and *second,* it is the liability to penalty, known as *reatus poenæ.* Actual sin includes both of these forms of guilt, while the second attaches only to original sin. Corruption or depravity likewise attaches to both the individual and the race. As it attaches to the sins committed by the individual, corruption is known as acquired depravity; as it attaches to the race it is called inherited depravity or original sin.

The Nature of Guilt and Penalty. The consequences of sin are to be found in guilt and penalty, which should be carefully distinguished in thought. Guilt is the personal blameworthiness which follows the act of sin, and involves the twofold idea of responsibility for the act, and a liability to punishment because of it. Penalty carries with it the thought of punishment which follows sin, whether as a natural consequence or a positive decree.

1. Guilt was originally a legal term, which in the course of history took on also, a moral significance. From debt as the primary meaning of the word, it came to mean liability for debt, then in the wider significance of a viola-

William Adams Brown points out that the consequences of sin must be described according to the point of view from which sin is regarded. Thus, looked at from the moral point of view sin issues in guilt; from the religious point of view in estrangement; from the point of view of man's own character and habits in depravity; from that of the divine government in penalty.—cf. *Chr. Th. in Outline,* p. 277.

tion of law, and finally as the state or condition of one who had transgressed the law. The law as here understood may mean in some instances objective law, but it cannot be limited to this. Nor can it be limited solely to a transgression against the attributes of divine justice. It must be regarded as a personal opposition to a personal God, in that degree and to that extent that He has been revealed to the offender. Guilt in this sense takes the form of condemnation based upon God's disapproval. Thus in conscience guilt is not a sense of transgression against divine justice or absolute law, but against the divine will. Guilt as personal blameworthiness must be distinguished from the consciousness of that guilt. The fact that a person has committed sin carries with it a sense of guilt, but varying circumstances may increase or diminish the consciousness of that guilt. Sin not only deceives but hardens the heart. Frequently a man feels less compunction of conscience the farther he goes into sin. But the guilt nevertheless remains, even though it is not fully realized in consciousness. Guilt must not only be viewed from the standpoint of personal responsibility for the act, but also as personal liability to punishment. In this sense guilt and penalty are correlative terms. However, a distinction must be made between liability to punishment on the part of the offender and the fact of punishment itself.

> The conscience in man bears its own clear testimony. This faculty of our nature, or representative of the Judge in our personality, is simply in relation to sin the registrar of its guilt. It is the moral consciousness, rather of instinct than of reflection, though also of both, faithfully assuming the personal responsibility of the sin and anticipating its consequences. Such is the scriptural meaning of the word. It is not the standard of right and wrong set up in the moral nature. St. Paul speaks of that written in the heart of universal man: the Gentiles *show the work of the law written in their hearts* (Rom. 2:15). He goes on to speak of "their conscience also bearing witness," by "accusing or else excusing," undoubtedly looking upward to a Judge and forward to a judgment. What St. Paul calls συνείδησις St. John calls καρδία, meaning, however, not the heart, in which St. Paul seats the law, but the consciousness of the inner man. The conscience is the self of the personality, in universal humanity never excusing, but always accusing, and is the *conscience of sins* (Heb. 10:2). It is enough to establish this distinction between the standard of right and wrong which may be defective and is not conscience proper, and that moral consciousness which infallibly unites the fault and its consequences in the consciousness of the sinner.—Pope, *Compend. Chr. Th.*, II, p. 34.

2. Penalty as related to guilt on the one hand, and the principles of God's moral government on the other, involves two questions, (1) What is the nature of penalty, that is, what part of the consequences of sin may be justly regarded as punishment for sin? (2) What is the function of penalty, that is, what is punishment intended to accomplish in the realm of God's moral government? As to the nature of penalty, it must be limited to those consequences which are adjudged to be evil, and which in God's moral government follow as inevitable and necessary consequences. Here again the word for penalty carries with it a legal significance and implies judicial and forensic relations. But we have seen that guilt implies something more than the violation of objective law; so also penalty must be regarded as broader in its significance. It must be made to include the consequences of all the various evils included in sin. Every form of sin has its own penalty. There are sins against law, against light and against love, and each has its own peculiar penalty. There are secret sins and sins against society, sins of ignorance and sins of presumption. Thus there may be degrees of both guilt and penalty as in the case of sins of ignorance or infirmity as over against sins of knowledge (cf. Matt. 10:15; 12:31; Mark 3:29; Luke 12: 47; John 19:11; Rom. 2:12). Penalty, therefore, is the punishment which follows sin, whether it be through the operation of natural, moral and spiritual laws, or by direct decree. God is not limited to His ordinary laws as a means of administration. He is a free Person, and may

The connection between sin and misery is universally felt, and not seriously disputed by any one. . . . . This connection is direct, since sin separates us from Him, in whom alone is our happiness, and on this account can but make us most miserable; reciprocal, because as misery springs from sin, so again does now sin spring continually from misery. Sin is the seed, misery the harvest, but this constantly brings with it new grains of seed; indeed, sin not merely produces, but itself is, the greatest misery. Every other sorrow is partly caused, partly increased, partly at length still more infinitely exceeded in wretchedness by it. Not only the suffering which comes direct from God, but the pain which men inflict on one another, even the calamity which we make for ourselves, must be regarded as its bitter fruit. The consciousness of sin increases on the one hand each load of life, and diminishes on the other the power to bear these with calmness. Just because sin is a much more general, shameful and pernicious evil than any other plague, ought it to be called the greatest cause of complaint.—Van Oosterzee, *Chr. Dogm.*, II, p. 434.

by direct action employ various means to vindicate Himself and His government. Penalty, however, in all its forms is God's reaction against sin, and is based ultimately on His holiness. As to the function of penalty, there are two general theories—the retributive and the reformative. These may be stated in the form of questions as follows: Does God punish sin solely to vindicate His justice? or, Does He seek the reformation of the sinner and the good of society? Where the dominant thought of theology has been the glory of God, the retributive theory is held as best displaying His justice, or mercy in relation to justice. Where the dominant thought has been the good of man, as in the idea of the kingdom of God, the disciplinary theory is the more prominent. But heredity and solidarity are both facts, and God has so created man that he cannot act apart from his social relations. The two theories, therefore, are not mutually exclusive and should not be set in too great contrast. Dr. William Adams Brown says the retributive theory of punishment may make a place incidentally for discipline, while the disciplinary theory clearly recognizes retribution as a necessary element in moral training (cf. WILLIAM ADAMS BROWN, *Chr. Th. in Outline*, p. 289). Penalty, therefore, must be considered in both relation to the individual and to the social structure, and consequently as it attaches to both actual and original sin. The chief penalty of sin is death. But since God loves all men, and seeks their salvation, the penalty of sin and the redemptive work of Christ are intimately bound up together and cannot be understood apart from each other.

Death as the Penalty of Sin. The Scriptures teach that the penalty of sin is death (Gen. 2:17), but the nature of this penalty has been interpreted in different ways. Arminian theologians have generally interpreted it to mean what is commonly known as the "fullness of death," that is, death physical, temporal and eternal. Four leading errors have appeared, (1) that death as a penalty for sin applies only to physical or bodily death. This is the position taken by the Pelagians and Socinians; (2) that the penalty is to be limited to spiritual death only, bodily death being regarded as merely a consequence of this; (3) that death is a natural law, and was given a penal significance when sin entered. Death, therefore, becomes a penal affliction and the fear and suffering which man endures become the penalties for his sin; (4) that death is to be regarded as the total annihilation of both soul and body. The first two are more speculative and theological, the last two more diffused and popular.

1. Physical death is included in the penalty of sin. Some writers such as Vaughan, Godet, and Meyer seem to make physical death the chief factor in the penalty. Thus Vaughan on *Romans* says, "Natural death, primarily, and as the punishment specially denounced; spiritual and eternal death, incidentally and secondarily, as the necessary consequence of the severance of the creature from the service and love of the Creator." Dr. Olin A. Curtis emphasizes the same view, regarding bodily death as neither a friendly nor useful event, but as abnormal, hostile and terrible. This position seems to be a reaction against the current scientific teaching that death is simply the expression of a biological law, and a beneficent arrangement to prevent the overpopulation of the earth. The fact that physical death is a

> Guilt has another meaning. It is the sure obligation to punishment; or what is sometimes called the *reatus poenæ*. We must remember that it is here regarded as absolute, without reference to any atoning provision; that it is the penalty of a living soul and not annihilation: and that it is the penalty of the human spirit informing a human body. The soul that sinneth is guilty of death, or of being sundered from the Holy Spirit of life: the death of the spirit separated from God, involving the separation of soul and body, and in its issue eternal. This is a hard saying, taken alone: but its mitigation will come in due time.—POPE, *Compend. Chr. Th.*, II, p. 36.

> Holy Scripture sums up all the disturbances of human life which are the result and punishment of sin in the designation "Death." "The wages of sin is death" (Rom. 6:23 and James 1:15; Rom. 5:12). There are various kinds of death; and Revelation means by the term not only the death which concerns the inward life—the spiritual semblance of life, the mock being which the sinner leads apart from God, not only the divided state of the inner man, the breaking up and dismemberment of the spiritual powers, which is the result of sin; but also the death which embraces the outward life, the whole array of sicknesses and plagues, which visit the human race, and "all the various ills that flesh is heir to," which are consummated in death, in the separation of the body and the soul.—MARTENSEN, *Chr. Dogm.*, p. 209.

penalty needs fresh emphasis, but that spiritual death is the chief factor needs to be kept constantly in view. Physical death is the consequence of the withdrawal of the Holy Spirit, and is therefore immediately connected with spiritual death. The branch separated from the vine is dead, in that it is no longer connected with its source of life. The moment of man's separation from God brought in the reign of death. That man's earthly existence did not end immediately was due to God's counsel for redemption. The "free gift" of divine grace began before the transgression took place. The virtue of the atonement issued forth from the Lamb slain before the foundation of the world. Hence the full strength of the condemnation was suspended and the consequences of the fall mitigated. The Scriptures lead us to believe, also, that not only man's nature, but also the nature which surrounds him, bears witness to the disorganizing principle of sin. Thus the creation ($\dot{\eta}$ $\kappa\tau\acute{\iota}\sigma\iota\varsigma$) itself, according to St. Paul, will be emancipated from the slavery of corruption into the freedom of the glory of the children of God (cf. Rom. 8: 19-22).

> Though a full and satisfactory explanation of the dark sayings of nature may be impossible in the present limits of our experience, yet a spiritual, a moral view of nature will always be led back to the words of the apostle that the creature is subject to vanity and sighs for redemption.—MARTENSEN, Chr. Dogm., p. 214.
>
> Physical death is the penalty of human sin: not, however, in itself, but as connected with death spiritual: connected with it in some sense as resulting from the same deprivation of the Holy Ghost, whose indwelling in regenerate man is the pledge of the physical resurrection, even as it is the principle of the spirit's resurrection to life. But it is declared to be expressly the penalty of sin in man; who was on its account subjected to the vanity that was the lot of the lower creatures, denied access to the Tree of Life, and surrendered to the dissolution that had already been the natural termination of the existence of the inferior orders of the inhabitants of the earth. . . . . Moreover, physical death in the sense of the annihilation of man's whole physical nature, as he is soul and spirit, is never once alluded to throughout the Scriptures. To die never in the Bible means extinction.—POPE, Compend. Chr. Th., II, p. 39.
>
> Weismann says that the organism must not be looked upon as a heap of combustible material, which is completely reduced to ashes in a certain time, the length of which is determined by its size and the rate at which it burns; but it should be compared to a fire, to which fresh fuel can be added, and which, whether it burns quickly or slowly, can be kept burning as long as necessity demands. . . . . Death is not a primary necessity, but it has been acquired secondarily, as an adaptation.—WEISMANN, Heredity, pp. 8, 24.

2. Spiritual death is due to the withdrawal of the Holy Spirit as the bond of union between the soul and God. By this withdrawal man lost immediately his fellowship with God. Negatively, this was the loss of original righteousness or primitive holiness; positively, it meant a depravation of those powers which in their united action we call man's moral nature. Thus fallen human nature is known as the *flesh* or σάρξ, a term which is used to indicate that the whole being of man, body, soul and spirit, have been separated from God and subjected to the creature. Evil consequences follow immediately, among which we may mention the following: (1) *Idolatry*. The loss of the Holy Spirit leaves the heart of man an abandoned temple. Nothing remains but for the self to become enthroned as its own god. Hence the world becomes "a vast pantheon" of lesser gods, all of which are made to minister to the enthroned self. (2) *The Self as the Ruling Principle of Life*. With the enthronement of the self, there begins the slavery of sin. *I am carnal,* said the apostle, *sold under sin* (Rom. 7:14); and again, *I see another law in my members, warring against the law of my mind, and bringing me into captivity to the law of sin which is in my members* (Rom. 7:23). Thus the flesh becomes the opposing principle of the Spirit. When, therefore, St. Paul refers to the carnal mind as *sarkikos* (σάρκικος), and the spiritual man as *pneumaticos* (πνευματικός), he portrays one whose whole nature is under the sway of the flesh, and the other as equally under the influence of the Spirit. (3) *The Concupiscence of the Flesh*. The self being in a false position, and still retaining its essentially active char-

The second consequence is, therefore, death spiritual, that moral state which arises from the withdrawment of that intercourse of God with the human soul, in consequence of its becoming polluted, and of that influence upon it which is the only source and spring of the right and vigorous direction and employment of its powers in which its rectitude consists; a deprivation, from which depravation consequently and necessarily follows. This, we have before seen, was included in the original threatening, and if Adam was a public person, a representative, it has passed on to his descendants, who in their natural state are therefore said to be "dead in trespasses and sins." Thus it is that the heart is deceitful above all things, and desperately wicked; and that all evils "proceed from it," as corrupt streams from a corrupt fountain.—WATSON, *Institutes*, II, p. 55.

acter, there arises what is known as concupiscence or inordinate desire. St. Paul in speaking of the carnal mind uses the term *phronema* (φρόνημα) or mind. St. James uses a cruder but stronger term, that of *epithumia* (ἐπιθυμία) which is generally translated lust (James 1:14, 15). St. John confirms this by referring to the sin of the world as being "the lust (ἐπιθυμία) of the flesh, the lust (ἐπιθυμία) of the eyes, and the pride (ἀλαζονία) of life (I John 2:16). (4) *Ungodliness.* The self is not only essentially active, but was created for unlimited progress. Under grace this becomes an ever increasing advancement in the divine likeness—a change from *glory unto glory* (II Cor. 3:18). In sin the increase is "unto more ungodliness" and hence a descent from shame to shame. It must be remembered, however, that sin is but an accident of man's nature and not an essential element of his original being. He retains his personality with all of its powers, but these are exercised apart from God as the true center of his being, and are therefore perverted and sinful. Sin is not some new faculty or power infused into man's being as the special organ of sin. It is rather the bias of all his powers—a darkening of the intellect, an alienation of the affections, and a perverseness of the will.

3. Eternal death is the final judgment of God upon sin. It is the separation of the soul from God made permanent. It is the punishment of sin apart from the mitigating influences of divine grace. From the standpoint of the individual sinner, it is the willful separation from God made final, the attitude of the soul's unbelief and sin made permanent. "But the highest sense of the term 'death,' in Scripture," says Mr. Watson, "is the punishment of the soul in a future state, by both a loss of happiness and separation from God, and also by a positive infliction of divine wrath. Now this is stated not as peculiar to any dispensation of religion, but as common to all—as the penalty of the transgression of the law of God in every degree. 'Sin is the transgression of the law'; this is its definition. 'The wages of sin is death'; this is its penalty" (WATSON, *Institutes,* II, p. 50).

CHAPTER XIX

ORIGINAL SIN OR INHERITED DEPRAVITY

We have seen that the penalty of sin is death. We have also seen that the effects of sin cannot be limited to the individual, but must include in their scope, the social and racial consequences as well. It is to these consequences that theology applies the terms Original Sin or Inherited Depravity. Following our usual procedure, we shall first examine the Scriptures themselves in order to establish the fact of human depravity; and from the facts thus gained, we shall attempt to construct a doctrine which will be in harmony with both the Scriptures and human experience. Two questions immediately arise. *First*, do these consequences attach to Adam as the federal head, or official representative of the race; or are they to be regarded simply as the natural consequences of the race's connection with Adam? *Second*, in what sense are these consequences to be viewed as

Mr. Wesley's treatise on Original Sin has been characterized as one of the most faithful and stern reflections of the scriptural doctrine that our language contains. His sermon on "Sin in Believers" is equally true to the facts of Christian experience. The latter was the result of his conflict with Moravianism. When he emerged from his maze of doubts and perplexities, he made a declaration of the following principles as summarized by Harrison. "Although the soul begins a new life at the hour of conversion, there remains not only the capacity for, but a tendency to, sin. The old Adam of active sin, of resistance to God and antagonism to holiness, is gone—buried with Christ by the regenerating grace of the Holy Spirit. But the Adamic fall is more than the ordering of a life, and the new birth is more than a change from one set of motives to another. After we have passed from death unto life, we are conscious that there remains a diseased moral nature whose allies are flesh and blood; and though these are conquered, they are not annihilated by the change which makes us children of God. . . . . The sagacious mind of Mr. Wesley analyzed his own experience, and finding himself not actually free from the warfare between good and evil, he searched the Scriptures, and was led thereby into the deep things of God. The aspirations of his soul for the higher life were accentuated by the doubts into which he had fallen; and when he once more threw himself upon the mercy of God in Christ Jesus, the Spirit of power and love and of a good conscience, undefiled manifested itself to him, and once more he was clothed with the spirit of rejoicing, having the peace that the world cannot give and cannot take away."—HARRISON, *Wesleyan Standards*, I, pp. 256, 257.

sin, and in what sense as inherited depravity? Since the term Original Sin seems to furnish a more direct connection with the subject discussed in the previous chapter, we shall examine the Scriptures which treat, (1) of Original Sin; and (2) of Inherited Depravity.

Original Sin. The Scriptures teach that the presence of death in the world, with all its attendant evils, is due to man's sin. *Wherefore, as by one man sin entered into the world, and death by sin; and so death passed upon all men, for that all have sinned: (For until the law sin was in the world: but sin is not imputed when there is no law. Nevertheless death reigned from Adam to Moses, even over them that had not sinned after the similitude of Adam's transgression, who is the figure of him that was to come. . . . . For if by one man's offence death reigned by one; much more they which receive abundance of grace and of the gift of righteousness shall reign in life by one, Jesus Christ.) Therefore as by the offence of one judgment came upon all men to condemnation; even so by the righteousness of one the free gift came upon all men unto justification of life* (Rom. 5: 12-14, 17, 18). Here it is clearly taught, that before the fall of Adam, there was neither sin nor death; after his fall there were both, and these are regarded as the direct consequences of sin. It seems clear also from this statement, that natural evil is the consequence of moral evil—for death is by sin. The apostle further declares, that death as a consequence of sin passed upon all men, that is, through racial propagation. Hence original sin and inherited depravity seem to be separated in thought only, but identified in fact. The propagation of the race from Adam was, therefore, not only in his physical likeness but also in his moral image. As if anticipating the error that Adam's sin constituted all men transgressors, he added the words, "for that all have sinned." By the apostle's own admission, however, death reigned even over those who had not sinned after the similitude of Adam's transgression, that is, by overt act of disobedience. Hence if the penalty of death was imputed to all men, because all had sinned, then this sin must have been a state of the heart, that is, a depraved nature. This is confirmed by such scriptures as *Behold the Lamb of God, which taketh away the sin of the world* (John 1: 29); *and the blood of Jesus Christ his Son cleanseth us from all sin* (I John 1: 7).

Inherited Depravity. Not only are all men born under the penalty of death, as a consequence of Adam's sin, but they are born with a depraved nature also, which in contradistinction to the legal aspect of penalty, is generally termed inbred sin or inherited depravity. This is defined in the language of the creed as "that corruption of the nature of all the offspring of Adam, by reason of which every one is very far gone from original righteousness" (Article V). We are now concerned, however, only with the scriptural teaching on this subject.

The Scriptures assert that man is born in a state of spiritual death; and while full provision is made for remitting the guilt and condemnation for which man is not directly responsible, it still remains that he is liable for the consequences of this sin. We make this statement in order to show the actual condition of man apart from the mitigating influences of divine grace. The first scripture which indicates the inherited depravity of man's nature is found in Genesis 5: 3, where it is stated that *Adam . . . . begat a son in his own likeness.* Here a distinction is made between the likeness of God, and Adam's own likeness in which his son was begotten. Another scripture of similar import is found in Genesis 8: 21 where it is said that *the imagination of man's heart is evil from his youth.* Since this word was spoken when there were no other human beings on earth except righteous Noah and his family, it must refer to the hereditary tendency of men toward evil. Closely related to these texts are the words of Job, *Who can bring a clean thing out of an unclean? not one* (Job 14: 4). Here again it is clearly indicated that the human race is defiled or polluted by sin, and hence every one born of the race is defiled. This is definitely stated by the psalmist as follows: *The Lord looked down from heaven upon the children of men, to see if there were any that did understand, and seek God. They are all gone aside, they are all together become filthy: there is none that doeth good, no, not one* (Psalms 14:2, 3). This scripture is later used by St. Paul as indicating a universally depraved state of mankind. Two other passages from the Psalms may be used as proof texts. *Behold, I was shapen in iniquity; and in sin did my mother conceive me* (Psalms 51:5); and *The wicked are estranged from the womb: they go astray as soon as they be born, speaking lies* (Psalms 58:3). The word iniquity as used here, cannot under any circumstances refer to actual sin, but carries with it the thought of a perverted or twisted nature from the very inception of life. The second verse carries the thought still farther as an estrangement or alienation from God. Since this estrangement is from birth, it must be regarded, not as acquired but as inherited depravity. The Prophet Jeremiah declared that *The heart is deceitful above all things, and desperately wicked: who can know it?* (Jer. 17:9). Here the strongest of terms is used to express the natural depravity of the human heart.

The New Testament references to the morally depraved character of the human race are numerous, but we need give here only a few of the stronger proof texts. Our Lord said, *That which cometh out of the man, that defileth the man. For from within, out of the heart of men, proceed evil thoughts, adulteries, fornications, murders, thefts, covetousness, wickedness, deceit, lasciviousness, an evil eye, blasphemy, pride, foolishness: All these evil things come from within, and defile the man* (Mark 7:20-23). Here our Lord clearly affirms that these evil traits come from within, that is, they have their original source in the natural heart of man. Again He says, *Except a man be born of water and of the Spirit, he cannot enter into the kingdom of God. That which is born of the flesh is flesh; and that which is born of the Spirit is spirit* (John 3:5, 6). Here the word *flesh* refers not only to the physical condition of mankind as born into the world, but implies also that his moral condition is such, that it becomes the ground of necessity for a new or spiritual birth. These words of our Lord are sufficient evidence of the morally depraved state of the natural man, and to the Christian there can be no higher authority. St. Paul uses the term *flesh* perhaps more than any other New Testament writer; and as he uses it, the term refers to the depraved nature of man—especially to the propagation of a corrupted nature. We can give only a few of these references. *For they that are after the flesh do mind the things of the flesh* (Rom. 8:5); *So then they that are in the flesh cannot please God* (Rom. 8:8); *But ye are not in the flesh, but in the Spirit* (Rom. 8:9); *If ye live after the flesh, ye shall die* (Rom. 8:13); *They that are Christ's have crucified the flesh with the affections and lusts* (Gal. 5:24). The outstanding passage, however, in this connection, is that from which the Church has derived the term "Indwelling Sin." *Now then it is no more I that do it, but sin that dwelleth in me. For I know that in me (that is, in my flesh,) dwelleth no good thing* (Rom. 7:17, 18). All of these terms show that the bias to sin belongs to fallen human nature as such. The term flesh as here used, is representative of the fallen estate of mankind generally—not the destruction of any of its essential elements, but the *deprivation* of its original spiritual life, and hence the *depravation* of its tendency.

THE DEVELOPMENT OF THE DOCTRINE IN THE CHURCH.

The doctrine of man's depravity rests upon the solid foundation of Scripture and the universal testimony of human experience. It is implied both in the penalty of the Adamic law and in the natural relation which Adam sustained to his posterity. The doctrine has never been seriously denied in the Church, except by the Pelagians and the Socinians. Mr. Wesley attached great importance to this fundamental belief. He says, "All who deny this (call it original sin or any other title) are but heathens still, in the fundamental point which distinguishes heathenism from Christianity. But here is our *Shibboleth;* Is man by nature filled with all evil?

Is he wholly fallen? Is his soul totally corrupted? Or, to come back to the text, is every imagination of the thoughts of his heart only evil continually? Allow this and you are so far a Christian. Deny it and you are but a heathen still" (WESLEY, *Sermon on Original Sin*). It will serve the purpose of better presenting this important doctrine, if we first make a brief survey of the various views which have been held in the Church, setting them forth in broad outline. Following this we shall indicate the finer distinctions which have served to guard the scriptural position.

The Early Christian Church. As with many other of the important doctrines of the Church, this fundamental truth was not questioned, and hence the early Church had no clearly defined doctrine of original sin. However, there soon appeared here and there, those variations which proved in their later developments, to be the germs of widely different systems of theology. The universality of sin was recognized from the beginning. Justin (A.D. 165) says, "Every race knows that adultery, and murder, and such like are sinful: and though they all commit such practices, they cannot escape from the knowledge that they act unrighteously whenever they do so." As to the proper explanation of this universality of sin, Justin appears to be uncertain. He speaks at one time of the "human race, which from Adam, had fallen under the power of death and the guile of the serpent, and each one of which has committed personal transgression"; but at another time, he says of the posterity of Adam, that "they becoming like

The early Christian Church exhibits the truth as it has been educed from the Scripture, but with the germ of every subsequent error here and there appearing. Before the Pelagian heresy the Greek and Latin fathers generally held the *Vitium Originis*, as Tertullian first called it, but laid stress upon the co-operation of the human will enlightened by teaching and grace. The Latins were still more decided as to both.—POPE, *Compend. Chr. Th.*, II, p. 74.

Tertullian (200) laid down the theory of natural depravity, which seems closely connected with his views about the traduction of souls. He is generally looked upon as the author of the doctrine of "Original Sin," which he formulates as follows: "There is, besides the evil which comes on the soul from the intervention of the evil spirits, an antecedent, and in some sense natural, evil which arises from its corrupt origin." This doctrine was afterward elaborated by Cyprian and Augustine, and gave rise to much angry controversy.—CRIPPEN, *Hist., Chr. Doct.*, p. 90.

Adam and Eve, work out death for themselves." Clement appears to have held the position which later came to be known as Pelagianism. He repudiates the idea of any hereditary taint. The later Greek theologians who generally follow Origen, took the same position. They maintained that original sin was merely physical corruption, and therefore could not be regarded as truly culpable. Sin, therefore, had no origin in Adam, but only in the human will. Thus Cyril says of original sin, that "when we come into the world we are sinless, but now we sin from choice." Chrysostom held a similar position. We may say, therefore, that in general, the Eastern Church regarded original sin as attaching only to the physical and sensuous nature and not to the voluntary and rational. Hence original sin was displaced by a belief in original evil.

The Pelagian Controversy. The controversy between Pelagius and Augustine was in reality, the focusing of two great systems of theology in their opposition to each other—the East and the West. Pelagius placed extreme emphasis upon the self-determination of the individual to good or evil, and denied that Adam's sin affected anyone but himself. Hence he denied inherited depravity or racial sin of any sort. The descendants of Adam were born in the same condition in which Adam was created, and like him, sinned by direct transgression. The prev-

The seven points of Pelagianism as given by Wiggers are as follows: (1) Adam was created mortal, so that he would have died even if he had not sinned; (2) Adam's sin injured, not the human race, but only himself; (3) newborn infants are in the same condition as Adam before the fall; (4) the whole human race neither dies on account of Adam's sin, nor rises on account of Christ's resurrection; (5) infants, even though not baptized, attain eternal life; (6) the law is as good a means of salvation as the gospel; and (7) even before Christ some men lived who did not commit sin. (These men were Abel, Enoch, Joseph, Job, and among the heathen, Socrates, Aristides and Numa.) The errors of Pelagianism may be refuted both from the Scriptures and from history. It has been held only sporadically by individuals, and has been regarded in the church as heresy.

Pelagianism as related to the denial of "original sin" and death as the effect of sin, was formally condemned as heretical by the General Council of Ephesus in 431 A.D. But this did not settle the controversy. Augustinianism was never fully received in the East, for its divines rejected predestination and held to the doctrine of original sin, side by side with human liberty. In the West, Augustinianism gained favor. Some of the monks of Adrumentum went to the extreme lengths of declaring that God predestinated even the sins of the wicked.

alence of sin, he held, was due to wrong example. Augustine on the other hand, emphasized racial sin or depravity to the exclusion of any true individual freedom. He adopted an extreme realism, maintaining that Adam and the race were the *one* that sinned—all being in Adam when he sinned, and, therefore, all actually sinning in him. This racial sin beginning in Adam was of the nature of *concupiscentia* or the ascendancy of the flesh over the spirit. This introduced the necessity of sinning; and the nature transmitted to his descendants made them not only depraved, but guilty in themselves as well as Adam. Semi-Pelagianism sought to mediate between the two extremes, by maintaining that original sin was merely vitiosity, or a weakening of the power to will and do. It held that there was sufficient power remaining in the depraved will to initiate or set in motion the beginnings of salvation but not enough to bring it to completion. This must be done by divine grace.

The Mediæval Transition. The discussions of the schoolmen were largely transitional, although several applications of the doctrine were developed. The Augustinian idea that the posterity of Adam must be considered guilty as well as depraved, found its logical development in the doctrine of the damnation of infants. Since baptism was regarded as the ground of remission for the guilt of original sin, Gregory applied the principle to the full. He maintained that to the *pœna damni* or loss, was added the *pœna sensus* or conscious suffering, and hence the damnation of all unbaptized infants. Another question which greatly divided the opinions of the schoolmen was that of the immaculate conception of Mary. Some maintained that unless Mary had been free from original sin, Christ would not have been born sinless. They held, therefore, that Mary was prenatally sanctified—the one exception to the universality of sin, original as well as actual. Others held that no one could be made holy without the intervention of the atonement. The subject was one of debate for almost a century. The doctrine of the immaculate conception, however, was made an article of faith in the Roman Catholic Church by Pope

Pius IX in 1854. The question as to the origin and transmission of original sin was likewise a matter of debate during this period. Peter Lombard maintained the position of Creationism. He held that God created each individual soul pure, but this immaterial spirit infused into the begotten organism of the body, contracted defilement and became guilty. Anselm and Thomas Aquinas, held to Traducianism as the best explanation of inherited depravity, that is, that Adam's person corrupted the nature; and in his posterity, the nature corrupts the person.

The Tridentine Development. The theologians of the Roman Catholic Church were as definite as the Reformers in their position concerning the penalty of sin. They maintained that the sin of Adam had entailed upon his posterity, not only the consequences of sin, but sin itself. They affirmed also, that free will had been weakened by the fall, but repudiated the idea that the freedom of the will had been extinguished or lost. They were, therefore, semi-Pelagian in their beliefs. The denial of original sin and of the freedom of the will were both alike anathematized by the Council of Trent in 1560 A.D. The peculiarity of the Tridentine doctrine, however, consists in the belief that original righteousness was a superadded gift. This we have previously pointed out in our discussion concerning the image of God in man. The loss of original righteousness, therefore, by the sin of Adam, threw the race back to its original con-

The dogma defined in the Council of Trent combines the Augustinian Realistic identification of Adam and the race with the semi-Pelagian negative idea of the effect of the fall. Adam created in the image of God, with the endowment of free will, and perfect harmony in the purely natural elements, had the gift of original righteousness added: *conditus in puris naturalibus,* he was then *in justitia et sanctitate constitutus.* Original righteousness was a supernatural added gift, and the loss of it threw the race back into its created condition of contrariety between flesh and spirit, without the superadded restraint. In baptism the guilt of the original offense which incurred the loss is taken away, and yet the concupiscence that sprang from transgression and leads to transgression remains untaken away, not having, however, itself the essential quality of evil. . . . . Against this the Reformed Confessions all protested, asserting that concupiscence has in it the nature of sin. For the rest, the Roman theory admits that the natural image has been clouded through the fall; man's whole nature being wounded, and propagated as such.—Pope, *Compend. Chr. Th.,* II, p. 77.

dition of a contrariety between flesh and spirit. From the deprivation of the original gift, concupiscence sprang up, in which the flesh dominated the spirit. The Tridentine doctrine maintains that the guilt which attaches to original sin is taken away by baptism, but the concupiscence remains. This, however, they do not regard as sin. "The concupiscence, which the apostle sometimes denominates sin, the Holy Synod declares the Catholic Church never understood to be called sin because it is really and truly sin in the regenerate, but because it is from sin and inclines to sin." It is admitted, however, that the natural image has been clouded through the fall, and that man's whole nature being wounded, is propagated as such.

The Lutheran Standards. The Lutheran theologians generally recognized two elements in original sin — corruption of the nature of man, and guilt as attaching to this corruption. The Augsburg Confession states that "All men begotten after the common course of nature are born in sin; that is, without the fear of God, without trust in Him, and with fleshly appetite; and this disease or original fault is truly sin, condemning and bringing eternal death now also upon all that are not born again by baptism and the Holy Spirit" (Art. II). Nothing is said here as to the nature of this imputation, whether mediate or immediate, but the theory necessarily identifies inherited depravity and original sin. Lutheranism has always strongly maintained the moral inability of fallen man. The Formula of Concord (1577) served to check two opposite tendencies — the synergists who held that there was a certain co-operation of the human will in the matter of salvation; and the theory of Flacius, that original sin is the very substance of fallen man. Against Lutheran Synergism, the creed affirmed that in

---

Melanchthon defined original sin as a corruption of nature flowing from Adam, but held rather to the mediate than to immediate imputation of this sin to the race. He says, "On account of which corruption men are born guilty and children of wrath, that is condemned by God, unless remission is obtained. If anyone wishes to add that men are born guilty by reason of Adam's fall, I do not object." Calixtus among the Lutheran theologians denied that guilt attached to original sin. Both Gerhard and Quensted favored mediate imputation.

natural things man may do good, but in spiritual things his will is entirely bound; against the theory of Flacius, it maintained that original sin was an accident of human nature, and not of the essence of the human soul. In the language of the schools, original sin is *accidens* rather than *substantia*.

The Reformed Confessions. Calvin and the Reformed Churches generally, made no distinction between imputed guilt and inherited depravity. Original sin included both elements—guilt and corruption. The guilt of original sin was explained in various ways; sometimes by the representative mode, or legal headship of Adam; sometimes by the realistic mode, or the virtual existence of the race in Adam; and sometimes by the genetic mode, or the natural headship of the race in Adam. With few exceptions, the reformers accepted the two former positions, that is, they believed that sin was imputed to the race by virtue of the relation which it sustained to Adam as its legal representative; and they held that the race being in Adam when he sinned, it sinned also, and, therefore, became guilty with him in the first sin. After the time of Cocceius (1603-1669), the federal notion took on greater prominence but did not entirely supplant the realistic position. The imputation was, therefore, sometimes regarded as legal and sometimes as moral. Frequently both elements were retained, giving rise to the Placæan Controversy over mediate or immediate imputation. Calvin and the reformers generally held to an immediate or antecedent imputation, which made the sin of Adam as the federal head of the race, the exclusive and prior ground of condemnation. Placæus on the other hand, advanced the theory of a mediate or consequent imputation, which held that condemnation followed and was dependent upon individual corruption as its ground. His doctrine involved the idea of creationism. The soul he maintained, is created immediately by God and as such is pure, but becomes corrupt as soon as it is united with the body. Inbred sin, therefore, according to this theory, is the consequence but not the penalty of Adam's transgression.

Zwingli (1484-1531) differed very materially from the other reformers in his conception of inbred sin, especially in excluding from it the element of guilt. Sin proper he defined as a transgression of the law. Concerning original sin he says, "Whether we wish it or not, we are compelled to admit that original sin, as it is in the descendants of Adam, is not properly sin, as has already been explained, for it is not a transgression of the law. It is therefore properly a disease and a condition. He holds, indeed, that men are by nature the children of wrath, but he interprets this to mean that men are not actually adjudged guilty, but that naturally we are without the birthright to immortality, just as the children of one who is made a slave inherit a condition of slavery." This conception of inbred sin is essentially the same as that which later was accepted by Arminius.

The Arminian Position. The position of James Arminius (560-1609) on the question of original sin, differed greatly from that of his followers, especially Limborch (1633-1702) and Curcellæus (1586-1659), who in the controversy with Dort leaned too far toward Pelagianism. For this reason we shall reserve the term "earlier Arminianism" as applying to the teachings of Arminius himself, and also to those teachings as reaffirmed by John Wesley (1703-1791). The position of the Remonstrants is best known as "Later Arminianism." In its purest and best forms, Arminianism preserves the truth found in the Reformed teaching without accepting its errors. With the Reformers it holds to the unity of the race in Adam, that "in Adam all have sinned," and that all men "are by nature the children of wrath." But over against this, it holds that in Christ, the second Man who is the Lord from heaven, "the most gracious God has provided for all a remedy for that general evil which was derived to us from Adam, free and gratuitous in His beloved Son Jesus Christ, as it were a new and another Adam. So that the baneful error of those is plainly apparent who are accustomed to found upon that original sin the decree of absolute reprobation invented by themselves." The Apology of the Remonstrants further declares that "there is no ground for the assertion that the sin of Adam was imputed to his posterity in the sense that God actually judged the posterity of Adam to be guilty of and chargeable with the same sin and crime that Adam had committed." "I do not deny that it is sin," said Arminius, "but it is not actual sin. . . . . We must distinguish between actual sin and that which is the cause of other sins, and which on that very account may be denominated sin."

The Wesleyan Doctrine. John Wesley greatly improved the later Arminian position, purging it from its Pelagian elements and putting it upon a more scriptural basis. Wesleyanism, therefore, more nearly approaches the positions of James Arminius himself. It must be recognized, however, that there are certain differences in the teachings of Arminius and those of Wesley. One of these is quite marked. Arminius regarded the ability bestowed upon our depraved nature which enabled it to co-operate with God, as flowing from the justice of God, without which man could not be held accountable for his sins. Wesley on the other hand, regarded this ability as solely a matter of grace, an ability conferred through the free gift of prevenient grace, given to all men as a first benefit of the universal atonement made by Christ for all men. The differences between the Wesleyans and the Remonstrants are thus summed up by Dr. Charles Hodge: "Wesleyanism (1) admits entire moral depravity; (2) denies that any men in this state have any power to co-operate with the grace of God; (3) asserts that the guilt of all through Adam was removed by justification of all through Christ; and (4) ability to co-operate is of the Holy Spirit, through the universal influence of the redemption of Christ" (HODGE, *Syst. Th.*, II, pp. 329, 330). Dr. Pope in his theology more nearly follows Wesley and Watson; while Whedon and Raymond

The order of the decrees in the Arminian system is as follows: (1) to permit the fall of man; (2) to send the Son to be a full satisfaction for the sins of the whole world; (3) on that ground to remit all original sin, and to give such grace as would enable all to attain eternal life; (4) those who improve that grace and persevere to the end are ordained to be saved.

better represent the type of Arminianism as held by the Remonstrants. Since it is our purpose to more fully present the Arminian position, we need not at this time, give the subject any extended treatment.

The Origin and Transmission of Original Sin

Granting that original sin or inherited depravity had its origin in the sin of Adam, we must now consider the manner in which this is transmitted to the individual members of the race, and the character which attaches to it. The theories are generally known as "modes of transmission," or in Calvinistic theology, "theories of imputation." There are three principal theories. *First*, there is the Realistic Mode, which regards Adam as the natural head of the race, and his posterity as identified with him in the original transgression. *Second*, there is the Representative Mode, which regards Adam as the legal head of the race, and, therefore, being the legal representative of the race, his sin was imputed to them as their sin. Here the emphasis is upon original sin, rather than upon inherited depravity. *Third*, there is the Genetic Mode, which is based upon the natural headship of Adam, but regards the consequences of his sin, chiefly in the light of inherited depravity instead of original sin.

The Realistic Mode of Transmission. This theory was first advanced by Augustine (354-430), although it appears in germinal form in the writings of Tertullian (d. 220), Hilary (350) and Ambrose (374). For this reason it is commonly known as the Augustinian theory of imputation, or the "theory of Adam's Natural Headship." With the exception of Zwingli (1484-1531), this was the generally accepted theory of the Reformers. As a mode of transmission, realism holds to the solidarity of the race; and as a theory of imputation, it maintains the constituted personal identity of Adam and his posterity. Three forms or degrees of realism are recognized in philosophical and theological thought. (1) Extreme Realism, which holds to a single generic nature in which individuals have no separate existence, but which are regarded as mere modes or manifestations of the one substance. This is pantheism and can have no proper place in the Christian System. (2) Moderate or Higher Realism, which also holds to a single generic nature, but which maintains that this one substance through a process of individualization may become separated into distinct individuals, each of which possesses a portion of the original nature or substance. (3) Lower Realism, which holds to the existence of the entire race in Adam, but only in a germinal manner. It is thus closely related to the genetic mode. The theory, however, identifies Adam's posterity with himself in the one original sin.

1. The Higher Realism is constructed upon the scholastic distinction between genera and species, between nature and the individual. It is the Augustinian theory of "generic existence, generic transgression, and generic condemnation." Dr. Shedd and Dr. Strong are the best modern representatives of this position, although the former is more pronounced in his realism than the latter. Dr. Shedd has given us by far the clearest statement of the realistic mode of transmission. "Human nature," he says, "is a specific or general substance created in and with the first individuals of the human species, which is not yet individualized, but which by ordinary generation is subdivided into parts, and these parts are formed into distinct and separate individuals

Dr. Shedd holds that "A species or a specific nature, is that primitive, invisible substance, or plastic principle, which God created from nonentity, as the rudimental matter of which all the individuals of the species are to be composed." "Though an invisible principle," it is "a real entity, nor a mere idea. When God creates a primordial substance which is to be individualized by propagation, that which is created is not a mental abstraction or general term having no objective correspondent. A specific nature has a real existence, not a noumenal." "Realism, then is true within the sphere of the specific, organic, and propagated being: and nominalism is true within that of non-specific, inorganic, and unpropagated being. . . . . man as a general conception, denotes not only the collective aggregate of all the individual men that ever exist, but also that primitive human nature of which they are fractional parts, and out of which they have been derived. The individual in this instance, is not the only actual and objective reality. The species is real also. The one human nature in Adam was an entity, as truly as the multitude of individuals produced out of it. The primitive unity 'man' was as objective and real as the final aggregate 'men.'"—SHEDD, *Dogmatic Theology*, II, pp. 68-71.

of the race. The one specific substance, by propagation, is metamorphosed into millions of individual substances, or persons. An individual man is a fractional part of a human nature separated from the common mass, and constituted a particular person having all the essential properties of human nature." He quotes Augustine as follows: "God the author of nature, but not of sin (*vitium*), created man upright, but he having through his own will become depraved and condemned, propagated depraved and condemned offspring. For we were all in that one man, since we were all that one man who lapsed into sin through that woman who was made from him, previous to transgression. The particular form in which we were to live as individuals had not yet been created and assigned to us man by man, but that seminal nature was in existence from which we were to be propagated..... All men at that time sinned in Adam, since in his nature all men were as yet that one man." Upon such statements as these, Dr. Shedd builds his own theory. Thus, the total life of mankind was in Adam, since the race as yet had its only being in him. Its essence was not yet individualized, and his will was as yet the will of the species. It was in Adam's free act, that the race revolted from God and became corrupt in its nature. Considered as an essence human nature is intelligent, rational and voluntary; and accordingly, its agency in Adam partakes of the corresponding qualities. Hence generic or

The question respecting the priority of the universal (the species) and the individual (res) arises here. Whether the universal is prior to the individuals, depends upon what individuals are meant. If the first two individuals of a species are in mind, then the universal, i.e., the species, is not prior, but simultaneous (universale in re). The instant God created the first pair of human individuals, he created the human nature or species in and with them. But if the individuals subsequent to the first pair are in mind, then the universal, i.e., the species is prior to the individuals (universale ante rem). God created the human nature in Adam and Eve before their posterity were produced out of it. Accordingly, the doctrine of "universale ante rem" is the true realism, in case "res" denotes the individuals of the posterity. The species as a single nature is created and exists prior to its distribution by propagation. The universal as a species exists before the individuals (res) formed out of it. And the doctrine of "universale in re" is the true realism, in case "res" denotes only the first pair of individuals. The specific nature as created and existing in these two primitive individuals (res) is not prior to them, but simultaneous with them.—SHEDD, *Dogmatic Theology*, II, p. 74.

original sin is truly and properly sin because it represents moral agency. On the realistic ground, therefore, Adam's sin is imputed directly to his posterity, not as something foreign to them, but because all men were in Adam as one moral whole, and all sinned in him. And having sinned in him, human nature at its source was corrupted and all became partakers of that one corrupt nature. Not merely that we inherit the same kind of nature, but that identical corrupt nature is individualized in us, so that by virtue of our own sin we have all corrupted ourselves. There is then, on the Augustinian ground of realism, a threefold imputation—the original act of sin; the corrupt nature as a consequence of that act; and eternal death as the penalty for both the act and the depraved nature.

The objections usually raised to this theory may be summarized briefly as follows: (1) The assumption of a generic nature is without ground in either philosophy or the Scriptures. Realism never has been fully accepted as a philosophical theory, and has generally found its logical issue in the higher forms of pantheistic monism. (2) If the whole generic nature were personalized in Adam, endowed with and capable of free moral agency, it must have existed in the unity of spiritual essence and personality. If the unity of personality be allowed, it is

Dr. Charles Hodge, the chief representative of the Federal Theory, raises strong objections to this theory. These may be summarized as follows: (1) Realism is a mere hypothesis; (2) It has no support from the Scriptures; (3) It has no support from the consciousness of men, but contradicts the teachings of consciousness as interpreted by the vast majority of our race. Every man is revealed to himself as an individual substance. (4) Realism contradicts the doctrine of the Scriptures in so far as it is irreconcilable with the Scripture doctrine of the separate existence of the soul. (5) It subverts the doctrine of the Trinity in so far that it makes the Father, Son and Spirit one God only in the sense in which all men are one man. The answers which the Trinitarian realists give to this objection are unsatisfactory, because they assume the divisibility, and consequently the materiality of Spirit. (6) It is difficult, if not impossible, to reconcile the realistic theory with the sinlessness of Christ. If the one numerical essence of humanity became guilty and polluted in Adam, how can Christ's human nature have been free from sin if He took upon Him the same numerical essence which sinned in Adam. (7) The above objections are theological or scriptural; others of a philosophical character have availed to banish the doctrine of realism from all modern schools of philosophy, except so far as it has been merged in the higher forms of pantheistic monism.—HODGE, *Systematic Theology*, II, pp. 221, 222.

hardly conceivable that it should be regarded as divisible and distributable. (3) Sin can be predicted of persons only. If in Adam "we sinned all," then there must have existed in him, not the unitary essence of a single personality, but an aggregate of individuals, which no one allows. The general objection to the realistic mode as we see it, is that it appears to be a strained attempt to prove what may be more simply accounted for on other grounds.

2. The Lower Realism differs from the higher in that it does not hold to the numerical unity of the generic nature, but is based upon the principle of the germinal **existence of the race in Adam.** In harmony with the higher realism, however, it maintains the common participation of the race in Adam's sin. The most frequent illustration of this relation is that which exists between the root and the branches of a tree, or between the head and the members of the body. John Owen (1616-1685) who with Richard Baxter and Thomas Ridgely, represented the intermediate group which attempted to reconcile the Realists and the Federalists, gives us the following explanation: "We say that Adam, being the root and head of all human kind, and we all the branches from that root, all parts of that body, whereof he was the head, his will may be said to be ours. We were then all that one man—we were all in him, and had no other will but his; so that though that be extrinsic unto us, considered as particular persons, yet it is intrinsical, as we are all parts of one common nature. As in him we sinned, so in

In his comment upon the above passage from Owen, Dr. Miley says that "close inspection discovers in it serious logical deficiencies, the pointing out of which will further show the groundlessness of the theory. The argument starts with the assumption of a rudimentary existence of all men in Adam, and respecting the soul as well as the body. Whether the soul so existed in Adam is still an open question with theologians. Augustine himself was always in serious doubt of it. Calvin rejected it, and the Reformed theologians mostly agreed with him. It has no place in the church creed. When so doubtful a principle takes the vital place of a logical premise the whole argument must be weak. On the ground of such an assumed existence in Adam the argument proceeds: 'his will may be said to be ours.' May be said! Many things may be said without proper warrant for the saying. With a doubtful premise and a merely hypothetical inference as the best support that can be given to the theory, its weakness is manifest"—MILEY, *Systematic Theology*, I, pp. 490, 491.

him we had a will of sinning." Here again, we may say that the theory is inadequate. It is intended to identify the posterity of Adam with himself in such a oneness that his sin would be chargeable to them, but this responsibility cannot be explained on the theory of germinal existence in Adam.

The Representative Mode of Imputation. This is usually known as the Federal Theory, or the "Theory of Condemnation by Covenant." The doctrine as held by the Reformed Churches is a combination of the covenant system of Cocceius (1603-1669), with the theories of immediate imputation held by Heidegger and Turretin (1623-1687). In American theology, this theory was developed by the Princeton theologians in opposition to the so-called "New School" of nonimputation in New England. The real impulse to federalism, whether earlier or later, grew out of the difficulty on the Augustinian theory, of accounting for the nonimputation to his posterity, of Adam's subsequent sins. The Federal Theory is therefore one of imputation, as is the Realistic Theory, but it accounts for this imputation in a distinctly different manner. Augustinianism as we have shown, accounted for guilt and depravity on the ground of an actual participation in Adam's first sin; the Federal Theory accounts for it on the purely legal ground of a covenant, in which Adam became the divinely appointed representative of the race. Hence his obedience was reckoned or imputed to his posterity as their obedience, and his transgression as their transgression.

1. We have first to consider, under the Representative Mode, the Theory of Immediate Imputation, commonly known as the Federal Theory. Dr. Charles Hodge is regarded as the ablest exponent of this theory in modern times, and gives us its clearest and most concise statement. He says, "The union between Adam and his posterity which is the ground of the imputation of his sin to them, is both natural and federal. He was their natural head. Such is the relation between parent and child, not only in the case of Adam and his descendants, but in all other cases, that the character and conduct of

the one, of necessity to a greater or less degree affect the other. No fact in history is plainer than that children bear the iniquities of their fathers. They suffer for their sins. But there was something peculiar in the case of Adam. Over and beyond this natural relation which exists between a man and his posterity, there was a special divine constitution by which he was appointed the head and representative of his whole race." "The scriptural solution of this fearful problem is," he says, "that God constituted our first parent the federal head and representative of his race, and placed him on probation not only for himself, but also for all his posterity. Had he retained his integrity, he and all his descendants would have been confirmed in a state of holiness and happiness forever. As he fell from the estate in which he was created, they fell with him in his first transgression so that the penalty of that sin came upon all them as well as upon him. Men, therefore, stood their probation in Adam. As he sinned, his posterity came into the world in a state of sin and condemnation. They are by nature the children of wrath. The evils which they suffer are not arbitrary impositions, nor simply the natural consequences of his apostasy, but judicial inflictions. The loss of original righteousness, and death spiritual and temporal under which they commence their existence, are the penalty of Adam's first sin" (HODGE, *Systematic Theology*, II, pp. 196, 197).

In order to greater clarity, we may with profit indicate some of the similarities and contrasts of the Realistic and Federal theories. *First*, the two theories are similar in this—both maintain that inherited depravity is condemnable. They explain this, however, in different ways. The Realistic theory maintains that Adam's posterity sinned in him, and are, therefore, guilty on account of their own sin. The Federal theory holds that

Professor Moses Stuart very aptly characterized this theory as one of "fictitious guilt, but veritable damnation." Dr. Baird said, "Here is a sin, which is no crime, but a mere condition of being regarded and treated as sinners; and a guilt, which is devoid of sinfulness, and which does not imply moral demerit or turpitude." Hollaz held that God treats men in accordance with what He foresaw they would do, if they were in Adam's place (cf. STRONG, *Syst. Th.*, II, p. 615).

Adam's posterity did not participate in his sin, but were nevertheless liable to his penalty, in that he was legally their representative. This penalty was the infliction of depravity upon the descendants of Adam, and death as a consequence of that corruption. Thus original sin is essentially a punitive matter. *Second,* they show marked contrast in this—that the former maintains that guilt in the sense of culpability attaches to depravity, while the latter distinguishes sharply between guilt and demerit. "When it is said that the sin of Adam is imputed to his posterity, it is not meant that they committed his sin, or were the agents of his act, nor is it meant that they were morally criminal for this transgression; but simply that in virtue of the union between him and his descendants his sin is the judicial ground of the condemnation of the race" (HODGE, *Systematic Theology,* II, p. 195). Thus a distinction is made between guilt which is simply amenability to punishment without personal culpability; and guilt to which personal demerit and moral turpitude are attached. The latter alone affects moral character.

There are many objections urged against this theory. (1) The Federal headship by virtue of a specific covenant is pure assumption without any support from the

In his reference to the theory of immediate imputation, Dr. Sheldon says, "What is this but the apotheosis of legal artifice? The same God whose penetrating glance burns away every artifice with which a man may enwrap himself, and reaches at once to the naked reality, is represented as swathing His judgment with a gigantic artifice, in that He holds countless millions guilty of a trespass which he knows was committed before their personal existence, and which they could no more prevent than they could hinder the fiat of creation. If this is justice, then justice is a word of unknown meaning. Sane men condemn the savagery of the tribe which treats all of a nation as enemies because one or more of its representatives has offended. Shall sane men, then, think of the holy God as condemning a race in advance of its existence because of the sin of one?"—SHELDON, *Syst. of Chr. Doct.*, p. 320.

This theory denies all direct sharing of the race in either the act or the demerit of Adam's sin. This is its distinction from the realistic theory, which, in its higher form, asserts both. As the race had no part in the agency of Adam, his sinning could have no immediate consequence of demerit and guilt upon them as upon himself. Hence, until the judicial act of immediate imputation, all must have been innocent in fact, and must have so appeared even in the view of the divine justice as it proceeded to cover them from the guilt of an alien sin, a sin in no sense their own, and then on the ground of such gratuitous guilt to inflict upon them the penalty of moral depravity and death. Thus the race though innocent in fact, is made the subject of guilt and punishment.— MILEY, *Syst. Th.,* II, p. 503.

Scriptures. That Adam is the natural head of the race, and that legal responsibilities attach to this headship is not denied, but the theory is too mechanical and too artificial to be true. (2) It is contrary to the general teaching of the Scriptures. The descendants of Adam are not sinners because God accounts them as such; God regards them as sinners because they are such. St. Paul is explicit—*death passed upon all men, for that all have sinned* (Rom. 5:12). (3) The theory confuses justice with sovereign power. If God by a sovereign act imputes guilt to the innocent, then He becomes an arbitrary ruler who treats the innocent as though they were guilty, and subordinates justice to legal fiction. (4) If the race had no part in either the agency or demerit of Adam's sin, it is evident that until the judicial pronouncement, they were in fact, innocent before the divine justice. Hence by a judicial act there is imputed to them a sin which is not their own, and on the ground of this gratuitous guilt, there is inflicted upon them the penalty of moral depravity and eternal death. This violates all sense of justice, and calls in question, the fundamental idea of God as a Perfect Being.

2. We have next to consider, under the Representative Mode, the Theory of Mediate Imputation, commonly known as the "Theory of Condemnation for Depravity." It was first advanced by Placeus (1606-1655) of the

---

The arbitrariness of the covenant system is shown in the fact that it is held in a variety of forms. Cocceius, the originator of the system, and Burmann, one of his immediate followers and an able exponent of the system, held that the covenant of grace was between God and the elect, the office of Christ being merely that of a Mediator. Witsius held that the covenant of grace was primarily an eternal covenant between the Father and the Son, and secondarily only, a covenant between God and the elect. Turretine and Hodge, who were advocates of the covenant-imputation scheme, held that in the covenant of works there were God and the first Adam; in the covenant of grace, God and the last Adam.

Dr. E. C. Robinson thinks that it is perfectly certain that Jonathan Edwards did not hold the doctrine of immediate imputation, and that there is no decisive evidence that he held to the mediate imputation of Placeus. He believed in "a real union between the root and the branches of the world of mankind established by the Author of the whole system of the universe"; "the full consent of the hearts of Adam's posterity to the first apostasy." And therefore the sin of the apostasy is not theirs, merely because God imputes it to them; but it is truly and properly theirs, and on that ground God imputes it to them.—AUGUSTINE, *Original Sin*. Cf. ROBINSON, *Christian Theology*, p. 155.

School of Saumur in France. At first he denied that Adam's sin was in any sense imputed to the race, but this position having been condemned by the Reformed Church in 1644 A.D., he afterward proposed the theory which now bears his name. According to this view, the posterity of Adam are counted guilty, not because of their representative, but because they are born physically and morally depraved. While the corrupted nature comes by natural descent, it is nevertheless considered a sufficient cause for condemnation. On the Federal theory, imputation is the cause of depravity; on the Placean theory, depravity is the cause of imputation. The chief objection to this theory is, that it gives no explanation of man's responsibility for his inborn depravity; and since this corrupt nature cannot be charged to man's account, it must therefore be viewed in the light of an arbitrary divine infliction. This brings it under the same objections as those which are urged against the theory of immediate imputation.

The Genetic Mode of Transmission. Stated in other words, this is simply the natural law of heredity. It is the law of organic life that everything reproduces its own kind, and that not only as to anatomical structure and physical characteristics, but also as to mental life and disposition. The Augustinian anthropology with its realistic mode of accounting for original sin, is based upon this law of genetic transmission. The Federal theory of imputation regarded Adam as the representative of the race, solely on the ground of his natural headship. So, also, Arminianism has made much of this genetic law in its explanation of native depravity. Dr. Miley says, "On the obedience and the maintenance of his own holiness of nature, his offspring would have received their life and begun their probation in the same primitive holiness. There would still have been the possible lapse of individuals, with the corruption of their own nature and the consequent depravity of their offspring; but apart from this contingency, or so far as the Adamic connection is concerned, all would have been born in the primitive holiness. Under what law would such have been the consequence? Unquestionably, the law of genetic transmission .... as the law of genetic transmission rules in all the forms of propagated life and determines the likeness of the offspring to the parentage, and as it was sufficient for the transmission of the primitive holiness to all the race, it must be a sufficient account of the common native depravity" (MILEY, *Systematic Theology*, II, p. 506). The manner in which Arminianism, earlier and later, is related to this mode of transmission, must be reserved for a later paragraph.

DOCTRINAL ASPECTS OF ORIGINAL SIN

Original Sin or Inherited Depravity are terms applied to the subjective moral state or condition of man by birth, and therefore express the moral condition of man in his natural estate. This depravity must not, however, be regarded as a physical entity or any other form of essential existence added to man's nature. It is rather, as its name implies, a deprivation of loss. Some theologians have attempted to locate depravity in the human will, but all such attempts are simply forms of the error of attempting to endow the will with personal powers. Depravity belongs to the whole person of man, and not merely to some form of personal manifestation, whether through the will, the intellect or the affections. It is a state or condition in which the person exists, and thus may be said to be a nature—a term which in its metaphysical form is not easily grasped, but which is very real in actual existence. By a "nature" we may mean either of two things, (1) the constituent elements of man's being which distinguish him from every other order of existence. In this sense human nature remains as it was originally created. (2) The moral development of his being as a growth from within, apart from external influences. It is in this sense only, that we speak of man's nature as corrupt. This corruption is inherent and not merely accidental. Sin, however, in the former sense of the word nature, is not inherent but simply accidental. It was not a constituent element of man's being as he was originally created. For this reason, sin is not in harmony with man's true nature, as is witnessed by conscience and the profounder law of reason, which is an element of man's natural image. This corrupt nature, therefore, is something alien to the primitive holiness of man's nature by creation, and in thought at least is separable from the person whose condition it represents. Depravity is "deeper down and farther back" than the intellect, the feelings or the will, and therefore metaphysically below consciousness. It is the condition or state in which the person exists, and affects man in both his sensuous and moral nature. By the sensuous nature, we must understand something more than the merely physical; we refer to those sensibilities on the borderline, where the physical condition affects the mental life, or the mental life in turn influences bodily conditions. From this disordered condition, there arise evil tendencies, inordinate sensibilities or affections, and vicious impulses. Likewise the moral nature is so affected that the light of conscience shines dimly, and moral duty is not properly enforced.

While most orthodox creeds regard man's moral condition as the loss of original righteousness, the theories of explanation differ widely. Pelagianism and Calvinism represent the extremes of thought, the former

The sensuous nature, as we here use the term, is much broader than the physical nature, and the seat of many other sensibilities than the appetencies regarded as more specially physical. These manifold feelings have their proper functions in the economy of human life. In a healthful tone and normal state of the sensuous nature, these feelings are subordinate to the sense of prudence and the moral reason, and may thus fulfill their functions consistently with the spiritual life. There may be a disordered state of the sensuous nature, with the result of inordinate sensibilities. Thus arise evil tendencies and vicious impulses and appetencies, inordinate forms of feeling—all that may be included in "the lust of the flesh, and the lust of the eyes, and the pride of life" (I John 2:16). There are in human life many instances of such perverted and inordinate sensibilities as clearly evince a disordered state of the sensuous nature. Such a disordered state is a part of the depravity of human nature. The moral nature is the seat of the conscious and the moral reason. There may be a disordered state of the moral nature, just as of the sensuous; a state in which the moral reason is darkened or perverted, and the conscience voiceless or practically powerless. In such a state moral duty is neither clearly seen nor properly enforced. God is far away, or so dimly seen that the vision of Him has little or no ruling power; for, while in the reality of His existence He still might be apprehended in the intuitive or logical reason, it is only in the apprehension of the moral consciousness that He becomes a living presence.—MILEY, *Systematic Theology*, I, pp. 443, 444.

denying any evil consequences as derived from the fall, the latter making it an effect of a participation in Adam's sin. Arminianism arose as a *via media* or mediating position, but sometimes leaned too far one way or the other. Mr. Wesley made every possible effort to live peaceably with the Calvinists, consistent with the scriptural positions which he held. Mr. Fletcher was always consistent, and his *"Checks to Antinomianism"* was a work so thorough and comprehensive, that it is still the best refutation of the Calvinistic positions. They are deserving of profound study by all who would be informed concerning the truest and best in Arminianism. We greatly prefer the Wesleyan type of Arminian doctrine, for two reasons: (1) it not only teaches, but makes one feel that sin is exceedingly sinful; and (2) it magnifies the atoning work of Jesus Christ. The doctrine of original sin is such, that it cannot be properly understood apart from the free gift of righteousness. Furthermore, if inherited depravity is not of the essence of sin, how can we understand such texts as *the Lamb of God which taketh away the sin of the world;* or *the blood of Jesus Christ his Son cleanseth us from all sin?* To weaken our position on sin, is to weaken it on holiness also. Consequently in the following pages, we have endeavored to set forth the positions of earlier Arminianism as held by Mr. Wesley himself, Mr. Watson, Mr. Fletcher, Wakefield, Sumners, Fields, Banks and Pope.

Definitions of Original Sin. "We believe that original sin, or depravity, is the corruption of the nature of all the offspring of Adam, by reason of which every one is very far gone from original righteousness, or the pure state of our first parents at the time of their creation, is averse to God, is without spiritual life, and is inclined to evil, and that continually; and that it continues to exist with the new life of the regenerate, until eradicated by the baptism with the Holy Spirit" (Article V). This article is historically related to Article VII of the Twenty-five Articles of Methodism, and Article IX of the Thirty-nine Articles of the Anglican Church. Mr.

Wesley omitted from the English Article, the word "fault" as applied to original sin, and also the words "so that the flesh lusteth always contrary to the Spirit, and therefore, in every person born into this world it deserves God's wrath and damnation." Furthermore, he omitted the words "And this infection of nature doth remain, yea in them that are regenerated," which we have retained in a similar statement. These omissions are significant, but cannot be made to support the idea of nonimputation of penalty as Dr. Miley suggests. As to the Calvinistic definitions, the following from the Westminster Confession will be sufficient. "By this sin (our first parents) fell from their original righteousness and communion with God, and so became dead in sin, and wholly defiled in all the faculties and parts of soul and body. They being the root of all mankind, the guilt of this sin was imputed, and the same death in sin and corrupted nature conveyed to all their posterity, descending from them by ordinary generation. From this original corruption, whereby we are utterly indisposed, disabled, and made opposite to all good, and wholly inclined to all evil, do proceed all actual transgressions. This corruption of nature, during this life, doth remain in those that are regenerated; and although it be through Christ pardoned and mortified, yet both itself, and all the motions thereof, are truly and properly sin."

The Nature of Original Sin. While with few exceptions, a belief in original sin has been uniform in the church, there has been a wide variety of opinion as to its nature. (1) By the Greek fathers, the Semi-Pelagians

As commonly understood, the expression "original sin" denotes "the inherent corruption in which all men since the fall are born." The corresponding term in science as distinguished from theology, is "heredity"; as such only, can science know it, and so far as this knowledge goes it is correct. We must go beyond science, into Scripture, and affirm that this hereditary corruption is not a mere "uncondemnable vitiosity." If this hereditary corruption comes at all under the view of God, considered as a moral Being, it must be regarded by him as something either agreeable or obnoxious. If it be regarded as the former, then it is not moral corruption, which is contrary to our hypothesis; but if it be regarded as the latter, then it is condemnable. With a mere physical vitiosity, or corruption, the moral government of God, and hence the plan of redemption, has nothing directly to do. Hence we conclude that original sin is not merely hereditary corruption, but it is with this quality of condemnableness attached thereto.—FOSTER, *Theology,* p. 406.

and some Arminians, emphasis was placed upon inherited depravity instead of original sin. Depravity was thus regarded as physical rather than moral—that is, *vitium* or weakness instead of *peccatum* or sin. Adam's physical condition having deteriorated as a consequence of his sin, this weakened or vitiated nature was communicated to his descendants. Thus the "New School" held that original sin was a vitiosity but not intrinsically sin. It was called such, only because it led to sin. Hence neither vitiosity nor death were regarded as penal inflictions, but only as natural consequences which God ordained to mark His displeasure at Adam's transgression. (2) Closely related to this, is the theory of original sin as concupiscence. By this is meant the native corruption which is the result of the ascendency of man's sensuous or animal nature, over the higher attributes of reason and conscience. It involves a proneness to sin, but is not regarded as intrinsically sinful. This is peculiarly the doctrine of the Roman Catholic Church, but is also held by some branches of Protestantism. (3) Some divines, through an undue emphasis upon the federal headship of Adam, have supposed that original sin was a positive evil infused into man's nature by a judicial act of God, and consequently transmitted to all Adam's posterity. (4) The generally accepted theory of theologians, both Calvinistic and Arminian, is that of privation—a depravity which is the result of deprivation. Two questions arise which demand our consideration, *first,* in what sense is depravity a deprivation; and *second,* in what sense may hereditary depravity be said to be hereditary guilt?

1. Original sin is to be considered as *privatio,* or a privation of the image of God. This is more in harmony with the tenor of the Scriptures than the notion of an infusion of evil qualities into the soul as a result of the divine degree. Arminius calls it "a privation of the image of God," but explains this privation as (1) a forfeiture of the gift of the Holy Spirit; and (2) in consequence of this, the loss of original righteousness. Depravity is therefore "a depravation arising from depriva-

tion." Connected with this deprivation is a positive evil also, which arises as a consequence of the loss of the image of God. Mr. Watson illustrates this by the analogy of physical death which has passed upon all men. He says, "For as the death of the body, the mere privation of the principle of life produces inflexibility of the muscles, the extinction of heat, and sense, and motion, and surrenders the body to the operation of an agency which life, as long as it continued, resisted, namely, that of chemical decomposition; so from the loss of spiritual life, followed estrangement from God, moral inability, the dominion of irregular passions, and the rule of appetite; aversion, in consequence, to restraint; and enmity to God. . . . . This accounts for the whole of man's corruption. The Spirit's influence in him, did not prevent the possibility of his sinning, though it afforded sufficient security to him, as long as he looked up to that source of strength. He did sin, and the Spirit retired; and, the tide of sin once turned in, the mound of resistance being removed, it overflowed his whole nature. In this state of alienation from God men are born, with all these tendencies to evil, because the only con-

The position of Arminius is as follows: "But since the tenor of the covenant into which God entered with our first parents was this, that if they continued in the favor and grace of God, by the observance of that precept and others, the gifts which had been conferred upon them should be transmitted to their posterity, by the like divine grace which they had received; but if they should render themselves unworthy of those favors, through disobedience, that their posterity should likewise be deprived of them, and should be liable to the contrary evils; hence it followed, that all men, who were to be naturally propagated from them, have become obnoxious to death temporal and eternal, and have been destitute of that gift of the Holy Spirit, or of original righteousness. This punishment is usually called a privation of the image of God, and original sin. But we allow this point to be made the subject of discussion—beside the want or absence of original righteousness, may not some other contrary quality be constituted, as another part of original sin? We think it is more probable, that this absence alone of original righteousness is original sin in itself, since it alone is sufficient for the commission and production of every actual sin whatsoever."

Mr. Watson thinks that the privation is not fully expressed by the phrase "the loss of original righteousness," unless that it be meant to include in it the only source of righteousness in even the first man, the life which is imparted and supplied by the Holy Spirit. Hence he says, "Arminius has more forcibly and explicitly expressed that privation of which we speak, by the forfeiture 'of the gift of the Holy Spirit' by which Adam, for himself and his descendants, and the loss of original righteousness as the consequence. This I take to be at once a simple and scriptural view of the case."—WATSON, *Theological Institutes* II, p. 80.

trolling and sanctifying power, the presence of the Spirit, is wanting, and is now given to man, not as when first brought into being, as a creature; but is secured to him by the mercy and grace of a new and different dispensation, under which the Spirit is administered in different degrees, times, and modes, according to the wisdom of God, never on the ground of our being creatures, but as redeemed from the curse of the law by Him who became a curse for us" (WATSON, *Theological Institutes*, II, pp. 79-83).

2. The next question concerns hereditary depravity and hereditary guilt. We have just seen that depravity is the loss of original righteousness in consequence of the withdrawal of the Holy Spirit. The curse threatened to disobedience was death. The sin of Adam incurred the penalty, and the penalty was inflicted. God withdrew from the soul of Adam. His descendants, therefore, were born under the curse of the law which has deprived human nature of the Spirit of God, and which can be restored only in Christ. Hereditary depravity, then, is not only the law of natural heredity, but that law operating under the penal consequence of Adam's sin. Consequently the church teaches, "that the whole race, descending by ordinary generation from the fallen first progenitors, inherit from them a morally tainted and vitiated nature; a nature in which there is no inclination to do anything truly good, but which, as soon as its dispositions or tendencies begin to unfold

In the discussion of the primitive holiness we fully recognize the presence of the Holy Spirit as the source of its highest form. We did not accept the papal view, that original righteousness was wholly a gracious endowment, superadded after the creation of man, but held the Adamic nature just as created to be upright in itself. In entire consistency with this view we held the presence of the Spirit as the source of the fuller strength and tone of that holiness. Provision was thus complete for the more thorough subordination of all sensuous impulses and appetencies, and the complete dominance of the moral and spiritual life. As the result of sin there was a deprivation of the Holy Spirit, and in consequence of this loss a depravation of man's nature. In addition to the more direct effect of this sin upon the sensuous and moral nature, there was a loss of all the moral strength and tone immediately arising from the presence and agency of the Holy Spirit. The detriment was twofold, and in consequence the depravation was the deeper. In this view we still find depravity as a disordered state of the sensuous and moral nature.—MILEY, *Syst. Th.*, I, pp. 444, 445.

themselves, shows itself evil in the production of evil thoughts, words and actions." For this reason Mr. Watson says that hereditary depravity arises from hereditary guilt; and Mr. Wesley interprets the scripture *for that all have sinned* (Rom. 5: 12), to mean that "they were so constituted sinners by Adam's sinning as to become liable to punishment threatened to his transgression" (WESLEY, *Works*, V, p. 535). But the term "guilt" as here used in Arminian theology, needs to be carefully guarded. It may mean, as we have shown, either culpability *(reatus culpœ)*, or mere liability to punishment *(reatus pœnœ)*. In this case, the culpability belonged solely to Adam, and resided in the first sinner as the natural head and representative of the race. The consequences of his sin were passed on to his descendants as the *reatus pœnœ*, or liability to punishment. The two ideas of responsibility for the act and liability for the consequences are not inseparable. Since Adam by his sin was separated from God, this state of separation or death has passed on to his descendants, who in their natural state are therefore said to be "dead in trespasses and sins," and "by nature the children of wrath." To this the testimony of the scriptures is explicit—*for the judgment was by one to condemnation*, and *by one*

The infliction of spiritual death, which we have already shown to be included in the original sentence, consisted, of course, in the loss of spiritual life, which was that principle from which all right direction and control of the various powers and faculties of man flowed. But this spiritual life in the first man was not a natural effect, that is, an effect which would follow from his mere creation, independent of the vouchsafed influence of the Holy Spirit. This may be inferred from the "new creation," which is the renewal of man after the image of Him who first created him. This is the work of the Holy Spirit; but even after this change, this being "born again," man is not able to preserve himself in the renewed condition into which he is brought, but by the continuance of the same quickening and aiding influence. No future growth in knowledge and experience; no power of habit, long persevered in, render him independent of the help of the Holy Spirit; he has rather, in proportion to his growth, a deeper consciousness of his need of the indwelling of God, and of what the apostle calls his "mighty working." The strongest aspiration of this new life is after communion and constant intercourse with God; and as that is the source of new strength, so this renewed strength expresses itself in a "cleaving unto the Lord," with a still more vigorous "purpose of heart." In a word, the sanctity of a Christian is dependent wholly upon the presence of the Sanctifier. We can work out our own salvation only as "God worketh in us to will and to do."—WATSON, *Th. Inst.*, II, p. 80

man's offence death reigned by one, but both in relation to the *free gift* which is *of many offences unto justification* (Rom. 5:16-18). In commenting upon the text *By one man sin entered into the world, and death by sin,* Dr. Ralston says, "Now, if all mankind are not involved in the penalty, we must flatly deny the Word of God, which plainly and repeatedly represents death, in every sense of the word, as a penal infliction—a judicial sentence pronounced upon the guilty as a just punishment for sin" (RALSTON, *Elements of Divinity,* p. 179). Both Mr. Watson and Mr. Howe argue the penal nature of depravity from the retraction of the Spirit, based upon Gal. 3:13, 14; *Christ hath redeemed us from the curse of the law, being made a curse for us: for it is written, Cursed is every one that hangeth on a tree: that the blessing of Abraham might come on the Gentiles through Jesus Christ; that we might receive the promise of the*

Watson, Raymond, Field and Banks lean more toward immediate imputation; Pope more toward the mediate idea. "And since Adam was a public person, a representative, this state of death, of separation from God, has passed on to his descendants, who, in their natural state, are therefore said to be 'dead in trespasses and sins,' aliens from God, and therefore filled with evil."—FIELD, *Handbook Chr. Th.,* p. 151. "The transmission of guilt, in the restricted sense already explained, is perfectly justifiable, if the representative or federal principle is justifiable in the moral as in other spheres. And then the transmission of guilt becomes the basis for the transmission of a corrupt nature."—BANKS, *Manual of Chr. Doct.,* p. 139. "The imputation of Adam's sin to his posterity is confined to its legal results. If a man has committed treason, and has thereby lost his estate, his crime is so imputed to his children that they with him, are made to suffer the penalty of his offense. We do not mean, however, that the personal act of the father is charged upon the children, but that his guilt or liability to punishment is so transferred to them that they suffer the legal consequences of his crime." —RAYMOND, *Chr. Th.,* p. 293.

It is to be observed that the Scripture never disjoins the condemnation from the depravity; the one is always implied in the other, while both are generally connected with the great salvation. It is impossible to conceive the two former apart from each other; though the precision of scriptural language suggests that those who are born with a sinful bias are therefore condemned rather than that being condemned they are necessarily depraved. There is one passage that strikingly illustrates this. The apostle speaks of the Ephesian converts as having been under the sway of the flesh, in the full sense as given above, and thus showing that they were by nature the children of wrath. The depravity and condemnation of the natural estate are here once brought together: it is the solitary instance in which man's nature is said to be under wrath; but the wrath is upon those who lived after that nature rather than upon the nature itself; and both are brought into close connection with Christ, the light of whose coming already shineth, though the darkness is not yet wholly past.—POPE, *Compend. Chr. Th.,* II, p. 54.

Spirit through faith. "If the remission of the curse carry with it the conferring of the grace of the Spirit then the curse, while it did continue, could but include and carry in it the privation of the Spirit. As soon as the law was broken, man was cursed, so as that thereby this Spirit should be withheld, should be kept off, otherwise than as upon the Redeemer's account, and according to His methods it should be restored" (cf. WATSON, *Institutes*, II, p. 81).

Total Depravity. The Scriptures as we have shown, represent human nature as being totally depraved. Since this term has been so grossly misinterpreted in popular speech, its theological use needs to be carefully guarded. As such, the term is not used *intensively*, that is, human nature is not regarded as being so thoroughly depraved that there can be no further degrees in wickedness; but *extensively*, as a contagion spread throughout man's entire being. No informed advocate of this doctrine has ever affirmed that all men are personally wicked in the same degree; or that wicked men may not "wax worse and worse." The term "total" is applicable to depravity in three different senses. (1) Depravity is total in that it affects the entire being of man. It vitiates every power

> It is a remarkable fact, and one which should not be overlooked, that nearly all Calvinistic divines who have attempted to state the Arminian doctrine upon this subject, have taken their views from the semi-Pelagian notions of Dr. Whitby, instead of deriving them from Arminius himself, or those who agree with him. Thus Dr. Dick asserts of the Arminians: "They do not admit that the effect of the fall was a total loss of what we call original righteousness." He represents them as holding that though man "fell from a state of innocence and integrity, and his appetite was now more inclined to evil than before," yet "he did not fall into a state of moral impotence, or lose entirely his power to do good." That these sentiments may be entertained by some who are called Arminians we will not deny; but to ascribe them to Arminius, or to any of his genuine followers, is a palpable misrepresentation. The first sin, according to that great divine, brought upon the offenders the divine displeasure, the loss of that primitive righteousness and holiness in which they were created, and liability to a twofold death. "Wherefore," he says, "whatever punishment was brought down upon our first parents, has likewise pervaded and yet pursues all their posterity; so that all men *are by nature the children of wrath* (Eph. 2:3), obnoxious to condemnation, and to temporal as well as eternal death. They are also devoid of original righteousness and holiness. With these evils they would remain oppressed forever, unless they were liberated by Jesus Christ." It must therefore be evident to every impartial mind, that Arminians as well as Calvinists hold to the doctrine of man's total depravity.—WAKEFIELD, *Christian Theology*, p. 299.

and faculty of spirit, soul and body. The affections are alienated, the intellect darkened, and the will perverted. Mr. Fletcher says that depravity is seen in the corruption of the powers that constitute a good head—the understanding, the imagination, the memory and the reason; and in the depravity of the powers which form a good heart—the will, the conscience and the affections. In the language of the prophet, *the whole head is sick, and the whole heart faint* (Isa. 1:5). (2) Depravity is total in that man is destitute of all positive good. St. Paul says, *For I know that in me (that is, in my flesh,) dwelleth no good thing* (Rom. 7:18). This is clearly stated also, in Article VII of the creed. "We believe that man's creation in godlikeness included ability to choose between right and wrong, and that thus he was made morally responsible; that through the fall of Adam he became depraved so that he cannot now turn and prepare himself by his own natural strength and works to faith and calling upon God; but the grace of God through Jesus Christ is freely bestowed upon all men, enabling all who will to turn from sin to righteousness, believe on Jesus Christ for pardon and cleansing from sin, and follow good works pleasing and acceptable in His sight." As in the case of demerit which attaches to inbred sin apart from the free gift in Christ, but is remitted through the universal diffusion of grace; so depravity apart from this communication of gracious ability, renders man totally unable in spiritual things. Pelagianism holds to a plenary ability of man in his natural state; the New School holds to natural ability; the Calvinistic churches to total inability apart from the election and effectual calling; while Arminians hold to a gracious ability extended to all men, so that in the words of Mr. Wesley, "the state of nature is in some sense a state of grace." (3) Depravity is total in a positive sense, in that the powers of man's being, apart from divine grace, are employed with evil continually (Gen. 6:5; Matt. 15:19). In the words of the creed, "Man is very far gone from original righteousness, and of his own nature inclined to evil, and that continually." Mr. Watson points out that some divines have attempted to soften this article, by availing themselves of the phrase "very far gone," as though it did not express a total defection from original righteousness. The articles were, however, subscribed by the two houses of convocation, in 1571 A.D., in Latin and English also, and therefore both copies are equally authentic. The Latin copy expresses this by the phrase *"quam longissime distet,"* which is as strong an expression as that language can furnish. It therefore fixes the sense of the compilers on this point, and takes away any argument which rests on the alleged equivocalness of the English version (cf. WATSON, *Th. Inst.*, II, p. 47).

ORIGINAL SIN IN RELATION TO CHRIST

The question of original sin cannot be understood apart from its counter truth, the free gift of righteousness. By the "free gift" is meant an unconditional diffusion of grace to all men, as a first benefit of the universal atonement made by Jesus Christ. This may be said to be the distinctive doctrine of earlier Arminianism, and was confirmed by the Wesleyan theologians from Fletcher to Pope. They allowed, with Calvin, that full penalty of death applied to both Adam and his posterity as a consequence of the fall; and that, therefore, apart from the grace of Christ, both guilt and demerit attached to

> This, therefore, is the general ground of justification. By the sin of the first Adam, who was not only the father, but likewise the representative of us all, we all fell short of the favor of God; we all became children of wrath; or, as the apostle expresses it, "judgment came upon all men to condemnation." Even so, by the sacrifice for sin made by the second Adam, as the representative of us all, God is so far reconciled to all the world, that He hath given them a new covenant; the plain condition whereof being once fulfilled, "there is no more condemnation" for us, but "we are justified freely by his grace, through the redemption that is in Christ Jesus."—WESLEY, *Sermon: Justification by Faith.*
>
> The teaching of the later scripture is summed up and confirmed by St. Paul, to the effect that Jesus Christ, the Second Adam, was given to the race of mankind, as the Fountain of an Original Righteousness that avails to efface and more than efface the effects of Original Sin in the case of all those who should be His spiritual seed. Hence this primitive gift was an objective provision for all the descendants of the first sinner, the benefits of which were to be applied to those whose faith should embrace the Saviour. But it is important to remember that it took the form of an original Free Gift to the entire race, before transgression began, and that it has in many respects affected the character of Original Sin: suspending the full strength of its condemnation, and in some degree counteracting its depravity.—POPE, *Compend. Chr. Th.*, II, p. 55.

inherited depravity. Mr. Wesley makes this assertion, but does not offer any explanation as to the manner in which original sin is transmitted. But they differed in this—Calvinism taught that the whole race having fallen in Adam, God might without any impeachment of His justice, predestinate some to salvation in Christ, and leave others to their deserved punishment. Over against this, the Arminians taught that there was a "free gift" of righteousness, unconditionally bestowed upon all men through Christ. Thus Dr. Summers says, "Representative theologians from the beginning until now, from

Fletcher's "Checks to Antinomianism" may well be called classic in Methodist theology. In his "Third Check" he sets forth the four degrees that make up a glorified saint's eternal justification. These are (1) Infant justification; (2) Justification, or the pardon of actual sins, consequent upon believing; (3) The justification by works of St. James; and (4) Justification at the day of judgment.

"All these degrees of justification," he says, "are equally merited by Christ. We do nothing in order to the first, because it finds us in a state of total death. Toward the second, we believe by the power freely given us in the first, and by the additional help of Christ's word and the Spirit's agency. We work by faith in order to the third. And we continue believing in Christ and working together with God, as we have opportunity, in order to the fourth.

"The preaching distinctly these four degrees of a glorified saint's justification is attended with peculiar advantages. The first justification engages the sinner's attention, encourages his hope, and draws his heart by love. The second wounds the self-righteous Pharisee, who works without believing, while it binds up the heart of the returning publican, who has no plea but 'God be merciful to me a sinner!' The third detects the hypocrisy and blasts the vain hopes of all Antinomians, who, instead of 'showing their faith by their works, deny in works the Lord that bought them, and put him to an open shame.' And while the fourth makes even a 'Felix tremble,' it causes believers to 'pass the time of their sojourning here in humble fear' and cheerful watchfulness.

"Though all these degrees of justification meet in glorified saints, we offer violence to Scriptures if we think . . . . that they are inseparable. For all the wicked who 'quench the convincing Spirit,' and are finally given up to a reprobate mind, fall from the first, as well as Pharaoh. All who 'receive the seed among thorns,' all who 'do not forgive their fellow-servants,' all who 'begin in the Spirit and end in the flesh, and all 'who draw back,' and become sons and daughters of 'perdition,' by falling from the third, lose the second and Hymenaeus, Philetus, and Demas. And none partake of the fourth but those who 'bear fruit unto perfection,' according to one or another of the divine dispensations: 'some producing thirty-fold,' like heathens, 'some sixty-fold,' like Jews, and 'some a hundred-fold,' like Christians.

"From the whole it appears, that although we can do absolutely nothing toward our first justification, yet to say that neither faith nor works are required in order to the other three, is one of the boldest, most unscriptural, and most dangerous assertions in the world; which sets aside the best half of the Scriptures, and lets gross Antinomianism come in full tide upon the Church."—FLETCHER, *Works*, I, pp. 161, 162.

Fletcher to Pope, have overthrown this fundamental teaching of Calvinism with the express statement of the Scriptures, setting over against the death-dealing first Adam the life-giving Second. If a decree of condemnation has been issued against original sin, irresponsibily derived from the first Adam, likewise a decree of justification has been issued from the same court, whose benefits are unconditionally bestowed through the Second Adam. *Therefore as by the offence of one judgment came upon all men to condemnation; even so by the righteousness of one the free gift came upon all men unto justification of life. For as by one man's disobedience many were made sinners, so by the obedience of one shall many be made righteous* (Rom. 5:18, 19). The first member of each of these verses is fully balanced and reversed by the second member. Had not the intervention of the Second Adam been foreseen, universally making and constituting righteous all who were made and constituted sinners, Adam would never have been permitted to propagate his species, and the race would have been cut off in its sinning head" (SUMMERS, *Syst. Th.*, II, p. 39). Thus the true Arminian position admits the full penalty of sin, and consequently neither minifies the exceeding sinfulness of sin, nor holds lightly the atoning work of our Lord Jesus Christ. It does so, however, not by denying the full force of the penalty, as do the semi-Pelagians, but by magnifying the sufficiency of the atone-

But the gift of righteousness to the race before the succession of its history began was of the nature of a provision to counteract the effects of sin, when original sin should become actual. It did not at once abolish the effects of the fall in the first pair, whose original sin was also in their case actual transgression; it did not place them in a new probation, nor did it preclude the possibility of a future race of sinners. The great Atonement had now become necessary: as necessary to these parents of the race as it was after they had spread into countless multitudes. The Redeemer was already the Gift of God to man; but He was still "the coming One," as St. Paul once calls Him in relation to this very fact: making the first sinner the first type of the Saviour from sin. The Atonement does not put away sin in the sovereignty of arbitrary grace, but as the virtue of grace pardoning and healing all who believe. It began at once to build the house of a new humanity—a spiritual seed of the Second Adam—the first Adam being himself the first living stone of the new temple. And with reference to the life bestowed on this new race St. Paul strains language to show how much it superabounds, how much it surpasses the effect of the Fall.—POPE, *Compend. Chr. Th.*, II, p. 56.

ment, and the consequent communication of prevenient grace to all men through the headship of the last Adam.

The Natural and Federal Headship of Adam. Arminianism accepts both the natural and federal headship of Adam, but rejects the extreme length to which these positions have sometimes been carried. It holds with realism, to the solidarity of the race, but rejects the idea of personal participation in Adam's sin. It holds also that Adam was legally or federally the representative of the race, but it always holds this in connection with the natural headship of Christ. Natural headship may have its consequences in hereditary depravity, but in no sense can these consequences be sinful, unless they are regarded as operating under penalty. Legal consequences flow only from legal relations. This the Scriptures specifically declare. The *locus classicus* is Romans 5:12-19, which has already been discussed in some of its phases. Omitting the italicized words in the summary, we have the following: *as by one offence, unto all men, to condemnation; even so, by one righteousness, unto all men, unto justification of life.* Here the sin of Adam and the merits of Christ are regarded as coextensive, the condemnation of the first being reversed by the righteousness of the second. St. Paul declares specifically that Adam was *the figure of him that was to come* (Rom. 5:14). Adam being the type of "the Coming One," his sin cannot be disjoined from the righteous obedience of Adam the Deliverer. "The redemption of man by Christ," says Wakefield, "was certainly not an afterthought, brought in upon man's apostasy. It was a provision, and when man

As to the case of Adam and his adult descendants, it will be seen that all became liable to bodily death. Here was justice. But by means of the atonement, which effectually declares the justice of God, this sentence is reversed by a glorious resurrection. Again, when God, the fountain of spiritual life, withdrew himself from Adam, he died a spiritual death and became morally corrupt; and, as "that which is born of the flesh is flesh," all his posterity are in the same condition. Here is justice. But spiritual life visits man from another quarter and through other means. The second Adam "is a quickening Spirit." Through the atonement which He has made the Holy Spirit is given to man, that he may again infuse into his corrupt nature the heavenly life and regenerate and sanctify it. Here is mercy. And as to a future state, eternal life is promised to all who perseveringly believe in Christ, which reverses the sentence of eternal death. Here again, is the manifestation of mercy.—WAKEFIELD, *Christian Theology*, p. 294.

fell he found justice in hand with mercy. If we look at the subject in this light, every difficulty will be removed" (WAKEFIELD, *Chr. Th.*, p. 294). The Lamb was slain from the foundation of the world, and the atonement began when sin began. The gospel was preached at the time the first sin was condemned; and the provision far exceeded the offense — for where sin abounded, grace did much more abound. Thus "original sin and original grace met in the mystery of mercy at the very gate of Paradise."

The Nature of the Free Gift. What, then, was the nature of this free gift, and what are the benefits from it which accrue to the race? We may broadly summarize these as follows: (1) The first benefit of the free gift was to preserve mankind from sinking below the possibility of redemption. It was the preservation of the race from utter destruction. Not only was the natural

But for the interposition of the plan of redemption, no other result could have followed the first transgression, at least, so it seems evident in the light of rational thought, than the immediate death of the first pair. Temporal death, or the death of the body, would have terminated their existence, and the second death must have instantly ensued. That the death of the body would render propagation impossible is too evident to require distinct statement. Human nature being what it is, the idea that souls without bodies can be propagated is too preposterous for a moment's indulgence. The only conception admissible in the case, is that, but for redemption, the race would have become extinct in the persons of our parents. For being and its blessings all mankind are indebted to the garden agonies, to the crucifixion and death of our Lord Jesus Christ. Consciousness of thought, emotion, and volition, all the pleasures of knowledge, love and hope, all we are or may hope to be, all we have, and all we enjoy, are the purchase of our Saviour's death. We are bought with a price, even the precious blood of the Son of God. Does any one conceive here an incongruity in calling existence a blessing, a gracious gift, the result of a benevolent interposition, in the case of those whose existence issues in eternal death?—RAYMOND, *Systematic Theology*, II, pp. 308, 309.

It is well known that the Methodist doctrine of sin is greatly modified by her doctrine of the atonement and the universality of its grace. We have ever held the doctrine of a common native depravity; that this depravity is in itself a moral ruin; and that there is no power in us by nature unto a good life. But through a universal atonement there is a universal grace—the light and help of the Holy Spirit in every soul. If we are born with a corrupt nature in descent from Adam, we receive our existence under an economy of redemption, with a measure of the grace of Christ. With such grace, which shall receive increase on its proper use, we may turn unto the Lord and be saved. With these doctrines of native depravity and universal grace there is for every soul the profoundest lesson of personal responsibility for sin, and of the need of Christ in order to salvation and a good life.—MILEY, *Syst. Th.*, I, pp. 532, 533.

image of man preserved, but the eternal sense of right and wrong, of good and evil were not effaced, and thus the moral image was in some sense shielded from violation. The fall was the utter ruin of nothing in our humanity; only the depravation of every faculty. The human mind retains the principles of truth; the heart the capacity for holy affections; the will its freedom, not yet the freedom of necessary evil. All this we owe to the Second Adam" (POPE, *Compend. Chr. Th.*, II, p. 52). (2) The second effect of the free gift was the reversal of the condemnation and the bestowal of a title to eternal life. *Judgment came upon all men to condemnation, so also, the free gift came upon all men unto justification of life.* Thus the condemnation which rested upon the race through Adam's sin is removed by the one oblation of Christ. By this we understand that no child of Adam is condemned eternally, either for the original offense, or its consequences. Thus we may say, that none are predestinated unconditionally to eternal damnation, and that culpability does not attach to original sin. We must believe that condemnation in the sense of the doom of the race, never passed beyond Adam and the unindividualized nature of man. It was arrested in Christ as regards every individual, and thereby changed into a conditional sentence. Man is not now condemned for the depravity of his own nature, although that depravity is of the essence of sin; its culpability we maintain, was removed by the free gift in Christ. Man is condemned solely for his own transgressions. The free gift removed the original condemnation and abounds unto many offenses. Man becomes amenable for the depravity of his heart, only when rejecting the remedy for it, he consciously ratifies it as his own, with all its penal consequences. (3) The free gift was the restoration of

The doctrine of natural depravity affirms the total inability of man to turn himself to faith and calling upon God. This being postulated, the affirmation that all have a fair probation involves the doctrine of a gracious influence unconditionally secured as the common inheritance of the race: this gracious influence is so secured; the same blood that purchased for mankind a conscious existence procured for them all grace needful for the responsibilities of that existence.—RAYMOND, *Syst. Th.*, II, p. 316.

the Holy Spirit to the race; not in the sense of the spirit of life in regeneration; or the spirit of holiness in entire sanctification, but as the spirit of awakening and conviction. We have seen that depravity is twofold—the absence of original righteousness, and a bias or tendency toward sin as a consequence of this deprivation. Both of these have their origin in the withdrawal of the Holy Spirit as the original bond of union between the soul and God. Hence the Spirit was as surely given back to the race as the atonement was given to it, that is, as a provisional discipline for the fuller grace of redemption.

The Mitigation of Inherited Depravity. The free gift has important bearings upon the question of original sin, and serves to reconcile some of the apparent contradictions in Arminian theology. Thus, both the earlier and later Arminians maintain that Adam's posterity are not to be held accountable for his sin, but they do it in very different ways. Earlier Arminianism holds that Adam's descendants came under the full penalty of his sin, that is, death, temporal, spiritual and eternal. But they hold that this penalty was remitted by the free gift imparted to all men as a first benefit of the atonement, made by the Lamb slain from the foundation of the world. The later Arminians with their Pelagianizing tendencies, reach the same result but in a less scriptural manner, by denying that the consequences of Adam's sin are penal in nature. The same apparent contradiction is seen in the different views as to the nature of inherited depravity. Both earlier and later Arminianism hold that guilt in the sense of culpability or demerit, does not at-

Mr. Watson in speaking of the rejection of the remedy for sin, has this to say: "Should this be rejected, he stands liable to the whole penalty, to the punishment of loss as to the natural consequence of his corrupted nature which renders him unfit for heaven: to the punishment of even pain for the original offense, we may also without injustice, say, as to an adult, whose actual transgressions, when the means of deliverance have been afforded him by Christ, is consenting to all rebellion against God, and to that of Adam himself; and to the penalty of his own actual transgressions, aggravated by his having made light of the gospel."—WATSON, *Institutes,* II, p. 57.

tach to it. Herein, the Arminian is distinguished from the Calvinist. But earlier Arminianism holds that inherited depravity is of the nature of sin, and that guilt originally attached to it, but was remitted by the free gift. Later Arminianism regards inherited depravity as merely natural heredity without demerit or culpability. Again, earlier Arminianism regards man as unable of himself to faith and calling upon God, but it regards this lack of natural ability as restored in the form of a gracious ability.

Original Sin in Its General Relations

We have seen that the connection between original sin and the Christian doctrine of salvation is fundamental and universal. The sin of Adam, its consequences for the race, the atonement in Christ and the grace of the Spirit are inextricably bound up together. Whatever the position which is taken toward one, whether theological or practical, affects all. Several general questions arise which must be given consideration: (1) What is the moral condition of man at birth; (2) In what sense is he in bondage to sin; (3) Is it possible to know the carnal mind apart from its manifestations; and (4) What is the difference between original sin and human infirmity?

The Corrupt Nature of Man. Man's nature as he is born into the world is corrupt, is very far gone from original righteousness, is averse to God, is without spiritual life, is inclined to evil, and that continually. However, for this depraved nature he is not responsible, and hence no guilt or demerit attaches to it. This is not because depravity is uncondemnable, but because through the grace of our Lord Jesus Christ, the free gift reversed the penalty as a consequence of the universal atonement. We hold, therefore, as truly as later Arminianism, that man as he comes into the world is not guilty of inbred sin. He becomes responsible for it, only when having rejected the remedy provided by atoning blood, he ratifies it as his own. We may say the same concerning free agency. All who will may turn from sin to righteousness, believe on Jesus Christ for pardon and cleansing from sin, and follow good works pleasing and acceptable in His sight. This free agency, however, is not mere natural ability, it is gracious ability. "Through the fall of Adam, man became depraved, so that he cannot now turn and prepare himself by his own natural strength and works to faith and calling upon God; but the grace of God through Jesus Christ is freely bestowed upon all men." Mr. Wesley calls attention to the fact that redemption was coeval with the fall. "Allowing that all the souls of men are dead by nature, that excuses none, seeing there is no man that is in a state of mere nature; there is no man, unless he has quenched the Spirit, that is wholly devoid of the grace of God" (WESLEY, *Sermon: On Working Out Our Own Salvation*).

The Bondage of Inbred Sin. The nature of inbred sin is that of a bondage of the higher nature to the lower. This lower nature in its entire being—body, soul and spirit—is called by St. Paul, the flesh or *sarx* ($\sigma\acute{a}\rho\xi$). In this sense, the "flesh" is the nature of man separated from God and become subject to the creature. That is, the Self or *autos ego* ($\alpha\grave{v}\tau\grave{o}\varsigma\ \grave{\epsilon}\gamma\acute{\omega}$) is without God, but only in the sense of being without Him as God: and being without God, it is in the world as a false sphere of life and enjoyment. This position which regards the flesh as depraved humanity enslaved to sense, is closely allied to the idea of concupiscence. In fact, St. Paul speaks of its working *all manner of concupiscence* (Rom. 7:8). He further declares that the one spiritual agent has the power to will, but is not able to carry this will into effect. Consequently there is impotence to good. "Therefore the one personality has a double character: the *inward man of the mind,* to which *to will is present,* and the flesh or the body of sin, in which *how to perform that which is good I find not.* But the one person, to whom these opposite elements belong—an inner man, a reason, a will to good; a carnal bias, an outer man, a slavery to evil—is behind all these, behind even the inner man. And in him, in the inmost secret of his nature, is the original vice which gives birth to these contradictions. . . . . It teaches most distinctly the freedom of the will, and at the same time the inability of man to do what is good. The harmony of these seeming opposites is most manifest; the faculty of willing is untouched in any case, and the influence of conscience prompts it to will the right; but this is bound up with a miserable impotence to good, and results in both a natural and moral inability to do what the law of God requires" (POPE, *Compend. Chr. Th.*, II, pp. 66, 67).

Filthiness of the Flesh and Spirit. St. Paul makes it clear, that in addition to the works of the flesh which are manifest (Gal. 5:19), there is also a secret filthiness of the flesh and spirit, which exists as the fountainhead or source of these outward carnal manifestations. He therefore urges the disciples to *cleanse* themselves *from all filthiness of the flesh and spirit, perfecting holiness in the fear of God* (II Cor. 7:1). Inbred sin as a principle can be known only through its personal and actual manifestation. Failure to remember this sometimes leads to confusion in the experience of those who seek deliverance from it. They see the "depths of pride, self-will and hell" in their own hearts through the illumination of the Holy Spirit, but they see it in the light of its past manifestations. This only do they see, that the works of the

> The Spirit's universal influence qualifies original sin as He is in every responsible soul a Remembrancer of a forfeited estate, the Prompter to feel after God and regain that communion which all history proves to be an inextinguishable yearning of mankind. He suffers not the spirit of man to forget its great loss. It is through this preliminary universal influence that guilt is naturally in man ashamed of its deformity. . . . . But conscience suggests the thought, at least in man, of recovery; and the same Spirit who moves toward God in conscience, through fear and hope, universally touches the secret springs of the will. Original sin is utter powerlessness to good; it is in itself a hard and absolute captivity. But it is not left to itself. When the apostle says that the Gentiles have the law written in their hearts, and in conscience measure their conduct by that standard, and may do by nature the things contained in the law, he teaches us plainly that in the inmost recesses of nature there is the secret mystery of grace which, if not resisted and quenched, prompts the soul to feel after God, and gives it those secret, inexplicable beginnings of the movement toward good which fuller grace lays hold on. In fact, the very capacity of salvation proves that the inborn sinfulness of man has been in some degree restrained; that its tendency to absolute evil has been checked; and that natural ability and moral ability—to use the language of controversy—are one through the mysterious operation of a grace behind all human evil.—POPE, *Compend. Chr. Th.*, II, p. 60.

flesh having been put off in conversion, there still remains the necessity of crucifying the flesh itself, that is, the carnal nature with its sinful tendencies and outreachings. *They that are Christ's,* in the full New Covenant sense, *have crucified the flesh with the affections and lusts* (Gal. 5:24).

Depravity and Infirmity. One more consideration demands our attention. We have seen that the "flesh" as St. Paul uses the term, includes both the spiritual and physical nature as under the reign of sin. The corruption extends to the body as well as the soul. The depravity of his spiritual nature may be removed by the baptism with the Holy Spirit, but the infirmities of flesh will be removed only in the resurrection and glorification of the body. Man in a general way has no difficulty in distinguishing between the soul and the body, but the fine line of demarcation, the exact arresting point between the spiritual and the physical, cannot be determined. Could we but know where this line of distinction lies, we could with ease distinguish between carnal manifestations which have their seat wholly in the soul, and physical infirmities which attach to his physical constitution still under the reign of sin. We are told that the body is dead because of sin, but the spirit is life because of righteousness. Since mental strain often weakens the physical constitution, and physical weakness in turn clouds the mind and spirit of man, there is ever needful, a spirit of charity toward all men.

> Fallen human nature is flesh or σάρξ: the whole being of man, body and soul, soul and spirit, separated from God, and subjected to the creature. . . . . The disturbance in the very essence of human nature may be regarded as affecting the entire personality of man as a spirit acting in a body. He is born with a nature which is—apart both from the external Evil One and from the external renewing power of the New Creation—under the bondage of sin. That bondage may be regarded with reference to the lower nature that enslaves the higher, and the higher nature that is enslaved.—POPE, *Compend. Chr. Th.,* II, p. 65.

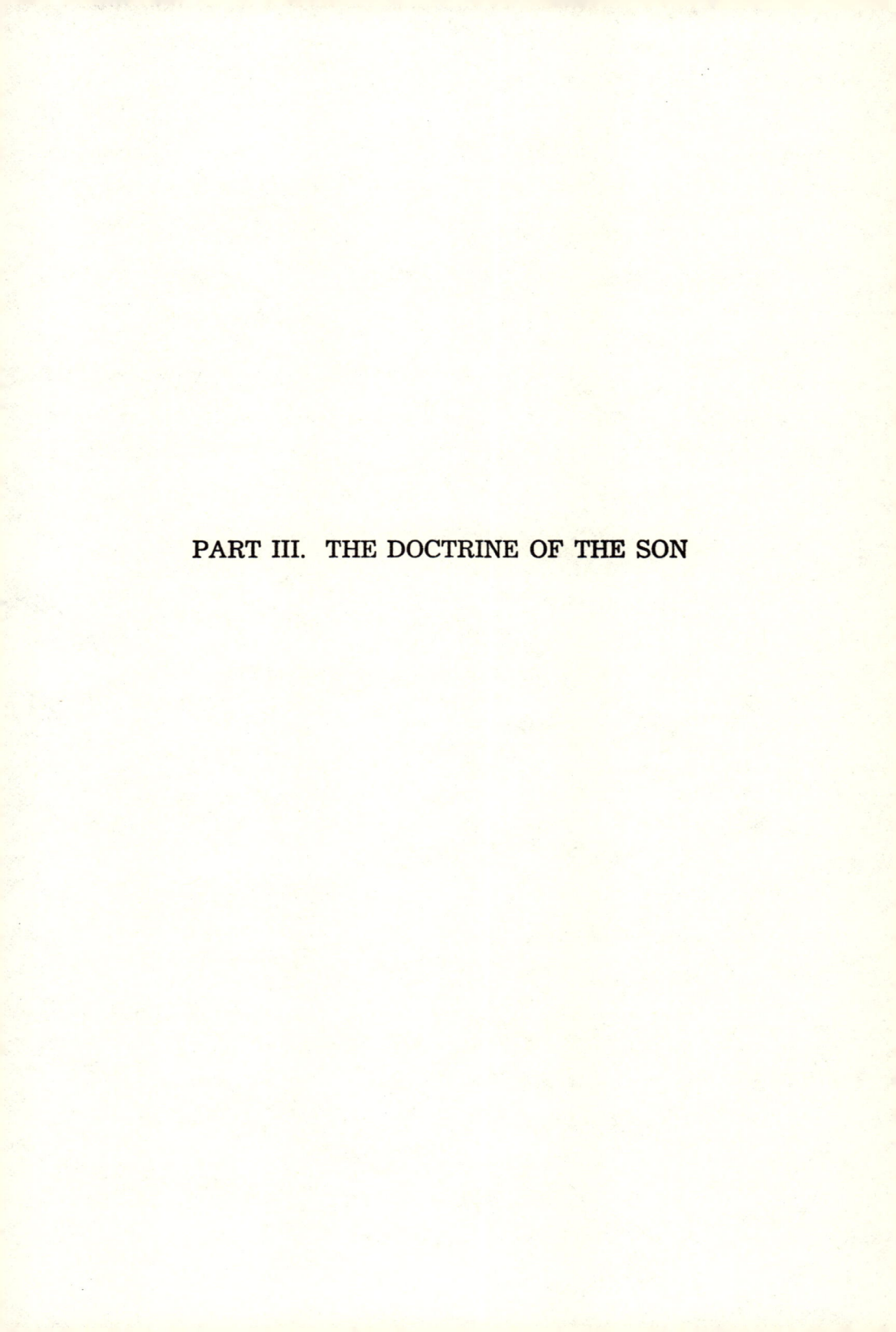

PART III. THE DOCTRINE OF THE SON

CHAPTER XX

CHRISTOLOGY

In approaching the subject of Christology, we may be permitted to emphasize the fact, that in this department we reach the very heart of Christianity. Here will be found those distinctive doctrines which mark Christianity as unique and universal; and which set it over against the ethnic religions in all of their forms. In our discussion of Religion, we pointed out the twofold ground of distinction between Christianity and the pagan religions as lying, *first,* in the difference of ethical quality; and *second,* in the character of the Founder. St. Paul recognized whatever of truth the ethnic religions contained, but condemned them because of their low moral tone. They were untrue to the creature, and untrue to the Creator. By way of anticipation also, we pointed out the superiority of Christianity as being founded by Jesus Christ, the Son of the only true and living God; and as being a religion of redemptive power and inward life. We are now to consider the distinctive doctrines of Christ in a more extended and critical manner.

Christology (Χριστοῦ λόγος), is that department of theology which deals with the Person of Christ as the Redeemer of mankind. The subject is sometimes enlarged to include both the Person and Work of Christ; but in general the term Soteriology is applied to the latter, and the term Christology limited to the former. The Advent of Christ is the central fact of all history, and with it is bound up the whole work of creation and redemption. Through Him, God sustains a twofold relation to mankind—one constituted by the creative Word in forming man after His own image; the other, as a consequence of sin having entered the world through the temptation and fall of Adam. A proper conception of the Advent, therefore, involves the two terms, *God* and *man,* and their reciprocal relations. As the Advent cannot be referred to God alone, or to man alone, so it may not be referred to merely legal and external relations existing between them. We must view it as an incarnation, in which God and man are conjoined in one Person—the eternal Son. In purpose it antedates, not only the fall of man and of angels, but the very beginning of the creative process. The cosmos included in its consummation the Lamb slain before the foundation of the world. In the very heart of God, is to be found that sacrificial love which gave the Son to be the propitiation for our sins. "Amongst all the works God intended before time, and in time effected," said Archbishop Leighton, "this is the masterpiece that is here said to be foreordained, the manifesting of God in the flesh for man's redemption."

As the doctrine of the Trinity is implicit in the Old Testament, so in the same manner, there is an Old Testament Christology. Thus, *Abraham saw my day, and was glad* (John 8:56). *Many prophets and righteous men have desired to see those things which ye see* (Matt. 13:17). *The prophets .... searched diligently .... what the Spirit of Christ which was in them did signify, when it testified beforehand the sufferings of Christ, and the glory that should follow* (I Peter 1:10-12). Only in the New Testament were these mysteries fully revealed. The Old Testament, therefore, must be viewed in the light of a preparatory economy, which comes to its perfect fulfillment in Christ. In the words of Dr. Schaff, "Genuine Judaism lived for Christianity and died with the birth of Christianity." We may note two lines of development—one objective and divine, the other subjective and human.

First, there is the objective fact of Divine Revelation. In the protevangelium, (Gen. 3:15) the promise that the seed of the woman shall bruise the serpent's head is as broad as the human race. Perhaps it was for this reason that the title "Son of man" was so frequently used by our Lord. Following this there was throughout the course of history added revelations, each in some sense an advent or a coming to God to His people. There was the Abrahamic covenant, in which God selected a people with whom He established personal communion, and through whom the promised Seed should come. Following this was the law given by Moses, which quickened the sense of sin and guilt. It served also as a tutor to bring men to a felt need for One who should be a propitiation for sin. Thus the community originated by the Abrahamic covenant, and taught by this higher revelation, was gradually transformed into a "peculiar people" (Deut. 14: 2; 26: 18, 19; I Peter 2: 9) with a nobler conception of the holiness of God, a deeper sense of the exceeding sinfulness of sin, and a new prophetic hope. They were, as St. Paul declares, *shut up unto the faith which should afterwards be revealed. Wherefore the law was our schoolmaster to bring us unto Christ, that we might be justified by faith* (Gal. 3: 23, 24). But Israel failed to grasp the spiritual significance of the law and contented themselves with external forms and ceremonial washings. Only the "remnant" understood its spiritual import, but out of this remnant the prophets arose. Prophetism in Israel was a distinct and far-reaching force. The prophets cultivated the Messianic hope and pointed the way to a new spiritual order. This prophetic line found its culmination and completion in John the Baptist, of whom our Lord said, *There hath not risen a greater than John the Baptist .... for all the prophets and the law prophesied until John* (Matt. 11: 11, 13). Immediately preceding the birth of Jesus prophetism had been reduced to a small, apocalyptic circle — Zacharias and Elisabeth, Joseph and Mary, Simeon the aged and Anna the prophetess—all of whom waited for the consolation of Israel.

Second, there is the subjective factor of human submission. Divine revelation is in some sense conditioned by the passive element of human receptivity. As the prophetic order culminated in John, so human submissiveness and trust found its highest Old Testament expression in Mary—the "highly favored" one of Israel, and blessed among women (Luke 1: 28). The character of Mary as it appears in the Gospel accounts is thus summarized by Dr. Gerhart: "Childlike simplicity is united with divine faith, holy self-surrender with womanly innocence, virgin purity with an obedient will. We detect a consciousness of spotless chastity, but no maiden prudery; a perception of the wonderful in the Annunciation, but no ecstatic excitement; a sense of extraordinary dignity of her vocation, but no proud elation; a deep joy, but no self-forgetfulness; an unwonted silence, but no fear; a becoming thoughtfulness, but no unbelief or doubt. The providence of God had in the process and through the conflicts of Messianic history formed a woman who by her moral and spiritual elevation was capable of becoming the mother of the ideal Man" (GERHART, *Inst. Chr. Relig.*, II, p. 201). It was in Mary, therefore, that the protevangelium given in Eden came to its fulfillment through the grace of the covenant. This Mary recognized in the Magnificat, when she declared that *he hath holpen his servant Israel, in remembrance of his mercy; as he spake to our fathers, to Abraham and to his seed forever* (Luke 1: 54, 55). It is applied directly to Christ by St. Paul, *Now to Abraham and his seed were the promises made. He saith not, And to seeds, as of many; but as of one, and to thy seed, which is Christ* (Gal. 3: 16). The nature of this covenant is given its spiritual interpretation by Zacharias in the Benedictus, *The oath which he sware to our father Abraham, That he would grant unto us, that we being delivered out of the hand of our enemies might serve him without fear, in holiness and righteousness before him, all the days of our life* (Luke 1: 73, 74). The announcement of the Advent to Joseph in the words, *She shall bring forth a son, and thou shalt call his name Jesus: for he shall save his people from their sins* (Matt. 1: 21), is by St. Matthew interpreted as a fulfillment of Isaiah's prophecy, *Behold, a virgin shall be with child, and shall bring forth a son, and they shall call his name Emmanuel, which being interpreted is, God with us* (Matt. 1: 23, Isa. 7: 14).

The study of Christology is best approached through its presentation in the Holy Scriptures, where the great events in the life of Christ are viewed in the light of the theological significance which attaches to them. Following this, the development of Christology in the Church will be considered, as furnishing the broad outlines under which the subject must be treated, and the dangers with which it is confronted. We shall then in this chapter consider (I) The Scriptural Approach to Christology; and (II) The Development of Christology in the Church.

The Scriptural Approach to Christology

The events in the life of Christ, which will be considered in their theological significance, are as follows: (1) The Miraculous Conception and Birth; (2) The Circumcision; (3) The Normal Development of Jesus; (4) The Baptism; (5) The Temptation; (6) The Obedience of Christ, His Passion and Death. The Descensus, the Resurrection, the Ascension and the Session, will be best considered in connection with His state of exaltation.

The Miraculous Conception and Birth. The account of the miraculous conception and birth of Jesus is given in the Gospel of Matthew as an exhibition of the fulfillment of prophecy, and in the Gospel of Luke as a fundamental historical fact in the work of redemption. This fact has been strongly assailed at times, but the preexistence of Christ demands it. Nor is it a matter of indifference as some have asserted, for its denial would reduce Christ to the level of a human being, and involve His person in the sin of the race. Those who deny the Virgin Birth involve themselves in greater problems than those who admit its miraculous nature. The appearance of Christ in the midst of history as the one and only sinless Being, cannot be explained except on the Scriptural basis that the Son of God became man (John 1:14). It is for this reason that the Church affirms that Jesus was conceived by the Holy Ghost and born of the Virgin Mary. From the human viewpoint, Mary conceives ac-

---

Bishop Pearson states that "As the Holy Ghost did not frame the human nature of Christ out of His own substance; so must we not believe that He formed any part of His flesh of any other substance than of the Virgin. For certainly He was of the fathers according to the flesh, and was as to that truly and totally the son of David and Abraham" —Pearson, *On the Creed*, p. 253.

cording to the natural law of motherhood but by miraculous agency, and thereby imparts to her child the same organic constitution which she possessed. Furthermore, the child was conceived with all the essential properties of original humanity, the accidental quality of sin in the fallen Adamic race being excluded. Sin is not an essential element of human nature, but an alien principle which falsifies the beginning of individual life (Psalms 51:5), and brings men into bondage through the law of sin and death which is in their members (Rom. 7:23).

But to establish the real and sinless humanity of Jesus, affirms but one aspect of the mystery of His person. His conception was also the assumption of human nature by the divine Son. As Hooker expressed it, "The flesh and the conjunction of the flesh was but one act" (HOOKER, *Eccl. Pol.*, Bk. 5, chaps. 52, 53). It is for this reason that the Scripture speaks of the new being as "that holy thing" which was to be born; implying thereby that a change was to be wrought in the very constitution of humanity. Jesus was not, therefore, merely the origin of a new individual in the race, but a pre-existent One coming into the race from above; He was not merely another individualization of human nature, but the conjoining of the divine and human natures in a new order of being—a theanthropic person. The instant human nature is conjoined with God in the person of Jesus it becomes a redeemed nature, and furnishes the principle of regeneration for fallen mankind. In Jesus there is the birth of a new order of humanity, a new man, *which after God is created in righteousness and true holiness* (Eph. 4:24). Hence in the person of Jesus Christ is to be found the ground of His mediatorial work, the principle of "eternal life" which through the Spirit is given to all who believe in Him.

The Circumcision. The rite of circumcision marked the official induction of a Jewish child into the blessing of the Abrahamic covenant. Jesus was therefore, in conformity to the Levitical law, circumcised on the eighth day (Luke 2:21). By His birth of the Virgin Mary, Jesus partook of the common human nature, and was therefore *the seed of David according to the flesh* (Rom. 1: 3). But He partook also of the life of the race as it had been elevated and disciplined through the Abrahamic covenant. Consequently He was not only the "seed of David," but also the "seed of Abraham." *For verily he took not on him the nature of angels; but he took on him the seed of Abraham.* And as the promise to Abraham included the gift of the Spirit (cf. Heb. 7: 6 and Gal. 3: 14); St. Paul affirms further, that He was *declared to be the Son of God with power, according to the spirit of holiness, by the resurrection from the dead* (Rom. 1: 4). The significance of these scriptures lies just here, that final perfection is not attainable through the kingdom of nature, but through the kingdom of grace. While the humanity of Jesus was spotless, and in some true sense already redeemed in the person of Christ, it was not true in the application of redemption to mankind apart from the incarnation. It could not, therefore, be the final perfecting of the Son for His redemptive office. It should be recalled that the promise to Abraham was that *in Isaac shall thy seed be called* (Gen. 21: 12). And although Isaac was the child of promise, prefiguring the birth of Christ, yet that promise was not made to Isaac after the flesh, but only when in a figure he had been received again from the dead. Hence St. Paul asserts that *he received the sign of circumcision, a seal of the righteousness of the faith which he had yet being uncircumcised: that he might be the father of all them that believe, though they be not circumcised; that righteousness might be imputed to them also. . . . . For the promise, that he should be the heir of the world, was not to Abraham, or to his seed, through the law, but through the righteousness of faith* (Rom. 4: 11, 13).

But a sound Christology must hold, that for Jesus circumcision was something more than an empty religious rite, devoid of meaning and spiritual power. For Him it was a covenant of grace, in which God's relation to man and man's relation to God was lifted to a unique and exalted level. It was for Him the communion of two natures in one Person—the divine and the human. Hence in this exalted communion with the Father through the Spirit, it was possible for the child Jesus to pass from the spotlessness and purity of His childhood, through perfect youth to an uncorrupted and undefiled manhood. In Him unconscious innocence was transformed into conscious obedience; and the holiness of His nature never knew either the contamination or experience of sin. We may say, then, that the personal fellowship of God with man promised in Abraham, received its perfect fulfillment in Christ without error or deficiency; and hence we read that Jesus *increased in wisdom and stature, and in favour with God and man* (Luke 2: 52).

The Normal Development of Jesus. We must regard that portion of the life of Jesus from the circumcision to the baptism, a period of about thirty years, as one of preparation for His great mediatorial work. Aside from the account of the visit to Jerusalem when Jesus became a child of the law, the Scriptures are silent; but we must not thereby assume that it was a period of inactivity. It must have been one of physical, ethical and spiritual development; for when our Lord took on Him our manhood, He took it under the law of natural development common to human nature. He might have taken it with all the glory of the Transfiguration, but He chose instead to take into communion with Himself the germ of all that is called man; that in Him human nature might unfold apart from sin, and consequently through the resurrection and ascension be brought to its glorious perfection. Early in the history of the Church Irenæus wrote that Christ "did not despise or evade any condition of humanity, nor set aside in Himself that law which He had appointed for the human race, but sanctified every age, by that period corresponding to it which belonged to Himself. For He came to save all through means of Himself, infants, and children, and boys, and youth, and old men. . . . . At last He came on to death itself, that He might be 'the firstborn from the dead, that in all things he might have the pre-eminence,' The Prince of life, existing before all and going before all."

There are two passages in the Gospel of Luke which refer to the growth and development of Jesus, one to His childhood (Luke 1: 80), and one to His youth as a "son of the law" (Luke 2: 52). Dr. Gerhart points out that in the first passage the child is represented as being passive and receptive rather than active. *The child grew, and waxed strong in spirit, filled with wisdom* [or becoming full of wisdom]: *and the grace of God was upon him* (Luke 2: 40). In the second it is stated that he "increased" or "advanced" in wisdom implying that this was a personal advance, due to the free action of His own powers. *And Jesus increased in wisdom and stature, and in favour with God and man* (Luke 2: 52). It should be further noted that in the first text the progress is from the physical to the spiritual; while in the second the order is reversed (cf. GERHARDT, *Inst. of Chr. Relig.*, II, p. 233ff). We must conclude that the uniqueness of Jesus as it concerns His growth and development, lies in this, that it was the unfolding of a pure and normal human nature apart from sin. In ordinary childhood there is the disintegrating force of inherited depravity, the bias due to sin and hence its development can never be wholly normal. But Jesus had none of the vitiating consequences of inbred sin. The outward pressures He must have felt, but in His being there were no alien forces, no biased dispositions. Under the tuition of the Holy Spirit, and in spiritual communion with the Father, His development was pre-eminently perfect.

The Baptism. The baptism of Jesus was His official induction into the office of the Messiah or Christ. As in the case of the circumcision, this rite was not merely a form devoid of significance, but marks the official beginning of His mediatorial ministry. Here again the objective and subjective lines of development come together in the one Mediator, the latter in the consecration of his perfect and mature manhood to the vocation of the Christ, the former in God's acceptance of the offering and the official anointing bestowed upon Him. In the circumcision, Christ had unconsciously submitted to the imputation of sin, now in conscious obedience to the will of

God He becomes the Representative of sinful mankind. Thus as He stood with the multitude awaiting baptism, the prophecy of Isaiah was fulfilled, *He was numbered with the transgressors; and he bare the sin of many, and made intercession for the transgressors* (Isa. 53:12). Having fulfilled all righteousness as required by the law (Matt. 3:15), Jesus, *when he was baptized, went up straightway out of the water: and, lo, the heavens were opened unto him, and he saw the Spirit of God descending like a dove, and lighting upon him: and, lo, a voice from heaven, saying, This is my beloved Son, in whom I am well pleased* (Matt. 3:16, 17). Here is the divine attestation to the Messiahship of Jesus, an attestation that sin had nothing in Him except as imputed to Him. Here also is the official anointing of the Spirit by which He was consecrated to the holy office of Mediator. One thing only remained, the prophet who was to prepare the way of the Highest must officially announce to the world His assumption of the office. This He did in words vitally related to the voluntary consecration of Jesus as the representative of sinners. When, therefore, he cried, *Behold the Lamb of God, which taketh away the sin of the world* (John 1:29), he officially announced the *death* of Jesus as a vicarious atonement for all sin.

The Temptation. The temptation of Jesus was a necessity of the mediatorial economy, and like the baptism, was of universal import. Two factors are involved. *First,* Jesus must personally triumph over sin by voluntary opposition to it, before He could become the Author of life to others. *For it became him, for whom are all things, and by whom are all things, in bringing many sons unto glory, to make the captain of their salvation perfect through suffering* (Heb. 2:10). *Second,* He must not only conquer for Himself, but He must secure dignity and strength for His kingdom. For this reason He became partaker of flesh and blood, that *through death he might destroy him that had the power of death, that is the devil; and deliver them who through fear of death were all their lifetime subject to bondage* (Heb. 2:14, 15). When, therefore, the Spirit "driveth" Him into the wilderness, this extreme urgency must imply that the temptation was an essential element in His mediatorial work.

The temptation was both external and internal. It was external in that it originated outside and apart from Himself. It was not merely a confusion of cross purposes in His own mind. He was confronted by a personality representing the kingdom of evil. The evangelists seem to indicate that since the first Adam was tempted on the threefold level of physical, intellectual and spiritual evil, the last Adam must be likewise tested. As the failure of the first found its issue in the spirit of the world, which St. John interprets as *the lust of the flesh, and the lust of the eyes, and the pride of life* (I John 2:16); so the triumph of the last issued in life and light and love which were to form the basic principles of the new kingdom. Internally, the temptation was a conscious pressure in the direction of evil. We must believe that Christ felt the full force of the suggestions of Satan, but the Gospels tell us that He repelled them immediately, relying for His strength upon the firm foundation of the truth as "it is written" in the Scriptures.

The temptation is closely connected also with another question—that of the peccability or impeccability of Jesus. Was it possible for Jesus to sin; and if not, how could He have been tempted? The question is purely academic. It rests upon a misapprehension of the theanthropic Person who conjoins in Himself the two natures —human and divine. It is an attempt to consider the natures separately and apart from the one Person. Unless there be first a tacit assent to the Nestorian position that two persons are conjoined in affiliation, instead of two natures in one inseparable union, the problem cannot arise. The two natures being conjoined in one Person, peccability as attaching to the human nature, and impeccability as a property of the divine nature, are complements of each other—much in the manner as finiteness and infinity, or time and eternity. The former is a metaphysical principle limited solely to the self-determination belonging to personality; while the latter is an ethical fact grounded in the divine nature. "He could not do wrong because He would not," says Dr. Gerhart. "It is, however, more scriptural and more philosophical to express the thought thus: wrong He could neither do nor will, because He constantly willed, and effectually willed to do the right. The ethical impossibility to commit sin is mightier and more ennobling than the physical impossibility. The physical finds its complement in the ethical" (GERHART, *Inst. Chr. Relig.*, II, p. 258). We may confidently affirm, then, that the peccability of Jesus was limited solely to the metaphysical autonomy of His own will, without which He would have been merely an automaton and incapable of voluntary sinlessness; while the impeccability lay in His positive ethical character. He was, as to His humanity, created in righteousness and true holiness. He said of Himself, *I am the way, the truth, and the life* (John 14:6). The eternal principles of truth, righteousness and holiness, being relative in man may be superseded; but being absolute in God, they can never be transmuted into unrighteousness and sin. Jesus Christ was not only the embodiment of truth, He was the truth; He was not only accepted as righteous, He was righteous; He was not only relatively holy, He was that *holy thing* which was born to be the Redeemer of mankind.

The Obedience, Passion and Death of Christ. The perfected humiliation of Christ is to be found in the circumstances of His death—particularly His death on the cross. This marks the fulfillment of His perfect obedience. It is evident that no sharp line of demarcation can be drawn between Christ's active and passive righteousness, for even his death was the consequence of His own free determination. Of His own life He said, *No man taketh it from me, but I lay it down of myself. I have power to lay it down, and I have power to take it again. This commandment have I received of my Father* (John 10:18). While the sufferings of Christ may be distinguished from the precise manner of His death, the death itself cannot be separated from the crucifixion. He was *obedient unto death, even the death of the cross* (Phil. 2:8). "Hence the cross was to our High Priest simply the awful form which His altar assumed. *His own self bare our sins in his own body on the tree* (I Peter 2:24). Isaac as "the most affecting type of the Eternal Son incarnate bore the wood on his shoulders to his Calvary, and that wood became the altar on which in a figure he was slain, and from which in a figure he was raised again..... But, while the cross on which human malignity slew the Holy One is really the altar on which He offered Himself, and we forget the tree in the altar into which it was transformed, the cross still remains as the sacred expression of the curse which fell upon human sin as represented by the Just One. *For he made him to be sin for us, who knew no sin; that we might be made the righteousness of God in him* (POPE, *Chr. Th.*, II, p. 162). The passion and death of Jesus furnished the ground for His redemptive work, and will be considered further in our study of the Atonement.

It is a significant fact that St. Luke in his introduction to the Acts, speaks of his former work as comprehending *all that Jesus began both to do and teach, until the day in which he was taken up*. He thus limits the earthly life of Jesus, not by His death but by His ascension. The descensus, the resurrection and the ascension are but events in the life of the Eternal One. The state of humiliation ended with the cry on the cross, *It is finished* and His death which immediately followed. The events above mentioned—the descensus, the resurrection, the ascension and the session—will be treated in connection with the state of exaltation.

THE DEVELOPMENT OF CHRISTOLOGY IN THE CHURCH

Since the subject of Christology is closely related to that of the Trinity, we need not refer at this time to those controversies by which the deity of Christ as the second Person of the Trinity was firmly established. Following the Trinitarian controversies however, another series arose, which were concerned especially with the integrity of the two natures and their union in the one

Person. After a brief review of the Primitive Period, we shall consider the subject under the threefold division of Nicene, Chalcedonian and Ecumenical Christology.

The Primitive Period. This period includes the thought of the Ante-Nicene fathers, from the earliest times to the Council of Nicea (325 A.D.); and is concerned primarily with the reality of the two natures in Christ.

1. The Ebionites denied the reality of the divine nature of Christ. This Jewish sect is said to have derived its name from the Hebrew word meaning "poor," which is presumed to be a reference to the poverty so characteristic of the Church at Jerusalem. They accepted the Messiahship of Jesus but rejected His deity, maintaining that at the time of His baptism an unmeasured fullness of the Spirit was given to him, thereby consecrating Him to the Messianic office.

2. The Docetæ take their name from the Greek word δοκέω which means "to seem" or "to appear." As a sect they were greatly influenced by Gnosticism and Manichæism, and therefore denied the reality of Christ's body. Since Gnosticism held that matter is essentially evil, they argued that Christ's body must have been merely a phantasm or appearance. Ebionism was the result of the influence of Judaism on Christianity, Docetism the result of the influence of pagan philosophy.

The Nicene Christology. The Nicene Christology dates from the Council of Nicea (325 A.D.) to about 381 A.D. or the time of the Second Ecumenical Council at Constantinople. Following this, controversies arose which demanded a further statement which was made at Chalcedon. The Nicene Christology was the outgrowth of the Arian and Semi-Arian controversies which for more than half a century agitated the eastern church. Arianism as it affected the trinitarian conception of God has already been discussed, but it had important bearings on Christology also and these must now be given consideration. Arius was a disciple of Lucian of Antioch. Lucian in turn, was a disciple of Paul of Samosata, but differed radically from the views of his master. He attempted to combine the adoptionism of Paul, his master, with the Logos Christology which Paul opposed. Hence he regarded Christ as an incarnation of a previously existent being—the Logos; but this Logos was an intermediate creature, and of another nature than either God or man. Arius accepted this doctrine and thereby came into conflict with Alexander, his bishop, the result being one of the most subtle and bitter controversies in church history. But the church saw and rejected his teaching which substituted an intermediate creature for the true deity of Christ. The Semi-Arians attempted a mediation between the *heter-ousia* of the Arians who regarded Christ as of a different nature, and the *homo-ousia* of the Athanasians who regarded Him as of the same nature of God. They affirmed a *homoi-ousia,* or like essence of Christ with the Father, but denied His numerical essence and therefore His proper deity. In opposition to these heresies the Council of Nicea was convened by Constantine, which affirmed the deity of the Son, and after a further struggle, reaffirmed it at the Second Ecumenical Council held at Constantinople in 381 A.D. The statement as found in the Nicæno-Constantinopolitan Creed is terse, but has become the standard of the orthodox faith since that time. The text is as follows: (We believe) "in one Lord Jesus Christ, the only begotten Son of God, begotten of the Father before all worlds, God of God, Light of Light, Very God of Very God, Begotten, not made, being of one substance with the Father: by whom all things were made; who for us men and for our salvation came down from heaven, and was incarnate by the Holy Ghost of the Virgin Mary."

The Chalcedonian Christology. While the Council of Nicea affirmed the Deity of Christ, it left the question of His humanity unsolved. Athanasius had taken for granted that Christ was truly man as well as truly God, and in the controversy had neglected the problem of the two natures. When the question of the Deity of Christ was solved by conciliar action, the problem of His humanity became even more insistent. The Chalcedonian Christology, therefore, is the answer to three heresies, all of which were concerned with the constitution of the theanthropic Person, (1) Apollinarianism; (2) Nestorianism; and (3) Eutychianism.

1. Apollinarianism was the first heresy which confronted the church during this period. Apollinaris (d. 390), Bishop of Laodicea, was one of the most learned men in the ancient church. He argued that if Christ possessed a rational human soul, He could not be truly God incarnate, but merely a God-inspired man. Otherwise one of two things would follow as a necessary consequence, either He must retain a separate will, in which case His manhood would not be truly united with the Godhead; or, the human soul would be deprived of its own proper liberty through union with the divine Word. He took the position that the divine Logos in becoming incarnate took on human nature, but not a human personality. On the basis of the Platonic trichotomy which he later held, he ascribed to Christ a human body ($\sigma\hat{\omega}\mu\alpha$), and an animal soul ($\psi\upsilon\chi\grave{\eta}\ \check{\alpha}\lambda o\gamma o\varsigma$), but not a human spirit or rational soul, ($\psi\upsilon\chi\acute{\eta}\ \lambda o\gamma \iota\kappa\acute{\eta}$ or $\pi\nu\epsilon\hat{\upsilon}\mu\alpha$). Instead, he held that the divine Logos took the place of the human spirit, thus uniting with soul and body to form a divine-human being, or the one theanthropic nature. He maintained that the active personal element in Jesus was divine, and the passive was composed of the human body and soul. While this position provided for both the fusion of the divine and human natures, and for the deification of human nature as required by the realistic theory of redemption, it was felt by the Church that Apollinaris had sacrificed the true humanity of Jesus in order to maintain His deity. As in the case of Arianism, Basil and the two Gregories opposed Apollinaris but offered no clear statement of their own. The chief opposition came from the Antiochan school which was represented at that time by Diodorus of Tarsus and Theodore of Mopsuestia—the latter being regarded as one of the great exegetes of the Church. The interest of the Antiochan school being primarily ethical, its representatives looked upon Christ as a moral example, meeting and overcoming temptation, and therefore building

up a character of His own—an ethical holiness. This He could not have done, had He not been completely human as well as perfectly divine. They therefore insisted that Christ must have had a genuine human personality, with freedom of the will and an independent moral character. Furthermore, they insisted that the human nature of Christ could not be merely impersonal nature apart from the rational soul, nor even human nature personalized by the divine Logos. The error of Apollinarianism lay in the fact that it presented a defective human nature in Christ, and was condemned at the Second Ecumenical Council, held in Constantinople, 381 A.D.

2. Nestorianism was the second great heresy of this period. The Antiochan theologians in their opposition to Apollinarianism, seemed to develop the doctrine of two persons in Christ—one the divine Logos, the other the human Jesus. Each of these they regarded as a perfect and complete personality. The Logos, they claimed, dwelt in man but did not become man. They especially objected to that form of union between the divine and the human which precluded any development in the person of Christ. Theodore went so far as to declare that the divine Logos and the human Jesus lived in perfect harmony with each other, not because of compulsion but by free choice. The controversy reached its climax when Nestorius became patriarch of Constantinople (428 A.D.); and while his teaching was no different from that of Theodore, his name became connected with the heresy because of the leading part which he took in the controversy. Nestorius attacked the Alexandrians for what he called their Apollinarianism. He objected especially to the word *Theotokos* or "Mother of God" which they applied to the Virgin Mary. The term was in common use among the Alexandrians and was also being used in Constantinople. Nestorius maintained the full deity of Christ and also His perfect humanity; but he regarded these rather as a loose connection or affinity than as an indissoluble union. The chief opponents of Nestorianism were found in the Alexandrian School, especially Cyril, patriarch of Alexandria (412-444 A.D.),

who resolutely supported the *Theotokos*. The controversy was bitter, and aggravated further by court intrigue. The emperor Theodosius endeavored to appease the parties by convening the general council of Ephesus (431 A.D.). This council, however, under the influence of Cyril, hastily condemned the doctrines of the Nestorians without waiting for the arrival of the Roman and Syrian delegates. When John, archbishop of Antioch, arrived with his delegation, they followed the example of Cyril and called a rival council, at which Cyril was condemned and the doctrines of the Nestorians approved. That peace might be restored, a so-called "union symbol" was prepared and signed by both Cyril and the Antiochans. In order to satisfy the Antiochans, Apollinarianism was condemned; while Cyril secured the recognition of the *Theotokos,* the one Person and the two natures. The formula, however, was very elastic, and each party interpreted it in its own peculiar manner. The union symbol is commonly known as the creed of Antioch, and is attributed to Theodoret of Cyrrhus (433 A.D.).

3. Eutychianism was the third and last Christological heresy of this period. It took its name from Eutyches, who at that time (444 A.D.) was the head of a monastery in Constantinople; and is a revival of the older Christology, in which the divine nature was so emphasized by the Alexandrians, as to make it a docetic absorption of His human nature. The "union symbol" or Creed of Antioch which was intended to reconcile the

The Creed of Antioch is as follows: "We, therefore, acknowledge our Lord Jesus Christ, the Son of God, the Only-begotten, complete God and complete man, of a rational soul and body; begotten of the Father before the ages according to (His) divinity, but in these last days .... of Mary the Virgin according to (His) humanity. For a union of the two natures has taken place; wherefore, we confess one Christ, one Son, one Lord. In accordance with this conception of the unconfounded union, we acknowledge the holy Virgin to be the mother of God, because the divine Logos was made flesh and became man, and from her conception united with himself the temple received from her. We recognize the evangelical and apostolic utterances concerning the Lord, making the characters of the divine Logos and the man common as being in one person, but distinguishing them as two natures, and teaching that the godlike traits are according to the divinity of Christ, and the humble traits according to His humanity" (cf. SEEBURG, *Textbook in the History of Doctrines*, p. 266).

Antiochan and Alexandrian schools was but a weak compromise, and resulted in further confusion. Eutyches taught that "after God the Word became man, that is, after the birth of Jesus, there was but one nature to be worshiped, that of God, who was incarnate and made man." It will be seen that this position is the direct opposite of that held by the Nestorians. Nestorianism preserved its belief in the distinctness of the two natures at the expense of the one person; Eutychianism maintained its belief in the unity of Christ's person at the sacrifice of the two natures. The absorption of the human by the divine was carried to such extreme length as to be in effect, a deification of human nature, even the human body. Hence the Eutychians held that it was permissible to use such expressions as "God was born," "God suffered," and "God died." Eutyches was deposed and excommunicated at a council held in Constantinople (448 A.D.) but appealed his case to Leo of Rome, as did also, Flavian, bishop of Constantinople. Dioscurus, the successor of Cyril had won the approbation of Theodosius, the emperor. A council was called to confirm the doctrine of Eutyches, and was presided over by Dioscurus, commonly known in church history as "the Robber Council" (449 A.D.). Dioscurus by brutal terrorism intimidated the delegates and forced his view upon the council. Theodoret, bishop of Cyrrhus was deposed, and Flavian who had deposed Eutyches was murdered. Leo's Tome was not read. The following year the emperor Theodosius died, and the Council of Chalcedon convened in 451 A.D. This was the largest council which had been called up to that time, and by it both Eutychianism and Nestorianism were condemned. Here also the various errors and deficiencies in the statement of the doctrine of Christ's person were corrected and the creed drawn up by this council has from that time to the present been acknowledged as the orthodox statement.

The Chalcedonian Statement. The Council of Chalcedon approved the two letters of Cyril and Leo's Tome, and these furnish the basis of the Chalcedonian statement. Cyril's First Letter (to John of Antioch) affirmed the unity of the Person of Christ as against Nestorianism; and his second letter (to Nestorius) was likewise opposed to it. Leo's Tome was concerned with the reality, the integrity and the completeness of Christ's manhood as against Eutychianism. The following is the text of the Chalcedonian Creed:

"Following the holy fathers we teach with one voice that the Son (of God) and our Lord Jesus Christ is to be confessed as one and the same (Person), that He is perfect in Godhead and perfect in manhood, very God and very man, a reasonable soul and (human) body consisting, consubstantial (ὁμοούσιον) with the Father as touching His Godhead, and consubstantial (ὁμοούσιον) with us as touching His manhood; made in all things like unto us, sin only excepted, begotten of His Father before the worlds (πρὸ αἰώνων) according to His Godhead; but in these last days for us men and for our salvation born (into the world) of the Virgin Mary, the Mother of God (Θεοτόκος) according to His manhood. This one and the same Jesus Christ, the only begotten son (of God) must be confessed in two natures, unconfusedly (ἀσυγχύτως), immutably (ἀτρέπτως), indivisibly (ἀδιαιρέτως), inseparably (ἀχωρίστως) (united) and that without distinction of natures being taken away by such union, but rather the peculiar property (ἰδιότης) of each nature being preserved and being united in one Person (πρόσωπον) and Hypostasis (ὑπόστασιν), not separated or divided into persons, but one and the same Son and Only Begotten, God the Word, our Lord Jesus Christ, as the prophets of the old time have spoken concerning Him, and as the Lord Jesus Christ hath taught us, and as the Creed our fathers hath delivered to us."

The statement against Eutyches as found in Leo's Tome is as follows: "For it confutes (1) those who presume to rend asunder the mystery of the Incarnation into a double Sonship, and it deposes from the priesthood (2) those who dare say that the Godhead of the Only Begotten is passible; and it withstands (3) those who imagine a mixture or confusion of the two natures of Christ; and it drives away (4) those who fondly teach that the form of a servant which He took from us was a heavenly or some other substance; and it anathematizes (5) those who feign that the Lord had two natures before the union, and that these were molded into one after the union."

The Post-Chalcedonian Christology. The Council of Chalcedon (451 A.D.) marked the close of the controversy in the West. The Eastern churches, however, refused to accept the decrees of the Council and called for a supplementary statement concerning the two wills of Christ. In 482 A.D., the emperor Zeno published a decree known as the *Henoticon,* in which both Nestorianism and Eutychianism were condemned, the Chalcedonian Creed abrogated, and the Creed of Constantinople declared to be the only standard of orthodoxy. Four leading tendencies appear, (1) Monophysitism; (2) Monothelitism; (3) Adoptianism; and (4) Socinianism.

1. Monophysitism was a revival of Eutychianism, or the doctrine that Christ had but one composite nature. His humanity was regarded merely as an accident of the divine substance. The liturgical shibboleth was "God has been crucified." While they were regarded as heretical, their beliefs were substantially those of Cyril and the Alexandrians of his time. Leontius of Byzantium attempted to appease those with Cyrillian sympathies by recasting the Chalcedonian formula in accordance with the categories of Aristotle, giving rise to his doctrine of the *Enhypostasia.* He asserted that one nature may combine with another in such manner, that it retains its peculiar characteristics, and yet have its substance in the second nature. It is not therefore without hypostasis, by *enhypostasis,* for "it has given of its attributes interchangeably, which continue in the abiding and uncommingled peculiarity of their own natures." Monophysitism was condemned by the Fifth Ecumenical Council of Constantinople (553 A.D.).

2. Monothelitism held that Christ possessed but one will, and is therefore closely related to Monophysitism. The emperor Heraclius who had become alarmed at the progress of Mohammedanism in Arabia, sought to reconcile the Monophysitists and the orthodox by suggesting

A distinction should be made between the terms *enhypostasia,* and *anhypostasia.* Theology uses the former to express the fact that Christ has the two natures but in one person—the one nature having its hypostasis in the other; it uses the latter term to express the idea that the human nature of Christ has no separate personality of its own.

the acceptance of a doctrine proposed a century previous in a book attributed to Dionysius the Areopagite. This teaching was to the effect that there were indeed two natures in Christ—the divine and the human, but these were united in a manner which admitted of but one will and one operation. The compromise was accepted for a short time but was unsatisfactory to both parties. The emperor issued an edict known as the *Ekthesis,* giving sanction to Monothelitism but this only increased the strife. His successor, Constans II in 648 A.D. abrogated the *Ekthesis* and by another decree, the *Typos,* prohibited both the affirmation and the denial of Monothelitism. Constantine Pognatus in 680 A.D. called the Sixth Ecumenical council at Constantinople to settle the controversy. The Council condemned Monothelitism and added a paragraph to the Chalcedonian Creed which affirmed not only two natures but two wills, the human will being subject to the divine in the Person of Christ.

3. Adoptianism was similar to the earlier Nestorianism, and arose in Spain during the latter part of the eighth century. Two bishops, Elipandus of Toledo and Felix of Urgel, attempted to reconcile the doctrines of the church with the Mohammedan Koran. They suggested that Christ was the Son of God naturally, only in respect to His deity; but that in respect to His humanity, He was merely the servant of God, as are all men, and was made the Son by adoption. According to His divine nature, He was the Only Begotten; according to His human nature, He was the First Begotten. His humanity was adopted into His divinity by a gradual process. Beginning with His miraculous conception, it was more fully manifested at His baptism, and perfected at the time of His resurrection. This was but a revival of Nestorianism. Christ was regarded as an ordinary man

The paragraph added to the Chalcedonian Creed is as follows: "And we likewise preach two natural wills in Him (Jesus Christ), and two natural operations undivided, incontrovertible, inseparable, unmixed, according to the doctrine of the holy fathers; and the two natural wills (are) not contrary, far from it! (as the heretics assert), but His human will follows the divine will, and is not resisting or reluctant, but rather subject to His divine and omnipotent will. For it was proper that the will of the flesh, should not be moved, but be subjected to the divine will, according to the wise Athanasius."

united to God in an ordinary manner, and was in no particular sense an incarnation. Charlemagne convened two synods in order to determine the orthodox faith. At Frankfort (794 A.D.) Adoptianism was condemned; at Aix-la-Chapelle (799 A.D.) it was again condemned, and in addition, Felix was deposed.

4. Socinianism belongs to the earlier part of modern church history and is related to the ancient Arianism. A crude unitarianism had previously appeared among the Italian humanists, whose views seem to have embodied the various modifications of Arianism and Ebionism. In 1546 a secret confraternity of rationalistic reformers is said to have held meetings in Vicenza. Two Italians of noble birth, Lælius Socinus, the uncle, and Faustus Socinus, the nephew, appear to have been the leaders. The former elaborated a system of unitarianism in which he regarded Jesus as supernaturally conceived and born of a virgin, so that He was truly the Son of God; but as to His nature, He was regarded simply as a man to whom God gave extraordinary revelations, exalted Him to heaven after His death, and committed to Him the government of the Church. He was, therefore, a divinized man. Early Socinianism held that Christ received the Spirit at the baptism, and since He was carried to heaven to receive special instructions, was therefore to be worshiped. Later Socinianism under the pressure of rationalism, developed into Deism and Unitarianism, which in its liberalistic forms regards Jesus Christ as no more than a man of exceptional character and power. Lælius Socinus died in Zurich in 1562, and Faustus Socinus soon after organized a Unitarian Society in Transylvania.

Ecumenical Christology. The development of ancient catholic Christology was practically closed at the time of the Sixth Ecumenical Council, held at Constantinople in 680 A.D. As we have indicated, Adoptianism and Socinianism appeared later, but these were only variations of the ancient heresies condemned by the Creed of Chalcedon. John of Damascus in the Eastern church, and Thomas Aquinas in the West, were perhaps the ablest exponents of the Chalcedonian Christology. The former offered an explanation of the two natures and the two wills in relation to the one Person, but otherwise made no further contribution. His great work was the systematizing and preserving of the results already gained. In the Western church, the scholastic theologians confined themselves largely to a discussion of incidental matters connected with the creed and cannot be said to have made any real progress. Peter Lombard, Bishop of Paris (1164), whose *Four Books of Sentences* were sanctioned by the Fourth Lateran Council (1215) became the standard of orthodoxy. His assertion that "the human nature of Christ was impersonal," was challenged by Walter of St. Victor (c. 1180) who accused him of maintaining "that Christ had become nothing." This gave rise to the "Nihilian Heresy." The mystics,

John of Damascus endeavored to answer the question, "How can the doctrine of two natures and two wills in Christ be reconciled with the unity of His Person?" His solution was as follows: first, he regarded the divine nature as that which constituted the person; and second, he supposed a kind of interpenetration or perichoresis, which brought about an interchange of properties between the two natures (cf. CRIPPEN, *Hist. Chr. Th.*, p. 116).

The Augsburg Confession: "Also they teach that the Word, that is, the Son of God, took unto Him man's nature in the womb of the blessed Virgin Mary, so that there are two natures, the divine and the human, inseparably joined together in the unity of the person; one Christ, true God and true man: who was born of the Virgin Mary, truly suffered, was crucified, dead and buried that He might reconcile the Father unto us, and might be a sacrifice, not only for original guilt, but also for the actual sins of men."

The Second Helvetic Confession: "We acknowledge, therefore, that there are in one and the same Jesus Christ our Lord, two natures, the divine and the human nature; and we say that these two are so conjoined or united, that they are not swallowed up, confounded or mingled together, but rather united or joined together in one person, the properties of each nature being safe and remaining still: so that we worship one Christ our Lord, and not two; I say, one, true God and man; as touching His divine nature, of the same substance with the Father, and as touching His human nature, of the same substance with us, and 'like unto us in all things, sin only excepted.'"

The Westminster Confession: "The Son of God, the second person in the Trinity, being very and eternal God, of one substance and equal with the Father, did when the fullness of time was come, take upon Him man's nature, with all the essential properties and common infirmities thereof, yet without sin; being conceived by the Holy Ghost in the womb of the Virgin Mary, or her substance: so that two whole, perfect, and distinct natures, the Godhead and Manhood, were inseparably joined together in one person, without conversion, composition, or confusion. Which person is very God, and very man, yet one Christ, the only Mediator between God and men." This is usually considered the clearest and strongest expression of the Calvinistic churches.

Tauler (d. 1361) and Ruysbroek (c. 1381) emphasized Christ as the Divine Representative, or the "Restored Prototype of humanity." The Lutheran and Reformed Churches also built upon the Chalcedonian statement. The Lutherans leaned more toward the Eutychian position of the unity of the Person, and the Reformed toward the Nestorian distinction between the two natures, but both denied these ancient heresies. Protestantism, however, uniformly rejected the *Theotokos*, regarding the expression, "Mother of God" as objectionable and misleading. Otherwise the Chalcedonian statement has become the orthodox creed of Protestantism, whether Lutheran, Reformed or Anglican. Dr. Shedd maintained that "the human mind is unable to go beyond it in the endeavor to unfold the mystery of Christ's complex Person." Dr. Schaff states that "the Chalcedonian Christology is regarded by the Greek and Roman, and the majority of orthodox English and American divines as the *ne plus ultra* of Christological knowledge attainable in this world. The statements of the Protestant position are to be found in the various creeds and confessions, especially the Augsburg Confession (1530), the Second Helvetic confession (1566), and the Thirty-nine Articles (1571). Later creeds, including the Twenty-five Articles of Methodism are generally abridgments or revisions of the former creeds.

In more modern times, there developed what is known as the *communicatio idiomatum*, or communion of the two natures, a doctrine which apparently found its germ in the perichoresis of John of Damascus. In connection with the two estates of Christ, there arose the Kenotic and Kryptic theories which may best be considered in connection with the subject of Christ's humiliation. Modern Christology has been greatly influenced

The Thirty-nine Articles of the Church of England: "The Son, which is the Word of the Father, begotten from everlasting of the Father, the very and eternal God, and of one substance with the Father, took man's nature in the womb of the blessed Virgin, of her substance; so that two whole and perfect natures, that is to say, the Godhead and manhood, were joined together in one Person, never to be divided, whereof is one Christ, very God and very man; who truly suffered, was crucified, dead and buried, to reconcile his Father to us, and to be a sacrifice not only for original guilt, but also for the actual sins of men."

by the rationalistic and critical philosophies of our times, as has every other department of theology; and while the attacks were severe, they have failed to shake the firm foundations of the Christian faith. We must admit that the creeds are inadequate, for the finite can never express the Infinite; but we may still exclaim with St. Paul, *Great is the mystery of godliness: God was manifest in the flesh, justified in the Spirit, seen of angels, preached unto the Gentiles, believed on in the world, received up into glory* (I Tim. 3: 16).

The Twenty-five Articles of Methodism: "The Son, who is the Word of the Father, the very and eternal God, of one substance with the Father, took man's nature in the womb of the blessed Virgin; so that two whole and perfect natures, that is to say, the Godhead and Manhood, were joined together in one person, never to be divided; whereof is one Christ, very God and very Man, who truly suffered, was crucified, dead and buried, to reconcile his Father to us, and to be a sacrifice, not only for original guilt, but also for the actual sins of men." It will be noticed that the only difference between this and the statement found in the Thirty-nine Articles, is the omission of the phrase, "of her substance."

Articles of Faith, Church of the Nazarene: "We believe in Jesus Christ, the second person of the Triune Godhead: that He was eternally one with the Father; that He became incarnate by the Holy Spirit and was born of the Virgin Mary, so that two whole and perfect natures, that is to say the Godhead and manhood, are thus united in one person very God and very man, the God-man. We believe that Jesus Christ died for our sins, and that He truly arose from the dead and took again His body, together with all things appertaining to the perfection of man's nature, wherewith He ascended into heaven and is there engaged in intercession for us."

CHAPTER XXI
THE PERSON OF CHRIST

Our historical approach to the subject of Christology shows that the doctrine of the Person of Christ has not always been properly limited and defined. We have seen that a sharp distinction must be made between the two "natures" and the one "Person," and that there must be neither a division of the person nor a confusion of the natures. We have seen, also, that the Church through its councils sought to carefully guard the orthodox teaching from heretical opinions—the Chalcedonian Christology, and the Athanasian or Third Ecumenical Creed being the authoritative conciliar statements. The right faith according to the Athanasian symbol is *That our Lord Jesus Christ, the Son of God, is God and Man; God, of substance: but by unity of Person. For as the reasonworlds: and Man, of the substance of His mother, born into the world; perfect God, and perfect Man: of a reasonable soul and human flesh subsisting; equal to the Father, as touching His Godhead: and inferior to the Father, as touching His Manhood; Who although He be God and Man: yet He is not two but one Christ; One, not by conversion of the Godhead into flesh: but by taking the Manhood into God; One altogether, not by confusion of substance: but by unity of Person. For as the reasonable soul and flesh is one man: so God and Man is one Christ*. The doctrine, therefore, involves the following truths which must be given proper consideration, (I) The Deity of Christ; (II) The Manhood of Christ; (III) The Unity of Christ's Person; and (IV) The Diversity of the Two Natures.

The Deity of Christ

The deity of the Son, as eternal in the essence of the Godhead, was considered at length in our discussion of the Trinity; now we have to do with a consideration of the deity of the Son in the Person of Christ. Two avenues of approach to this subject are found in the history of doctrine—the textual and the historical. The *textual* method approaches the subject through the numerous proof texts, classified in various ways but usually including those scriptures which refer to His Divine Titles, Divine Attributes, Divine Acts and Divine Worship. With its many advantages, this method has one distinct disadvantage—the reliance upon proof texts is always open to the objection that they may be interpreted in a wrong manner by those whose minds are biased or prejudiced against the proper deity of Christ. It is the *historical* method, however, by which men have been convinced of the supernatural character of Christ and have been led to the persuasion that He is very God. This is the method of the Gospels, and any attentive reader may share the wonderment of the disciples, their insight and their conclusions as to the deity of their Lord. Dr. Johnson points out that any idea formed of Christ in this manner, "will neither be wavering nor vague, but as our conception of His personality grows clear and firm, insight into His nature deepens, and His divinity is revealed before our eyes" (JOHNSON, *Outline of Systematic Theology*, pp. 159, 160). Rothe likewise points out the necessity of apprehending the divine nature of Christ from the study of the picture of His human life. "To speak of recognizing and acknowledging the divine element in Christ," he says, "without having observed it shine forth from what is human in Him, or having caught its reflection in the mirror of His humanity, is merely to bandy idle words." We shall not attempt, therefore, any elaborate system of proof texts in this connection, but will refer the reader to the collation of scriptures concerning the deity of Christ, which has already been furnished in connection with our discussion of the Trinity. It is sufficient here to consider only those points which involve the incarnation and its relation to the redemptive work of Christ.

The Pre-existence of Christ. The Church in all ages has affirmed the doctrine of the true deity of Christ, and hence His eternal existence—the *Messiah* of the Old

Testament, and the *Christos* of the New Testament. Was Jesus of Nazareth the Christ? Did the Christ of the Gospels have an eternal personal existence before His birth of the Virgin Mary? If so, what was the nature of this existence? Did He exist as man or as God? If the latter, did He exist as the sole God—a simple and absolute personal unity; or did He exist as one of the essential and infinite Persons of the Triune Godhead? The Holy Scriptures and the conciliar actions of the Church, both affirm that Jesus of Nazareth was the Christ, the Son of the living God. Jesus speaking of Himself said, *Before Abraham was, I am* (John 8: 58); and *No man hath ascended up to heaven, but he that came down from heaven, even the Son of man which is in heaven* (John 3: 13). Isaiah called Him *the everlasting Father* (Isa. 9: 6), and St. Paul declares that *he is before all things, and by him all things consist* (Col. 1: 17).

The mere fact of existence, however, does not necessarily carry with it the evidence of deity. It does not furnish a proof against Arianism which maintains that Christ was of like essence with the Father, but not identical in essence and therefore not truly God. Nor does the fact of pre-existence furnish proof against the modern so-called "idealistic theories." One of these theories maintains that Christ's pre-existence was only ideal—an impersonal principle or potency, which became personalized in Jesus. Another of these theories maintains that Christ was not an eternal being, but a premundane, created being, a perfect spiritual image of God and the prototype of humanity. Thus Pfleiderer, who held that Christ existed in another form previous to His earthly state, regarded this pre-existence not as an abstract, impersonal principle, but as a concrete personality, an image of God and thus a created Son of God. But this

Whenever the attempt is made to bring Christology to a logical conclusion, and formulate it, the difficulty of avoiding Ebionism or Docetism, Nestorianism or Monophysitism, which stand on either side like Scylla and Charybdis, will present itself, and the history of doctrines will require, to defend itself against the attacks of various forms of heresy, the manner best suited to repel the antagonizing error. The reason for this fact does not, however, lie in the doctrine itself, with its infinite significance, but in the human limitations which affect the dogmatics of each particular age.—CROOKS AND HURST, *Encycl. and Meth.*, p. 431.

pre-existent Christ he did not regard as true deity in any sense, but as man—a pre-existent "spiritual" man. It is evident that these theories are closely related to ancient Arianism, and must therefore be classified among the forms of modern Unitarianism. The fact of pre-existence does, however, refute Socinianism and all the purely humanitarian conceptions of Christ.

The Holy Scriptures teach, and the Church has believed that the pre-existent One was none other than the eternal Son of God, the second Person of the Trinity. Christology is, therefore, vitally related to Trinitarianism. "The anti-Trinitarian movements of recent times," says Dorner, "have made it perfectly clear that there consequently remains only the choice either to think of God in a Unitarian manner, and in that case to see even Jesus as a mere man; or if He is supposed to be the God-man, to hold eternal distinction in God, and therefore undertake to prove that the unity of God is quite consistent with such distinctions" (DORNER, *Syst. Chr. Doct.*, I, p. 415). This the Church does by maintaining that in the Trinity there are three Persons subsisting in one divine essence or nature; and that it was not that which was common to the three persons who assumed our human nature, but that which marks the distinctions in the Trinity. It was not the Godhead which became incarnate, but one of the persons of the Godhead. It was not the Father or the Spirit who became incarnate, but the Son—the Second Person of the Trinity. The pre-existent One, therefore, is not a mere abstraction or idealization; He is not a pre-existent creature, whether human or divine; He is "the only begotten Son of God, begotten of His Father before all worlds, God of God, Light of Light, very God of very God; begotten, not made; being of one substance with the Father; by whom all things were made." The Church finds its ground for this position in the Holy Scriptures. The classic passage is found in the prologue to John's Gospel (John 1: 1-5), *In the beginning was the Word, and the Word was with God, and the Word was God. The same was in the beginning with God. All things were made by him; and with-*

out him was not anything made that was made. In him was life; and the life was the light of men. And the light shineth in darkness; and the darkness comprehended it not. Here the Word or Logos is identified with Jesus, and to the description of this Logos the whole Gospel is devoted. This Logos was eternal—He existed in the beginning. But in the eternal world He was not alone, He was πρὸς τὸν θεόν, existing with God, whom as the incarnate Word He came to reveal. Furthermore, this Logos was not only eternal, existing in the beginning with God, but He was God. The *locus classicus* of St. Paul is to be found in his Epistle to the Philippians, where he distinctly declares that Christ, prior to His existence on earth as Jesus of Nazareth, existed to all eternity "in the form of God," and "equal with God" (Phil. 2:5). Likewise, also, the Epistle to the Hebrews places Christ as the Son above the angels (Heb. 1:5); and furthermore identifies the priestly office as coeternal with the Son himself. *Thou art a priest for ever after the order of Melchisedec* (Heb. 5:6). As the priesthood was considered to have no end, neither did it have a beginning. The two were coeternal—the Sonship and the priesthood.

Christ was the Jehovah of the Old Testament. The deity of Christ finds abundant support in the Old Testament Scriptures, as previously pointed out in our discussion of the Trinity. In order, however, to show the continuity of the redemptive mission of the Son, it seems necessary to point out the fulfillment of two prophetic utterances concerning the Messiah. The first is the prophecy of Jeremiah concerning the New Covenant. It will be recalled, that the Mosaic law was given by the dispensation of angels, referring more especially to the "angel of Jehovah," who was at once servant and Lord, angel and Jehovah; and that this law was given in His own name (Exod. 23:20, 21). Later Moses declared that *The Lord thy God will raise up unto thee a Prophet from the midst of thee, of thy brethren, like unto me; unto him ye shall hearken* (Deut. 18:15). Still later Jeremiah prophesied saying, *Behold, the days come, saith the Lord, that I will make a new covenant with the house of Israel, and with the house of Judah: not according to the covenant that I made with their fathers in the day that I took them by the hand to bring them out of the land of Egypt* (Jer. 31: 31, 32). The first of these prophecies was specifically declared by Stephen in his last address, to have been fulfilled in Christ; and he refers also to the law given by the dispensation of angels, a subject which receives its full development by the author of the Epistle to the Hebrews in his discussion of the New Covenant (cf. Acts 7: 53 with Heb. 8: 6-13, 10: 16-18). Closely related to this, but referring more specifically to the temple than to the covenant, is the prophecy of Malachi. *Behold, I will send my messenger, and he shall prepare the way before me; and the Lord, whom ye seek, shall suddenly come to his temple, even the messenger of the covenant, whom ye delight in; behold, he shall come, saith the Lord of hosts* (Mal. 3: 1). As the Lord of a temple is the Deity to whose worship it is consecrated, the act of our Lord in entering the temple makes it evident that He was the Jehovah of the Old Testament to whom it was consecrated.

The Unique Claims of Jesus for Himself. The highest testimony to the deity of Christ must, of necessity, be His own claims. If it be argued that a man's claims for himself are worthless, it must be answered that this depends upon the prior question as to who the man is. This was the objection of the Pharisees who said to Jesus, *Thou bearest record of thyself; thy record is not true. Jesus answered and said unto them, Though I bear record of myself, yet my record is true: for I know whence I came, and whither I go; but ye cannot tell whence I come, and whither I go. . . . . It is also written in your law, that the testimony of two men is true. I am one that bear witness of myself, and the Father that sent me beareth witness of me* (John 8: 13-18). It is possible here to enumerate only a few of the claims of Jesus—one of the most profound subjects that can engage the mind of man. Jesus claimed for Himself, (1) the possession of divine attributes, such as eternity (John 8: 58, 17: 5), omnipotence (Matt. 28:20, 18:20, John 3:13), omniscience (Matt. 11:27, John 2:23-25, 21:17), and omnipresence (Matt. 18:20, John 3:13). (2) He claimed, and manifested the power to work miracles, or to empower others to perform wonderful works (Matt. 10:8, 11:5, 14:19-21, 15:30, 31, Mark 6:41-44, Luke 8:41-56, 9:1, 2). (3) He claimed divine prerogatives, such as being Lord of the Sabbath (Mark 2:28); the power to forgive sins and to speak *as* God or *for* God (Matt. 9:2-6, Mark 2:5-12, Luke 5:20-26). (4) He claimed to know the Father in a direct and perfect manner, as no other being can; (Matt. 11:27, Luke 10:22) and to be the Son of God in a unique manner (Matt. 10:32, 33, 16:17, 27). (5) He spoke words of infinite wisdom, for He spake as never man spake. (6) He accepted the homage of worship (Matt. 14:33). And (7) He claimed to be the final judge of all men (Matt. 7:21-23, 13:41-43, 19:28, 25:31-33, Mark 14:62, Luke 9:26, 26:69, 70).

The Manhood of Christ

Christ became incarnate in a manner that made Him man. The Scriptures tell us that *the Word was made flesh, and dwelt among us* (John 1:14); and that as children *are partakers of flesh and blood, he also himself likewise took part of the same* (Heb. 2:14). We must, then, regard His human nature as true and entire, admitting no defect in any of its essential elements, nor acquiring any additions by virtue of its conjunction with Deity. Furthermore, our Lord's human nature was assumed under conditions which properly belong to man, and underwent a process of development in common with other men, sin only excepted. Hence in Him development was natural and normal, being free from the bias of inherited depravity or the blighting influence of

---

Here the prophet describes the coming Messiah, not only as the messenger of the covenant, but also as the Lord and Owner of the Jewish temple; and consequently, as a divine prince or governor—he shall "come to his temple." The Lord of any temple is the divinity to whose worship it is consecrated. The temple at Jerusalem of which the prophet here speaks, was consecrated to the true and living God; and we have therefore the express testimony of Malachi that the Christ, the Deliverer, whose coming he announced, was no other than the Jehovah of the Old Testament.—RAYMOND, *Chr. Theology,* p. 94.

sin. For this reason He is called the "Son of man" the perfect realization of the eternal idea of mankind.

The Human Nature of Christ. The Incarnation did not mean merely the assumption of a human body; for human nature does not consist in the possession of a body only, but in the possession of body and soul. Two facts stand out clearly. *First,* our Lord had a human body. This was at first denied by the Docetæ on the ground that matter is essentially evil, but this heresy soon disappeared. The Scripture proofs of His human nature are many and varied. There is the account of His birth, His circumcision, His visit to the temple, His baptism and temptation (Matt. 2:1—4:11, Luke 2:1—4:13). He was hungry (Matt. 4:2), thirsty (John 19:28), and weary (John 4:6). We are told of His bodily pain and of His bloody sweat in the garden (Luke 22:44); of His sinking under the weight of the cross (Luke 23:26); of the piercing of His hands and feet, His agony on the cross, His death and burial (Matt. 27:33-66, Mark 15:22-47, Luke 23:33-56, John 19:16-42). *Second,* our Lord had a human soul. The evidence for this is regarded as almost equally conclusive. It was called in question by Apollinarius, who substituted the divine Logos in place of the human soul; and it has appeared in various forms from time to time, but has never been an accepted doc-

There are several ancient accounts of the personal appearance of our Lord, but none of them can be accounted thoroughly trustworthy. The first is reported to be composed by Publius Lentulus, a Roman officer; while another, discovered by Tischendorf, is said to have been written by Epiphanius in Greek. We give the first only as translated from the Latin. "A man of tall stature, good appearance, and a venerable countenance, such as to inspire beholders with love and awe. His hair, worn in a circular form and curled, rather dark and shining, flowing over the shoulders, and parted in the middle of the head, after the style of the Nazarenes. His forehead, smooth and perfectly serene, with a face free from wrinkle or spot, and beautiful with a moderate ruddiness, and a faultless nose and mouth. His beard full, of an auburn color like his hair, not long but parted. His eyes quick and clear. His aspect terrible in rebuke, placid and amiable in admonition, cheerful without losing its gravity: a person never seen to laugh, but often to weep" (For both accounts cf. POTTS, *Faith Made Easy,* pp. 206, 207).

Find us a better answer to the questionings of our spirits than Christ has furnished! Show us a better ideal of manhood than He has given! Bring us a better testimony to the life beyond the grave than He has borne! Ah! for four thousand years the world has tried in vain to return to God, and now that He has come Himself to be the way, we will not give him up for any negation.—WILLIAM M. TAYLOR, D.D.

trine of the Church. In anticipation of His passion, Jesus said to His disciples, *Now is my soul* [ψυχή] *troubled* (John 12:27); and again in the garden, *My soul is exceeding sorrowful, even unto death* (Matt. 26:38). Jesus said of Himself, *I am meek and lowly in heart* (Matt. 11:29) and He *rejoiced in spirit* (Luke 10:21) when the disciples returned from their successful mission. Christ, therefore, had a human soul as well as a human body. To deny that the attributes, acts and experiences natural to a human soul are not evidences of a complete humanity is to lay the ground for a denial of His deity, as based on the divine acts, attributes and names ascribed to Him.

The Sinlessness of Christ. There was no original sin in Christ. Inherited depravity is the result of a natural descent from Adam; but Christ's birth was miraculous and hence He was born without the natural or inherited corruption which belongs to other men. Having God alone as His Father, the birth of Christ was not a birth out of sinful human nature, but a conjoining of human nature with Deity which in the very act sanctified it. Sin is a matter of the person, and since Christ was the preexistent Logos, the Second Person of the adorable Trinity, He was as such, not only free from sin but from the possibility of sin. Christ was, from His birth, perfect in His relation to His heavenly Father, and absolutely free from the sinful bias which characterizes every natural son of Adam. Christ was also free from actual sin. He *did no sin, neither was guile found in his mouth* (I Peter 2:22). His earthly life was free from fault or blemish. As a child He was filial and obedient (Luke 2:51); as a youth, respectful and docile (Luke 2:52); and as a man was holy, harmless, undefiled, separate from sinners, and made higher than the heavens (Heb. 7:26).

But Christ was made also *in the likeness of sinful flesh* (Rom. 8:3). The best expositors have always agreed that this passage means that Christ's flesh is like that which in us is sinful. "Neither the Greek nor the argument requires that the flesh of Christ shall be regarded as *sinful flesh,* though it is His flesh, His incarnation, which brought Him into contact with sin (SANDAY-HEADLAM, *Com. on Romans*). We may argue, with DeBose, that since the holiness of Jesus Christ was by the Holy Ghost, in Him, and not merely in His nature, He was therefore the cause of His own holiness and His sinlessness was His own (cf. DUBOSE, *Soteriology of the New Testament*). The mystery is that Christ should take our nature in such a manner, that while without sin, He bore the consequences of our sin. Furthermore, Christ had immortality in Himself. *In him was life* (John 1:4). This right to the immortality of His body He surrendered and of Himself laid down His life, that He might take it again. And while we may say that Christ, being the divine Son incarnate and not born after the manner of other men, was lifted above all those infirmities which exist in man as a consequence of sin, yet He voluntarily made Himself the partaker of human weaknesses and infirmities, *that he might be a merciful and faithful high priest in things pertaining to God, to make reconciliation for the sins of the people. For in that he himself hath suffered being tempted, he is able to succour them that are tempted* (Heb. 2:17, 18).

THE UNITY OF CHRIST'S PERSON

We have considered the scriptural proofs of the deity of Christ, and of His perfect manhood, and must now give attention to the union of these two natures in one person. This union was effected by the incarnation; and the result is a theanthropic person, or God-man, who unites in Himself all the conditions of both the divine and the human existence. This one personality is the pre-existent Logos, or the divine Son, who assumed to Himself human nature, and in this assumption both personalized and redeemed it. Four things are involved in our study, (1) The Nature of the Incarnation; (2) The Hypostatic Union; (3) The Incarnation and the Trinity; and (4) The Incarnation as a Permanent Condescension.

The Nature of the Incarnation. The Incarnation in the sense in which we shall now consider it, was not merely a stage in the mediatorial ministry of Christ, but the necessary basis of all. As it applies to "the Word made flesh," the incarnation must be distinguished from every form of transubstantiation. The apostle does not teach that the second Person of the Trinity ceased to be God when He became man. The expression is equivalent to saying that Christ came in the flesh, thereby assuming a human nature, that He might enter redemptively into the experiences of men. A scriptural view of the Incarnation involves the following facts. *First,* it was the Word, or second Person of the Trinity alone who became incarnate. One trinitarian Person may become incarnate, and yet that incarnation will not be of the whole Godhead, because the Godhead represents the divine essence in three modes; and the essence in all three modes did not become incarnate. Since the whole essence or divine nature exists in each of the three modes, as Father, Son and Holy Spirit, we may say that when the Son became incarnate, there dwelt in Him all the fullness of the Godhead bodily, but only in the mode of the second Person, or the divine Son. *Second,* the Incarnation was the union of a divine Person with human nature and not with a human person. The human nature which He assumed acquired personality by its union with Him. The Redeemer is therefore said to have laid hold on "the seed [σπέρμα] of Abraham" (Heb. 2:16); and further, was known both as the "seed of the woman" (Gen. 3:15), and the "seed of David" (Rom. 1:3). These expressions can only mean that the nature our Lord as-

While the Incarnate Person is the God-man, or manifestation of God in the flesh, the divine personality is only that of the Son, the second Person in the Trinity. As a distinct Person in the Godhead He brings the entire divine nature into humanity, and continues His eternal personality through all the processes of His development and mediatorial work forever.—POPE, *Chr. Th.,* II, p. 113.

The full truth of the Incarnation is not contained in the notion of a union of the divine nature, simply as such, with the human nature. The subject of the Incarnation was not a mere nature, but a person—the personal Son. The divine nature is common to the persons of the Trinity: therefore any limitation of the Incarnation to the divine nature would deny to the Son any distinct or peculiar part therein. This would contradict the most open and uniform sense of Scripture. The Father and the Holy Spirit had no such part in the Incarnation as the Son. Nor could any union of the divine nature, simply as such, with the human nature give the profound truth and reality of the Incarnation. It could mean nothing for the unique personality of Christ; nothing for the reality and sufficiency of the atonement.—MILEY, *Syst. Th.,* II, p. 17.

sumed was as yet not individualized. Christ's human nature was not impersonal except in this sense—it was not personalized out of the race by natural birth, but by becoming a constituent factor of the one theanthropic Person. *Third,* the body which the Son assumed was prepared for Him by the Holy Ghost. *Wherefore when he cometh into the world, he saith, sacrifice and offering thou wouldst not, but a body hast thou prepared me* (Heb. 10:5). The Son in the trinitarian sense, is the "only begotten" of the Father; but He is also that "holy thing" which was conceived by the Holy Ghost and born of the Virgin Mary. The Socinians supposed that some of the elements of His body were furnished by the Virgin, and some by the Holy Spirit, hence He was called the Son of God. Bishop Pearson says, that "As He was so made of the substance of the Virgin, so was He not made of the substance of the Holy Ghost, whose essence cannot at all be made. And because the Holy Ghost did not beget Him by communication of His essence, therefore He is not the father of Him, though He were conceived by Him. There were no material elements in the person of Christ except those He received from her." "There is nothing on which the Scripture is more explicit than this," says Dr. Summers, "that as His divinity was begotten without a mother, from eternity, so His humanity was begotten without a father. He was conceived by the Holy Ghost: not by any communication of His essence, as in human paternity, but by a miraculous operation which enabled the Virgin to perform the functions of maternity, and be a virgin still" (SUMMERS, *Syst. Th.,* I, p. 203).

The Hypostatic Union. The union of the divine and human natures in Christ is a personal one—that is, the union lies in their abiding possession of a common Ego or inner Self, that of the eternal Logos. In theology, this is termed the hypostatic union, and is derived from the use of the word *hypostasis,* a term which marks the distinction between personal subsistences in the Godhead, and their common substance or essence. The two natures meet and have communion with each other, solely through the self which is common to both. The term is understood, therefore, to guard against two errors—that of a confusion of the two natures in a third essence, neither divine nor human; and that of a loose conjunction or affiliation of natures which may be considered in separation from each other. The possession of the two natures does not involve a double personality, for the ground of the person is the eternal Logos and not the human nature. Christ, therefore, uniformly speaks of Himself in the singular person. Always and everywhere, the Agent is one. There is never any interchange of the "I" and the "thou" as in the Trinity. The varying modes of consciousness pass quickly from the divine to the human, but the Person is always the same. Hence He says, *I and my Father are one* (John 10:30), and again, *I thirst* (John 19:28). In the first instance, the form of the consciousness is divine; in the latter, human. Frequently there are passages where the person is designated by a divine title, and yet human attributes are ascribed to Him, such as *feed the church of God, which he hath purchased with his own blood* (Acts 20:28); *He spared not his own Son, but delivered him up for us all* (Rom. 8:32); *had they known it, they would not have crucified the Lord of glory* (I Cor. 2:8); and *in whom we have redemption through his blood* (Col. 1:14). Divine attributes are also predicated of the person designated by a human title. *No man hath ascended up to heaven, but he that came down from heaven, even the Son of man which is in heaven* (John 3:13); *What and if ye shall see the Son of man ascend up where he was before* (John 6:62); and *Worthy is the Lamb that was slain to receive power, and riches, and wisdom, and strength, and honour, and glory, and blessing* (Rev. 5:12).

The Incarnation and the Trinity. The question sometimes arises as to the relation existing between the Incarnation and the Trinity. Prior to the Incarnation the Trinity consisted of the Father, the unincarnate Son (λόγος ἄσαρκος) and the Holy Spirit; subsequent to the Incarnation, it consisted of the Father, the incarnate Son (λόγος ἔνσαρκος) and the Holy Spirit. But the incarnation makes no change in the Trinity, for the Son's assumption of human nature is not the addition of another Person to Him. The second Person of the Trinity was modified by the Incarnation, but the Trinity was not so modified; for neither the Father nor the Spirit became divine-human Persons. In becoming man, the Son remained God, for He still subsisted in the divine nature.

The Incarnation as a Permanent Condescension. The union of the two natures in the one theanthropic Person is indissoluble and eternal. Marvelous as it may seem, and mysterious beyond compare, our Lord took His human nature with Him into the depths of the Godhead. In His ascension, He carried His glorified humanity to the throne of God. "He became man once for all: our manhood is a vesture which he will not fold and lay aside. Immanuel is His name forever." His glorified human nature is now united with the eternal Son, so that the God-man is the middle Person of the Trinity. For

We must consider that the divine nature did not assume a human person, but the divine Person did assume a human nature; and that of the three divine Persons, it was neither the first nor the third that did assume this nature, but it was the middle person who was to be the middle one (mediator) that must undertake the mediation between God and us. For if the fullness of the Godhead should have thus dwelt in any human person, there should have been added to the Godhead a fourth kind of person; and if any one of the three persons besides the second had been born of a woman, there should have been two Sons in the Trinity. Whereas, now, the Son of God and the Son of the blessed Virgin, being but one Person, is consequently but one Son; and so no alteration at all made in the relations of the persons to the Trinity.—USHER, *Incarnation*, I, p. 580.

It is the infinite condescension of the Son of God and the glory of man that the union of the two natures in Christ is permanent. He became man once for all: our manhood is a vesture which we will not fold and lay aside. Immanuel is His name forever. This being so, it is scarcely right to speak of our Lord's alliance with our race as a part of His mediatorial humiliation: were it such, His humiliation would never terminate. It is true that the effect of His condescension will never cease. He will be one with mankind to all eternity: as it were expressly to declare this, to keep it in the minds of His people and prevent misconception, that one profound saying was placed on record: "Then shall the Son also himself be subject," or subject himself (I Cor. 15:28). His union with us, which is the same thing as His kingdom or His tabernacle with us, shall have no end. We know Him only as Immanuel.—POPE, *Chr. Th.*, II, pp. 141, 142.

It is the doctrine of the Church, as definitely formulated in the Chalcedonian symbol, that the union of the two natures in Christ is forever an inseparable one.—MILEY, *Syst. Th.*, II, p. 23.

this reason the Son stands in the closest possible relation to the redemption of mankind, and by His Spirit is ever present to secure the progress of His kingdom. Hence the Scriptures declare of Christ that He *is over all, God blessed forever* (Rom. 9:5); that *in him dwelleth all the fulness of the Godhead, bodily* (Col. 2:9); *Jesus Christ, the same yesterday, and today, and forever* (Heb. 13:8); and above all, *We have a great high priest, that is passed into the heavens* (Heb. 4:14, 15).

THE DIVERSITY OF THE TWO NATURES

The Unity of Christ's Person finds its complementary truth in the Diversity of the Two Natures. That the Godhead and the manhood each retains its respective properties and functions, without either alteration of essence or mutual interference is as necessary to a true conception of the Incarnation as is their hypostatic union in Jesus Christ. While the acts and qualities of either the divine or the human nature of Christ may be attributed to the theanthropic Person, it may not be said that they can be attributed to each other. The properties which belong to a nature are necessarily confined to it. A material substance can have only material properties, and an immaterial substance can have only immaterial or spiritual qualities. So, also, human nature can have only human properties, and the divine nature only divine properties. Natures, on the other hand, however heterogeneous, may belong to the same person. Thus, in the Trinity, three Persons or Hypostases subsist in one nature. In man, one person subsists in two natures—one immaterial or spiritual, the other material or physical. In Christ as a theanthropic Being, the one person subsists in two natures—the divine and the human; or, if we analyze more minutely, in three natures—the divine, the spiritual and the physical.

The Chalcedonian Creed. The Chalcedonian statement, previously mentioned in connection with the development of Christology in the Church, furnishes us with a true guide to the orthodox belief concerning the two natures. "This one and same Jesus Christ, the only begotten Son (of God) must be confessed in two natures, unconfusedly, immutably, indivisibly, inseparably (united) and that without the distinction of natures being taken away by such union, but rather the peculiar property of each nature being preserved and being united in one Person and Hypostasis." Dr. Shedd in his "History of Christian Doctrine" (Vol. I, p. 399ff) gives us a somewhat simpler translation as follows: "He is one Christ, existing in two natures without mixture, without change, without division, without separation—the diversity of the two natures not being at all destroyed by their union in the person." Here the two natures of Christ are not only affirmed, but their relations adjusted to each other in four main points—without mixture (or confusion); without change (or conversion); without division; and without separation. If then we would hold to the orthodox or catholic faith, (1) we must believe that the union of the two natures in Christ does not confuse or mix them in a manner to destroy their distinctive properties. The deity of Christ is as pure deity after the Incarnation as before it; and the human nature of Christ is as pure and simple human nature as that of His mother or of any other human individual—sin excluded. (2) We must reject as unorthodox any theory that would convert one nature into the other, either an absorption of the human nature by the divine as in Eutychianism; or the reduction of the divine nature to the human, as in some of the kenotic theories. (3) We must hold the two natures in such a union that it does not divide the person of Christ into two selves, as in Nestorianism, or such a blending of the two natures into a composite which is neither God nor man as in Apollinarianism. The resultant of the union is not two persons, but one person who unites in Himself the conditions of both the divine and human existence. (4) We must hold to a union of the two natures that is inseparable. The union of humanity with Deity in Christ is indissoluble and eternal. It is a permanent assumption of human nature by the second Person of the Trinity.

The Incarnation and the Redemptive Work of Christ. We have seen that the incarnation is the basic fact in the mediatorial economy; we must now indicate briefly its relation to the redemptive work of Christ. The primary purpose of our Lord's assumption of "flesh and blood" was to provide atonement by sacrificial death. It was the purpose of the Father, that *he by the grace of God should taste death for every man* (Heb. 2:9). By this death He effected three things—the abolishment of death itself, the reconciliation of offenders, and the propitiation necessary for both. This it is further stated, He accomplished by "taking hold on" or "rescuing" the "seed of Abraham," thereby becoming a *merciful and faithful high priest in things pertaining to God, to make reconciliation for the sins of the people* (Heb. 2:16, 17). Thus the primary purpose of the Incarnation was to provide an atonement. But the "seed of Abraham" refers also to a more remote purpose of the Incarnation. The atonement while perfected in Christ, requires to be applied by the Spirit. By taking to Himself the "seed of Abraham" it is implied that He assumed human nature in its capacity for development, or continuity as a race. Christ was, therefore, a racial man, the true Representative of the human race, and consequently is Himself called "the seed of Abraham," to whom the promises were made. (Gal. 3:16). Hence, *Christ hath redeemed us from the curse of the law, being made a curse for us .... that the blessing of Abraham might come on the Gentiles through*

This passage with its entire context (Heb. 2:10-18) impressively shows that the Incarnation was the way to the cross. Three terms are used, each of great importance. It was to abolish death, by taking his power from its representative and lord, that is, the devil. This, however, required that He should take our flesh in order that He might taste death for every man, and thus deliver them who through fear of death were all their lifetime subject to bondage: this deliverance being accomplished by His sacrifice of reconciliation, as the words ἀπαλλάξῃ and ἔνοχοι sufficiently prove. Only as man could He be a merciful and faithful High Priest in things pertaining to God to make expiation for the sins of the people, εἰς τὸ ἱλάσκεσθαι. In order to accomplish these results—the destruction of death, the reconciliation of the offenders subject to death, and the propitiation required in order to both—He taketh hold of the seed of Abraham: He taketh to Himself ἐπιλαμβάνεται humanity, or the blessed with faithful Abraham, and the seed of Abraham my friend. But it was that He might taste of death ὑπὲρ παντός.—POPE, *Chr. Th.*, II, p. 144.

Jesus Christ; that we might receive the promise of the Spirit through faith (Gal. 3:13, 14). St. Paul expresses this purpose with an ethical emphasis when he declares that *he hath chosen us in him before the foundation of the world, that we should be holy and without blame before him in love.* Christ then is the "seed" or vital center from which shall spring a redeemed and holy people, characterized by St. Peter as *a chosen generation, a royal priesthood, an holy nation, a peculiar people* (I Peter 2:9). But this remote purpose is to be succeeded by a final or ultimate purpose. *Having made known unto us the mystery of his will, according to his good pleasure which he hath purposed in himself: that in the dispensation of the fulness of times he might gather together in one all things in Christ, both which are in heaven, and which are on earth; even in him* (Eph. 1:9, 10). Here then the Incarnation is related, *first,* to the finished work of Christ, or the Atonement; *second,* to the more remote purpose found in the work of the Spirit, or the Administration of Redemption; and *third,* to the last things, or Eschatology.

CHAPTER XXII

THE ESTATES AND OFFICES OF CHRIST

A consideration of the estates and offices of Christ forms the natural transition between the doctrine of His Person and that of His finished work—commonly known as the Atonement. The estates of Christ are two—the State of Humiliation and the State of Exaltation. Theologically they represent varying emphases upon the two natures of the God-man. The doctrine of the two estates was formulated in the fourth century and was an outgrowth of the Apollinarian controversy. As to the limits of the humiliation, different positions are held. The Reformed Church holds that it extends from the miraculous conception to the close of the descent into Hades, while the Lutheran Church makes the descensus the first stage in the exaltation. The Arminian theologians have generally accepted the Lutheran position. The offices of Christ are three—that of prophet, priest and king. This threefold classification was worked out carefully by Eusebius at an early date, and was followed by both

There is no method of studying the theology of redemption at once so interesting and so effectual as that which connects it with the successive stages of our Lord's history. This does not, however, demand the presentation of what is commonly called The Life of Jesus..... Yet there is an historical review of the Saviour's career which may be made the basis of the entire system of evangelical theology. The life of our Lord was the manifestation of His Person and of His work, as begun below and continued above; and, remembering that the Acts and the Epistles and the Apocalypse supplement the Gospels, even as the Old Testament is their preface, we shall pursue our study of the Mediatorial Ministry in strict connection with the stages and processes of our Lord's history on earth and in heaven, before and at and after the fullness of time.—POPE, *Chr. Th.*, II, p. 140.

The work of Christ forms in itself one whole, completed as to its principle, when He left the earth (John 17:4). But that which for His consciousness was inseparable, must be divided in our presentation of it, on account of the extent and dignity of the subject. A sharp line of separation between the different parts would lead to one-sidedness; but correctness of distinction is here one of the requirements. Thus the old dogmatic mode of speaking of a twofold state (*duplex status*), in which the Lord accomplished His redeeming work, is to be approved in principle; and we cannot be surprised that traces of it present themselves even in the earliest fathers.—VAN OOSTERZEE, *Chr. Dogm.*, II, p. 540.

Calvin and Luther. In more modern times it has been the principle of distribution by Schleiermacher, Dorner, Martensen, Hodge, Pope and Strong. We shall, then, in this chapter, consider the following subjects: (I) The State of Humiliation; (II) The State of Exaltation; and (III) The Offices of Christ.

The State of Humiliation

The Scriptures present Christ in strikingly contrasted conditions. The prophets foresaw Him as subjected to the greatest indignities, and as seated on the most exalted of thrones. Unable to reconcile these contrasts, the Jewish exegetes sometimes affirmed the necessity of two Messiahs. Much of the opposition to Jesus during His earthly life, was based on His humble condition, and the reasons given by His opposers are in exact correspondence with the nature of the humiliation which the prophets had foretold concerning Him. If in the light of modern exegetical studies, we inquire as to the nature of the humiliation, we shall find that it pertains generally, though not exclusively to the limitations of His human nature, and its relation to the penalty of sin. The portion of scripture which has furnished the basis for numerous and widely divergent Christological theories is found in St. Paul's Epistle to the Philippians, *Let this mind be in you, which was also in Christ Jesus: who being in the form of God, thought it not robbery to be equal with God: but made himself of no reputation, and took upon him the form of a servant, and was made in the*

Perhaps the best rendering of Phil. 2:6-8 is as follows: "Who, existing in the form of God, counted not the being on an equality with God a thing to be grasped, but emptied himself, taking the form of a servant, being made in the likeness of men; and being found in fashion as a man, he humbled himself, becoming obedient even unto death, the death of the cross." The Emphatic Diaglot has the following translation: "Who, though being in God's Form, yet did not meditate a Usurpation to be like God, but divested Himself, taking a Bondman's form, having been made in the Likeness of Men; and being in condition as a Man, he humbled himself, becoming obedient unto Death, even the Death of the Cross." Rotheram in his "Emphasized New Testament" gives the text in the form of a transliteration, "Who in the form of God subsisting, not a thing to be seized accounted the being equal with God, but himself emptied taking a servant's form coming to be in men's likeness; and in fashion being found as a man humbled himself, becoming obedient as far as death, yea, death upon a cross."

likeness of men: and being found in fashion as a man, he humbled himself, and became obedient unto death, even the death of the cross (Phil. 2: 5-8). A sound exegesis reveals, in this text, two stages in the humiliation, *first*, from the divine to the human; *second*, from the glory of created manhood, to the ignominy of the cross. Each stage is marked by parallel steps in the decline. Subsisting in the form of God, there was (1) a self-renunciation, *He thought it not robbery to be equal with God*, or as frequently translated, *not a thing to be grasped and held on to*; (2) a self-emptying or kenosis, *He made himself of no reputation*, that is, He emptied Himself; and (3) He took upon Him the form of a servant, *and was made in the likeness of men*. Subsisting in the form of man, there are likewise three well-defined steps in the humiliation set in parallel to the preceding, (1) a self-renunciation, *He humbled himself;* (2) a subordination, *and became obedient unto death, and* (3) a perfection of His humiliation as the Representative of sinners, *even the death of the cross.*

There is a sense in which the Person of the Incarnate, as such, was incapable of abasement. His assumption of a pure human nature, by which the center of His being, that is, His personality, was not changed, was an act of infinite condescension, but not of humiliation strictly so-called. The self-determining or self-limiting act of the Godhead in creating all things cannot be regarded as a derogation; nor was it such in the specific union of Deity with manhood. But, as we shall hereafter see that the descent into Hades was the moment which united the deepest abasement and the loftiest dignity of the Christ, so the moment of the Incarnation in the womb of the Virgin united the most glorious condescension of the second Person with His most profound abjection. His work began as a suffering Redeemer, with the submission to conception and birth. Hence the Person and the work cannot be separated. And the humiliation which the Redeemer underwent must be regarded as the humiliation of the God-man. He assumed it, even as He assumed the nature that rendered it possible.—Pope, *Chr. Th.*, II, p. 164.

The whole activity of the Son of God before His Incarnation bears an exalted and beneficent character, but not yet actually a redeeming one. It is for this reason here mentioned simply as the basis and starting-point for that which He, after His appearing as the Redeemer of the world, both in the state of humiliation and in that of exaltation, has done, is doing, and will yet further do. As such, however, it must not be overlooked, since His activity after His incarnation becomes, to a certain extent, more intelligible to us, even on account of His previous activity. Yet, the incarnation of the Word, the true beginning of His work of redemption properly so-called, is, on the other hand, simply the continuation of that which the Logos had already earlier effected in order to bring in light and life.—Van Oosterzee, *Chr. Dogm.*, II, p. 542.

The Stages of Christ's Humiliation. From the scripture just cited it is evident that the two states of Christ's being—as pre-existent Logos, and as the Word made flesh, necessitated a twofold renunciation, from the divine to the human, and from the manger to the cross. The Reformed Christology generally applies the term *exinanition* to the first stage, and limits the *humiliation* to the second or earthly life of Jesus. If now we place the total process in its historical relations, we shall observe the following consecutive stages in the humiliation of the Redemptive Person: (1) The *Exinanition,* or self-renunciation on the part of the pre-existent Logos, who existing in the form of God, thought this not a thing to be grasped and maintained. It is not the divinity, however, that is relinquished, but the form under which the divine nature was to be manifested. Hence it must refer to what is termed in the high priestly prayer, "the glory"; by which is meant the free and independent exercise of His divine powers (John 17:5). (2) The *Incarnation* or submission to the laws of natural birth, thereby taking His human nature from the substance of the virgin. Being conceived by the Holy Ghost, His nature was sinless, yet He took it in such a manner that He bore the consequences of man's sin. (3) The *self-limitation* of human finiteness, by which He subjected Himself to the laws of natural growth and development, as a preparation for His office as Mediator. (4) The *subordination,* or the exercise of His divine powers in submission to the mediatorial will of the Father, and under the control of the Holy Spirit. (5) The *humiliation,* which began officially at His baptism when He became the Representative of sinners; and was followed through

The voluntary Incarnation of the Son of God must be regarded as the first step in the path of His humiliation. Apart from all the privations and sufferings which, as became later apparent, were for Him, from the beginning to the end, connected with being man among men, even the incarnation itself was for the Lord a self-denial in the natural and moral aspect. And indeed, it was not His fate only, but His own act, that He appeared as man upon earth, an act of grace (II Cor. 8:9) explicable only from the inexhaustible riches of His obedience and love (John 6:38; Heb. 10:5) in consequence of which He, who was God in God, placed Himself, as the Ambassador of the Father, to the Father in the lowly relation of a servant.—VAN OOSTERZEE, *Chr. Dogm.,* II, p. 543.

all the downward steps of temptation and suffering to its perfection—the death on the cross.

Following the Reformation, the Lutheran and Reformed Churches took widely different positions concerning the nature of the humiliation. We may summarize these briefly under four heads: (1) The *Communicatio Idiomatum;* (2) The Earlier Depotentiation Theories; (3) The Later Kenotic Theories; and (4) The Mystical Theories.

The Communicatio Idiomatum. This was peculiarly a Lutheran development, and signified the communication of the *Idiomata,* or attributes of the two natures of Christ to the one Person, and through that Person from one nature to the other. It does not involve the merging of one nature into the other, but it does hold that all the attributes, whether of the divine or human natures, are to be regarded as attributes of the one Person. The acts of Christ, therefore, are acts of the one Person and not of either nature independently of that one Person. This doctrine presupposes the *Communio Naturam* or Communion of Natures in such a manner that there is a communication of the attributes and powers of the divine to the human nature. This, however, is not reciprocal, for the human nature cannot communicate anything to the divine which is unchangeable and perfect. The divine nature is the higher and active, while the human is the lower and passive. Here, again, no confusion of the natures is allowed, but a permeation of the human by the divine on the basis of a perichoresis; this permeation taking place through the person which is the bond of union between the two natures. Thus

The Lutheran theologians further developed the *Communicatio Idiomatum* under three genera: (1) the *Genus Idiomaticum,* in which the peculiarities of either or both natures are predicated of the one Person. Thus "they crucified the Lord of glory," or "ye killed the Prince of life" (cf. I Cor. 2:8; Acts 3:15; John 3:13; Rom. 9:15). (2) The *Genus Majesticum* by which the Son of God communicates His divine majesty to the human nature which He assumed. The Lutherans interpreted this to mean that Christ possessed according to His human nature, such relative attributes as omnipresence, omniscience and omnipotence (cf. Matt. 11:27; 28:20). (3) The *Genus Apotelesmaticum* signifies that the mediatorial acts of Christ proceeded from the whole Godhead, and not from either the one or the other nature (cf. Luke 19:10; I John 1:7).

through the Person, the resources of the divine nature are placed at the disposal of the human. This position was denied by the Reformed Church. To the Lutheran maxim, "*Humana natura in Christo est capax divinæ,*" or human nature in Christ is capable of the divine, they opposed the formula, "*Finitum non est capax infiniti,*" or the finite cannot become the infinite.

The Earlier Depotentiation Theories. The development of the *Communicatio Idiomatum* led finally to a controversy within the Lutheran Church. Early in the seventeenth century two schools arose—the Giessen and the Tubingen, which took widely different positions as to the nature of the humiliation. Starting from the *communicatio* as a common basis, both schools held that from the moment of His conception Christ possessed the attributes of omnipresence, omniscience and omnipotence. But they interpreted the humiliation in different ways. The Giessen theologians held that there was a kenosis or emptying of the divine attributes during the earthly life of Christ, and hence were known as kenotists; while the Tubingen school maintained that the attributes were only concealed, and hence were known as kryptists. The kenotists, however, made a distinction between the possession of the attributes ($\kappa\tau\hat{\eta}\sigma\iota\varsigma$) and the use of the attributes ($\chi\rho\hat{\eta}\sigma\iota\varsigma$), the *kenosis* applying only to the latter. Hence the kryptists regarded the glorification as the first display of the divine attributes in the life of Christ, while the kenotists viewed it as a resumption of them. The depotentiation theories took various forms but there was a common element in them all—they believed that there was a literal merging of the Deity of Christ into the Spirit of the Man Christ Jesus.

<blockquote>
The general bearing of the question is well seen in the following words of Gerhard: "Not a part to a part, but the entire Logos was united to the entire flesh, and the entire flesh was united to the entire Logos; therefore, on account of the hypostatic union and intercommunion of the two natures, the Logos is so present to the flesh and the flesh so present to the Logos that neither is the Logos extra carnem, nor the flesh extra Logos; but wherever the Logos is, there it has the flesh most present, as having been assumed into the unity of the person." The controversy led to no definite results: indeed, to us who look at the question from the outside, there is but little difference between them.— POPE, *Chr. Th.*, II, p. 193.
</blockquote>

The Later Kenotic Theories. During the earlier part of the nineteenth century an attempt was made to unite the two great branches of German Protestantism—the Lutheran and Reformed churches, on the basis of the kenotic Christology. The substance of this new position was to the effect that Christ in becoming incarnate "emptied" Himself, and thereby brought the eternally pre-existent Logos within the limitations of finite personality. The form and degree of this kenosis or "self-emptying" was a matter of Dispute. Four more or less distinct types of kenotic theory appear in the Christological literature of the period—that of Thomasius, Gess, Ebrard and Martensen.

1. Thomasius (1802-1875), a Bavarian Lutheran was the earliest advocate of modern kenoticism. He held that the Lutheran conception of the two natures demanded, either that the infinite be brought down to the finite, or the finite raised to the infinite. Since the acceptance of the latter position had led to insuperable difficulties in Lutheran theology, he held that the *majestas* should be abandoned for the *kenosis*. According to Thomasius, the Son of God entered into the existence form of creaturely personality, and made Himself the ego of a human individual. His consciousness, therefore, had the same conditions and content as that which belonged to finite persons. The difference lay in this, that in Him the ego was not born out of human nature, but instead was born into it, that He might work His way through it to a complete divine-human being. We may say then, that the distinctive characteristic of the kenosis as held by Thomasius, was that the Logos emptied Himself of the

Bruce in his "Humiliation of Christ" arranges the modern kenotic theories in four groups as follows: (1) the absolute dualistic type represented by Thomasius; (2) the absolute metamorphic type represented by Gess; (3) the absolute semi-metamorphic type represented by Ebrard; and (4) the real but relative type represented by Martensen.

The link between the earlier kenoticism of the Giessen-Tubingen schools, and that of the modern schools, is generally found in the pietistic Christology of Zinzendorf (1702-1760). To him, Jesus was on the one hand the natural Son of God, of divine essence; and on the other, mere natural man. "These can be reconciled," says Dorner, "only if we assume Zinzendorf's idea to have been that the self-conversion into a human germ, which then appropriated to itself material elements from Mary, so that the Son of God woke up to life in Mary a man."

194   CHRISTIAN THEOLOGY

relative attributes of omnipresence, omniscience and omnipotence, while still retaining the immanent or *essential attributes* of Deity.

2. Gess (1819-1891), a Swabian theologian, was brought up under the influence of Bengel, Oetinger and Beck. Starting, therefore, from a background of theosophic biblical realism, he carries the kenotic theory still farther than Thomasius. He affirmed that the Logos not only emptied Himself of the relative attributes, but divested Himself also of the essential attributes. There was, therefore, an actual transformation of the Logos into a human soul. This theory holds still further, that while Christ assumed His flesh from the body of the Virgin, His soul was not so derived, but was the result of a voluntary kenosis.

3. Ebrard (1818-1888) was a Reformed theologian who first advanced his doctrine in connection with the Holy Supper. He agreed with Gess in regarding the incarnate Logos as taking the place of the human soul, but differs from him, in that he does not hold this to be a depotentiation. He held that the attributes of omnipresence, omniscience and omnipotence remained, and therefore the humiliation was a disguising of His divinity. The position very closely approaches the older orthodoxy of the Reformed Church.

4. Martensen (1808-1884), a Danish bishop and theologian, advanced the theory of "a real but relative" kenosis. By this he means that the depotentiation though real, applied only to the earthly life of Christ in the flesh, and not to His divine nature or attributes. "The manifestation of the Son of God in the fullness of the times points back to His pre-existence; by pre-existence understanding, not merely that He had been originally in the Father, but also that He had been originally in the world. As the mediator between the Father and the world, it appertains to the essence of the Son not only to have His life in the Father, but to live also in the world. As 'the heart of the Father,' He is at the same time the 'eternal heart of the world.' As the Logos of the Father, He is at the same time the eternal Logos of the world, through

whom the divine light shines into creation (John 1: 4). He is the ground and source of all reason in creation.... the principle of the law and the promises under the Old Testament, the eternal light which shines in the darkness of heathenism; and all the holy grains of truth which are found in heathenism were sowed by the Son of God in the souls of men" (MARTENSEN, *Chr. Dogm.*, p. 237). Bishop Martensen makes a distinction between the Logos revelation and the Christ-revelation, and confines the kenosis to the latter. The Logos while continuing as God in His general revelation to the world, enters at the same time into the bosom of humanity as a holy seed, that He may rise within the human race as a Mediator and Redeemer. As the Logos, He works in an all-pervading activity through the kingdom of nature; as Christ, He works in the kingdom of grace; and He indicates His consciousness of personal identity in the two spheres by referring to His pre-existence.

If now we add to these, the earlier kenotic and kryptic theories, we shall have at least a practical survey of the various kenotic theories in their relation to the humiliation of Christ. Julius Mueller (d. 1879) is a modern representative of the earlier kenoticism—holding that the Incarnation implied not only a renunciation of the use but of the possession of the divine attributes and powers. Kahnis (1814-1888) and Lange (1802-1884) returned more nearly to the older orthodox position, maintaining that the kenosis must be limited solely to the abandonment of the use of the divine attributes. Dorner criticizes the kenotic theories, and in their place sub-

---

The new feature in the revelation of Christ is not that union of the divine and human nature, which is involved in the idea of man as created in the image of God. The new feature is such a union of the two natures, that a man on earth appears as the self-revelation of the divine Logos. Although the word "God-man" is not found in the New Testament, the thought expressed by it lies at the basis of its Christological representations. Christ describes Himself as both the Son of God and Son of man. In styling Himself the Son of man, He sets Himself forth as the personal embodiment of human nature in its pure archetypal form (as the second Adam according to the explanation of the Apostle). And in styling Himself the Son of God, He assumes the position of the Only Begotten of the Father. (He is "the brightness of the Father's glory, and the express image of his person") (Heb. 1:3).—MARTENSEN, *Chr. Dogm.*, p. 240.

stitutes the idea of a progressive union consummated by an enlarging impartation from the Logos to the growing receptivity in the human nature. This theory applies the kenosis to the whole range of the earthly life of Jesus instead of limiting it to a single event. It follows also the pattern of the earlier kenoticism, in that there is no depotentiation of the Logos, which remains unchanged in being and reality; but finds the limitation in the human nature, to which according to a growing capacity, there is a self-communication of the Logos.

The Mystical Theories. As previously indicated, the teaching of Zinzendorf was in some sense, the germ from which the later kenotic theories developed. It also marked a stage in the development of the modern mystical theories. In its bearing upon Christology, mysticism was developed by Weigel, Arndt, and Boehme into what amounted to a Protestant philosophy in theosophical form. The Christology of the Confessions did not satisfy the friends of mysticism. They felt the need of a stronger emphasis upon the essential affinity of man with God, and also upon the notion of a mystic vision. The eye by which earthy knowledge becomes real, they held to be man himself. In the matter of supernatural knowledge, the eye is not man but God, who is both the light and the eye in us. This inner light, Weigel identified with Christ. Later there developed the doctrine of a pre-existent humanity or pre-temporal Incarnation, in which the Word and this ideal humanity were conjoined from eternity. It was not, therefore, the Son of God who directly became flesh, but the Son of God already in the heavenly nature of mankind. There are three representative types of this mysticism in modern times.

1. Barclay, the theologian of the Quakers, taught that the flesh of which St. John speaks under the symbol of "the bread of life which came down from heaven" (John 6:51) is a spiritual body, and therefore the pre-temporal humanity of Jesus. In order to maintain a belief in the historical Redeemer, Barclay was driven to

Lange points out the curious fact that the Labadism of the Reformed Church is on the one side connected with the Roman Catholic Jansenism, and on the other with Lutheran Spenerism.

posit two bodies of Christ — one heavenly, the other earthly. The peculiar tenet of Barclay, however, was his inclination to the view that the Word of God revealed Himself to men in all ages by means of the same body. The Old Testament theophanies were, then, manifestations of this body previous to the Incarnation. For this reason all men could become partakers of the life which is in Christ; and this is possible to faith, even apart from the Eucharist.

2. Zinzendorf was the founder of Herrnhut and the head of the Moravian Brethren. John Wesley was profoundly influenced by the spiritual experience of the Brethren, but reacted sharply against their peculiar doctrines. Zinzendorf shows in a marked manner the influence of the earlier mysticism as found in Weigel (1533-1588) and Boehme (1575-1624). He maintains that the human soul of Jesus was inbreathed as a glorious, holy, chaste, divine substance, by the Son himself. It took place, however, in such manner that His humanity was made subject to His divinity, His soul being a part of the divine essence. Jesus is, therefore, the natural Son of God. This family idea of Zinzendorf is applied to the Trinity and to the Church.

3. Oetinger interpreted the text "he came unto his own" (John 1:11), as indicating that man was fashioned after the pattern of the humanity of the pretemporal Christ, and, therefore, the Incarnation was a literal coming to His own in a physical sense. Hence he says, "Because Wisdom, before the Incarnation, was the visible image of the invisible God, therefore the Son, in comparison with the Being of all beings, is something relatively incorporeal although He, too, is pure spirit. The heavenly humanity which He had as the Lord from

> The one fundamental principle in these sporadic speculations—they have never been formulated in any Confessions—is that the pure humanity of our Lord was as independent of the race of man as that of Adam was when he came from the hand and breath of his Maker. Denying, with the Scripture, that Jesus owed anything to a human father, they deny, without or in opposition to Scripture, that He derived anything from a human mother. The Virgin was no more than the instrument or channel through which a divine humanity, existing before the foundation of the world or from eternity, was introduced by the Holy Ghost into human history.—POPE, *Compend. Chr. Th.*, II, p. 194.

heaven was invisibly present even with the Israelites. They drank out of the rock." It is thus the heavenly humanity of Jesus which takes on or assumes to itself an earthly body.

Summary and Critical Statement. The theories under discussion will be best understood by considering them in their relation to the development of modern thought. The older Lutheranism with its extreme emphasis upon the deity of Christ, had practically ignored His humanity. It had, as Dr. Schaff says, arrived at the brink of Docetism. The rationalism which arose at the close of the eighteenth century was a reaction against this scholastic and confessional Christology, and brought a renewed emphasis upon the humanity of Christ. However it went to the opposite extreme; it ignored the divine nature, and soon fell back upon a purely human or Ebionitic Christ. With the arrival of the evangelical faith in Germany, the divine element was again emphasized, followed by original modifications and reconstructions of the orthodox Christology. Two tendencies may be noted—the humanistic and the pantheistic; the former having its origin in the theology of Schleiermacher, the latter in the philosophy of Hegel and Schelling. The humanistic tendency includes, in addition to the Christology of Schleiermacher, those also of Channing, Bushnell and other unitarian developments. The pantheistic tendency is best represented by Daub, Marheineke and Goeschel.

It is evident from our discussion of the kenotic theories that some of them must be classed with the humanistic theories, and others with the pantheistic. We have seen that the earlier depotentiation theories limited the kenosis merely to the use, or the manifested use of the divine predicates. The later theories, however, applied the kenosis directly to the Logos, holding to such a depotentiation as in some instances reduced the divine Logos to a mere finite human being. Here must be mentioned the theories of Thomasius, Gess and Julius Mueller. These are unitarian, or at least humanitarian theories and cannot be held consistently with orthodox trinitarianism. Their error lies in this—that they carry the humiliation and self-limitation to the extent of a metaphysical impossibility, and consequently contradict the essential unchangeableness of God. The pantheistic tendency led to another type of Christology. Starting from the idea of an essential unity between the divine and the human, it held to a continuous incarnation of God in the human race as a whole. The peculiar position of Christ according to this theory, is that He was the first to awake to a consciousness of this unity, and represents it in its pur-

Schleiermacher's Christology may be said to mark the beginning of the nineteenth development in unitarian thought. While holding to the divine element in Christ, and emphatically asserting His sinlessness and absolute perfection, Schleiermacher nevertheless emphasizes Christ's humanity to the disparagement of His deity. He holds Christ to be a perfect man, in whom, and in whom alone, the ideal of humanity has been realized. He admits that Christ was a "moral miracle," and that there was in Him a peculiar and abiding indwelling of the Godhead, which marked Him as different from all other men. "He was willing," says Dr. Philip Schaff, "to surrender almost every miracle of action, to save the miracle of the person of Him whom he loved and adored, from his Moravian childhood to his deathbed, as his Lord and Saviour. He adopts the Sabellian view of the Trinity as a threefold manifestation of God in creation (in the world), redemption (in Christ), and sanctification (in the Church). Christ is God as Redeemer and originated an incessant flow of a new spiritual life, with all its pure and holy emotions and aspirations which must be traced to that source. Sabellian as he was, Schleiermacher did not hold an eternal pre-existence of the Logos which would correspond to the historical indwelling of God in Christ."—SCHAFF-HERZOG, *Enc.*, Art., Christology.

Richard Rothe was greatly influenced by Schleiermacher and Hegel. Next to Schleiermacher, he is generally considered the greatest speculative theologian of the nineteenth century. He held to the divine-human character of Christ, but abandoned the orthodox doctrine of the Trinity. God by a creative act called the last Adam into existence in the midst of the old natural humanity. Christ was born of Mary yet not begotten of man, but created by God as to His humanity, and hence free of all sinful bias as well as actual sin. He stood every moment of conscious life in personal union with God, but the absolute union took place only at the completion of His personal development. This took place at the time of His Perfect self-sacrifice in death. The death of Christ on earth was at the same time His ascension to heaven, and His elevation above the limitations of earthly existence.

The criticism urged against Bishop Martensen's twofold Logos revelation and Christ revelation, is that he fails to explain more clearly the unity of Christ's Person on this theory than does the orthodox creed with its two natures. As to the progressive idea of Dorner, if it be understood to make Christ more and more a theanthropic Person, we must reject it. Christ must be regarded as a theanthropic Person from His conception and birth; and His normal development, as we have previously pointed out, must be the law of natural development under which he assumes true human nature.

est and strongest form. But the idea of a racial Incarnation soon developed into a denial of the specific dignity of Christ as the only true God-man, and consequently the theory found its logical issue in rationalistic criticism and religious skepticism. The mediating theologians, Martensen and Dorner, attempted by their kenotic theories to harmonize orthodox Christology with this idealistic philosophy, but with doubtful success. As to the mystical theories, their tendency was toward Arianism as is shown in the position of Isaac Watts, and as actually affirmed in the case of Paul Maty.

If now we take into account the teaching of St. Paul that there was in the humiliation of Christ a kenosis or self-emptying (Phil. 2: 7); and if we set over against this the idea of a divestment of His pre-existent glory, as indicated by our Lord in His high priestly prayer (John 17: 5), we shall find some light on this perplexing problem. The mystery of the humiliation, however, must forever transcend human comprehension. Of this divestment, Dean Alford says, "He emptied himself of the $\mu o \rho \phi \hat{\eta}\ \Theta \epsilon o \hat{v}$, not the essential glory but the manifested possession .... the glory which He had with the Father before the world began and which was resumed at His glorification. He ceased while in the state of exinanition to reflect the glory which He had with the Father." Lightfoot takes practically the same position. "He divested Himself, not of His divine nature, for this was impossible, but of the glories, the prerogatives, of Deity" (LIGHTFOOT, *Comm. Phil.*, p. 110). We may then, with safety interpret this divestment of the glory to mean the giving up of the independent exercise of His own divine attributes during the period of His earthly life. We may also confidently believe: (1) That the pre-existent Logos gave up the glory which He had before the foundation of the world, in order to take upon Himself the form of a servant. (2) That during His earthly life He was subordinate to the mediatorial will of the Father in all things; yet knowing the will of the Father, He voluntarily offered Himself in obedience to this will. (3) That His ministry during this period was under the immediate control of the Holy Spirit, who prepared for Him a body, who instructed Him during the period of development, who anointed Him for His mission, and who enabled Him at last to offer Himself without spot to God.

The State of Exaltation

The Exaltation is that state of Christ in which He laid aside the infirmities of the flesh according to His human nature, and again assumed His majesty. As in the humiliation there were stages of descent, so also in the exaltation there are stages of ascent. These stages are as follows: (1) The *Descensus,* or descent into Hades; (2) The Resurrection; (3) The Ascension; and (4) The Session.

The Descent into Hades. The brief interval in redemptive history, between the death of Christ and the resurrection, is known as the *Descensus ad inferos,* or the Descent into Hades. The term is not found in the Scriptures but in the creeds, and as found there is expressed in the words, "He descended into hell." The doctrine of the *descensus* however, is based upon such scriptures as Psalms 16:10 quoted by the Apostle Peter in His sermon at Pentecost. *Thou wilt not leave my soul in hell, neither wilt thou suffer thine Holy One to see corruption. . . . . He seeing this before spake of the resurrection of Christ, that his soul was not left in hell, neither his flesh did see corruption* (Acts 2:27, 31). Closely con-

---

Various views have been held concerning the Descensus. It has been held (1) that Christ in His own person preached to the good in the spirit world. This view is attributed to Irenæus, Clement of Alexandria, Tertullian, Origen and Gregory the Great. It was advocated also by Anselm, Alburtus and Thomas Aquinas. Zwingli held that Christ preached the gospel of redemption to the "spirits in prison," that is, to the Old Testament saints, who could not be admitted into heaven proper, prior to the actual death of Christ. This is substantially the view of the Roman Catholic Church. (2) Christ preached to both the good and bad. This view was maintained by Athanasius, Ambrose, Erasmus and Calvin. (3) Christ preached to the wicked only, announcing their final condemnation. This was held by many of the Lutheran divines. (4) Christ in the person of the apostles preached to the spirits in prison, that is, to those yet in the prison of the body or flesh. This was the view of the celebrated Grotius, and also of Socinius. (5) Christ preached in the person of ancient Noah, to those who were alive on earth in his day. This view has been held by a number of eminent expositors, ancient and modern.

nected with these texts is another by the same apostle, which states that *he went and preached unto the spirits in prison; which sometime were disobedient, when once the longsuffering of God waited in the days of Noah, while the ark was a preparing, wherein few, that is, eight souls were saved by water* (I Peter 3:19, 20). The Greek word *Hades* ("Αιδης) and its Hebrew complement, *Sheol*, signifies the hidden or unseen state, that is, the realm of the dead. It has no reference to punishment endured while in this hidden state. It was into this realm of the dead that our Lord entered, while His body was concealed in the sepulcher, or "visible representative of the invisible Hades into which He entered as to His soul."

We must regard the *descensus* as the first stage in the exaltation. The Reformed Churches generally regard it as the last stage in the humiliation, although it is not made an Article of Faith. Calvin and the Heidelberg Catechism regarded the creedal expression "he descended into hell" as referring to the intensity of Christ's sufferings on the cross, where he may be said to have tasted the pains of hell for sinners. The Westminster divines held that the expression meant merely that Christ continued

Cremer says that "θάνατος is not an isolated occurrence or fact merely, it is also a state, just as life is a state: it is the state of man as liable to judgment. It is the antithesis of that eternal life which God has purposed for man, and which man may yet obtain through Christ. . . . . We find that, according to the context, the reference of θάνατος is either to death as the objective sentence and punishment accounted for man, or to death as the state in which man is as condemned through sin (cf. Rom. 6:23; I John 3:14-16).—CREMER, *Lexicon of New Testament Greek*.

Christ's humiliation after His death consisted in His being buried and continuing in the state of the dead and under the power of death until the third day, which hath been otherwise expressed in these words, He descended into hell.—*Larger Westminster Catechism*, Question 50.

We simply believe that the whole person of Christ, including both His divine and human natures, after His burial, descended into hell (*ad inferos*), conquered Satan, overturned the power of hell, and broke down all the strength and power of the devil. But in what manner Christ did this, it is not possible that we should ascertain, whether by argumentation or by sublime imaginings.—*Formula of Concord*, Art. ix. 2.

The Roman Catholic Church holds that Christ descended into an intermediate state known as the *Limbus Patrum;* His purpose being to deliver the righteous dead whom He led on high as captives when He ascended after the resurrection. This assumes that the ordinances of salvation in the Old Testament were not effacious, and that no Old Testament saint could be admitted into heaven proper on the basis of a Christ not yet historically come.

dead as far as this world is concerned, for the period of three days. The Lutheran Church, on the other hand, held that the *descensus* belongs to the exaltation of Christ and is a constituent element in His redemptive work. This is the teaching of the Formula of Concord (Art. ix., 2). The older theologians based their doctrine chiefly upon the words of St. Peter (I Peter 3: 18, 19) and likewise regarded it as the first stage in the exaltation. It took place, according to their belief, immediately after the quickening in the tomb and just preceding the visible resurrection. We may safely believe, then, that when our Lord uttered the cry, "It is finished!" the humiliation ended and in the same instant His exaltation began. His death was His triumph over death, consequently death had no more power over Him (Rom. 6: 8, 9). When, therefore, He entered into the realm of the dead it was a Conqueror. Descending into the lower parts of the earth (Eph. 4: 8, 9), *He led captivity captive, and gave gifts unto men.* "Quickened by the Spirit," He went and preached to the spirits in prison (I Peter 3: 18, 19), a scripture which "Indicates, and will allow no other interpretation, that in the interval the Redeemer asserted His authority and Lordship in the vast region where the congregation of the dead is the great aggregate of man-

The word Hades is derived from α meaning "not"; and εἶδος to see and therefore means etymologically the "not seen." It occurs ten times in the New Testament, Matt. 11:23; 16:18; Luke 10:15; 16:23; Acts 2:27, 31; Rev. 1:18; 6:8; 20:13, 14.

Calvin maintained that "If Christ had merely died a corporeal death, no end would have been accomplished by it; it was requisite also that He should feel the severity of the divine vengeance, in order to appease the wrath of God, and satisfy His justice. Hence it was necessary for Him to contend with the powers of hell and the horror of eternal death" (cf. CALVIN, *Institutes*, II, xvi, 10). This makes the *descensus* a part of the humiliation, against which Arminian theologians generally have protested.

Godet in his comment on Rom. 14:9 has the following: "With the view of securing the possession of His own, whether as living or dead, Jesus began by resolving in His own person the contrast between life and death. He did so by dying and reviving. For what is one raised again except a dead man living? Thus it is that He reigns simultaneously over the two domains of being through which His own are called to pass, and that He can fulfill His promise to them, John 10:28, 'None shall pluck them out of my hand.'"

Bengell remarks (Rev. 1:18), He might have said, ἀπέθανον, "I died," but with singular elegance it is ἐγενόμην νεκρὸς, "I became dead," to denote the difference of times, and of the events in them.

kind, the great assembly to which also we may apply the words *In the midst of the congregation will I praise thee"* (cf. POPE, *Compend. Chr. Th.*, II, pp. 168, 169). We must believe also, that Christ's body was preserved inviolate, and consequently *saw no corruption* (Acts 13: 37). As through the Incarnation, the Son of God took upon Him flesh and blood and thereby entered into the state of human life, so in the *descensus* He entered triumphantly the hitherto unknown state of the dead.

The Resurrection. The second stage in the exaltation of Christ is the resurrection, or that act by which our Lord came forth alive from the tomb. As previously indicated, St. Luke in his introduction to the Acts, makes the span of Christ's earthly life to end, not at His death but at His ascension, *the time when he was taken up* (Acts 1:2). The ascension marked the transition from His earthly to His heavenly state. The resurrection therefore, was the last and crowning event of our Lord's earthly mission. Two phases of this truth must be given brief consideration; *first,* the historical fact of the resurrection; and *second,* the dogmatic significance, or meaning of the resurrection.

First, the fact of the resurrection was attested by *many infallible proofs* (Acts 1:3). The testimony of the apostles and first disciples is of great value, and the historical significance of the resurrection must not therefore, be undervalued. Jesus having been crucified, dead and buried, His body on the third day disappeared from the tomb; and this despite the fact that the tomb was sealed and a Roman guard set before it. To the women who early visited the tomb an angel declared that He had risen and gone before them into Galilee (Matt. 28:1-7). Our Lord's clothes were found in the tomb, in positions

In His one Person He kept inviolate His human body, which did not undergo the material dissolution of its elements: not because, as is sometimes said, He was delivered from the grave before corruption had time to affect His sacred flesh; but because the work of death was arrested in the very instant of the severance of soul and body. As His spirit dieth no more, so His body saw no corruption. The unviolated flesh of our Lord was still the moment He was quickened a silent declaration of perfect victory: His divinity never left His body, any more than it forsook His spirit in its passage into the world of spirits.—POPE, *Compend. Chr. Th.,* II. p. 168.

which suggested that the body was exhaled in a manner which left them undisturbed, except causing them to collapse. He appeared alive to His disciples in tangible "flesh and bones" by which they recognized His body as that in which He had been crucified. Added to this, they recognized that he had acquired new and mysterious powers, which transcended those manifested during His earthly life in the flesh. During the forty days, the following appearances are recorded: to Mary in the garden (John 20:15, 16); to Peter (Luke 24:34); to the two disciples on the way to Emmaus (Luke 24:13ff); to the ten gathered together, Thomas being absent (John 20:19); to the eleven (John 20:24-29); to the disciples as they were fishing on the Sea of Tiberias (John 21:1ff); to above five hundred brethren at once (I Cor. 15:6); to James (I Cor. 15:7); at the ascension (Luke 24:50, 51); and last of all, to the Apostle Paul (I Cor. 15:8). One of the strongest evidences of the resurrection, therefore, was the complete and instantaneous change which took place in the minds of the disciples. From discouragement and unbelief, they were suddenly transformed into joyous believers. The supreme evidence of the resurrection, however, must ever be the gift of the Holy Spirit to the disciples, making of them flaming evangels of the gospel, and giving them power in the preaching of the Word (cf. Acts 4:33; 5:32; 10:44 and Heb. 2:4).

Second, the resurrection must also be considered in its dogmatic relations. Here may be mentioned, (1) the self-verification of Jesus, or the evidential power of the resurrection; (2) the new humanity as the basis and consummation of the atoning sacrifice; (3) The resurrection as the ground of our justification; (4) The glorified humanity in Christ as the basis of a new spiritual fellow-

The denial of the miracle of the resurrection is not, therefore, the bare denial of a single historical fact, it is the denial of the entire prophetic aspect of the world which Christianity presents; which finds in the resurrection its beginning in fact. A view of the world which makes the present order of things perpetual, and which considers the eternal to be only a continual present, naturally allows no room for the resurrection of Christ, which is an interruption of the order of this world by the higher order of creation still future; and which is a witness to the reality of a future life.—MARTENSEN, *Chr. Dogm.*, p. 319.

ship; and (5) The resurrection of Christ as the guaranty of our future resurrection.

1. The resurrection of Christ was the self-verification of the claims of Jesus. He was declared to be the Son of God with power, *by the resurrection from the dead.* The resurrection, therefore, was an event of supreme evidential value, and afforded the apostles a new significance of the Person and work of Christ. In turn, it made possible the fuller revelation of the Holy Spirit (Luke 24: 45, John 20: 22, 23). We must regard it, therefore, as the divine attestation of Christ's prophetic ministry, by which not only His claims were vindicated, but by which His mission was interpreted to the apostles and evangelists.

2. The new humanity of Jesus being sinless, furnished the ground of the atoning sacrifice. In the Incarnation our Lord assumed flesh and blood that He might taste death for every man; in the resurrection He achieved victory over death. It is for this reason that the resurrection is called a birth (Col. 1: 18, Rev. 1: 5). It was in reality a birth out of death, and therefore the death of death. By taking our nature and dying in it, then reviving or quickening it, this new and glorified humanity becomes the ground of an eternal priesthood, His death and resurrection being the consecrating basis. It is therefore an event of progress, in which the Redeemer passes from a lower to a higher plane in the new creation. The resurrection was not merely a return from the grave to the natural status of human life. It was a

All the four Gospel accounts of the resurrection seem to introduce two contrasted representations concerning the nature of the resurrection body of the Lord. The risen One seems to live a natural human life, in a body such as He had before His death. He has flesh and bones, He eats and drinks: again, on the contrary, He seems to have a body of a spiritual transcendental kind, which is independent of the limitations of time and space; He enters through closed doors, He stands suddenly in the midst of the disciples, and as suddenly becomes invisible to them. This contradiction, which occurs in the appearances of the risen Saviour during the forty days may be explained upon the supposition, that during this interval His body was in a state of transition and of change, upon the boundary of both worlds, and possessed the impress or character of both this world and the next. Not until the moment of the ascension can we suppose that His body was fully glorified and freed from all earthly limitations and wants, like the spiritual body of which Paul speaks (I Cor. 15: 44).—Martensen, *Chr. Dogm.*, p. 321.

transcendent event. For this reason two classes of phenomena appear—natural and supernatural. The natural phenomena served to identify Him, such as the nail prints, the wound in His side (John 20: 26-29), and the fact that He ate with them (Luke 24: 39-43). With these were connected such supernatural phenomena as suddenly standing before the disciples, the door being shut, and as mysteriously appearing from time to time. Our Lord plainly distinguished His resurrected state from His previous mode of existence, when in speaking to His disciples He said, *while I was yet with you* I spake of the things which must needs be fulfilled (Luke 24: 44). The resurrection as it pertains to the mode of existence during the forty days, must therefore, be regarded as an intermediate stage in the history of the exaltation, looking forward to the ascension and His final and perfect glorification.

3. The resurrection furnished the ground for our justification. Christ *was delivered for our offences, and raised again for our justification* (Rom. 4: 25). It becomes, therefore, a vindication, not only of His prophetic work, but also of His priesthood; and this both as to the character of the offering and the efficiency of the offerer. His birth or emergence out of death, established a new and unchangeable priesthood. For this cause He is the mediator of a better covenant (Heb. 9: 11-15). He died for the transgressions that were under the first testament; He arose to become the executor of the new covenant—by the which will, or covenant, we are *sanctified through the offering of the body of Jesus Christ once for all* (Heb. 10: 9, 10). The resurrection, therefore, furnishes a new and vital principle—a power for righteousness, which is the abiding source of justifying and sanctifying grace. *For by one offering he hath perfected forever them that are sanctified. Whereof the Holy Ghost also is a witness to us* (Heb. 10: 14, 15). Here the resurrection is directly related to the ascension and session, as it pertains both to His Person and to His work.

4. The glorified humanity of Christ formed the basis of a new spiritual fellowship. He was *the image of the in-*

visible God, the firstborn of every creature. . . . . And he is the head of the body, the church: who is the beginning, the firstborn from the dead; that in all things he might have the pre-eminence. For it pleased the Father that in him should all fulness dwell (Col. 1:15, 18, 19). This new humanity in Christ, which made Him *the firstborn among many brethren* (Rom. 8:29), furnishes the bond between Him and those who are adopted as children *by Jesus Christ to himself, according to the good pleasure of his will* (Eph. 1:5). This new humanity is ethical and spiritual (Eph. 4:22-24, Col. 3:9, 10), and as the basis of a new and holy fellowship becomes the Church, or the body of Christ.

5. The resurrection of Christ is the guaranty of our future resurrection. Christ was the *firstfruits of them that slept. For since by man came death, by man came also the resurrection of the dead. . . . . But every man in his own order: Christ the firstfruits; afterward they that are Christ's at his coming* (I Cor. 15:20-23). It is a vital part of the redemptive purpose of God in Christ, that man should not only be delivered from sin spiritually, but that he should be made free from the consequences of sin physically.

The Ascension. The Ascension is the third stage in our Lord's exaltation, and marks the close of His life on

In the resurrection is anticipated the perfecting of the world. That regeneration, including renewal and glorification, which mankind and all creation look forward to as the consummation of the world's development, in which spirit and body, nature and history, are perfectly reconciled—human nature being glorified into a temple for the Holy Ghost, and material nature being brought into the glorious liberty of the children of God—that regeneration which necessarily involves and demands the belief, that the contradiction between the physical and the ethical, between the kingdom of nature and that of grace shall not continue as if eternal and indissoluble—is revealed ideally in the resurrection of the Lord. The resurrection of the Lord is not the mere sign of that regeneration, it is itself the actual beginning of it. It is the sacred point where death has been overcome in God's creation; and from this point the spiritual as well as the bodily resurrection . . . . proceeds. Now, for the first time, as a risen Saviour can Christ become the real Lord and Head of His Church. Now that the perfecting of the world is in His person ideally accomplished, he becomes the actual Perfecter of the world, and can replenish this present world with the energies of the future.—MARTENSEN, *Chr. Dogm.*, p. 318.

Cf. also Rom. 8:18-23; I Cor. 15:24-28, 49-57; Eph. 1:9, 10: Col. 1:16-20.

earth. It is noticeable that St. Luke alone records the event in its historical order (Luke 24:50, 51; Acts 1:9-11), although St. Mark mentions it as a fact in the concluding verses of his Gospel (Mark 16:19). Christ's removal from earth to heaven must not be understood to mean merely a transference of His presence from one portion of the physical universe to another, but a local withdrawal into what is known as the *Presence of God*. The ascension was the passing into a new sphere of mediatorial action, the taking possession of the Presence of God for us and is, therefore, immediately associated with His High Priestly intercession. It signifies our Lord's entrance into the holy place, there to *appear in the presence of God for us* (Heb. 9:24). Here He offers His living manhood, perfected through sufferings (Heb. 5:6-10), *as the propitiation for our sins: and not for ours only, but also for the sins of the whole world* (I John 2:2). Here also He has consecrated a new and living way for us through the veil, *that is to say, his flesh;* His glorified body becoming the way of access through which His people have liberty or boldness *to enter into the holiest by the blood of Jesus* (Heb. 10:19, 20). Lastly, the ascension signifies the withdrawal of Christ in the flesh in order to establish conditions under which the Holy Spirit could be received as a gift to the Church. *Nevertheless I tell you the truth; it is expedient for you that I go away: for if I go not away, the Comforter will not come unto you: but if I depart, I will send him unto you* (John 16:7).

The pentecostal gift of the Holy Ghost was at once the immediate proof of the verity of the ascension, and demonstration of the authority to which it led. The prediction of the psalmist, *Thou hast received gifts for men; yea, for the rebellious also, that the Lord God might dwell among them,* was interpreted by both our Lord and by St. Paul of the supreme gift of the Holy Spirit (Psalms 68:18). *I will send him unto you* (John 16:7) was the promise before the Saviour's departure; it was confirmed after His resurrection and it was fulfilled on the Day of Pentecost once for all and for ever..... The Gift itself was the demonstration of the Session of Christ at the right hand of God (Acts 2:33; Eph. 4:8, 12). But the great prophecy in the Psalms (Psalms 68:18), *that the Lord God might dwell among them,* had its plenary fulfillment when the Holy Ghost came down as the Shekinah, the symbol of God manifest in the flesh, resting upon the Church and abiding within it as the indwelling presence of the Holy Trinity. Thus the glory within the veil, and the candlestick outside, symbols of the Son and the Spirit, were blended when the veil was removed, into one and the same fullness of God.—Pope, *Compend. Chr. Th.,* II, p. 182.

The Session. The fourth and last stage of the exaltation is known as the Session. It is closely connected with the ascension, and signifies, primarily, the place of Christ at the right hand of God as an intercessory presence. St. Mark connects the ascension and the session when he says of Christ that *he was received up into heaven, and sat on the right hand of God* (Mark 16:19). Our Lord referred indirectly to the session when He quoted the prophecy of David, *The Lord said unto my Lord, Sit thou on my right hand, till I make thine enemies thy footstool* (Matt. 22:44); and later directly in the words, *Hereafter shall ye see the Son of man sitting on the right hand of power* (Matt. 26:64). Both St. Peter and St. Paul speak of Christ as being at the right hand of God (I Peter 3:22; Eph. 1:20-23). As the prophetical office of Christ was merged into His priestly work by His death and resurrection, so His priestly office is merged into His Kingship by the ascension and session. And as the resurrection was the divine attestation of His prophetical office, so the gift of the Holy Spirit is the divine attestation of both the ascension and the session. As prophet, our Lord foretold the coming of the Holy Spirit as the *Comforter* (John 15:26; 16:7, 13); as priest, *He received of the Father the promise of the Holy Ghost;* and as King he *shed forth this, which ye now see and hear* (Acts 2:33). Christ's presence on the throne is the beginning of a supreme authority which shall end only when He *hath put all enemies under his feet* (I Cor. 15:25). He is not only the Head of the Church, but the Head over all things to the Church (Eph. 1:20-23). From the session our Lord will return to the earth a second time, without sin unto salvation (Heb. 9:28); and the ascension is the pattern of this return (Acts 1:11).

The Offices of Christ

The mediatorial process which began historically with the incarnation, and was continued through the humiliation and exaltation, reached its full perfection in the session at the right hand of God. The estates and offices therefore, form the transition from a consideration of the complex Person of Christ, to that of His finished work in the Atonement—the former relating the mediatorial work more directly to His Person, the latter more immediately to the Finished Work. As Mediator, the work of Christ is resolved into the threefold office of Prophet, Priest and King. Into these offices He was inducted at His baptism, and by a specific anointing with the Holy Spirit became officially the Mediator between God and man. But before directly considering the prophetical, priestly and regal offices of Christ, it will be necessary to consider some of the more general characteristics of Christ as Mediator. This will serve to prevent any misconception as to the nature of the mediatorial work as a whole.

1. Christ as mediator between God and men cannot be God only, or man only, for a mediator supposes two parties between whom he intervenes. *Now a mediator is not a mediator of one, but God is one* (Gal. 3:20). *For there is one God, and one mediator between God and men, the man Christ Jesus* (I Tim. 2:5). The man to which the apostle refers is *Christ Jesus,* and therefore the theanthropic or God-man. The Logos was not actually and historically the Mediator until He assumed human nature. In the Old Testament Christ was Mediator by anticipation, and men were saved through His mediatorial work in view of His future Advent. In the New Testament the types and shadows through which the Word manifested Himself are done away, being superseded by the fuller revelation of the incarnate Word.

2. The Mediatorship of Christ is an assumed office. We must regard Creatorship as a primary function of Deity. The Son never assumed it and He will never lay it down. But the mediatorship as an office is not inherent in Deity, although we may say that it is inherent in His nature as sacrificial love (Eph. 1:4; I Peter 1:19, 20; Rev. 13:8). The Son voluntarily assumed the office of Mediator, being sent of the Father; and being found in fashion as a man, humbled Himself and became obedient even to the death of the cross (Phil. 2:5-11). Because the office was voluntary and involved the carrying out of

a commission, His condescension and humiliation are deserving of reward. Wherefore, *God also hath highly exalted him, and given him a name which is above every name: that at the name of Jesus every knee should bow, of things in heaven, and things in earth, and things under the earth; and that every tongue should confess that Jesus Christ is Lord, to the glory of God the Father* (Phil. 2: 9-11). Furthermore, the office of Mediator because it was assumed will also end—in this sense, that there will be a time when the work of redemption will cease. And while the God-man will forever exist, and the relations of His people to the Father will be eternally mediated through Him, the work of redeeming sinners will be superseded by the judgment of all things. *As it is appointed unto men once to die, but after this the judgment: so Christ was once offered to bear the sins of many; and unto them that look for him shall he appear the second time without sin* (that is, without a sin-offering) *unto salvation* (Heb. 9: 27, 28).

3. Christ is represented as the Mediator of a Covenant. In a strict sense, there can be but two forms of a covenant—the legal and evangelical. The first is based upon justice, the second upon mercy. Man having sinned in the fall, the first became inoperative; consequently the evangelical covenant alone could be established. This is sometimes known as the covenant of redemption, and sometimes as the covenant of grace. The evangelical covenant existed first under the Old Dispensation, and as such was known as the "first covenant" (Heb. 8: 6-13). It exists now in a second form under the New Testament, and is known as the "new" or "better covenant" (cf. also Heb. 8: 6-8). The first was more external, and was administered through animal sacrifices and visible types and symbols. It was therefore ceremonial and national. The second is an internal covenant of life, and therefore spiritual and universal. In the first covenant the words were spoken to the people in the form of external law; in the new covenant the law is written within, upon the hearts and minds of the people (Heb. 8: 8-13: 10: 16-18).

4. Christ, as the Mediator of the New Covenant, discharges three offices, that of prophet, priest, and king. Under the Old Testament, Samuel was a prophet and a priest; David a prophet and a king; and Melchisedec, a priest and a king; Christ alone, unites in Himself the threefold office. His prophetical office is mentioned in Deut. 18: 15, 18, *For Moses truly said unto the fathers, A prophet shall the Lord your God raise up unto you of your brethren, like unto me; him shall ye hear in all things whatsoever he shall say unto you* (Acts 3: 22). His priestly office is foretold in Psalm 110: 4, *Thou art a priest forever after the order of Melchisedec* (Heb. 5: 6, 4: 14, 15). Since Melchisedec was a king-priest, Christ's priesthood involved also His kingship. This is directly stated in Isaiah 9: 6, 7, where He is called the *Prince of Peace;* and again in the Psalms, *I have set my king upon my holy hill of Zion* (Psalms 2: 6).

The Prophetic Office. Christ as a prophet is the perfect revealer of divine truth. As the Logos, He was the true Light, which lighteth every man that cometh into the world (John 1: 9). In the Old Testament He spoke through angels, through theophanies, through types, and by means of the prophets, to whom He communicated His Holy Spirit. As the Incarnate Word He faithfully and fully revealed to men the saving will of God. He spoke with inherent authority (Matt. 7: 28, 29) and was recognized as a teacher come from God (John 3: 2). After His ascension He continued His work through the Holy Spirit, who now dwells in the Church as the Spirit of truth. In the world to come His prophetic work will be continued, for we are told that the *city had no need of the sun, neither of the moon, to shine in it: for the glory of God did lighten it, and the Lamb is the light thereof* (Rev. 21: 23). It will be through His glorified manhood that we shall see and enjoy the vision of God to all eternity.

The Priestly Office. The priestly office of Christ is concerned with objective mediation, and includes both sacrifice and intercession. *He offered up himself* (Heb. 7: 27). He was at once the offering and the Offerer, the one corresponding to His death, the other to His resurrection and ascension, and together issuing in the Atonement. Based upon His sacrificial work in His office of Intercession and Benediction, which are together connected with the Administration of Redemption. It was on the eve of the crucifixion that our Lord formally assumed His sacrificial function—first by the institution of the Lord's Supper, and following this by His high priestly prayer of consecration (John 17:1-26). After Pentecost the priestly office became more prominent. Consequently the cross becomes the center of the apostolic gospel (I Cor. 1:23; 5:7); His death is the establishment of a new covenant (I Cor. 10:16; 11:24-26); and His sacrifice is regarded as a voluntary act of atonement and reconciliation (Eph. 5:2, I Peter 2:24, Rom. 5:10, Col. 1:20). After Pentecost the priestly work of Christ is continued through the Holy Spirit as a gift of the risen and exalted Saviour; and in the world to come our approach to God must be ever through Him as the abiding source of our life and glory.

The Kingly Office. The kingly, or regal office of Christ is that activity of our ascended Lord which He exercises at the right hand of God, ruling over all things in heaven and in earth for the extension of His kingdom. It is based upon the sacrificial death, and therefore finds its highest exercise in the bestowment of the blessings secured for mankind by His atoning work. As our Lord formally assumed His priestly work on the eve of the crucifixion, so He formally assumed His kingly office at the time of the ascension. We must not overlook the fact, however, that by anticipation Christ assumed to Himself the office of king during His earthly life, particularly at the time just preceding His death. But at the ascension, He said, *All power is given unto me in heaven and in earth. Go ye therefore, and teach all nations, baptizing them in the name of the Father, and of the Son, and of the Holy Ghost: teaching them to observe all things whatsoever I have commanded you: and, lo, I am with you alway, even unto the end of the world. Amen* (Matt. 28:18-20). Having already proclaimed His rule over the dead in the *descensus:* and having declared it to His brethren on earth, He ascended to the throne, there to exercise His mediatorial power until the time of the judgment, when the mediatorial economy shall end. God's efforts to save men then have been exhausted, and the fate of all men, whether good or evil, will be fixed forever. This is the meaning of St. Paul, when he says, *Then cometh the end, when he shall have delivered up the kingdom to God, even the Father; when he shall have put down all rule and all authority and power. For he must reign, till he hath put all enemies under his feet* (I Cor. 15: 24, 25). It is obvious that the kingly office as exercised for the redemption of mankind applies only to that era of extending and perfecting the kingdom; and the regal office in this sense will end when that era is completed. Nor does this mean that the Son shall not continue to reign as the Second Person in the Trinity; nor that His theanthropic Person shall cease. He shall forever reign as the God-man, and shall forever exercise His power for the benefit of the redeemed and the glory of His kingdom.

The Names and Titles of Our Lord

In our discussion of "The Divine Names and Predicates" we pointed out the practical value of a study of the names through which God had revealed Himself, and also the misuse which had been made of this subject by the so-called "Higher Criticism" of modern times. There is likewise a practical value in the study of "The Names and Titles of Our Lord." "It is the divine method of teaching us the doctrines of the economy of redemption; he who understands the derivation, uses and bearings of the rich cluster of terms, in their Hebrew and Greek symbols especially, ... will have no mean knowledge of this branch of theology and of theology in general. For this study will also tend to give precision to the language of the theologian, especially the preacher, who will observe with what exquisite propriety every epithet is used by evangelists and apostles in relation to the person and work and relations of the Redeemer. There can be no better theological exercise than the study of evangelical doctrine as based upon the titles of Jesus. No study more surely tends to exalt our Lord. We cannot range in thought over the boundless names given by inspiration to our adorable Master without feeling that there is no place worthy of Him below the highest, that He cannot be less than God to our faith and reverence, and devotion and love" (POPE, *Compend. Chr. Th.,* II, p. 261ff). Dr. Pope classifies the names and titles under the following six general heads: (I) Names of the supra-human Being who became man; (II) Names that express the union of the divine and human; (III) Names that express the official aspects of Christ; (IV) Names which designate the specific offices of the Redeemer; (V) Names resulting from the changes and combinations of the titles of the Redeemer; and (VI) Names which refer to our Lord's relations with His people.

CHRISTIAN THEOLOGY

The various helps to the study of the Bible generally give lists of the Names, Titles and Offices of Christ. (Those found in the Oxford Bibles are excellent.) The following list is not intended to be exhaustive, but merely to furnish the student with a classification and guide to the direct study of the Scriptures.

Adam, the last, I Cor. 15:45, 47; Advocate, I John 2:11; Alpha and Omega, Rev. 1:8; 22:13; Amen, Rev. 3:14; Author and Finisher (or Perfecter) of our faith, Heb. 12:2; Beginning of the creation of God, Rev. 3:14; Blessed and only Potentate, I Tim. 6:15; Branch, Zech. 3:8; 6:12; Bread of God, John 6:33; Bread of Life, John 6:35; Captain of our Salvation, Heb. 2:10; Child, Holy, Acts 4:27; Child, little, Isa. 11:6; Christ, Matt. 16:16; Mark 8:29; Luke 9:20; John 6:69; Cornerstone, Eph. 2:20; I Peter 2:6; Counsellor, Isa. 9:6; David, Jer. 30:9; Dayspring, Luke 1:78; Deliverer, Rom. 11:26; Desire of all nations, Hag. 2:7; Emmanuel, Isa. 7:14; Matt. 1:23; Everlasting Father, Isa. 9:6; Faithful witness, Rev. 1:5; 3:14; First and Last, Rev. 1:17; First begotten (Firstborn) of the dead, Rev. I:5; God, Isa. 40:9; I John 5:20; God blessed forever, Rom. 9:5; Good Shepherd, John 10:11; Governor, Matt. 2:6; Great High Priest, Heb. 4:14; High Priest, Heb. 5:10; Holy Child Jesus, Acts 4:27; Holy One, Luke 4:34; Holy Thing, Luke 1:35; Horn of Salvation, Luke 1:69; I AM, Exod. 3:14; Image of God, II Cor. 4:4; Jehovah, Isa. 26:4; Jesus, Matt. 1:21; I Thess. 1:10; Just One, Acts 3:14; King of Israel, John 1:49; King of the Jews, Matt. 2:2; King of kings, I Tim. 6:15; Lamb of God, John 1:29, 36; Law-giver, Isa. 33:22; Life, the, John 14:6; Light of the World, John 8:12; Light, the true, John 1:9; Lion of the tribe of Judah, Rev. 5:5; Living stone, I Pet. 2:4; Lord, Matt. 3:3; Lord God, Almighty, Rev. 15:3; Lord of all, Acts 10:36; Lord of Glory, I Cor. 2:8; Lord of lords, I Tim. 6:15; Lord our righteousness, Jer. 23:6; Mediator, I Tim. 2:5; Messiah, Dan. 9:25; John 1:41; Mighty God, Isa. 9:6; Mighty One of Jacob, Isa. 60:16; Nazarene, Matt. 2:23; Passover, I Cor. 5:7; Priest forever, Heb. 5:6; Prince, Acts 5:31; Prince of Peace, Isa. 9:6; Prince of the kings of the earth, Rev. 1:5; Prophet, Deut. 18:15; Luke 24:19; Redeemer, Job 19:25; Righteous, the, I John 2:1; Root and offspring of David, Rev. 22:16; Root of David, Rev. 5:5; Ruler in Israel, Mic. 5:2; Same yesterday, today, and forever, Heb. 13:8; Saviour, Luke 2:11; Acts 5:31; Shepherd and Bishop of souls, I Pet. 2:25; Shepherd of the sheep, Great, Heb. 13:20; Shiloh, Gen. 49:10; Son, a, Heb. 3:6; Son, the, Psalms 2:12; Son, my beloved, Matt. 3:17; Son, only-begotten, John 3:16, Son of David; Son of God, Matt. 8:29; Luke 1:35; Son of man, Matt. 8:20; John 1:51; Son of the Highest, Luke 1:32; Star, Bright and Morning, Rev. 22:16; Star and sceptre, Num. 24:17; Truth, the, John 14:6; Vine, the true, John 15:1, 5; Way, the, John 14:6; Witness, Rev. 3:14; Wonderful, Isa. 9:6; Word, John 1:1; Word of God, Rev. 19:13.

CHAPTER XXIII

THE ATONEMENT: ITS BIBLICAL BASIS AND HISTORY

A few general remarks are necessary in order to prepare the mind for a satisfactory study of the Atonement. (1) It is important to include in this study, the various phases of the scriptural presentation, such as expiation, propitiation, redemption, reconciliation, and others of like character. Since the subject may be approached from so many angles, our knowledge of it will be unbalanced and fragmentary, unless we give due consideration to the wide range of material found in the New Testament. (2) It is important to guard against the fallacies which arise through abstract processes of thought. There is not a leading idea of this important subject that has not been drawn out into unprofitable abstractions. Thus the idea of penalty has been so stated as to make it necessary to regard Christ as a sinner. The idea of substitution has been so conceived as to make the atonement merely a commercial transaction. Errors have arisen also by abstracting one attribute of God from the others, and treating it as if it were the whole divine nature. Socinianism exalted the will of God, Calvinism, the justice of God. (3) A sharp distinction should be made between the fact of the atonement, and the various theories which are advanced for its explanation. Some have questioned the value of any attempt to formulate a theory of the atonement; but the word *theory* as it is here used simply expresses meaning, and no moral fact can be properly related to an intelligent being without it. Otherwise priestcraft would become the dominant factor in religion. Then, too, we are commanded to be able to give a reason for the hope that is within us. Christianity must stimulate, not abjure, intelligence. (4) The literature on this subject is enormous, and apart from basic facts becomes confusing and unprofitable. We shall, therefore, give primary attention to this subject as presented in the Scriptures; and following this, we shall study the various explanations as found in the history of Christian doctrine.

Foreshadowing of the Atonement in the Old Testament. The doctrine of the atonement was gradually unfolded to the world. Three principal stages in its development may be mentioned, (1) The Primitive Sacrifices; (2) The Sacrifices of the Law; and (3) The Predictions of the Prophets.

1. The Primitive Period is everywhere characterized by sacrifices. In the patriarchal story, the altar is always prominent. It is regarded as an essential element in any approach to God. While the Scriptures give us no account of the origin of sacrifice, they do give us a record of sacrificial worship, from the earliest dawn of history to the time when the sacrifices were done away by the atoning work of our Lord Jesus Christ. We may note here, (1) *The Divine Origin of the Sacrifices.* This is evidenced by the nature of sacrifice itself, and also from the fact, that previous to the deluge, animals were classified as clean and unclean. The strongest argument, however, is to be found in the historical record of particular sacrifices. The first is that of Cain and Abel. *Cain brought of the fruit of the ground an offering unto the Lord. And Abel, he also brought of the firstlings of his flock and the fat thereof. And the Lord had respect unto Abel and his offering* (Gen. 4:3, 4). This scripture taken in connection with Hebrews 11:4, reveals two facts: one, that the sacrifice was offered in faith; the other, that it was divinely approved. The second is the sacrifice of Noah, which he offered immediately upon leaving the ark. *And Noah builded an altar unto the Lord; and took of every clean beast, and of every clean fowl, and offered burnt offerings on the altar. And the Lord smelled a sweet savour; and the Lord said in his heart, I will not again curse the ground any more for man's sake* (Gen. 8:20, 21). Here it is asserted that the sacrifice was marked by divine approbation. The third patriarchal sacrifice is that of Abraham, as recorded

in an interesting account found in Genesis 15: 9-21. Here it is expressly stated that Abraham offered up animal sacrifices in obedience to the command of God. The acceptance of the offering is indicated by the "burning lamp" which passed between the pieces and hallowed them. (2) *The Sacrifices were regarded as Expiatory in Character.* This is evidenced primarily by the prohibition of blood in the use of animal food. *But the flesh with the life thereof, which is the blood thereof, shall ye not eat* (Gen. 9: 4). To this was added later, the Mosaic explanation, *I have given it to you upon the altar, to make an atonement for your souls."* Furthermore, the end of Abel's offering was pardon and acceptance with God, for he *obtained witness that he was righteous* (Heb. 11: 4). In the sacrifice of Noah, the ground was no more to be cursed for man's sake; and it is said of Abraham, that he *believed God, and it was counted unto him for righteousness* (Rom. 4: 3). To this was added, also, the confirmatory and declaratory witness of circumcision, as *a seal of the righteousness of the faith which he had yet being uncircumcised* (Rom. 4: 11). While these sacrifices had no power in themselves to atone for sin, as is clearly set forth in Hebrews 10: 1-4; yet it is wrong to speak of the Old Testament sacrifices as purely ceremonial. Their efficacy lay in the power of Christ's sacrifice, to which as types and symbols, they pointed forward in faith.

2. The Sacrifices of the Law include those of the Mosaic economy. In Israel the consciousness of a need for reconciliation took on an earnest and energetic manifestation. This is shown in its distinction between evil and sin. Instead of regarding evil as unavoidable suffering, as is done in the dualistic theories; or identifying it

---

A type, in a theological sense, is a sign or example prepared and designed by God to prefigure some future person or thing. It is required that it should represent this future object with more or less clearness, either by something which it has in common with the antitype, or in being a symbol of some property which it possesses; that it should be prepared and designed by God thus to represent its antitype, which circumstance distinguishes it from a simile and from a hieroglyphic; that it should give place to the antitype as soon as it appears; and that the efficacy of the antitype should exist in the type in appearance only, or in a lower degree.—WAKEFIELD, *Christian Theology,* p. 352.

with finitude or corporeity in creation, Hebraism refused to stop at physical evil and traced it back to its root in sin. It was the work of the patriarchs to keep alive this sense of dependence upon God, as the Creator of a universe at harmony with Himself. Hence the presence of evil they regarded as being due to the disorganization and ill-adjustment consequent upon disobedience and sin. It was this consciousness of dependence upon God's power, that made possible the further advance to a stage of law, in which it becomes a dependence upon God's will. Thus it took on a moral character. In the new economy, also there was a further appeal to man's freedom. The universal law of conscience necessarily took on added importance, and at the same time developed a consciousness of sin and a need for atonement. We may note three things in this connection. (1) *The Law demanded Holiness.* It said, *Ye shall therefore keep my statutes, and my judgments: which if a man do, he shall live in them* (Lev. 18:5). This might have been understood to mean that man was to obtain righteousness solely by his own efforts, had the law regarded him as being free from sin. But this the law did not do. It regarded all men as guilty before God, and demanded an expiation for past sins. Since holiness was demanded by present obligation, past guilt could not be expiated by mere amendment of life. It necessitated forgiveness. It was found also, that the law but increased the knowledge of sin, and therefore revealed increasingly, the need for expiation. (2) *The Institution of Sacrifice.* It was

> It was the object of God in appointing these sacrifices, (a) That they should release from the civil punishment of certain crimes. The commission of a crime rendered one unworthy of the community of holy people, and excluded him from it. The offering of sacrifice was the means by which he was externally readmitted to the Jewish community, and rendered externally pure; although he did not, on this account, obtain the pardon of his sin from God. It was designed that all who offered sacrifice should by this act, both make a public confession of their sins, and at the same time see before them, in the sacrifice, the punishment which they had deserved, and to which they acknowledged themselves exposed. Hence sins were said to be laid upon the victim, and borne away by it when sacrificed. (b) Another end of the sacrifices appointed by Moses was, as we are taught in the New Testament, to point the Israelites to the future, and to prefigure by types the greater divine provision for the recovery of the human race, and to excite in the Israelites a feeling of their need for such a provision.—KNAPP, *Chr. Th.*, p. 381.

through the stated sacrifices for the people that the entire national life of Israel was environed by a gracious presence of the divine Spirit. There is deep significance in the fact that the atonement attached to the religious community, and that the sacrifices did not avail for those who separated themselves. It is indicated here that there is a common racial depravity out of which all personal transgressions spring; and that it was for this "sin of the world" that the Lamb of God was to make atonement. Dr. Dorner thinks that the notion of expiatory sacrifice as a real self-efficient substitute for man is baseless. Also that the idea is false which would make the words "to cover" apply in the sense of an equivalent, and thus *pay* the debt by *multa*. This, he says, would break down completely the idea of expiatory sacrifice; for one could scarcely speak of forgiveness if full satisfaction had been made (cf. DORNER, *Syst. Chr. Doct.*, III, pp. 404, 405). The word which is translated sacrifice, or atonement, signifies in Hebrew "to cover" or "to hide." Since the holiness of Jehovah is His unapproachable majesty, it is thought that the word "to cover" is intended to convey the idea of a defensive covering for those who would approach Him. The primary idea of sacrifice then, is propitiation. After the imposition of hands, the slaying of the sacrifice had reference to the significance of death as a fundamental concept of the Old Testament. Following this, the offering of the blood had a two-fold significance: it was a representation of the pure life which the sinner should have; and it was an atonement made expiatory through death only. Thus the sacrificial lamb became a symbol of the Lamb slain from the foundation of the world, whose life poured out in its richer, fuller measure, atoned for the sin of the world. Him, God hath set forth to be a *propitiation through faith in his blood, to declare his righteousness for the remission of sins that are past, through the forbearance of God* (Rom. 3: 25).

But we must not pass by the fact also, that it was the life poured out that was pleasing to God. It was the life separated from the body that commanded the attention of God as He saw it in the blood. This was a "sweet savour" to Him. The continuation of His anger, however, is shown in the continuation of the penalty of death in respect to the body. Thus St. Paul declares that *the body is dead because of sin; but the Spirit is life because of righteousness* (Rom. 8:10). But he follows this immediately with another declaration, that in the resurrection of Jesus, the consequences of sin still remaining in the physical realm, shall be removed in the restoration of all things. *But if the Spirit of him that raised up Jesus from the dead dwell in you, he that raised up Christ from the dead shall also quicken your mortal bodies by his Spirit that dwelleth in you* (Rom. 8:11); *For the earnest expectation of the creature* [the whole creation] *waiteth for the manifestation of the sons of God. . . . . Because the creature itself also shall be delivered from the bondage of corruption into the glorious liberty of the children of God* (Rom. 8:19, 21). (3) *The Messianic Idea.* The animal sacrifices of the Mosaic economy, not only pointed to Christ as the great antitype, but they were a revelation of the true nature of human sacrifice. They taught not merely the sacrifice of man himself in a subjective sense, but also that he himself should be the offerer, that is, self-sacrifice. Human sacrifices were prohibited, for these would merely have sacrificed others, and thus have been a mere caricature of the sacrificial idea. And even were it possible for man to offer himself as a perfect sacrifice, he is not qualified as a perfect offerer. Hence, from both the objective and subjective viewpoint, no man could atone for his own sins. Further still, it was impossible upon this ground, for the Old Testament priesthood and kingship to furnish expiatory security for the nation. This could be done only by the Righteous Servant of Jehovah. Hence there developed in Israel, the Messianic idea. It was the Messiah alone who could become the security for the nation, because he was absolutely the Righteous one. He alone could satisfy the righteousness of God, for He only as the incarnate One could personally manifest the unity of God and man. Thus the nation's center must be in Him as the personal manifestation of the covenant, the seed that should come. Since then, the divine thought of the nation centered in Him, there was given to Him also, the power to call forth a new and holy race—not now limited to Israel only, but extended to all mankind. It was only as Christ became a light to lighten the Gentiles, that He became the glory of Israel. The sacrifices of the law revealed the vicarious death of the Messiah, but this was fully developed only in the prophetic era. Outwardly, the Messiah bore the punishment due our sins, and inwardly suffered the chastening of His Spirit in intercession. But since He answered for man's guilt, righteousness may also be implanted by Him. Thus through the restoration of the Holy Spirit, given again to the race in Christ, holiness and righteousness are again made possible, and the idea of kingship is reborn by the inner communication of strength through the Spirit.

3. The Predictions of the Prophets supplemented the sacrifices of the law. The prophets developed more fully the Messianic idea, and with it the idea of His sacrificial sufferings and death. They saw in Him a living totality of truth. Being the God-man, in whom are conjoined Deity and humanity, there is in His consciousness the full range of all truth. His individual words and acts, therefore, spring from that indivisible whole. Thus

There is one other application of the high-priestly function of our Lord to which it is important in this place to refer, however slightly. The entire scheme of the Christian atonement belongs to this office of Messiah. Not as the Teacher, nor as the Ruler, does He save the world: save as teaching the principles of His sacrificial work and administering the blessings it has purchased. It will hereafter be shown how much the doctrine of the atonement is bound up with the divine government of a Lawgiver who administers His law in a new court, the Court Mediatorial. There He exacts and receives what theological language terms satisfaction. But it must always be remembered that the temple is the true sphere of atoning sacrifice. The evangelical hall of judgment is no other than a court of the temple. And it is something more than a mystical fancy which regards the veil as separating between the outer sanctuary where the oblation that satisfies justice is offered, and the holiest where it is presented for divine acceptance. Our Lord's Atonement is the sacrificial obedience, or the obedient sacrifice which hath put away sin: the obedience was rendered in the outer court where blood reigns unto death, the sacrifice was offered in the inner shrine where mercy reigns unto life. In Christ all these things are one. And the unity is the main object of the evangelical discussion of the Epistle to the Hebrews.—POPE, *Compend. Chr. Th.*, II, pp. 247, 248.

particular truths are blended with the universal, and the individual is set in proper relation to the race. It was for this reason that it is written, *He knew what was in men.* It is because all men have an essential relation to Him, that His words have so piercing and familiar a tone. "This is the wondrous charm of His words," says Dorner, "their unfathomable, mysterious depth despite all their simplicity, that they are ever uttered, so to speak, from the heart of the question; for the harmony which binds together and comprehends in one view the opposite ends of things, is livingly and consciously present to Him, since everything is related to His kingdom. Other words of men this or that man might have spoken; nay, most that is spoken or done by us is merely a continuation of others through us, we are simply points of transmission for tradition. But the words which He drew from within—these precious gems, which attest the presence of the Son of man, who is the Son of God—have an originality of a unique order; they are His, because taken from that which is present in Him" (DORNER, *Syst. Chr. Doct.,* III, pp. 397, 398). For this reason, He fills out the Old Testament types and forms, giving to them their true spiritual content. He is the manifestation of personal truth and eternal life, and therefore becomes the goal toward which all men should strive. This profound truth He himself declared when He said, *I am the way, the truth, and the life: no man cometh unto the Father, but by me* (John 14:6).

Perhaps the highest reach of spiritual truth in the Old Testament is to be found in Isaiah's remarkable prophecy concerning the suffering Servant of Jehovah. *Surely he hath borne our griefs, and carried our sorrows: yet we did esteem him stricken, smitten of God and afflicted. But he was wounded for our transgressions, he was bruised for our iniquities: the chastisement of our peace was upon him; and with his stripes we are healed. All we like sheep have gone astray; we have turned every one to his own way; and the Lord hath laid on him the iniquity of us all. . . . . Yet it pleased the Lord to bruise him; he hath put him to grief: when thou shalt make his soul an offering for sin, he shall see his seed, he shall prolong his days, and the pleasure of the Lord shall prosper in his hand. He shall see of the travail of his soul, and shall be satisfied: by his knowledge shall my righteous servant justify many; for he shall bear their iniquities* (Isaiah 53: 4-6, 10, 11). Nothing greater has ever been written. While Isaiah speaks of Christ primarily under the figure of a lamb there is doubtless also an allusion to the scapegoat upon which the priest laid his hands, confessed over it the sins of the people and sent it away into the wilderness. But no language can be plainer than that He bore the punishment due our sins, and hence His sacrifice was vicarious and expiatory. He was stricken, smitten, wounded, bruised, and chastised—language which can only indicate that His sufferings were penal inflictions for our sins. And since by His stripes we are justified and healed, His death must in the truest and deepest sense be regarded as propitiatory.

The New Testament Conception of Sacrifice. The conception of Christ's atoning sacrifice as found in the New Testament is simply the completion of that foreshadowed in the Old Testament. For this reason, Christ is described as having died according to the Scriptures. Our Lord himself represents His death as a ransom for men. He laid down His life voluntarily, for no man had power to take it from Him. Hence we must regard the crucifixion not merely as an occurrence brought about by mere circumstances, but as the great end for which He came into the world. He was not merely a martyr to truth; His death was sacrificial and propitiatory. Perhaps the most elaborate treatment of the expiatory death of Christ, is that set forth by St. Paul in Romans 3: 21-26. Here Christ is regarded as a propitiatory sacrifice which is accepted of God for all men in such a manner that He is Himself shown to be just, and yet can be the Justifier of all those who put their faith in the efficacy of that

It is therefore evident that the Prophet Isaiah, six hundred years before the birth of Jesus; that John the Baptist, on the commencement of His minsitry; and that St. Peter, His friend, companion and apostle, subsequent to the transaction; speak of Christ's death as an atonement for sin, under the figure of a lamb sacrificed.—WATSON, *Dictionary.*

death. The word which is here used for propitiation is *hilasterion* (ἱλαστήριον), a word which was employed by the Septuagint to signify the lid of the ark, or the mercy-seat. As this was sprinkled with the blood of the sacrifice, so the mercy-seat of the gospel is that which is sprinkled with the precious blood of Christ. The substitute endures the punishment which otherwise would fall upon the guilty themselves. According to this use, the blood of Christ becomes an expiation or a covering which protects the offerer from the wrath of God through the substitution of another life. While the voluntariness of Christ's sacrifice is held out as a constraining motive for the loving self-surrender of men to God, we must never relax our belief in the priestly work of Christ, as offering less than a real objective sacrifice to God. The death of Christ is never represented as merely a means of propitiation, but as an actual propitiatory sacrifice. That the Passover lamb was an objective sacrifice cannot be doubted, and the sprinkling of the blood essential to salvation. So also it is said, that Christ appears *in the presence of God for us* (Heb. 9:24), or in our behalf. There is no vicarious substitution in the sense of a discharge of all its beneficiaries from an obligation to righteousness. Christ appears for us, that is as the second Adam, the representative of the human race, and the Head of the new creation. It is on this basis of representation that the idea of substitution must be considered. It is impossible, therefore, to interpret the atoning work of Christ apart from His person. The Scriptures

Christ our Passover was sacrificed for us, as it were on the 14th Nisan, and rose the First Fruits, as it were on the 16th Nisan—and marking that the Synoptists speak of the day of crucifixion as the preparation of the great Sabbath of 15th Nisan, and not on the feast day itself, we are led to the conclusion that the Last Supper was, as St. John records, before the Feast of the Passover, and that the Crucifixion took place on Friday, the 14th Nisan. The disciples who, according to the Synoptists, on the first day of the Feast of Unleavened Bread, put their question, "Where wilt Thou that we prepare for Thee to eat the Passover?" prepared the meal on the 14th Nisan, but before the 13th had ended, that is, on the evening of Thursday, the 13th Nisan, and on that same evening the Lord anticipated the Passover which He so much desired to eat with them. The exact date of the world's redemption may, with near approach to absolute certainty, be assigned to the Friday, 18th of March, 14th Nisan, in the year of Rome 782, A.D. 29.—POPE, *Compend. Chr. Th.*, II, p. 160.

nowhere teach that the sinlessness of Christ merely gave Him a unique position as an individual in the race. They teach that Christ takes the place of sinners as a whole. His sacrifice was the equivalent for all who had come under the penalty of death by reason of sin. His death, therefore, has a universal significance, and this because of His divine nature. By virtue of this divine nature, the sinless humanity of the God-man reaches as far and as wide as the humanity to which it belongs. The death of Christ is not, therefore, to be limited merely to moral influence as an external and constraining power, but must be regarded as a propitiatory offering which avails for the remission of sins. Since the doctrine of the atonement must be drawn largely from the teachings of the New Testament, we shall give the subject more extended treatment in our next division.

THE BIBLICAL BASIS OF THE ATONEMENT

It is to the Scriptures that we must turn in order to establish the Christian idea of atonement through the sufferings and death of Jesus Christ. Having considered *first,* the Foreshadowing of the Atonement in the Old Testament; and *second,* made some general statements concerning the New Testament Conception of Sacrifice, we turn now to a more critical examination of the Scriptures on this important subject. We shall consider (1) The Motive of Atonement; (2) its Vicariousness; and (3) its Scriptural Terminology.

The Motive for the Atonement Is Found in the Love of God. This is sometimes known as the moving cause of redemption. The most prominent text in this connection is the epitome of the gospel found in John 3:16. *For God so loved the world, that he gave his only begotten Son;* and again in the following verse, *For God sent not his Son into the world to condemn the world; but that the world through him might be saved* (John 3:17). This is shown also in the following verses from the epistles of St. Paul and St. John. *But God commended his love toward us, in that, while we were yet sinners, Christ died for us* (Rom. 5:8); and *In this was mani-*

fested the love of God toward us, because that God sent his only begotten Son into the world, that we might live through him (I John 4:9). The atonement, whether in its motive, its purpose, or its extent must be understood as the provision and expression of God's righteous and holy love. Christ's life and death are the expression of God's love for us, not the producing cause of that love.

The Death of Christ Was a Vicarious Sacrifice. In the words of Mr. Watson, "Christ suffered in our room and stead, or as a proper substitute for us." This is shown by those scriptures which declare that He died for men, or that connect His death with the punishment due our offenses. There are two Greek prepositions which are translated "for" in the Scriptures. The first is *hyper* (ὑπέρ) and is found in the following verses: *It is expedient for us, that one man should die for the people* (John 11:50); *Christ died for the ungodly..... While we were yet sinners, Christ died for us* (Rom. 5:6, 8); *if one died for all, then were all dead* [or died]..... *And that he died for all, that they which live should not henceforth live unto themselves, but unto him that died for them, and rose again..... For he hath made him to be sin for us, who knew no sin; that we might be made the righteousness of God in him* (II Cor. 5:14, 15, 21); *who gave himself for our sins* (Gal. 1:4); *Christ hath redeemed us from the curse of the law, being made a curse for us* (Gal. 3:13); *hath given himself for us an offering and a sacrifice to God for a sweetsmelling savour..... Christ also loved the church, and gave himself for it*

The second Adam also takes the place of humanity; and His sacrificial work must be looked upon as the actual work of humanity itself (*satisfactio vicaria*). But our innermost consciousness demands that the righteousness and obedience rendered, should not only be without us in another, but should also become personally our own. Now this demand is satisfied by the fact that Christ is our Redeemer as well as our Reconciler: our Saviour who removes sin by giving a new life to the race, by establishing a living fellowship between Himself and mankind. All merely external and unspiritual confidence in the atonement arises from a desire to take Christ as Reconciler without taking Him as Redeemer and Sanctifier. The gospel, "God was in Christ reconciling the world unto himself," must not be separated from the following call, "Be ye reconciled to God!" that is, "appropriate to yourselves the reconciliation accomplished in Christ, by the healing and purifying, the life-giving and sanctifying power which emanates from Christ!—MARTENSEN, Chr. Dogm., pp. 307, 308

(Eph. 5:2, 25); *our Lord Jesus Christ, who died for us* (I Thess. 5:9, 10); *who gave himself a ransom for all* (I Tim. 2:6); *that he by the grace of God should taste death for every man* (Heb. 2:9). The second Greek preposition is *anti* (ἀντὶ) and is found in such verses as Matt. 20:28 and Mark 10:45, where Christ is said *to give his life a ransom for many*. It is sometimes objected that these Greek prepositions do not always signify substitution; that is, that they do not always mean *instead of*, but are sometimes used as *in behalf of*, or *on account of*. Thus we have the expression "Christ died for our sins," which cannot of course mean instead of in this instance. However, that these prepositions are generally used in the sense of substitution, both Watson and Wakefield clearly show (cf. Note, WAKEFIELD, *Chr. Th.*, p. 359). The vicarious or substitutionary death of Christ is known in theology as the "procuring cause" of salvation.

The Scriptures regard the sufferings of Christ as a propitiation, a redemption, and a reconciliation. As being under the curse of the law, the sinner is guilty and exposed to the wrath of God; but in Christ his guilt is expiated and the wrath of God propitiated. The sinner is under the bondage of Satan and sin, but through the redemptive price of the blood of Christ, he is delivered from bondage and set at liberty. The sinner is estranged from God, but is reconciled by the death on the cross. These scriptures are peculiarly rich and satisfying.

1. Propitiation is a term drawn from the Kapporeth or Mercy-seat as used in the Old Testament scriptures. To propitiate is to appease the wrath of an offended person, or to atone for offenses. The term *hilasmos* (ἱλασμός) is used in three different senses in the New Testa-

---

With reference to the use of the Greek prepositions translated "for," Dr. Wakefield makes the following statement: "All this may be granted, but it is nevertheless certain that there are numerous texts of scripture in which these particles can be interpreted only when taken to mean 'instead of,' or 'in the place of.' When Caiaphas said, 'It is expedient for us that one man should die for the people, and that the whole nation perish not' (John 11:50) he plainly taught that either Christ or the nation must perish; and that to put the former to death would be to cause Him to perish instead of the latter. In Romans 5:6-8, the sense in which 'Christ died for us' is indubitably fixed by the context."—WAKEFIELD, *Chr. Th.*, p. 359.

ment. (1) Christ is the ἱλασμός, at once the Propitiator and the virtue of that propitiation. *He is the propitiation for our sins: and not for ours only, but also for the sins of the whole world* (I John 2:2); *He loved us, and sent his Son to be the propitiation for our sins* (I John 4:10). (2) He is the *hilasterion* (ἱλαστήριον) or Mercy-seat as the word is used in the Septuagint. *Whom God hath set forth to be a propitiation through faith in his blood* (Rom. 3:25). (3) Where the adjective is used, then the term *thuma* (θῦμα) is understood as in Hebrews 2:17, where the High Priest is said to *make reconciliation for the sins of the people.* Here the term is *hilasterion* (ἱλαστήριον) and the correct meaning is *"to make propitiation for the sins of the people."*

2. Redemption is from the word which means literally "to buy back." The terms *lutroo* (λυτρόω) and *apolutrosis* (ἀπολύτρωσις) meaning to redeem and redemption respectively, were used by the ancient Greeks and also by the New Testament writers, to signify the act of setting a captive free through the payment of a *lutron* (λύτρον) or redemptive price. The terms therefore came to be used in the broader sense of a deliverance from every kind of evil, through a price paid by another. This is the true scriptural meaning as shown in the following texts: *Being justified freely by his grace through the redemption that is in Christ Jesus* (Rom. 3:24); *For ye are bought with a price: therefore glorify God in your body, and in your spirit which are God's* (I Cor. 6:20); *Christ hath redeemed us from the curse of the law, being made a curse for us: for it is written, Cursed is every one that hangeth on a tree* (Gal. 3:13); *In whom we have redemption through his blood, the forgiveness of sins, according to the riches of his grace* (Eph. 1:7); *Ye were not redeemed with corruptible things, as silver and gold, ... but with the precious blood of Christ, as of a lamb without blemish and without spot* (I Peter 1:18, 19); *For thou wast slain, and hast redeemed us to God by thy blood out of every kindred, and tongue, and people, and nation* (Rev. 5:9). The death of Christ is the redemptive price, who gave *his life a ransom* (λύτρον)

for many (Matt. 20:28); and *He gave himself a ransom* (ἀντίλυτρον) *for all* (I Tim. 2:6). Here the idea of substitution is clearly evident—one thing is paid for another, the "blood of Christ" for the redemption of captives and condemned men.

3. Reconciliation is from the verbs *katallasso* (καταλλάσσω) or *apokatallasso* (ἀποκαταλλάσσω), both of which are translated "to reconcile." Primarily they denote a change from one state to another, but as used in the Scriptures, this is a change from a state of enmity to one of reconciliation and friendship. The Apostle Paul uses this term freely. *For if, when we were enemies, we were reconciled to God by the death of his Son, much more, being reconciled, we shall be saved by his life. And not only so, but we also joy in God through our Lord Jesus Christ, by whom we have now received the atonement* [or reconciliation, καταλλαγήν] (Rom. 5:10, 11); *And all things are of God, who hath reconciled us unto himself by Jesus Christ, and hath given to us the ministry of reconciliation; to wit, that God was in Christ, reconciling the world unto himself, not imputing their trespasses unto them; and hath committed unto us the word of reconciliation* (II Cor. 5:18, 19); *And that he might reconcile both unto God in one body by the cross, having slain the enmity thereby* (Eph. 2:16); *And having made peace through the blood of his cross, by him to reconcile all things unto himself; by him, I say, whether they be things in earth, or things in heaven. And you, that were sometime alienated and enemies in your mind by wicked works, yet now hath he reconciled in the body of his flesh through death, to present you holy and unblameable and unreproveable in his sight* (Col. 1:20-22). Here it is clearly evident that the reconciliation between God and men is effected by Christ. But reconciliation means more than merely laying aside our enmity to God. The relation is a judicial one, and it is this judicial variance between God and man that is referred to in the idea of reconciliation. Moreover, the reconciliation is effected, not by the laying aside of our enmity but by the nonimputation of our trespasses to us. This previous reconciliation of the

world to Himself by the death of His Son, is to be distinguished also from "the word of reconciliation" which is to be proclaimed to the guilty, and by which they are entreated to be reconciled unto God.

EARLIER HISTORY OF THE ATONEMENT

The Patristic Doctrine. The apostolic fathers taught that Christ gave himself for our sins, but they did not formulate their views into any definite theory of the atonement. Their successors held every variety of opinion, and on this subject variety was tolerated. The most popular view was that which regarded the atonement as a victory over Satan. This position seems to have been first advanced by Irenæus (c. 200 ?) and was based upon such scriptures as Colossians 2:15 and Hebrews 2:14. It was Origen (185-254), however, who first converted the idea into the theory of a ransom paid to Satan. He held that men had surrendered to Satan and could not, therefore, be delivered from captivity without his consent. Satan was deluded when he accepted Christ as a ransom. The humanity of Christ was the bait, and His divinity the hook by which Satan was caught. Fearing the effect on his captives of the life and teachings of Jesus, and seeing the divine glory of the Lord through the veil of His flesh so obscurely as to be deceived, Satan undertook to rid himself of the danger by putting Christ to death. But to cause the crucifixion was

---

The earlier fathers followed very closely the words of scripture in their references to the atonement. Thus Clement of Rome, sometimes identified with the Clement mentioned by St. Paul in Philippians 4:3, says, "On account of the love He bore us, Jesus Christ gave His blood for us by the will of God; His flesh for our flesh, and His soul for our souls" (Chap. xlix). The doctrine of Paul is faithfully reproduced also in the Epistle of Barnabas, where it is stated that "The Lord endured to deliver his body to death, that we might be sanctified by the remission of sins which is the shedding of that blood" (Epistola, 5). Ignatius (c. 116) the pupil of St. John declares that we "have peace through the flesh and blood, and passion of Jesus Christ" (Ad Ephesos, 1). Polycarp (c. 168) likewise acquainted with St. John is more specific. "Christ is our Saviour; for through grace we are righteous, not by works; for our sins, He has even taken death upon Himself, has become the servant of us all, and through His death for us our hope, and the pledge of our righteousness. The heaviest sin is unbelief in Christ; His blood will be demanded of unbelievers; for to those to whom the death of Christ, which obtains the forgiveness of sins, does not prove a ground of justification, it proves a ground of condemnation" (Ad. Philippos, 1, 8).

to accept the ransom; the captives were released and the Deliverer escaped. This position finds even more exact statements in Gregory of Nyssa (c. 395). Dr. Banks thinks that this theory in its unqualified form was held only by Gregory, and that it was qualified in the writings of Irenæus and Augustine, either by being shorn of its objectional features, or by being held in conjunction with a propitiation made to God. Dorner, Kahnis and Sheldon hold to the same opinion. Thus, Augustine says, "God the Son, being clothed with humanity, subjugates even the devil to man, extorting nothing from him by violence, but overcoming him by the law of justice; for it would have been injustice if the devil had not had the right to rule over the beings whom he had taken captive." While the approach to this subject is made through the concepts of war and conquest, there are two terms which stand out clearly, that of "honor" and "satisfaction"; and in the later period of chivalry, these took on even greater meaning in their religious application. In the Latin Church, however, the theory of a ransom offered

The position of Irenæus (c. 200) is thus given in his own words. "The Word of God (the Logos), omnipotent and not wanting in essential justice, proceeded with strict justice even against the apostasy or kingdom of evil itself (*apostasiam*) redeeming it (*ab ea*) that which was his own originally, not by using violence, as did the devil in the beginning, but by persuasion (*secundum suadelam*), as it became God, so that neither justice should be infringed upon, nor the original creation of God perish" (Adversus Hæreses i.1). Dr. Shedd points out that two interpretations of this phraseology are possible. The "persuasion" may be referred to Satan, or to man; and the "claims" alluded to, may be regarded as those of the devil, or of law and justice. Against the first interpretation which is urged by the rationalistic school, Dr. Shedd in common with most orthodox writers, maintains that the second interpretation is without doubt the correct one.

Christ's sacrifice is frequently referred to as offered to God for a propitiation. Eusebius says, "That as a victim of God, and a great sacrifice, He might be offered to the Most High for the whole world." Basil also says, "The only begotten Son, who gives life to the world, since He offers himself to God as a victim and oblation for our sins, is called the Lamb of God." "The blood of Christ," says Ambrose, "is the price paid for all, by which the Lord Jesus, who alone has reconciled the Father, has redeemed us." "We were enemies of God through sin, and God had decreed that the sinner should die. One of two things, therefore, was necessary: either God, remaining true, must destroy all, or, using clemency, must annul the sentence issued. But behold the wisdom of God. He maintained both the sentence and the exercise of His goodness. Christ bore our sins in His own body on the tree, so that we, through His death, dead to sins, might live unto righteousness."—CYRIL OF JERUSALEM.

to Satan never became current, although it was generally admitted that Satan had usurped rights over the apostate race. Leo regarded this usurpation as a tyrannical right, and Gregory the Great held that it was only a seeming right. They maintained, however, that these rights were lost, not by virtue of a contract but through the death of Christ. "Certainly it is just," says Augustine, "that we whom he held as debtors should be dismissed free by believing in Him whom he slew without any debt" (*De Trin.* xiii, 14).

Athanasius (325-373) is supposed to have been the first to propound the theory that the death of Christ was the payment of a debt due to God. His argument may be briefly stated as follows: God having threatened death as the penalty of sin, would have been untrue, had He not fulfilled His promise. But it would have been unworthy of divine goodness, had He allowed rational beings to whom He had imparted His Spirit to incur death as a consequence of an imposition practiced on them by Satan. Seeing, then, that nothing but death could solve the dilemma, the Word, who could not die, assumed a mortal body, and having fulfilled the law by His death, offered His human nature a sacrifice for all.

It is during this earlier period also, that we first notice a trend toward belief in predestination and a limited atonement. Apart from Augustine and his followers, it was the common belief that Christ died for all, and that it was the unfeigned will of God that all men should partake of salvation through Him. The fact that some are saved and some are not, was explained by reference to man's free agency and not by electing grace. Augustine, himself, distinctly advocated this position at first, but in his controversy with the Pelagians adopted a strictly monergistic system. He held to the total inability of man to exercise good works, and hence, until the individual

Dr. Sheldon thinks that it is a gross and amazing persistent slander, that for a thousand years the Church knew no other theory of the redemptive work than that which teaches the payment of a ransom to Satan. He says that in both the Greek and Latin churches, the relation of the redemptive work to Satan was only one aspect among many which received attention.—Cf. SHELDON, *His. Chr. Doct.*, I, pp. 121-124, 251-257, 362-367.

was regenerated, there was no power to exercise faith. Grace, therefore, was bestowed solely upon the elect through effectual calling, and the atonement limited to those for whom it availed. Previous to this time, synergism had been the dominant theory, i. e., that the individual in his recovery from sin, works with God through grace universally bestowed as a free gift, in such a manner as to condition the result.

The Anselmic Theory of the Atonement. Anselm (1033-1109) in the latter part of the eleventh century, published his epoch-making book *"Cur Deus Homo,"* in which he gave the first scientific statement to those views of the atonement, which from the beginning had been held implicitly by the fathers. Here the idea of satisfaction to divine justice became the leading formula, and the "satisfaction theory" of the atonement is still called by his name. While giving even a more prominent place than the earlier fathers to such terms as "honor," "justice," "satisfaction" and "merit," Anselm rejected wholly, the theory of a ransom paid to Satan. This he disposed of in the following brief words: "Was it the law of Satan we had transgressed? Was he the judge that cast us into prison? Was it he to whom we were indebted? Was it ever heard that the ransom price of redemption was paid to the jailer? Whether any of the ancients said so or not, I shall not now trouble myself to inquire, or in what sense they said it; the thing in itself is ridiculous and blasphemous." Anselm's own theory may be stated as follows: Sin violates the divine honor, and deserves infinite punishment since God is infinite. Sin is guilt or a debt, and under the government of God, this debt must be paid. This necessity is grounded in the infinite perfections of God. Either adequate satisfaction must be provided, or vengeance must be exacted. Man cannot pay this debt, for he is not only

The church at large, as in the previous period, regarded predestination, so far as it is connected with man's moral destiny, as conditioned by foreknowledge. Augustine himself at one time distinctly advocated this position, saying that God chose those who He foreknew would believe, and conjoining with this statement that believing lies in man's power. First man believes, he said, and then God gives grace for good works.—SHELDON, *Hist. Chr. Doct.*, I, p. 258.

finite, but morally bankrupt through sin. Adequate satisfaction being impossible from a being so inferior to God as man is, the Son of God became man in order to pay the debt for us. Being divine, He could pay the infinite debt; and being both human and sinless, could properly represent men. But as sinless He was not obliged to die, and owing no debt on His own account, He received as a reward of His merit, the forgiveness of our sins. "Can anything be more just," he says, "than for God to remit all debt, when in this way He receives a satisfaction greater than all debt, provided it be offered only with the right sentiment?" It should be noted here, that Christ renders satisfaction to divine justice, not by bearing the penalty of a broken law in the sinner's place, but indirectly by the acquisition of merit. The sacrifice of Christ being infinite, was of greater value than the demerit of sin, and consequently this merit accrues to Christ, and overflows to all who believe. This merit when received in faith becomes the justification of men, and is transferred to them or placed to their account. As such it offsets the demands of justice, in so far as those demands were a fixed barrier against the forgiveness of sins. Thus the divine justice was satisfied, but only in the sense that it secured the honor of that justice, notwithstanding the offer of the forgiveness of sins. Anselm, it will be seen, makes the redeeming work of Christ to center in His voluntary death.

Dr. A. A. Hodge states Anselm's doctrine of the atonement as follows: "He taught that sin is debt (guilt); that, under the government of God, it is absolutely necessary that his debt should be paid, i.e., that the penalty incurred by the guilt of sin should be suffered; that this necessity has its ground in the infinite perfections of the divine nature; that this penalty must be inflicted upon the sinner in person, unless a substitute can be found having all legal qualifications for his office. This was alone realized in Jesus Christ, a divine person embracing a human nature."

Dr. Sheldon states the theory in these words: "Christ incarnate, then, appears as perfect God and perfect man. As a sinless being, He is under no obligation to die. Consequently, in voluntarily surrendering Himself to death He establishes a merit—a merit proportioned to the dignity of His person, and fully adequate to offset man's demerit. So great a merit deserved an extraordinary reward. But Christ, as being already possessor of all things, needed no gift for Himself. It remained accordingly, that He should be allowed to elect man to receive the benefits which had been purchased by His sacrifice.—SHELDON, *Hist. Chr. Doct.*, I, p. 363.

The Theory of Abelard. Abelard (1079-1142) differed widely from Anselm in his theory of the atonement. He maintained that it was the rebellion of man that needed subduing, and not the wrath of God that needed propitiating. In place of a satisfaction to divine justice, he held that the atonement should be regarded as a winning exhibition of the divine love. To him, benevolence was the only attribute concerned in redemption. Redemption like creation was by divine fiat, and therefore sin could be abolished and the sinner restored to favor by the will of God, without any need of satisfaction or propitiation. Christ died for the twofold purpose of subduing the opposition of sinners and removing their guilty fears, through a transcendent exhibition of divine love. Abelard's position became the basis of the later Socinianism, and was adopted also by those trinitarian divines, who in modern times have held some form of the moral influence theory of the atonement.

Scholastic Developments. In the history of the atonement, the scholastic period is of importance in that it marks the beginning of those trends which later devel-

Dr. Sheldon says that Abelard did not discard altogether the sacrificial aspect of Christ's work, or the idea of imputed merit. He recognized in some sense, a vicarious efficacy in the merit acquired by Christ, inasmuch as this comes into supplement, in the sight of God, the deficiency of merit in the elect, or the imperfection of that love which is called forth in them by the revelation of divine love. But this is a subordinate consideration. Love revealed and drawing to returning love, this is the essence of Abelard's theory of the redemptive work of Christ. "Our redemption," says Abelard, "is that supreme love wrought in us by the passion of Christ, which not only frees us from the servitude of sin, but acquires for us the true liberty of the sons of God; so that we fulfill all requirements rather through love than the fear of Him who has exhibited toward us so great a grace—a grace than which there is no greater, according to His own testimony, cannot be found."—SHELDON, *Hist. Chr. Doct.*, I, p. 365.

Abelard was the chief opponent of Anselm; and may be said to have been the founder of a theory of the atonement which shuts out the deepest mystery of the cross. He referred the Christian redemption only to the love of God as its source; and taught that there could be nothing in the divine essence which absolutely required satisfaction for sin. Redemption like creation was a fiat: equally sure, equally free, and equally independent of anything in the creature. The influence of the work of Christ, as accomplished on the cross, and carried on in His intercession, is moral only subduing the heart, awakening repentance, and leading the soul to the boundless mercy of God whose benevolence is the only attribute concerned in the pardon of sin.—POPE, *Compend. Chr. Th.*, II, 305.

oped into the Tridentine Soteriology of the Roman Catholic Church, and the strict penal satisfaction theory of the earlier Protestant reformers. Peter Lombard (1100-1164) accepted the position of Abelard and opposed that of Anselm. He held that the work of Christ must be supplemented by baptism and penance, and in this we find the secret of the popularity of his *Liber Sententiarum* in the Roman Catholic Church. Bernard of Clairvaux (1091-1153) and Hugh of St. Victor (c. 1097-1141) adopted in the main, the position of Anselm. Bernard, however, hesitates to denominate sin as an "infinite evil," and as a consequence does not distinctly assert the intrinsic necessity for an atonement. He prefers to hold with Augustine, a relative necessity founded upon the optional will and arrangement of God. Hugo more nearly approached the Anselmic position, combining both the legal and sacrificial elements in his idea of propitiation. "The Son of God," he says, "by becoming a man, paid man's debt to the Father, and by dying expiated man's guilt." It was Bonaventura (1221-1274) and Thomas Aquinas (c. 1225-1274) who largely shaped the theology of the Roman Catholic Church. The teachings of the two are very similar, but Thomas Aquinas being the stronger systematizer, occupies the more prominent position. Several new developments are found in his theology. (1) He held that merit and demerit are strictly personal, and therefore in order to substantiate the idea of vicarious satisfaction, he advanced his idea of the *unio mystica,* or mystical union existing between Christ and the

Aquinas attached great importance to the substitutionary value of the pain which Christ endured. In one of his eucharistic hymns he says,
"Blood, of which one drop, for human-kind outpoured,
Might from all transgression have the world restored."
This was characteristic of the age immediately preceding the Reformation. In several hymns of the fifteenth century, not only the cross, but the nails, the spear and other instruments of His passion appear as the actual objects of worship. Later in Protestantism, the suffering of Christ attaches more to His mental anguish. Æpinus (1533) declares that Christ's soul endured the punishments of hell while His body lay in the grave! The Heidelberg Catechism (1563) affirms that He bore the divine wrath during the whole period of His earthly life. Calvin rejected altogether, the ancient doctrine of Christ's descent into hell, explaining the passages bearing on this point as referring to the extreme anguish of His soul. (Cf. CRIPPEN, *Hist. Chr. Doct.,* pp. 136, 138.)

Church. He based his doctrine upon the statement in Ephesians 5:30, maintaining that this relation is different from any existing in secular life. It is not the external relation which exists between individuals, but is one in which there is a communion of interest and moral life. Thus a sinner united by faith to the Saviour may become the ground and cause of judicial infliction upon his atoning Substitute, and in turn, the incarnate Word may become the sinner's propitiation. This idea of the mystical oneness of Christ and the Church pervades his soteriology. (2) He made a distinction also, between *satisfactio* and *meritum,* the former applying to the sufferings of Christ as a satisfaction to divine justice, the latter to the merit of His obedience, by which the redeemed are entitled to the rewards of eternal life. He thus anticipated the later distinction in Calvinistic theology, between the "active" and "passive" righteousness of Christ. (3) He taught the doctrine of the superabundance of the merits of Christ. While this seemed to honor the atonement, in reality it resulted in a lower estimate of sin, and led directly to the Roman Catholic theory of supererogation, with a treasury of merit at the command of the Church. (4) He departed from the Anselmic theory of an absolute as distinguished from a relative satisfaction. This resulted in a theory of justification, resting partly upon the work of Christ and partly upon the works of the individual. The lax theory gradually gained in the Roman Catholic Church until it finally obtained ecclesiastical authority in the Soteriology of Trent. But there were developing also, those forces which finally led to the Reformation. The mediating theologians, such as Bonaventura, Alexander of Hales, and many of the later mystics paved the way for this reform, (1) by admitting a relative view of the atonement,

Duns Scotus opposed Anselm, arguing that the passion of Christ owed its efficacy, not to its intrinsic merit, or to its voluntary endurance, but to its voluntary acceptance by God. The controversy ran high between the adherents of Aquinas and Scotus. The Nominalists in philosophy naturally favored the views of Scotus, for his theory was that of a nominal satisfaction in distinction from that which was real and objective. The views of Thomas Aquinas, however, were more nearly in harmony with the Protestant view and feeling.

but showing that it could not supersede the absolute idea of satisfaction without great peril to the Church; and (2) by keeping alive the Anselmic idea of absolute satisfaction through Christ alone.

The Tridentine Soteriology. The soteriology of the Roman Catholic Church, as we have shown, was largely the outgrowth of the theological principles of Bonaventura and Thomas Aquinas. The *unio mystica* gave rise to two fundamental errors: (1) it limited redemption to the believer configured to his Lord, in that the guilt of the sinner was transferred to Christ in the same sense that Christ's merit was transferred to the sinner. This contradicted the universality of the atonement and marked the further development of the theory of predestination. (2) In the case of sin after baptism, the believer must be configured to his Lord by personal penance. This penance was of course imperfect, but it was regarded as an expiation joined to that of Christ. The distinction between satisfaction and merit, and the further distinction between an absolute and a relative atonement, made possible the *superabundans satisfactio* or the superabundance of Christ's merit. This, added to the idea of a superfluous merit of the saints, constituted the source of the mediæval system of indulgences. However, it is chiefly in its subjective character that the error of Roman Catholic theology appears, and this in its individual aspect will be further treated in our discussion of justification.

The Reformation Period. In their reaction against the theology of the Roman Catholic Church, the Reformers revived the Anselmic theory of the absolute necessity for satisfaction in the divine nature. The ideas of satisfaction and merit as held by Anselm were both retained, but given a distinctly different direction. Thus satisfaction became a penal substitutionary offering instead of an accumulation of merit which was imputed to the elect; and merit was viewed in the sense of becoming the ground of their righteousness. That is, the voluntary death of Christ removed the penalty from the elect, and His active obedience assured their personal righteousness. The Reformed churches differed from the Lutheran in this, that while the Lutherans held that the satisfaction of Christ was sufficient for all sins, both original and actual, the Reformed limited the scope of the atonement to the elect. Both Lutherans and Reformed, however, made the death of Christ the center of the atoning work, flanked by the incarnation and the resurrection on either side. With the voluntary death of Christ as the procuring cause of salvation, they associated the merit of His active obedience to law. This they urged on the ground that He was not a subject but the Lord of the law. Over against the Lutheran and Reformed churches the Socinians revived the theory of Abelard, and in a measure that of Duns Scotus. These find their modern expression in the numerous moral influence theories. The Arminians aimed at a middle ground between the extremes of the penal satisfaction theory and the moral influence theories. Grotius argued against Socinus, that God punishes sin, not as an act of retaliation, but as the Ruler of the universe in the upholding of His government. These theories will be discussed in our next division.

Modern Theories of the Atonement

We propose to give in this division, not a chronological history of the various theories of the atonement held in modern times, but rather a classification of the principal forms which such theories have taken. These we shall treat under the following classification: (1) The Penal Satisfaction Theory; (2) The Governmental or Rectoral Theory; (3) The various Moral Influence Theories; (4) The Ethical Theory; and (5) The Racial Theory.

The Penal Satisfaction Theory. This is the theory held by the Reformed churches, and generally known as the Calvinistic theory. It is sometimes referred to also, as the Anselmic theory; and although related to it, the Anselmic theory underwent important changes at the hands of the Reformers. In the first place, Anselm taught that the sacrifice of Christ secured such merit as was capable of being imputed to the guilty; while the Reformers held that the satisfaction of Christ was to be considered in the sense of a penal substitution for the sinner. Thus they took over from Anselm the idea of satisfaction but gave it the meaning of substitution instead of merit. In the second place, the Reformers included Christ's active obedience as a part of the redemptive price, as well as His voluntary death, while Anselm maintained that the satisfaction which Christ offered could not have been His obedience, for this He owed to God as a man. We may say then, that while the Socinian theory sets forth the sufferings of Christ as designed to produce a moral effect upon the heart of the individual sinner; and the governmental theory claims that it was designed to produce a moral effect upon an intelligent universe; the Satisfaction theory maintains that the immediate and chief end of Christ's work was to satisfy that essential principle of the divine nature which demands the punishment of sin. Dr. A. A. Hodge, a Calvinist theologian of the federal type, sums up this theory in the following essential points: (1) Sin for its own sake deserves the wrath and curse of God. (2) God is disposed, from the very excellence of His nature, to treat His creatures as they deserve. (3) To satisfy the righteous judgment of God, His Son assumed our nature, was made under the law, fulfilled all righteousness, and bore the

---

The Penal Theory is sometimes known also as the "Judicial Theory," in that God is considered in the character of a judge, and satisfaction must be rendered to His justice. Men appear before Him as guilty, but having agreed to accept satisfaction in the person of a substitute, God is obliged on the ground of justice to acquit those for whom it was made. Dr. Charles Hodge says that, "All the benefits which accrue to sinners in consequence of the satisfaction of Christ are to them pure gratuities; blessings to which in themselves they have no claim. They call for gratitude and exclude boasting. Nevertheless it is a matter of justice that the blessings which Christ intended to secure for His people should be actually bestowed upon them. This follows for two reasons: First, they were promised to Him as the reward of His obedience and sufferings. God covenanted with Christ that if He fulfilled the conditions imposed, if He made satisfaction for the sins of His people, they should be saved. It follows, secondly, from the nature of satisfaction. If the claims of justice are satisfied they cannot again be enforced. This is the analogy between the work of Christ and the payment of a debt. The point of agreement between the two cases is not the nature of the satisfaction rendered, but one aspect of the effect produced."—Hodge, *Syst. Th.*, II, p. 472.

punishment of our sins. (4) By His righteousness, those who believe are constituted righteous, His merit being so imputed to them that they are regarded as righteous in the sight of God (A. A. HODGE, *Outline of Theology*, p. 303). Dr. J. P. Boyce, the eminent Baptist theologian, says that the Calvinistic theory of the atonement is, that in the sufferings and death of Christ, He incurred the penalty of the sins of those whose substitute He was, so that He made a real satisfaction to the justice of God for the law which they had broken. On this account, God now pardons all their sins, and being fully reconciled to them, His electing love flows out freely toward them. The doctrine as thus taught involves the following points: (I) That the sufferings and death of Christ were a real atonement. (II) That in making it Christ became the substitute of those whom He came to save. (III) That as such He bore the penalty of their transgression. (IV) That in so doing He made ample satisfaction to the demands of the law, and to the justice of God. (V) That thus an actual reconciliation has been made between them and God (cf. BOYCE, *Abstract of Syst. Th.*, p. 317).

This type of theory contains a valuable element of truth. Any theory of vicarious satisfaction must admit the idea of the substitutionary work of Christ, but it matters much whether this substitution be regarded merely externally as "instead of," or whether it may be said to be "in behalf of" also. Both Arminian and Calvinistic divines admit that the theory conceives of substitution in too formal and external a manner, and as exalt-

To the Calvinistic principle that sin must be punished, either in the principal or the substitute, Dr. Miley attaches the following consequences. "Nothing could be punished in Christ which was not transferred to Him, and in some real sense made His. Hence, if sin, with its demerit, could not, as now admitted, be put upon Christ by imputation, no punishment which He suffered fell upon such demerit, or intrinsic evil of sin. And we think it impossible to show how sin is punished according to its demerit, and on that ground, in the total absence of such demerit from the substitute in punishment." To the distinction which the Federalists make between guilt as liability to punishment, and guilt as demerit or culpability, he says, "With the imputation of such an abstract guilt to Christ, while sin, with its turpitude and demerit, with all that is punishable and all that deserves to be left behind, how can the redemptive suffering which He endured be the merited punishment of sin?"—MILEY, *Syst. Th.*, II, pp. 146, 147.

ing the divine honor instead of the divine holiness in which it is grounded. Dr. Miley calls attention to the perplexities in its treatment, and the vacillations and diversities of opinion given in its explanation. He says, "The effect of the imputation of sin to Christ, and the nature and degree of His penal sufferings, are questions entering deeply into the difficulties of the subject. Did imputation carry over sin, with its turpitude and demerit, or only its guilt to Him? Did He suffer, instead of the elect, the same punishment, otherwise, they must have suffered? Did He endure penal suffering equal in amount though differing in kind, to the merited punishment of the redeemed? Did He suffer an equivalent punishment, less in amount but of higher value, and thus a penal equivalent with justice? Did He suffer the torment of the finally lost? Was His punishment potentially or intensively eternal? Such questions have been asked and answered affirmatively; though a negative is now mostly given to those of more extreme import. The boldness of earlier expositors is mainly avoided in the caution of the later. The former are more extravagant, the latter less consistent. But the theory, in every phase of it, asserts the just punishment of sin in Christ; and therefore, asserts or implies all that is requisite to such punishment. A denial of any such requisite is suicidal" (MILEY, *Syst. Th.*, II, p. 142). While these questions will be treated more at length in our consideration of the nature of the atonement, it is necessary here to state broadly, some of the weaknesses of this theory.

1. A study of the principles of Calvinism as found in the various creedal statements reveals that it is fundamental to the theory, that sin must be punished on its own account. If it ought to be punished, then God is under obligation to punish it. It is a necessity of the judicial rectitude of God. The divine justice must have penal satisfaction. For this reason the position of Calvinism is sometimes known as the "judicial theory." The penalty must be inflicted upon the sinner or a substitute. Christ, the Son of God, became our Substitute. Whether He bore the identical penalty or its equivalent, Calvinists

have never been able to decide, but it is not essential to the theory. The inconsistency lies in this, that if sin is to be punished on its own account, and if Christ became our Substitute, then our sin must in some sense have been transferred to Him, or He did not merit the punishment inflicted upon Him. Now Calvinists are generally careful to maintain the distinction between the demerit or culpability of sin *(reatus culpæ)*, and guilt as liability to punishment *(reatus poenae)*, a distinction which it is proper to observe. But this very distinction nullifies their idea of substitution, for the Substitute becomes liable to penalty without demerit, and, therefore, the sin is not actually punished. Its substitute is only an innocent victim. It is in this attempt to impute our sin to Christ as His own, that the weakness of this type of substitution appears. Even the Calvinistic Dr. Strong admits that this theory "is defective in holding to a merely external transfer of the merits of Christ's work, while it does not clearly state the internal ground of that transfer, in the union of the believer with Christ" (STRONG, *Syst., Th.*, II, p. 748).

2. It is frequently claimed by its advocates, that the penal substitutionary theory is the only theory which admits of the substitutionary work of Christ, and therefore to deny it, is to deny Christ as our Substitute. But the Governmental or Rectoral theory holds this fact as fully and as firmly as does the Penal theory. Dr. Miley, its strongest representative among modern theologians, gives proper emphasis to Christ's substitutionary work.

Dr. Miley in his criticism of this theory states "that the necessary satisfaction of justice, as maintained in this theory, respects not merely a punitive disposition in God, but specially and chiefly an obligation of His justice to punish sin according to its demerit, and on that ground. It is because the punishment of sin is a necessity in the rectitude of divine justice that the only possible atonement is by penal substitution."— MILEY, *Syst. Th.*, II, p. 143.

Ebrard says, "If I bear the chastisement of another instead of him, the same suffering which for him would have had the moral quality of a punishment has not for me, who am innocent, the moral quality of a punishment. For the notion of punishment contains, besides the objective element of suffering inflicted by the judge, also the subjective element of the sense of guilt or of an evil conscience endured by the guilty, or the relation between the evil act committed and the consequent suffering inflicted." (cf. VAN OOSTERZEE, *Chr. Dogm.*, p. 603.)

Nor is the idea of penal substitution a distinctive fact of this theory. Other theories admit also of the penal sufferings of Christ as the conditional ground of forgiveness. The moderate rectoral theory of Mr. Watson holds firmly to the vicariousness of Christ's sufferings, but grounds this in the ethical character of God as well as in the essentials of government. The deeper and more scriptural approach to this subject is recognized instantly in the words of Dr. Pope. "As the atonement avails for the human race, and is therefore ours, it must be viewed as a vicarious satisfaction of the claims of divine justice or the expiation of the guilt of sin, and propitiation of the divine favor..... The substitutionary idea is in their case qualified by that of representation on the one hand, and the mystical fellowship of his saints on the other..... The doctrine is not that a penalty has been endured by Christ instead of His people; that He has occupied their legal place and borne their legal responsibility; and, therefore, that they are forever discharged. It is rather that a sacrificial offering has been presented by Him instead of the race; and that He, making the virtue of His atonement the strength of His plea, represents all that come unto God by Him. The propitiation offered for all men, and accepted, becomes effectual only for the penitent who embraces it by trusting in Him whom God has set forth to be a propitiation in His blood through faith" (POPE, *Compend. Chr. Th.*, II, p. 271).

3. The Penal substitutionary theory leads of necessity, either to universalism on the one hand, or unconditional election on the other. Dr. Miley makes the charge that "such an atonement, by its very nature, cancels all punitive claims against the elect, and by immediate result forever frees them from all guilt as a liability

---

Watson holds that the design of God in the gift of His Son is "that he should die in the place and stead of all men as a sacrificial oblation, by which satisfaction is made for the sins of every individual, so that they become remissible upon the terms of the evangelical covenant, i.e., upon the condition of faith."—WATSON, *Theol. Inst.*, II, chap. 25.

Dr. A. A. Hodge says that "the Arminian view, therefore, differs from the Calvinistic in two points. They maintain that Christ died, first, for the relief of all men; second, to make salvation possible. We hold, on the other hand, that Christ died, first, for His elect; second, to make their salvation certain."—HODGE, *Outlines of Th.*, p. 313.

to the penalty of sin. We know that such a consequence is denied, though we shall show that it is also fully asserted." In proof of his assertion he cites such authorities as Hodge, Dick, Symington and Turretin. Thus Dr. Charles Hodge says, "If the claims of justice are satisfied they cannot again be enforced. This is the analogy between the work of Christ and the payment of a debt. The point of agreement between the two cases is not the nature of the satisfaction rendered, but one aspect of the effect produced. In both cases the persons for whom the satisfaction is made are certainly freed. Their exemption or deliverance is in both cases, and equally in both, a matter of justice." So also, Dr. Symington declares that "the death of Christ being a legal satisfaction for sin, all for whom he died must enjoy the remission of their offenses" (MILEY, *Syst. Th.*, II, p. 151; HODGE, *Syst. Th.*, II, p. 472; SYMINGTON, *Atonement and Intercession*, p. 190). It is evident then, that the penal substitutionary theory of the atonement involves the question of its extent also. If Christ died for all men, then all are unconditionally saved as universalism maintains. If all are not saved, as the Scriptures clearly teach, then the only alternative is a belief in the atonement as limited to the elect. Thus there is developed as a natural consequence of the theory, an unscriptural and false notion of its application. It must accept either universalism or a limited atonement. This fact is also borne out by the history of Christian doctrine.

4. In its historical development, the penal theory is associated with the Calvinistic ideas of predestination and limited atonement. We object to the theory on the ground that its application necessarily represents the atonement as limited to the elect, whereas the Scriptures declare that Christ died for all. We object further,

The following statement from Dr. A. A. Hodge confirms the above position. He says, "If it is involved in the very nature of the atonement . . . . that all the legal responsibilities of those for whom he died were laid upon Christ; if he suffered the very penalty which divine justice exacted of them, then it follows necessarily that all those for whom he died are absolved, since justice cannot demand two perfect satisfactions, nor inflict the same penalty once upon the substitute and again upon the principal."—A. A. HODGE, *Outlines of Theology*, p. 313.

on the ground that the Scriptures declare that the propitiatory offering of Christ became effective through faith (Rom. 3: 22-25); whereas this theory depends solely upon effectual calling, or God's electing grace. This Dr. Boyce admits in his argument against Arminianism. He says that "it does not accord with justice that any should suffer for whom a substitute has actually borne the penalty and made full satisfaction"; and again, "It makes salvation the result in part of faith; but faith is the result of reconciliation, not its cause; it is the gift of God." He then states his own position in these words, "That this limitation is one of purpose; that God designed only the actual salvation of some; and that, whatever provision has been made for others, He made this positive arrangement by which the salvation of certain ones is secured (BOYCE, *Abstract of Systematic Theology*, p. 337). Here we see the substitutionary theory in its unadulterated form. Christ died in the place of some, who must therefore be saved, since it would be wrong to punish both the sinner and his substitute. Christ died for the elect, who are not only foreknown, but foreordained to this state of salvation by the decree of God. Those who are so predestinated, are unconditionally saved by the bestowal of regenerating grace, out of which arise repentance, faith, justification, adoption and sanctification.

5. Our final objection to the satisfaction theory is based upon the fact that it leads logically into antinom-

Dr. Gammertsfelder offers the following objections to the penal theory: (1) It holds that justice lies deeper in the nature of God than love and mercy, while the Bible as well as reason teaches that love and not justice was the moving cause of redemption. (2) It violates the moral principle which holds that guilt and penalty are not transferable. Salvation is an ethical process and cannot be determined by mere commercial, governmental or juridicial principles. The demerit of sin cannot be transferred; neither can righteousness be transferred. (3) Another objection to the theory is, that no place is left for forgiveness. Now if sins are removed by penal substitution, there is no room for forgiveness. If a debt is paid, there is no room for remission. If God must punish, then He must punish according to absolute justice and cannot punish by fiction. Forgiveness and penalty mutually exclude each other. (4) The fourth objection is found in the quality of unreality in the whole procedure. The satisfaction for sin on which the theory rests, is an unreal satisfaction. Mere physical suffering can never atone for sin; for penalty is more than physical suffering. There must be all the elements of sorrow, shame and contrition enter into it, and these are not transferable.—GAMMERTSFELDER, *Syst. Th.*, pp. 277-279.

ianism. This its advocates usually deny, but historically, antinomianism has always been held in connection with this type of belief in the atonement. (1) It holds that Christ's active obedience is imputed to believers in such a manner that it is esteemed by God as done by them. They are, therefore, righteous by proxy. (2) This imputation in reality makes Christ's sufferings superfluous; for if He has done for us all that the law requires, why should we be under the necessity of being delivered from penalty by His death. (3) If Christ's active obedience is to be substituted for that of believers, it shuts out the necessity of personal obedience to the law of God. Thus it transfers the requirement of obedience from the subjects of the divine government, to Christ as the substitute, and leaves man without law and God without dominion. Man is therefore left in the position of being tempted to license of every kind, instead of being held strictly accountable for a life of righteousness. (4) This type of satisfaction cannot be called such in truth, for it is merely the performance of all that the law requires by one person substituted for another.

THE PRINCIPLES OF CALVINISM

We give the following brief summary of the principles of Calvinism, for the purpose of showing the entire system in its logical arrangement. This summary is condensed from the positions of A. A. Hodge, a Calvinist of the federal type. It is against the ideas of predestination, limited atonement, effectual calling and final perseverance as here set forth, that Arminianism has so strongly objected.

1. *The Relation of the Creator to Creation.* Calvinism teaches Christian theism. It holds that His creatures are momentarily dependent upon the energy of His will for substance, and for the possession of the powers communicated to them as second causes in all their exercises. Before the apostasy, the spirit of man depended for spiritual life and moral integrity upon the concurrence of the Spirit of God, the withdrawal of which is the immediate cause of spiritual death and moral impotence. This divine influence, in one degree, and in one mode or another, is common to all creatures and all their actions; and it is called "grace" when, as undeserved favor, it is in a supernatural manner restored to the souls of sinful men, with the design of affecting their moral character and action.

2. *The Design of God in Creation.* This is declared to be the manifestation of His own glorious perfections, and becomes a principle of interpretation for all God's dealings with mankind.

3. *The Eternal Plan of God.* (1) The eternal and immutable plan of God has constituted man a free agent, and consequently can never interfere with the exercise of that freedom of which the exercise of that freedom is itself the foundation. (2) This created free will is not, however, independent, but ever continues to have its ground in the con-

serving energies of the Creator. (3) In case of an infinitely wise, powerful and free Creator, it is obvious that the certain foreknowledge of all events from the absolute beginning virtually involves the predetermination of each event without exception; for all the causes and consequences, direct and contingent, which are foreseen in creation are of course, determined by creation. (4) Since all events constitute a single system, the Creator must embrace the system as a whole, and every infinitesimal element of it, in one all-comprehensive intention; ends more or less general must be determined by ends which are made dependent upon them; hence while every event remains dependent upon its causes, and contingent upon its conditions, none of God's purposes can possibly be contingent, because in turn, every cause and condition is determined in that purpose, as well as ends which are suspended upon them; all the decrees of God are hence called absolute, because they are ultimately determined always, by "the counsel of His own will," and never by anything exterior to Him which has not in turn been previously determined by Him. (5) This determination, however, instead of interfering with, maintains the true causality of the creature, and the free self-determination of men and angels. Since the holiness of the created moral agent is conditioned upon the indwelling of divine grace, and its turning from grace is the cause of sin, it follows that all the good in the volitions of free agents is to be referred to God as its positive source; but all the evil (which originates in defect or privation) is to be referred simply to his permission. In this view all events, without exception, are embraced in God's eternal purpose; even the primal apostasies of Satan and Adam, as well as those consequences which have flowed from them. The charge of fatalism so often made does not really lie against Calvinism; for the energizing will of the personal Jehovah, at once perfect Light and Love, is very different from fate. It is one thing to be borne along by irresistible yet utterly blind force, and quite another to be led by our heavenly Father's hand.

4. *God's Benevolence, Justice and Grace.* Justice as well as benevolence is an essential and ultimate property of the divine nature, and hence lies back of and determines the character of, the divine volitions. By the perfection of God's character He is always benevolent to the innocent, and just as equally certain is he determined to punish the guilty. Hence He has exercised both justice and benevolence—justice to the sin and the law, benevolence to the sinner, which benevolence is undeserving in sovereign grace.

5. *The Effect of Adam's Apostasy upon the Race.* The entire soul with its constitutional faculties and acquired habits is the organ of volition, the agent willing. It possesses the inalienable property of self-determination, the moral character of which depends upon the indwelling of the Holy Spirit, and it needs, therefore, divine help to will rightly. Adam was created in fellowship with God, and hence with a holy tendency of heart, with full power not to sin, but also, for a limited period of probation, with power to sin; and when he sinned the Holy Spirit was withdrawn from the race, and he and his descendants lost the original power not to sin, and gained the necessity to sin; in other words, total moral inability. . . . . Hence Calvinists hold (1) Human sin, having originated in the free apostatizing act of Adam, deserves God's wrath and curse, and immutable justice demands their infliction. (2) Such, moreover, was the relation subsisting between Adam and his descendants, that God righteously regards and treats each one as he comes into being as worthy of the punishment of that sin, and consequently withdraws his life-giving fellowship from him. The whole race, therefore, and each individual it embraces, is under the just condemnation of God; and hence the gift of Christ, and the entire scheme of redemption in its conception, execution, and application, are throughout and in every

sense a product of sovereign grace. God was free to provide it for few or for many, for all or for none, just as He pleased; and in every case of its application the motives determining God cannot be found in the object, but only in the good pleasure of the will of the Divine Agent. (3) As to original sin—since every man comes into the world in a condition of ante-natal forfeiture, because of Adam's apostasy, he is judicially excluded from the morally quickening energy of the Holy Ghost, and hence begins to think, feel and act without a spontaneous bias to moral good. (4) But since moral obligation is positive, and the soul is essentially active, it instantly develops in action, a spiritual blindness and deadness to divine things, and a positive inclination to evil. This involves the corruption of the whole nature; and the absolute impotency of the will to good is, humanly speaking, without remedy, and necessarily tends to the indefinite increase, both of depravity and guilt. It is therefore said to be total.

6. *The Nature and Necessity of Regenerating Grace.* Grace is free, sovereign favor to the ill-deserving. Calvinists distinguish (1) "common grace," or the moral and suasory influence on the soul, of the Spirit acting through the truth, as the result of Christ's work, which tends to restrain evil passions, but which may be resisted, and is always prevailingly resisted by the unregenerate, from (2) "effectual calling" which is a single act of God, changing the moral character of the will of the subject, and implanting a prevailing tendency to co-operate with future grace in all forms of holy obedience. By reason of the new creative energy within it, the soul spontaneously embraces Christ and turns to God. Afterwards this same divine energy continues to support the soul, and prepare it for, and concur with it in, every good work. This grace is now prevailingly co-operated with by the regenerated soul, and at times resisted, until the status of grace is succeeded by the status of glory.

7. *The Application of the Plan of Redemption.* Predestination, or the purpose of God to secure the salvation of some men, and not all, has been popularly regarded as the distinguishing feature of Calvinism, and one of the most revolting to the moral sense. Some Calvinists reasoning downward from the nature of God as absolute, and developing this doctrine in a strictly speculative manner, have made it the foundation of their system. These have necessarily conceived of it in the high and logically coherent supralapsarian sense (election before creation; the decree to create, and permit men to fall, in order to carry out their predestined salvation or perdition), which has been rejected by the great body of Reformed theologians as unscriptural, and revolting to the moral sense. The vast majority of Calvinists, however, are influenced by practical, and not speculative considerations, and therefore hold to the infralapsarian (election after creation) view. God, they say, elects His people out of the mass of guilty sinners, and provides redemption for them, thus securing for them faith and repentance whereby they may be saved. These gifts cannot, therefore, be conditions of salvation, as Arminians hold: rather they are its predetermined and graciously effected results. Gottschalk taught a double predestination—the elect to salvation and the reprobate to damnation. But this theory is not taught in the recognized standards of Calvinism. God elects of free grace all those He purposes to save, and actually saves them; while those whom He does not elect are simply left under the operation of the law of exact justice, whatever that may be. Calvinistic "particularism" admits the actual results of salvation in their widest scope, and refers all to the gracious purpose and power of God, but does not restrict it within the limits determined by the facts themselves.

The Governmental Theory. This theory as developed by Grotius, held that the atonement was not a satisfaction to any internal principle of the divine nature, but to the necessities of government. It arose as a protest against the rigorous penal substitution theory on the one hand, and the Socinian rejection of all vicarious intervention on the other. The theory was first advanced by James Arminius and his follower Hugo Grotius, although later, Grotius departed from the earlier position. Together they agreed to uphold, not the exactitude of divine justice wholly, or even mainly, as in the Anselmic theory, but also the just and compassionate will of God as a true element in the atonement. They thus sought to lay emphasis upon the love of God as well as His justice. Grotius differed from Arminius in the later development of these principles, by limiting the satisfaction which was made by Christ, to the dignity of the law, the honor of the lawgiver and the protection of the universe. The death of Christ and His sufferings became, therefore, not an exhibition of love to draw men to God, as in the moral influence theories, but a deterrent to sin through an exhibition of its punishment.

Hugo Grotius (1583-1645) was a distinguished Dutch jurist, and patterned his idea of the atonement after the method of civil law. His great work was entitled, "A Defense of the Catholic Faith Concerning the Satisfaction of Christ Against Faustus Socinus" (1617). But while

The Grotian Theory was adopted in England by Richard Baxter (1615-1691) and Samuel Clarke (1675-1729). His first work published in 1617 was translated into English by Dr. F. H. Foster, the historian of New England Theology, and published at Andover in 1889. Dr. Foster shows, however, that Grotius' theological writings were in Yale College library in 1733. These were published in four folio volumes at London and Amsterdam in 1679 and at Basle in 1732. The theory was advocated by the New England theologians since the days of Jonathan Edwards, but to what extent, it has been difficult to determine. Many of them advocated only the governmental demand for an atonement, making this the point of departure for a further demand. Dr. Dickie states that the New England divines developed their doctrine of the atonement from Grotius, much as the Schoolmen used the Sentences of Lombard, and were likewise soon lost in the fog of speculation. The leading New England discussions were collected and published at Boston, with an Introductory Essay by Dr. E. A. Park of Andover. The views of Dr. R. W. Dale, and Dr. J. Scott Lidgett are but modernizations of the Grotian Theory.

seeking to defend the orthodox faith, he really transformed it into a new theory, commonly known as the Governmental or Rectoral Theory. Here the central idea of the defense was that God must not be regarded as the offended or injured party, but as the moral Governor of the universe. He must therefore uphold the authority of His government in the interests of the general good. Consequently the sufferings of our Lord are to be regarded, not as the exact equivalent of our punishment, but only in the sense that the dignity of the divine government was as effectively upheld and vindicated, as it would have been if we had received the punishment we deserved. This truth, the great jurist regarded as self-evident in the sphere of jurisprudence, and it is difficult to understand his position unless this fact be taken into account. It was at this point, however, that the satisfactionists urged their criticism of his position. He taught that the law under which man is held, both as to penalty and precept, is a positive product of the divine will; and therefore He may, as a moral Governor, relax its demands. It was this position as to the relaxation of the demands of the law that subjected him to criticism. He introduced the term *acceptilatio*, which Duns Scotus had used against the Anselmic position, and was therefore accused of conceding too much to the Socinians. The *acceptilatio* in Roman law was an acquittance from obligation by word of mouth without real payment. Grotius, however, insisted that his theory of satisfaction was far more than the *acceptilatio* of Roman jurisprudence; that it was of infinite value, though not the precise equivalent. Thus there was a relaxation of the claims of the law in one sense, though not in another. Dr. Pope makes the remark that "the most rig-

But Grotius, its later representative, did not agree with the Arminian theology when he limited the satisfaction to the dignity of the law, the honor of the Lawgiver, the protection of the interests of the universe, and the exhibition of a deterrent example. Grotius founded what has been called the Rectoral or Governmental Theory of the Atonement, which dwells too exclusively on its necessity for the vindication of God's righteousness as the Ruler of all. Not to speak of the invincible repugnance felt by every reverent mind to the thought that our Lord was thus made a spectacle to the universe, this theory errs by making a subordinate purpose supreme.—POPE, *Compend. Chr. Th.*, II, p. 313.

orous Anselmic theory must admit the principle, so far as the acceptance of a substitute goes; why not then carry the principle a little farther and make the interfering act extend to the *value* of the thing substituted, as well as to the *principle* of substitution; especially as the value here is infinite?" (POPE, *Compend. Chr. Th.*, II, p. 313). Dr. Miley attributes the *acceptilatio* to the Anselmic position, rather than to that of Grotius, holding that the latter does not admit of a theory of the atonement based on any such sense of debt and payment.

Richard Watson (1781-1823) taught a modified form of the governmental theory. He held that the atonement is a satisfaction to the ethical nature of God, as well as an expedient for sustaining the majesty of His government. This he did on the ground that there should be

The following summary of the Governmental Theory as held by Grotius is taken mainly from the account of it as stated by Dr. Charles Hodge.

1. That in the forgiveness of sin God is to be regarded neither as an offended party, nor as a creditor, nor as a master, but as a moral governor. A creditor can remit the debt due him at pleasure; a master may punish or not punish as he sees fit; but a ruler must act, not according to his feelings or caprice, but with a view to the best interests of those under his authority.

2. The end of punishment is the prevention of crime, or the preservation of order and the promotion of the best interests of the community.

3. As a good governor cannot allow sin to be committed with impunity, God cannot pardon the sins of men without some adequate exhibition of His displeasure, and of His determination to punish it. This was the design of the sufferings and death of Christ. God punished sin in Him as an example. This example was the more impressive on account of the dignity of Christ's person, and therefore in view of His death, God can consistently with the best interests of His government remit the penalty of the law in the case of penitent believers.

4. Punishment is defined as suffering inflicted on account of sin. It need not be imposed on account of the personal demerit of the sufferer; nor with the design of satisfying justice, in the ordinary sense of that word. It was enough that it should be on account of sin. As the sufferings of Christ were caused by our sins, inasmuch as they were designed to render their remission consistent with the interest of God's moral government, they fall within the comprehensive definition of the word punishment. Grotius, therefore, could say that Christ suffered the punishment of our sins, as His sufferings were an example of what sin deserved.

5. The essence of the atonement, therefore, according to Grotius consisted in this, that the sufferings and death of Christ were designed as an exhibition of God's displeasure against sin. They were intended to teach that in the estimation of God, sin deserves to be punished; and that, therefore, the impenitent cannot escape the penalty due to their offenses.—HODGE, *Syst. Th.*, II, pp. 573-575.

no moral chasm between the laws and the nature of God; and that what satisfies the one is agreeable to the other. Mr. Watson states his position as follows: "The death of Christ, then, is the satisfaction accepted; and this being a satisfaction to justice, that is, a consideration which satisfied God, as a being essentially righteous, and as having strict and inflexible respect to the justice of His government; pardon through, or for the sake of that death, became, in consequence, 'a declaration of the righteousness of God,' as the only appointed method of remitting the punishment of the guilty; and if so, satisfaction respects not, ... the honor of the law of God, but its authority, and the upholding of that righteous and holy character of the Lawgiver, and of his administration, of which that law is the visible and public expression. Nor is this to be regarded as a merely wise and fit expedient of government, a point to which even Grotius leans too much, as well as many other divines .... and that it is to be concluded, that no other alternative existed but that of exchanging a righteous government for one careless and relaxed, to the dishonor of the divine attributes, and the sanctioning of moral disorder; or the upholding of such a government by the personal and extreme punishment of every offender; or else the acceptance of the vicarious death of an infinitely dignified and glorious being, through whom pardon should be offered, and in whose hands a process for the moral restoration of the lapsed should be placed" (WATSON, *Institutes,* II, p. 139).

Dr. John Miley (1813-1895) is the outstanding representative of the governmental theory in modern times. In accepting this theory, however, he does so, not in any particular exposition which has been given to it, but that which he constructs himself, out of its fundamental prin-

Dr. Sheldon says that Watson stood on the ground of the governmental theory, and that this may be regarded as largely current among Methodist theologians. Here he classifies also Dr. Henry B. Smith, and also many of the more orthodox Lutheran theologians of modern times. These regard the satisfaction of Christ as referring to general rather than distributive justice. In opposition to the Grotian theory, therefore, these theologians agree with Mr. Watson in finding a ground for it in the ethical nature of God, and not merely in the demands of administration. (Cf. SHELDON, *Hist. Chr. Doct.,* II, p. 356.)

ciples. He holds with good reason, that the theory has not always been fortunate in its exposition, particularly in its beginning. Alien elements have been retained, and vital facts either omitted or wrongly placed. From the premises which he lays, Dr. Miley builds up a strong and logical system, although he stands almost alone among modern theologians. He holds, however, that Mr. Watson grounds the necessity of the atonement in the governmental theory, although he differs from him in his exposition of it. He holds further, that while Dr. Whedon has never given his theory of the atonement in the style of the governmental, yet it is in principle the same. Dr. Raymond he understands to hold the same idea of the atonement as Dr. Whedon. Dr. Tigert, in Summers' *Systematic Theology,* especially criticizes the theory of Dr. Miley, the most serious objection being his lack of emphasis upon the idea of propitiation.

Dr. Miley's governmental theory of the atonement briefly summarized is as follows: (1) *Substitution by Atonement.* The sufferings of Christ are an atonement for sin by substitution, in the sense that they were intentionally endured for sinners under judicial condemnation, and for the sake of their forgiveness. They render forgiveness consistent with the divine justice. (2) *Conditional Substitution.* The forgiveness of sin has a real conditionality. An atonement for all by absolute substitution would inevitably achieve the salvation of all. Therefore a universal atonement, with the fact of

The question now arises, Is Dr. Miley's the Methodist doctrine of the atonement? Can we regard it as fortunate that the only express Methodist treatise on atonement should ground its theory exclusively in a governmental necessity? Does Dr. Miley's theory adequately interpret Scripture in those profound texts which represent the demand for propitiation and reconciliation as arising among the divine attributes in the innermost recesses of the divine nature? Or is Dr. Summers nearer the truth of Scripture, and nearer the Methodist doctrine as taught by Watson, the first, and Pope, the last, of great Methodist writers on systematic theology? Can the atonement be represented as a satisfaction to God, a harmonization of the divine nature and attributes, and a reconciliation of God and the world, without the errors of the Calvinistic theory of commercial substitution? . . . . Watson, Pope, and Summers seem to think that those scriptures teach that the atonement is a real satisfaction to the demands of the divine nature, and that this is consistent with the true Arminian doctrine of the atonement, Dr. Miley to the contrary notwithstanding."—SUMMERS, *Syst. Th.,* I, p. 272.

a limited actual salvation, is conclusive of a real conditionality in its saving grace. (3) *Substitution in Suffering*. The substitution of Christ must be of a nature agreeing with the provisory character of the atonement. It could not, therefore, be a substitution in penalty as the merited punishment of sin, for such an atonement is absolute. The substitution, therefore, is in suffering without the penal element. (4) *The Atonement Must Be Related to Public Justice*. As in the satisfaction theory, so in the rectoral, the sufferings of Christ are an atonement for sin only as in some sense they take the place of penalty. In the one they take its place as a penal substitute, thus fulfilling the office of justice in the actual punishment of sin; in the other they take its place in the fulfillment of its office as concerned with the interests of moral government. (5) *Remissibility of Its Penalties*. There is no sufficient reason why sin must be punished solely on the ground of its demerit. The forgiveness of the actual sinner, as a real remission of penalty at the time of his justification and acceptance in the divine favor, is proof positive to the contrary. (6) *The Place of Atonement*. Thus the way is open for some substitutional provision which may replace the actual infliction of penalty upon sin. The theory of satisfaction really leaves no place for vicarious atonement. Its most fundamental and ever asserted principle, that sin as such must be punished, makes the punishment of the actual sinner an absolute necessity. But as penalties are remissible so far as a purely retributive justice is concerned, so, having a special end in the interest of moral government, they may give place to any substitutional measure equally securing that end. Here is a place for vicarious atonement. (7) *Nature of the Atonement*. The nature of the atonement in the sufferings of Christ follows necessarily from the above principle. It cannot be of the nature required by the principles of the satisfaction theory. In asserting the absoluteness of divine justice in its purely retributive element, the theory excludes the possibility of a penal substitution in atonement for sin. And, therefore, the sufferings of Christ are not, as they cannot be, an atonement by penal substitution. But while His sufferings could not take the place of penalty in the actual punishment of sin, they could, and do, take its place in its strictly rectoral end. And the atonement is thus determined to consist in the sufferings of Christ, as a provisory substitute for penalty in the interest of moral government (MILEY, *Systematic Theology*, II, pp. 155-156).

The objections to this theory will be given consideration in our constructive treatment of the atonement. It is sufficient here to mention only briefly, the objections which are usually urged against it. (1) It does not attach sufficient importance to the idea of propitiation, and therefore minifies the idea of a real satisfaction of the divine attributes. (2) It emphasizes the mercy of God in much the same sense that Calvinism emphasizes the justice of God. A true theory of the atonement must satisfy all the attributes of the divine nature. (3) It is built upon a false philosophical principle that utility is the ground of moral obligation. (4) It practically ignores the immanent holiness of God, and substitutes for the chief aim of the atonement, that which is only subordinate. Dr. Miley is called in question also by Dr. Tigert, for his assumption that there is no true middle ground between the Calvinistic idea of satisfaction and the strict rectoral theory. He thinks that the satisfaction theory can be held apart from its Calvinistic additions. "Watson, Pope, and Summers are certainly satisfactionists," he says, "but this is not their theory. Miley denies that there is any scientific place for them." They must either be Calvinists or deny their adhesion to the pure rectoral

Dr. Tigert says, "It is strange that all these Methodist theologians (referring to Watson, Pope and Summers) some of whom are certainly possessed of as much exegetical skill, metaphysical acumen, and logical power as Dr. Miley has manifested in any part of his treatise, should have all lodged in an unscientific and indefensible half-way position, unable to see that if they abandoned the Calvinistic theory of commercial substitution their principles must carry them over to the governmental theory of atonement. Dr. Miley is free to essay the rescue of Methodism and of these uncritical theologians from an inconsistent doctrine; but undoubtedly, the whole ground must be carefully reviewed before he can be permitted to hold the field unchallenged. He must make good his position."—SUMMERS, *Syst. Th.*, I, p. 273.

theory. Dr. Strong objects to this theory on the ground that it is an exhibition of justice which is not justice; and an exhibition of regard for law, which will make it safe to pardon the violators of law. But it must be admitted that the governmental factor is essential to any true theory of the atonement. It is only the undue emphasis upon this element to the disparagement of other equally essential elements, which makes the theory wrong. This whole subject will be given further consideration in our next chapter.

The Moral Influence Theories. The moral influence theories take their name from the basic assumption, that salvation comes through the appeal of divine love. They limit the efficacy of Christ's death to Adam's race, making its value consist, not in its influence upon the divine mind, nor upon the universe at large, but upon the power of love to subdue the enmity of the human heart. They do not hold that the sacrifice of Christ expiated sin, or placated the divine wrath by suffering; or that the atonement in any wise satisfied divine justice. They maintain that the sole obstacle to the forgiveness of sins, is to be found in the sinner's own unbelief and hardness of heart. This Christ's death was designed to remove by a display of God's love in the death of His Son. With this hardness of heart removed, God can be just and the justifier of him who believes in Jesus. They look upon God, therefore, as exhibiting nothing but complacent love, upon sin as its own punishment, and upon men as saved by becoming good. The work of Christ tends to save men by assuring them of God's love, and by persuading them to love Him. These theories are numerous, but they are all one in emphasizing the basic idea of moral influence. We shall mention briefly, only four general types: (1) The Socinian Theories; (2) The Mystical Theories; (3) Bushnell's Theory of Moral Influence; and (4) The New Theology of McLeod Campbell and the Andover School.

1. *Socinianism.* Socinianism was the precursor of modern unitarianism. Dr. Strong calls it "The Example Theory of the Atonement," for it altogether denies any

idea of propitiation or satisfaction. Its sole method of reconciliation is to better man's moral condition, and this can be effected only by man's own will through repentance and reformation. The death of Christ is regarded as that of a noble martyr. His loyalty to truth and faithfulness to duty provide us with a powerful incentive to moral improvement. Socinianism like Calvinism is based upon the idea of divine sovereignty, but in a very different manner; in Calvinism, predestination applies to the destinies of men; in Socinianism, it governs the attributes of God. That is, it holds that God is free to do that which He wills, and refuses to admit of any immutable qualities in the divine nature, whether of mercy or justice. His occasional will is called out by the conduct of men. He is free to forgive sin without any satisfaction to divine justice, if He desires to do so, simply on the ground of repentance. The death of Christ is designed to remove the hardness of the sinner's heart as the obstacle to repentance. The theory advanced by Lælius Socinus, the uncle, and Faustus Socinus, the nephew, represents the seventeenth century attack of rationalism on the penal satisfaction theory of the atonement. As such it

Dr. Alvah Hovey characterizes the moral influence theories as those "which affirm that the atonement made by Christ benefits and saves men by its moral influence on their characters, and by that alone."

According to the teaching of early Socinianism—as distinguished from that of modern Unitarianism—the Saviour's priestly office was only figuratively on earth, and began in heaven where He uses His exalted authority to plead for mankind. "The sacerdotal office consists in this, that as He can in royal authority help us in all our necessities, so in His priestly character; and the character of His help is called by a figure His sacrifice." But it may be said that forgiveness is never represented as bestowed save through a real sacrifice: God is in Christ reconciling the world to Himself; and for Christ's sake forgives sins which only the spirit obtained by the atonement enables us to confess and forsake.—POPE, *Compend. Chr. Th.*, II, p. 311.

In the Socinian theory Christ is a prophet, a teacher. He saves His people as a teacher saves his pupils—by instruction, He saves them from the evils of ignorance, and blesses them with the immunities and benefits of knowledge. Christ teaches the will of God and the way to heaven, and thus saves them who heed His instructions. . . . . But man has other needs besides instruction. . . . . The Saviour of mankind must be more than a teacher, more than a prophet; He must be a priest, a king; indeed He must be as Saviour all in all. Man as a sinner is lost; so far as his own resources are concerned, irretrievably lost. He is nothing, has nothing, can do nothing, without a Saviour.—RAYMOND, *Syst. Th.*, II, pp. 222-224.

consisted almost wholly of an array of arguments against Anselmic principles.

2. *The Mystical Theories.* These represent the type of the moral influence theory as held by Schleiermacher, Ritschl, Maurice, Irving and others. Dr. Bruce calls it "Redemption by Sample." The mysticism lies in the identification of Christ with the race in the sense that He rendered to God, the perfect devotion and obedience which we ought to render; and which in some sense mankind offered in Him. This it holds, is the only meaning of sacrifice in the Scriptures—self-sacrifice by self-consecration to God's service. These theories are sometimes known also, as "redemption by incarnation."

Schleiermacher (1769-1834) held that the atonement is purely subjective, and denied any objective satisfaction to God by the substitutionary work of Christ. Such ideas as reparation, compensation, substitution, satisfaction and propitiation, he held to be wholly Jewish. His conception of the work of Christ consisted in this—that being one with God, Christ taught men that they could be one with God; and His consciousness of being in God and knowing God, gave Him the power to communicate it to others. For this reason, He became a Mediator and a Saviour.

Ritschl (1822-1889) was one of the most influential representatives of the moral influence in Germany. He did not, like Schleiermacher, set aside historical revelation, but nevertheless held inadequate views of the Redeemer. To him, Christ was a Saviour in much the same sense as Buddha—achieving His lordship over it by His indifference to it. He was the Word of God only in so far as He revealed this divine indifference to things. The sense of sin was regarded as an illusion which it was the work of Christ to dispel.

Maurice (1805-1872) held that Christ was the archetype and root of humanity, and in His own body offered an acceptable sacrifice to God for the race. This was not a substitutionary offering in the commonly accepted sense of the term, but such a mystical union of the race with Christ, that it could make a perfect offering through

Him. The sacrifice of Christ consisted in a complete renunciation of that human self-will which is the cause of all men's crimes and miseries. This he held, was the meaning of the ancient sacrifices—not as substitutes for the offerer, but as symbols of his devotion. These found their fulfillment in Christ, who in His life and death, offered up the one and only complete sacrifice ever offered, a perfect surrender to the divine will. Hence in Him, the archetypal man, the race offered a sacrifice acceptable to God.

On Irving's theory, evil inclinations are not sinful. Sinfulness belongs only to evil acts. The loose connection between the Logos and humanity savors of Nestorianism. It is the work of the person to rid itself of something in the humanity which does not really render it sinful. If Jesus' sinfulness of nature did not render His person sinful, this must be true of us, which is a Pelagian element, revealed also in the denial that for our redemption we need Christ as an atoning sacrifice. It is not necessary to a complete incarnation for Christ to take a sinful nature, unless sin is essential to human nature. In Irving's view, the death of Christ's body works the regeneration of His sinful nature. But this is to make sin a merely physical thing, and the body the only part of man needing redemption. Penalty would thus become a reformer, and death a savior.—DORNER, *Syst. Chr. Doct.*, III, p. 361.

Dr. Strong points out, that according to this theory, the glory of Christ was not in saving others, but in saving Himself, and so demonstrating the power of man through the Holy Spirit to cast out sin from his heart and life.—STRONG, *Syst. Th.*, II, p. 746.

Freer, one of Irving's followers, modified this doctrine, stating that "unfallen humanity needed not redemption, therefore, Jesus did not take it. He took fallen humanity, but purged it in the act of taking it. The nature of which He took part was sinful in the lump, but in His person most holy."

The Mystical Theory, while existing in numerous forms, may be stated as follows: The reconciliation effected by Christ is brought about by a mysterious union of God and man, accomplished by His incarnation. The theory was held by the Platonizing fathers, by the followers of Scotus Erigena during the Middle Ages, by Osiander and Schwenkfeld at the Reformation, and the disciples of Schleiermacher among modern German theologians. One reason why the mystical theory seems so vague, is due to the fact that it has not been held as an exclusive theory, but differently colored by different writers.

Thomas Erskine taught that "Christ came into Adam's place. This is the real substitution. . . . . We are separated from each other by being individual persons. But Jesus had no human personality. He had the human nature under the personality of the Son of God. And so His human nature was more open to the commonness of men; for the divine personality while it separated Him from sinners in point of sin, united Him to them in love. And thus the sins of other men were to Jesus what the affections and lusts of his own particular flesh are to each individual believer. Every man was a part of Him, and He felt the sins of every man—just as the new nature in every believer feels the sins of the old nature—not in sympathy, but in sorrow and abhorrence."— ERSKINE, *The Brazen Serpent*.

Irving (1792-1834) held what is commonly known as the "Theory of Gradually Extirpated Depravity." According to Irving, Christ took upon Himself our human nature, not in its purity, but in its likeness after the Fall. Hence there was in Him, a fallen nature with its inborn corruption and predisposition to moral evil. He held that there were two kinds of sin—guiltless sin and guilty sin. Passive depravity he did not regard as guilty, but became such only when expressed in action. The passive sin Christ took, and through the power of the Holy Spirit, not only kept His human nature from manifesting itself in actual sin, but through struggle and suffering, gradually purified this passive sinful nature, until in His death, He completely extirpated it, and reunited the spirit to God. This is subjective purification, but there is no idea of a substitutionary atonement.

3. *Bushnell's Theory of Moral Influence.* This is frequently regarded as the clearest and best statement of moral influence in relation to the atonement. Dr. Miley

Bruce says, "Unless we are to treat the Epistle to the Hebrews as a portion of scripture practically meaningless, as possessing no permanent value for the Church, as being indeed nothing more than an ingenious piece of reasoning for a temporary purpose, we must regard Christ's priesthood as a great reality."—BRUCE, *Humiliation of Christ.*

Dr. Miley calls attention to the fact that in the analogy of certain pathologies, such as personal resentment against sin, "the scheme lowers God into the likeness of men; so that in Him, as in them, the great hindrance to forgiveness is in these same personal resentments. Thus 'one kind of forgiveness matches and interprets the other, for they have a common property. They come to the same point when they are genuine, and require also the same preparations and conditions precedent.' The theory commands no lofty view of the divine goodness. Nor can it give any proper significance to the sacred proclamation of the divine love as the original of the redemptive economy. Such a love is held in no bonds of personal resentment. The theory has no profound and glorious doctrine of divine love; and indeed, is found on a true sounding to be shallow."—MILEY, *Syst. Th.,* II, p. 118.

In recent times Socinian principles have been introduced into the Latitudinarian theology of many who do not reject the doctrine of the Trinity. And it is here that they are most dangerous. In the works of some divines, the love of God alone is introduced into the atoning sacrifice, which on Christ's part is a sublime and supreme act of repentance for man, His amen to the sentence of the law, and to man himself an affecting representative sorrow which he must make his own by adding to it the personal consciousness of guilt. The latter idea links it with the Romish doctrine of human additional expiation; and, as to the former, a representative sorrow that does not taste the wrath of God against sin falls immeasurably below the scriptural illustrations of the atoning passion in which our Lord was made a curse for us.—POPE, *Compend. Chr. Th.,* II, p. 312.

calls it the theory of "Self-propitiation by Self-sacrifice." It belongs to the class of mystical theories, in that it regards the race as identified with Christ, but is given separate mention because of its distinct character. Dr. Bushnell resolves Christ's priesthood into "sympathy"; that is, there are certain moral sentiments similar in God and in man, such as the repulsiveness of sin and resentment against wrong, which must not be extirpated, but mastered and allowed to remain. God, therefore, forgives just as man does. "They come to the same point where they require exactly the same preparations and conditions. So God must propitiate the cost and suffering for our good. This He did in sacrifice on the cross, that sublime act of cost, in which God has bent himself downward in loss and sorrow, over the hard face of sin, to say, and in saying to make good, 'Thy sins be forgiven thee' " (BUSHNELL, *Forgiveness and Law*, p. 35). There is here no propitiation by Christ's death, but only suffering in and with the sins of His creatures. The theory, therefore, is strictly Socinian and Unitarian, although Bushnell was himself a trinitarian.

4. *The New Theology.* The New Theology is a term applied to the more systematized forms of the mystical theory of the atonement, as found in the writings of McLeod Campbell of Scotland, and the Andover School of New England. The theory is essentially the same as that held by Maurice, Robertson, Bushnell and R. J. Campbell.

John McLeod Campbell (1800-1872) in his *Nature of the Atonement* (1856) advocated that Christ made a perfect confession and an adequate repentance of sin for us. He saw as we cannot, the depths of sin, and therefore was enabled to make full acknowledgment for us, this reparation being in some sense, an act of vicarious re-

---

Horace Bushnell's moral influence theory as set forth in his "Vicarious Sacrifice" failed to satisfy his mind, and in his "Forgiveness and Law" he held that "reconciliation" not only applies to what happens in men, but also to that which in a certain measure applies to the divine attitude toward men. That is, as we by making cost to ourselves for an enemy, overcome our reluctance to forgive, so God by entering into a sacrifice for sinners, becomes in His own feeling, fully at peace with Himself in extending grace to them.

pentance. It is for this reason that Dr. Dickie calls it the theory of "Vicarious Repentance." He held also, that Christ became the Head of a new humanity, in which He lives as a quickening spirit, imparting to it the same attitude toward God's holiness and love, as were realized in His own life of obedience and love. As the root of this new life in humanity, there was revealed in it, an inestimable preciousness, brought into manifestation by the Son of God, for the Revealer of the Father was also the Revealer of man made in His image. "Therefore," he continues, "there must be a relation between the Son of God and the sons of men, not according to the flesh only, but according to the Spirit—the second Adam must be a quickening Spirit, and the head of every man be Christ." This was interpreted to mean, whether rightly or wrongly, that man has in him an element of the divine, and that a difference in degree and not in kind, marked the dividing line between man and Christ. As a consequence, the New Theology came into immediate conflict with the older orthodox beliefs. The attempt to break down the dividing line between man and Christ gave rise to two errors, (1) it lowered the conception of Christ as Deity and led directly to unitarianism; and (2) it precluded the idea of total depravity, and therefore minified both sin and redemption. Here again we have unitarian principles held by a trinitarian divine.

The Andover School or "New Theology" is another form of the moral influence theory, and takes its name from the prominence given to the "New Theology" by the Andover divines. The theories held by this school were first advanced in a series of articles on "Progressive Orthodoxy" published in the fourth volume of the *Andover Review* in 1885. The third of this series is on the atonement. Dr. Dickie connects this theory with the Rectoral or Governmental theory. Dr. Boyce treats it as a separate theory of the atonement, but connects it with the moral influence theory as advocated by Bushnell and McLeod Campbell. It holds more nearly to the cosmological than the soteriological view of Christ's work, regards Christ as a representative of the race in the suffering for sin and repenting of it, denies any imputation or transfer of man's sins to Christ, or Christ's righteousness to man, maintains that love is the source of appeal to man, and holds that even the wrath of God is but one form of the manifestation of His love.

Aside from the three historical theories, there are two modern theories of the atonement which combine the three essential elements—satisfaction, governmental and moral influence, in a manner deserving of special consideration. These are the Ethical Theory of Dr. A. H. Strong, and the Racial Theory of Dr. Olin A. Curtis. Both give prominence to the idea of holiness in the nature of God and the necessity for propitiation. The Ethical Theory of Dr. Strong should not, however, be confused with the moral influence theories.

The Ethical Theory. Dr. A. H. Strong has sought to combine the essential elements of atonement in what he calls the Ethical Theory. He arranges his material according to two main principles. (1) *The atonement as related to the holiness of God.* The Ethical Theory holds that the necessity for atonement is grounded in the holiness of God, of which conscience in man is a finite reflection. The ethical principle in the divine nature demands that sin shall be punished. Aside from its results, sin is essentially ill-deserving. As those who are made in God's

The following is a summary of the principles of the Andover School. (1) Christ is the universal Mediator, and therefore must appear wherever there is need for His aid in any portion of the universe; (2) That Christ would probably have come as the incarnate one, even if there had been no sin from which to be redeemed; (3) The work of Christ changed the relation of God to man, and therefore man's relation to God; (4) There is no imputation in the work of the atonement—neither of man's sins to Christ, or of Christ's righteousness to man; (5) Christ as the substitute for the race approaches God as a representative of man through a mystical union, and therefore offers a vicarious suffering and adequate repentance; (6) This substitutionary suffering, however, is not available apart from man's own repentance; (7) The sufferings and death of Christ can be considered vicarious only in the sense that it expressed fully God's abhorrence of sin; (8) The application of the gospel is made by the Spirit who regenerates men, but not apart from their personal knowledge and experience of it; (9) Justice to God's own love requires that the gospel be preached to every sinner; (10) The judgment does not come until the gospel is preached to all nations. This last is interpreted to mean, not merely a proclamation of the truth within certain geographical bounds, but only when in reality all individuals of all nations have known it. (For further study, cf. BOYCE, *Abstract of Syst. Th.*, pp. 298ff.)

image, mark their growth in purity by their increasing hatred of impurity, so infinite purity is a consuming fire of all iniquity. Punishment is, therefore, the constitutional reaction of God's being against moral evil—the self-assertion of infinite holiness against its antagonist and would-be destroyer. In God this demand is devoid of all passion, and is consistent with infinite benevolence. The atonement then, must be regarded as the satisfaction of an ethical demand in the divine nature, through the substitution of Christ's penal sufferings for the punishment of the guilty. On the part of God, it has its ground (a) in the holiness of God, which must visit sin with condemnation, even though this condemnation brings death to His Son; and (b) in the love of God which provides the sacrifice, by suffering in and with His Son for the sins of men, but through this suffering opening a way of salvation. (2) *The atonement as related to the humanity of Christ.* The Ethical Theory maintains that Christ stands in such relation to humanity, that what God's holiness demands Christ is under obligation to pay, longs to pay, inevitably does pay, and pays so fully, in virtue of His twofold nature, that the claim of justice is satisfied, and the sinner who accepts what Christ has done is saved. If Christ had been born into the world by ordinary generation, He too, would have had depravity, guilt and penalty. But He was not so born. In the womb of the virgin, the human nature which He took was purged from its depravity. But this purging of depravity did not take away guilt, in the sense of liability to punishment. Although Christ's nature was pure, His obligation to suffer still remained. He might have declined to join Himself to humanity, and then He need not have suffered. But once born of the virgin, once possessed of the human nature that was under the curse, He was bound to suffer. The whole weight of God's displeasure against the race fell on Him, when once He became a member of the race. The atonement on the part of man, therefore, is accomplished, (1) through the solidarity of the race; of which (2) Christ is the life, and so its representative and surety; and (3) justly yet voluntarily bearing its guilt and shame and condemnation as His own. Christ as the incarnate One, in some sense, rather revealed the atonement than made it. The historical work was finished upon the cross, but that historical work only revealed to men the atonement made both before and since the extramundane Logos. The theory is stated and discussed at length by Dr. Strong in his *Systematic Theology* (Vol. II, pp. 750-771).

The Racial Theory. This is the theory of Dr. Olin A. Curtis, in his excellent work entitled *The Christian Faith* (pp.316-334). As in the Ethical Theory, holiness in God becomes the supreme factor in determining the nature of the atonement. Dr. Curtis introduces the subject by giving an account of his dissatisfaction with the three historical theories, and his attempt to combine the essential qualities of each by the method of eclectic synthesis. The result, however, was so mechanical that it had to be given up. Then came the vision of the full Christian meaning of the human race—a vision which not only vitalized but transformed the entire theological situation. From that time he studied the Bible more profoundly, being impressed with the tremendous emphasis placed upon the event of physical death as abnormal in human experience; and finding in St. Paul's teachings a racial view of our Lord's redemptive work. He found also, to his astonishment, that the elements in the old theories which he desired to preserve, appeared in a stronger light when viewed from the racial standpoint. The satisfaction theory required that justice be

Dr. Strong holds that the guilt which Christ took upon Himself by His union with humanity was: (1) not the guilt of personal sin—such guilt as belongs to every adult member of the race; (2) not the guilt of inherited depravity—such as belongs to infants, and to those who have not come to moral consciousness; but (3) solely the guilt of Adam's sin, which belongs prior to personal transgression, and apart from inherited depravity, to every member of the race who has derived his life from Adam. This original sin and inherited guilt, but without the depravity that ordinarily accompanies them, Christ takes, and so takes away. He can justly bear penalty, because He inherits guilt. And since this guilt is not His personal guilt, but the guilt of that one sin in which "all sinned"—the guilt of the common transgression in Adam, the guilt of the root sin from which all other sins have sprung—He who is personally pure can vicariously bear the penalty due to the sin of the fall.—STRONG, *Syst. Th.*, II, pp. 757, 758.

exchanged for holiness, and the automatic necessity be exchanged for the personal need of structural expression. The governmental idea required a profounder conception of the moral law, making it reach into the structure of the divine nature, and granting it a racial goal. The moral influence theory required that its conception of love should be so united to moral concern as to furnish a new atmosphere for holiness. That is, it should be holy love.

The main points of the theory may be summed up as follows: (1) The new race is by the death of Christ, so related to the Adamic race, penally, that it must express in perfect continuity, God's condemnation of sin; (2) the center of the new race is the Son of God himself, with a human racial experience completed by suffering; (3) the new race is so constituted that it can be entered only on the most rigid moral terms; (4) the race moves through history as the one thoroughly reliable servant of the moral concern of God; (5) this new race makes it possible for each human being to find a holy completion of himself in his brethren and in his Redeemer in perfect service, rest and joy; and (6) this new race will finally be the victorious realization of God's original design in creation.

CHAPTER XXIV

THE ATONEMENT: ITS NATURE AND EXTENT

Having considered the biblical basis of the atonement, and having traced the development of its leading ideas in the history of the Church, we are now ready to consider more fully, its nature and extent. The word *atonement* occurs but once in the New Testament (Rom. 5:11), the Greek term καταλλαγὴν from which it comes being usually translated reconciliation. The word is of frequent occurrence, however, in the Old Testament, and is from *kaphar* which signifies primarily to cover or to hide. When used as a noun it signifies a covering. In theology it is used to express the idea of satisfaction or expiation. This is the sense in which it is used by the most critical lexicographers. In the English language, it is made to cover a wide range of thought. (1) It denotes that which brings together and reconciles estranged parties, making them at-one-ment, or of the same mind. (2) It denotes also, the state of reconciliation, or the one-mindedness which characterizes reconciled parties. (3) It is sometimes used in the sense of an apology or *amende honorable*. This is a penitential confession, as for instance, the suffering in connection with the beloved dead, because we cannot make "atonement" to them for the wrongs committed against them while they were with us. (4) The word is most frequently used in the sense of a substitute for penalty—a victim offered as a propitiation to God and hence an expiation for sin. (5) The Old Testament idea as indicated, is that of a covering, and therefore applies to anything which veils man's sins from God. (6) It reaches its highest expression in the New Testament where it is used to signify the propitiatory offering of Christ.

The Nature of the Atonement

We shall consider in this division, (1) Definitions of the Atonement; (2) The Ground or Occasion of the Atonement; (3) The Vital Principle of the Atonement; and (4) The Legal Aspects of the Atonement.

Definitions of the Atonement. Mr. Watson defines the atonement as follows: "The satisfaction offered to divine justice by the death of Christ for the sins of mankind, by virtue of which all true penitents who believe in Christ are personally reconciled to God, are freed from the penalty of their sins, and entitled to eternal life" (WATSON, *Dictionary*, p. 108). The definition of Dr. Summers is similar in its import but more specific. "The atonement is the satisfaction made to God for the sins of all mankind, original and actual, by the mediation of Christ, and especially by His passion and death, so that pardon might be granted to all, while the divine perfections are kept in harmony, the authority of the Sovereign is upheld, and the strongest motives are brought to bear upon sinners to lead them to repentance, to faith in Christ, the necessary conditions of pardon, and to a life of obedience, by the gracious aid of the Holy Spirit" (SUMMERS, *Syst. Th.*, I, pp. 258, 259).

Dr. Miley's definition is as follows: "The vicarious sufferings of Christ are an atonement for sin as a conditional substitute for penalty, fulfilling, on the forgiveness of sin, the obligation of justice and the office of penalty in moral government" (MILEY, *The Atonement in*

The idea of the atonement may accordingly be defined as the solution of a certain antithesis in the very life of God as revealed to man, or the apparent opposition between God's love and God's righteousness. Though these attributes are essentially one, yet sin has produced a tension or apparent variance between these two points in the divine mind. Though God eternally loves the world, His actual relation to it is not a relation of love, but of holiness and justice, a relation of opposition, because the unity of His attributes is hindered, restrained. There exists also, a contradiction between the actual and essential relations of God to mankind; a contradiction which can be removed only by the destruction of the interposing principle of sin.—MARTENSEN, *Chr. Dogm.*, p. 303.

Dr. E. H. Johnson thus summarizes the atonement: "The Lord Jesus, by what He was and is, by what He did and bore, has made every provision required by the holy nature of God and the fallen estate of man to deliver men from sin, its penalties and its power."—JOHNSON, *Outline of Syst. Th.*, p. 223.

Christ, p. 23). Dr. Pope does not give a condensed definition of the atonement, but summarizes his position in the following statement: "The teaching of the scripture on this subject may be summed up as follows: The finished work, as accomplished by the Mediator himself, in His relation to mankind, is His divine-human obedience regarded as an expiatory sacrifice: the atonement proper. Then it may be studied in its results to God, as to God and man, and as to man. *First,* it is the supreme manifestation of the glory and consistency of the divine attributes; and, as to this, is termed the righteousness of God. *Second,* as it respects God and man, it is the reconciliation, a word which involves two truths, or rather one truth under two aspects: the propitiation of the divine displeasure against the world is declared; and therefore the sin of the world is no longer a bar to acceptance. *Third,* in its influence on man, it may be viewed as redemption: universal as to the race, limited in its process and consummation to those who believe" (POPE, *Compend. Chr. Th.*, II, p. 263). These definitions set forth the main factors in the atonement.

The Ground or Occasion of the Atonement. "We believe that Jesus Christ, by His sufferings, by the shedding

We have in our possession, an article entitled "The Methodist Doctrine of the Atonement," by Dr. J. J. Tigert, published in the *Methodist Quarterly Review,* April, 1884. This gives one of the best comparative studies of the atonement which we have seen. Dr. Tigert compares Dr. Miley's theory with that held by Dr. Summers and Dr. Pope. In this article the following comparisons, or contrasts are made. In his definition of the atonement, Dr. Summers calls it a satisfaction made to God, which form of expression Dr. Miley not only excludes, but carefully avoids, and stringently opposes since he identifies the theory of satisfaction with the penal substitution theory. Again, Dr. Summers gives the atonement relation to original as well as actual sin, as is done in the second article of the creed. This Dr. Miley's definition ignores, and his whole essay does not touch the question except when he glances at the relation of the atonement to infant salvation. Furthermore, Dr. Summers makes the atonement to consist of the entire mediation of Christ, especially of His sufferings and death, while Dr. Miley speaks only of vicarious sufferings, though he is doubtless in accord with Dr. Summers as is evinced by his masterly treatment of the great passage in the second chapter of Philippians.

Dr. Raymond states his position as follows: "The death of Christ is declarative; is a declaration that God is a righteous Being and a righteous Sovereign. It satisfies the justice of God, both essential and rectoral, in that it satisfactorily proclaims them and vindicates them by fully securing their ends—the glory of God and the welfare of His creatures."—RAYMOND, *Syst. Th.*, II, p. 259.

of His own blood, and by His meritorious death on the cross, made a full atonement for all human sin, and that this atonement is the only ground of salvation, and that it is sufficient for every individual of Adam's race." (Creed: Article IV.) Article II of the Twenty-five Articles as revised by Mr. Wesley, states the purpose of the incarnation in these words: "The Son, who is the Word of the Father, the very and eternal God, of one substance with the Father, took man's nature in the womb of the virgin; so that two whole and perfect natures, that is to say, the Godhead and manhood, were joined together in one person, never to be divided, whereof is one Christ, very God and very man, who truly suffered, was crucified, dead and buried, to reconcile the Father to us, and to be a sacrifice, not only for original guilt, but also for the actual sins of men." The ground or the occasion of the atonement then, is the existence in the world of both original and actual sin, together with the necessity for propitiation. As we have previously indicated, it may be said to be grounded in three necessities: (1) the nature and claims of the Divine Majesty; or the propitiatory idea; (2) the upholding of the authority and honor of the Divine Sovereign, or the governmental idea; and (3) the bringing to bear upon the sinner, the strongest possible motive to repentance, or the moral influence theory.

1. The atonement is grounded in the nature and claims of the Divine Majesty. The nature of God is holy love. In our discussion of the moral attributes (vol. I, pp. 365ff), we pointed out that holiness as it relates to

There are three views of the atonement in Scripture. It is sometimes regarded as the result of a mystery that had been transacted in the divine mind before its manifestation in time. Sometimes, again, it is exhibited as a demonstration of God's love to mankind, and self-sacrifice in Christ for their sake: as it were to move the hearts of men with hatred of sin and desire to requite so much mercy. Strictly speaking, this is not given as an explanation of the atonement. The New Testament does not sanction the idea that our Lord's self-sacrifice is made an argument with sinners. . . . . Lastly, it is set forth as an expedient for upholding the dignity of the Ruler of the universe and Administrator of law. These three views, or to use modern language, theories of the atonement are combined in the Scriptures: neither is dwelt upon apart from the rest. The perfect doctrine includes them all. Every error springs from the exaggeration of one of these elements at the expense of the others.—POPE, *Compend. Chr. Th.*, II, p. 280.

the Father, expresses the perfection of moral excellence, which in Him exists unoriginated and underived; while love is that by which He communicates Himself, or wills a personal fellowship with those who are holy, or capable of becoming holy. By His very nature, He could have no fellowship with sinful beings; and yet His love yearned for the creatures which He had made. Sin rent the heart of God. We may now enter more fully into the profound truth, that sin made man an orphan and left God bereaved. His holiness prevented sinful man from approaching Him, while His love drew the sinner to Him. Propitiation became necessary in order to furnish a common ground of meeting, if holy fellowship was again to be established between God and man. The thought of drawing near is involved in the very nature of propitiation. God himself provided the propitiatory offering. Holy love devised the plan. *Herein is love, not that we loved God, but that he loved us, and sent his Son to be the propitiation for our sins* (I John 4: 10). The Son voluntarily offered himself to do the will of the Father. To His distressed disciples on the way to Emmaus He said, *Ought not Christ to have suffered these things, and to enter into his glory?* (Luke 24: 26). The atonement, therefore, had its origin in God, and propitiation satisfies the infinite depths of His nature as holy love. That propitiation is intended to satisfy the vindictiveness of a wrathful Being, is the false charge of those who would make the nature of God to consist in benevolence instead of holy love, and who, therefore, exalt His goodness to the disparagement of His holiness. Hold firmly to the nature

The expression, the "wrath of God," simply embodies this truth, that the relations of God's love to the world are unsatisfied, unfulfilled. The expression is not merely anthropopathic, it is an appropriate description of the divine pathos necessarily involved in the conception of a revelation of love restrained, hindered, and stayed through unrighteousness. For this wrath is holy love itself, feeling itself so far hindered because they have turned away from its blessed influence whom it would have received into its fellowship. This restrained manifestation of love, which in one aspect of it may be designated wrath, in another aspect is called grief, or distress, in the Holy Spirit of love; and wrath is thus turned into compassion. It is only when the wrath of God is allowed that any mention can be made of His compassion.—MARTENSEN, *Chr. Dogm.*, p. 303.

of God as holy love, and propitiation becomes the deepest fact of the atonement.

2. The atonement is also grounded in a governmental necessity. God as the infinite moral Being, is characterized by the absolute and essential principles of the true, the right, the perfect and the good. These cannot be abrogated, altered or set aside. He has created a race of beings endowed with the same principles of rational intuition. Moral law, therefore, becomes imperative, and moral government a necessity. As moral Governor, God cannot dispense with the sanctions of those eternal and immutable laws under which alone, His creatures can exist. To repeal the sanctions would be to break down the distinctions between right and wrong, give license to sin, and introduce chaos into a world of order and beauty. God cannot, therefore, set aside the execution of the penalty. He must either inflict retributive justice upon the sinner himself, or maintain public justice by providing a substitute. The governmental theory of the atonement, therefore, makes prominent the sacrifice of Christ as a substitute for penalty. It maintains that the death on the cross marked God's displeasure against sin, and therefore upholds the divine majesty and makes possible the forgiveness of sins. On

Dr. Summers presents this phase of the atonement in a strong statement as follows: "Mankind constitute a species: all are 'made of one blood'; they are viewed as a solidarity; all were seminally contained in the primal pair. When our first parents fell, the species fell. If the penalty of the law had been enforced the species would have been cut off. To prevent this disastrous result the atonement was provided. This secured the perpetuation of the species. But it did not so take effect that Adam's posterity are not born in sin. They all partake of his fallen nature. The depravity of mankind is inherited, inherent, universal. But as it would be unjust and cruel to bring multiplied millions of responsible and immortal beings into existence, in this miserable condition, without furnishing them a remedy, the atonement was so devised as to meet all the demands of the case. There is no inherited and inherent depravity in man for which atonement has not been made by Christ. But with the nature they possess and the influences brought to bear upon them, actual, personal transgressions will certainly be committed by them, and this liability to sin will remain as long as they remain in their probationary state. Hence, it were better for them that they had never been born—that everyone had died seminally, as he sinned seminally, in Adam—than that they should be brought into the world with this liability to actual sin, if no provision were made to reach the case; therefore, the atonement is made 'not only for original guilt, but also for the actual sins of men'."—SUMMERS, *Syst. Th.*, I, pp. 261, 262.

this theory, the sacrifice of Christ is regarded as the substitute for public rather than retributive justice.

3. The atonement is further grounded in the appeal of divine love. *Hereby perceive we the love of God, because he laid down his life for us* (I John 3:16). Love is the strongest force in the universe. *We love him, because he first loved us* (I John 4:19). Love is not only God's appeal *to* the sinner; it is also a transforming power *within* him. *God is love; and he that dwelleth in love dwelleth in God, and God in him. Herein is our love made perfect, that we may have boldness in the day of judgment: because as he is, so are we in this world. There is no fear in love; but perfect love casteth out fear: because fear hath torment. He that feareth is not made perfect in love* (I John 4:16-18). The cross of Christ represents at once, the greatest exhibition of God's love for man, and the culmination of man's rebellion against God. Those who view this cross from the standpoint of rebellion shall feel the weight of its eternal condemnation; those who view it from the standpoint of love, find Him to be the propitiation for their sins, and not only so, *but also for the sins of the whole world* (I John 2:2).

The Vital Principle of the Atonement. We must consider the atonement also, as God's method of becoming immanent in a sinful race. We distinguish here between metaphysical and ethical immanence. God is everywhere present in nature; and in so far as his bodily and spiritual constitution are concerned, is immanent in man also. This is the deep meaning of the Apostle

Dr. Sheldon points out that the governmental theory has great advantage over the judicial in that it holds that the work of Christ instead of satisfying distributive justice for any man or number of men, established simply a suitable basis for the proffer of salvation to all men upon equal conditions. But he indicates also that it is quite possible to push the theory too far. He insists that there is no occasion for any disjunction between the personal and governmental in God. In self-consistency He is in the identical plane as Moral Ruler and Divine Person. What is agreeable to His feeling in the one character is agreeable to that feeling in the other. If the ends of good government forbid an unconditional display of indulgence, so also does His personal holiness and justice. He concludes that the governmental theory ought to be so modified in so far as it gives place to the anthropomorphic conception that God is other in His governmental position than He is in His intrinsic nature, or that there is only a lax connection between the two, (cf. SHELDON, *Syst. Chr. Doet.*, pp. 399, 400).

Paul when he says, *in him we live, and move, and have our being* (Acts 17:28). This immanence is not pantheistic. Man is not a mode of the divine existence. He has substantial being in himself, having been created through the Divine Word. But God is not immanent in man's sin or guilt consciousness. Sin has separated between them. And yet, if man is to become God's spiritual son, this divine immanence must be re-established. There must come into his innermost consciousness, the Spirit of His Son, *crying, Abba, Father* (Gal. 4:6). This vital element in the atonement can be brought back into the race only through Jesus Christ. We may further consider this principle under the following aspects:

1. The pre-existent Logos is the ground of unity between Christ and the race, and therefore a fundamental factor in the atonement. As Romans 3:24-26 most completely sets forth the atonement from its Godward and ethical side, so Colossians 1:14-22 most perfectly expresses the cosmical or metaphysical relations between God and man. St. Paul introduces the subject by a reference to the redemptive power of Christ, and then describes His cosmical relations to the world and man as the pre-existent Logos. Christ is *the image of the invisible God, the first born of every creature: for by him were all things created, that are in heaven, and that are in earth, visible and invisible, whether they be thrones, or dominions, or principalities, or powers: all things were created by him, and for him: and he is before all things, and by him all things consist. And he is the head of the body, the church: who is the beginning, the first born from the dead; that in all things he might have the pre-eminence. For it pleased the Father that in him should all fulness dwell; and, having made peace through the blood of his cross, by him to reconcile all things unto himself: by him, I say, whether they be things in earth, or things in heaven* (Col. 1:15-20). Here we have given us, the metaphysical ground of the atonement, in the relations of the Logos to the race. These relations are the closest that can possibly exist short of pantheistic identification. Mankind as a race

depends upon Him, (1) for its origin (through the creative Word); (2) for its continued existence (*consistere,* to stand together, or subsist); (3) for its goal or purpose (all things were made for him); and (4) for its completion or perfection (that He might have the preeminence). These relations, it will be seen, are all-inclusive up to the point of His interposition for the redemption of mankind. Certainly they are deep enough, and wide enough to lay a foundation for anything the Logos may undertake in behalf of men. It is on the ground of this solidarity of the God-man and the race of mankind, or His consubstantiality with us, that it is possible for Him to become a true Representative of the race, and, therefore, bear the penalty due its sin; and (5) having become incarnate, He brings back into the race, the Spirit, of which it had been deprived—the Spirit of life and holiness. Becoming immanent in the race, Christ becomes the efficient ground of both our justification and our sanctification.

2. The Incarnate Logos, or the Word made flesh, represents this vital principle of the atonement in another aspect. What He now undertakes in this immanent relation to mankind, has particular reference to the redemption of the race whose nature He has

Dr. Johnson states, that while we need not be embarrassed by the speculative realism of the scholastics, there is nevertheless, a scientific realism which sees in human nature the common basis of all human existence—a *universalia in re,* a realism which finds in Christ's assumption of our nature, the condition of bearing our evils, and even of drawing more closely that earlier and divine bond, by virtue of which, personally He might stand in our place before God. . . . . Natural science is essentially realistic. The descent of individuals from a common origin, testifies that species is more than succession of individuals; it is an entity perpetuated through individuals. The real existence of species is testified positively by the persistence of type, negatively by the uniform inability of animal hybrids to perpetuate a breach of type. This physical evidence for the entity of race is corroborated by the moral sentiment of solidarity. Nor does it rest solely on the physical fact of a common origin. It would acknowledge as a man a creature just like ourselves from any other world. It is a prudent sentiment because the highest and best of our faculties as earthly beings are the social faculties whose actions knit us together. We are next to nothing except as parts of a whole. In no hazy, speculative sense then, but in conscious and felt reality, human nature is a vast unit, capable of receiving the Divine Logos, and suitable for Him to put on. As He did so, pre-existent relations of His being to ours, made it impossible for Christ to be merely a specimen man, or less than the Son of man, the second Adam, the true Representative of all mankind.—Johnson, *Out. Syst. Th.,* p. 230ff.

assumed. For this reason it is known as the procuring cause of redemption, when applied to its culmination in the death on the cross. All-inclusive as His pre-existent relations were, there is not one which did not through the incarnation attain a new and higher significance. As the Logos, He was the Creator of all things; as the incarnate Christ, He creates men anew. As He gave existence to the race, so now He gives it life. The unjust objection to the atonement as a transfer of penalty from the guilty to the innocent, loses its force when it is seen that this new Representative is the Creator of all men. We are made in His image; we are constituted persons only in Him. We are, therefore, bound to Him in a unique manner, and this new relationship underlies His whole redemptive work. But the pre-existent Logos not only created the universe and man as a part of it, He has so constituted it also, that it must express the holiness of His nature. This He did by connecting happiness with righteousness, and suffering with sin. Therefore, as the Incarnate One, Christ not only brings life back into the race; but having assumed the likeness of sinful flesh, He must endure also, the penalty which comes from the reaction of God's holiness to its sin.

3. The restoration of the Spirit is a further aspect of this vital principle in the atonement, and is generally known as the efficient cause of salvation. As depravity is a consequence of the deprivation of the Spirit, so the bestowal of the Spirit restores man's inner spiritual relations with God. This is shown (1) in the re-establishment of the moral ideal. Man in his fallen condition perceives the right as an ideal, but finds no way to perform that which is good. Depravity did not root out the

> The second Adam also takes the place of humanity; and His sacrificial work must be looked upon as the actual work of humanity itself (*Satisfactio vicaria*). But our inmost consciousness demands that the righteousness and obedience rendered, should not only be without us in another, but should also become personally our own. Now this demand is satisfied by the fact that Christ is our Redeemer as well as our Reconciler: our Saviour who removes sin by giving a new life to the race, by establishing a living fellowship between Himself and mankind. All merely external and unspiritual confidence in the atonement arises from a desire to take Christ as Reconciler without taking Him as Redeemer and Sanctifier.—MARTENSEN, *Chr. Dogm.*, p. 307.

ideal for which man hungers and thirsts, but it did bring him into the bondage of sin and death. Consequently the moral ideal transcends him. It is beyond his experience at every point. The incarnation, then, must be regarded as the supreme embodiment of the moral ideal in human form. The death on the cross was the overcoming of the principle of sin and death in the race, and the establishing of the law of the Spirit of life in Christ Jesus. (Rom. 8:2). Thus the divine immanence through the incarnation, becomes a new life force, operating in an ethical and spiritual manner for the redemption of mankind. (2) Furthermore, the gift of the Spirit made possible the inner reconciliation of the individual believer with God, through sanctification. *For both he that sanctifieth and they who are sanctified are all of one* (Heb. 2:11). Pentecost is the necessary sequel to Calvary. The atonement made objectively by Christ, is applied subjectively by the Spirit. The historic act issues in personal experience. The atonement became a reconciliation within as well as without. By His incarnation and death on the cross, Christ became one with sinners; in justification and sanctification, He becomes legally and vitally one with every individual believer. Thus through redeemed individuals, Christ builds up a new race after the pattern of His own resurrection.

The Legal Aspects of the Atonement. We have dealt with the vital principle in the atonement as God's immanence in the race, through the pre-existent Logos, the incarnation and the bestowal of the Spirit. There is a legal aspect also. By this we do not mean any artificial or merely external arrangement, but simply that the vital principle is the expression of moral and spiritual law. Upon this view, the atonement becomes the transformation and glorification of law. Two questions arise, (1) In what sense did Christ fulfill the law? and (2) In what sense does He absolve us from it?

 1. Christ fulfilled the whole range of moral demand. It was the satisfaction of those laws which were involved in the atoning act itself, or which He encountered in the

work of redemption. We may, however, regard the law as a unity, or a single moral demand, in which case we must consider it in at least four different aspects. (1) Christ fulfilled the moral law generally, including the Mosaic expression of it. The principles of truth, righteousness, perfection and goodness were embodied in Him as a perfect expression of the moral ideal. (2) By taking upon Himself the likeness of sinful flesh, He came under the operation of the law of sin and death. Regarded negatively, this is the law of holiness. Christ suffered death at the hands of sinners, and bore in Himself the consequences of their sin. (3) He obeyed the law of filial love and devotion. Though a Son, He was made perfect through sufferings, and in no instance did His perfect Sonship please the Father more than in His vicarious death for sinners. (4) Thus He fulfilled at once the claims of love and of justice.

2. Christ delivers us from the law. But in what sense? Certainly not in the antinomian sense of abrogating all law. Why abrogate that which He came to fulfill? St. Paul gives us the true sense. *God sent forth his Son, made of a woman, made under the law, to redeem them that were under the law, that we might receive the adoption of sons* (Gal. 4: 4, 5). The atonement therefore does not do away with the law, but it does deliver men from its legal consciousness by becoming the ground of justification. Thus the idea of justification in the New Testament is lifted above mere external legalism in that it is "by faith." Justification by faith is God's plan of enabling sinful men to pass from the legal to the filial consciousness—a redemption from the law in order to the adoption of sons. This is St. Paul's way of deliverance from Jewish legalism. The faith principle changes the formal and legal side of justification into something vital and spiritual. The vital-life-union is thus combined with the formal declaration and the whole process is lifted from the lower plane of legal bondage, to the new and higher plane of spiritual sonship.

The Vicarious Expiation

By vicarious suffering or punishment, we do not mean merely that which is endured for the benefit of others, but that which is endured by one person instead of another. The two ideas of substitution and satisfaction necessarily belong to the word in its common acceptation. We have seen, both from the Scriptures and from the history of Christian doctrine, that the idea of satisfaction rests in the twofold nature of Christ as a theanthropic Being. It was upon this basis of the surrender and obedience of Christ that the scholastics built up their theory of merit. Reacting against the exaggerated position given to the church in Roman Catholicism, the Protestant Reformers again fell back upon the teachings of the Scriptures and the early fathers, and Christ alone was made the central principle of redemption. Satisfaction, therefore, was rendered by One who was both God and man. His human nature involved the penal suffering of which the divine was incapable; and the Divine Person gave infinite worth to the sacrifice.

> Dr. E. H. Johnson takes the position that Christ bore our sins (I) Historically, in that coming to recover a revolted race, He declared the law of God fully, and consequently received the full force of sin's opposition. It was a bearing of all sin, not through a reckoning to Christ of our several acts of sin, but by virtue of the fact that the principle of sin as antagonism against God, went all the length against Him whom God had sent (cf. John 6:29, 3:18). (II) Ethically, Christ bore the sin of the world. (1) As one of the limitations imposed by the human upon the divine in His person, Christ accepted whatever moral evils were compatible with His paternity. The only such evil of which we have evidence was that of temptation. Note how extreme were the temptations in the wilderness renewed at the close of his mission, each corresponding to each, in the suggestion that possibly the cup might pass from Him; in the knowledge that twelve legions of angels were ready to deliver Him; and in the particular satanic challenge of priests and scribes, "Let him now come down from the cross" (Matt. 27:42). That to be thus tempted was inconceivably painful, none can doubt. He "suffered being tempted" (Heb. 2:18). (2) But that union which imposed limitation upon the divine, so enlarged the powers of the human, that Christ bore the burden of human sin upon His sympathies to an extent impossible to man. He felt the extent of the calamity which He sought to repair. (3) A woe for which we cannot with certainty account, and at which He was Himself astonished, deepens the mystery of His death. He lost the sense of His Father's presence. The fact is not affected by the attempted explanations. It is certain that His soul was filled with the horror of "outer darkness." In any case it was occasioned by the sins of men. Human guilt could lay upon Him no further burdens. He had tasted of the second death, and the sacrifice was complete.—JOHNSON, *Out. Syst. Th.*, p. 230ff.

Guilt was regarded as of infinite magnitude, in that it was an offense against the absolute holiness of God. Christ as the God-man, was then, the only being capable of making an atonement for sinners.

This argument was sustained by a further reference to the incarnation. These two natures, the human and the divine, were in His person, perfect and complete. His Godhead was neither impaired nor reduced by His personal union with human nature; and His humanity was likewise full and complete, in that no quality was omitted in order to make place for the divine nature. Therefore, in Him, humanity had received God, and God had received humanity. Consequently He represents before God, all that sinful humanity is to God and owes to God; and He represents to man, all that God means to him in redeeming grace. This representation the Scriptures regard as both subjective and vital, and as outward and legal. Subjectively, Christ is perfectly identified with the human race and therefore qualified in every way to be its true Representative; objectively, by His death on the cross, He fully propitiates the divine nature, and thereby expiates human sin. Propitiation, therefore, becomes the dominant idea of the atonement; and this because it is the ground of restored fellowship, is seen to be the deepest fact in holy love. The Scriptures declare of Christ, that He is our propitiation, and through faith in His blood, there is granted the remission of sins that are past (cf. Rom. 3:25).

The Propitiatory Aspect of the Atonement. In asserting that the propitiatory aspect of the atonement gives us the true idea of satisfaction and expiation, we do not deny that other aspects are involved. But we do hold that these grow out of, and are subsidiary to, the dominant idea of propitiation. We give as our reasons, the following:

1. Propitiation has reference to the divine nature. This nature is holy love. God cannot tolerate sin, nor can He hold fellowship with sinners. This is true, not on

the mere caprice of will, but as an essential and eternal verity. *For what fellowship hath righteousness with unrighteousness? and what communion hath light with darkness?* (II Cor. 6:14). God's nature being that of holy love, He cannot exhibit this love apart from righteousness, and therefore, must maintain the honor of His divine sovereignty. This He does, not from any external expediency, but from His essential and eternal nature. Furthermore, love cannot be exhibited apart from holiness. The moral influence theories, therefore, which overlook the fact that there can be no fellowship between God and man except on the plane of holiness, are to say the least inadequate if not false. There can be no possible objection then, to the governmental idea, if it is not given prominence above propitiation; nor can there be any criticism of the idea of the moral influence, if this be considered as holy love.

That the idea of propitiation is the dominant note in the Wesleyan type of Arminian theology is shown by the following statement, and the appended notes. "Our Saviour's sacrifice on the cross finished a perfect obedience which He offered in His divine-human person. This was His own obedience, and therefore of infinite value or worthiness; but it was vicarious, and its benefit be-

The necessity for propitiation arises out of the separation produced by sin between God and man. As this separation certainly concerns God as well as man, the necessity for propitiation is not only a human but a divine necessity. . . . . The living action of God's love in His world has been hindered and stayed by sin; and consequently it hovers round the divine holiness and rectitude as a demand which has not been fulfilled in the world of unrighteousness; a requirement which finds expression in this—that the divine love, which must be manifested actively, must yet remain in abeyance; that God must retain the revelation of His love in the depths of possibility instead of allowing it to flow forth freely. . . . . But though we also teach that the essence of God is unchangeable love, we at the same time maintain that the active life of God's love in the world must needs have been interrupted by sin, and that a love, whose holy and righteous claims could not thus be injured and wounded would not be true love. The notion of God's greatness, which considers Him too high to require an atonement, differs nothing from the notion that He is too high to be grieved by sin, that as the atonement does not affect Him, so neither does sin affect Him. We, on the contrary, believe that sin is against God, that it does concern Him, that it disturbs His divine relations toward us, and therefore we cannot rest satisfied with that seeming reconciliation which is effected on earth but not in heaven. He has only a superficial perception of sin who can rest satisfied with it.—MARTENSEN, *Chr. Dogm.*, pp. 302, 305.

longs absolutely to our race, and on certain conditions, to every member of it. As availing for man, by the appointment of God, it is no less than satisfaction, provided by divine love, of the claims of divine justice upon transgression: which may be viewed, on the one hand, as an expiation of the punishment due to the guilt of human sin: and, on the other, as a propitiation of the divine displeasure, which is thus shown to be consistent with infinite goodwill to the sinners of mankind. But the expiation of guilt and the propitiation of wrath are one and the same effect of the atonement. Both suppose the existence of sin and the wrath of God against it. But, in the mystery of the atonement, the provision of eternal mercy, as it were, anticipates the transgression, and love always in every representation of it has the pre-eminence. The passion is the exhibition rather than the cause of the divine love to man" (POPE, *Compend. Chr. Th.*, II, p. 264).

2. Not only is propitiation concerned with the nature of God as holy love, it involves a consideration of the divine attributes as well. The tendency to exalt one attribute above another, has been the source of much error in theology. If we bear in mind that the attributes are to be regarded as modes, either of the relation or the

In speaking of the death of Christ as a governmental expedient, Dr. Raymond says, "This theory is objectional, not because it teaches that the death of Christ is a governmental measure, but because it teaches that it is solely that, and implies that it is only one of several expedients that might have been adopted. Beyond all question, the death of Christ secures governmental ends, the same ends as would be secured by the execution of the penalty, and secures them as fully and effectually as the actual infliction of penalty would do, if not more so. But a demonstration that the government of God is a righteous government, or that God is a righteous governor, is not itself necessarily a complete and adequate declaration of God's righteousness. He is just, not only in the administration of law, but is also essentially just in inherent character." —RAYMOND, *Syst. Th.*, II, pp. 253, 254.

Viewed as His own, the expiatory work of Christ was a perfect spontaneous obedience and a perfect spontaneous sacrifice to the will of the Father imposed upon Him. The two terms may be regarded in their difference and in their unity as constituting the act and the virtue of the atonement. Its worthiness, or what is sometimes called its merit, connects it with the human race, and depends on two other truths: it was not due for Himself, but was the act of infinite charity for man; and that act was divine, both in its value and in its efficiency. The offering of the Redeemer had infinite efficacy for the human race.—POPE, *Compend. Chr. Th.*, II, p. 265.

operation of the divine essence, it will be seen that they must of necessity be in harmony with each other. There can be no strife between mercy and justice, no lack of harmony between truth and righteousness. *Mercy and truth are met together; righteousness and peace have kissed each other* (Psalms 85:10). The nature of God as perfection is all-harmonious. Hence every attribute or perfection of His nature sanctions also His law. Wisdom is vindicated in the creation of moral beings, and power in His sovereign righteousness. Truth cannot be set aside. Goodness and mercy have their place. But true goodness cannot allow anything which in the slightest degree connives at sin or reflects upon the holiness of God. Benevolent love is as much concerned in law and order as are justice and truth. Thus the nature of God as expressed in the revelation of His perfections, not only demands, but devises a method of propitiation. *Herein is love, not that we loved God, but that he loved us, and sent His Son to be the propitiation for our sins* (I John 4:10).

An Exposition of the Scripture Terms Used to Express the Idea of Atonement. In our study of the Biblical Basis of the Atonement, we grouped together certain scriptures according to the Greek terms, or family of terms, from which the translations were made. These terms were propitiation (ἱλασμός), redemption (λύτρον), and reconciliation (καταλλάσσω). We arranged them in this order to show (1) the sacrifice made to God as the ground of redemption, (2) the redemptive price paid for the salvation of men; and (3) the consequent reconciliation effected between God and mankind. It is evident, however, that the word reconciliation, having both a Godward and manward aspect, is in the former sense

---

The attributes of God are glorified both singly and unitedly, and in a transcendent manner, by the mediation of the Incarnate. This indeed is included in the meaning of the prayer that the name of God might be glorified in His Son; for that name is not only the triune name, but the assemblage of the divine perfections. Throughout the Old Testament and the New the divine glories, especially those which we may in this connection call the glories of the moral attributes, are condensed over the mercy-seat: receiving from it their highest illustration. There is a gradational display of the eternal majesty.—POPE, *Compend.*, II, p. 277.

closely related to the idea of propitiation. It is for this reason that Dr. Pope says that "there are two Greek terms, or families of terms, on which hang all the details of the doctrine just laid down: ἱλασμός and καταλλαγή are their representatives. The relations of these are clear and distinct in the original scriptures; but they are to some extent confused in our present English translation. . . . . Both these verbs have God for the subject and not for the object. The Supreme Being reconciles the world to Himself; it is not said that He is reconciled: this simply gives expression to the great truth that the whole provision for the re-establishment of peace is from above. God is reconciled to man, but *in Christ* who is Himself God: He therefore is the Reconciler while He is the reconciled. So also the word expiate refers to an act of God: it is not said that He is propitiated, but that He propitiates Himself or brings Himself near by providing an expiation for the sin. Strictly speaking the atoning sacrifice declares a propitiation already in the divine heart" (POPE, *Compend. Chr. Th.*, II, pp. 271, 272).

In Romans 3:25, the word for propitiation is *hilasterion* (ἱλαστήριον), which is the neuter form of the adjective *hilasterios* (ἱλαστήριος), and when used as a noun, is translated propitiatory or expiatory. It refers to the lid or covering of the ark of the covenant which stood in the holy of holies. This is the place where God manifested Himself, the Shekinah appearing between the cherubim and over the mercy-seat. Here it was that the blood was sprinkled, and consequently it came to be known as the propitiatory or place of atonement. Two things must be noted: (1) the atonement or propitiation was made in the presence of God; and (2) the sprinkling of the blood made possible the exhibition of mercy, and a drawing near to God. The word ἱλαστήριον is by Robinson, and most lexicographers, translated sin-offering, or an expiatory sacrifice. Since the word is used in connection with redemption "through faith in his blood," it shows clearly that both propitiation (ἱλαστήριον) and the redemptive price (ἀπολύτρωσις) refer to the sacrificial death of Jesus. The atonement, therefore, is the propitiation made, and the price paid down, for the salvation of men. Christ Jesus is the true propitiatory—the divine and human meeting in Him as the one theanthropic person. The sacrifice was His own blood. Beneath that sprinkled blood, mercy is extended to all mankind. All men may draw near in full assurance of faith. Above that sprinkled blood is the Shekinah, the living flame guarded by holiness and righteousness. Zacharias the priest seems to have blended together all the symbolism of the holy of holies in an interpretative passage of marvelous spiritual insight. Being filled with the Holy Spirit, he prophesied saying, *The oath which he sware to our father Abraham, that he would grant unto us, that we being delivered out of the hand of our enemies might serve him without fear, in holiness and righteousness before him, all the days of our life* (Luke 1: 73-75).

In Hebrews 9: 28 we have another expression which clearly shows the expiatory character of Christ's ministry. Here the word is *anaphero* ($\dot{\alpha}\nu\alpha\phi\acute{\epsilon}\rho\omega$), which according to Robinson means "to bear up our sins, to take upon oneself and bear our sins, i.e., to bear the penalty of sin, to make expiation for sin." The reference is to the active phase of Christ's priestly work. He is regarded as the Offerer rather than as the offering, as Priest rather than as sacrifice. Under the Old Testament economy, it was the function of the high priest to make atonement, or expiation for the sins of the people. By this means they were restored to favor with God, and became the recipients of the blessings of the covenant. So also Christ laid hold of our nature, that in all things *he might be a merciful and faithful high priest in things pertaining to God, to make reconciliation* [$\iota\lambda\acute{\alpha}\sigma\kappa\epsilon\sigma\theta\alpha\iota$ or propitiation] *for the sins of the people* (Heb. 2: 17). Thus He secured for them the blessings of a better covenant of which He became the Mediator, that is, the promise of the Spirit, and the law written within their hearts. The active phase of Christ's work as propitiator in bringing God near to men, is further set forth by the writer of this epistle in these words, *And having an high priest over the house of God; let us draw near with a true heart in full assurance of faith, having our hearts sprinkled from an evil conscience, and our bodies washed with pure water* (Heb. 10: 21, 22).

In Hebrews 10: 10, we have the counter truth, or the passive phase of Christ's work as a propitiatory offering. He is here regarded not as a priest but as a sacrifice. It is the subjective rather than the objective aspect of the atonement. Hence a new set of terms is introduced. These deal not so much with justification or the work of Christ done *for* us, as with sanctification, or the work wrought *in* us by the Holy Spirit. Sin as we have seen, not only entails guilt but defilement. In actual sins, there is guilt in the double sense of culpability *(reatus culpœ)* and liability to punishment *(reatus pœnœ)*. In original sin there is guilt only in the sense of liability to punishment *(reatus pœnœ), the guilt of culpability (reatus culpœ)* having been removed by the free gift of grace. The defilement which attaches to actual sin is known as acquired depravity. This is removed by initial sanctification, which is concomitant with justification and regeneration. The defilement which attaches to original sin is known as inherited depravity, and is removed by entire sanctification. Hence the guilt of sin, whether as attaching to actual or original sin, is removed by the propitiatory or expiatory offering of Christ's blood; while the consequences or defilement of sin—either acquired or original, is removed by the renewing of the Holy Spirit in His sanctifying power. We have, therefore, another set of terms, *katharizein* (καθαρίζειν) and *hagiazein* (ἁγιαζέιν), one applying to the cleansing from guilt, the other to the cleansing from defilement. Thus *The blood of Jesus Christ his Son cleanseth* [καθαρίζει] *us from all sin* (I John 1: 7); that is as a sacrifice which removes the guilt of sin by expiation. Again, *By the which will we are sanctified* [ἡγιασμένοι] *through the offering of the body of Jesus Christ once for all* (Heb. 10: 10). This latter is the cleansing from the defilement of original sin or depravity, as is shown further by the statement that *by one offering he hath perfected for ever them that are sanctified. Whereof the Holy Ghost also is a witness to us* (Heb. 10:14, 15). Here is a removal of defilement by the renewing of the Holy Spirit in his sanctifying offices.

The last set of terms we shall mention in this connection, are those from which we have our word reconciliation. Here the Greek word is *katallassein* (καταλλάσσειν) which means to exchange, or to change the relation of one person to another, generally in the sense of an exchange of enmity for friendship. This is the word from which we have atonement, in its strict literal sense of an at-one-ment, or reconciliation. The word καταλλαγὴν is translated atonement in Romans 5:11 *by whom we have now received the atonement.* In reality, it carries with it the idea of reconciliation, and would have been better so translated. In Hebrews 2:17 *to make reconciliation for the sins of the people,* the word ἱλάσκεσθαι may well have been translated atonement, or to be more exact, propitiation. In Ephesians 2:16, and Colossians 1:20, 21, the word used is *apokatallassein* (ἀποκαταλλάσσειν) which is an intensive form and signifies to reconcile fully. Dr. Pope indicates that the verb *katallassein* (καταλλάσσειν) signifies the virtue of the mediation of Christ as composing a difference between man and God; while *katallage* (καταλλαγή) applies to the result, or the new relation in which the world stands to God. This term must be given further consideration in a later paragraph.

The Godward and Manward Aspects of the Atonement

We have seen that the words propitiation, reconciliation and redemption are used in the scriptures to set forth the atonement, (1) in relation to God; (2) in relation to God and man; and (3) in relation to man. Propitiation deals with the divine aspect of the atonement; reconciliation with the double aspect of its Godward and manward relations; and redemption with the manward aspect. In our discussion of the propitiatory aspect of the atonement, we endeavored to show that the high priestly work of Christ served as the one great oblation both for the remission of sins, and as the satisfaction of the claims of divine justice. We must now consider the atonement as an accomplished fact, that is, as reconciliation and redemption.

The Atonement as Reconciliation. Reconciliation is that aspect of the finished work which expresses the restored fellowship between God and man. It must be viewed, therefore, both in its Godward and manward relations. But since God provided the atonement or propitiatory offering, he must be regarded as both the Reconciler and the Reconciled. Man must also be regarded as reconciled, but this aspect of the atonement is best treated under the head of redemption.

1. God is the Reconciler and the Reconciled. It is sometimes objected that God could not both demand and provide an atonement, but this objection is only apparent. Man was created both as dependent upon God and as a free and responsible creature. The atonement satisfies both of these relations. The Scriptures are specific at this point. *All things are of God, who hath reconciled ($καταλλάξαντος$) us to himself by Jesus Christ, and hath given to us the ministry of reconciliation ($καταλλγῆς$); to wit, that God was in Christ, reconciling ($καταλλάσσων$) the world unto himself; not imputing their trespasses unto them; and hath committed unto us the word of reconciliation* [$καταλλαγῆς$] (II Cor. 5:18, 19). Here it is said that God has not only provided the propitiatory offering Himself, but He has associated His people with Him in the proclamation, having committed to them the word of reconciliation. Two errors need to be guarded against at this point. (1) We must not regard God as having been angry with us in the sense of a hostility to be overcome by the sacrifice of an innocent victim, for God himself is the Reconciler. (2) We must not suppose that God was induced to feel compassion for man, only after Jesus had by His suffering fulfilled the demands of violated law. It was His love that gave the Son, that *whosoever believeth in him should not perish, but have everlasting life* (John 3:16). Love has never acted more freely than in providing through the incarnation and

atonement, the breaking down of all the barriers between man and God. Here it is "love outloving love," a grace that superabounded where sin abounded.

2. The reconciliation refers also to the state of peace existing between God and man. In this sense it is sometimes used as one of the titles of our Lord's work. Thus *we also joy in God through our Lord Jesus Christ, by whom we have now received the atonement* (or reconciliation) (Rom. 5: 11). As Christ is called "the Lord of our righteousness," so also He is known as our "reconciliation" or our "peace" (Eph. 2: 14-16). We may say then, that in the Old Testament an amnesty was established, *through the forbearance of God* (Rom. 3: 25); but in the New Testament, this amnesty becomes an established peace. Furthermore, we are to understand that through the vicarious sufferings and death of Jesus Christ, God reconciled the world to Himself, removing from it, as a world, His displeasure. Thus a general peace was established as the basis for God's acceptance of the believer into the rights and privileges of the new order. The reconciliation of individual believers is the acceptance through faith of this general reconciliation, and is therefore always regarded as the revelation of God's mercy in the souls of believers. This St. Paul definitely teaches us. *For if, when we were enemies, we were reconciled to God* [κατηλλάγημεν] *by the death of his Son, much more, being reconciled* [καταλλαγέντες], *we shall be saved by his life* (Rom. 5: 10). When, therefore, the reconciliation is received in faith, it becomes a personal state of righteousness and peace.

The Atonement as Redemption. The term redemption from λυτρόω, to buy back, and λύτρον, a purchase price, represents Christ as buying back, or laying down a purchase price for the deliverance of men from the bondage of sin. Like reconciliation, redemption also has its objective and subjective aspects. Objectively, the entire race is redeemed in that the purchase price has been paid for all mankind. Subjectively, as it applies to the individual, redemption is provisional and is made effective only through faith in the atoning blood. Dr. Pope arranges the terms which apply to redemption in four classes as follows: (1) those in which the *lutron* (λύτρον) or ransom price is included; (2) those which mean purchase generally, such as *agorazein* (ἀγοράζειν); (3) those which imply only release, as from *luein* (λύειν); and (4) those which indicate the notion of forcible rescue, as *ruesthai* (ῥύεσθαι). It is evident that we are more concerned with the first class of terms, since we are discussing the atonement solely in relation to the finished work of Christ. We shall consider (1) the ransom price, and (2) the bondage from which men are delivered.

1. The ransom price is the blood of Christ, although our Lord speaks of giving His *life a ransom for many* (Matt. 20:28), and St. Paul says, He gave *himself a ransom for all* (I Tim. 2:6). Doubtless the sense of these passages is that He laid down His life as being in the blood, and therefore as the God-man, who "being dead still lived" became the ever-blessed Substitute, suffering vicariously in the stead of all men, and making full satisfaction for the sins of the people. The sacrifice which He offered was not the blood of irrational animals, but His own precious blood (I Peter 1:18, 19). By this *one offering he hath perfected for ever* [τετελείωκεν, made a perfect expiation for] *them that are sanctified* (Heb. 10:14). Therefore those who reject this method of salvation must eternally perish, for there remaineth no more sacrifice for sins. By this is meant, not that God refuses to save any who come to Him, but those who reject the only way of salvation provided, must by virtue of this rejection, forever remain in their sins.

2. The ransom price secured for mankind the deliverance from the bondage of sin. This deliverance is sometimes mentioned as a redemption, (1) from the curse of the law (Gal. 3:13); (2) from the law itself (Gal. 4:4, 5, cf. Rom. 6:14); (3) from the power of sin (John 8:34, cf. Rom. 6:12-23); and (4) from the power of Satan (Heb. 2:15). If we use the expression "bondage to sin" in the broader sense, we shall see the force of the earlier Wesleyan position that we are redeemed (1) from the

guilt of sin; (2) from the reigning power of sin; and (3) from the inbeing of sin. The first results in justification; the second in regeneration, and the third in entire sanctification. Thus we make the transition from our study of the atonement proper, to a consideration of its benefits. In closing this section, we need only mention that Christ does not lay down the purchase price merely to redeem us from wrath and release us to our own ways. He ransoms us back into His own rights over us, which thus marks the connection between His priestly and His kingly offices.

Theological Modification of Terms. Our historical survey has given the broader outlines in the doctrinal development of the atonement, and we need now to give only a brief summary of some of the later and more specific changes. (1) *Atonement.* The word as used in the New Testament is from καταλλαγή which in most places is translated reconciliation. It is, therefore, rather a legal term and in its exact signification is best expressed as at-one-ment, or reconciliation. In theological terminology, however, it has come to mean the whole economy of our Lord's sacrificial ministry, with special emphasis upon the virtue of the sacrifice by which the reconciliation is effected. Theology, therefore, uses the term in its Old Testament significance. (2) *Satisfaction.* During the Reformation period the idea of satisfaction was added to that of expiation, and was given a specific meaning. It is not used in theology now to express the general idea of merit, but to express the relation which the work of Christ sustains to the demands of law and justice. The character and degree of this satisfaction as held in theology, ranges from the full exaction of the penalty of the law inflicted upon a substitute, through the equivalent of that penalty, or a substitute for penalty, on down to the *acceptilatio* of the Socinians, who held that forgive-

---

Propitiation, from *prope,* near, indicates in the Bible that the favor and good pleasure of God is attracted to the sinner by the mediation of Jesus. He is the propitiation because in Him God is brought nearer to man the sinner than even to man the unfallen. The fact that holy wrath is turned away through the atoning satisfaction is a secret behind the incarnation: in the very essence of the Triune God.—POPE, *Compend. Th.,* II, p. 275.

ness of sins was merely by word of mouth without the requirement of satisfaction. (3) *Expiation*. This term differs from that of satisfaction, in that instead of referring the sacrifice to the claims of the law and the honor of the Lawgiver; it refers it to sin and the sinner. By expiation is meant the doing away with guilt and the cancelling of the obligation to punishment. (4) *Propitiation*. This term bears almost the same relation to expiation as does satisfaction. The wrath or displeasure of God is propitiated, the sin is expiated. But propitiation differs from satisfaction in its primary significance in that it is not a satisfaction of the claims of justice—for justice cannot be propitiated, but is an appeasement of wrath or an allaying of displeasure. The word comes from *prope,* meaning near, and indicates that God and man are brought near to each other through the satisfaction of the atonement.

The Extent of the Atonement

The atonement is universal. This does not mean that all mankind will be unconditionally saved, but that the sacrificial offering of Christ so far satisfied the claims of the divine law as to make salvation a possibility for all. Redemption is therefore universal or general in the provisional sense, but special or conditional in its application to the individual. It is for this reason that the universal aspect is sometimes known as the sufficiency of the atonement. While the claims of reason may anticipate the universality of the atonement, it is to the positive assertion of Scripture that we must turn for our final authority. Two scripture texts taken in their relation to each other, stand out with peculiar distinctness. The first is the statement of our Lord, that *the Son of man came . . . . to give his life* [ψυχὴν] *a ransom* [λύτρον] *for many* [πολλῶν] (Matt. 20:28). The second is generally considered to be the last statement of St. Paul on this subject, and is evidently a quotation from the previous Scripture. *Who gave himself* [ἑαυτον] *a ransom* [ἀντίλυτρον] *for all* [πάντων] (I Tim. 2:6). Note that each of the principal words is given in a stronger connotation—

the life becomes the self, the purchase price, the personal Redeemer, and the many, the all.

The scripture passages bearing upon this subject have already been presented in a general way, and we need here merely to give additional references. We group them according to the following simple outline. (1) Those scriptures which speak of the atonement in universal terms: (John 3:16, 17; Rom. 5:8, 18; II Cor. 5:14, 15; I Tim. 2:4, 4:10; Heb. 2:9; Heb. 10:29; II Peter 2:1; I John 2:2, 4:14). (2) Those which refer to the universal proclamation of the gospel and its accompaniments: (Matt. 24:14; 28:19; Mark 16:15; Luke 24:47. Cf. also Mark 1:15; Mark 16:16; John 3:36; Acts 17:30); (3) Those which distinctly declare that Christ died for those who may perish: (Rom. 14:15; I Cor. 8:11; Heb. 10:29).

Arminianism with its emphasis upon moral freedom and prevenient grace, has always held to the universality of the atonement; that is, as a provision for the salvation of all men, conditioned upon faith. Calvinism on the other hand, by its doctrine of the decrees, its unconditional election, and its penal satisfaction theory, has always been under the necessity of accepting the idea of a limited atonement. Thus Turretin says, "The mission and death of Christ are restricted to a limited number—to His people, His sheep, His friends, His Church, his body; and nowhere extended to all men severally and collectively" (TURRETIN, *The Atonement*, pp. 125, 126). It should be said, however, that the Calvinistic idea of a limited atonement does not grow out of a belief in its insufficiency; for Calvinists as well as Arminians believe in the sufficiency of the atonement. "All Calvinists agree," says Dr. A. A. Hodge, "in maintaining earnestly that Christ's obedience and sufferings were of infinite intrinsic value in the eyes of the law, and that there was no need for Him to obey or suffer an iota more nor a moment longer, in order to secure, if God so willed, the salvation of every man, woman and child that ever lived" (A. A. HODGE, *The Atonement*, p. 356). The difficulty, therefore, does not lie in the insufficiency of the atonement, but in their belief in predestination. "By the decree of God, for the manifestation of His glory, some men and angels are predestined unto everlasting life, and others foreordained to everlasting death" (*Westminster Confession*). The primary question, then, concerns the doctrine of grace and not the sufficiency of the atonement. We shall, therefore, take up the subject of predestination in connection with our discussion of prevenient grace and effectual calling.

The Benefits of the Atonement. Closely related to the question as to the extent of the atonement, is that of the benefits of the atonement. Within the range or scope of the redemptive work, all things are included, both spiritual and physical. Every blessing known to man is the result of the purchase price of our Lord Jesus Christ, and comes down from the Father of lights. These benefits are generally considered under two main heads, (1) The Unconditional Benefits; and (2) The Conditional Benefits.

1. The Unconditional Benefits include, (1) The continued existence of the race. It is hardly conceivable that the race would have been allowed to multiply in its sin and depravity, had no provision been made for its salvation. Yet had it not been for the divine intervention, the immediate death of the first pair would doubtless have taken place, and with it the termination of their earthly career. (2) The restoration of all men to a state of salvability. The atonement provided for all men unconditionally, the free gift of grace. This included the restoration of the Holy Spirit to the race as the Spirit of enlightenment, striving and conviction. Thus man is not only given the capacity for a proper probation, but is granted the gracious aid of the Holy Spirit. Both of these subjects have been given extended treatment in our discussion of the problem of sin. (3) The salvation of those who die in infancy. We must regard the atonement as accomplishing the actual salvation of those who die in infancy. This we may admit is not stated explicitly in the Scriptures, and in the past, has been the subject of much debate. The general tenor of the Scriptures, how-

ever, when viewed in the light of divine love and the universal grace of the Spirit, will allow no other conclusion. When our Lord declared that *Except ye be converted, and become as little children, ye shall not enter into the kingdom of heaven* (Matt. 18:3); and again, *Suffer little children, and forbid them not, to come unto me: for of such is the kingdom of heaven* (Matt. 19:14), there can be no reasonable doubt as to His meaning. Dr. Raymond sums up the generally accepted Arminian position as follows: "The doctrine of inherited depravity involves the idea of inherited disqualification for eternal life. The salvation of infants, then, has primary regard to a preparation for the blessedness of heaven—it may have regard to a title thereto; not all newly created beings, nor those sustaining similar relations, are by any natural right entitled to a place among holy angels and glorified saints. The salvation of infants cannot be regarded as a salvation from the peril of eternal death. They have not committed sin, the only thing that incurs such a peril. The idea that they are in danger of eternal death because of Adam's transgression, is, at most, nothing more than the idea of a theoretic peril. But if it be insisted that 'by the offense of one, judgment came upon all men to (a literal and actual) condemnation,' we in-

Dr. Fairchild, a Calvinistic theologian, takes this position on the question of infant salvation. "The case of infants dying before moral agency begins is not set forth in the Scriptures. Our ideas on the subject must be wholly speculative, inference from our ethical philosophy. In the first place we can affirm, without misgiving, that such an infant is not a sinner, and cannot need forgiveness; yet he may have a share in the atonement in a variety of ways. . . . . If the race had been propagated without an atonement, it would have been a doomed race. No one could be punished without sin; but all, upon attaining responsibility, would fall into sin, and die without hope. We may conceive that the benefit of the atonement reaches the infant in the other world. He passes into that world without an established character of righteousness; he finds himself in the society of the redeemed, of those who in this life have been recovered from sin, and forgiven through the atonement. The character and experience of these saints may be of advantage to him; he may be brought up in righteousness under their care, and thus become directly a partaker of the atonement. . . . . Without the atonement, heaven might have been to infants what Eden was to the human race: a place where there was no experience, and where the moral influences were feeble; but received into the family of the redeemed in heaven, these infants are surrounded by all the experiences and moral forces which have accumulated in the Church below and the Church above. Thus the infant, dying before moral agency begins, may have a part in the song of Moses and the Lamb."—FAIRCHILD, *Elements of Theology*, pp. 165, 166.

sist that from that condemnation, be it what it may, theoretic or literal, all men are saved; for *by the righteousness of one the free gift came upon all men unto justification of life,* so that the condition and relations of the race in infancy differ from those of newly created beings solely in that, by the natural law of propagation, a corrupted nature is inherited. As no unclean thing or unholy person can be admitted into the presence of God and to the society of holy angels and glorified saints, it follows that if infants are taken to heaven some power, purifying, sanctifying their souls, must be vouchsafed unto them; the saving influence of the Holy Spirit must be, for Christ's sake, unconditionally bestowed. Not only their preparation for, but also their title to, and the enjoyment of the blessedness of heaven comes, as came their existence, through the shed blood of our Lord Jesus Christ" (RAYMOND, *Systematic Theology,* II, pp. 311, 312).

2. The Conditional Benefits of the Atonement are (1) Justification, (2) Regeneration, (3) Adoption, (4) The Witness of the Spirit, and (5) Entire Sanctification. These must furnish the subjects for our discussion of the states of salvation. Before taking up these subjects, however, we must first give attention to the offices and work of the Holy Spirit as the Administrator of the great salvation purchased through the atonement of our Lord Jesus Christ.

The Intercession of Christ. There is another transitional point which needs to be mentioned, in addition to the conditional benefits of the atonement enumerated above. This is the intercession of Christ. The New Testament does not teach that the work of Christ ceased with the coming of the Holy Spirit. It teaches that His finished work of atonement was only the ground for the work of administration, which He himself was to continue through the Spirit. He died for the sins of the past, that He might establish a new covenant; He arose that He might become the executive of His own will. His continued activity consists in carrying into effect through the Spirit, the merits of His atoning death. *He ever liv-*

eth to make intercession for them (Heb. 7:25); *It is Christ that died . . . . who also maketh intercession for us* (Rom. 8:34); and *If any man sin, we have an advocate with the Father* (I John 2:1). As a consequence of Christ's intercession for us, the Holy Spirit is given as an intercessory presence within the hearts of men. *Likewise the Spirit also helpeth our infirmities: for we know not what we should pray for as we ought: but the Spirit itself maketh intercession for us with groanings which cannot be uttered. And he that searcheth the hearts knoweth what is the mind of the Spirit, because he maketh intercession for the saints according to the will of God* (Rom. 8:26, 27). The intercession of Christ at the right hand of God, and the intercession of the Spirit within, are in perfect harmony, for the Spirit takes the things of Christ and shows them to us. It is to this rich field of the Holy Spirit's offices and work, that we now turn our attention.

PART IV. THE DOCTRINE OF THE HOLY SPIRIT

CHAPTER XXV
THE PERSON AND WORK OF THE HOLY SPIRIT

As the incarnate Son is the Redeemer of mankind by virtue of His atoning work, so the Holy Spirit is the Administrator of that redemption; and as there has been in the Holy Scriptures a progressively unfolding revelation of the Son, so also, there has been a corresponding revelation of the Spirit. We may note then, in an introductory manner, the four following propositions concerning the Holy Spirit. *First*, the Holy Spirit is a Person. That He is not merely a sacred influence, but the third Person of the adorable Trinity, is everywhere admitted in the Scriptures and in the creeds. For while both the Father and the Son are holy; and while both are called Spirit, yet the term "Holy Spirit" as a title is applied to neither of them. *Second*, the Holy Spirit has been progressively revealed to the Church. The Holy Spirit could not be fully revealed until after the Incarnation, and that for two reasons, (1) the Holy Spirit is the Person who completes the Godhead, as indicated in our study of the Trinity; and therefore of necessity is the last to be made manifest. (2) There is no analogy or counterpart in nature, as in the case of the Father and the Son, to assist us in interpreting the ineffable distinction of the Holy Spirit. Hence it was only as a resting-place for human thought had been provided by the Incarnation, that the threefold distinctions of the Godhead could come clearly into view, and thus the personality of the Holy Spirit be made known. *Third*, the Holy Spirit could not come as the Administrator of Christ's atoning work until His earthly ministry was completed. Hence the Holy Spirit could not be fully revealed until after the death, resurrection and glorification of Christ. *Fourth*, the Holy

William Newton Clarke says that a practical definition of the Holy Spirit is "God in man." It is God working in the spirit of man, and thereby accomplishing the results that are sought in the mission and work of Christ.—WILLIAM NEWTON CLARKE, *Outline of Chr. Th.*, p. 369.

Spirit as a Person was fully revealed at Pentecost. We must therefore regard Pentecost as the inauguration day of the Holy Spirit, at which time He came in His own proper Person as the inner Advocate of the Church—the Paraclete or Comforter. We may therefore in the words of the creed, declare that "In no respect do we separate the Holy Spirit, but we adore Him, together with the Father and the Son, as perfect in all things, in power, honor, majesty and Godhead" (Creed of 369 A.D.).

The Holy Spirit as a Person. The Scriptures abound with references to the personality of the Holy Spirit, but these have been previously considered in our discussion of the Trinity, and need not be repeated here. One question, however, which often proves troublesome, needs explanation. "Why is the Spirit sometimes referred to in the neuter gender?" Dr. George B. Stevens states that "since the word πνεῦμα or spirit is grammatically neuter, all pronominal designations of the Spirit which have πνεῦμα for their immediate antecedent, must, of course, be neuter. These words obviously have no bearing upon the question of the personality of the Spirit. That which is of especial importance in this connection is that as soon as πνεῦμα ceases to be the immediate antecedent of pronouns designating the Spirit, masculine forms are employed" (STEVENS, *Johannine Theology*, pp. 195, 196). As an illustration of this, two scripture references may be cited (John 14:26 and 15:26), which show the force of this change in pronouns—*the Holy Spirit which* [ὅ] *the Father will send in my name, he* [ἐκεῖνος] *shall teach you all things; and the Spirit of truth, which* [ὅ] *proceedeth from the Father, he* [ἐκεῖνος] *shall bear witness of me* (R.V.). It is evident that when

According to William Adams Brown, the doctrine of the Holy Spirit, historically considered is an inheritance from Israel. Originally denoting the energy of God which came upon men to fit them for special work connected with the upbuilding of the divine kingdom (Exod. 31:3; Judges 6:34; 14:6), the Spirit came to be conceived as the immanent life of God in the soul of man. Its marks became prevailingly ethical and spiritual, and the convincing proof of its presence is a character acceptable to God. The conception of the Spirit of God as an abiding presence is further developed in Christianity, and finds its clearest expression in the writings of John and Paul.—WILLIAM ADAMS BROWN, *Chr. Th., in Outline*, p. 397

not prevented from doing so by the grammatical construction, St. John always designates the Spirit by masculine pronouns which denote personality. We may say, then, that the personality of the Spirit as separate and distinct from Christ, may be summed up in two general statements: (1) the Holy Spirit is described by personal designations; and (2) various personal activities are predicated of Him.

The Holy Spirit in His Preparatory Economy. While the full dispensation of the Holy Spirit does not begin until Pentecost; the Spirit himself, as the Third Person of the Trinity, was from the beginning, operative in both Creation and Providence. It was the Spirit who brooded over the waters, and brought order and beauty out of chaos (Gen. 1:2); and it was the Spirit who breathed into the face of man and made him a living soul (cf. Gen. 2:7, Job 33:4). He has been the Agent in the production of all life, and is therefore, by prophetic anticipation, the Lord and Giver of life. But it is in the specific preparations of the gospel economy that His agency is set forth. We have seen in our discussion of the Person of Christ, that the revelation of the Son was mediated by the Spirit of Christ which was in the prophets (I Peter 1:10-12); and that the record of the gospel in the Old Testament was given by His inspiration. The Spirit, therefore, no less than the Son, was the promise of the Father, and this in a twofold manner. There is both a forward and a backward look—the Spirit being given in fulfillment of the promise; and given also as the earnest of a promise yet unfulfilled. The crowning promise of the Father was the gift of the Holy Spirit at Pentecost.

The work of the Holy Spirit in His relation to mankind after the fall assumes four principal forms, of which Abel, Abraham, Moses and the prophets are representa-

Dr. George B. Stevens tells us that the rendering "the Comforter" for ὁ παράκλητος, dates back to Wycliffe's translations, and has been perpetuated in almost all later versions of English Bibles, including our Revised Version. It is formed from the Latin *con* and *fortis*, *confortare* and means "one who strengthens." While in these various versions the word παράκλητος, is rendered "Comforter" in the Gospel of John, it is translated "Advocate" in the First Epistle (2:1), a fact which is probably due to a similar variation in the rendering found in several ancient versions.—STEVENS, *Johannine Theology*, p. 190.

tive types. There is *first,* the direct striving of the Spirit with the consciences of men, in a purely personal and private manner. Abel yielded to these strivings and offered the sacrifice of faith, thereby obtaining witness that he was righteous; while Cain, offering the fruits of his own labor, was rejected. The wickedness of men increased, until at the time of the flood, the condemnation of God was expressed in these fearful words, *My spirit shall not always strive with man, for that he also is flesh* (Gen. 6: 3). The family of Noah linked the old world to the new, and the Spirit still continued his striving under new and less degenerate conditions. *Second,* there is the operation of the Spirit through the family. The promises were made to *Abraham and his seed* (Gal. 3: 16); and hence Abraham looked forward to the "City of God" (Heb. 11: 8-10). The family forms a new order, a new locality for the Spirit's communications, and implies a more definite hold upon the race. The success of the Spirit in the Chosen Family is thus summed up by St. Paul, *to whom pertaineth the adoption, and the glory, and the covenants, and the giving of the law, and the service of God, and the promises; whose are the fathers, and of whom concerning the flesh Christ came, who is over all, God blessed forever* (Rom. 9: 4, 5). The called out family was the *ecclesia* or the Church in germ; and therefore the first historical beginning of a religious community.

The *third* stage in the operations of the Spirit is to be found in the giving of the law. To the internal strivings, therefore, was added an external mode of appeal. The moral law within man's nature demanded an objective stimulus in order to revive its operations and set it forth in clearer light. Hence St. Paul declares that the law was added *because of transgressions, till the seed should come to whom the promise was made; and it was ordained by angels in the hand of a mediator* (Gal. 3: 19). In the process of history, the inner light became dim and variable, and the Chosen Family enslaved and degraded. God therefore sent Moses to deliver His people from social bondage and give them the guidance of a written law to supplement the inner workings of the conscience, which no longer operated with strength and precision. This law was moral, ceremonial and judicial. That portion known as the Ten Commandments is said to have been given by "the finger of God," an expression which is interchangeable with "the Spirit of God" (cf. Matt. 12:28 and Luke 11:20). The law served to give permanence to the moral ideal. Further, its violation involved guilt, for by the law is the knowledge of sin (Rom. 3:20). The law being given by the voice of God from heaven, sin not only clashed with the sense of right within, but also with the external voice of the law. It became, therefore, in a very manifest sense, an offense against God. Man's sense of sin having been dulled, God in the law gave him a written transcript from His own moral nature. The *fourth* and last method of the Spirit's operations in the preparatory economy, is found in the voice of the prophets, *Holy men of God spake as they were moved by the Holy Ghost* (II Peter 1:21). The law being a fixed instrument, men soon began to give more attention to its outward forms than to its inward spirit. Hence the prophets arose, who appealed to the hopes and fears of men, and thus gave inward content to the outward forms. While these revelations were transient, given at sundry times and in divers manners, the body of prophecy itself was cumulative and expansive. The prophetic order, therefore, marked a distinct advance by appealing to the law, by furnishing a devotional literature and especially by directing men's attention to the promised Redeemer. The order became permanent only in Christ to whom all the prophets pointed and in whom all their prophecies were fulfilled (Luke 1:70).

The Holy Spirit and the Incarnation. Having traced the operations of the Spirit to the time of the Incarnation, we must now consider His part in this great mystery for which all other dispensations were but preparatory. The Incarnation was accomplished by the Holy Spirit. As the bond of union between the Father and the Son, it was appropriate that He should effect the high and singular union between the uncreated and the created natures in the One Person of Christ. And being the bond of love between the Father and the Son, the Holy Spirit as the Minister of this union, becomes thereby the highest expression of the love of God for His creatures. And further still, the Holy Spirit being the perfecting Person of the Godhead, prepares and perfects the Mediator for His official work, and thereby effects the salvation of men. In this way alone are men restored to communion and fellowship with God.

The mystery of the Incarnation made possible the unveiling of the Holy Spirit as the Third Person of the Trinity. Until the Annunciation, the Holy Spirit had never been revealed as a distinct Personal Agent. Never before had He been called by His own name. Previous to that time He was always mentioned in connection with the other Divine Persons. In the penitential Psalm it is *take not thy holy spirit from me* (Psalms 51:11); and in Isaiah, *they rebelled, and vexed his holy Spirit* (Isa. 63:10). Consequently the term is used relatively and not in the absolute sense. The full disclosure of His personality and perfections was not made until the set time for His inauguration. Only when Christ had been fully glorified at the right hand of the Father could the Holy Spirit come in the fullness of His pentecostal glory.

The Holy Spirit and the Earthly Ministry of Jesus. During His mediatorial ministry, the Son alone did not act through His humanity. This humanity was also the temple of the Holy Spirit, which God gave to Him without measure (John 3:34). We may say, then, by way of

Paræus in his *Notes on the Athanasian Creed,* gives the following reasons for the incarnation of the second Person of the Trinity, rather than the first or the third. First, that by the incarnation the names of the Divine Persons should remain unchanged; so that neither the Father nor the Holy Spirit should have to take the name of a Son. Second, it was fitting that by the Incarnation men should become God's adopted sons, through Him who is God's natural Son. Third, it was proper that man, who occupies a middle position between angels and beasts, in the scale of creatures, should be redeemed by the middle Person in the Trinity. Last, it was proper that the fallen nature of man which was created by the Word (John 1:3) should be restored by Him. In addition to these reasons, it is evident that it is more fitting that a father should commission and send a son upon an errand of mercy, than that a son should commission and send a father (cf. SHEDD, *Dogm. Th.,* II, p. 266).

discrimination, that whatever in the Incarnation belonged to the Son as the Representative of Deity, was the act of His own eternal Spirit as the Son; whatever belonged to Him as the Representative of man was under the immediate direction of the Holy Spirit. Not only was Christ's body prepared for Him by the Holy Spirit, but His entire earthly ministry was likewise presided over by the Spirit. Hence, as Christ was the theanthropic or God-man, made like unto His brethren in order to become a merciful and faithful High Priest (Heb. 2:17); so the Holy Spirit, who guided and sustained Him in every experience of His earthly life, became in a peculiar sense the Spirit of the incarnate Christ. Dwelling in the human nature of the theanthropic Person, the Spirit searched not only the deep things of God (I Cor. 2:10-13), but also the full depths of human nature. As the Son was perfected officially for His mediatorial ministry through suffering (Heb. 2:10-13), so the Holy Spirit became the prepared Agent, who as the Spirit of Christ was able to take hold of the whole being of man "by its very roots." While this subordination of the Son to the Spirit ceased when the Redeemer laid down His life of Himself, and through the eternal Spirit—or His own essential deity, offered Himself without spot to God (Heb. 9:14); it was not until the session that He was restored to the full glory which He had with the Father before the world was (John 17:5). Here He received of the Father the promise of the Holy Spirit; and by a strange reversal, He who was presided over by the Spirit during His humiliation, now in His exaltation becomes the Giver of that same Spirit to the Church (Acts 2:33).

The Holy Spirit as the future Agent of Christ's ministry was the object of prophecy during our Lord's

Christ was under the guidance of the Holy Spirit during His earthly life rather than under the independent agency of His divine personality. Our Lord's human nature was sealed and consecrated and enriched with sevenfold perfection by the Spirit given to Him not by measure. This particular subordination ceased when the Redeemer laid down His life of Himself, and through the Eternal Spirit, His own essential divinity, offered Himself to God for us. Until then, however, the Son as such did not act through His human nature alone. His own divine supremacy is in abeyance, and, as the Representative of man, He is, like us, led of the Spirit.—POPE, *Compend. Chr. Th.*, II, p. 155.

earthly life. This appears first in the words, *How much more shall your heavenly Father give the Holy Spirit to them that ask him?* (Luke 11:13), which, as Dr. Pope indicates, bears the same relation to the Holy Spirit as the protevangelium bears to the work of the Son. It is the dawn of the pentecostal day. The second prediction took place at the close of the great day of the feast, when Jesus stood and cried, saying, *If any man thirst, let him come unto me, and drink* (John 7:37). In a parenthetical expression St. John explains that our Lord referred to the Spirit, *which they that believe on him should receive: for the Holy Ghost was not yet given: because that Jesus was not yet glorified* (John 7:39). The full and complete foreannouncement, however, was not given until the eve of the crucifixion, and is found in the farewell discourses of Jesus (John 14:16, 17, 26). Here it is distinctly declared that the Comforter, as the Spirit which dwelt in Christ, should dwell in His people also. This Comforter or Paraclete, is the Spirit of truth, and as such is the Revealer of the Person of Christ. He will not speak of Himself during the Pentecostal age, but will glorify only the Son, taking the things of Christ and making them known to the Church. As the Son came to reveal the Father, so the Holy Spirit comes to reveal the Son. The farewell discourses of Jesus, therefore, in a peculiar sense, furnish us with a revelation of the Trinity —the unity of the one God in the distinction of the three Persons.

The Dispensation of the Holy Spirit

Pentecost marks a new dispensation of grace—that of the Holy Spirit. This new economy, however, must not be understood as in any sense superseding the work of Christ, but as ministering to and completing it. The New Testament does not sanction the thought of an economy of the Spirit apart from that of the Father and the Son except in this sense—that it is the revelation of the Person and work of the Holy Spirit, and therefore the final revelation of the Holy Trinity. Here, too, the economical aspect of the Trinity is the more prominent as emphasizing the distinction in offices. *All things that the Father hath are mine: therefore said I, that he shall take of mine, and shall shew it unto you* (John 16:15). As the Son revealed the Father, so the Spirit reveals the Son and glorifies Him. *No man can say that Jesus is the Lord, but by the Holy Ghost* (I Cor. 12:3). The mediatorial Trinity, one in essence and distinct in office, affords the true explanation of the dispensation of the Holy Spirit. His work as the Third Person of the Trinity is therefore in connection with His offices as the Representative of the Saviour. He is the Agent of Christ, representing Him in the salvation of the individual soul, in the formation of the Church, and in the witnessing power of the Church to the world. But He is not the Representative of an absentee Saviour. He is our Lord's ever-present other Self. This is the meaning of the promise, *I will not leave you comfortless: I will come to you* (John 14:18). It is through the Spirit, therefore, that our Lord enters upon His higher ministry—a ministry of the Spirit and not merely of the letter. For this reason He said, *It is expedient for you that I go away: for if I go not away, the Comforter will not come unto you* (John 16:7). In the Old Testament God used history to teach spiritual truth by means of divinely given symbols; in Christ as the historical Person, this truth was actualized in human experience; in the New Testament the fullness of grace and truth revealed in Christ is through the Holy Spirit universalized and made available to the Church.

There is a sense in which Pentecost introduced a new economy: that of the Holy Ghost, as the final revelation of the Holy Trinity. The One God, known in the Old Testament as Jehovah, a name common to the Three Persons, was then made known in the Third Person: the Lord the Father, the Lord the Son, is the Lord the Spirit (II Cor. 3:17). Hence the glory of the Day of Pentecost, excelling in glory every former manifestation of the Supreme. The Shekinah, the ancient symbol of the future incarnation of the Son tabernacling in flesh, becomes the fire of the Holy Ghost, disparted into tongues, and without a veil, resting on the entire Church. The perfect God is perfectly revealed; but revealed in the Trinity of Redemption, the Economical Trinity. The Church is the "habitation of God through the Spirit." From that day forward the Holy Ghost is essential to every exhibition of God as revealed among men.—POPE, *Compend. Chr. Th.*, II, p. 326.

The Inaugural Signs. Pentecost was the inauguration day of the Holy Spirit. As in the Old Testament the Passover marked the deliverance of Israel from Egyptian bondage, and Pentecost celebrated the giving of the law fifty days later; so in the New Testament Christ our Passover was sacrificed for us, and the Pentecost which followed marked the ushering in of a dispensation of inward law (Heb. 8:10; 10:16). The pentecostal Gift was the gift of a Person—the Paraclete or Comforter. This Gift Jesus promised to His disciples as the Agent through whom He would continue His office and work in a new and more effective manner. As the Advent of Christ was attended by miraculous signs, so also the inauguration of the Holy Spirit was attended by signs indicative of His Person and Work. These signs were three, *first,* the sound as of a rushing mighty wind; *second,* the cloven tongues like as of fire resting upon the disciples; and *third,* the gift of other tongues. We may say, then, that the first sign was the harbinger of His coming; the second indicated His arrival; and the third marked at

When our Lord cried *It is finished!* He declared that His work of atonement was accomplished. But it was accomplished only as a provision for the salvation of men. The application of the benefit remained for the administration of the Spirit from heaven; whose sole and supreme office it is to carry into effect every design of the redemptive economy or undertaking. As the Spirit of the Christ had from the foundation of the world administered the evangelical preparations, so now He acts on behalf of the fully revealed Christ. Through Him our Lord continues His prophetic office: the Holy Ghost is the Inspirer of the new Scriptures and the Supreme Teacher in the new economy. Through Him the priestly office is in another sense perpetuated: the ministry of reconciliation is a ministration of the Spirit. And through Him the Lord administers His regal authority.—Pope, *Compend. Chr. Th.,* II, p. 328.

The Holy Spirit is called an Advocate because He transacts the cause of God and Christ with us, explains to us the nature and importance of the Great Atonement, shows the necessity of it, counsels us to receive it, instructs us how to lay hold on it, vindicates our claim to it, and makes intercessions in us with unutterable groanings. Our Lord makes intercession for us by negotiating and managing, as our Friend and Agent, all the affairs pertaining to our salvation. And the Spirit of God maketh intercession for the saints, not by supplication to God in their behalf, but by directing and qualifying their supplications in a proper manner, by His agency and influence upon their hearts; which according to the gospel scheme, is the peculiar work and office of the Holy Spirit. So that God, whose is the Spirit, knows what He means when He leads the saints to express themselves in words, desires, groans, sighs, or tears; in each God reads the language of the Holy Ghost, and prepares the answer according to the request.—Adam Clarke, *Chr. Th.,* p. 174.

once the assumption of His office as Administrator, and the beginning of His operations.

The first inaugural sign was that of the *rushing mighty wind* which filled all the house where they were sitting (Acts 2:2). While the account is brief, we may draw the following conclusions from the data at hand: (1) The sound came suddenly, not as winds ordinarily arise by increased intensity, but was at its height immediately. (2) The sound came from heaven, probably as thunder, heard not only by the disciples but throughout the city. The Revised Version reads as follows: *When the sound was heard, the multitude came together* (v. 6), indicating that it was the sound that attracted them and not the reports of the disciples as is sometimes urged. This sign is indicative of the inner, mysterious, spiritual power of the Holy Spirit which was to characterize His administration in the Church and in the world. There is another rendering of this text which brings out added beauties of the Spirit of grace. It may be translated, *the sound of a mighty wind, rushing along,* conveying the thought of an intense eagerness on the part of the Spirit, to carry into effect the great salvation purchased by the blood of Christ.

The second inaugural sign was the appearance of *cloven tongues like as of fire* which sat upon each of them (Acts 2:3). From the use of the singular pronoun, it has been argued that the holy fire like a living flame hovered over the entire company, parting or cleaving into tongues which reached out to each of the waiting company. The generally accepted position, however, is that a cloven or forked tongue sat independently upon each of the disciples. These tongues "like as of fire" were glowing, lambent and quivering flames which gleamed like a corona above the heads of the spiritual Israel, recalling the signs at Mount Sinai, when the Lord descended in fire and the whole mount quaked greatly (Exod. 19:18). The significance of this symbol is to be found in the purifying, penetrating, energizing and transforming effect of the Spirit's administration; while the cloven tongues signify the different gifts communicated by the

314   CHRISTIAN THEOLOGY

one Spirit to the different members of the mystical body of Christ.

The third inaugural sign occupies a unique position in the events of the day. It must be regarded not only as a sign of the Spirit's coming, but in some sense also, as the actual beginning of the Spirit's operations. It is described as follows: *And they were all filled with the Holy Ghost, and began to speak with other tongues as the Spirit gave them utterance* (Acts 2:4). It is a significant fact that the words *heterais glossais* (ἑτέραις γλώσσαις) or "other tongues" appear only in this scripture which describes the phenomena of Pentecost. In the account of the gift of the Spirit to the Samaritans, ten years after Pentecost (Acts 10:46); and to the Ephesians, about twenty-three years after Pentecost (Acts 19:6, the word *heterais* (ἑτέραις) does not appear. In the Greek language, the word *glotta* (γλῶττα) or tongue, always stands in strong contrast with the word *logos* (λόγος) or reason. Hence the contrast between the *logos* and the *glotta,* is the difference between that which a man thinks with the mind, and that which he utters with the vocal organs. Ordinarily of course, the *glotta* follows the *logos;* but at Pentecost the Holy Spirit by a miraculous operation enabled the disciples to declare the wondrous works of God in such a manner that the representatives of the nations heard them in their own languages. As the word *logos* (λόγος) connotes the idea of reason or intelligence, so the word *glotta* (γλῶττα) connotes the idea of rational utterance or an intelligible language. It may and often does signify an ecstatic utterance, but never a mere jargon of sounds without co-

The word γλῶσσα or γλῶττα means "tongue" and is so translated in James 1:26 and 3:5-8. The word γλῶτται or λγῶσσαι or "tongues" is hence a language as in Acts 2:11 and I Cor. 12:10, 28. "A man's thinking," says Dr. Kuyper, "is the hidden, invisible, imperceptible process of the mind. Thought has a soul, but no body. But when the thought manifests itself and adopts a body, then there is a word. And the tongue being the movable organ of speech, it was said that the tongue gives a body to the thought. Hence in the Greek word, from which this word is taken, the word λγῶτται or γλῶσσαι means tongues, and hence language."

Hutchings points out that Protestantism accepted this interpretation, and hence in the Preface for Whitsun-Day, speaks of the Spirit as giving to the disciples "the gift of **divers languages.**"

herence or intelligibility. The Church has always maintained that the true interpretation of the phenomena of Pentecost is that the "other tongues" referred to the miraculous gift of "divers languages."

The Offices of the Holy Spirit. The Holy Spirit is both Gift and Giver. He is the Gift of the glorified Christ to the Church, and abides within it as a creating and energizing Presence. This center of Life and Light and Love is the Paraclete or the abiding Comforter. Following His inauguration at Pentecost, the Holy Spirit be-

Dr. Kuyper maintains that since speech in man is the result of his thinking, and this thinking in a sinless state is an inshining of the Holy Spirit, speech, therefore, in a sinless state would be the result of inspiration, the inbreathing of the Holy Spirit. But sin has broken the connection, and human speech is damaged by the weakening of the organs of speech, the separation of tribes and nations, by the passions of the soul, by the darkening of the understanding, and principally by the lie which has entered in. Hence that infinite distance between this pure and genuine human language, which as the direct operation of the Holy Spirit upon the human mind, should have manifested itself, and the empirically existing languages which separate the nations. But the difference is not intended to remain. Sin will disappear. What sin destroyed will be restored. In the day of the Lord, at the wedding feast of the Lamb, all the redeemed will understand one another. In what way? By the restoration of a pure and original language upon the lips of the redeemed, which is born from the operation of the Holy Spirit upon the human mind. And of that great, still tarrying event, the Pentecost miracle is the germ and the beginning; hence it bore its distinctive marks. In the midst of the Babeldom of the nations, on the day of Pentecost the one pure and mighty human language was revealed which one day all will speak, and all the brethren and sisters from all the nations and tongues will understand. And this was wrought by the Holy Spirit. They spake as the Spirit gave them utterance. They spoke a heavenly language to praise God, not of angels, but a language above the influence of sin. Hence the understanding of this language was also a work of the Holy Spirit.—KUYPER, *Person and Work of the Holy Spirit,* p. 137ff.

Dr. Hutchings in his "Person and Work of the Holy Spirit" states that the gift of tongues on the day of Pentecost was a gift of divers languages, and that the difficulty of believing the literal truth will not be great to those who hold that language from the first was the gift of God to man, and who further accept the history of the building of Babel and view the distinctions of language as connected with that event. Those who attempt to minimize the miraculous element in Holy Scripture, reduce the gift of tongues to a sort of ecstatic utterance, the deliverance of certain inarticulate sounds; or suppose that the miracle was in the hearers rather than in the speakers, which, if it were so, would only make it more wonderful. Extraordinary gifts accompanied the founding of the Church, and lingered on through the Apostolic age more or less, and perhaps afterward. As they were the distinct results of the Spirit's presence and operation, they are still latent in the temple of the Spirit, only their exercise may be suspended. They have, however, their natural counterparts. The Apostle Paul enumerates nine such gifts of the Spirit (p. 114).

came the Executive of the Godhead on earth. While He abides perpetually in the Church, this does not imply that He is not still in eternal communion with the Father and the Son in heaven. As we have previously pointed out, arrival in one place does not with God necessitate the withdrawal from another. It does mean, however, that the Holy Spirit is now the Agent of both the Father and the Son, in whom they hold residence (John 14: 23), and through whom men have access to God. There is therefore a twofold intercession. As the Son is the Advocate at the right hand of the Father, so the Holy Spirit is the Advocate within the Church; and as the Son was incarnate in human flesh, so the Spirit of God becomes incarnate in the Church—but with this difference; in Christ the divine and human natures were immediately conjoined, while in the Church as the body of Christ, they are mediated through the Living Head. Christ is the "only begotten" Son of God; men are sons by the adoption of Jesus Christ to Himself (Eph. 1: 5, 6).

The Holy Spirit as the *Giver*, or Administrator of redemption, ministers in two distinct though related fields—that of the fruit of the Spirit, and that of the gifts of the Spirit. In his enumeration of the graces and gifts, St. Paul catalogs nine graces (Gal. 5: 22, 23), and nine gifts (I Cor. 12: 8-10), the former referring to character, and the latter to personal endowments for specific vocations.

Dr. A. J. Gordon says that when Christ, our Paraclete with the Father, entered upon His ministry on high, it is said that He "sat down at the right hand of God." Henceforth heaven is His official seat until He returns in power and great glory. So also when He sent another Paraclete to abide with us for the age, He took His seat in the Church, the Temple of God, there to rule and administer till the Lord returns. There is but one "Holy See" upon earth: that is, the seat of the Holy One in the Church, which only the Spirit of God can occupy without the most daring blasphemy.—GORDON, *The Ministry of the Spirit*, pp. 130, 131.

Dr. Abraham Kuyper mentions the presence of the Holy Spirit in three modes: (1) there is the omnipresence of the Holy Spirit in space, the same in heaven and in hell, among Israel and among the nations; (2) there is a spiritual operation of the Holy Spirit according to choice, which is not omnipresent: active in heaven but not in hell: among Israel, but not among the nations; and (3) this spiritual operation works either from without, imparting losable gifts, or from within, imparting the gift of salvation.—KUYPER, *Person and Work of the Holy Spirit*, pp. 119, 120.

The fruit of the Spirit is the communication to the individual of the graces flowing from the divine nature, and has its issue in character rather than in qualifications for service. It is the outflow of divine life which follows as a necessary consequence of the Spirit's abiding presence. The apostle may have had in mind the parting parable of our Lord concerning the Vine and the branches. *I am the true vine, and my Father is the husbandman. Every branch in me that beareth not fruit he taketh away: and every branch that beareth fruit, he purgeth it, that it may bring forth more fruit ...I am the vine, ye are the branches. He that abideth in me, and I in him, the same bringeth forth much fruit: for without me ye can do nothing* (John 15:1-5). Here the Spirit is not mentioned, but is assumed as the life of the vine, giving character and quality to the fruit. That which obstructs the free flow of life affects the fruit; hence there must be a purging in order to an increased fruitage. This fruit is not named, but St. Paul catalogs nine graces—a trinity of trinities as follows: (1) in relation to God, love, joy and peace; (2) in relation to others, longsuffering, gentleness and goodness; and (3) in relation to ourselves, faithfulness, meekness and temperance (or self-control). These qualities the apostle sets in strong contrast with the *works* of the flesh (Gal. 5:19-23). Fruit grows by cultivation. It receives its life from the vine and takes its character from that life. Works are the result of effort and human striving; fruit is the consequence of the Spirit's abiding. It is not of man's producing, it grows by the life that is in the Vine.

The gifts of the Spirit are known in Scripture as *charismata* (χαρίσματα) or gifts of grace. Hence there is an internal connection between the graces and the gifts in the administration of the Spirit. The gifts are the divinely ordained means and powers with which Christ endows His Church in order to enable it to properly perform its task on earth. Paul summarizes the teachings of the Scriptures concerning spiritual gifts as follows: *Now there are diversities of gifts, but the same Spirit. And there are differences of administrations, but the same Lord. And there are diversities of operations, but it is the same God which worketh all in all. But the manifestation of the spirit is given to every man to profit withal. For to one is given by the Spirit the world of wisdom; to another the word of knowledge by the same Spirit; to another faith by the same Spirit; to another the gifts of healing by the same Spirit; to another the working of miracles; to another prophecy; to another discerning of spirits; to another divers kinds of tongues; to another the interpretation of tongues: but all these worketh that one and the selfsame Spirit, dividing to every man severally as he will* (I Cor. 12: 4-11). There are two other scriptures from the same writer which refer to the gifts of the Spirit in a more official capacity. The first is found in the Epistle to the Ephesians and is concerned with the general order of the ministry. *And he gave some, apostles; and some, prophets; and some, evangelists; and some, pastors and teachers* (Eph. 4: 11). The second is concerned with the gifts which attach to the ordinary service of the Church. *Having then gifts differing according to the grace that is given unto us, whether prophecy, let us prophesy according to the proportion of faith; or ministry, let us wait on our ministering: or he that teacheth, on teaching; or he that exhorteth, on exhortation: he that giveth, let him do it with simplicity; he that ruleth, with diligence; he that sheweth mercy, with cheerfulness* (Rom. 12: 6-8).

The gifts of the Spirit, then, are supernatural endowments for service, and are determined by the character of the ministry to be fulfilled. Without the proper functioning of these gifts, it is impossible for the Church to succeed in her spiritual mission. Hence the subject is of great importance, not only to theology, but to Christian experience and work. It will, however, be impossible to deal adequately with the subject here, and hence we can give only a brief summary of the more important truths concerning spiritual gifts. (1) The gifts of the Spirit must be distinguished from natural gifts or endowments, although there is admittedly, a close relation between them. While they transcend the gifts of nature, yet they function through them. Grace quickens the powers of the mind, purifies the affections, and enables the will to energize with new strength; and yet the gifts of the Spirit transcend even sanctified human powers. The strength of the Church is not in the sanctified hearts of its members, but in Him who dwells in the hearts of the sanctified. It is the indwelling Spirit who divides to every man severally as He will, and then pours His own energy through the organism which He has created. (2) There is a diversity of gifts in the Church. Not all members are similarly endowed. Hence in a series of rhetorical questions St. Paul asks, *Are all apostles? are all prophets? are all teachers? are all workers of miracles?* (I Cor. 12:29, 30). Nine such gifts are mentioned—wisdom, knowledge, faith, miracles, healing, prophecy, discernment of spirits, tongues, interpretation of tongues (I Cor. 12:7-11). Doubtless the Spirit takes into account the ability of sanctified nature, and its capacity to receive and function spiritually, but the energizing power is not the natural spirit alone, it is *the power that worketh in us* (Eph. 1:19). (3) The gifts of the Spirit take their character from the positions which the various individual members occupy in the mystical body of Christ. St. Paul compares the Church as a spiritual organism, to the natural human body with its many and varied members. As the functions of the several members of the body are determined by the nature of the organs—the eye for seeing and the ear for hearing, so it is in the body of Christ. The Spirit who

Dr. Adam Clarke refers to the parallel drawn by Bishop Lightfoot between the offices and the gifts mentioned in I Cor. 12:8-10, 28, 29, 30, these texts being arranged in three columns. Dr. Clarke then remarks that if the reader thinks this is the best way of explaining these different offices and gifts, he will adopt it, and he will in that case consider, (1) That the word or doctrine of wisdom comes from the apostles. (2) The doctrine of knowledge, from the prophets. (3) Faith, by means of the teachers. (4) That working of miracles includes the gifts of healing. (5) That to prophesy, signifying preaching which it frequently does, has helps as the parallel. (6) That discernment of spirits, is the same with governments, which Dr. Lightfoot supposes to imply a deeply comprehensive, wise and prudent mind. (7) As to the gift of tongues, there is no variation in either of the three places. (ADAM CLARKE on I Cor. 12:31.)

creates the spiritual body, of necessity creates the members which compose that body, *for the body is not one member, but many* (I Cor. 12:14). God has set the members in the natural body as it has pleased Him (I Cor. 12:18); so also the Spirit divides to every man severally as He will in the spiritual body (I Cor. 12:11). The gifts of the Spirit, therefore, are those divine bestowments upon individual members which determine their functions in the body of Christ. Consequently *the eye cannot say unto the hand, I have no need of thee: nor again the head to the feet, I have no need of you.... that there should be no schism in the body; but that the members should have the same care one for another* (I Cor. 12:21-25). (4) The gifts of the Spirit are exercised in conjunction with, and not apart from, the body of Christ. The human body cannot function through maimed and lifeless members, nor can members separated from the body exist, much less perform their natural functions. So, also, God does not bestow extraordinary gifts upon men to be administered through mere human volition, and for self-glory and aggrandisement. The true gifts of the Spirit are exercised as functions of the one Body, and under the administration of the one

Dr. George B. Stevens states that the gifts of the ministry here mentioned are to set forth the basis of unity, rather than as a description of the various offices in the Church. Prophecy or preaching—the gift of clear, luminous exposition of Christian truth under the influence of the Holy Spirit was the endowment which Paul most highly prized, and deemed most serviceable to the Church (I Cor. 14:1-5, 24, 25). Other *charismata* are more incidentally alluded to, such as "the word of wisdom" and the "word of knowledge" (I Cor. 12:8)—terms which are not easily defined, but which doubtless refer to the enunciation and apprehension of those deep truths and mysteries, such as the sacrifice of Christ (I Cor. 1:22-24), that constitute the true Christian wisdom which may be taught to those of spiritual maturity (I Cor. 2:6), but which the worldly and carnal mind cannot receive (I Cor. 2:14). Paul mentions also, "helps," which most naturally refers to the duties of the diaconate, and "governments" which is best understood as the counterpart of "helps," and would therefore designate the functions of government which are exercised in the local church by the elders or bishops.—STEVENS, *Pauline Theology*, pp. 326, 327.

Quesnel observes that there are three sorts of gifts necessary to the forming of Christ's mystical body. (1) Gifts of power, for the working of miracles, in reference to the Father. (2) Gifts of labor and ministry, for the exercise of government and other offices, with respect to the Son. (3) Gifts of knowledge for the instruction of the people, with reference to the Holy Ghost. (ADAM CLARKE, *Com.* I Cor. 12:31.)

Lord. (5) The gifts of the Spirit are essential to the spiritual progress of the Church. As physical ends can be accomplished only by physical means, or intellectual attainments by mental effort, so the spiritual mission of the Church can be carried forward only by spiritual means. From this it is evident that the gifts of the Spirit are always latent in the Church. They did not cease with the apostles, but are available to the Church in every age.

The Soteriological Function of the Spirit. In addition to the gifts and graces of the Spirit, there are certain other acts or functions of His administrative work which demand brief attention before taking up more directly His work as related to the individual, the Church and the world. These pertain especially to the work of salvation, and may be classified broadly under two general heads—the Holy Spirit as "the Lord and Giver of Life," and the Holy Spirit as "a sanctifying Presence." To the former belongs the "birth of the Spirit" or the initial experience of salvation; to the latter, the "baptism with the Spirit"—a subsequent work by which the soul is made holy. This is known as entire sanctification, which as our creed states "is wrought by the baptism with the Holy Spirit, and comprehends in one experience the cleansing of the heart from sin and the abiding, indwelling presence of the Holy Spirit, empowering the believer for life and service." (*Article X.*) Analyzing this state of holiness from the viewpoint of the Agent rather than the work wrought, we notice a threefold operation of the Spirit in the one experience of the believer: the *baptism,* which in its restricted sense refers to the act of purifying, or making holy; the *anointing,* or the indwelling Spirit in His office work of empowering for life and service; and the *sealing,* or the same indwelling Presence in His witness-bearing capacity. When, therefore, we speak of the birth, the baptism, the anointing and the sealing, as four administrative acts or functions of the Spirit, we are referring only to the two works of grace, but are considering the latter under a threefold aspect. We are to be understood as referring (1) to the birth of the Spirit as the bestowment of life in the initial experience of salvation—an experience which will be considered later under the head of regeneration and its concomitants, justification and adoption. We shall then consider the subsequent work of the Spirit as sanctifier, under the threefold aspect of (2) the baptism; (3) the anointing, and (4) the sealing—an experience which we shall treat later under the head of "Christian Perfection" or "Entire Sanctification."

1. *The Birth of the Spirit* is the impartation of divine life to the soul. It is not merely a reconstruction or working over of the old life; it is the impartation to the soul, or the implantation within the soul, of the new life of the Spirit. It is therefore a "birth from above." As the natural birth is a transition from fœtal life to a life fully individualized, so the Holy Spirit infuses life into souls dead in trespasses and sins, and thereby sets them up as distinct individuals in the spiritual realm. These individuals are children of God. To them is given the Spirit of adoption by which they are constituted heirs of God and joint-heirs with Christ (Rom. 8: 15-17). The apostle defines specifically the nature of this inheritance. It is the blessing of Abraham, which God gave him by promise, that is, the promise of the Spirit through faith (Gal. 3: 14-18). While the child of God as an individual possesses life in Christ, there is in him also, the "carnal mind" or inbred sin, and this prevents him from entering fully into his New Testament privileges in Christ. Jesus as the "Lamb of God" came to take away "the *sin* of the world." There must therefore be a purification from sin. Until then he *differeth nothing from a servant, though he be lord of all; but is under tutors and governors until the time appointed of the father* (Gal. 4: 1, 2). He is an heir, but he has not yet entered into his inheritance. The time appointed of the Father, is the hour of submission to the baptism of Jesus—the baptism with the Holy Spirit which purifies the heart from all sin. With the cleansing of the heart from inbred

While the baptism with the Spirit is usually considered as the act by which regenerated men are made holy, it is sometimes used also in the broader sense of the state of holiness flowing from that act. The former appears to be the more exact position.

sin, the son is inducted into the full privileges of the New Covenant; through this baptism he enters into the *fulness of the blessing of the gospel of Christ* (Rom. 15:29).

2. *The Baptism with the Spirit,* as we have indicated, is the induction of newborn individuals into the full privileges of the New Covenant. *This is the covenant that I will make with them after those days, saith the Lord, I will put my laws into their hearts, and in their minds will I write them; and their sins and iniquities will I remember no more. Now where remission of these is, there is no more offering for sin* (Heb. 10:16-18). Both the individual and social aspects of personality are involved. As by the natural birth each individual comes into possession of a nature common to others, and thereby becomes a member of a race of interrelated persons; so also the individual born of the Spirit has a new nature which demands a new spiritual organism as the ground of holy fellowship. The old racial nature cannot serve in this capacity, for it is *corrupt according to the deceitful lusts* (Eph. 4:22). The new nature in Christ, *created in righteousness and true holiness* (Eph. 4:24), can alone supply this spiritual nexus. Hence we are commanded to *put off the old man* and to *put on the new man*. The baptism with the Spirit,

> Now this baptism with the Holy Ghost is *the blessing of Christ* spoken of in the text. Someone may still ask, "Why is it called 'the blessing of Christ'?" Because it is; "why is it?" It is the crowning glory of the work of the soul's salvation. All that ever went before was preparatory for it. Did prophets speak and write; did sacrifices burn; were offerings made; did martyrs die; did Jesus lay aside His glory; did He teach and pray and stretch out His hands on the cross; did He rise from the dead and ascend into heaven; is He at the right hand of God? It was all preparatory to this baptism. Men are convinced of sin, born again and made new creatures that they may be baptized with the Holy Ghost. This completes the soul's salvation. Jesus came to destroy sin—the work of the devil—the baptism with the Holy Ghost does that. Jesus sought for Himself fellowship, communion and unity with human souls, by this baptism He is enthroned and revealed in man.—Dr. P. F. BRESEE, *Sermon: The Blessing.*
>
> To us the clear teaching of the Bible is that a man quits sinning when he begins to repent; that God freely forgives the repentant sinner and that the child of God goes with Jesus without the camp bearing His reproach, and, putting his arms of faith about the will of God, believes God and the old man is crucified by the power of God—the inherited fountain of evil is taken away, and the new man Christ Jesus becomes the fountain of life. This brings an end to sin in the soul.—Dr. P. F. BRESEE, *Sermon: Death and Life.*

therefore, must be considered under a twofold aspect; *first,* as a death to the carnal nature; and *second,* as the fullness of life in the Spirit. Since entire sanctification is effected by the baptism with the Spirit, it likewise has a twofold aspect—the cleansing from sin and full devotement to God.

3. *The Anointing with the Spirit* is a further aspect of this second work of grace—that which regards it as a conferring of authority and power. It refers, therefore, not to the negative aspect of cleansing, but to the positive phase of the indwelling Spirit as "empowering the believers for life and service." Prophets, priests and kings were in the Old Testament dispensation, inducted into office by an anointing with specially prepared oil. This administrative act of the Spirit, therefore, bears an official as well as a personal relation to Christ. As previously indicated, purification from sin is in order to the full devotement of the soul to God. But this devotement is not merely human energy exercised toward God. It is the inwrought power of the Holy Spirit—the operation of the abiding Comforter who dwells within the holy heart. Hence we read, that *God anointed Jesus of Nazareth with the Holy Ghost and with power: who went about doing good, and healing all that were oppressed of the devil; for God was with him* (Acts 10:38). While it is recorded that Jesus was baptized with water by John, it is not stated that He was baptized with the Holy Spirit. This is significant. The reason is plain—baptism implies cleansing, and Jesus had no sin from which to be cleansed; neither could He in this sense be filled with the Spirit, for the Spirit already dwelt in Him without measure. But He was anointed with the Spirit at the time of His baptism by John, and thereby inducted into the office and work of the Messiah or Christ. As we become the sons of God by faith in Jesus Christ, so also, because we are sons, God gives us the Holy Spirit as a sanctifying and empowering Presence. This Spirit, our Lord tells us, the world cannot receive, because *it seeth him not, neither knoweth him* (John 14:17). St. John further declares that this anointing abides in us as the

personal Paraclete or Comforter, and consequently is ever present to confer authority, and to supply the needed power for the accomplishment of every divinely appointed task.

4. *The Sealing with the Spirit* is a further aspect of this second work of grace. The seal to which St. Paul refers in his letter to Timothy, had two inscriptions— *The Lord knoweth them that are his,* or ownership; and *let every one that nameth the name of Christ depart from iniquity,"* or holiness. The pentecostal gift of the Holy Spirit, which under one aspect is the baptism which purifies the heart; and under another, the anointing which empowers for life and service, is under still another aspect, the seal of God's ownership and approval. This approval is not only a claim upon the service of the sanctified as involved in ownership, but the seal of approval upon that service as rendered through the Holy Spirit. The seal is also the guaranty of full redemption in the future. Hence St. Paul says that after *ye believed, ye were sealed with that holy Spirit of promise, which is the earnest of our inheritance until the redemption of the purchased possession, unto the praise of his glory* (Eph. 1:13, 14). Here the Spirit is not only the promised Gift, but the gift of promise, which in connection with the earnest, is the guaranty of future perfection. The "earnest" was a portion of the inheritance given in advance as a sample and guaranty of that which later was to be had in its perfection—*for if the first fruit be holy, the lump is also holy* (Rom. 11:16). The earnest of the Spirit then, is given to us for our present enjoyment until the end of the age, and is the seal of assurance that the purchased possession will then be fully re-

Dr. A. J. Gordon says that the inscription on the seal "Let every one that nameth the name of Christ depart from iniquity," is in Hebrew substantially the same as that upon the forehead of the high priest— "Holiness unto the Lord."—GORDON, *The Ministry of the Spirit.*

The seal is also said to refer to a custom of the Jewish priests, who when they examined the sacrifices offered for worship, stamped those which were acceptable. "But whatever the source of the figure," says Dr. Lowrey, "it represents one of the precious offices of the Holy Spirit. He himself comes into the heart and gives us grace—a pledge of glory, or rather, gives us a part of the glory as a pledge of the whole."— LOWREY, *Possibilities of Grace,* p. 363.

deemed—all of which shall redound to the praise of His glory.

In this connection, also, it may be well to note the close relation which the work of the Spirit bears to that of Christ. These four administrative acts belong at once to Christ and the Spirit. It is Christ who quickens dead souls into life by the Spirit; it is Christ who baptizes men and women with the Holy Spirit; and it is Christ, also, who both anoints and seals His people with the Spirit.

The Holy Spirit and the Individual. As the Spirit formed the body of the incarnate Christ, and took up His abode in the new nature thus formed, so He thereby becomes the Intermediary between Christ and the human soul. There are therefore two sources of life in Christ—the fullness of the Spirit, and the redeemed human nature through which the Spirit is mediated, and by means of which He unites Himself to the individual soul. This will appear more evident, if we take into consideration the fact that while Christ was free from sin

Dr. Asbury Lowrey says that the anointing is "an inward, evidential, abiding light, which serves as a sure guide to the truth—a spiritual discernment of spiritual things. It does not discount the Word, nor set aside the ordinary means of edification, but it does detect and reject much that claims to be religious thought and instruction. It discriminates between the chaff and the wheat, the form and the power; between the *charity that never faileth*, and the *sounding brass and tinkling cymbal*. It accompanies entire sanctification, and is one with it, and in a large measure inseparable from it; and yet there may be, so to speak, reapplications of the anointing oil. This anointing inducts into the office, and confers authority and power. It is the gift which invests a man with ministerial rights, and makes him effective. A man who has not by such anointing received the credentials of the Holy Ghost has no right in the ministry. The apostles were commanded to *tarry at Jerusalem* until they had received this enduement of power. With a perishing world around them they were held back until thus empowered from on high."—Lowrey, *Possibilities of Grace*, p. 370.

The allusion to the seal as a pledge of purchase would be peculiarly intelligible to the Ephesians, for Ephesus was a maritime city, and an extensive trade in lumber was carried on there by the ship masters of the neighboring ports. The method of purchasing was this: The merchant, after selecting his timber, stamped with his own signet, which was an acknowledged sign of ownership. He often did not carry off his possession at the time; it was left in the harbor with other floats of timber; but it was chosen, bought and stamped; and in due time the merchant sent a trusty agent with the signet, who finding that timber which bore a corresponding impress, claimed and brought it for the master's use. Thus the Holy Spirit impresses on the soul now, the image of Jesus Christ: and this is the sure pledge of the everlasting inheritance."—Bickersteth, *The Spirit of Life*, quoted in Gordon, *The Ministry of the Spirit*.

in both nature and act, yet this new Man appeared in the midst of a sinful race, and dwelt in the likeness of sinful flesh (Rom. 8:3). He that had no sin, by His birth into a fallen race, thereby took upon Himself the penalty due its sin, and died without the camp that He might sanctify the people with His own blood (Heb. 13:12; cf. Titus 2:14). Only by death could He be freed from the old race into which He was born; and only by the resurrection from the dead could He establish a new, unique and spiritual people. He was therefore, the *first begotten from the dead,* uniting in Himself as did the first Adam, both the individual and the race.

If now we refer briefly to the question of original sin already discussed, we may note that the sin of Adam not only brought penalty but entailed consequences, both for himself and for his posterity. Two effects followed the first transgression—a criminal act and a subjective change. When man consented to sin, God withdrew the fellowship of His presence through the Spirit. Deprived of life, only corruption and impurity remained. This fallen nature is continued in the posterity of Adam as "inbred sin" or "inherited depravity," an element utterly foreign to the original character and life of man. Sin therefore exists in a twofold manner, as an act and as a state or condition back of that act; and while guilt does not attach to the latter, it is nevertheless of the nature of sin. In Adam depravity followed as a consequence of sin; in his posterity sin exists as a nature before it issues in sin as an act. As a state or quality which is the racial inheritance of every man born into the world, sin is the root or essence of all spiritual impurity and corruption. It is the primal cause of every transgression and the fountain of all unholy activities; but it must not be confused with these activities, or with any one of them. It is the nature back of the act, the generic or racial idea of sin, to which St. John refers when he says, *All unrighteousness is sin* (I John 5:17); and again, *the blood of Jesus Christ his Son cleanseth us from all sin* (I John 1:7). It is this to which John the Baptist referred when he cried out and said, *Behold the Lamb of God, which taketh away the sin of the world* (John 1:29). St. Paul uses the word in the same sense when he says, *Likewise reckon ye also yourselves to be dead indeed unto sin, but alive unto God through Jesus Christ our Lord* (Rom. 6:11); and he refers to the same elementary antagonism to holiness when he uses the terms "the body of sin," the "old man" or the "carnal mind."

We must hold firmly to the fact that in the teaching of Christ there is a moral condition antecedent to the act of sin. *A good tree cannot bring forth evil fruit, neither can a corrupt tree bring forth good fruit* (Matt. 7:18). There is therefore not only human personality as a free and responsible agent, but there is a nature or character which attaches to this agent, which in thought at least is distinguishable from it—that is, the person may be either good or bad, may exist in the state of holiness or in the state of sin. If we may be permitted to use the technical terms applied usually only to the Trinity; we may say, that as in the Godhead, the Three Persons subsist in one Divine Nature; and as angels subsist in angelic nature; so also human beings are persons who subsist in human nature. Previous to the fall, man subsisted in holy human nature; since that time he subsists in a fallen and depraved human nature. As persons, each human being is by the very nature of personality forever separate and distinct from every other; as members of a common race each individual possesses a nature in common with every other individual, and this furnishes the common bond of racial union. *What man knoweth the things of a man, save the spirit of man which is in him? even so the things of God knoweth no man, but the Spirit of God* (I Cor. 2:11). It is evident, then, that Christ as the theanthropic Person furnishes the source of life for both the person and the race. Since in Him human nature was conjoined in vital union with the divine, this new life becomes in the administration of the Holy Spirit the principle of regeneration in respect to the person; and since Christ not only died for sin but unto sin, His shed blood becomes the principle of sanctification as it respects the sinful nature inherited from

Adam. But this matter will be given fuller treatment in our consideration of the states of grace; here it must now be considered in relation to the Church as the body of Christ.

The Holy Spirit and the Church. Pentecost was the birthday of the Christian Church. As Israel redeemed from Egypt, was formed into a church-state by the giving of the law at Sinai; so also from individuals redeemed by Christ our Passover, the Holy Spirit formed the Church at Pentecost. This was accomplished by the giving of a new law, written upon the hearts and within the minds of the redeemed. As the natural body is possessed of a common life which binds the members together in a common organism; so the Holy Spirit sets the members in the spiritual body as it pleases Him, uniting them into a single organism under Christ its living Head. God did not create men as a string of isolated souls, but as an interrelated race of mutually dependent individuals; so also the purpose of Christ is not alone the salvation of the individual, but the building up of a spiritual organism of interrelated and redeemed persons. This new organism is not destructive of the natural relationships of life, but lifts them up and glorifies them. Hence the Church is *a chosen generation, a royal priesthood, an holy nation, a peculiar people;* and the purpose of this organization is to *shew forth the praises of him,* who has called us out of darkness into His marvelous light (I Peter 2:9, 10).

As the Intermediary between the Saviour and the individual soul the Spirit has two classes of office: one more external and one more internal. And these functions He discharges in respect to two orders of men: Those not yet in Christ and those who are by faith united to Him. (1) His external function is that of bearing witness, or applying the truth to the mind: to the unconverted for the conviction of sin, the awakening of desire for Jesus and His salvation, and the revelation to penitence of the promises of grace; to the believer for the assurance of acceptance, the unfolding of the knowledge of Christ, the application of the several promises of grace, and all that belongs to His personal instruction and guidance through the Word. (2) His internal function is the exercise of divine power on the heart, or within the soul: to the unconverted in infusing the grace of penitence and the power of faith, issuing in an effectual inward conversion; to the believer in renewing the soul by communicating a new spiritual life, and carrying on the entire work of sanctification to its utmost issues.—Pope, *Comp. Chr. Th.,* II, p. 329.

The Holy Spirit is therefore not only the bond which unites the individual soul to Christ in a vital and holy relationship; but He is the common bond which unites the members of the body to each other, and all to their living Head. The spirit is the life of the body, and since His inauguration at Pentecost, has His "See" or seat within the church. This may be made clearer by an illustration from Dr. Kuyper, who calls attention to the fact that in earlier times, when rain fell, each householder collected the water for himself in a cistern, in order to supply his own needs and those of his family. In a modern city each house is supplied with water from a common reservoir, by means of mains and laterals. Instead then of the water falling upon every man's roof, it streams through an organized system into every man's house. Previous to Pentecost the mild showers of the Holy Spirit descended upon Israel in drops of saving grace; but in such a manner that each gathered only for himself. This continued until the time of the Incarnation, when Christ gathered into His one Person the full stream of the Holy Spirit for us all. When, after His ascension, He had received of the Father the promise of the Holy Spirit; and when the channels of faith were completed and every obstacle removed, the Holy Spirit on the day of Pentecost came rushing through the connecting channels into the heart of every believer. Formerly there was isolation, every man for himself; now it is an organic union of all the members under their one Head. This is the difference between the days before and after Pentecost (cf. KUYPER, *The Work of the Holy Spirit*, pp. 123, 124).

The Church in its corporate life is a kingdom of the incarnation as well as a kingdom of the spirit. We must remind ourselves here, that there was in the manhood of Christ, two mysteries, the union of human nature with the divine, and the unmeasured fullness of the Spirit which dwelt in that holy nature; the one administered through the other. When, therefore, the Spirit administers the pure human nature of Christ, He is said to make us members of His spiritual and mystic Body;

when He ministers in His own proper Personality as the Third Person of the Trinity, He is said to dwell within the holy temple thus constructed. It may be readily seen, then, that the Church is not merely an independent creation of the Spirit, but an enlargement of the incarnate life of Christ. He is the head of the Church, whether militant, expectant or triumphant. The Church is complete, not through the presence of pure Godhead, but is complete in Christ (Col. 2:10). Christ is *the first begotten of the dead* (Rev. 1:5; Rom. 1:4; Col. 1:15); and as such is "the seed" (Heb. 2:16) from which the Church grows by expansion, through the operation of the Spirit. Christ is a new spring of pure human life. The first Adam was made a "living soul," the last Adam was made a "quickening spirit." Christ is the Lord from heaven (I Cor. 15:45-47). He is, therefore, by virtue of His resurrection, a new order of being, a holy humanity, free from every taint of sin and pollution. This new humanity is the channel of the Spirit's descent; and the rent veil of Christ's flesh forms the new and living way into the presence of God (Heb. 10:19-22). It is this holy humanity which becomes the spiritual nexus in the corporate life of the Church. The Spirit's illuminations flow through the mind and heart of Jesus, and therefore perpetuate the pure energies of His sacred manhood. He is the firstborn among many brethren.

The Holy Spirit and the World. The Spirit represents Christ to the world. But since the world does not know the Holy Spirit and cannot receive Him in the fullness of His dispensational truth, Christ is therefore limited in His operations to the preliminary stages of grace. The nature of this work is given to us by our Lord in His farewell address as follows: *When he is come, he will reprove the world of sin, and of righteousness, and of judgment: of sin, because they believe not on me; of righteousness, because I go to my Father, and ye see me no more; of judgment, because the prince of this world is judged* (John 16:8-11). The sin referred to here is the formal rejection of Jesus Christ as the Saviour; the righteousness is His finished work of atonement as the only ground of acceptance before a righteous God; while the judgment is the dethronement of Satan as the prince of this world, and hence the final separation of the righteous and wicked at the last day. If the prince be judged, then all of his followers must suffer condemnation. It is evident, therefore, that the Spirit must be regarded in this connection, as primarily the Spirit of truth, and His instrument the Word of God. The relation of the Church to the Spirit's efficiency through the Work, finds its highest expression in the great commission. Here the gospel is the proclamation of salvation, and leads directly to the vocation or call of the Spirit.

Emblems of the Holy Spirit

As the names and titles applied to Christ are numerous and varied, so also the emblems used in the Scriptures to portray the office and work of the Holy Spirit are presented in great variety. These can be presented only in a brief manner, but further study will richly repay the efforts of the student.

1. The dove is the symbol of the Spirit in both the Old and New Testaments. In Gen. 1:2 the Spirit is said to have "brooded" over the waters, bringing order and beauty out of chaos. There is an interesting parallel between the dove of Noah and the appearance like that of a dove at the baptism of Jesus. (a) The dove when first sent out returned because there was no resting place. So also in the Old Testament the Spirit found no place of rest in the hearts of men because of their sinfulness. (b) The second time the dove returned with an olive leaf "plucked off"—this word signifying in other instances, a violent death. Hence the Spirit gives hope to the world in the violent death of Christ on the cross. (c) At the baptism of Jesus the Spirit like a dove lighted upon Him (Matt. 3:16); or as given in John's account, the Spirit "abode" upon Him (John 1:32). In Jesus the Spirit found an abiding place, and was given to Him without measure. The dove is primarily the symbol of peace, and signifies the gentleness of the Spirit's operations (Matt. 10:16; Phil. 2:15). It is said that the dove has no gall, and consequently signifies the lack of bitterness. The dove was constant in love (Cant. 5:12); swift and strong of wing (Psalm 55:6); and clean in its nature. Someone has written that under this emblem the Holy Spirit is the Spirit of truth to sanctify (John 14:17); the Spirit of grace to beautify (Acts 6:5-8, R.V.); the Spirit of love to intensify (Col. 1:6); the Spirit of life to fructify (I Peter 1:11); the Spirit of holiness to purify (Acts 15:9); the Spirit of light to clarify (Eph. 1:17); and the Spirit of prophecy to testify (Rom. 1:4).

2. Water was used as an emblem of the Spirit by our Lord. He spoke of a well of water springing up into everlasting life (John 4:14). Here it is the sign of effectiveness and sufficiency (John 4:13, 14). Jesus indicated the abundance of the spirit as "rivers of living water," living water being that which is ever connected with its source (John 7:38, 39). Rain signifies the refreshing and reviving influences of the Spirit (Deut. 32:2; Psalms 72:6; Hosea 6:3; Zech. 10:1). The dew represents the mellowing and enriching influences of the Spirit (Isa. 18:4; Hosea 14:5). The baptism with the Holy Spirit is peculiarly set forth by

Ezekiel under the symbol of the "sprinkling of clean water" and the impartation of the Spirit (Ezek. 36:25-27).

3. The fire was one of the emblems of Pentecost. John prophesied of Jesus, saying, "He shall baptize you with the Holy Ghost, and with fire" (Matt. 3:11). Doubtless the pillar of cloud and fire in the Old Testament was a prophetical symbol of Pentecost. This is a reference to an ancient custom of armies carrying lighted torches when crossing an enemy's territory at night. It served the double purpose of lighting the way and of striking terror to the enemies. On the Day of Pentecost tongues like as of fire sat upon each of the disciples, indicating that they were to go forth as an army of living flames. Fire signifies the purifying, penetrating and energizing influence of the Holy Spirit (Mal. 3:1-3; Matt. 3:11, 12).

4. The atmosphere is likewise an emblem of the Holy Spirit. On the Day of Pentecost there was the sound as of a rushing mighty wind, which marked the coming of the Holy Spirit. God breathed life into the face of man at his creation (Gen. 2:7); and Jesus breathed upon the disciples and said, "Receive ye the Holy Ghost" (John 20:22). As the atmosphere is necessary to sustain life, so in the creeds the Holy Spirit is called "the Lord and Giver of Life." The atmosphere exerts a pressure of approximately fifteen pounds to the square inch, or about 32,000 pounds upon an ordinary man. So the Spirit is said to have fallen upon the disciples, the term indicating pressure (cf. Acts 8:16; 10:44; cf. Mark 3:10). The balance of pressure within and without maintains a proper equilibrium. Without the inward pressure of the Spirit, the outward pressures of life would crush men; with the true inward strength of the Spirit, man needs outward tasks to challenge his efforts. The atmosphere is the medium of communication, hence there is the communion of the Spirit. The atmosphere revives the earth by drawing up vast stores of water which it returns in refreshing showers.

5. Oil is a symbol of the Spirit's official anointing for service. Prophets, priests and kings were inducted into office by a ceremony of anointing with oil. The formula of the anointing oil is given in Exodus 30:23-33, and is as follows: (1) The myrrh of the Spirit's excellence; (2) the sweet cinnamon of the Spirit's grace; (3) the sweet calamus of the Spirit's worth; (4) the cassia of the Spirit's righteousness; and (5) the olive oil of the Spirit's presence. Also there was the shekel of the Spirit's word—the exact measurements given for the compounding of the formula. The anointing oil could not be used for profane purposes, and it was a criminal act to counterfeit it. The oil could never be placed upon the flesh, only as that flesh had been previously touched with the blood of sacrifice. So also the oil of the Spirit's presence must follow the atoning sacrifice of Jesus Christ.

There are many other emblems of the Spirit given in the Old Testament such as the flaming sword at the gate of Eden, the seal, the earnest or pledge and others of a like nature. A knowledge of the divinely given emblems in the Old Testament will give added meaning and value to many of the New Testament Scriptures.

CHAPTER XXVI
THE PRELIMINARY STATES OF GRACE

The finished atonement of Jesus Christ becomes effective for the salvation of men, only when administered to believers by the Holy Spirit. The former is known in theological science as objective soteriology, the latter as subjective soteriology. The work of the Holy Spirit done *in* us, is as necessary to salvation, as the work of Christ done *for* us. But it would be truer to fact to say, that the redemption which Christ wrought for us in the flesh becomes effective only as He works in us through the Spirit. It is a mistake to view the work of the Holy Spirit as superseding that of Christ; it is to be viewed rather as a continuation of that work on a new and higher plane. The nature of this work is now to be considered, and consequently we turn our attention to what in theology is generally known as the benefits of the atonement. We shall consider these, first in their objective form as the *words* of the covenant, and second in their subjective aspect as the inner *grace* of the covenant. Our subjects then will be: (I) The Vocation or Call; and (II) Prevenient Grace. Following this we shall consider (III) Repentance, (IV) Faith and (V) Conversion.

The Gospel Vocation

The Holy Spirit as the Agent of Christ, makes known His divine purpose for the salvation of the world, through a Proclamation, commonly known in theology, as the Vocation or Call. The Word comes from the Greek κλῆσις, which means a vocation or calling; hence the word καλεῖν, *to call*, carries the thought backward to the Agency of that call; while the word κλητός, *the called*, carries the thought forward to those who have accepted the invitation, and who are, therefore, the elect. In this sense, the Church is the *ecclesia*, or called out ones. The

Vocation or call is further distinguished as the Indirect or universal call, and the Direct or immediate call—a distinction similar to that between General and Special Revelation. By the Universal Call, or *Vocatio Catholica*, is meant that secret influence exerted upon the consciences of men, apart from the revealed Word as found in the Holy Scriptures. We have already pointed out that in the earlier dispensation the Spirit strove with men (Gen. 6:3); and St. Paul later affirms, both that the law of God was written in the hearts of the Gentiles (Rom. 1:19; 2:15), and that God has never, in any age, left Himself without a witness (Acts 14:17). The Direct, or immediate call refers to that which is made through the Word of God revealed to mankind. "In the Old Testament it was limited to one race, first elected and then called; in the New Testament it is universally to all men, first called and then elected: a distinction of great importance" (POPE, *Compend. Chr. Th.*, II, p. 338). The call of Abraham is the central point of vocation in the Old Testament (cf. Amos 3:1-2, Hosea 11:1). However, God's choice of Abraham must be considered, both in relation to moral character, and in its prophetical connection with the universal call of the gospel. In the New Testament, especially after Pentecost, the gospel call is freed from the nationalism of the previous period, and consequently becomes the divine means of election for all people.

Election and Predestination—Vocation or Calling is closely related to predestination. Predestination as we have seen, has an intimate connection with the doctrine of the atonement in regard to the extent of its benefits. The *elect* in either the Arminian or Calvinistic view of grace are the called or chosen ones, but the two systems differ widely as to the manner of this election. Those who hold to the former view regard it as dependent upon the personal acceptance of a universal call, and therefore conditional; the latter regard it as unconditional and dependent upon predestination, or the exercise of sovereign grace. "Predestination," says Calvin, "we call the eternal decree of God, by which he has determined in Himself what He would have become of every individual of mankind, for they are not all created with a similar destiny; but eternal life is foreordained for some, and eternal damnation for others. Every man, therefore, being created for one or the other of these ends, we say he is predestinated either to life or to death..... In conformity, therefore, to the clear doctrine of Scripture, we assert that, by an eternal and immutable counsel God has once for all determined both whom He would admit to salvation and whom He would condemn to destruction" (CALVIN, *Institutes*, III, Chap. 21). Dr. Dick says that "It is applicable according to the import of the term, to all the purposes of God which determine beforehand what is come to pass; but it is usually limited to those purposes to which the spiritual and eternal state of man is the object" (DICK, *Lecture*

Dr. Wakefield analyzes the Westminster teaching on election as follows: (1) That the decrees of God are eternal, being called "his eternal purpose." (2) That predestination is all-comprehensive as to its objects, embracing "whatsoever comes to pass in time." (3) That "some men and angels are predestinated unto everlasting life, and others foreordained to everlasting death." (4) That the decree both of election and reprobation is personal and definite, its objects being "particularly designed, and their number certain." (5) That election to eternal life is unconditional, being "without any foresight of faith or good works, or any other thing in the creature." (6) That Christ atoned for those only who were ordained to everlasting life, and (7) That faith and obedience are the fruits of election, while unbelief and sin result from reprobation. —WAKEFIELD, *Christian Theology*, p. 389.

The extent to which belief in reprobation was carried by earlier Calvinistic theologians may best be illustrated by a paragraph from the lectures of Dr. Hill. He says, "From the election of certain persons, it necessarily follows that all the rest of the race of Adam are left in guilt and misery. The exercise of the divine sovereignty in regard to those who are not elected is called reprobation; and the condition of all having been originally the same, reprobation is called absolute in the same with election. In reprobation there are two acts which Calvinists are careful to distinguish. The one is called preterition, the passing by of those who are not elected, and withholding from them the means of grace which are provided for the elect. The other is called condemnation, the act of condemning those who have been passed by for the sins which they commit. In the former act God exercises His good pleasure, dispensing His benefits as He will; in the latter act He appears as a judge, inflicting upon men that sentence which their sins deserve. If He had bestowed upon them the same assistance which He prepared for others, they would have been preserved from that sentence; but as their sins proceeded from their own corruption, they are thereby rendered worthy of punishment, and the justice of the Supreme Ruler is manifested in condemning them, as His mercy is manifested in saving the elect."—HILL, *Lectures IV*, 7. It was against such positions as these that the Remonstrants objected, and Arminian theologians since that time have lifted their voices in protest.

XXV). Predestination, according to this view, includes two great branches of the divine purpose toward man— Election and Reprobation. Election in the Calvinistic sense is defined by Dr. Dick as that "choice which God, in the exercise of sovereign grace, made of certain individuals of mankind to enjoy salvation by Jesus Christ." This necessarily involves the unconditional reprobation of all the rest. This is stated in the Westminster Confession as follows: "The rest of mankind God was pleased according to the unsearchable counsel of His own will, whereby He extendeth or withholdeth mercy as He pleaseth, for the glory of His sovereign power over His creatures, to pass by, and to ordain them to dishonor and wrath for their sin, to the praise of His glorious justice."

In opposition to this, Arminianism holds that predestination is the gracious purpose of God to save mankind from utter ruin. It is not an arbitrary, indiscriminate act of God intended to secure the salvation of so many and no more. It includes provisionally, all men in its scope, and is conditioned solely on faith in Jesus Christ. *For God so loved the world, that he gave his only begotten Son, that whosoever believeth in him should not perish, but have everlasting life* (John 3:16). Election differs from predestination in this, that election implies a choice, whereas predestination does not. In Eph. 1:4, 5, 11-13 it is said that God *hath chosen us in him before the foundation of the world, that we should be holy and without blame before him in love.* This is election. The gracious plan by which this is to be accomplished is predestination, *having predestinated us unto the adoption of children by Jesus Christ to himself, according to the good pleasure of his will.* Thus predestination is God's general and gracious plan of saving men, by adopting them as children through Christ; election pertains to the chosen ones who are holy and blameless before Him in love. The proofs of election are not in the secret counsels of God, but in the visible fruits of holiness. Election is the foundation of the Church, and predestination the basis of providence. The Church is both predestinated and elected, the former referring to the plan of redemption as manifested in the universal call; the latter to the elect or chosen ones who have closed in with the offers of mercy. The elect are chosen, not by absolute decree,

Mr. Wesley published a pamphlet entitled, "Serious Considerations on Absolute Predestination" in which his views on this subject are stated as follows:

"1. God delighteth not in the death of a sinner, but would that all should live and be saved, and hath given His Son, that all that believe on Him should be saved. He is the true light which lighteth every man which cometh into the world. And this light would work out the salvation of all, if not resisted.

"2. But some assert, that God by an eternal and unchangeable decree, hath predestinated to eternal damnation the far greater part of mankind, and that absolutely, without any regard to their works, but only for the showing the glory of His justice; and that for the bringing this about, He hath appointed miserable souls necessarily to walk in their wicked ways, that so His justice may lay hold on them.

"3. This doctrine is novel. In the first four hundred years after Christ, no mention is made of it by any writer, great or small, in any part of the Christian Church. The foundations of it were laid in the later writings of Augustine, when unguardedly writing against Pelagius. It was afterward taught by Dominicus, a popish friar, and the monks of his order, and at last, it was unhappily taken up by John Calvin. This doctrine is, First, injurious to God, because it makes Him the author of all sin. Second, it is injurious to God, because it represents Him as delighting in the death of sinners, expressly contrary to His own declaration (Ezek. 33:11; I Tim. 2:4). Third, this doctrine is highly injurious to Christ, our mediator, and to the efficacy and excellency of His gospel. It supposes His mediation to be necessarily of no effect with regard to the greater part of mankind. Fourth, the preaching of the gospel is a mere mockery and delusion, if many of those to whom it is preached, are by an irrevocable decree, shut out from being benefited by it. Fifth, this doctrine makes the coming of Christ, and His sacrifice upon the cross, instead of being a fruit of God's love to the world, to be one of the severest acts of God's indignation against mankind: it being only ordained (according to this doctrine) to save a very few, and for the hardening and increasing the damnation of the far greater number of mankind: namely, all those who do not believe: and the cause of this unbelief, according to this doctrine, is the counsel and decree of God. Sixth, this doctrine is highly injurious to mankind; for it puts them in a far worse condition than the devils in hell. For these were some time in a capacity to have stood. They might have kept their happy estate, but would not. Whereas, according to this doctrine, many millions of men are tormented forever, who never were happy, never could be and never can be. Again, devils will not be punished for neglecting a great salvation: but human creatures will. In direct opposition to this, we affirm, that God hath willed all to be saved; and hath given His only begotten Son, that whosoever believeth on Him might be saved. There is hardly any other article of the Christian faith so frequently, plainly and positively asserted. It is that which makes the preaching of the gospel 'glad tidings to all,' (Luke 10:2), otherwise, had this salvation been absolutely confined to a few, it had been 'Sad tidings of great sorrow to most people.' Read Col. 1:28; I Tim. 2:1-6; Heb. 2:9; John 3:17—12:47; II Peter 2:3, 9; Ezek. 33:11; I John 2:1, 2; Psalms 17:14; Isa. 13:11; Matt. 18:7; John 7:7, 8, 26; 12:19; 14:17; 15:18, 19; 18:20; I Cor. 1:21; 2:12; 6:2; Gal. 6:14; James 1:27; II Peter 2:20; I John 2:15; 3:1; 4:4, 5."

but by acceptance of the conditions of the call. And as the character of the elect consists of holiness and blamelessness before Him in love, so election is by those means which make men righteous and holy. Hence our Lord says, *I have chosen you out of the world* (John 15:19). St. Paul explains it by saying, *God hath from the beginning chosen you to salvation, through sanctification of the Spirit and belief of the truth* (II Thess. 2:13). St. Peter's teaching is to the same effect—*elect according to the foreknowledge of God the Father, through sanctification of the Spirit unto obedience and sprinkling of the blood of Jesus Christ* (I Peter 1:2).

Arminian theology has generally treated the subject of election under a threefold aspect as follows: (1) Election of individuals to perform some particular service. Thus Moses was chosen to lead Israel out of Egypt and Aaron to be the priest of the sanctuary. Cyrus was elected to aid in rebuilding the temple, Christ chose the twelve as apostles, and St. Paul was chosen as the apostle of the Gentiles. These offices were ordained to assist others, and not to exclude them from saving grace. (2) Election of nations or other bodies of men to special religious privileges. Thus Israel was chosen as God's first representative of the visible Church on earth. It is this to which St. Paul refers in Ephesians 1:11-13. The words "who first trusted in Christ" refer to believing Israel; while the words in the following verse "In whom ye also trusted" refer to the extension of the Jewish privileges to the Gentiles. The calling and election of

Nothing is more grievous in the predestination theory than the way in which it shadows the love of God. Between love as a nature or disposition, and an arbitrary choice of its beneficiaries, there is an irreconcilable antithesis. To assign to love its direction by fiat is to displace the very notion of love, and to put caprice in its stead. Suppose a father standing upon the deck of a ship should see his children struggling in the sea, in imminent peril of drowning. In the worth or worthiness of the children there is no ground of discrimination. The father has ample means to save all, for aplenty of life-preservers is immediately at hand. But instead of saving all he casts means of rescue to only two out of four, thus leaving half of his children to sink into the depths. Who would ascribe parental love to such a father? His unnatural conduct denies the very conception, and leaves in view only mad caprice and appalling eccentricity. It is not the nature of holy love to be subject to arbitrariness any more than it is the nature of sunlight to fill only selected portions of an open expanse.—SHELDON, *Syst. Chr. Doct.*, pp. 432-433.

the Christian Church, therefore, was not the choice of another nation to succeed the Jews, but the election of believers in all nations, wherever the gospel should be preached. Thus the Christian Church rises above the narrow limits of nationalism and extends the call to all nations and tongues and people. (3) The election of particular individuals to be the children of God and heirs of eternal life, which Arminianism always regards as conditional upon faith in Christ, and as including all who believe. Thus we are brought to the consideration of election as a factor in the beginnings of salvation.

The Beginnings of Salvation. The first step toward salvation in the experience of the soul, begins with vocation or the gracious call of God which is both direct through the Spirit and immediate through the Word. This is followed by awakening and conviction. Conversion, in the narrower sense of the term, is sometimes used in this connection also.

The vocation or call is God's offer of salvation to all men through Christ. This is the gracious beginning of salvation. The call is universal and includes three things —the proclamation, the conditions upon which the offer of salvation is made, and the command to submit to the authority of Christ. Thus St. Peter in speaking of the crucifixion and exaltation of Christ says, *We are his witnesses of these things; and so is also the Holy Ghost, whom God hath given to them that obey him* (Acts 5: 32 cf. 13: 38-40). Here we have the testimony, the terms or conditions of salvation, and the command to submission. The Agent of the call is the Holy Spirit, and the Word is the instrument of His operations. The Word, however, is not limited to the letter but includes the Spirit of Truth as well. While the Scriptures are God's authoritative revelation, and the instrumentality which the Spirit ordinarily uses, these themselves seem to indicate that there is a substantial truth of which the Word itself is but the vehicle. This is indicated in St. Paul's reference to the prophecy of Isaiah. He says, *Have they not heard? Yes verily, their sound went into all the earth, and their words unto the ends of the world.*

. . . . But Esaias is very bold, and saith, I was found of them that sought me not; I was made manifest unto them that asked not after me (Isaiah 65:1). This seems to indicate that God's Word is in some sense universally uttered, even when not recorded in a written language.

Awakening is a term used in theology to denote that operation of the Holy Spirit by which men's minds are quickened to a consciousness of their lost estate. In this quickening, the Spirit not only works through the medium of objective truth, but by a direct influence upon the minds and hearts of men. There are two errors which should be mentioned in this connection. The first denies the personality of the Holy Spirit, and maintains that the truth is effective in and of itself. This reduces the power of the Word to the mere influence of the letter. The second does not deny the personality of the Holy Spirit, but holds that since Pentecost, His operation is limited to a mediate and indirect influence through the Word. In this sense, the influence of a holy life goes on after the death of a saint. Thus Wesley and Fletcher, Luther and Melanchthon are still exerting an influence through their writings, although they have long since departed this life. The failure here, is to distinguish between a medium as instrumental and passive on the one hand, or as efficient and active on the other. An officer may use his own sword to destroy an enemy, or he may order a company of soldiers into battle. In the first instance, the officer is the sole agent and his sword the passive instrument; in the second, he is only

The impulse to turn toward communion with God depends on the impact of divine agency upon the human spirit. This initial agency may be described by the term awakening, which thus denotes a pressure from the divine side which is unsought by men, but whose intent they can either follow or resist. Awakening is not so much regeneration as a preparation for the same. It is true that some theologians, especially of the strict Calvinistic school, have preferred to understand by regeneration the primary act of God in man's spiritual recovery, in which almighty power operates upon a purely passive subject, and creates therein a new spiritual sensibility. But this view, as will be shown a little farther on, is not in harmony with the scriptural representation, which assumes a conditioning agency in man, or a consenting rather than a purely passive subject of regeneration. The office of awakening is to produce the sense of need and the measure of aspiration and desire which are requisite to make one a willing subject in the consummation of his spiritual sonship.—SHELDON, *Syst. Chr. Doct.*, pp. 453, 454.

indirectly the agent. So, also, the apostle speaks of the Word as the sword of the Spirit, in which sense the Spirit is the sole Agent of operation, and the Word His instrument. Those, therefore, who hold that the influence of the Spirit is limited solely to the mediate power of the Word, thereby reject His direct spiritual influence upon the hearts of men. There is a third theory which we believe expresses the true scriptural doctrine. This admits the indirect influence of the Spirit through the Word, but maintains that in addition to this, there is an immediate or direct influence upon the hearts of men, not only accompanying the Word, but also the providences and the various means of grace. In support of this, we may refer to the following scriptures: *The king's heart is in the hand of the Lord: as the rivers of water; he turneth it whithersoever he will* (Prov. 21:1); *Open thou mine eyes, that I may behold wondrous things out of thy law* (Psalms 119:18); *Create in me a clean heart, O God; and renew a right spirit within me* (Psalms 51:10). In the New Testament we find the following scriptures: *Then opened he their understanding, that they might understand the scriptures* (Luke 24:45); and again, *Whose heart the Lord opened, that she attended unto the things that were spoken of Paul* (Acts 16:14). In these texts it is distinctly declared that the understanding and the heart were opened by the Lord and not by the Scriptures. Here then we have a direct influence exerted, *first,* in awakening to a knowledge of the truth; and *second,* in attendance upon the things which were spoken.

Conviction is that operation of the Spirit which produces within men, a sense of guilt and condemnation because of sin. To the idea of awakening, there is added that of personal blame. Conviction is specifically stated to be one of the offices of the Spirit during the pentecostal dispensation. *And when he is come, he will reprove the world of sin, and of righteousness, and of judgment* (John 16:8). The threefold conviction mentioned here has been previously discussed in connection with the offices of the Holy Spirit. There are, however, two things which need additional emphasis. (1) The word "convict" as here used, indicates a moral demonstration, and not merely a convincing of the intellect. It involves personal relations with Christ, and hence applies to the conscience as well as the reason. (2) This conviction is one of hope and not of despair. The Spirit not only reveals the sinfulness of human hearts, but the fullness and freeness of salvation through Christ. His purpose is not only to turn men from sin, but to lead them to a living faith in Christ. The conviction of the Spirit, therefore, is one of hope for all who truly repent of their sins and believe on the Lord Jesus Christ.

Effectual Calling and Contingency. Those who hear the proclamation and accept the call are known in the Scriptures as the elect. St. Paul speaks of *the called of Jesus Christ* (Rom. 1:6); and St. Peter states that the nature of election is *according to the foreknowledge of God the Father, through sanctification of the Spirit, unto obedience and sprinkling of the blood of Jesus Christ* (I Peter 1:2). In the Old Testament the call was chiefly that of a nation or a people to some specific mission. The call of the individual was subordinate, although we must believe that even then, the matter of character was important. In the New Testament the gospel call is mainly to the individual, the national or racial being subordinate. The gospel is committed to the Church as a whole, but especially to the ministry set apart for its proclamation. The word *evanggelion* (εὐαγγέλιον) signifies a joyful announcement of Good Tidings, and the word *evanggelizein* (εὐαγγελίζειν) has reference to the preaching of those good tidings. In this sense the gospel has come to indicate the central idea of the Redeemer's mission and work.

<small>Of a *Vocatio Interna,* as distinguished from the *Vocatio Externa,* there is no trace in Scripture: internal calling and effectual calling are phrases never used. The distinction implies such a difference as would have been clearly stated if it existed; and all that is meant by the internal call finds its expression, as we shall see, in other offices of the Holy Spirit of enlightenment, conviction and conversion. Each of these terms carries the meaning of an external summons made effectual by interior grace; but never in the sense that sufficient interior grace is denied to any. It may be said that the true internal vocation is election in the strict sense.—Pope, *Compend. Chr. Th.,* II, p. 345.</small>

Effectual calling, as the term is used in Calvinistic theology, denotes an interior grace or compelling power, by which the mind is led to accept the invitation of the gospel, and yield to the solicitations of the Spirit. A sharp distinction is usually made between the external call which is regarded as universal, and "effectual calling" which pertains only to the elect. Since the elect, in this use of the term indicates only those who by the decree of God are predestinated to salvation, efficacious grace is given only to them, and withheld from those who are not thus predestinated. This is one of the pivotal points in the controversy between Calvinism and Arminianism. We are not to believe that God gives a universal call to all men, and then secretly withholds the power to believe or accept the call from all those He has not especially chosen to salvation. The divine intention is that all men shall avail themselves of their blood bought privileges in Christ Jesus. The call is not fictitious but genuine. It is not only an external offer of salvation, but is accompanied by the internal grace of the Spirit sufficient for its acceptance.

The element of contingency also enters into the question of vocation or calling. The call may be resisted; and even after having been accepted, obedience may be forfeited. Of such, the term reprobation is used, but never in the sense of a fiat or arbitrary decree. The reprobate, *adokimoi* (ἀδόκιμοι) are those who do not retain the knowledge of God, or who finally resist the truth. *Know ye not your own selves how that Jesus Christ is in you, except ye be reprobates?* (II Cor. 13:5). The word has reference primarily, to failure under test. Since many of the vital problems connected with this subject will appear also in our discussion of "Prevenient Grace," they may be properly reserved for later consideration.

Prevenient Grace

Before taking up the discussion of prevenient grace, it may be well to call attention to the fact that the grace of God is in itself infinite, and therefore cannot be limited to His redemptive work, unspeakably great as this may be. (1) Grace is an eternal fact in the inner relations of the Trinity. (2) It existed in the form of sacrificial love before the foundation of the world. (3) It extended order and beauty to the process and product of creation. (4) It devised the plan for the restoration of sinful man. (5) It is manifested specifically through revealed religion as the content of Christian theology; and, (6) it will find its consummation in the regeneration of all things, of which our Lord testified. The absolute holiness of the Creator determines the nature of divine grace. Its laws ever operate under this standard. Once grasp and hold this conception of the infinity of divine grace, and the regal and judicial acts of God in justification and adoption can never be questioned.

Prevenient grace, as the term implies, is that grace which "goes before" or prepares the soul for entrance into the initial state of salvation. It is the preparatory

> Augustine and the theologians of his period distinguished five kinds of grace, as follows: (1) Prevenient grace which removed natural incapacity and invited to repentance; (2) Preparing grace which restrained natural resistance and disposed the will to accept salvation by faith; (3) Operating grace which conferred the power of believing and kindled justifying faith; (4) Co-operating grace which followed justification, and served to promote sanctification and good works; and (5) Conserving grace, by which faith and holiness were conserved and confirmed.
> At a later period in the history of Christian thought, the theologians regarded faith as constituting a fourfold office as follows: (1) Elenchtical, or the awakening to a knowledge of sin; (2) Didactic, or instruction in the way of salvation; (3) Pedagogical, or the conversion of the sinner; and (4) Paracletic, or the consoling and strengthening of the converted.
> The Holy Ghost is here the Author of preliminary grace; that is, of the kind of preparatory influence which is imparted outside of the temple of Christ's mystical body, or rather in the outer court of that temple. When He bestows the full blessings of personal salvation, as they are the result of a union with Christ, He is simply and solely the Administrator and Giver: the object of this grace in the nature of things can only receive. Forgiveness, adoption, sanctification are necessarily divine acts: nothing can be more absolute than the prerogative of God in conferring these blessings. This does not imply that the influences which prepare the soul for these acts of perfect grace are not from a divine Source alone. It must be remembered that it is "the grace of our Lord Jesus Christ" flowing from and revealing the "love of God" that is dispensed even to the outer world in the communion of the Holy Ghost. But it must also be remembered that this prevenient influence is literally bound up with the human use of it being without meaning apart from that use; and, moreover, that of itself it is not saving, though it is unto salvation. The present department of theology is beset with peculiar difficulties, and has been the arena of some of the keenest controversies.—POPE, *Compend. Chr. Th.*, II, pp. 358, 359.

grace of the Holy Spirit exercised toward man helpless in sin. As it respects the guilty, it may be considered mercy; as it respects the impotent, it is enabling power. It may be defined, therefore, as that manifestation of the divine influence which precedes the full regenerate life. The subject is beset with peculiar difficulties and should be given careful study. We shall consider, (1) the Historical Approach to the Subject, and (2) the Nature of Prevenient Grace. Following this we shall analyze the subject more carefully by considering (3) Prevenient Grace and Human Agency.

The Historical Approach to the Subject. The idea of grace or *charis* ($\chi\acute{\alpha}\rho\iota\varsigma$) is fundamental in both the Old and the New Testaments. In the Old Testament it is found in such texts as *My spirit shall not always strive with man* (Gen. 6:3), and *Not by might, nor by power, but by my spirit, saith the Lord of hosts* (Zech. 4:6). In the New Testament, the texts are numerous. Our Lord said, *No man can come to me, except the Father which hath sent me draw him* (John 6:44), and again, *Without me ye can do nothing* (John 15:5). St. Paul uses the term frequently. *For when we were yet without strength* [$\dot{\alpha}\sigma\theta\epsilon\nu\hat{\omega}\nu$, *helpless*], *in due time Christ died for the ungodly* [$\dot{\alpha}\sigma\epsilon\beta\hat{\omega}\nu$, *godless*] (Rom. 5:6). *God commended his love toward us, in that, while we were yet sinners* [$\dot{\alpha}\mu\alpha\rho\tau\omega\lambda\hat{\omega}\nu$, *transgressors*], *Christ died for us* (Rom. 5:8). *For if, when we were enemies* [$\dot{\epsilon}\chi\theta\rho o\grave{\iota}$, *under wrath*], *we were reconciled to God by the death of his Son, much more, being reconciled, we shall be saved by his life* (Rom. 5:10). *My preaching was not with enticing words of man's wisdom, but in demonstration of the Spirit and of power: that your faith should not stand in the wisdom of men, but in the power of God* (I Cor. 2:4, 5). *Not that we are sufficient of ourselves . . . . but our sufficiency is of God* (II Cor. 3:5). *You hath he quickened, who were dead in trespasses and sins* (Eph. 2:1). *By grace are ye saved through faith; and that not of yourselves: it is the gift of God* (Eph. 2:8). *It is God which worketh in you both to will and to do of his good pleasure* (Phil. 2:13). *For our gospel came not unto you in word only, but also in power, and in the Holy Ghost, in much assurance* (I Thess. 1:5). *God hath from the beginning chosen you to salvation through sanctification of the Spirit and belief of the truth* (II Thess. 2:13, cf. I Peter 1:2). *For the grace of God that bringeth salvation hath appeared to all men, teaching us that, denying ungodliness and worldly lusts, we should live soberly, righteously, and godly, in this present world* (Titus 2:11, 12). These are but a few of the many references which might be cited as presenting the fundamental truth of salvation through grace.

1. During the period of the earlier fathers, the doctrine of prevenient grace seems never to have been questioned, except by the Gnostics and Manichæans. Justin (c. 165) says, "That we may follow those things that please Him .... He both persuades and leads to faith." Tertullian (c. 220) writes that "the greatness of some good things is insupportable, so that only the greatness of the divine inspiration is effectual for attaining and practicing them." Clement of Alexandria (c. 220) bears the same testimony. "It is not without eminent grace," he says, "that the soul is winged, and soars, laying aside all that is heavy..... Neither is God involuntarily good, as fire is warm; but in Him the imparting of good things is voluntary, even if He first receive the request. Nor shall he who is saved be saved against his will..... God ministers salvation to those who co-operate for the attainment of knowledge and good conduct." Origen (c. 254) makes the statement that "our perfection is brought about not as if we ourselves did nothing; yet it is not completely by ourselves, but God produces the greater part of it." So also Cyprian (c. 258) writes to the same effect. "If, depending on God with your whole strength," he says, "and with your whole heart, you be only what you have begun to be, power to do so is given you in proportion to the increase of spiritual grace." We may say then, that in a broad sense, the doctrine of prevenient grace was held by all the earlier fathers. The lax interpretation of it, however, by the Greek fathers, led to Pelagianism; while the extreme emphasis upon the

divine element was, in the West, developed into Augustinianism. Thus arose the great controversy between the two types of theology—the East represented by Pelagianism, the West by Augustinianism.

2. Pelagianism marked a radical departure from the orthodox faith. Early in the fifth century, Pelagius, a British monk of high rank, and Celestius his friend, traveled to Rome where they opposed with some warmth, the commonly received doctrines of original sin and prevenient grace. They denied original sin, and regarded prevenient grace as the innate and undestroyed capacity of the soul for good. This natural sanctity of the mind, needed only the aid of instruction in order to attain holiness. The grace of the Holy Spirit, therefore, was not absolutely but only relatively necessary to salvation. That this doctrine was new, needs no other proof than the impression which it made on the minds of the great majority of learned theologians of that day. Jerome ascribes the new opinions to Rufin, who he alleges borrowed them from Origen. Isidore, Chrysostom and Augustine strenuously opposed the new doctrines, and the latter secured their condemnation at the Synod of Carthage in 412 A.D.

3. Augustinianism represents the opposite extreme of thought. Instead of denying original sin as did Pelagius, Augustine made it the foundation of his entire system of theology. The fall having bereft mankind of all capacity for good, salvation must be solely of grace without any admixture of human co-operation. He maintained the freedom of the will, but only in the sense of freedom to evil. Grace, therefore, operates directly upon the will. This necessitated a belief in a divine decree which determined the exact number of those who were to be saved. To these as the elect, efficacious grace was applied, which included irresistible grace for the beginning of the Christian life and persevering grace for its close. Augustine, therefore, was the first to lay down the principle that "Predestination is the preparation of grace; grace the bestowment itself." From these views of the necessity of divine grace, there gradually grew

up a theory of predestination. At first this was not regarded as unconditional, but was made to depend upon a belief in God's foreknowledge. Thus Justin says, "If the Word of God foretells that some angels and men shall certainly be punished, it did so because it foreknew that they would be unchangeably wicked. So also Irenæus, "God, foreknowing the number of those who will not believe, since he foreknows all things, has given them over to unbelief." With Augustine, however, the system of divine decrees amounted to a form of fatalism. He overlooked apparently, the fact that the first benefit of the atonement was coextensive with the ruin of man, and that universal grace mitigated depravity and preserved the freedom of the will. Augustine was not able to carry out logically, his scheme of predestination, for he had no solution of the difficulty that electing grace should be bound up with a sacramental system of external ordinances. Almost a thousand years later, John Calvin (1509-1564), a man of extraordinary ability and sternness of character, systematized the doctrines of Augustine, unhindered by the sacramentarianism of the church which had so restricted the thought of his great predecessor. His doctrine of predestination, revived from Augustine, was developed in opposition to the lax views of sin and grace held by the Roman Catholic Church. In this he was joined by the other reformers —Luther, Melanchthon and Zwingli, but in his supralapsarian views he stood alone.

4. Arminianism represents a mediating position between Pelagianism and Augustinianism. Against the doctrines of Augustine as systematized by Calvin, the Arminians or "Remonstrants" protested. They were

The following is the supposed order of the decrees according to the Calvinistic system of theology. I. According to the supralapsarians; (1) The first decree was that of predestination, that is, the salvation of some men and angels and the damnation of others. (2) The decree to create follows next in the accomplishment of this. (3) The fall is then decreed. (4) Following this the plan of redemption is decreed into existence in order to accomplish the salvation of some. (5) Lastly, the vocation or call of these is decreed. II. According to the sublapsarians, the order of the decrees is as follows: (1) The decree to create; (2) The decree to permit the fall; (3) The decree of redemption; (4) The decree of predestination; and (5) The vocation, or decree to call the predestinated.

especially opposed to the rigid predestinarianism of the system. James Arminius (1560-1609) while a professor of theology in the University of Leyden, was openly attacked by his strictly Calvinistic opponent, Francis Gomarus (1563-1641), and a long and bitter discussion followed. James Arminius died in 1609, but the controversy continued under Simon Episcopius (1583-1643), a dogmatist of high repute who championed his position. Under the leadership of Episcopius, the Arminians formulated a statement known as the "Five Points of Remonstrance" which was laid before the Dutch States in 1610. It was due to this fact that they came to be known as Remonstrants. A conference was held for the settlement of the dispute, but ended without any definite results. In 1618 to 1619, a synod was called, known as the Synod of Dort, which met November 13, 1618, and continued until May 9, 1619—a total of one hundred and fifty-four sessions. Before this synod the Remonstrants appeared in the person of thirteen deputies, headed by Episcopius. To all appearances their

The doctrine of predestination is set forth in the Westminster Confession of Faith as follows:

"By the decree of God for the manifestation of His glory, some men and angels are predestinated unto everlasting life, and others foreordained to everlasting death.

"These men and angels, thus predestinated and foreordained, are particularly and unchangeably designated; and their number is so certain and definite that it cannot be either increased or diminished.

"Those of mankind that are predestinated unto life, God, before the foundation of the world was laid, according to His eternal and immutable purpose, and the secret counsel and good pleasure of His will, hath chosen in Christ unto everlasting glory, out of His mere free grace and love, without any foresight of faith and good works, or perseverance in either of them, or any other thing in the creature, as conditions or causes moving Him thereto, and all to the praise of His glorious grace.

"As God hath appointed the elect unto glory, so hath He, by the eternal and free purpose of His will, foreordained all the means thereunto. Wherefore, they who are elected being fallen in Adam, are redeemed by Christ; are effectually called unto faith in Christ by His Spirit working in due season; are justified, adopted, sanctified and kept by His power through faith unto salvation. Neither are any other redeemed by Christ, effectually called, justified, adopted, sanctified, and saved, but the elect only.

"The rest of mankind God was pleased, according to the unsearchable counsel of His own will, whereby He extendeth or withholdeth mercy as He pleaseth, for the glory of His sovereign power over His creatures, to pass by, and to ordain to dishonor and wrath for their sin, so the praise of His glorious justice."

cause was lost. The synod drew up ninety-three canons, combating the principles tenets, and developing more thoroughly the Calvinistic system. The Canons of Dort, therefore, constitute an important portion of Calvinistic symbolics.

In addition to Arminianism, there were two other mediating positions—that of Semi-Pelagianism, and Lutheran Synergism. The former held that divine assistance, or prevenient grace, was necessary, not for the beginning but only for the progress and consummation of grace in the soul. This developed later into the idea of merit. Synergism grew out of the Lutheran doctrine of a universal atonement. Its watchword was that the human will is a *causa concurrens*. This was drawn from the words of Chrysostom, "He that draweth draweth a willing mind." Dr. Pope points out that the Lutheran teaching on this point is vitiated by two errors; first, it ascribes that good in man which converting grace appeals to nature not wholly debased by the fall, without laying stress on the redeeming gift of our Saviour to the world; and second, it makes the preliminaries of grace depend too much on baptism.

THE FIVE POINTS OF CONTROVERSY

The doctrine of the Remonstrants is set forth in five propositions. These are known as the "Five Points of Controversy between the disciples of Arminius and Calvin." They are given by Mosheim as follows:

1. "That God, from all eternity, determined to bestow salvation on those who, as He foresaw, would persevere unto the end in their faith in Jesus Christ, and to inflict everlasting punishment on those who should continue in their unbelief, and resist, to the end of life, His divine succors.

2. "That Jesus Christ, by His death and suffering, made an atonement for the sins of mankind in general, and of every individual in particular; that, however, none but those who believe in Him can be partakers of that divine benefit.

3. "That true faith cannot proceed from the exercise of our natural faculties and powers, or from the force and operation of free will, since man, in consequence of his natural corruption, is incapable of thinking or doing any good thing; and that therefore it is necessary to his conversion and salvation that he be regenerated and renewed by the operation of the Holy Ghost, which is the gift of God through Jesus Christ.

4. "That this divine grace or energy of the Holy Ghost, which heals the disorders of a corrupt nature, begins, advances, and brings to perfection everything that can be called good in man; and that, consequently, all good works, without exception, are to be attributed to God alone, and to the operation of His grace; that, nevertheless, this grace does not force the man to act against his inclination, but may be resisted and rendered ineffectual by the perverse will of the impenitent sinner.

5. "That they who are united to Christ by faith are thereby furnished with abundant strength and succor sufficient to enable them to triumph over the seductions of Satan, and the allurements of sin; nevertheless they may, by the neglect of these succors, fall from grace, and, dying in such a state, may finally perish. This point was started at first doubtfully, but afterward positively as a settled doctrine."

From the Calvinistic standpoint, the Five Points are stated as follows: (1) Unconditional Election; (2) Limited Atonement; (3) Natural Inability; (4) Irresistible Grace; and (5) Final Perseverance. Sometimes they are expressed in the following terms: (1) Predestination; (2) Limited Atonement; (3) Total Depravity; (4) Effectual Calling; and (5) Final Perseverance.

The *Nature of Prevenient Grace.* We come now to a consideration of the doctrine of prevenient grace as advanced by the earlier Arminians, and as given its distinct and final form by the Wesleyans. The original statement is found in the fourth article of the Five Points of the Remonstrants, as follows: "That this divine grace or energy of the Holy Ghost, which heals the disorders of a corrupt nature, begins, advances, and brings to perfection everything that can be called good in man; and that, consequently, all good works, without exception, are to be attributed to God alone, and to the operation of His grace; that, nevertheless, this grace does not force the man to act against his inclination, but may be resisted and rendered ineffectual by the perverse will of the impenitent sinner." This article is analyzed and set forth in propositional form by Mr. Watson in his *Institutes,* as follows:

1. Everything which can be called good in man, previous to regeneration is to be attributed to the work of the Spirit of God. Man himself is totally depraved and not capable of either thinking or doing any good thing, as shown by the previous article.

2. That the state of nature in which man exists previous to regeneration, is in some sense a state of grace —preliminary or prevenient grace.

3. That in this preliminary period there is a continuity of grace—the Holy Spirit, beginning, advancing and perfecting everything that can be called good in man. The Spirit of God leads the sinner from one step to another, in proportion as He finds response in the heart of the sinner and a disposition to obedience.

4. That there is a human co-operation with the divine Spirit, the Holy Spirit working with the free will of man, quickening, aiding and directing it in order to secure compliance with the conditions of the covenant by which man may be saved.

5. That the grace of God is given to all men in order to bring them to salvation through Jesus Christ, but that this grace so given, may be resisted by the free will of man, so as to be rendered ineffectual.

From this analysis it appears that the main points in the Arminian system of grace are the following: (1) the inability of man as totally depraved; (2) the state of nature as in some sense a state of grace through the unconditional benefit of the atonement; (3) the continuity of grace as excluding the Calvinistic distinction between common and efficacious grace; (4) synergism, or the co-operation of grace and free will; and (5) the power of man to finally resist the grace of God freely bestowed upon him. These points must now be given more specific attention.

The powerlessness and inability of man is everywhere assumed in the Scriptures. The question of total depravity, therefore, or the loss of the moral image of God, does not mark the dividing line between Arminianism and Calvinism. In this they agree, with the exception that Calvinism attaches to depravity the idea of guilt, which Wesleyanism in harmony with Arminianism rejects. The following paragraph from Watson's *Institutes* will substantiate this. "The Calvinists contend that the sin of Adam introduced into his nature such a radical impotence and depravity, that it is impossible for his descendants to make any voluntary effort (of themselves) toward piety and virtue, or in any respect to correct and improve their moral and religious character; and that faith and all the Christian graces are communicated by the sole and irresistible operation of the Spirit of God, without any endeavor or concurrence on the part of men" (Watson, *Institutes*, II, p. 48). In commenting on this paragraph Mr. Watson says, "The latter part of this statement gives the Calvinistic peculiarity; the former is not exclusively theirs." On the natural state of man, Arminius in his forcible manner said that "man is so totally overwhelmed as with a deluge,

---

The doctrine of natural depravity affirms the total inability of man to turn himself to faith and calling upon God. This being postulated, the affirmation that all have a fair probation involves the doctrine of a gracious influence unconditionally secured as the common inheritance of the race: this gracious influence is so secured; the same blood that purchased for mankind a conscious existence procured for them all grace needful for the responsibilities of that existence.—Raymond, *Syst. Th.*, II, p. 316.

354   CHRISTIAN THEOLOGY

that no part is free from sin and, therefore, whatever proceeds from him is accounted sin." **The true Arminian as fully as the Calvinist, admits the depravity of human nature, and thereby magnifies the grace of God in salvation.** He is in fact able to carry through his system of grace with greater consistency than the Calvinist himself. For while the latter is obliged, in order to account for certain good dispositions and occasional religious inclinations in those who never give evidence of actual conversion, to refer them to nature or "common grace," the former refers them to grace alone.

The state of nature is in some sense a state of grace, according to Arminian theology. Thus Mr. Wesley says, "Allowing that all the souls of men are dead in sin by nature, this excuses none, seeing there is no man that is in a mere state of nature; there is no man, unless he has quenched the Spirit, that is wholly devoid of the grace of God. No man living is entirely destitute of what is vulgarly called natural conscience. But this is not natural: it is more properly termed preventing grace. Every man has a greater or less measure of this, which waiteth not for the call of man" (WESLEY, Sermon: *Working Out Our Own Salvation*).

Arminianism holds to a belief in the continuity of grace. This is another point to which Mr. Wesley attaches peculiar emphasis. In his sermon on the *Scrip-*

Arminianism holds "that there is a state of nature, as distinguished from the state of grace and the state of glory, that state of nature, however, being itself a state of grace, preliminary grace, which is diffused throughout the world, and visits all the children of men: not merely the remains of good untouched by the fall, but the remains as the effect and gift of redemption. The special grace of enlightenment and conversion, repentance and faith, it holds to be prevenient only, as resting short of regeneration; but as flowing into the regenerate life. It therefore asserts, in a certain sense, the principle of a continuity of grace in the case of those who are saved. But in its doctrine all grace is not the same grace in its issues, though all is the same in its divine purpose. It distinguishes measures and degrees of the Spirit's influence, from the most universal and common benefits of the atonement in life and its advantages up to the consummation of the energy of the Holy Ghost which fits for the vision of God. It rejects the figment of a common grace not χάρις σωτήριος; and refuses to believe that any influence of the Divine Spirit procured by the atonement is imparted without reference to final salvation. The doctrine of a continuity of grace, flowing in some cases uninterruptedly from the grace of Christian birth, sealed in baptism, up to the fullness of sanctification, is alone consistent with Scripture."—POPE, *Compend. Chr. Th.*, p. 390.

ture Way of Salvation, he says, "The salvation which is here spoken of might be intended to be the entire work of God, from the first dawning of grace in the soul till it is consummated in glory. If we take this in its utmost extent it will include all that is wrought in the soul by what is frequently termed natural conscience, but, more properly, prevenient grace; all the drawings of the Father; the desires after God, which if we yield to them, increase more and more; all that is light, wherewith the Son of God 'enlighteneth everyone that cometh into the world'; all the convictions which His Spirit, from time to time, works in every child of man; although it is true the generality of men stifle them as soon as possible, and after a while forget or at least deny, that they ever had them at all."

Synergism, or the co-operation of divine grace and the human will, is another basic truth of the Arminian system. The Scriptures represent the Spirit as working through and with man's concurrence. Divine grace, however, is always given the pre-eminence, and this for two reasons: (1) The capacity for religion lies deep in the nature and constitution of man. The so-called "natural conscience" is due to the universal influence of the Spirit. It is preliminary grace in the very roots of man's nature, to which he may yield, or which he may resist. The fact that man since the fall is a free moral agent, is as much the effect of grace as it is a necessity of his moral nature. (2) The influence of the Spirit connected with the Word is irresistible as claiming the attention of the natural man. He may resist it, but he cannot escape it. This grace moves upon the will through the affections of hope and fear, and touching the deepest recesses of his nature, disposes him to yield to the appeals of the Word, whether presented directly or indirectly. But this divine grace always works within man in a manner that does not interfere with the freedom of his will. "The man determines himself," says Pope, "through divine grace to salvation; never so free as when swayed by grace."

356   CHRISTIAN THEOLOGY

Finally, Arminianism holds that salvation is all of grace, in that every movement of the soul toward God is initiated by divine grace; but it recognizes also in a true sense, the co-operation of the human will, because in the last stage, it remains with the free agent, as to whether the grace thus proffered is accepted or rejected.

Prevenient Grace and Human Agency. The relation of free grace to personal agency demands a further analysis. This relation may be briefly summed up in the following propositions: (1) Prevenient grace is exercised upon the natural man, or man in his condition subsequent to the fall. This grace is exercised upon his entire being, and not upon any particular element or power of his being. Pelagianism regards grace as acting solely upon the understanding, while Augustinianism falls into the opposite error of supposing that grace determines the will through effectual calling. Arminianism holds to a truer psychology. It insists that grace does not operate merely upon the intellect, the feelings or the will, but upon the person or central being which is beneath and behind all affections and attributes. It thus preserves a belief in the unity of personality. (2) Prevenient grace has to do with man as a free and responsible agent. The fall did not efface the natural image of God in man, nor destroy any of the powers of his being. It did not destroy the power of thought which belongs to the intellect, nor the power of affection which pertains to the feelings. So, also, it did not destroy the power of volition which belongs to the will. (3) Prevenient grace has to do further, with the person as enslaved by sin. Not only is the natural heart depraved,

God does not compel man by a mechanical force, but draws him on and moves him by the moral power of His love. Nowhere does either Scripture or the Church teach that the sinner is entirely passive at the commencement of his repentance. The voice which cries awake! comes not to corpses, but to the spiritually dead, in whom a capacity for life remained, a receptivity, even where we cannot think of any spontaneity without the influence of the preparing grace of God. The grace of God leads the sinner to faith, but always in such wise, that the latter's believing surrender to Christ is his own personal act.—Van Oosterzee, *Chr. Dogm.*, II, p. 682.

Never does man appear to be more powerfully determined by God, than in the summons to grace, and yet it is that very summons which calls his freedom from its latent form into actual existence.—Lange.

but added to this is the acquired depravity which attaches to actual transgression. This slavery is not absolute, for the soul is conscious of its bondage and rebels against it. There is, however, a sinful bias, commonly known as a "bent to sinning" which determines the conduct by influencing the will. Thus grace is needed, not to restore to the will its power of volition, nor thought and feeling to the intellect and sensibility, for these were never lost; but to awaken the soul to the truth upon which religion rests, and to move upon the affections by enlisting the heart upon the side of truth. (4) The continuous co-operation of the human will with the originating grace of the Spirit, merges prevenient grace directly into saving grace, without the necessity of any arbitrary distinction between "common grace" and "efficacious grace" as in the Calvinistic system. Because of their insistence upon the co-operation of the human will, Arminian theologians have been charged with being Pelagian, and of insisting upon human merit rather than divine grace in salvation. But they have always held that grace is pre-eminent, and that the power by which man accepts God's proffered grace is from God (Banks); and "the power by which man co-operates with grace is itself grace" (Pope). In opposition to Augustinianism which holds that man has no power to co-operate with God until after regeneration, Arminianism maintains that through the prevenient grace of the Spirit, unconditionally bestowed upon all men, the power and responsibility of free agency exist from the first dawn of the moral life.

Repentance

The doctrine of repentance is fundamental in the Christian system, and should be carefully studied in the light of God's Word. Christ said of himself, *I am not*

Calvinism with its belief in predestination finds it necessary to make a distinction in kinds of grace and thereby breaks the continuity of the Spirit's manifestations. It holds that the good in man before conversion is due to "common grace," but holds also that this can never become saving grace. Common grace belongs to all, efficacious grace only to the elect. "Such a distinction," says Dr. Banks, "can never be reconciled with Scripture, with divine justice or with human responsibility" (BANKS, *Manual Chr. Doct.*, p. 228).

come to call the righteous, but sinners to repentance (Matt. 9:13). Both John the Baptist and Jesus preached repentance as a basic condition of entrance into the kingdom of God (Matt. 3:2, 8; 4:17). God seeks to lead men to repentance, both by His admonitions (Rom. 2:4; II Tim. 2:25; Rev. 2:5, 16), and by His judgments (Rev. 9:20, 21; 16:9). As the conditions of salvation, however, repentance toward God and faith in our Lord Jesus Christ are always conjoined. Both proceed from prevenient grace, but they differ in this, that the faith which saves is the instrument as well as the condition of salvation, and as such, must of necessity flow from grace and follow repentance. For this reason it is frequently stated that faith is the sole condition of salvation, and repentance the condition of faith. Thus Mr. Wesley says that "Repentance and its fruits are only remotely necessary; necessary in order to faith; whereas faith is immediately and directly necessary to justification. It remains that faith is the only condition which is immediately and proximately necessary to justification" (WESLEY, *Sermon xliii*). Both are properly introductory to the state of salvation, but saving faith is alone the point of transition where conviction passes into salvation.

The Greek word *metanoia* (μετάνοια) which in English is rendered repentance, properly "denotes the soul recollecting its own actions, and that in such a manner as to produce sorrow in the review, and a desire of amendment. It is strictly a change of mind, and includes the whole of that alteration with respect to views, disposition and conduct which is effected by the power of the gospel." The word *metameleia* (μεταμέλεια) is also translated *repent*, as in Matt. 27:3, II Cor. 7:8; Heb. 7:21. The distinction between the two verb forms μεταμέλομαι and μετανοέω is this, the former refers more properly to contrition, and signifies a sorrowful change of mind; while the latter carries with it the idea of a sorrow that leads to the forsaking and turning away from sin. Macknight says that "the word *metanoia*, properly denotes such a change of one's opinion concerning some action which he hath done, as produceth a change in his conduct to the better. But the word *metameleia,* signifies the grief which one feels for what he hath done, though it is followed with no alteration of conduct." In the Vulgate, the word *metanoia* is rendered "doing penance." When Luther discovered that repentance meant a change of mind instead of "doing penance," it changed his whole outlook upon religion, and was one of the chief factors in ushering in the Reformation.

Definitions of Repentance. Among the many definitions of repentance, we may note the following: Mr. Wesley says, "By repentance I mean conviction of sin, producing real desires and sincere resolutions of amendment." According to Mr. Watson, "Evangelical repentance is a godly sorrow wrought in the heart of a sinful person by the Word and the Spirit of God, whereby from a sense of his sin, as offensive to God, and defiling and endangering his own soul, and from an apprehension of the mercy of God in Christ, he with grief and hatred of all his known sins, turns then to God as his Saviour and Lord." "Repentance," says Dr. Adam Clarke, "implies that a measure of divine wisdom is communicated to the sinner, and that he thereby becomes wise to salvation; that his mind, purposes, opinions, and inclinations, are changed; and that, in consequence, there is a total change in his conduct." Dr. Pope gives us the following statement: "Repentance is a divinely wrought conviction of sin, the result of the Holy Spirit's application of the condemning law to the conscience or heart. It approves itself in contrition, which distinguishes it from mere knowledge of sin; in submission to the judicial sentence, which is the essence of true confession; and in sincere effort to amend, which desires to make reparation to the dishonored law. Hence it must needs come from God and go back to Him: the Holy Spirit, using

Dr. Nevin says that "Real repentance consists in the heart's being broken for sin and from sin." Mason, "Repentance begins in the humiliation of the heart and ends in the reformation of the life." Dr. Field says that the two words translated "repent" and the two corresponding nouns derived from them, signify "after-concern" and "after-thought." "After-concern" on account of something that has been amiss; and "afterthought" signifying such a change or alteration of mind as implies a return to right views, right feelings and right conduct.

the law, being the Agent in producing this preliminary divine change." These definitions sufficiently set forth the true nature of repentance.

The Divine and Human Elements in Repentance. A study of the definitions just given, makes it clear that there are two factors involved in genuine repentance—the divine and the human. To suppose that repentance is a purely human act, accomplished by the unassisted exercise of the sinner's own powers, is to presume upon God; while to look upon it as the work of God alone, is to sink in carelessness or despair. A correct understanding of this subject is necessary in order to preserve one from either extreme. God is said to be the author of repentance. But He does not repent for us, He gives or grants repentance (Acts 4:31; 11:18) in the sense of making repentance possible. Thus as our creed expresses it, "The Spirit of God gives to all who will repent the gracious help of penitence of heart and hope of mercy, that they may believe unto pardon and spiritual life" (Article VIII). Several controversial points need attention here.

1. Repentance presupposes the sinful condition of mankind. It presupposes, also, both the total depravity of man in his natural state, and the necessity of prevenient grace. Mr. Wesley and Mr. Watson emphasized both of these elements, never allowing themselves to slip over into the Calvinistic idea of irresistible grace on the one hand, or Pelagian moralism on the other. Allowing for the depravity of mankind, Mr. Watson declares that the "gift" comes upon all in prevenient grace—"the influences of the Holy Spirit removing so much of their spiritual death as to excite in them various degrees of religious feeling, and enabling them to seek the face of God, to turn at His rebuke, and by improving that grace, to repent and believe the gospel."

We believe that repentance, which is a sincere and thorough change of mind in regard to sin, involving a sense of personal guilt and a voluntary turning away from sin, is demanded of all who by act or purpose become sinners against God. The Spirit of God gives to all who will repent the gracious help of penitence of heart and hope of mercy, that they may believe unto pardon and spiritual life.—*Manual*, Article VIII.

2. Repentance is the result of the gracious work of the Holy Spirit upon the souls of men. The goodness of God leads to repentance (Rom. 2:4). The means by which it is effected is the divinely wrought application of the holy law. The first effect of the Spirit's work is *contrition*, or godly sorrow for sin. In the Old Testament, this condition was known as "a broken and contrite heart" (Psalms 51:17), the heart being the inmost personality and not merely the affections, the intellect or the will. Thus true repentance is not a sorrow for sin apart from forsaking it, which St. Paul terms "the sorrow of the world" (II Cor. 7:10); nor is it a reform apart from godly sorrow which worketh repentance to salvation. Furthermore, contrition is a conviction of sin as universal, and not merely of particular sins, although the latter may be, and generally are the focal points of the Spirit's convicting work. In its truest and deepest sense, however, contrition is a new moral consciousness of sin, in which the sinner identifies himself with God's attitude toward sin, and thinks God's thoughts about it. He hates sin, and from the center of his being, repudiates and abhors it. Herein lies the ethical significance of true repentance. The second effect of the Spirit's work takes the form of confession. This in essence, is personal submission to the law as applied by the Spirit, and must be viewed under two aspects, (1) as condemnation, in which the sinner accepts the judgment as just; and (2) as impotence, or a conviction of his utter helplessness before the law. *When the commandment came, sin revived, and I died* (Rom. 7:9). True repentance, therefore, "absolutely withers all hope in self as to present or future ability."

3. Repentance is finally, an act of the sinner himself in response to the conviction and appeals of the Spirit.

Repentance, like conversion, is generic, comprehensive in its character; it covers sin as sin. It is impossible to repent of a particular sin without repenting of sin as such—of all sin. The repentance may begin with a particular sin, probably often does; but when the sin is abandoned it must be abandoned as sin; and this involves a renunciation of all sin; that is, of the carnal mind which is the essence of all sin. . . . . Hence in repentance it cannot be necessary to recall every past sin; such repentance would be impossible. The sinful mind, the self-indulgent will, is renounced, and thus all sin is repudiated, even if a particular act of sin be not at the moment recalled.—FAIRCHILD, *Elements of Theology*, p. 250.

The power indeed is given to him of God, but the act is necessarily his own. This power is not given arbitrarily, nor is the agency of the Spirit one of compulsion. God by His Spirit, applies the truth to the sinner's heart, and unveils to his mind the number and aggravations of the sins which he has committed, and the exposure to everlasting wrath which he has incurred. And in view of this revelation, and of the grace bestowed upon him, he is commanded to repent and turn to God. He may accept the truth or he may resist it; but if he does not repent, it is because he will not. We may say then that repentance implies (1) a conviction that "we have done the things we ought not to have done, and left undone those things which we ought to have done"; that we are guilty before God and if we die in this state must be turned into hell; (2) that repentance includes contrition of sin, and that the remembrance of sins will always be grievous and the burden intolerable; (3) that true repentance will produce confession of sin; and (4) that true repentance implies reformation, a turning from sin to God and a bringing forth of fruits meet for repentance. It is for this reason that Mr. Finney defines repentance as "a turning from sin to holiness, or more strictly from a state of consecration to self, to a state of consecration to God"; while Dr. Steele says that "Evangelical repentance is called a repentance toward God because it consists in turning from sin to holiness, implying a sense of, and hatred of sin and a love of holiness."

The State of Penitence. Repentance is an act, penitence is a state of the soul consequent upon that act. Penitence, therefore, is that attitude which belongs to every moral being recovered from sin, and as such will not only exist in every subsequent stage of life, but will have place also in heaven. "It is generally supposed," says Wesley, "that repentance and faith are only the gate of religion; that they are necessary only at the beginning of our Christian course, when we are setting out in the way to the kingdom..... But notwithstanding this, there is also a repentance and faith (taking the words in another sense, a sense not quite the same, nor yet entirely different) which are requisite after we have believed the gospel; yea, and in every subsequent stage of our Christian course, or we cannot run the race which is set before us. And this repentance and faith are full as necessary, in order to our continuance and growth in grace, as the former faith and repentance were, in order to our entering into the kingdom of God" (WESLEY, *Sermon: The Repentance of Believers*). True repentance works a radical change of mind—a change which is manifested in the intellect, the feelings and the will. In a literal sense of course, the true penitent has the same mind and the same mental faculties as before, but they have undergone an inner revolution. He has the same intellect, but this now functions in a different sphere. As a natural man, he was spiritually blind, but now he sees truths which had never before penetrated his mind. He also sees many things in a new light, for he now sees them in a new perspective. There is also a change in his feelings or affections. Once he rested in a false security, and was callous to the threats of the law; now his feelings have been strangely reversed. He now hates what he once loved, and loves what he formerly hated. There is a change also in his will. Once he was bound by the chains of darkness and sin, now he finds his will freed from its fetters and able to function in the spiritual realm. Thus true repentance brings a change of mind, which followed by an act of saving faith, brings the soul into the state of initial salvation; and the continuance of penitence as a state makes possible the reception of further benefits and an abiding communion with God.

The Necessity of Repentance. Repentance is essential to salvation. This has appeared from the previous discussion and needs no extended treatment here. From Christ, our highest possible authority, we have the words, *Except ye repent, ye shall all likewise perish* (Luke 13:3). This is not an arbitrary requirement, but arises from the nature of sin itself. Sin is rebellion against God. There can be no salvation, therefore, without a renunciation of sin and Satan. Sin is as inconsistent with happiness as it is with holiness. But there can be no deliverance from either without true repentance. Until there is a deep feeling of the evil of sin, and an utter renouncement of it, the soul is unprepared for spiritual exercises and holy joy. Repentance is indeed bitter; yet the remembrance of the bitter cup will be an occasion of praise to the redeemed forever. In its adaptation to human needs, therefore, it strikingly exhibits the divine wisdom and benevolence.

Saving Faith

Repentance leads immediately to saving faith, which is at once the condition and the instrument of justification. Faith therefore forms the connecting link between prevenient grace and the initial state of salvation. The term *saving faith*, however, is used in a particular sense, and must be distinguished on the one hand, from the principle of faith generally as it belongs to human nature, and on the other, from the assurance of faith which is the outflow of the Christian life. We shall consider then, (1) The Nature of Faith in General; (2) Saving Faith, or Faith as the Condition and Instrument of Salvation; and (3) Faith as a Grace of the Christian life.

The Nature of Faith in General. Faith has been defined as "credit given to the truth," or "a full assent of the mind to a declaration or promise, on the authority of the person who makes it" (cf. WEAVER, *Chr. Th.*, p. 156). It is that principle of human nature which accepts the unseen as existing, and which admits as knowledge, that which is received on evidence or authority. This general principle of faith, when directed to the gospel and exercised under the prevenient grace of the Spirit becomes saving faith. The Christian idea of faith roots

Impenitence is the state opposed to penitence. It is persistence in sin—in an unbenevolent purpose and life; a state rather than an act; the state of the sinner under light and motives which should induce repentance, and do not (cf. Rom. 2:4, 5). Impenitence does not imply any special emotion or positive feeling of resistance or repugnance or opposition to God. Mere immobility, under motives which should turn the soul from sin, from worldliness, is all that is necessarily involved. Every sinner has motives before him which should lead to repentance. Every persistent sinner is an impenitent sinner.—FAIRCHILD, *Elements of Theology*, p. 251.

back into the Old Testament, and has been modified also by Greek and Roman usage. The Hebrew word translated faith in its simple form, means "to support, to sustain, or to uphold." In the passive form, it means "to be firm, stable and faithful." The use of the word carries with it in almost every instance, the idea of reliance upon the Jehovah of the ancient covenant. For this reason Dr. Oehler defines faith as it is used in the Old Testament to be "the act of making the heart firm, steadfast and sure in Jehovah." The Greek word for faith is *pistis* ($\pi \iota \sigma \tau \iota \varsigma$ from $\pi \epsilon \iota \theta \omega$, to persuade), which means "to trust" or "to be persuaded" that its object, whether a person or a thing, is trustworthy. The Latin word *credere* means "to believe" or "to trust" another. From it we have our word "credit" as belief in the statement of another as true, or the placing confidence in another. This word is usually translated "believe" and refers more especially to the intellectual assent to truth. The word *fides* is another Latin term, and also means "to exercise trust in" or "place confidence in" another. It emphasizes, not so much the intellectual, as the volitional and emotional aspects of faith. In its various forms, the word is usually translated "faith," "faithfulness" or "fidelity." The English word "faith" is supposed to have come from the Anglo-Saxon *faegan* to covenant. From the derivation of these words, it is evident that the primary element of faith is trust. The older theo-

Though much is said in the sacred Scriptures in regard to faith, there is only one passage in which it is particularly defined. This is Hebrews 11:1, "Now faith is the substance of things hoped for; the evidence of things not seen." As this is the only inspired definition of faith, it will be proper to examine with suitable attention the terms in which it is expressed. The word $\upsilon \pi \delta \sigma \tau \alpha \sigma \iota \varsigma$, which is rendered substance, means literally something placed under—a basis or foundation. But in its metaphorical application it means a certain persuasion, an assured expectation, a confident anticipation. We think the latter sense, "confident anticipation," is the true import of the word in the passage before us, as the apostle connects it with "things hoped for." So also, in Hebrews 3:14, the same term is translated "confidence." The term $\epsilon \lambda \epsilon \gamma \chi o \varsigma$, which is rendered evidence, means primarily whatever serves to convince or confute—an argument, proof or demonstration. But when it is used metonymically, it means refutation or conviction—firm persuasion. The last we take as the true import of the word in the present case. The apostle's definition, therefore, may be stated thus: Faith is the confident anticipation of things hoped for, the firm persuasion of things not seen.— WAKEFIELD, *Chr. Th.*, pp. 481, 482.

logians commonly defined faith as (1) the assent of the mind; (2) the consent of the will; and (3) recumbency or reclining, by which was meant the element of trust. But the comprehensive meaning of faith must ever be trust—that which sustains our expectations and never disappoints us. It is, therefore, opposed to all that is false, unreal, deceptive, empty and worthless. Faith is what it purports to be, and is therefore worthy of both credence and trust.

Several deductions must be made in order to better understand the various elements entering into the true nature of belief or faith. (1) Faith implies a previous knowledge of its object. This applies to the intellectual element in faith, or the assent of the mind. It is in this sense of "belief" that knowledge must be regarded as antecedent to faith, but it is only so as to specific acts. A proposition to be believed, must be either expressed or implied; and it must carry with it sufficient evidence, either real or supposed. Faulty judgments are due to a failure to distinguish, between real and supposed evidence. Furthermore, the constitution of the mind is such that it cannot withhold assent to a proposition, if it be sustained by a sufficient amount of evidence. (2) Faith operates in the emotional and volitional life to the degree that the fact or proposition believed is judged to be important. Thus a thing near at hand may be judged to be of more importance than a greater thing farther removed. If faulty judgments arise from a failure to discriminate between real and supposed evidence, so the emotional and volitional elements of the mind may sometimes be moved more by false judgments than the true. Herein is the deceptiveness of the human heart. It puts far

Dr. Whedon says that saving faith is that "belief of the intellect, consent of the affections and act of the will, by which the soul places itself in the keeping of Christ as its ruler and Saviour" .... it is, therefore "our self-commitment to God and to all goodness."

Dr. Fairchild says that "there are three elements which may be distinguished in the general exercise called faith. (1) The intellectual element; that is, an apprehension and conviction of the truth, of some truth which involves obligation. (2) The moral acceptance of that truth, a voluntary treatment of it as true. (3) The emotional results, the peace and assurance and confidence which follow a yielding of the heart to truth."—FAIRCHILD, *Elements of Theology*, pp. 255, 256.

away the evil day. It sells its birthright for a mess of pottage. Only grace can awaken the mind to the truth as it is in Jesus. It was under this illumination of the Spirit that St. Paul wrote, *We look not at the things which are seen, but at the things which are not seen: for the things which are seen are temporal; but the things which are not seen are eternal* (II Cor. 4:18). (3) There are degrees in faith. This is due, not only to a limited apprehension of the truth but also to varying degrees of strength in faith itself. Our Lord said to His disciples, *O ye of little faith* (Matt. 6:30); while to the woman of Canaan, He said, *O woman, great is thy faith* (Matt. 15:28). St. Paul likewise speaks of *him that is weak in the faith* (Rom. 14:1); and again, of the righteousness of God being revealed *from faith to faith,* which can only mean, from one degree of faith to another. To his brethren at Thessalonica, he said, *your faith groweth exceedingly* (II Thess. 1:3). So, also, we find the disciples praying to the Lord, *Increase our faith* (Luke 17:5). From this it follows that we must admit of different degrees of faith in the progress of the Christian life.

Saving Faith. By the term "saving faith" we do not mean a different kind of faith, but faith considered as the condition and instrument of salvation. We have seen that the primary element in faith is trust; hence saving faith is a personal trust in the Person of the Saviour. We may say in this connection that the efficient cause of this faith is the operation of the Holy Spirit, and the instrumental cause is the revelation of the truth concerning

Mr. Wesley says that the word ἔλεγχος translated in Heb. 11:1 means literally a divine evidence and conviction..... It implies both a supernatural evidence of God, and the things of God; a kind of spiritual light exhibited to the soul, and a supernatural sight or perception thereof..... "It is by this faith we are saved, justified and sanctified." "Faith is the condition, and the only condition of justification. It is the condition: none is justified but he that believes: without faith no man is justified. And it is the only condition: this alone is sufficient for justification. Everyone that believes is justified, whatever else he has or has not. In other words: no man is justified till he believes; every man, when he believes, is justified." As to repentance and its fruits, he says, these "are only remotely necessary; necessary in order to faith; whereas faith is immediately and directly necessary to justification. It remains that faith is the only condition which is immediately and proximately necessary to justification.—WESLEY, *Sermon on the Scripture Way of Salvation.*

the need and possibility of salvation. Here we are indebted to Mr. Wesley's clear thought not only for a correct theological statement, but for such a practical interpretation as renders it vital in the experience of men. In his sermon on "The Scripture Way of Salvation" he deals with the subject of faith in relation to both justification and sanctification. He says, "Faith is a divine evidence and conviction not only that 'God was in Christ, reconciling the world unto himself,' but also that Christ loved *me,* and gave Himself for *me.*" Mr. Watson states that "the faith in Christ, which in the New Testament is connected with salvation is clearly of this nature; that is, it combines assent with reliance, belief with trust." "The faith by which 'the elders obtained a good report,' united assent to the truth of God's revelations, to a noble confession in His promises. 'Our fathers trusted in Thee,

Man lives and moves and has his being, as a spiritual creature, in an element of belief or trust in the unseen; in that sense also, "We walk by faith, not by sight." Belief is a primary condition of all knowledge and of all reasoning on knowledge. It may be said that without it there can be no full assent given to any proposition that deals with other than the matter of sense. Hence the propriety of Anselm's *crede ut intelligas,* in opposition to Abelard's *intellige ut credas;* the two watchwords of Christian faith and rationalism respectively.—POPE, *Compend. Chr. Th.,* II, p. 377.

He who will not believe till he receives what he calls a reason for it is never likely to get his soul saved. The highest, the most sovereign reason, that can be given for believing, is that God has commanded it. —DR. ADAM CLARKE, *Chr. Th.,* p. 135.

Faith must be regarded as a form of knowledge. It deals with the invisible, while science deals with the natural and visible world. This, however, does not involve any contradiction between faith and knowledge. The underlying principles of science, such as the uniformity of nature, and the law of causation are, after all, not demonstrated knowledge, but great acts of faith. Faith in spiritual things, deals with realities as truly as does physical science. It is by faith that we know God, and enter into spiritual union with Christ. No form of knowledge can be more genuine than this.

Dr. Fairchild points out that the opposing of faith to reason is entirely without justification. Faith depends on reason, and is only following reasonable evidence; any belief beyond this is arbitrary presumption, or prejudice, not faith. The only foundation for the idea of such opposition is that in the exercise of faith we receive divine revelation, and thus reach truth which lies beyond our reason. We accept God's Word, and take as true what He teaches us, instead of relying on our own unaided reason. In doing this we do not abandon reason, or go in opposition to it; we follow it. Reason brings us to God; we accept His Word as truth, because we have reason to do so in the evidence we have of its truth. A child who takes his father's wisdom as his guide is following reason. He who rejects a higher wisdom, and claims to walk only by his own, is commonly called a rationalist: but he is not following reason (cf. FAIRCHILD, *Elements of Theology,* p. 257).

and were not confounded' " (WATSON, *Institutes*, II, p. 244). Dr. Pope bears witness also to this twofold aspect of faith. "Faith as the instrument of appropriating salvation," he says, "is a divinely wrought belief in the record concerning Christ and trust in His person as a personal Saviour: these two being one" (POPE, *Compend. Chr. Th.*, II, p. 376). We may analyze this subject further, as follows:

1. There is both a divine and a human element in faith. It is a "divine evidence and conviction" or a "divinely wrought belief." The question immediately arises, "Is faith the gift of God, or is it the act of the creature?" The question itself is ambiguous, and each of its clauses has been carried to extreme lengths, the former to an Antinomian faith apart from any operation of the believer; and second to a mere mental assent to truth. Between these extremes of Calvinistic Antinomianism, and Pelagian rationalism, both the earlier and later Arminian theologians have sought a mediating position. Dr. Adam Clarke gives perhaps the clearest and best statement of the Wesleyan position. He says, "Is not faith the gift of God? Yes, as to the grace by which it is produced; but the grace or power to believe, and the act of believing are two different things. Without the grace or power to believe no man ever did or can believe; but with that power the act of faith is a man's own. God never believes for any man, no more than He repents for him; the penitent, through this grace

Dr. Harrison in his "Wesleyan Standards" sums up Mr. Wesley's teaching on faith as follows: (1) A divine evidence and conviction that God hath promised this in His Holy Word. (2) A divine evidence and conviction that what He hath promised He is able to perform. (3) A divine evidence and conviction that He is able and willing to do it now. (4) A divine evidence and conviction that He doeth it. In that hour it is done.—HARRISON, *Wesleyan Standards*, II, p. 340.

In Scripture, faith is presented to us under two leading views. The first is that of assent or persuasion; the second that of confidence or reliance. That the former may be separated from the latter, is also plain, though the latter cannot exist without the former. Faith, in the sense of intellectual assent to truth, is allowed to be possessed by devils. A dead inoperative faith is also supposed, or declared, to be possessed by wicked men, professing Christianity (cf. Matt. 25:41-46). As this distinction is taught in Scripture, so it is also observed in experience, that assent to the truths of revealed religion may result from examination and conviction, while yet the spirit and conduct may be unrenewed and wholly worldly.—WATSON, *Institutes*, II, p. 245.

enabling him, believes for himself: Nor does he believe necessarily or impulsively when he has that power; the power to believe may be present long before it is exercised, else, why the solemn warnings with which we meet everywhere in the Word of God, and threatenings against those who do not believe? Is not this a proof that such persons have the power, but do not use it? They believe not, and therefore are not established. This, therefore, is the true state of the case: God gives the power, man uses the power thus given, and brings glory to God: Without the power no man can believe; with it, any man may" (cf. CLARKE, *Ch. Th.*, pp. 135, 136. Also *Commentary,* Heb. 11:1).

2. Faith has both a negative and a positive aspect, that is, it is both receptive and active. As negative, faith makes the whole soul empty and ready for Jesus; as active, it reaches forth with all its powers to embrace Him and His salvation. Faith in its negative aspect may be regarded as the understanding affecting the heart; in its active aspect, it is that of the understanding affecting the will. The former is the operation of the Holy Spirit, convincing the mind of sin and awakening in the heart strong desires after salvation; the latter, the active instrument by which the soul lays hold of Christ, and is enabled to believe unto the salvation of the soul.

> Bishop Weaver simplifies this position by saying that we have the power to walk; that power is the gift of God. We have the power to see; this also is the gift of God. But God does not walk for us, nor see for us. We may refuse to walk, or we may close our eyes (cf. WEAVER, *Chr. Th.*, p. 158). Dr. Ralston uses practically the same illustration, limiting the "gift of God" to what he terms a "merciful arrangement" not independent of, but in connection with, the free moral agency of man. In this sense, God is "the author and finisher of our faith" because through this merciful arrangement and by the aid of the divine grace imparted, we are enabled to believe. We may say then that in these acceptations faith is the gift of God; but this is far from admitting that faith is in no sense the act of the creature. (cf. RALSTON, *Elements of Divinity,* p. 358).
>
> Christ dwells in the heart only by faith, and faith lives only by love, and love continues only by obedience; he who believes loves, and he who loves obeys. He who obeys loves; he who loves believes; he who believes has the witness in himself; he who has this witness has Christ in his heart, the hope of glory; and he who believes, loves, and obeys, has Christ in his heart, and is a man of prayer.—DR. ADAM CLARK, *Chr. Th.*, p. 141.

3. Faith is the act of the entire being under the influence of the Holy Spirit. It is not merely the assent of the mind to truth, nor a feeling arising out of the sensibilities; nor is it alone the consent of the will to moral obligation. True faith is the act of the whole man. It is the highest act of his personal life—an act in which he gathers up his whole being, and in a peculiar sense goes out of himself and appropriates the merit of Christ. It is for this reason the Scriptures declare that, *with the heart man believeth unto righteousness* (Rom. 10:10). Here the heart is understood as the center of personality, and as involving all of its powers. Thus, saving faith is far more than a mere assent of the mind to truth; it is more than the consent of the will giving rise to mere outward reformation; and it is more than a comfortable state of the emotions. It is admitted that saving faith must embrace all of these, but in its highest exercise it is an unshaken trust in God. It is the acceptance of the propitiatory offering of Christ which is set forth for the salvation of both Jews and Gentiles, and a firm reliance upon the merits of the blood of atonement. This firm and unshaken trust in the atoning work of Jesus Christ must ever be the crowning exercise of saving faith.

4. Saving faith is based upon the truth revealed in the Word of God. It is for this reason that St. Paul defines the gospel as *the power of God unto salvation to every one that believeth* (Rom. 1:16). Our Lord laid the foundation for faith in revealed truth when He said, *Neither pray I for these alone, but for them also which shall believe on me through their word* (John 17:20). St. John says of his own gospel, that *these are written, that ye might believe that Jesus is the Christ, the Son of God; and that believing ye might have life through his name* (John 20:31). St. Paul also declares that God hath chosen us to salvation *through sanctification of the Spirit and belief of the truth* (II Thess. 2:13); and consequently inquires, *How then shall they call on him in whom they have not believed? and how shall they believe in him of whom they have not heard? and how shall they hear without a preacher? And how shall they*

preach, except they be sent? So then faith cometh by hearing, and hearing by the word of God (Rom. 10:14, 15, 17). God, therefore, gives to mankind, through His providence and His grace, the ground of saving truth in His eternal and immutable Word. He gives, also, the gracious influences of the Holy Spirit, to awaken, convict, and lead the soul to Christ. But the Word must not be understood in the sense of the letter only, which we are told, kills; but in the Spirit which gives life. Thus a firm belief in the Christian revelation leads the soul to trust in the Christ who is the object of that revelation. We may say then, that the proper and ultimate ideal of faith is a Divine Person. "When a living faith has arisen in a Divine Person," says Dr. Sheldon, "then, by necessary consequences, there follows reliance upon that which has rational warrant for being regarded as representative of His thought or good pleasure. Faith in the Bible can be, in advance of trust in God who is back of the Bible, only superficial and conventional. The greater here includes the less. Hearty reliance upon God first prepares for genuine repose upon His oracles. Through trustful self-surrender to a personal will we are made ready to rely upon everything which is approved to us as an authentic manifestation of that will" (SHELDON, *System Chr. Doct.*, pp. 438, 439). In this sense, belief is often made perfect by personal trust; and personal trust is the means of strengthening mere belief.

> Dr. Fairchild defines faith "as the voluntary acceptance of truth which calls for moral action: or as treating truth as true; respecting as truth what we have reason to believe to be true in regard to God and our relations to Him, or to any moral duty. The truth must pertain to God, and to duty, because the acceptance of no other truth touches moral character, or can have any bearing on our acceptance with God." In this connection, he points out that faith in its subjective moral nature involves not so much any particular form or amount of truth embraced, as the disposition to know and do the truth. The devils have more truth in their knowledge than many of the saints; they "believe and tremble," but they have no faith; they do not treat the truth as true, are not adjusted to the truth in their voluntary attitude; they resist and reject it. Pilate and Herod knew much about Jesus. Pilate knew Him to be a righteous man; but he did not act according to his knowledge. It is not a question of more or less light or knowledge, but a disposition to obey the light. The feeblest light which is consistent with moral agency lays the foundation for faith. It is not necessary to know the gospel in its highest revelation, in order to the possibility and obligation of faith (cf. FAIRCHILD, *Elements of Theology*, pp. 254-255).

5. **Saving faith is vitally related to good works.** The relation of faith to works has been the subject of much controversy in the history of the Church. Too frequently, Calvinists in their insistence upon salvation by faith only, have denied works, both as a merit and as a condition. Arminians deny the merit of good works but insist upon them as a condition of salvation. Mr. Wesley's formula was, "works, not as a merit, but as a condition." But it must be borne in mind that the works of which he speaks, are regarded, not as springing from unassisted human nature, but from the prevenient grace of the Spirit. This position is set forth in Article X of Methodism, which with a few verbal changes, is the same as Article XII of the Anglican Confession. "Although good works, which are the fruits of faith, and follow after justification, cannot put away our sins, and endure

Mr. Wesley wisely omitted Article XIII of the Anglican Creed which follows this and is entitled "Of Works Before Justification." This was probably written in opposition to the Romanist doctrine of merit, and reads as follows: "Works done before the grace of Christ, and the inspiration of his Spirit, are not pleasant to God, forasmuch as they spring not of faith in Jesus Christ: neither do they make men meet to receive grace, or (as the school authors say) deserve grace of congruity: yea rather, for that they are not done as God hath willed and commanded them to be done, we doubt not but they have the nature of sin."

Mr. Fletcher in his "Checks to Antinomianism" has given us perhaps our strongest argument for good works as a condition of salvation. These are not to be understood as meriting salvation; nor are they to be regarded as the immediate condition of salvation, which both Mr. Fletcher and Mr. Wesley held to be faith alone. They are however, remote conditions, and are set over against the Antinomian position, that the sinner is to do nothing toward his salvation. He says, "Please to answer the following questions, founded upon the express declarations of God's Word. 'To him that ordereth his conversation aright will I show the salvation of God.' Is ordering our conversation aright, doing nothing? 'Repent ye and be converted that your sins may be blotted out.' Are repentance and conversion nothing? 'Come unto me all ye that....are heavy laden, and I will give you rest'—I will justify you. Is coming doing nothing? 'Cease to do evil, learn to do well. Come now, let us reason together: though your sins be red like crimson, they shall be as white as snow"—you shall be justified. Is ceasing to do evil, and learning to do well doing nothing? 'Seek ye the Lord while he may be found, call upon him while he is near. Let the wicked forsake his way, and the unrighteous man his thoughts, and let him return unto the Lord, who will have mercy upon him, and to our God for he will abundantly pardon.' Is seeking, calling, forsaking one's way, and returning to the Lord a mere nothing? 'Ask and ye shall receive; seek and ye shall find; knock, and it shall be opened unto you.' Yea, take the kingdom of heaven by force. Is seeking, asking, knocking, and taking by force absolutely nothing? When you have answered these questions, I will throw one or two hundred more of the like kind in your way."

the severity of God's judgment; yet they are pleasing and acceptable to God in Christ, and spring out of a true and lively faith, insomuch that by them a lively faith may be as evidently known as a tree is discerned by its fruit." The good works here mentioned are pleasing to God, (1) because they are performed according to His will; (2) because they are wrought through the assistance of divine grace; and (3) because they are done for the glory of God.

Throughout the gospel, grace and faith are regarded as correlative terms. *For by grace are ye saved through faith; and that not of yourselves: it is the gift of God* (Eph. 2:8). The Jews had come to consider salvation as a matter of works, which carried with it the idea of debt on God's part. St. Paul, however, set the idea of faith over against that of works, and the idea of grace over against that of debt. Faith on man's part he did not regard as a work of merit, but as a condition of salvation. Hence man could be saved only by faith, apart from the meritorious deeds of the law. It may be well to note that this principle of faith operated in the Old Testament also. It is sometimes stated that men were saved by law in the Old Testament, but by grace in the New Testament. But salvation has always been by grace through faith. St. Paul distinctly states that the law could not annul the promise or make it of none effect. For him the idea of obedience as meriting salvation was inconceivable. In Galatians 3:15-22, he sets forth the meaning of the law in relation to the gospel, but makes it clear that no law could have given life, for all are under sin. Hence the law could only serve as a schoolmaster to bring us to Christ. If men had possessed the

Dr. Pope in his Higher Catechism expresses the relation of faith and works as follows:
(1) Faith is opposed to works as meritorious, and the formula is: "A man is not justified by works of law, but only through faith in Jesus Christ" (Gal. 3:16).
(2) Faith lives only in its works, and the formula is: "Faith without works is dead" (James 2:26).
(3) Faith is justified and approved by works, and the formula is: "I will shew thee my faith by my works" (James 2:8).
(4) Faith is perfected in works, and the formula is: "By works was faith made perfect" (James 2:22). (Cf. POPE, *Higher Catechism*, p. 233.)

moral power to perfectly obey the law, even then salvation would have been due to the living union with God through faith. Hence salvation is now, and always has been, by grace through faith. The act of faith by which man is saved, becomes the law of his being as saved; and hence good works flow from the principle of living faith.

Faith as a Grace of the Christian Life. Saving faith is that act by which the prevenient grace of the Spirit passes over into the regenerate life of the believer. Thus the faith which saves becomes the faith which is a law of our being. The initial act becomes the permanent attitude of the regenerate man. *As ye have therefore received Christ Jesus the Lord, so walk ye in him: rooted and built up in him, and stablished in the faith* (Col. 2: 6, 7). This faith becomes *the law of the Spirit of life in Christ Jesus* (Rom. 8: 2), which St. Paul declares *works by love* (Gal: 5: 6). He also mentions faith as the seventh fruit of the Spirit (Gal. 5: 22), and further catalogues it as one of the gifts of the Spirit (I Cor. 12: 9). As the former, it is a quality of the regenerate life and, therefore, a gracious result and an abiding privilege of believers; as the latter, it is a special gift bestowed by the Spirit for the profit of those to whom it is given (I Cor. 12: 7). Closely associated with saving faith is the so-called "assurance of faith." Arminian theologians, however, have always regarded assurance as an indirect, or reflex action of saving faith, and not that faith

Concerning assurance, Mr. Wesley says, "But is this faith of assurance, or the faith of adherence? The Scripture mentions no such distinction. The apostle says, 'There is one faith, and one hope of your calling'; one Christian saving faith: 'as there is one Lord,' in whom we believe, and 'one God and Father of us all." And it is certain, this faith necessarily implies an assurance (which is here only another word for evidence, it being hard to tell the difference between them) that Christ loved me, and gave Himself for me. For 'he that believeth' with the true, living faith 'hath the witness in himself'; 'the Spirit witnesses with His Spirit that He is a child of God.' 'Because he is a son, God hath sent forth the Spirit of his Son into his heart, crying, Abba, Father'; giving him an assurance that he is so, and a childlike confidence in Him. But let it be observed, that in the very nature of the thing, the assurance goes before the confidence. For a man cannot have a childlike confidence in God till he knows he is a child of God. Therefore, confidence, trust, reliance, adherence, or whatever else it be called, is not the first, as some have supposed, but the second branch or act of faith."—WESLEY, *Sermon: The Scripture Way of Salvation.*

itself. Thus Dr. Pope says, "Assurance belongs to this trust only in an indirect manner, as its reflex action and its gracious result, and its abiding privilege in the regenerate life. As faith is the highest negative work of repentance and passes into the energy of regeneration, so confidence in its object, relying upon it as an objective, passes into the faith of subjective assurance. But the assurance is the fruit, and not the essence of faith. ....That He is my actual Saviour, and that my belief is saving, cannot be the object of faith direct; it is the reflex benefit and gift of the Holy Ghost. It is the full assurance of faith, the πληροφορία πιστέως in which worshipers are exhorted to draw near" (POPE, *Compend. Chr. Th.*, II, pp. 383, 384). Again, faith as the law of the Christian life, is always operative. "It works by love and purifies the heart." Otherwise there is danger of faith becoming merely a formal assent to the conditions of salvation. It is this against which St. James warns us. *Thou believest that there is one God; thou doest well......But wilt thou know, O vain man, that faith without works is dead? For as the body without the spirit is dead, so faith without works is dead also* (James 2: 19, 20, 26). True faith is, therefore, a working faith.

Conversion

Conversion is the term used to designate the process by which the soul turns from sin to salvation. It is commonly used in a narrower sense in theology, but in common speech is used as a general term to express the initial state of salvation, as including in an undifferentiated manner, justification, regeneration and adoption. In the Scripture, however, conversion is generally used in the narrower sense of the term, sometimes being connected with repentance, and sometimes with faith. Once the term is used as the antecedent of repentance, *Surely after that I was turned, I repented* (Jer. 31: 19). More frequently, however, it is used in close connection with repentance, as the human act in turning away from sin. Thus our Lord quotes the prophecy of Isaiah, that *they should not see with their eyes, nor understand with their heart, and be converted, and I should heal them* (John 12:40). He also said, *Except ye be converted, and become as little children, ye shall not enter into the kingdom of heaven* (Matt. 18:3). To Peter He said, *When thou art converted, strengthen thy brethren* (Luke 22:32). St. Peter himself uses the term twice in his sermon at Pentecost—the first as an exhortation, *Repent ye therefore, and be converted, that your sins may be blotted out* (Acts 3:19); and once in recounting the mission of Jesus, *in turning away every one of you from his iniquities* (Acts 3:26). It is used also in connection with the mission of St. Paul, *to turn them from darkness to light, and from the power of Satan unto God, that they may receive forgiveness of sins, and inheritance among them which are sanctified by faith that is in me* (Acts 26:18). Usually, however, it is used in the Acts in connection with faith, to designate the company of believers. Thus, *all that dwelt at Lydda and Saron saw him, and turned to the Lord* (Acts 9:35); and *a great number believed, and turned unto the Lord* (Acts 11:21). St. Peter uses the term in the wider sense, when he said, *But ye are now returned unto the Shepherd and Bishop of your souls* (I Peter 2:25); while St. James uses it in the narrower sense of a

The term conversion stands here for a few equivalents in Hebrew and Greek which express the same religious idea: that of the change by which the soul is turned from sin to God. The fact that it is thus common to the two Testaments gives it great importance. It is the general description of the restoration of the sinner that runs through the Bible; and, therefore, has been very often regarded as including much more than the mere crisis of moral and religious change. Sometimes it is thought to represent the whole course, through all its stages, of the return of the soul to God: this is the case especially in the works of mystical writers, and of some who are not mystical. By those for instance, who recognize no saving influence before regeneration, out of which repentance and faith flow, conversion is of necessity made to include all the moral blessings of the state of grace: in fact, it must have a very indeterminate meaning in every system of Calvinism. The theology that may be called Sacramentarian generally regards conversion as the process of recovery from a state in which the regenerating grace conferred in baptism has been neglected and might seem to be lost. Sometimes, by a very loose employment of the term, it is made synonymous with the experience of forgiveness and the assurance of reconciliation. But we must remember that it simply means the turning point of the religious life: its turning from a course of sin to the commencement of seeking God. Hence the crisis that it marks is not in the religious life of a believer, but in the life of the soul, redeemed indeed, but not yet a new creature in Christ.—POPE, *Compend. Chr. Th.*, II, pp. 367, 368.

merely human change, when he says, *Brethren, if any of you do err from the truth, and one convert him; let him know, that he which converteth a sinner from the error of his way, shall save a soul from death, and shall hide a multitude of sins* (James 5: 19, 20).

In Calvinistic theology, "Conversion is the human side or aspect of that fundamental spiritual change, which, viewed from the divine side, we call regeneration." Holding as they do that regeneration is an effectual calling by the decree of God, men are first regenerated, and then are able to turn themselves to God. In this sense it is simply man's turning (cf. STRONGE, *Syst. Th.*, III, p. 829). Dr. A. H. Strong defines conversion as "that voluntary change in the mind of the sinner in which he turns, on the one hand, from sin, and on the other hand, to Christ. The former or negative element in conversion, namely, the turning from sin, we denominate repentance. The latter or positive element in conversion, namely, the turning to Christ, we denominate faith." Dr. Pope takes almost the same position, when he defines it as "the process by which the soul turns, or is turned, from sin to God, in order to its acceptance through faith in Christ. This is its strict meaning, as distinguished from that broader sense in which it is applied to the entire history of the soul's restoration" (POPE, *Compend. Chr. Th.*, II, p. 367). While these definitions are similar, and are in fact essentially the same, there is a vast difference in the two views. Calvinism, as indicated, holds that man is regenerated by absolute decree, and then turns to God; Arminianism holds that through grace, preveniently bestowed, man turns to God and is then regenerated. Thus conversion in its truest scriptural meaning, is the pivotal point, wherein through grace, the soul turns from sin, and to Christ, in order to regeneration.

CHAPTER XXVII
CHRISTIAN RIGHTEOUSNESS

Christian righteousness or justification by faith is a cardinal doctrine in theology, and for this reason occupies a controlling position in the entire Christian system. It is the particular point in saving grace, where the soul is brought into an acceptable relation to God through Christ, and therefore determines all further advances in the Christian life. Martin Luther spoke of justification as the *articulus stantis aut cadentis ecclesiæ* or the "article of a standing or falling church." "It spreads its vital influence through all Christian experience, and operates in every part of practical godliness." The practical importance of this truth is ably set forth by Bishop Merrill in his *Aspects of Christian Experience*. He says, "Here His life and spirit and power come into efficient contact with awakened consciences and penitent hearts, bringing the throbs of a new life and the gleams of a new day to the soul lost in darkness and sin. Destroy this link of the chain and the whole is useless. The name of Christ, if retained, will have lost its charm. His blood will be robbed of its meritorious efficacy, and His Spirit will be reduced to a sentiment or a temper, with no power to quicken the soul into the life of righteousness. Along with this displacement of Christ will come an undue exaltation of human virtues and the diminution of the turpitude of sin, till the presence of guilt shall cease to alarm, and the need of humiliation become a dream. Then the pomp of worship will take the place of inward groaning for salvation, and the services of the sanctuary will be required to charm the senses, to minister to

---

The first reformers regarded justification by faith as the central question in their gigantic assault upon corrupt Christendom: induced proximately by the abuse of indulgences, and ultimately by the fervent study of St. Paul's doctrine of righteousness. They made this the starting point of all controversy, and relied upon its settlement for the removal of every abuse.—POPE, *Compend. Chr. Th.*, II, p. 439.

the esthetic tastes, and to nourish the vanity of the heart, without disturbing the emotions or stirring the depths of the soul with longings after God and purity."

Definitions of Justification. Arminius gives us this definition: "Justification is a just and gracious act of God by which, from the throne of His grace and mercy, He absolves from his sins man, who is a sinner but who is a believer, on account of Christ, and His obedience and righteousness, and considers him righteous to the salvation of the justified person, and to the glory of the divine righteousness and grace." Mr. Wesley defines justification as "that act of God the Father, whereby, for the sake of the propitiation made by the blood of His Son, He sheweth forth His righteousness (or mercy) by the remission of the sins that are past." According to Wakefield, "Justification is an act of God's free grace, by which He absolves a sinner from guilt and punishment, and accepts him as righteous, on account of the atonement of Christ." A definition found in Watson's *Dictionary,* and quoted by Wakefield, Ralston and Pope, is that of Dr. Bunting. He says, "To justify a sinner is to account and consider him relatively righteous; and to deal with him as such, notwithstanding his past unrighteousness, by clearing, absolving, discharging and

Watson speaks of justification as "being the pardon of sin by a judicial sentence of the offended Majesty of heaven, under a gracious constitution."—WATSON, *Institutes,* II, p. 215.

Wakefield quotes favorably the definition of Dr. Schmucker, that "Justification is that judicial act of God by which a believing sinner, in consideration of the merits of Christ, is released from the penalty of the law, and is declared to be entitled to heaven."—WAKEFIELD, *Chr. Th.,* p. 406.

Among the Calvinistic definitions may be mentioned the following: Strong defines justification as "that judicial act of God, by which, on account of Christ, to whom the sinner is united by faith, He declares that the sinner is no longer exposed to the penalty of the law, but to be restored to His favor" (*Syst. Th.,* III, p. 849). Boyce defines it as "a judicial act of God, by which on account of the meritorious work of Christ, imputed to a sinner and received by him through that faith which vitally unites him to his substitute and Saviour, God declares that sinner to be free from the demands of the law, and entitled to the rewards due to the obedience of that substitute" (*Syst. Th.,* p. 395). According to Fairchild, justification as a fact under the gospel, is "the pardon of sin that is past; and the doctrine of justification is simply the doctrine of the pardon of sin" (*Elements of Th.,* p. 277). E. Y. Mullins defines justification as a "judicial act of God in which He declares the sinner free from condemnation, and restores him to divine favor" (*Chr. Relig.,* p. 389).

releasing him from various penal evils, and especially from the wrath of God, and the liability to eternal death, which by that past unrighteousness he had deserved; and by accepting him as if just, and admitting him to the state, the privileges, and the rewards of righteousness." Our own Article of Faith, while intended primarily as a statement of belief, is nevertheless definitive in its nature. "We believe that justification is that gracious and judicial act of God, by which He grants full pardon of all guilt and complete release from the penalty of sins committed, and acceptance as righteous, to all who believingly receive Jesus Christ as Lord and Saviour" (Article IX). We may now sum up these various aspects of truth and express them in the following definition: "Justification is that judicial or declarative act of God, by which He pronounces those who believingly accept the propitiatory offering of Christ, as absolved from their sins, released from their penalty, and accepted as righteous before Him."

The Scriptural Development of the Doctrine. Concerning the doctrine of justification, various opinions have been asserted and defended by theologians. But before considering these positions, it will be well to give attention to those Scriptures which bear directly upon this subject, in order to apprehend as clearly as possible, the light in which divine inspiration has presented it. A variety of terms is used—justification, righteousness, nonimputation of sin, reckoning or imputation of righteousness, and like terms, all of which have substantially the same import, but with various shades of meaning. The seed thought of the new and divine righteousness is given us in the following words from our Lord himself, *Seek ye first the kingdom of God and his righteous-*

The Wesleyan statement as found in Article IX of the Twenty-five Articles is as follows: "We are accounted righteous before God, only for the merit of our Lord and Saviour Jesus Christ by faith, and not for our own works or deservings; wherefore, that we are justified by faith only is a most wholesome doctrine, and very full of comfort." This is the same as Article XI of the Thirty-nine Articles, with the omission of the words "as more largely is expressed in the Homily of Justification." The Methodist Catechism has the following statement. "Justification is an act of God's free grace, wherein He pardoneth all our sins, and accepteth us as righteous in His sight, only for the sake of Christ."

ness (Matt. 6: 33). This was later developed by St. Paul. The following are the more important passages. (1) *Be it known unto you therefore, men and brethren, that through this man is preached unto you the forgiveness of sins: and by him all that believe are justified from all things, from which ye could not be justified by the law of Moses* (Acts 13: 38, 39). Here it is evident that forgiveness and justification are synonymous terms, the one explanatory of the other but with a shade of difference. (2) *Being justified freely by his grace through the redemption that is in Christ Jesus: whom God hath set forth to be a propitiation through faith in his blood, to declare his righteousness for the remission of sins that are past, through the forbearance of God; to declare, I say, at this time his righteousness: that he might be just, and the justifier of him which believeth in Jesus* (Rom. 3: 24-26). This is considered one of the classical passages on justification, and sets forth the Pauline position in a variety of terms. Another passage also considered classical is the following: (3) *But to him that worketh not, but believeth on him that justifieth the ungodly, his faith is counted for righteousness. Even as David describeth the blessedness of the man, unto whom God imputeth righteousness without works, saying, Blessed is the man whose iniquities are forgiven, and whose sins are covered. Blessed is the man to whom the Lord will not impute sin* (Rom. 4: 5-8). St. Paul's Epistle to the Galatians deals with the subject of justification also, but emphasizes more especially the relation of faith and works.

The Nature of Justification

The term justification has several applications. *First,* it is applied to one who is personally just or righteous, and against whom no accusation is brought. This is personal justification, or justification on the ground of perfect obedience or personal worthiness. The word *dikaioo* (δικαιόω) is frequently used in the New Testament in this forensic sense of pronouncing a person just or righteous. Thus, *Wisdom is justified of her children* (Matt.

11:19). *And all the people that heard him, and the publicans, justified God* (Luke 7:29); and *the doers of the law shall be justified* (Rom. 2:13). *Second,* the term may be applied to one against whom accusation has been made but not sustained. *If there be a controversy between men, and they come unto judgment, that the judges may judge them; then they shall justify the righteous, and condemn the wicked* (Deut. 25:1). This is legal justification on the ground of innocence or the righteousness of the cause. *Third,* it is applied to one who is accused, is guilty and condemned. How can such a one be justified? In one sense only—that of pardon. By the act of God, his sins are pardoned for Christ's sake, his guilt canceled, his punishment remitted, and he is accepted before God as righteous. He is therefore declared righteous, not by legal fiction, but by judicial action, and stands in the same relation to God through Christ, as if he had never sinned. This is evangelical justification, and is possible only through the redemption that is in Christ Jesus.

Evangelical justification is the remission of sins. The importance of acquiring and maintaining this simple and distinct view of justification, will appear on further consideration of the subject. "The first point which we find established by the language of the New Testament," says Mr. Watson, "is that justification, the pardon and remission of sins, the nonimputation of sin, and the imputation of righteousness, are terms and phrases of the same import" (WATSON, *Institutes,* II, p. 212). But this position must be carefully guarded. While the remission of sins is an act of mercy, it is not an exercise of the divine prerogative apart from law, but consistent with law. It is thus distinguished from mere forgiveness. This position must be further distinguished on the one hand, from the mere imputation of Christ's righteousness as taught by the Antinomians; and on the other, from the idea of justification upon the ground of inherent righteousness as held by the Roman Catholic Church. That justification means the pardon or remission of sins, is not only a tenet of Arminianism, but is the "vital fact" in the teaching of all orthodox Protestant divines.

Justification is both an act and a state. It is an act of God whereby men are declared to be just or righteous; and it is a state of man, into which he is introduced as a consequence of this declaration. But whether as an act or as a state, the word in its true connotation, is never used in the sense of making men righteous, but only in the sense of declaring or pronouncing them free from the guilt and penalty of sin, and therefore righteous. Thus salvation is a broader term than justification, and includes regeneration, adoption and sanctification. The terms used in the Scriptures carry a certain exactness of meaning, indicating an act, an act in process, an act as fully accomplished or perfected, and a state following the accomplishment of the act. (1) δικαιόω or the simple verb form is expressive of the act of justification. *Who shall lay anything to the charge of God's elect? It is God that justifieth* (Rom. 8:33). (2) δικαίωσις signifies the act in process of completion. *Who was delivered for our offences, and was raised again for our justification* (Rom. 4:25). *The free gift came upon*

Mr. Wesley states that "the plain scriptural notion of justification is pardon, the forgiveness of sins." "It is that act of God the Father, whereby, for the sake of the propitiation made by the blood of His Son, He 'showeth forth His righteousness (or mercy) by the remission of the sins that are past.' This is the easy, natural account of it given by St. Paul, throughout this whole epistle."—WESLEY, *Sermon, Justification by Faith.*

Knapp takes the position that "one who is guilty is said to be justified when he is declared and treated as exempt from punishment, or innocent, or when the punishment of his sins is remitted to him. This is called *justificatio externa*. The terms justification, pardon, accounting righteous, occur in the Bible much more frequently in this sense than in any other, and so are synonymous with forgiveness of sin."—KNAPP, *Chr. Th.*, p. 387.

The words forgiveness and remission have, sometimes, each a specific sense. The word pardon is sometimes specifically synonymous with remission, and sometimes equal to both forgiveness and remission. When an aggrieved party forgives the aggressor, there is a change in the feelings of the aggrieved toward the aggressor; he regards him, feels toward him, and treats him the same as though he had never done him an injury. This may occur between private individuals in cases where the offense is not a violation of public law, where the aggrieved has not authority to inflict penalty. Remission has respect not to the feelings of the aggrieved, or to the personal feelings of the magistrate, but to the penalty incurred by the transgression. To remit sin is to release from obligation to punishment; it is to order authoritatively the nonexecution of penalty.—RAYMOND, *Syst. Th.*, II, p. 323.

all men unto justification of life (Rom. 5: 18, last clause). (3) δικαίωμα signifies the act as already accomplished. *The free gift is of many offenses unto justification* (Rom. 5: 16); *Even so by the righteousness of one* [the act completed] *the free gift came upon all men unto justification of life* [the act in process] (Rom. 5: 18). The meaning of the two terms as used in this latter verse is, that the "righteousness or justification" of Christ as fully accomplished, becomes the ground by which this righteousness avails, and is continuously available to men. As a completed act, this word is translated "ordinance" in Romans 2: 26 and Hebrews 9: 1, and hence conveys the meaning of a legal decision, or statute of law. (4) δικαιοσύνη refers to the state of one who has been justified or declared righteous. *The Spirit is life because of righteousness* (Rom. 8: 10). *But of him are ye in Christ Jesus, who of God is made unto us wisdom, and righteousness, and sanctification, and redemption* (I Cor. 1: 30). The necessity of distinguishing between justification as an act and a state, will appear as we further study the subject.

Justification is a relative change, and not the work of God by which we are made actually just and righteous. Justification being the pardon of sin, we must guard against the notion that it is an act of God by which we are made actually just and righteous (cf. WATSON, *Institutes*, II, p. 215). Here also we must refer to Mr. Wesley's clear and discriminating thought on this subject. "But what is it to be justified? What is justification? ....It is evident from what has been already observed

Justification changes our relation to law—it removes condemnation, but does not change our nature or make us holy. "This is sanctification, (or in its incipient state, regeneration), which is indeed, the immediate fruit of justification; but nevertheless, is a distinct gift of God and of a totally different nature."—RALSTON, *Elements of Divinity*, p. 371.

As justification is distinguishable from sanctification, so also is it from regeneration, which, in reality, is but the inception of sanctification. Justification is that gracious act of God, as the moral Governor of the world, by which we are released from the guilt and punishment of sin; regeneration is a work of the Holy Spirit, by which we experience a change of heart, being made "partakers of the divine nature," and "being created in Christ Jesus unto good works, which God hath before ordained that we should walk in them."—WAKEFIELD, *Chr. Th.*, p. 409.

that it is not the being made actually just and righteous. This is *sanctification;* which is, indeed, in some degree, the immediate fruit of justification, but, nevertheless, is a distinct gift of God, and of a totally different nature. The one implies what God does *for us* through His Son; the other what He works *in us* by His Spirit. So that, although some rare instances may be found wherein the term justified or justification is used in so wide a sense as to include sanctification also; yet, in general use, they are sufficiently distinguished from each other, by both St. Paul and the other inspired writers" (WESLEY, *Sermon on Justification by Faith*). In viewing justification as a relative change, and sanctification as a real change,

In anticipation of our discussion of entire sanctification, we may say that as Mr. Wesley used the term sanctification, and as used generally in theology, it refers to the whole inner work of cleansing from sin. As it pertains to the cleansing from guilt and acquired depravity, it is known as "initial" sanctification, and as such, is concomitant with justification, regeneration and adoption; as it pertains to the cleansing from inbred sin, it is a subsequent work, known in Wesleyan theology as "entire" sanctification. When, therefore, the term sanctification is used in contradistinction to justification, the latter as Mr. Wesley indicates, "implies what God does for us through His Son; the other, what He works in us by His Spirit." This use of the terms should be kept clearly in mind.

Is holiness a condition of justification? If so, the individual is holy before he is justified. What then are we to do with such passages as the following: Gal. 2:17; Rom. 5:10) "When we were enemies, we were reconciled to God by the death of his Son"? Again, how are any to become holy but through Christ. It should not be supposed that persons may be justified and still remain enemies to God. Their moral state is changed at the time of their justification. Holiness does not precede justification, but such a state of mind is induced in the sinner that it is consistent for God to pardon him.—DUNN, *Syst. Th.*, p. 249.

The fathers in the ministry of the Methodist Church, in public discourse, used frequently to speak of salvation in three regards: *first*, salvation from the guilt of sin; *second*, from the reigning power of sin; and *third*, from the inbeing of sin. The first they called justification; the second, regeneration, or initial sanctification; and the third, entire sanctification. That they intended, by the guilt of sin obligation to punishment admits of no manner of doubt; indeed, there is no other sense in which a man can be saved from the guilt of sin. . . . . The deed being done, it can never come to pass that it was not done; and so also of the responsibility and demerit of the doer. To save them from the guilt of sin is to exempt the sinner from the punishment due, from the penalty incurred. To justify is to order, authoritatively, the nonexecution of penalty—just this, and nothing more.—RAYMOND, *Syst. Th.*, II, p. 326.

The grand object of our redemption was to accomplish human salvation; and the first effect of Christ's atonement, whether anticipated before His coming, as "the Lamb slain from the foundation of the world," or when effected by His passion, was to place man in that new relation from which salvation might be derived to the offender.—WAKEFIELD, *Chr. Th.*, p. 404.

we must clearly understand the use of these terms. We do not mean by the term *relative* and *real,* that one is fiction and the other fact. In this sense justification is as much a reality as is sanctification. What we mean is this, that justification is an actual change in relationship to God, while sanctification is a change in the moral nature of the individual. The relation of a sinner to God is that of condemnation; when justified, this relation is changed through pardon to acceptance or justification. Now it is evident that if sanctification or the inward change preceded the outward, then we should have holiness or inward righteousness in those who stood in a relation of condemnation before God. For this reason Protestantism has always held that the first act of God in the salvation of men must be justification or a change of relation from condemnation to righteousness. It holds also, that concomitant with the act of justification, there is the inward change of sanctification, or the impartation of righteousness. But in thought at least, justification must precede, and upon this change in relation, all else, however immediate or remote, must ultimately depend.

This failure to make a sharp distinction between justification as a declarative act in the mind of God, and sanctification as a moral change within the soul consequent upon the new relation of justification, lies at the basis of the whole Tridentine theology. Even in the New Testament we find an attempt to reconcile faith and works; and the earlier fathers frequently used the term justification in the broader sense of applying the atonement to the whole nature and life of the sinner. Faith also came to be regarded, not only as the principle which apprehends Christ's merit for forgiveness, but that which unites the soul to him in the inner work of renewal. Hence two kinds of faith were distinguished— the *fides informis,* or an intellectual assent to the articles of faith; and *fides formata charitate* which manifests itself in love and virtue. It was an easy matter, therefore, to transfer the imputation of Christ's righteousness from the individual to faith itself, as having in it the germ of all good. Faith thus had virtue, and consequently merit, a position which leads directly to the idea of justification as an infusion of righteousness rather than a remission of sins.

It was in the Tridentine Decrees (1547 A.D.) of the Roman Catholic Church that the doctrine took shape in opposition to the positions of the Reformers. Here it is distinctly stated that "Justification is not the mere remission of sins, but also the sanctification and renovation of the inward man through the voluntary reception of grace and gifts of grace; whereby an unjust man becomes just, the enemy a friend, so that he may be an heir according to the hope of eternal life. The only cause of formal justification is the justice of God, not that by which He himself is just, but that by which He makes us just . . . . receiving justice into ourselves, each one according to his own measure, which the Holy Spirit imparts to each as He pleases, and also according to each one's own disposition and co-operation." How rapid and steep is the decline, when once the forensic idea of justification is rejected, is shown by two other statements of the Tridentine Council—one denying the instantaneousness of justification, the other its assurance. The first is as follows: "By mortifying their fleshly members, and yielding them as instruments of righteousness unto sanctification, through the observance of the commands of God and of the Church, their righteousness itself being accepted through the grace of Christ, and their faith co-operating with their good works, they grow and are justified more and more." This

The controversies of the fourth and fifth centuries led to a general confounding of faith with orthodoxy. John Damascene (750 A.D.) was the first theologian who clearly apprehended the distinction between "faith that cometh by hearing" or assent to a creed, and "faith the substance of things hoped for," or the personal application so as to produce the fruits of faith. Hugh of St. Victor in the West also distinguished between faith as a form of knowledge and faith as an affection.

Augustine said, "We ascribe faith itself, from which all righteousness taketh beginning . . . . not to the human will, nor to any merits going before, but we confess it to be the free gift of God." His *catena* or chain of grace is as follows: "Faith is the first link of the gracious chain which leads to salvation. By the law comes the knowledge of sin, by faith the attainment of grace against sin, by grace the healing of the soul from the stain of sin, by the healing of the soul full freedom of the will, by the freed will love to righteousness, and by love to righteousness the fulfilling of the law."

increase of justification the holy Church seeks when she prays: "Give unto us, O Lord, increase of faith, hope and charity." The next statement carries this position of the council further in its logical development. "Although it is necessary to believe that no sin is, or ever has been remitted except gratuitously by the divine mercy on account of Christ, yet no one affirms with confidence and certainty that his sins are remitted, and who rests in this confidence alone, is to be assured of remission."

Justification is a forensic or judicial act. The term forensic is from *forum,* a court. A forensic proceeding, therefore, belongs to the judicial department of government; and a judicial act is a declaration or pronouncement, either of condemnation or justification. The act of justification in a theological sense, is judicial, for God does not justify sinners merely of his own good pleasure, but only on account of the righteousness of Christ. In the forensic proceeding, two forms or constitutions of righteousness are before God, the Supreme Judge of all men, as the ground of justification. There is the righteousness which is of the law, and the righteousness which is by faith. The sinner standing before God under the legal constitution or law of works, receives through the justice of God, the sentence of condemnation; for *by the deeds of the law there shall no flesh be justified*

The anathemas are as follows: "If anyone shall say that the sinner is justified by faith alone, in the sense that nothing else is required which may co-operate toward the attainment of the grace of justification, and that the sinner does not need to be prepared and disposed by the motion of his own will: let him be accursed. If anyone shall say that men are justified either by the sole imputation of the righteousness of Christ, or by the sole remission of sin, to the exclusion of that grace and charity which is shed abroad in their hearts by the Holy Spirit, and which inheres in them, or shall say that the grace whereby we are justified is merely and only the favor of God: let him be accursed. If anyone shall say that justifying faith is nothing but confidence in the divine mercy remitting sin on account of Christ, or that this faith is the sole thing by which we are justified: let him be accursed."

Hence justification was dispossessed of all that was forensic, and became *actio Dei physica*—righteousness infused, making a man just instead of unjust. Therefore it could never be regarded as a settled and fixed act of God, and never as a matter of certain assurance to its possessor. Justification in this system confirmed at Trent, is the process of a transmutation from a state of righteousness, in virtue of which the justified can accomplish works entitling to eternal life.—POPE, *Compend. Chr. Th.,* II, p. 424.

in his sight: for by the law is the knowledge of sin (Rom. 3:20). But St. Paul tells us of a new constitution which he calls *the righteousness of God without the law* (Rom. 3:21), *Even the righteousness of God which is by faith of Jesus Christ unto all and upon all them that believe* (Rom. 3:22). Now that same sinner standing before God under the constitution of faith, receives through the justice of God, the sentence of acquittal, *being justified freely by his grace through the redemption that is in Christ Jesus* (Rom. 3:24). The act which pronounces the sinner justified, is authoritative solely because it is a judicial act. Anyone might lay claim to having received the rewards of Christ's merit, but such a proclamation would not be justification. It becomes such, only when uttered as an authoritative pronouncement by God as Judge. A sovereign may pardon, but only a judge can pronounce righteous. His word is final.

In the later controversy concerning *imputation,* a certain class of Arminian theologians sought to avoid the

The best account of the development of the mediæval doctrine is given by Dr. Pope (Vol. II, p. 425). He says, "The present and eternal acceptance of the sinner for the sake of Christ alone, never rejected absolutely, was denied by implication: the absolute supremacy of the Saviour's merit was reserved for the original fault of the race; for sin committed after its first imputed benefit, human expiation was demanded. Second, the peculiarity of the apostolical term justification, as referring to a sinner's relation to law, was all but entirely abolished. Justification was said to make the sinner a saint and meet for heaven; and thus the word did duty for the renewal and entire sanctification of the soul. It was forgotten that, because the law will forever have its charge against him—as apart from Christ—he must ever be justified by grace through faith. Third, the fatal dogma of Supererogation, based upon the figment of a possible superfluous merit acquired by observance of the Counsels of Perfection, laid the broad and deep foundation of the practice of indulgence. This profoundly affected the doctrine of justification, whether viewed as pardon or righteousness. Fourth, and this was the climax of the mediæval error, the one eternal and finished sacrifice of Christ was taken from the direct administration of the Holy Ghost, and changed into a sacrifice offered by the Church through her priests, with special application according to the intention of the human administrator. The combination of all these influences gradually introduced another gospel, preached no longer to a faith that brings neither money nor price.—POPE, *Compend. Chr. Th.,* II, p. 425.

They are wrong inasmuch as they deny that there is a distinction between the acceptance for Christ's sake and the acceptance of the inward work of holiness wrought by His Spirit. The Scriptures teach, what common sense confirms, that the present, constant and final acceptance of a sinner must be a sentence of righteousness pronounced for Christ's sake independent of the merit of works.—POPE, *Compend. Chr. Th.,* II, p. 432.

evil consequences of Antinomianism by making justification a sovereign rather than a forensic act. Thus Dr. Miley makes the statement that "forgiveness really has no place in a strictly forensic justification." But then, he interprets forensic justification in his own peculiar manner as "simply an authoritative judgment of actual righteousness." Hence he says that "forgiveness and forensic justification can neither be the same thing nor constituent parts of the same thing"; and "there must be error in any theory which omits forgiveness as the vital fact of justification." He admits one fact, however, in which the divine forgiveness is closely akin to forensic justification, that is "the result of forgiveness is a justified state. With respect to the guilt of all the past

Justification is the divine judicial act which applied to the sinner, believing in Christ, the benefit of the Atonement, delivering him from the condemnation of his sin, introducing him into a state of favor, and treating him as a righteous person. Though justifying faith is an operative principle which through the Holy Spirit's energy attains to an interior and perfect conformity with the law, or internal righteousness, it is the imputed character of justification which regulates the New Testament use of the word. Inherent righteousness is connected more closely with the perfection of the regenerate and sanctified life. In this more limited sense, justification is either the act of God or the state of man.—POPE, *Compend. Chr. Th.*, II, p. 407.

Justification, being the pardon of sin by judicial sentence of the offended Majesty of heaven, under a gracious constitution, the term affords no ground for the notion, that it imports the imputation or accounting to us the active and passive righteousness of Christ, so as to make us both relatively and positively righteous.—WATSON, *Institutes*, II, p. 215.

Mr. Wesley in his sermon on "The Lord Our Righteousness" thus deals with the question of imputation. "But when is this righteousness imputed? When they believe. In that hour the righteousness of Christ is theirs. It is imputed to everyone that believes, as soon as he believes. But in what sense is this righteousness imputed to believers? In this: all believers are forgiven and accepted, not for the sake of anything in them, or of anything that ever was, that is, or ever can be, done by them, but wholly for the sake of what Christ hath done and suffered for them. But perhaps some will affirm that faith is imputed to us for righteousness. St. Paul affirms this; therefore, I affirm it too. Faith is imputed for righteousness to every believer—namely, faith in the righteousness of Christ; but this is exactly the same thing which has been said before; for by that expression I mean neither more nor less than that we are justified by faith, not by works, or that every believer is forgiven and accepted merely for the sake of what Christ had done and suffered."

Dr. Ralston points out that Calvin taught imputation in a strict sense, that the obedience of Christ was accepted for us as if it were our own; while Wesley teaches an imputation in an accommodated sense, that is the righteousness of Christ is imputed to us in its effects—that is, in its merits. We are justified by faith in the merits of Christ.—RALSTON, *Elem. of Divinity*, p. 385.

sins, the forgiveness sets the sinner right with the law and with God" (MILEY, *Syst. Th.*, II, pp. 311, 312). The Wesleyans—Watson, Adam Clarke, John Fletcher, and John Wesley himself—while laying stress on the forgiveness of sins, do not forget also, that justification, strictly speaking, is more than mere forgiveness. One of the earliest statements of Methodism was this, "To be justified is to be pardoned and received into God's favor; into such a state that, if we continue therein, we shall finally be saved" (Minutes, 1744). Methodist theologians also grasped the fact that in the act of justification, both the sovereign and judicial factors were involved.

Mr. Watson in his *Institutes* gives us a suggestion which is worthy of more elaborate treatment. He says "that in the remission or pardon of sin, Almighty God acts in His character of Ruler and Judge, showing mercy upon terms satisfactory to His justice, when He might in rigid justice have punished our transgressions to the utmost. The term justification especially is judiciary, and taken from courts of law and the proceedings of magistrates; and this judiciary character of the act of pardon is also confirmed by the relation of the parties to each other, as it is constantly exhibited in Scripture. God is an offended Sovereign; man is an offending subject. He has offended against public law, not against private obligations; and the act therefore by which he is relieved from the penalty, must be magisterial and regal. It is also a further confirmation that in this process Christ is represented as a public Mediator and Advocate." Mr. Watson also points out that some of the older divines properly distinguish between *sententia legis* and *sententia judicis*, that is between legislation and judgment; between the constitution under which the sovereign decides, whether it be rigidly just or softened by mercy, and his decisions in his regal and judicial capacity themselves. Justification is therefore a decision under a gracious legislation, "The law of faith"; but not this legislation itself. "For if it be an act of legislation, it is then only promise, and that looks toward none in particular; but to all to whom the promise is made, in general, and presupposeth a condition to be performed. But justification presupposeth a particular person, a particular cause, a condition performed, and the performance, as already past, pleaded; and the decision proceeds according" (cf. WATSON, *Institutes*, II, pp. 213, 214).

If we take into account the various factors of justification found in the above statements, we shall see that the one act of justification when viewed negatively is the forgiveness of sins; when viewed positively, is the acceptance of the believer as righteous. Furthermore, we shall see that in the work of justification, God acts in His character as both Ruler and Judge, by His sovereign grace forgiving the sins of the penitent believer, and by a judicial act remitting the penalty and pronouncing him righteous. To separate between these too sharply is to lay the foundation for error. Overemphasis upon the first, as we have seen, leads to a denial of imputation, and laid the ground for the Tridentine theology; overemphasis upon the second, led to the opposite error of Antinomianism. This seems to be the position of Dr. Pope, although here again, no special treatment is accorded it. He says, "The state of δικαιοσύνη is that of conformity to law, which, however, is always regarded as such only through the gracious imputation of God who declares the believer to be justified negatively from the condemnation of his sin, and positively reckons to him the character, bestowing also the privileges of righteousness. The former or negative blessing is pardon distinctively, the latter or positive blessing is justification proper. Whether the act or the state is signified, the phraseology of justification is throughout Scripture faithful to the idea of imputation. The verb is not used of making righteous save as the notion of declaring or reckoning is bound up with it" (POPE, *Compend. Chr. Th.*, II, p. 409).

Justification is an instantaneous, personal and comprehensive act. Justification is an actual work performed, in which God changes the relation of the sinner from that of condemnation under law, to that of righteousness in Christ. This work is instantaneous in that it is a definite and immediate decision consequent upon faith, and hence is not a sentence extending through years. The moment a true penitent believes on the Lord Jesus Christ he is justified. *He that believeth on the Son hath everlasting life* (John 3: 36). It is personal as distinguished from "that gracious constitution of God, by which, for the sake of Christ, He so delivers all mankind from the guilt of Adam's sin as to place them in a salvable state. Justification is a blessing of a much higher and more perfect character, and is not common to the human race at large, but experience by a certain description of persons in particular" (BUNTING, *On Justification*). Those who would be justified, therefore, must seek it by earnest prayer and faith, and experience this grace for themselves. It is comprehensive, in that it is the remission of all the sins of the past, through the forbearance of God.

THE GROUND OF JUSTIFICATION

In our treatment of the nature of justification, we found it necessary to constantly assume that the ground of justifying faith was the mediatorial work of Jesus Christ. The two subjects are so closely interwoven, that it is impossible to draw any sharp line of demarcation between them. The one necessarily gives character

We have a familiar parallel to the above in the act of sanctification, which we define to be negatively, the cleansing from sin; positively, perfect love or the infilling of the Spirit. And yet there are not two acts, but one act. To disparage the former, or cleansing aspect leads to Antinomianism—a legal standing without an inward state of purity. To disparage the latter, is to rest in the work of God instead of in God himself.

Dr. Sheldon says, "It was the verdict of early Protestant theology that Paul used the word justification ($\delta\iota\kappa\alpha\iota\omega\sigma\iota\varsigma$, $\delta\iota\kappa\alpha\iota o\hat{\upsilon}\nu$) in the objective or judicial sense, denoting thereby not the inner quality of its subject but his standing with God as being freed from condemnation. That this verdict was the true one is very largely the conclusion of free scholarship in the present, that is, of scholarship which is not under the constraint of an inflexible ecclesiastical authority. It may be accepted as representing the actual usage of the apostle, provided the intimate association between the objective and subjective phase of salvation which subsisted in his thought is not overlooked. This interpretation rests upon no technical etymological ground, but is involved in the texture of the Pauline arguments."—SHELDON, *Syst. Chr. Doct.*, p. 441.

to the other. The evangelical plan of justifying the ungodly rests upon three things: *first,* the full satisfaction of the divine justice through the propitiatory offering of Christ as man's Representative; *second,* the divine honor placed upon the merit of Christ by virtue of His redeeming work; and *third,* the union of these two in a righteous and gracious economy, wherein it is possible for God as Ruler and Judge, to show mercy in the forgiveness of sins, on terms consistent with justice. The sole ground of justification then, according to the evangelical plan, is the propitiatory work of Christ received in faith. This has already been set forth in our discussion of the atonement, and needs now to be restated only in its immediate reference to the work of justification.

The sole ground of justification being faith in the blood of Christ as a propitiatory offering, all theories based upon personal righteousness through the works of the law are immediately excluded. *First,* it excludes Socinianism which holds to a form of justification—not on the ground of faith in Christ as a condition of forgiveness, but as an act of the highest obedience. Unitarianism and Universalism, which generally regard repentance as in itself a sufficient ground for forgiveness, are likewise excluded as essentially attempts at justification by works. *Second,* it excludes also the Roman Catholic theory of inherent righteousness, as already presented in our discussion of the nature of justification.

The method of orthodox Protestantism in its attempt to relate the work of Christ to the justification of the believer, is known as imputation. The word is derived from the Greek verb $\lambda o\gamma \acute{\iota} \zeta o\mu a\iota$ which means to reckon or to account. However, we may say at this point that it is never used in the sense of reckoning or accounting the actions of one person to have been performed by another. A man's sin or righteousness is imputed to him when he is actually the doer of the sinful or righteous acts. In this sense the word repute is frequently used, that is, a man is reputed to be sinful or righteous. In a legal sense, the consequence of a man's sin or righteousness is imputed to him in the matter of punishment or reward. To impute sin or righteousness is to take account of it, either to condemn or acquit, and hence to punish or to exempt from punishment. There are three theories of imputation which have been held as the ground of justification by Protestant theologians. (1) Justification by the imputation of Christ's active obedience; (2) Justification by the imputation of Christ's active and passive obedience combined; and (3) Justification by the imputation of faith for righteousness.

Imputation of the Active Obedience of Christ. This is generally known as the Hyper-Calvinistic or Antinomian theory of justification. It maintains that the active obedience of Christ is substitutionary, and is so imputed to the elect, as to render them legally as righteous as if they had themselves rendered perfect obedience to the law of God. The elect are therefore righteous by proxy. The Antinomian tendencies of this type of theology are peculiarly subtle and dangerous. It rightly makes a distinction between the "standing" of the believer legally, and his "state" or condition spiritually; but too frequently it has so widely separated between the two, and so strongly emphasized the former, as to overlook and undervalue the subjective work of the Spirit in the impartation of righteousness. The faith by which we are justified is a *fides formata,* or a faith which has in it the inherent power of righteousness. It is as the Wesleyans commonly expressed it, "a faith which works by love and purifies the heart." Arminianism holds that while the act of imputation is logically precedent, actually it is always accompanied by inward sanctification. It maintains that justification, regeneration, adoption and initial sanctification are concomitant blessings, all of which are included in the broader sense of conversion. Antinomianism, however, has usually been content with what the older theologians termed *fides informis,* or a mere intellectual assent to truth stated in confessional form.

Mr. Wesley objected strongly to this theory of imputation. "The judgment of an all-wise God," he says, "is always according to truth; neither can it ever consist with His unerring wisdom to think that I am innocent, to judge that I am righteous or holy because another is so. He can no more confound me with Christ than with David or Abraham" (WESLEY, *Sermon on Justification*). From this Dr. Wakefield argues as follows: "If the obedience of Christ is to be accounted ours in the sense of this theory, then it must be supposed that we never sinned, because Christ never sinned; and if we are accounted to have perfectly fulfilled in Christ the whole law of God, why are we required to ask for pardon? Should it be said that when we ask for pardon we ask only for a revelation of our eternal justification, the matter is not altered, for what need is there of pardon, either in time or eternity, if we are accounted to have perfectly obeyed God's holy law? And why should we be regarded as having suffered, in Christ, the penalty of sins which we are accounted never to have committed?" (WAKEFIELD, *Chr. Th.*, p. 410). Other objections which Arminianism has raised against the above position may be summarized as follows: (1) It is unsupported by Scripture. Such verses as *the Lord our righteousness* (Jer. 33:16), can only mean that He is the Author of our righteousness, as He is made also unto us wisdom and sanctification and redemption. (2) The personal acts of Christ were of too lofty a character to be imputed to mankind. "He who claims for himself the righteousness of Christ presents himself to God, not in the habit of a righteous man, but the glorious attire of the Divine Redeemer." This attitude is not characteristic of the humility of the genuine Christian. (3) It shifts the meritorious cause of justification from the death of Christ to the obedience of His life. His death then is made unnecessary, and men are still under the covenant of works, by which St. Paul says, *Shall no flesh be justified* (Rom. 3:20).

Imputation of the Active and Passive Obedience of Christ. Both Calvinism and Arminianism are united in maintaining that the active and passive obedience of Christ are never separated in fact and should not be separated in thought. Calvin states his position as follows: "We simply explain justification to be an acceptance, by which God receives us into His favor and esteems us as righteous persons, and we say it consists in the remission of sins and the imputation of the righteousness of Christ .... He must certainly be destitute of a righteousness of his own, who is taught to seek it out of himself. This is most clearly asserted by the apostle when he says, 'He hath made him to be sin for us who knew no sin, that we might be made the righteousness of God in him.' We see that our righteousness is not in ourselves but in Christ. 'As by one man's disobedience many were made sinners, so by the obedience of one shall many be made righteous.' What is placing our righteousness in the obedience of Christ, but asserting that we are accounted righteous only because His obedience is accepted?" (CALVIN, *Institutes*, Bk. 3, Chap. 11). Arminius makes this statement, "I believe that sinners are accounted righteous solely by the obedience of Christ; and that the righteousness of Christ is the only meritorious cause on account of which God pardons the sins of believers, and reckons them as righteous as if they had perfectly fulfilled the law. But since God imputes the righteousness of Christ to none except believers, I conclude, that in this sense, it may be well and properly said, to man who believes, faith is imputed for righteousness, through grace, because God hath set forth his Son Jesus Christ to be a propitiation, through faith in His blood. Whatever interpretation may be put upon these expressions, none of our divines blame Calvin, or consider him to be heterodox on this point; yet my opinion is not so widely different from his, as to prevent me employing the signature of my own hand in subscribing to those things which he has delivered on this subject in the third book of his *Institutes*." So also Mr. Wesley, in his sermon entitled, "The Lord Our Righteousness," almost repeats Arminius' words; but though these eminent divines seem to agree substantially with Calvin, it is clear that, in their interpretation of the phrase, the "imputed righteousness of Christ," they would not entirely follow him (WATSON, *Institutes*, II, pp. 222-224).

While the phraseology of Calvin and Arminius is similar, their interpretations are widely different, as the following considerations will show. Calvin makes no distinction between the active and passive righteousness of Christ. His idea of imputation seems to be that the righteousness of Christ, both His doing and His suffering, is accounted or imputed to us "as if it were our own." Here Mr. Watson remarks, "We may conclude that he admitted some kind of transfer of the righteousness of Christ to our account; and that believers are considered so to be in Christ, as that He should answer for them in law, and plead His righteousness in default of theirs. All this we grant, is capable of being interpreted in a good and scriptural sense; but it is also capable of a contrary one." It is the Antinomian abuse of the doctrine that has rendered it suspicious. Hence Dr. Pope warns us to be on our guard "against surrendering precious truths, merely because they have been perverted. So long as we hear the apostle's trust as to the past, *I am crucified with Christ,* and his present experience and hope for the future of being *found in Christ, not having mine own righteousness,* we must be cautious how we recoil from the imputation of the righteousness of Christ. To this it must in some sense come at last; for even when our own conformity to the law is raised to the highest perfection heaven can demand, we must in respect to the demand of righteousness upon our whole history and character be *found in Christ* or be lost. But the language of Scripture should be adhered to in every statement on such a subject" (POPE, *Comp. Chr. Th.,* II, pp. 447, 448). These are wholesome words. The Antinomianism that would lead a soul to a reliance upon the imputed righteousness of Christ, without the concomitant inward impartation of righteousness by the Spirit, is a dangerous perversion of the truth. But neither can self-righteousness stand in the presence of God. Only as Christ is made unto us wisdom, and righteousness, and sanctification, and redemption, do we rest securely in the grace of God.

The Imputation of Faith for Righteousness. This is the only view of the subject which fully accords with the Scriptures and with the great tenet of the Reformation that we are justified by faith alone. This is proved by the scriptures already mentioned and by many others. Thus, *by him all that believe are justified from all things* (Acts 13: 39). *Abraham believed God, and it was counted* [ἐλογίσθη] *unto him for righteousness* (Rom. 4: 3). *Faith was reckoned* [imputed] *to Abraham for righteousness* (Rom. 4: 9). *Therefore it was imputed unto him for righteousness* (Rom. 4: 22); and *for us also, to whom it shall be imputed, if we believe on him that raised up Jesus our Lord from the dead* (Rom. 4: 24). In this connection it may be well to observe also that the word *righteousness* (δικαιοσύνη) is frequently used in the passive sense for justification itself. *If righteousness* [justification] *come by the law, then Christ is dead in vain* (Gal. 2: 21). *For if there had been a law given which could have given life, verily righteousness* [justification] *should have been by the law* (Gal. 3: 21); and *Christ is the end of the law for righteousness* [justification] *to every one that believeth* (Rom. 10: 4).

From these Scriptures it appears, (1) that it is faith itself, as a personal act of the believer, and not the object of that faith that is imputed for righteousness. Those who hold to the antinomian view of imputation are under the necessity of interpreting these scriptures in a metonymical manner, that is, making faith to be a figure of speech which includes the whole of Christ's active and passive righteousness. But the Scriptures are clear that faith is imputed or reckoned for righteousness only to him whose personal act it is, and in no sense the imputation of the personal act of another. (2) Faith is the condition of righteousness. Faith is not to be identified with righteousness in the Tridentine sense, that faith constitutes righteousness. Faith cannot constitute personal righteousness. This would be to make faith a subtle form of works, to which merit would be attached, and would take away from us the atonement of Christ as the only ground of justification. St. Paul insists that faith is the condition of righteouness, and therefore "of faith" simply means the legal state consequent upon the remission of sins through faith. (3) The faith that justifies is not faith in general, but a particular faith in the propitiatory work of Christ. *Being justified freely by his grace through the redemption that is in Christ Jesus: whom God hath set forth to be a propitiation through faith in his blood* (Rom. 3: 24, 25). Christ becomes the Saviour by virtue of the blood of the atonement which He shed for all men; but the faith which brings the assurance of salvation is that faith alone which accepts Him as the Saviour through an atonement in His blood.

CHAPTER XXVIII
CHRISTIAN SONSHIP

Christian sonship, involving as it does, both regeneration and adoption, is vitally related to Christian righteousness. There are, however, real points of difference between them. The necessity for justification lies in the fact of guilt and penalty, while that of regeneration is due to the moral depravity of human nature after the fall. The former cancels guilt and removes penalty; the latter renews the moral nature and re-establishes the privileges of sonship. The two, however, are coincident in time, for they are accomplished in answer to the same act of faith. We may say, then, that Christian righteousness and Christian sonship, involving justification, regeneration, adoption and initial sanctification, are concomitant in personal experience, that is, they are offered as inseparable blessings and occur at the same time. The regenerate man is justified, and the justified man is re-

The leading blessings concomitant with justification are regeneration and adoption; with respect to which we may observe generally, that although we must distinguish them as being different from each other, and from justification, yet they are not to be separated. They occur at the same time, and they all enter into the experience of the same person; so that no man is justified without being regenerated and adopted, and no man is regenerated and made a son of God, who is not justified. Whenever they are mentioned in Scripture, they, therefore, involve and imply each other.—WATSON, *Theological Institutes*, II, p. 266.

No terms are more strictly correlative than regeneration and adoption. They describe the same blessing under two aspects: the former referring to the filial character, the latter to the filial privilege. But they are not thus closely connected as cause and effect: they are co-ordinate, and the link between them is the common sonship. The assurance of filial adoption does not produce the regenerate life nor does the infusion of the perfect life of regeneration of itself invest the children of God with all the prerogatives of heirship. Moreover, they are as distinct from the other leading blessings in the economy of grace as they are themselves united. The justified state does not involve of necessity the special privileges of adoption; nor does regeneration as such imply the specific relation to God which sanctification signifies. The two terms we now consider embrace in their unity an entirely distinct department of the Spirit's administration of the New Covenant; they lead us into the household of faith and the family of God. Touching at many points those other departments, they are nevertheless perfect and complete in themselves.—POPE, *Compend. Chr. Th.*, III, pp. 3, 4.

generated. The terms are not, however, synonymous, and in the development of theological thought gradually became more sharply defined—justification being limited to a change in relations, and regeneration to a change in the moral state. Regeneration and adoption are more nearly correlative terms than regeneration and justification. The former describes sonship in reference to its filial character, while the latter presents it from the viewpoint of filial privilege. However, these terms are not related as cause and effect, but find their union in the common fact of sonship. Our study will embrace the following subjects: (1) Regeneration; (2) Adoption; and (3) The Witness of the Spirit.

Regeneration

The term *regeneration* is derived from the Greek word *palingenesia* (παλινγενεσία or παλιγγενεσία) which is compounded of πάλιν "again" and γένεσις 'to be," so that the word means literally "to be again." It is, therefore, to be understood as a reproduction or a restoration. Theologians and biblical commentators have generally applied the terms to the moral change set forth in the Scriptures as "born again" (John 3:3, 5, 7; I Peter 1:23); "born of God" (John 1:13; I John 3:9; 4:7; 5:1, 4, 18); "born of the Spirit" (John 3:5, 6); "quick-

> Crowther in his portraiture of the Wesleyan position says, "That all who repent and believe, are, (1) Justified, and have peace with God; that we are accounted righteous, only through the sacrifice and intercession of our Lord and Saviour Jesus Christ. But although faith, receiving and resting upon Christ, is the sole condition and instrument of justification; yet this faith in the justified person, 'worketh by love,' and produces inward and outward holiness. They believe (2) That all persons who are thus justified, are adopted into the family of God, have a right to all the privileges of His children, and may come boldly to the throne of grace; receiving the spirit of adoption, they are enabled to cry, Abba, Father; and, as His children are loved, pitied, chastened, protected, and provided for; they are heirs of God, and jointheirs with Jesus Christ; and that continuing in this state they shall inherit all the promises, and obtain everlasting life. They believe also, (3) That those who are thus justified and made children of God, are assured of this; and that this blessed assurance arises from 'The Spirit of God bearing witness with their spirits that they are the children of God.' They believe that no person, under the gospel dispensation is excluded from this privilege, except through unbelief, lukewarmness, the love of the world, or some other sin. . . . . But they believe that every person possessed of this justification, adoption, and witness of the Spirit, hungers and thirsts after righteousness."—Crowther, *Portraiture*, pp. 171, 172.

ened" (Eph. 2:1, 5; Col. 2:13); and "passed from death unto life" (John 5:24; I John 3:14). In the conversation with Nicodemus, Jesus uses the words γεννηθῇ ἄνωθεν which means literally, "to be born from above." St. John indicates also, that the change wrought by the Spirit in regeneration is, like that of justification and adoption, conditioned on faith. Thus, to *as many as received him, to them gave he power* [ἐξουσίαν or authority] *to become the sons of God, even to them that believe on his name* (John 1:12). St. Paul uses more indirect terms than St. John, but his meaning is the same. Thus *if any man be in Christ, he is a new creature* (II Cor. 5:17). *And you, being dead in your sins and the uncircumcision of your flesh, hath he quickened together with him, having forgiven you all trespasses* (Col. 2:13). In all his epistles, St. Paul stresses faith as the sole condition of salvation.

The word regeneration occurs but twice in the New Testament. The first use of the term is in our Lord's conversation concerning future rewards, where He said to His disciples, *that ye which have followed me, in the regeneration when the Son of man shall sit in the throne of his glory, ye also shall sit upon twelve thrones, judging the twelve tribes of Israel* (Matt. 19:28). Commentators generally admit the correctness of the punctuation as found in the Authorized Version and, therefore, connect the word regeneration with that which immediately follows. They differ, however, as to the application—some referring it to the millennial state, and others to the resurrection or the general judgment. Dr. Ralston refers it to the perfected gospel dispensation. However the passage be interpreted, it cannot be made to refer to the moral and spiritual renovation by which men are constituted the children of God. The second

---

Regeneration, like justification, is a vital part of Christian soteriology. It must be such, since native depravity is a reality, and regeneration a necessity to a truly spiritual life. It follows that a truthful doctrine of regeneration must be profoundly important. Yet it is one respecting which error has widely prevailed, and greatly to the detriment of the Christian life. However, as between evangelical systems, the doctrine of regeneration has been far less in issue than that of justification, mostly because it is less directly concerned in the doctrinal view of the atonement.—MILEY, *Syst. Th.*, II, p. 327.

use of the term is found in the statement of St. Paul to the effect that men are saved *by the washing of regeneration, and renewing of the Holy Ghost* (Titus 3:5). Here the "washing of regeneration" is an allusion to the rite of baptism, although in a narrower sense, the "washing" may refer to the rite, and the "regeneration" to the spiritual renovation which it symbolizes. The "renewing of the Holy Ghost" must be regarded as a comprehensive term, referring in one sense to the basic work of regeneration, and in another to the subsequent work of entire sanctification. As related to regeneration, this renewing is a restoration to the moral image of God in which man was originally created and, therefore, the re-establishment of the primal pattern. But it is more than this. It is also the renewing of the original purpose of man's life in its full devotement to God. Hence we are exhorted by St. Paul to *put on the new man, which after God is created in righteousness and true holiness* (Eph. 4:24); and again to *put on the new man, which is*

Dr. Shedd points out that the term "regeneration" has been used in a wide, and in a restricted sense. "It may signify the whole process of salvation, including the preparatory work of conviction and the concluding work of sanctification. Or it may denote only the imparting of spiritual life in the new birth, excluding the preparatory and concluding processes. The Romish Church regards regeneration as comprehending everything in the transition from a state of condemnation on earth to a state of salvation in heaven, and confounds justification with sanctification. The Lutheran doctrine, stated in the Apology for the Augsburg Confession and in the Formula Concordiæ, employs regeneration in the wide meaning, but distinguishes carefully between justification and sanctification. In the Reformed Church, the term regeneration was also employed in the wide signification. Like the Lutheran, while carefully distinguishing between justification and sanctification, the Reformed theologian brought under the term 'regeneration' everything that pertains to the development as well as to the origination of the new spiritual life. Regeneration thus included not only the new birth, but all that issues from it." "The wide use of the term passed into the English theology. The divines of the seventeenth century very generally do not distinguish between regeneration and conversion, but employ the two as synonyms." "But this wide use of the term regeneration led to confusion of ideas and views. Consequently, there arose gradually a stricter use of the term regeneration, and its discrimination from conversion. Turretin defines two kinds of conversion, as the term was employed in his day. The first is 'habitual' or 'passive' conversion. It is the production of a habit or disposition in the soul. The second kind is 'actual' or 'active' conversion. It is the acting out in faith and repentance of this implanted habit or disposition." This shows the manner in which Calvinism was led to adopt such a sharp distinction between regeneration and conversion. (Cf. SHEDD, *Dogmatic Theology*, II, pp. 41-49).

renewed in knowledge after the image of him that created him (Col. 3:10). Here it is evident that man is "renewed" or created anew in regeneration (τὸν κατὰ θεὸν κτισθέντα); and that the subsequent knowledge, righteousness and holiness is the end for which he was renewed. He is, therefore, exhorted to "put on the new man" of perfect inward holiness and righteousness. We may note in this connection also, that the word ἀνακαινώσις translated "renewing" is found only twice in the New Testament—once the "renewing of the Holy Ghost" as here used (Titus 3:5); and once as the "renewing of your mind" (Rom. 12:2). While the former as indicated, bears a relation to regeneration, the latter can refer only to the transformation effected by the Holy Spirit in entire sanctification.

Definitions of Regeneration. Mr. Wesley defines regeneration as "that great change which God works in the soul when He brings it into life; when He raises it from the death of sin to the life of righteousness. It is the change wrought in the whole soul by the Almighty Spirit of God, when it is created anew in Christ Jesus; when it is renewed after the image of God in righteousness and true holiness" (WESLEY, *Sermon on the New Birth*). According to Mr. Watson, "Regeneration is that mighty change in man, wrought by the Holy Spirit, by which the dominion which sin had over him in his natural state, and which he deplores and struggles against in his penitent state, is broken and abolished; so that with full choice of will and the energy of right affections, he serves God freely, and runs in the way

---

The change in regeneration consists in the recovery of the moral image of God upon the heart; that is to say, so as to love Him supremely and serve Him ultimately as our highest end, and to delight in Him superlatively as our chief good. . . . . Regeneration consists in the principle being implanted, obtaining the ascendancy, and habitually prevailing over its opposite. . . . . It is all effected by the word of truth, or the gospel of salvation, gaining an entrance into the mind, through divine teaching, so as to possess the understanding, subdue the will, and reign in the affections. In a word, it is faith working by love that constitutes the new creature, the regenerate man. . . . . Regeneration is to be distinguished from our justification, although it is connected with it. Everyone who is justified, is also regenerated; but the one places us in a new relation, and the other in a new moral state.—WATSON, *Dictionary*, Art. Regeneration.

of His commandments" (WATSON, *Th. Inst.*, II, p. 267). "Regeneration," says Dr. Pope, "is the final and decisive work wrought in the spirit and moral nature of man when the perfect principle of spiritual life in Christ Jesus is imparted by the Holy Ghost" (POPE, *Compend. Chr. Th.*, III, p. 5). Dr. Ralston says that "Regeneration may be defined to be a radical change in the moral character from the love and practice, and dominion of sin, to the love of God, and to the internal exercise and external practice of holiness" (RALSTON, *Elements of Divinity*, p. 420). Dr. Hannah defines regeneration as "that spiritual change which is wrought in believing man by the Holy Spirit of God, and which, though it may be mysterious and inexplicable in its process, is sufficiently plain and obvious in its effects" (Cf. FIELD, *Handbook of Chr. Th.*, p. 217). We prefer the following simple definition, "Regeneration is the communication of life by the Spirit, to a soul dead in trespasses and sins."

Characteristics of Regeneration. What is the nature of the new birth? "We are not," says Mr. Wesley, "to expect any minute, philosophical account of the manner of this. This our Saviour told Nicodemus, when he said, *The wind bloweth where it listeth, and thou hearest the sound thereof, but canst not tell whence it cometh, and whither it goeth: so is every one that is born of the Spirit* (John 3:8). Thou mayest be as absolutely assured of

Dr. Julius Kafton says, "Regeneration is the entrance of the new life that is connected with the rise of the Christian faith. This is the conception of regeneration in the narrower sense; in the wider sense, it includes justification and sanctification." This definition has in it something of the confusion which attaches to the Roman Catholic position, especially in its wider aspect. Kafton is usually classified as Ritschlian in his Theology.

The Calvinistic position is shown in the following definitions: "Regeneration is that act of God by which the governing disposition of the soul is made holy, and by which, through the truth as a means, the first holy exercise of this disposition is secured."—DR. A. H. STRONG. "Regeneration may be defined as that work of the Holy Spirit in man by which a new life of holy love, like the life of God, is initiated."—WILLIAM NEWTON CLARKE.

Dr. A. M. Hills defines regeneration as "the work of God and man co-operating, by which man resolutely turns from a life of self-gratification, and makes the supreme choice to live for the glory of God and the good of being; having been previously incited thereunto by the convicting and enlightening influence of the Holy Spirit who graciously inclined him to the love of God and holiness."—HILLS, *Fund. Chr. Th.*, II, p. 200.

the fact, as of the blowing of the wind: but the precise manner how it is done, how the Holy Spirit works this in the soul, neither thou nor the wisest of the children of men are able to explain" (WESLEY, *Sermon on the New Birth*). The subject may be approached from a twofold point of view, (1) that of the operation of God; and (2) the nature of the work wrought in the regenerate.

From the viewpoint of the operation of God there are three terms used to denote the work of regeneration. (1) The first and simplest is that of a begetting, as in I John 5:1—*every one that loveth him that begat* [γεννήσαντα] *loveth him also that is begotten of him* [τὸν γεγεννημένον]. St. Peter (I, 1:3) uses the expression *begotten us again* [ἀναγεννήσας]; while St. James declares that *Of his own will begat he us with the word of truth* (James 1:18). While it is veiled in the translation, the word used by St. James is expressive of the maternal [ἀπεκύησεν] rather than the paternal [γεννήσαντα] function. The word is the same as the translated "bringeth forth" in verse 15. (2) Another term used in this connection is that of a "quickening" or "making alive." Thus, *the Son quickeneth* [ζωοποιεῖ or makes alive] *whom he will* (John 5:21); and again, He *hath quick-*

Professor Burwash says that it is the soul's entrance on the new life which Mr. Wesley specifically regards as the new birth. In the latter part of the sermon, he allows that the term "new birth" is used in all the standards of the Church of England in a different sense from this, to designate the new relationship in which a man is placed before God and the Church in the ordinance of baptism. But whatever may have been his interpretation of the church formulary, he puts it aside and preaches only the Arminian doctrine of the new birth and this is "an inward change of nature, inseparably associated with a change of relation to God, and a profound crisis of religious experience." Professor Burwash also maintained that it was to "this view of regeneration, with the corresponding views of justification, justifying faith," and assurance, that the power of revival preaching was largely due. He says, "This entire system of doctrine of salvation sets before men something so definite as the test of their moral and religious condition that every man's conscience must respond with a definite 'Yes' or 'No' to the question, 'Am I saved?' It is throughout the doctrine of a present and conscious salvation. Any doctrine of an election from all eternity, or of a personal redemption completed unconditionally in Christ, or of a sacramental salvation, the germ of which is implanted in baptism, and which is gradually and unconsciously carried forward to perfection by the means of grace, can never be made the basis of such appeal to the unconverted as is founded upon the doctrine before us." (Cf. HARRISON, *Wesleyan Standards*, I, p. 364).

ened us together [συνεζωοποίησε] *with Christ* (Eph. 2:5). (3) The third term presents this work as "a creating" or "a creation." *Therefore if any man be in Christ, he is a new creature* [κτίσις creation] (II Cor. 5:17); and again, *we are his workmanship* [ποίημα, *creation*] *created* [κτισθέντες] *in Christ Jesus unto good works* (Eph. 2:10). In this connection, Dr. Pope reminds us that "we must remember the analogy of the genesis of all things at the beginning: there was an absolute creation of matter, or calling that which was not into being; and there was a subsequent fashioning of that matter into forms which constitute the habitable cosmos. The latter is the creation on which the scripture most dwells: whether it regards the physical or spiritual order. Just as the sleeper is dead, and the dead is only asleep—*awake thou that sleepest, and arise from the dead*—so creation is only a renewal, while the renewal is no less a creation. The two are sometimes united" (POPE, *Compend. Chr. Th.*, III, p. 6).

As viewed from the nature of the work wrought in the souls of men, regeneration is described in the Scriptures by a series of terms comparable to those which express the operation of God. Hence instead of the terms begetting, quickening and creating, we have such terms as the new birth, a spiritual resurrection, and a new creature. (1) The first of these, or the "new birth" is taken from the conversation of our Lord with Nicodemus. The statement is emphatic, *except a man be born again, he cannot see the kingdom of God* (John 3:3, 6, 7). This is His only formal statement on this subject and must, therefore, be given pre-eminence. As previously indicated in our discussion of the work of the Holy Spirit (Chapter XXV), regeneration must be regarded as that impartation of life to the souls of men, which sets them up as distinct individuals in the spiritual realm. Evidently our Lord intended by His use of the term "born from above," to make a distinction between the prevenient grace which is given to all men, and the mysterious issue of this grace in individual regeneration. That regeneration is thus a distinct and completed act is shown by St. John's use of the term. The word for born is ὁ γεγεννημένος, and being used in the perfect form, denotes the completion of a process. Our Lord also emphasizes the distinct moral quality of the new birth. He says, *That which is born of the flesh is flesh; and that which is born of the Spirit is spirit* (John 3:6). This "new birth" carries with it, therefore, the idea of a bestowment of life, and is the result of that divine operation by which the souls of men are restored to fellowship with God. (2) The second term used to describe the regenerate life is that of a spiritual quickening or resurrection. While the "new birth" carries with it the idea of the origin and moral quality of the new life, the "resurrection" in a spiritual sense, sets this new life in contrast with the previous state of sin and death. St. Paul emphasizes this contrast in a twofold manner. He

Mr. Wesley points out the analogy between the natural and spiritual birth as follows: "A man's being spiritually born again, bears a near analogy to the natural birth. Before a child is born, it has eyes, but does not see: and ears, but it does not hear. It has a very imperfect use of any other sense. It has no knowledge of anything, nor any understanding. To that existence we do not even give the name of life. It is only when a child is born that it begins to live. He then begins to see the light, and the various objects which surround him. His ears are opened, and he hears sounds. And all the other senses begin to be exercised upon their proper objects, and he breathes and lives in a manner, very different from what he did before. In like manner, before a man is born of God, he has eyes, but in a spiritual sense, does not see. Hence he has no knowledge of God, or of the things of God, either of spiritual or eternal things. But, when he is born of God, the eyes of his understanding are opened. He sees the light of the knowledge of the glory of God. He is conscious of a peace that passeth all understanding, and feels a joy unspeakable and full of glory. He feels the love of God shed abroad in his heart by the Holy Ghost which is given to him. And all his spiritual senses are exercised to discern spiritual good and evil. Now he may be properly said to live: God having quickened him by his Spirit, he is alive to God through Jesus Christ."—WESLEY, *Sermon on the New Birth*.

Regeneration is for the individual man, what the coming of Christ is for the human race: it is the absolute turning point, where the earlier development of character is broken off and terminated, and a new and holy development of life begins; a turning point which has been heralded by a series of external and internal workings of preparatory grace. Regeneration may be described as the breaking out of grace in the man; or, with equal propriety, as the breaking out of freedom in the man, for regeneration denotes precisely that these two factors have henceforward found their living point of union, and that a new personality is established, a copy of the divine and human personality of Christ. "If any man be in Christ," says the apostle, "he is a new creature: old things are passed away; behold all things are become new." —MARTENSEN, *Christian Dogmatics*, p. 383.

says, *You hath he quickened, who were dead in trespasses and sins* (Eph. 2:1); and *you, being dead in your sins and the uncircumcision of your flesh, hath he quickened together with him, having forgiven you all trespasses* (Col. 2:13). In the former, the contrast is between the new life, and death under the condemnation of the law; in the latter, between the new life, and the idea of death as a defilement. Regeneration, then, is a spiritual quickening, by which the souls of men dead in trespasses and sins are raised to walk in newness of life. It is an introduction into a new world, where there are new tastes, new desires and new dispositions. St. Paul exhorts them, therefore, to yield themselves to God, as those that are alive from the dead, and declares that sin shall not have dominion over them (Rom. 6:13, 14). From this it is evident that while regeneration is the infusion of divine life into the soul, it must not be regarded as the removal of anything infused by sin into the nature of the spirit. (3) The third term used in this connection, is that of a "new creation" or a "new creature." *If any man be in Christ, he is a new creature* (II Cor. 5:17). As a "birth from above" regeneration must be understood to be a sharing of the life of Christ. *I am come,* He said, *that they might have life* (John 10:10). As a quickening or spiritual resurrection, regeneration is the communication of the life of Christ glorified. St. Paul declares that *like as Christ was raised from the dead by the glory of the Father, even so we also should walk in newness of life* (Rom. 6:4). As a new creature, man is restored to the original image in which he was created. Christ is the great pattern or

Dr. Miley lays it down as a principle, that "the offspring is in the likeness of the parentage." "This is the principle," he says, "which opens the clearer view of regeneration. As by natural generation we inherit from the progenitors of the race a corruption of the moral nature, so by the new birth we receive the impress and likeness of the Holy Spirit. This is our interpreting principle. Nor is it fetched from afar, but is right at hand in the classical passage on regeneration: 'That which is born of the flesh is flesh; and that which is born of the Spirit is spirit.' In the first part the truth is deeper than the derivation of a body of flesh in the form and likeness of the parental body: it means the inheritance of a corrupt nature. As the depravity of the original parentage is transmitted through natural generation, so through regeneration we are transformed into the moral likeness of the Holy Spirit."—MILEY, *Syst. Th.*, II, pp. 330-331.

archetype, and man is *renewed in knowledge after the image of him that created him* (Col. 3:10, 11).

Errors respecting regeneration. Before beginning a systematic discussion of the errors respecting regeneration, it may be well to note briefly, some of the more popular misconceptions of this basic experience. (1) Regeneration is not a stage in naturalistic evolution. The assertion that regeneration is merely the unfolding of previously existing spiritual elements in a man is false. Man apart from the grace of God, is destitute of spiritual life. A power from above must enter his soul. A wholly new beginning must be made. (2) Regeneration is not the transition from childhood to manhood, as is frequently advocated by certain psychologists. It is true that the period of adolescence is one of marked changes, but this does not in itself produce spiritual life. The latter is not merely a process of natural development, but a special work of the Spirit in creating the soul anew in Christ. (3) Regeneration is not a change of the higher in distinction from the lower powers of the soul. It is not a partial work but a change in the entire nature of the being. (4) Regeneration is not repentance. The latter is a preparatory process leading to regeneration, but must not be identified with it. Regeneration is such a renewal of the whole heart, as to bring dominion over sin. With penitents, this is still the object of search, and, therefore, confessedly unattained. (5) Regeneration is not water baptism. Baptism is the outward sign of an inward grace, and for this very reason cannot be regeneration. St. Peter tells us that baptism is *not the putting*

Those who have attempted to explain the work of regeneration on the ground of trichotomy, have fallen into the error of partial regeneration. Trichotomy as an assumption of three distinct and essential elements in the constitution of man, holds that the first is material, the second animal and the third spiritual. As it respects regeneration, one class holds that sin has its seat in the soul, and regards the πνεῦμα as uncorrupted by the fall. Another class regards the soul and body as without moral quality, and places sin in the πνεῦμα or spirit. This they regard as paralyzed by the fall. In either case, regeneration consists in restoring the πνεῦμα to its place as the controlling factor. This it is readily seen is only a partial regeneration. In reply to this objection, we say that trichotomy as above held is not accepted in the church. There are not two spiritual essences in man, one sinful and the other holy. Furthermore, it makes the human πνεῦμα the controlling principle instead of the Holy Spirit.

away of the filth of the flesh, but the answer of a good conscience toward God (I Peter 3:21); and this good conscience cannot be attained apart from an inward spiritual renewal. (6) Regeneration is not to be identified with either justification or initial sanctification. It is true that they are concomitant, but they are not identical. This is the error of the Roman Catholic Church.

The theological errors respecting regeneration may be systematically treated under the following general heads: (1) Sacramentarianism; (2) Pelagianism; and (3) Calvinistic monergism. Philosophically considered, these errors arise from an undue emphasis upon one aspect of personality, either that of the mystical, the rational or the volitional.

1. Sacramentarianism represents, perhaps, the earliest error respecting regeneration. Since the inner spiritual transformation and the outward symbolic representation of it were so closely related in thought, early patristic literature came to identify the two. In this, Jewish influence was prominent. During the intertestamental period, the convert of Judaism was said to be "born again." As such, he became a proselyte, either of the gate, which admitted him to the civil privileges and a place in the court of the Gentiles; or of righteousness, which bound him to the whole law. It is thus seen that regeneration was used in the sense of adoption, or an induction into the outward privileges of the covenant. It was in this sense that the idea of regeneration was introduced into the church. This is shown by our Lord's use of the term as referring to the future regeneration of all things. In the development of the doctrine, the following stages may be noted: (1) As in the case of Jewish proselytes, the "new birth" came to represent initiation by baptism into the mysteries of the Christian estate. While the inner spiritual renewal was faithfully taught, it was not always connected with the term, and hence regeneration came to be used in the sense of adoption. Baptism, therefore, was looked upon as the completing act in the appropriation of Christianity, and the seal of positive adoption into the family of God. (2) Re-

generation being confused with adoption, the latter came to be viewed as the precursor of the new life, instead of being concomitant with it. It was held to be the state out of which the new life should flow if preliminary grace was used aright. Hence regeneration came to be regarded as sacramentally pledged by virtue of the grace preveniently bestowed upon all men. Baptism, then, was the sign of the blessing into which this grace was expected to mature. It was in this sense that infant baptism was generally understood. As such, it was the seal of adoption into the privileges of the covenant by virtue of Christian parentage, and the pledge of divine grace which should later prompt them to personal dedication. They were thus regarded as being made outwardly holy, and given the sign and seal of the impartation of inward blessings in so far as they were capable of receiving them. To adults, baptism was the sign and seal of pardon and renewal. (3) Baptism being so closely related to adoption and regeneration, came to be further regarded as the instrument by which the inner transformation was effected. As early as the middle of the second century, it may be said that baptismal regeneration had become prevalent in the teachings of the church. Furthermore, baptism was regarded as securing the "remission of sins" and, therefore, regeneration was not only confused with adoption, but with justification and sanctification as well. Thus according to the Nicene Creed, there is "one baptism for the remission of sins," and this was interpreted as being unto pardon, regeneration and sanctification. The confusion of this position was more or less removed by the Reformers, especially as it concerned the distinction between justification and sanctification.

Dr. Pope gives the following in defense against the error of baptismal regeneration. (1) It should be remembered that baptism is the seal of all the blessings of the covenant, and not of the new birth apart and alone; the term baptismal may as well be applied to justification and sanctification as to regeneration. (2) Scripture connects the new birth with baptism, which is its ordained seal and pledge; but the covenant seal may assure the believer of a past fact, a present gift, or of a blessing yet to come. Union with Christ is symbolized in this sacrament, which, however, is like circumcision, of no avail apart from faith. In Christianity there is no grace *ex opere operato* or dependent upon official acts.—POPE, *Higher Catechism*, p. 249.

2. Pelagianism represents the rationalistic tendency in the early church. During the fifth century, the controversy between Pelagianism and Augustinianism marked the extremes of thought concerning the doctrines of grace. The former was synergistic, but stressed the human element almost to the exclusion of the divine; the latter was monergistic, emphasizing the divine to the exclusion of the human. Between these extremes were various mediating positions, such as Semi-Pelagianism and Semi-Augustinianism. (1) Pelagianism regarded the change effected by regeneration as an act of the human will. Regeneration was not, therefore, a renewal of the will by the operation of the Holy Spirit, but the illumination of the intellect by the truth. God's grace was designed for all, but man must make himself worthy, by choosing the right and fully fixing his purpose on the good. As we are imitators of Adam in sin, so we must become imitators of Christ in order to salvation. (2) Semi-Pelagianism maintained that fallen man was graciously restored by the redemptive work of Christ to that extent, that the will was given its freedom and power. Hence regeneration was regarded as the divine blessing upon human volition. (3) At a later time, the Latitudinarians held that all men were regenerated in Christ, and, therefore, no subsequent regeneration was necessary. (4) In modern times, this rationalistic tendency is found in those churches which hold that regeneration is effected by the power of truth alone. The error in all these positions is to be found in the de-

Pelagianism which denied original sin, regarded regeneration as merely the renewal of human nature through Christian discipline. Semi-Pelagianism taught that man's power was only weakened by the fall, and this finds expression in some modern theories which hold that regeneration is the right exercise of our own faculties under the influence of grace.

Lutheran Synergism rightly taught that there is a co-operation of the human will with divine grace, but it did not trace this with sufficient distinctness to the special grace of the Spirit restored in redemption. Wesleyanism, even more than earlier Arminianism developed the doctrine of prevenient grace, asserting that man is not now found in the fallen state of nature simply, but that very nature itself is grace; that the Spirit works through the word with His own preliminary influences, deepening and bringing them to perfection; and that this continuous prevenient grace is in salvation consummated by the gift of regenerate life (Cf. POPE, *Higher Catechism*, p. 220).

nial of the immediate agency of the Holy Spirit, who alone can effect the new birth.

3. Calvinistic monergism represents the opposite extreme of thought in relation to the work of regeneration. It holds that regeneration is the first step in the *ordo salutis,* or order of salvation; that this is effected unconditionally by the Holy Spirit apart from any preparatory steps; and that the mind of man is, therefore, perfectly passive in its reception. Thus the Westminster Confession of Faith declares that "this effectual call is of God's free and special grace alone, not from anything at all foreseen in man, who is altogether passive therein, until, being quickened and renewed by the Holy Spirit, he is thereby enabled to answer this call, and to embrace the grace offered and conveyed in it." So also Witsius, after defining regeneration as "that supernatural act of God whereby a new and divine life is infused into the elect person spiritually dead," states that "there are no preparations antecedent to the first beginning of regeneration; because, previous to that, nothing but mere death, in the highest degree is to be found in the person of the regenerated." "You will say, then, that there are no preparatory dispositions to the first regeneration? I confessedly answer, there are none." It is evident that if regeneration is the first effect of saving grace on the heart, then it precedes both repentance and faith. The Calvinistic order is (1) regeneration; (2) faith; (3) repentance; and (4) conversion.

Against this position, Arminianism has always strenuously objected, on both theological and practical grounds. (1) It objects to making regeneration the first step in the process of salvation, in that this is a virtual denial of any gracious influence upon the heart previous

In Buck's *Theological Dictionary,* under the article "Conversion," the position of Calvinism is stated as follows: "In regeneration, man is wholly passive; in conversion, he is active. The first reviving in us is wholly the acts of God, without any concurrence of the creature; but after we are revived, we do actively and voluntarily live in His sight. Regeneration is the motion of God in the creature; conversion is the motion of the creature to God, by virtue of that first principle: from this principle all the acts of believing, repenting, mortifying, quickening, do spring. In all these a man is active; in the other he is merely passive."

to regeneration. Nothing is clearer in the Scriptures than this, that before one can be made the child of God by regenerating grace, he must first make use of prevenient grace by repenting, believing and calling upon God. *As many as received him, to them gave he power to become the sons of God, even to them that believe on his name* (John 1:12); *For ye are all the children of God by faith in Christ Jesus* (Gal. 3:26); and *Repent ye, therefore, and be converted, that your sins may be blotted out, when the times of refreshing shall come from the presence of the Lord* (Acts 3:19). Since this doctrine, therefore, conflicts with the Bible doctrine of prevenient grace, we cannot admit its truth. (2) Closely related to this, is the objection that Calvinism does in fact, identify regeneration with incipient grace instead of making it concomitant with justification and adoption. It maintains that the first act of grace upon the heart of the sinner regenerates him. Following this are faith, repentance and conversion. Thus we have according to this system, a regenerated person who has not yet repented, who has not been pardoned, and hence is still a sinner. The mere statement of this position is its own refutation. (3) Objection is further made to the Calvinistic idea of passivity. That regeneration is solely the

The work of regeneration is synergistic and not monergistic, as is affirmed by the Augustinian anthropology. From the standpoint in which the above discussion places us, the controversy between monergists and synergists is reduced to narrow limits, is confined to a single view. Monergism affirms that the work of regeneration is the sole work of the Spirit. Synergism affirms that the will of man co-operates in this work. Now, of course, to affirm that the Spirit does what He does is an identical proposition; there can be no controversy so far. Again, that creating anew is a divine work; that the only agency competent to effect the change we call regeneration is the omnipotent will of God is also evident; all evangelical Christians are agreed on this point. The point of controversy is found in the question, "Is the work of regeneration conditioned upon any volition of the human mind, or is it wholly unconditioned?" The work is divine—wholly divine—but whether the doing, the fact of its being done, depends solely upon the sovereign will of God, entirely separate from, and independent of, the human will, or is made dependent upon the co-operating consent of both the human and the divine will, is the question. The human agency is not employed in the work of regenerating—this is God's work—but in the performance of antecedent conditions; in hearing the word and giving good heed thereto, in repenting of sin and doing works meet for repentance, and in believing and trusting in the grace and mercy of God through Jesus Christ.—RAYMOND, *Syst. Th., II*, pp. 356, 357.

418   CHRISTIAN THEOLOGY

work of the Spirit is not denied, but that it is absolutely so, apart from all conditions, is not according to the Scriptures. We are commanded to seek, to ask, to repent, to open the heart, and to receive Christ. These are requisites which cannot be met apart from human agency. There can be no regeneration without them, and yet they are not possible to the unaided resources of fallen human nature. While this help is graciously bestowed upon man by the Spirit, yet with every communication of saving grace, there must be the co-operation of the human will. The soul may resist and be lost, or it may accept and be born of the Spirit. This is the uniform testimony of Scripture. (4) To deny all conditions as prerequisites to regeneration, is to link the doctrine with unconditional election. Hence all the five points of Calvinism follow immediately, predestination, limited atonement, natural inability, irresistible grace and final perseverance. These we trust have been sufficiently discussed in connection with the atonement and prevenient grace. (5) There is a final objection drawn from practical considerations. If men are made to feel that there are no conditions to regeneration on their part, they are led into either carelessness or despair. Only as men have been made sensible of the presence of the Holy Spirit, and the necessity of obedience to His awakening and convicting influences, have revivals been promoted, and the work of salvation accomplished. We are, therefore, exhorted to seek the Lord while He may be found, and to call upon Him while He is near.

Summary of the Arminian Doctrine. The doctrine of regeneration as held by Arminian theologians may be summarized under two general heads as follows: (1) It is a work wrought in the souls of men by the efficient operation of the Holy Ghost. (2) The Holy Spirit ex-

Through the whole process of salvation, man receives grace for grace; the grace of faith is given when the grace of repentance has been improved; and the power to believe given by grace, being used, the grace of justification, regeneration, and adoption succeeds; each succeeding is conditioned upon the proper improvement of antecedent grace. Man works out what God works in, and on condition of his so working, God works farther, and thus man grows in grace, from the first enlightening of the understanding, to the full completion of the preparation for heaven.—RAYMOND, *Syst. Th.,* II, p. 358.

erts His regenerating power only on certain conditions, that is, on the conditions of repentance and faith. These positions may be amplified to cover the following statements of belief.

1. Regeneration is a moral change wrought in the hearts of men by the Holy Spirit. This change is neither physical nor intellectual, although both the body and the mind may be affected by it. It is not a change in the substance of the soul, nor is it the addition of any new powers. Regeneration is not a metamorphosis of human nature. Man does not receive a new *ego*. His personal identity is the same in essence after regeneration as before. He has the same powers of intellect, feeling and will, but these are given a new direction. God does not undo in the new creation what He did in the first creation. The change is, therefore, not in the natural constitution of man, but in his moral and spiritual nature. Furthermore, it is important to believe that the whole man, and not merely certain powers of his being, is the subject of this spiritual renewal.

2. This radical change is wrought by the efficient agency of the Holy Spirit. It is an act of God. Whatever means may be used to bring the soul to Christ, the work itself is wrought solely by the direct, personal agency of the Spirit. The nature of the work indicates this. It

Dr. Pope in his *Higher Catechism*, thus sums up some of the less prevalent errors concerning regeneration. (1) The ancient Gnostic heresy, still found in its subtle influence, that the spirit in man was not affected by sin, and that the sensuous soul only is renewed. (2) The modern theory that regeneration is itself the gift of a spirit through the Spirit: here, as the opposite of the former, the loss of the spirit is held to have been the effect of sin, which virtually reduced man to a mere body and soul. These two are together refused as follows: "Regeneration is the spirit of new life imparted by the Spirit to the entire personality and nature of man." (3) Another error is that of those who suppose the Holy Spirit to give such an ascendancy to the renewed spirit that no sin remains in the regenerate, supposed to preserve his union with Christ. This is refuted by "the Apostle's testimony that the flesh lusteth against the Spirit, and the Spirit [the Holy Spirit in our spirit, or our spirit under the Holy Spirit] lusteth against the flesh" (Rom. 7:23; 8:2). This is not to be interpreted as merely a conflict between the state of conviction and that of regeneration. "In the state of preliminary grace the conflict is between the flesh and 'the law of my mind' still in bondage; in the state of regeneration it is between the flesh and 'the Spirit' who makes 'free from the law of sin and death'" (Cf. POPE, *Higher Catechism*, p. 248).

is not an act of the soul. It is a new birth. Arminianism maintains that there are conditions which must precede this operation of the Spirit, such as repentance and faith, but these only bring the soul to God. It then becomes passive, as clay in the hands of the potter, while the Holy Spirit by His omnipotent power breathes new life into the soul dead in trespasses and sins. It is through this infusion of life that the moral and spiritual nature of the soul is changed.

3. Regeneration is concomitant in experience with justification and adoption. Both Calvinists and Arminians hold that regeneration is the infusion of life into

> Regeneration does not consist in a change of the substance of the soul. This the Church has universally rejected as Manichæism, which it regards as inconsistent with the nature of sin and holiness. This ancient error was revived by Flacius (1510-1575), who held that original sin was a corruption of the substance of the soul, and that regeneration was such a change of that substance as to restore the soul to its normal purity. The Formula of Concord condemned these views as a virtual revival of Manichæism, maintaining that if the substance of the soul be sinful, God by whom each individual soul is created, must be the author of sin, and that Christ who assumed our nature must have been a partaker of sin. While the error of Flacius is to be condemned, and has never been held by the Church, it is noticeable that the Formula of Concord condemns it on the assumption of creationism, or that each individual soul is created immediately by God. This position has itself been one of the disputed doctrines of the church.
> Regeneration must not be regarded as a change in some one power of the soul, such as the intellect, the feelings or the will. While most Protestant theologians maintain that regeneration affects the entire man, they have placed the emphasis in various places. Thus, Dr. Raymond says, "Its chief effect is, therefore, upon the volitionary faculty. To regenerate, then is, primarily and chiefly, to strengthen the will. But it must be evident, from the manifest fact that man is a unit, so that whatever affects one faculty of his nature, in some measure and in some degree affects all, that this change we call regeneration has some relation to the entire human nature" (III, p. 353). Dr. Pope on the other hand, holds that this grace moves upon the will through the affections of fear and hope, but likewise guards the unity of personality.
> Once more, and this is of great moment, the object of this change, or the subject of this renewal, is the whole spiritual nature of man. Not his body; for its regeneration will be its resurrection; the body is (and remains) dead because of sin (Rom. 8:10), and must undergo its penalty. Doomed as it is to dissolution it must be presented in ceaseless oblation as the instrument of the spirit which is life because of righteousness, laid on the altar of service for the present and of hope for the future. But the spirit as the seat of reason, or the immortal principle in man, and the soul, as the same spirit linked with the phenomenal world by the body, are in all their complex faculties which are a unity in diversity, brought under the regenerating power of the Holy Ghost. Neither is the soul without the spirit, nor the spirit without the soul, the seat of sin or the subject of regeneration. It is the man who is renewed.—POPE, *Compend. Chr. Th.*, III, p. 11.

souls dead in trespasses and sins, but the former regard it as the incipient bestowal out of which all further spiritual acts grow; while the latter regard it as that work of the Spirit by which grace preveniently bestowed issues in a new spiritual life for the individual soul. Calvinists confuse regeneration with prevenient grace and, therefore, deny the latter. They reject the idea of any preparatory work preceding regeneration, and consequently regard it as unconditionally bestowed upon the elect by the decree of God. Arminians hold firmly to the doctrine of prevenient grace and, therefore, regard regeneration as conditionally bestowed upon graciously aided penitents through the instrumentality of faith.

4. Regeneration is a complete work and therefore perfect in its kind. While concomitant with justification and adoption, it is nevertheless distinct from them. Justification is a work which God does for us in the for-

Dr. Emmons held that both sin and holiness consisted in acts, and that regeneration therefore, is the commencement of a series of holy acts. Dr. Charles G. Finney limited moral character and responsibility to voluntary acts. "If any outward action or state of feeling exists, in opposition to the intention or choice of the mind, it cannot," he says, "by any possibility have moral character." Dr. Finney never thought himself through to the Wesleyan position on holiness, as did his colaborer, Dr. Asa Mahan. Consequently he regarded regeneration as a simple change of purpose, and, therefore, "an instantaneous change from entire sinfulness to entire holiness." Dr. Taylor of New Haven agreed with Dr. Finney in making free agency include plenary power, and of limiting regeneration to a change of purpose. He differed from him in that he did not regard it as simply a change from selfishness to benevolence, but a change from sin, as seeking happiness in the creature, to holiness, or a seeking of happiness in God. Dr. Charles Hodge (*Syst. Th.*, III, p. 7ff) gives an interesting account of these positions, but sums them up by saying that "all these speculations are outside the Bible."

It is perhaps in reference to these teachings that Dr. Pope has the following paragraphs. "In certain American schemes, which represent regeneration as the right ultimate choice of the soul, there are some errors to be noted. (1) This choice is a conviction and desire before regeneration, and may be called conversion; or, in its higher form of entire consecration of the will, it is the fruit of renewal. It cannot be regeneration itself. (2) The state of the soul before God is more than merely its present will and act or exercise: it has a disposition or character underlying this with which the new birth has most to do. (3) Therefore, in common with almost all the errors on this subject, these Semi-Pelagian rather than Arminian theories imply a failure to distinguish between the preliminary grace of life and the life of regeneration." "The error in every Semi-Pelagian theory is that of forgetting that the Holy Spirit always ends, even as He always begins, the work of goodness in man without human concurrence. He begins before cooperation joins Him; and co-operation must cease at the crisis where He finishes the work."—Pope, *Compend. Chr. Th.*, III, pp. 24, 25.

giveness of our sins and in the changing of the relation which we bear to Him; regeneration is the renewal of our fallen nature through the bestowment of life on the ground of this new relationship; while adoption is the restoration of the privileges of sonship by virtue of the new birth. The necessity for justification is found in the fact of guilt; that of regeneration in the fact of depravity; that of adoption in the loss of privilege. Arminianism holds that all three, while distinct in nature and perfect in their kind, are nevertheless bestowed by the same act of faith and consequently concomitant in personal experience.

5. *Regeneration is accomplished through the instrumentality of the Word.* The Holy Spirit uses means, for St. James declares specifically, that *Of his own will begat he us with the word of truth, that we should be a kind of first-fruits of his creatures* (James 1:18). We need to guard against an error which has frequently been current in the church, namely, that it is the power of truth alone which regenerates. We need to grasp and hold

It is true that some theologians, especially of the strict Calvinistic school, have preferred to understand by regeneration the primary act of God in man's spiritual recovery, in which almighty power operates upon a purely passive subject, and creates therein a new spiritual sensibility. But this view, as will be shown a little farther on, is not in harmony with the scriptural representation, which assumes a conditioning agency in man, or a consenting rather than a purely passive subject of regeneration. The office of awakening is to produce the sense of need and the measure of aspiration and desire which are requisite to make one a willing subject in the consummation of his spiritual sonship.—SHELDON, *Syst. Chr. Doct.,* p. 454.

Regeneration must not be confounded with awakening, though there is a striking similarity between them, and they are often blended together in real life. Awakening precedes regeneration, but it does not constitute it. Awakening is certainly a work of grace, affecting the entire personality of the man, raising his consciousness to a higher religious state, a state to which he could not raise himself by his own natural powers. The awakened man is as yet only aroused by grace, he is not actually endowed with grace: he is still one of the called, not the chosen. There is still wanting a decided resolve on his own part. Awakening, as such, is only a state of religious distress, a pathos, in which the man is involuntarily influenced; it must be viewed as analogous to those congenial circumstances in a person's life, which must not be identified with his own free discretion and action. Grace cannot advance toward its goal except through a voluntary act of surrender on the part of the man himself.—MARTENSEN, *Chr. Dogm.,* p. 384.

Mr. Wesley says that "Justification relates to that great work which God does *for us,* in forgiving our sins; and that regeneration relates to the great work which God does *in us,* in renewing our fallen nature."

clearly in mind that it is not the truth apart from the operation of the Spirit which regenerates, nor is it the action of the Spirit apart from and independently of the truth. That the Spirit uses the truth as the instrument in both regeneration and sanctification is clearly set forth in the Scriptures (cf. Acts 16:14; Eph. 6:17; I Peter 1:23). Perhaps one of the best guarded statements concerning the relation of the Spirit and the truth in regeneration is that of Dr. Daniel Fiske, published in the *Bibliotheca* in 1865. He says, "In regenerating men, God in some respects acts directly and immediately on the soul, and in some respects He acts in connection with and by means of the truth. He does not regenerate them by the truth alone, and He does not regenerate them without the truth. His mediate and immediate influences cannot be distinguished by consciousness, nor can their respective spheres be accurately determined by reason."

6. Regeneration is related to sanctification. The life bestowed in regeneration is a holy life. It is for this reason that Mr. Wesley spoke of it as the gateway to sanctification. In its relation to regeneration, however, a distinction must be made between initial and entire sanctification. Initial sanctification is, in the Wesleyan scheme, concomitant with justification, regeneration and adoption, while entire sanctification is subsequent to it. The distinction arises from the fact that guilt which as condemnation for sin is removed by justification, carries with it also, an aspect of pollution which can be removed only by cleansing. For this reason Wesleyanism has always held that sanctification begins with regeneration, but it limits this "initial sanctification" to the work of cleansing from the pollution of guilt and acquired depravity, or, the depravity which necessarily attaches to sinful acts. Entire sanctification, then, is subsequent to this, and from the aspect of purification, is a cleansing of the heart from original sin or inherited depravity. The distinction, therefore, is grounded in the twofold character of sin—sin as an act, and sin as a state. Those who hold to the doctrine of entire sanctification frequently take a position concerning regenera-

tion which is logically opposed to it. They regard regeneration as such a "change of heart" as amounts to only a renovation of the old life. This renovation is regarded as complete, and hence no place is found for a further work of grace. But this is a misconception of the work of regeneration. It is not a remaking of the old life, but an impartation of new life. Regeneration, therefore, "breaks the power of cancelled sin and sets the prisoner free," but it does not destroy the inbeing of original sin. "What has occurred," says Dr. Raymond, "is not a complete removal of what is called the flesh, or its weakness, not an entire removal of the carnal mind, but a bestowment of power to conquer it, to walk not after it, but to walk after the Spirit, and so to conquer the flesh and live after the Spirit as to maintain a constant freedom from condemnation. The thing done is salvation from the reigning power of inbred or original sin; it is deliverance from captivity; he is free whom the Son maketh free; it is a bestowment, by the grace and power of God by which man is empowered to volitionate obedience" (RAYMOND, *Syst. Th.*, II, p. 358).

Regeneration in Its Larger Relations. The Christian privilege of sonship, whether regarded as regeneration or adoption, connects the Holy Trinity in a particular

The relation of regeneration to the order of grace and other privileges, is thus stated by Dr. Pope: (1) As to the Christian life generally, regeneration takes the middle place between the life of release from condemnation and the life everlasting which follows the resurrection. (2) As to preliminary grace, regeneration is not merely its full development, but a new gift of life in Christ, for which that grace only prepares: the preparation may be mistaken for the gift, inasmuch as it shows many signs of a life of its own. (3) As to original sin, regeneration brings entire freedom from its power: "For the law of the Spirit of life in Christ Jesus hath made me free from the law of sin and death" (Rom. 8:2). (4) To justification and sanctification it is related as the new life is related to the righteousness and holiness of that life. (5) It is the substratum of all ethics, which are in this relation viewed as the growth of the new man, or fruits of a new nature, or the gradual renewal into the original image of God lost or defaced through sin. As to the conditions and means of regeneration, he gives the following: "(1) The preliminary grace of repentance and faith, used under the influence of the Spirit, is the condition. (2) The efficient cause is the Spirit using the Word of God. (3) The sacraments are the seals and pledges of the new life: baptism of its bestowment, and the Eucharist of its continuance and increase. Channels, strictly speaking, they are not. (4) But the formal cause is the formation of Christ in the soul as the principle and element of its new life."—POPE, *Higher Catechism,* pp. 244, 245.

manner with the administration of redemption. Each of the Persons is vitally involved. It is said of the Father, that *Of his own will begat he us with the word of truth* (James 1: 18); of the Son, *I am come that they might have life* (John 10: 10); and of the Holy Spirit, *That which is born of the Spirit is spirit* (John 3: 6). The Father is the pattern of all true paternity, and His relation to the eternal Son, becomes in some sense, the type of His relation to His created sons. The Son as the Logos of creation takes on a new aspect in respect to the filial creation, in that we are regenerated by the life of Christ imparted through the Holy Spirit; while the Holy Spirit himself becomes in the truest and deepest sense, "the Lord and Giver of life." That we may understand how central this doctrine is, it must be considered briefly in relation to the other great doctrines of the gospel.

1. Regeneration makes possible to mankind the personal knowledge of God. The regenerated soul is changed fundamentally in moral and spiritual quality, and this change becomes the ground of a new personal relationship. The life communicated by the Spirit is a reproduction of the life of Christ in man. Its quality is of the nature of God. Hence only as man becomes the partaker of the divine nature, does he learn through experience the kind of a being God is. Previous to this he may have had a theoretical knowledge of God; or he may have been given to metaphysical speculation as to the nature of the reality back of all phenomenal experi-

> We cannot review these various aspects of the new life without being impressed with the feeling that it is in some sense the central blessing of the Christian covenant. Justification is unto life, and this life is devoted to God in sanctification. But the life, as the life is in Jesus, is the unity of all. . . . . This specific blessing is in relation to justification and sanctification what the Son is in relation to the Father and the Holy Ghost. . . . . He who is the Logos to creation generally is the Son toward the filial creation. But this special relation to the Son extends to both aspects of sonship as adoption and regeneration. We are adopted into the relation which the Son occupies eternally: hence the term which expresses this prerogative is υἱοθεσίῳ, where the υἱός is preserved as the solitary word that is ever used to signify the Son's relation to the Father. We are regenerated by the life of Christ imparted through the Spirit: hence it is παλιγγενεσία, and we are τέκνα, both terms as it were reproducing in time the eternal generation. Our regeneration answers to the eternally Begotten, our adoption to the eternally Beloved.—POPE, *Compend. Chr. Th.*, III, pp. 4, 11.

ence, but only through the character and quality of the life given in regeneration, can man have a positive acquaintance with God. It is through this experience, that we *taste and see that the Lord is good* (Psalms 34:8).

2. Regeneration is vitally related to the revelation of God in Christ. Jesus Christ is the supreme revelation of God. In Him the truth of God becomes visible, as if projected for us upon the screen of humanity. He may be viewed as a Teacher, a Prophet or a Revealer, but He is more. He is our life (Col. 3:4). It is for this reason that men miss the true conception of the gospel when they view it merely as a system of ideas instead of a series of spiritual forces. It is indeed, a system of truth, but it is truth vitalized into reality. The doctrinal system is but an attempt to give expression to this reality in a unified and systematic manner. Since Christ is the supreme revelation of God, it is evident that the truth remains outside and apart from man experientially, until Christ is revealed in him as the hope of glory. This explains the fact that unregenerate man frequently fails to accept the revelation of Christ as set forth in the Holy Scriptures. With such it is purely a matter of intellectual investigation, but Christ can be understood only as we are made spiritually like Him. Hence these rationalists have closed the spiritual avenues of approach to the truth, and shut themselves off from that inner affirmation which comes solely through the new birth. It is for this reason that St. Paul declares that *if our gospel be hid, it is hid to them that are lost: in whom the God of this world hath blinded the eyes of them which believe not, lest the light of the glorious gospel of Christ, who is the image of God, should shine unto them* (II Cor. 4:3, 4).

3. Regeneration is also related to the enabling power of the Holy Spirit. He not only reproduces the life of Christ in the regenerate as a Revealer, but also as the Agent of enabling grace. The life bestowed in regeneration is not only manifested in new light but in new power. It is a new spiritual beginning for man. It is an ethical change. It is a revitalizing of truth. It

lifts the whole process out of the realm of theory into the realm of reality. Not only is a new goal set for man's

Bishop Merrill endeavors to explain the change in the soul made by regeneration, by a distinction between the technical use of the "soul" and the "spirit." He assumes the unity of our spiritual nature and the oneness of our essential selfhood. The ego in which consciousness inheres is not an aggregation of distinct substances or essences, but is simple and uncompounded. We call this entity the soul, and then it is the soul that remembers, wills and imagines. It is the soul acting in different directions, or exercising its different powers. Thus all the natural faculties, attributes and powers of the soul, have a common nature, essence and being. Now it is possible, he says, to conceive of the soul as existing with all its natural attributes, and yet as destitute of moral character. The soul does not so exist in fact, but when we so conceive by abstracting in the mind, everything from the soul that gives it character, leaving it possessed only of its natural attributes, we leave it in possession of all that the word "soul" expresses, when that word is used in connection with the word "spirit," so as to require in thought a distinctition between soul and spirit. But since the soul does not exist without something to give it character, we must recognize as belonging to it a different set of powers, or attributes, distinct and yet not separate, in quality and manifestation. These additional are moral, and determine character, because they give bent or inclination to all the powers of the soul and determine the life and conduct of the person with reference to goodness or badness. They are qualities in the natural faculties, giving them tone, inclination, impulse and affinity. They are to the soul what temper is to steel, or fragrance to the flower, or heat to the sunlight. We describe them as passions, impulses, desires and affections. They are not the soul but its vesture, its tone, its character. Any change in them is a change in the soul, for they are the soul's properties. As distinct from the "soul" they are the "spirit." "Do the Scriptures sustain this distinction?" he inquires. "When the word 'soul' occurs in the Bible without the word 'spirit,' or any other term conjoined with it requiring a limitation of its meaning, to its exact import, it expresses all that belongs to our spiritual nature, including the natural attributes and moral qualities and dispositions. So also, when the word 'spirit' occurs alone, or unconnected with the soul, or any other word that suggests or requires limitation to its more specific meaning, it expresses all that is included in soul and spirit both. It then denotes all our nature that is not material, expressed by the word body. But when the two words are conjoined in the same sentence, each has its own meaning, and must be restricted to its specific import. The word 'soul' means the conscious self, the substratum of being, including the natural attributes; and the 'spirit' means the tone or disposition of the soul, with its leanings, aversions, and affinities, with reference to the eternal law of righteousness." He points out also that the word "mind" and "heart" are used in the same manner, either of the terms when used alone referring to the immaterial part of our nature, but when used together, the word "mind" refers more especially to the intellectual powers, and the "heart" to the moral and passional elements within us. Consequently he argues, that the change is in the "spirit" and the "heart," which are the subjects of cleansing, renewal and change. "The soul with its natural attributes remains the same through all the experiences of sin and pardon, of pollution and washing, or death and life, retaining its identity and its essential aptitudes and powers; but the spirit, the seat and sphere of depravity, and of renewing and sanctifying influences, passes through these changes of character and condition, determining always the moral state of the man. A new soul is impossible, but a new heart and a new spirit are plainly promised, and graciously realized" (Cf. MERRILL, *Aspects of Christian Experience*, pp. 117ff).

attainment, but power is also given to free him from the bondage of sin, and to cause him to always triumph in Christ. This new life is devoted to God in sanctification, and he needs now to advance to the goal of entire sanctification, in which the heart is purified from all sin by the baptism with the Holy Spirit.

Adoption

Adoption is the declaratory act of God, by which upon being justified by faith in Jesus Christ, we are received into the family of God and reinstated in the privileges of sonship. Adoption as we have previously indicated, is concomitant with justification and regeneration, but in the order of thought, logically follows them. Justification removes our guilt, regeneration imparts spiritual life, and adoption actually receives us into the family of God. Like the term *regeneration,* adoption has a wider application in the Scriptures, than that which is concerned immediately with the restoration of the individual. St. Paul uses the term broadly to express, (1) the special election of Israel from among the nations, *to whom pertaineth the adoption* (Rom. 9:4); (2) the purpose of the incarnation, *that we might receive the adoption of sons* (Gal. 4:5; and (3) the full assurance of a future inheritance, *waiting for the adoption, to wit, the redemption of our body* (Rom. 8:23). It will be noticed that this last scripture bears a close relation to

Adoption is an act of God's free grace, whereby, upon the forgiveness of sins, we are received into the number, and have a right to all the privileges, of the sons of God.—*Wesleyan Catechism.* Adoption is the term occasionally used to signify the divine declaratory act by which those who are accepted in Christ are reinstated in the privileges of forfeited sonship for the sake of the Incarnate Son. It is used also of the state to which these privileges belong.—Pope, *Compend. Chr. Th.,* III, p. 13. Adoption is "that act of God's free grace by which, upon our being justified by faith in Christ, we are received into the family of God, and entitled to the inheritance of heaven."—Ralston, *Elem. of Divinity,* p. 435.

In civil government sonship by adoption is sonship by provision of law, not on the ground of parentage. In the absence of such ground, adoption is the only mode of sonship. Now there is a sense in which we are alien from God; out of filial relation to Him. Hence, when we are so viewed as the subjects of a gracious affiliation, our sonship may very properly be represented as in the mode of adoption. But it is never really such in fact. The new birth always underlies this sonship.—Miley, *Syst. Theology,* II, pp. 337, 338.

Matt. 19:28, where our Lord speaks of the final regeneration of all things. Both terms refer to man's restoration to his original estate. The word *adoption* is characteristic of St. Paul, and is used to express the privileges to which regeneration introduces believers under the terms of the new covenant. He uses both the words υἱός and τέκνον of the Christian, while St. John, who is concerned with the community of life, uses only τέκνον, reserving the word υἱός for the sonship of Christ. The term υἱοθεσία or *adoptio* meant in ordinary usage, the act of a man in taking into his household as his own, children which were not born to him. Civil adoption, however, always requires the consent of the person to be adopted, which was publicly demanded and expressed.

The Benefits of Adoption. The blessings which flow from adoption into the family of God are many and desirable. These may be summarized as follows: (1) The privilege of sonship. We become *the children of God by*

Dr. Wakefield includes in his treatment of this subject, the following interesting account of the ceremony of adoption. He says, "Among the Romans the ceremony of adoption consisted in buying the child to be adopted from his parents for a sum of money formally given and taken. The parties appeared before the magistrate in the presence of five Roman citizens: and the adopting father said to the child, 'Art thou willing to become my son?' to which the child replied, 'I am willing.' Then the adopter, holding the money in his hand, and at the same time taking hold of the child, said, 'I declare this child to be my son according to Roman law, and he is bought with this money,' which was given to the father as the price of his son." "Thus the relation was formed according to law; and the adopted son entered into the family of his new father, assumed his name, became subject to his authority, and was made a legal heir to the whole of the inheritance, or to a share of it if there were other sons." "Of the same nature is that transaction in the divine economy by which men are acknowledged to be the children of God. We may, therefore, define adoption, according to the scriptural sense of the term, to be that gracious act of God by which we are acknowledged to be of the number and become entitled to all the privileges of His children."—WAKEFIELD, *Chr. Th.*, p. 483.

"Betwixt civil and sacred adoption," says John Flavel, "there is a twofold agreement and disagreement. They agree in this, that both flow from the pleasure and good will of the adoptant; and in this, that both confer a right to the privileges which we have not by nature; but in this they differ; one is an act imitating nature, the other transcends nature; the one was found out for the comfort of them that had no children, the other for the comfort of them that had no Father. Divine adoption is in Scripture either taken properly for that act or sentence of God by which we are made sons, or for the privileges with which the adopted are invested. We lost our inheritance by the fall of Adam; we receive it by the death of Christ, which restores it again to us by a new and better title."

faith in Christ Jesus (Gal. 3:26); *And if children, then heirs; heirs of God, and joint-heirs with Christ* (Rom. 8:17); *And because ye are sons, God hath sent forth the Spirit of his Son into your hearts, crying, Abba, Father. Wherefore thou art no more a servant, but a son; and if a son; then an heir of God through Christ* (Gal. 4:6, 7). The kingdom of heaven has been described as "a parliament of emperors, a commonwealth of kings; every humble saint in that kingdom is coheir with Christ, and hath a role of honor and a scepter of power and a throne of majesty and a crown of glory." (2) Filial confidence toward God. *For ye have not received the spirit of bondage again to fear; but ye have received the Spirit of adoption, whereby we cry, Abba, Father* (Rom. 8:15). The Spirit of adoption brings deliverance from the bondage of sin. Condemnation is removed, spiritual darkness dispelled, and God's approval placed upon the soul. (3) The unity of the soul with Christ. *For both he that sanctifieth and they who are sanctified are all of one: for the which cause he is not ashamed to call them brethren* (Heb. 2:11). This unity is wrought by the Holy Spirit, a gift promised by our Lord to all His disciples. Those who have been born of the Spirit become candidates for the baptism with the Spirit. Through Him as the Comforter or Paraclete, we are to be blessed *with all spiritual blessings in heavenly places in Christ* (Eph. 1:3). (4) A proprietary right in all that Christ has and is. *All things are yours..... And ye are Christ's and Christ is God's* (I Cor. 3:21, 23). (5) The right and title to an eternal inheritance. St. Peter speaks of this inheritance as *incorruptible, and undefiled, and that fadeth not away* (I Peter 1:4). It is called a "kingdom" (Luke 12:32; Heb. 12:28); a "better country" (Heb. 11:16) a "crown of life" (James 1:12); a "crown of righteousness" (II Tim. 4:8); and an "eternal weight of glory" (II Cor. 4:17). "Whatever God now is to angels and glorified saints," says Dr. Dick, "and whatever He will be to them through an endless duration, for all this the adopted sons of God are authorized to hope. Even in this world, how happy does the earnest of the inheritance make them! How divine the peace which sheds its influence upon their souls! How pure and elevating the joy which in some select hour, springs up in their bosoms! How are they raised above the pains and pleasures of life, while, in the contemplations of faith, they anticipate their future abode in the higher regions of the universe! But there are only an earnest" (Lecture 73).

The Evidence of Adoption. The doctrine of assurance is one of the precious doctrines of the gospel. Nor is there any doctrine more clearly taught in the Scriptures than that of experiential religion. As in the case of the new birth, we may not understand the Spirit's operations, yet we may and can know the fact. Theologians sometimes make a distinction between the "witness of the Spirit" and the doctrine of "assurance," yet in the conscious experience of the believer, they are substantially the same. We shall, therefore, follow the practice common to Arminian theologians, and treat this subject under the head of the "Witness of the Spirit."

THE WITNESS OF THE SPIRIT

By the *Witness of the Spirit* is meant that inward evidence of acceptance with God which the Holy Spirit reveals directly to the consciousness of the believer. This doctrine is held by the great majority of evangelical Christians, but may be said in a peculiar sense to have been revived in modern times by Mr. Wesley and his coadjutors. Mr. Wesley in turn, receiving it from the Moravians, although it was contained in the doctrinal standards of his own church. When, however, his mind was fully awakened to the truth, he found he could no longer follow the Moravian guides, and so turned to the Scriptures, which he studied with that tireless energy which was so characteristic of his labors. He had proved beyond question that the earlier fathers taught this doctrine, and sustained his position by quotations from Origen, Chrysostom, Athanasius and Augustine; but it was only in the Scriptures that he found the true principles of its defense. "The Methodists, in proof of the doctrine of the witness of the Spirit," wrote Dr. Adam

Clarke, "refer to no man, not to Mr. John Wesley himself. They appeal to none—they appeal to the Bible, where this doctrine stands as inexpugnable as the pillars of heaven." Added to this was the practical and experiential aspects of the doctrine which they so fully developed. "There is nothing more usual," continues Dr. Clarke, "among even the best educated and enlightened of the members of the Methodist society, than a distinct knowledge of the time, place and circumstances, when and where, and in which way, they were deeply convinced of sin, and afterward had a clear sense of God's mercy to their souls, in forgiving their sins, and giving them the witness in themselves that they were born of God" (CLARKE, *Chr. Th.*, p. 169). It is for these reasons that the best in the literature on this subject must be drawn from the writings of the fathers of Methodism.

The Scriptural Basis of the Doctrine. The Scriptures afford many illustrations of men who enjoyed the witness of the Spirit. In the Old Testament we have the record of Abel (Heb. 11:4); Enoch (Heb. 11:5); Job (19:25); David (Psalms 32:5; 103:1, 3, 12); Isaiah (6:7); and Daniel (9:23). The New Testament likewise abounds with references to this doctrine (cf. Acts 2:46; 8:39; 16:34). As proof texts supporting this position, the following may be mentioned, *The Spirit itself* [αὐτὸ τὸ πνεῦμα or *the same Spirit*] *beareth witness with our spirit, that we are the children of God* (Rom. 8:16); *ye*

Of this doctrine Mr. Wesley wrote, "It more nearly concerns the Methodists, to call, clearly to understand, explain, and defend the doctrine; because it is one great part of the testimony which God has given them to bear to all mankind. It is by His peculiar blessing upon them in searching the Scriptures, confirmed by the experience of His children, that this great evangelical truth has been recovered, which had been for many years well-nigh lost and forgotten."—WESLEY, *Works*, Vol. I, p. 93.

The direct teaching of Mr. Wesley upon this subject is found in Sermon X on the Witness of the Spirit, written in 1747. Sermon XII on the Witness of Our Own Spirit, was written in 1767, twenty years later. Sermon XI, likewise on the Witness of the Spirit was written in 1771, and interposed between Sermons X and XII, in order to present the aspect of the continuous state of assurance, arising out of the initial assurance described in Sermon X. Mr. Watson deals at length with this doctrine in his Institutes, and with "assurance" in his Theological Dictionary. Dr. Adam Clarke emphasizes the witness of the Spirit in his Christian Theology and in his commentaries.

have received the Spirit of adoption, whereby we cry, Abba, Father (Rom. 8:15); *God hath sent forth the Spirit of his Son into your hearts, crying, Abba, Father* (Gal. 4:6); *He that believeth on the Son of God hath the witness in himself* (I John 5:10); *And it is the Spirit that beareth witness, because the Spirit is truth* (I John 5:6). These passages clearly teach that the Spirit testifies concerning the relation of the believers to God.

The Twofold Witness of the Spirit. The classical passage on this subject is that found in Romans 8:16, *The Spirit itself beareth witness with our spirit, that we are the children of God.* It is evident that the apostle teaches here, a twofold testimony, the witness of the divine Spirit, and the witness of our own spirit. The first is commonly known as the direct witness, the second as the indirect witness. In addition, the use of the Greek word συμμαρτυρεῖ seems to imply a conjoint testimony of these two witnesses, the Spirit itself (αὐτὸ τὸ Πνεῦμα or *the same Spirit*), being a fellow-witness with our own spirit. The word συμμαρτυρεῖ means literally, "to testify or bear witness together, or at the same time with another, or to add one's testimony to another" (cf. WAKEFIELD, *Chr. Th.*, p. 437). The passage is sometimes rendered "bear witness to" instead of "bear witness with" our spirit. This, however, does not change the meaning, but rather strengthens the former position. In maintaining the doc-

> I should never have looked for the "witness of the Spirit," had I not found numerous scriptures which most positively assert it, or hold it out by necessary induction; and had I not found that all the truly godly of every sect and party, possessed the blessing, a blessing which is the common birthright of all the sons and daughters of God. Wherever I went among deeply religious people, I found this blessing. All who had turned from unrighteousness to the living God, and sought redemption by faith in the blood of the cross, exulted in this grace. It was never looked on by them as a privilege with which some peculiarly favored souls were blessed: it was known from the scripture and experience to be the common lot of the people of God. It was not persons of a peculiar temperament who possessed it; all the truly religious had it, whether in their natural dispositions sanguine, melancholy or mixed. I met with it everywhere, and met with it among the most simple and illiterate, as well as among those who had every advantage which high cultivation and deep learning could bestow. Perhaps I might with the strictest truth say that, during the forty years I have been in the ministry, I have met with at least forty thousand who have had a clear full evidence that God, for Christ's sake, had forgiven their sins, the Spirit himself bearing witness with their spirit that they were the sons and daughters of God.—DR. ADAM CLARKE, *Christian Theology*, p. 163.

trine of the direct witness of the Spirit, Wesleyanism has had to contend against the mediate or single witness theory. This position is that the Holy Spirit does not bear direct or immediate testimony to the human consciousness, but only mediately through our own spirit. It is argued that the Holy Spirit works certain moral changes in the heart, such as "illuminating our understanding, and assisting our memory in discovering and recollecting those arguments of hope and comfort within ourselves," and that these are the evidence of our sonship. But it will be seen that this but reduces the testimony to that of our own spirit; and the Holy Spirit is not brought in at all except to qualify our own testimony. This theory does in fact do away with the direct testimony of the Holy Spirit, and reduces the whole process to mere inference from subjective changes.

1. The Witness of the Divine Spirit. Mr. Wesley held that "the testimony of the Spirit is an inward impression on the soul, whereby the Spirit of God directly witnesses to my spirit that I am the child of God: that Jesus Christ hath loved me, and given Himself for me; and that all my sins are blotted out, and I, even I, am reconciled to God" (*Sermon X*). He points out that the question is not whether there is a testimony of the Spirit, but whether or not this is a direct testimony; "whether there is any other than that which arises from a consciousness of the fruit of the Spirit. We believe there is.... because, in the nature of the thing, the testimony

It must be evident from what has been already said that to the fact of our adoption two witnesses and a twofold testimony must be allowed. But the main consideration is, whether the Holy Spirit gives His testimony directly to the mind by impression, suggestion, or otherwise, or mediately by our own spirit, in some such way as is described by Bishop Bull in the extract above given; by "illuminating our understanding, and assisting our memory in discovering and recollecting those arguments of hope and comfort within ourselves," which arise from "the graces which he has produced in us." But to this statement of the doctrine, we object, that it makes the testimony of the Holy Spirit, in the point of fact, nothing different from the testimony of our own spirit; and that by holding but one witness it contradicts St. Paul, who, as we have seen, holds two. For the testimony is that of our own consciousness of certain moral changes which have taken place no other is admitted; and, therefore, it is but one testimony. Nor is the Holy Spirit brought in at all except to qualify our own spirit to give witness.—WAKEFIELD, *Chr. Th.*, p. 437.

must precede that which springs from it..... Does not the Spirit cry, 'Abba, Father,' in our hearts the moment it is given, antecedently to any reflection upon our sincerity? Yes, to any reasoning whatsoever! And is not this the plain natural sense of the words which strikes anyone as soon as he hears them? All these texts, then, in their most obvious meaning, describe a direct testimony of the Spirit" (WESLEY, *Sermons*, pp. 94, 99). The value of absolute certainty in matters of such vital importance as the eternal salvation of the soul, cannot be overestimated. Here we must have the highest form of testimony. If there be no direct witness of the Holy Spirit, then the whole matter becomes one of mere inference. But God has not left His people in darkness. He has given us of His Spirit that we may know the things that are freely given to us of God. For this reason Mr. Wesley exhorted his people not to "rest in any supposed fruit of the Spirit without the witness. There may be foretastes of joy, peace and love, and those not delusive, but really from God, long before we have the witness in ourselves: before the Spirit of God witnesses with our spirits that we have 'redemption in the blood of Jesus, even the forgiveness of sins.'" "If we are wise," he continues, "we shall be continually crying to God, until his Spirit cry in our heart, Abba, Father! This is the privilege of all the children of God, and without this we can never be assured that we are His children. Without this we cannot secure a steady peace, nor avoid perplexing doubts and fears, but when we have once received the Spirit of Adoption, this 'peace

Meantime let it be observed, I do not mean hereby that the Spirit of God testifies this by any outward voice; no, nor always by the inward voice, although He may do this sometimes. Neither do I suppose that He always applies to the heart (though He often may) one or more texts of scripture. But He so works upon the soul by His immediate influence, and by a strong though inexplicable operation that the stormy wind and troubled waves subside, and there is a sweet calm, the heart resting as in the arms of Jesus, and the sinner being clearly satisfied that God is reconciled that all His "iniquities are forgiven, and his sins all covered..... Now what is the matter of dispute concerning this? Not whether there be a witness or testimony of the Spirit; not whether the Spirit does testify with our spirit, that we are the children of God; none can deny this, without flatly contradicting the Scriptures, and charging a lie upon God."—WESLEY, *Sermons*, II, p. 94.

which passes all understanding,' will 'keep our hearts and minds in Christ Jesus' " (WESLEY, *Sermons*, II, p. 100).

2. The Witness of Our Own Spirit. This is the indirect witness of the Spirit, and consists in the consciousness that individually we possess the character of the children of God. Mr. Wesley held that "it is nearly, if not exactly, the same with the testimony of a good conscience toward God; and is the result of reason and reflection on what we feel in our own souls. Strictly speaking, it is a conclusion drawn partly from the Word of God and partly from our own experience. The Word of God says everyone who has the fruit of the Spirit is a child of God; experience or inward consciousness tells me that I have the fruit of the Spirit; and hence I rationally conclude, therefore, I am a child of God..... Now, as this witness proceeds from the Spirit of God, and is grounded on what He works in us, it is sometimes called the Spirit's indirect witness, to distinguish it from the other testimony, which is properly direct" (*Sermon XI*). Furthermore, this indirect witness is confirmatory, rather than fundamental. "We love him because he first loved us" (I John 4:19). "Since, therefore, this testimony of His Spirit must precede the love of God and

---

Referring to the Spirit's cry in the soul, Dr. Adam Clarke says that "crying" is not only the participle of the present tense, denoting the continuation of the action; but, being neuter, it agrees with the Spirit of his Son; so it is the divine Spirit which continues to cry, 'Abba, Father!' in the heart of the true believer. And it is ever worthy to be remarked that when a man has been unfaithful to the grace given, or has fallen into any kind of sin, he has no power to utter this cry. The Spirit is grieved and has departed, and the cry is lost! Were he to utter the words with his lips, his heart would disown them."—CLARKE, *Chr. Th.*, p. 161.

To suppose that through the infinite love of God the eternal Logos became incarnate, suffered and died; that the eternal Spirit visits man with enlightening, sanctifying, guiding, comforting, and saving influences; that holy angels are commissioned to minister unto men; that the Scriptures have been divinely inspired; that the Christian ministry has been divinely appointed; and that the Church, with all its ordinances and appliances is divinely employed—all for the accomplishment of man's personal salvation—and at the same time to suppose that at best the result of all this in the mind of man is but a doubtful impression—a ground for only an uncertain hope—is, to say the least, a great incongruity, and precisely the opposite of all reasonable expectations.—RAYMOND, *Syst. Th.*, II, p. 362.

all holiness, of consequence it must precede our inward consciousness, thereof, or the testimony of our spirit concerning them." Filial love springs from the knowledge of filial relationships, and the direct witness of the Spirit must therefore, precede the indirect. But the indirect is not thereby of less consequence. It is as indispensable as the first, for by it the direct testimony of the Spirit is fully confirmed. "How am I assured," continues Mr. Wesley, "that I do not mistake the voice of the Spirit? Even by the testimony of my own spirit; by 'the answer of a good conscience toward God.' Hereby I shall know that I am in no delusion, that I have not deceived my own soul. The immediate fruits of the Spirit, ruling in the heart, are 'love, joy, peace, bowels of mercies, humbleness of mind, meekness, gentleness, long-suffering.' And the outward fruits are the doing of good to all men, and a uniform obedience to all the commandments of God" (WESLEY, *Works*, I, p. 92). We may

"These fruits (love, joy, and peace) cannot result from anything but manifested pardon; they cannot themselves manifest our pardon, for they cannot exist till it is manifested. God, conceived of as angry, cannot be the object of filial love; pardon unfelt supposes guilt and fear still to burden the mind; and guilt, and 'joy,' and 'peace' cannot 'coexist.'"—WATSON, *Institutes*, II, Chap. XXIV.

"Again, it is asked if a man be conscious of love, joy and peace, may he not infer therefrom that he is a child of God? We answer, a consciousness of the fruits of the Spirit is the testimony of our own spirit and not of the divine Spirit. It is confirmatory, but it is not primary—not first in order—not basal or fundamental. The love which evidences adoption is filial love; but filial love is conditioned upon a knowledge of filial relations; one does not love God as his father, until he knows God as his father; when the Spirit is given, and the recipient in heart says Abba, Father, then, and not until then, he loves as a child. The witness of the Spirit, then must be antecedent to filial affections. The same may be said of joy and peace. These spring from a sense of salvation; they do not arise till the assurance of adoption has been given; they are evidences of adoption, but evidently do not render the divine testimony useless; so far from rendering a divine testimony unnecessary, they are founded upon and flow from it."—RAYMOND, *Syst. Th.*, II, p. 370.

Our own spirit can take no cognizance of the mind of God as to our actual pardon, and can bear no witness to that fact. The Holy Spirit only, who knows the mind of God, can be this witness; and if the fact that God is reconciled to us can be known only to Him, by Him only can it be attested to us. But we are competent witnesses, from our own consciousness, that such moral effects have been produced within us as it is the office of the Holy Spirit alone to produce; and thus we have the testimony of our own spirit that the Holy Spirit is with us and in us, and that He who bears witness to our adoption is, in truth, the Spirit of God.—WAKEFIELD, *Chr. Th.*, p. 441.

say, then, that these two witnesses taken together, establish the assurance of salvation. The one cannot exist without the other, and taken together, no higher evidences can exist.

The Common Privilege of Believers. We have gone carefully over the scriptural grounds for belief in the witness of the Spirit; we have shown that this testimony is inseparably connected with the Spirit of Adoption; that it is indeed essential to filial love; and therefore, that it is as much a part of the common salvation as adoption itself. For this reason, we may safely affirm that the witness of the Spirit is the common privilege of all believers. It is in some peculiar sense, their divine birthright. Closely related to this is the question as to whether or not, the witness of the Spirit can be held in uninterrupted enjoyment. As a matter of observation, it is well known that there are wide differences in the spiritual experiences of believers. Consequently, we should expect the assurance of sonship to vary accordingly. This whole subject, Mr. Wesley reviews with his usual spiritual insight, in his sermon on "The Wilderness State." Finally, the Scriptures speak of the "full assurance of understanding" (Col. 2: 2); the "full assurance of hope"

> This doctrine has been generally termed the doctrine of assurance; and perhaps the expressions of St. Paul, "the full assurance of faith," and "the full assurance of hope" may warrant the use of the word. But as there is a current and generally understood sense of this term among persons of the Calvinistic persuasion, implying that the assurance of our present acceptance and sonship is an assurance of our final perseverance, and of our indefeasible title to heaven, the phrase, a comfortable persuasion or conviction of our justification and adoption, arising out of the Spirit's inward and direct testimony, is to be preferred; for this has been held as an indubitable doctrine of Holy Writ by Christians who by no means receive the doctrine of assurance in the sense held by the followers of Calvin. There is also another reason for sparing the cautious use of the term assurance, which is that it seems to imply, though not necessarily, the absence of all doubt, and shuts out all those lower degrees of persuasion which may exist in the experience of Christians. For, as our faith may not at first, or at all times, be equally strong, the testimony of the Spirit may have its degrees of strength, and our persuasion or conviction be proportionally regulated. Yet if faith be genuine, God respects its weaker exercises, and encourages its growth, by affording measures of comfort, and degrees of this testimony. Nevertheless, while this is allowed, the fullness of this attainment is to be pressed upon everyone that believes, according to the Word of God: "Let us draw near," says St. Paul to all Christians, "with full assurance of faith."—WATSON, *Institutes*, II, pp. 407, 408.

(Heb. 6: 11); and the "full assurance of faith" (Heb. 10: 22). These refer to a perfect persuasion of the truth as it is in Christ, the fulfillment of the promise of a heavenly inheritance, and entire trust in the blood of Christ. From these Scriptures we must conclude, therefore, that the full assurance of understanding, faith and hope is the privilege of every Christian, and that none ought to rest short of his high calling in Christ Jesus.

CHAPTER XXIX
CHRISTIAN PERFECTION OR ENTIRE SANCTIFICATION

Christian perfection, or entire sanctification are terms used to express the fullness of salvation from sin, or the completeness of the Christian life. Entire sanctification has been defined as a comprehensive word which bridges the chasm between hell and heaven, sin and holiness, guilt and glorification. To understand the spiritual significance of this work of grace it must be experienced, for spiritual things can be known only by experience. Holiness has been called "the central idea of the Christian system, and the crowning accomplishment of human character." To convey to the mind of man the riches of this grace, the entire Levitical system of the Old Testament is laid under tribute. The terms used embrace the altar and its sacrifice, the priesthood, the ritual with its

Bishop Foster says of holiness that "it breathes in the prophecy, thunders in the law, murmurs in the narrative, whispers in the promises, supplicates in the prayers, sparkles in the poetry, resounds in the songs, speaks in the types, glows in the imagery, voices in the language, and burns in the spirit of the whole scheme, from alpha to omega, from its beginning to its end. Holiness! holiness needed! holiness required! holiness offered! holiness attainable! holiness a present duty, a present privilege, a present enjoyment, is the progress and completeness of its wondrous theme! It is the truth glowing all over, webbing all through revelation; the glorious truth which sparkles and whispers, and sings and shouts in all its history, and biography, and poetry, and prophecy, and precept, and promise, and prayer; the great central truth of the system. The wonder is that all do not see, that any rise up to question, a truth so conspicuous, so glorious, so full of comfort."—Foster, *Christian Purity*, p. 80.

Dr. Phineas F. Bresee regarded holiness as the goal of the redemptive process. He says, "Now this baptism with the Holy Ghost is 'the blessing of Christ' spoken of in this text. . . . It is the crowning glory of the work of the soul's salvation. All that ever went before it was preparatory for it. Did prophets speak and write; did sacrifices burn; were offerings made; did martyrs die; did Jesus lay aside the glory; did He teach and pray and stretch out His hands on the cross; did He rise from the dead and ascend into heaven; is He at the right hand of God: It was all preparatory to this baptism. Men are convinced of sin, born again and made new creatures that they may be baptized with the Holy Ghost. This work completes the soul's salvation."—P. F. Bresee, *Sermons*, p. 100.

sprinklings and washings, the ceremonies of presentation and dedication, the hallowing and consecration, the sealing and the anointing, the fasts and the feasts—all these point to this New Testament standard of piety.

While this subject is a fundamental doctrine of Christianity, and of vast importance to the church, there are few subjects in theology concerning which there is a greater variety of opinion. All evangelical Christians hold that it is a Bible doctrine, that it includes freedom from sin, that it is accomplished through the merits of Christ's death, and that it is the heritage of those who are already believers. They differ widely, however, as to its nature, and the time of its attainment. There are four general positions concerning the subject: (1) that holiness is concomitant with regeneration and completed at that time. This is frequently known as the Zinzendorfian theory. (2) Another class regards it as a growth extending from the time of regeneration until the death of the body. (3) Others hold that man is made holy only in the hour and article of death; while (4) another class believes that holiness begins in regeneration, but is completed as an instantaneous work of the Holy Spirit subsequent to regeneration. It is this view, commonly known as the Wesleyan position, which we shall endeavor to set forth in the following pages. A subject so sacred, however, and an experience so high and holy, forbids in any degree the spirit of controversy. We tread here upon sacred ground; we are through the blood of Jesus to enter into the holiest *by a new and living way, which he hath consecrated for us, through the veil, that is to say, his flesh* (Heb. 10:19). This truth has a large place in the confessions and the theologies, the catechisms and

---

The doctrine of a purgatorial cleansing from sin, as held by the Roman Catholic Church is sometimes included in the theories of deliverance from sin. The doctrine of purgatory, however, is so far from Protestant thought, that no account need to be taken of it here.

That this is an experience here and now I need not wait to argue. The New Testament dispensation rests upon it. This is the keystone to the arch of redemption. Take it away and the arch crumbles into decay and ruin. Build the arch and crown it with this all embracing fact and it shines in this world in glorious reflection of the rainbow about the throne, full of the unbraided colors of divine glory.—Dr. P. F. Bresee, *Sermons*, p. 164.

hymnologies of the church, whether eastern or western, Catholic or Protestant. Needless to say, the whole tenor of the inspired Scriptures is *holiness unto the Lord.*

We shall discuss this subject under the following divisions: (I) The Scriptural Basis for the Doctrine; (II) The Historical Approach to the Subject; (III) The Meaning and Scope of Sanctification; and (IV) Progressive Sanctification. Following this we shall discuss the finished work under two aspects, (V) Entire Sanctification; and (VI) Christian Perfection.

THE SCRIPTURAL BASIS FOR THE DOCTRINE

A careful study of the Holy Scriptures is the best apologetic for the doctrine and experience of entire sanctification. Here, however, we must limit this study to the more prominent proof texts, which we shall arrange according to the following classification: (1) those which speak of Holiness as the New Testament Standard of Christian Experience; (2) those which specifically teach that Entire Sanctification Is a Second Work of Grace; (3) the Tense Readings of the Greek Testament; and (4) Scripture Texts used in Opposition to the Doctrine. For the sake of brevity, texts properly belonging to more than one division, will not generally be duplicated.

Holiness as the New Testament Standard of Christian Experience. Here we shall notice those scriptures which refer to the will of God, His promises and His commands.

1. It is the will of God that His people shall be holy. (1) *Wherefore be ye not unwise, but understanding*

A very extensive class of terms—perhaps the most extensive—exhibits the Christian estate as one of consecration to God. The entire range of phraseology has been transferred from the ancient temple service to the use of the new temple or church. It embraces all aspects of the Christian privilege as one of dedication to God, whether the dedication be external or internal, effected by the Spirit or presented by the believer. But sanctification is here viewed as a blessing bestowed freely under the covenant of grace; and we must therefore to some extent, though not altogether, omit its ethical relations. As a privilege of the covenant, its principle is twofold: purification from sin, consecration to God; holiness being the state resulting from these. As a gift of grace, it is declared to be perfect in the design of the Spirit; and full provision is made for the entire sanctification of the believer in the present life, even as full provision is made for His finished righteousness and perfect Sonship.—POPE, *Compend. Chr. Th.,* III, p. 28.

CHRISTIAN PERFECTION OR ENTIRE SANCTIFICATION 443

what the will of the Lord is. And be not drunk with wine, wherein is excess; but be filled with the Spirit (Eph. 5:17, 18). This refers to the promised gift of the Holy Spirit, which the disciples received at Pentecost, and of whom it was said, *they were all filled with the Spirit.* It implies (a) that the disciples had some measure of the Spirit previous to Pentecost; (b) that to be filled with the Spirit necessitates a cleansing from sin; (c) that it is mandatory; (d) that it not only means to be filled to the exclusion of all sin, but to be continuously filled in an ever-enlarging capacity. This is possible because of the property of the Spirit as *procession*. (e) Lastly, it implies a passive submission to the Spirit in all His offices. (2) *For this is the will of God, even your sanctification* (I Thess. 4:3). Here holiness or "the sanctification" is set in contrast to the misuse of the body. God's will is that His people shall be cleansed from all uncleanness, whether of the soul or the body. The text implies that the grace of God can deliver from those fleshly appetites which bind the world in sin. (3) *By the which will we are sanctified through the offering of the body of Jesus Christ once for all* (Heb. 10:10). The one great act of atonement finds its supreme purpose in the sanctification of His people. The blood of Jesus Christ not only furnishes the ground of our justification, but is the medium of our sanctification also.

2. God has promised to sanctify His people. (1) *Come now, and let us reason together, saith the Lord: though your sins be as scarlet, they shall be as white as snow; though they be red like crimson, they shall be as wool* (Isa. 1:18). Scarlet is known as one of the most indelible of the dyes, and is here used to designate the stain of sin in the soul. The guilt of actual sin, and the pollution of inbred sin, can be cleansed only by the blood of Jesus Christ. (2) *Then will I sprinkle clean water upon you, and ye shall be clean: from all your filthiness, and from all your idols, will I cleanse you* (Ezek. 36:25). The work of the Holy Spirit is here represented by the symbol of water as a cleansing agent. It is to this scripture doubtless that St. Paul refers in II Cor. 7:1. (3)

For he is like a refiner's fire, and like fuller's soap: and he shall sit as a refiner and purifier of silver: and he shall purify the sons of Levi, and purge them as gold and silver, that they may offer unto the Lord an offering in righteousness (Mal. 3:2, 3). Christ is portrayed by the prophet as the Great Refiner of His people. It should be noted (a) that it is the sons of Levi who are to be purged; and (b) the purpose of this purging is to enable them to make an offering in righteousness. This is a reference doubtless to the baptism with the Holy Ghost and fire. (Matt. 3:11, 12). (4) *I indeed baptize you with water unto repentance: but he that cometh after me . . . . he shall baptize you with the Holy Ghost, and with fire. Whose fan is in his hand, and he will throughly purge his floor, and gather his wheat into the garner; but he will burn up the chaff with unquenchable fire* (Matt. 3:11, 12). Nothing can be more evident than that (a) the baptism with the Holy Ghost effects an internal and spiritual cleansing which goes far deeper than John's baptism. One was for the remission of sins, the other for the removal of the sin principle. (b) This baptism is applicable to Christians only, not to sinners. (c) The separation is not between the tares and the wheat, but between the wheat and the chaff, or that which clings to it by nature. Sinners are never regarded as wheat, but always as tares. (d) The wheat thus separated, will be gathered into the garner and preserved; the chaff will be burned, or destroyed with unquenchable fire. The chaff referred to here is not the wicked, but the principle of sin which cleaves to the souls of the regenerate, and which is removed by Christ's purifying baptism.

3. God commands His people to be holy. These commands embrace the three terms commonly applied to entire sanctification—holiness, perfection, and perfect love. (1) *Be ye holy; for I am holy* (I Peter 1:16). This text is a reference to Lev. 19:2. God requires His people to be holy and enjoins it by precept and example. Evangelical holiness is positive and real, not merely typical or ceremonial. There is a relative aspect of holiness as we shall show later, but it is never separated from that

which is inwrought by the Spirit. Holiness in God is absolute, and in man is derived, but the quality is the same in God and man. (2) *The Lord appeared to Abram, and said unto him, I am the Almighty God; walk before me, and be thou perfect* (Gen. 17:1); *Be ye therefore perfect, even as your Father which is in heaven is perfect* (Matt. 5:48). This is the perfection of love, which comes from the purging of all the antagonisms of the soul, which war against it. (3) *And thou shalt love the Lord thy God with all thy heart, and with all thy soul, and with all thy mind, and with all thy strength: this is the first commandment* (Mark 12:30). *And the Lord thy God will circumcise thine heart, and the heart of thy seed, to love the Lord thy God with all thine heart, and with all thy soul, that thou mayest live* (Deut. 30:6). Dr. Adam Clarke says that "the circumcision of the heart implies the purification of the soul from all unrighteousness." The love mentioned here is not merely natural human love or friendship ($\phi\iota\lambda\iota\alpha$), but holy love ($\dot{\alpha}\gamma\dot{\alpha}\pi\eta$), or the love created and shed abroad in the hearts of men by the Holy Spirit (Rom. 5:5).

Entire Sanctification as a Second Work of Grace. Of the numerous texts which could be cited in this connection, we limit ourselves to three only. (1) *I beseech you therefore, brethren, by the mercies of God, that ye present your bodies a living sacrifice, holy, acceptable unto God, which is your reasonable service. And be not conformed to this world: but be ye transformed by the renewing of your mind, that ye may prove what is that good, and acceptable, and perfect, will of God* (Rom. 12:1, 2). Nothing can be clearer than (a) that this exhortation is addressed to those who were at the time

The love of God is the secret presence of God himself in our souls whilst in eternal blessedness He gives Himself to His saints as the Manifested one. Accordingly, the love of God is not the inward life of man in a state of exaltation, the life of feeling heightened in intensity, but it is a higher principle which has been grafted into man—the Holy Spirit. These words express the substantial cause, love the actual effect: but essentially they are the same, for the love of God cannot be regarded as separate from the essential being of God in its highest manifestation, that is, the Holy Ghost—God's love is there only where God himself is, for He is love, and does not have love as something in or beside Himself.—OLSHAUSEN.

Christians; (b) that an appeal to the mercies of God would mean nothing to those who had not already experienced His pardoning grace; (c) that the sacrifice was to be presented holy, as initially sanctified by the cleansing from guilt and acquired depravity; (d) that it was to be acceptable, that is, those who presented it must have been justified; all of which the apostle deems a reasonable service. In the second verse it is admitted, (e) that there remained in the hearts of the believers, a bent toward worldliness, or a bias toward sin; (f) that this tendency to conform to the world was to be removed by a further transformation, or a renewal of their minds; and (g) that they were thereby to prove, or experience, the good, and acceptable, and perfect will of God. (2) *Having therefore these promises, dearly beloved, let us cleanse ourselves* (καθαρίσωμεν) *from all filthiness of the flesh and spirit, perfecting holiness* (ἐπιτελοῦντες) (present) ἁγιωσύνην (or a personal purification) *in the fear of God* (II Cor. 7:1). Regeneration as we have seen, is the impartation of a life that is holy in its nature; and concomitant with it, is an initial holiness or cleansing from guilt and acquired depravity. Now this holiness already begun is to be perfected by the cleansing at a single stroke from inbred sin, and brings the soul to a constantly existing state of perfected holiness. This cleansing applies to the body as well as to the soul. (3) *Therefore leaving the principles of the doctrine of Christ, let us go on unto perfection* (Heb. 6:1). The word for perfection is *teleioteta* (τελειότητα) from the adjective *teleios* (τέλειος). Dr. Clarke says, "The verb teaches the idea of our being borne on immediately into the experience." Dr. Whedon makes a similar statement as follows: "When Hebrews 6:1 is adduced as an exhortation to advance to a perfected Christian character, it is no misquotation."

Tense Readings of the Greek Testament. Dr. Daniel Steele in his *Milestone Papers* has an excellent chapter on this important subject (cf. STEELE, *Milestone Papers*, Chapter V). He points out the contrast between the use of the present tense, as *I am writing*, or the imperfect as denoting the same continuity in the past, as *I was writing*, with the aorist tense, which in the indicative expresses simple momentary occurrence of an action in past time, as *I wrote*. In all other moods, the aorist is timeless, or what is styled "singleness of act." When, therefore, the present tense is used, it denotes continuous action; but when the aorist is used, it denotes a momentary, completed act without reference to time. There is in the English no tense like it, and hence the translators found it difficult to translate it without circumlocution. .... A proper understanding of this will greatly aid in the interpretation of important texts. We shall mention but a few of these. (1) *Sanctify* [aorist imperative] *them* (once for all) *through thy truth:* [that is, through faith in the distinctive office and work of the Comforter] .... *And for their sakes I sanctify* [present tense—am sanctifying or consecrating] *myself, that they also might be sanctified through the truth* (or truly sanctified) (John 17:17, 19). Dr. C. J. Fowler points out, that in the Greek text, verse 17 reads *en tei aletheia* (ἐν τῇ ἀληθείᾳ), through the truth, or in the use of the truth; but verse 19 omits the *tei* (τῇ) and reads *en aletheia* (ἐν ἀληθείᾳ) which means *in truth,* since omitting the article makes it equivalent to an adverb. (2) *Purifying* [aorist — instantaneously] *their hearts by faith* (Acts 15:9). "This verse," says Dr. Steele, "is a key to the instantaneous sanctifying work of the Holy Spirit wrought in the hearts of believers on the day of Pentecost, since the words, *even as he did unto us,* refer to that occasion." (3) *I beseech you therefore, brethren, by the mercies of God, that ye present* [aorist—a single act not needing to be repeated] *your bodies a living sacrifice* (Rom. 12:1). (4) *Put ye on* [aorist—a single definite act] *the Lord Jesus Christ, and make* [present tense] *not provision* [that is, quit making provision] *for the flesh* (Rom. 13:14). (5) *Now he which stablisheth* [present—who is continually establishing] *us with you in Christ, and hath* [aorist, as a single definite act] *anointed us, is God; who hath also sealed us* [aorist]; *and given* [aorist—gave as a single definite act] *the earnest of the Spirit in our hearts* (II Cor. 1:21, 22). Here the establishing is constant, or continuous, while the anointing, the sealing and the earnest of the Spirit are momentary and completed acts of the one experience of entire sanctification. (6) *And they that are Christ's have crucified* [aorist—a single definite and completed act] *the flesh* [σάρξ not σῶμα or body], *with the affections and lusts* (Gal. 5:24). A distinction is made here between the carnal mind as the principle of sin, and the works of the flesh which flow from it. These works of the flesh are put off in conversion. But now the carnal mind itself, as the underlying principle of sin (the flesh or σάρξ with its inordinate affections and outreachings, which though existing are not allowed to express themselves in works, or actual sinning) is to be crucified (from σταυρόω implying destruction accompanied with intense pain). (7) *In whom also after that ye believed,* [aorist] *ye were sealed* [aorist] *with that holy Spirit of promise* (Eph. 1:13). Here both the believing and the sealing are definite, completed acts. (8) *Mortify* (aorist —kill outright) *therefore your members which are upon the earth* (Col. 3:5). "Let nothing live inimical to your true life, hidden in Christ. Kill at once (aorist) the organs and media of a merely earthly life."—Bishop Ellicott (cf. STEELE, *Milestone Papers*, p. 80). (9) *Put on* [aorist] *the new man* (Col. 3:10). *Put on,* .... [aorist] *as the elect of God*.....*bowels of mercies, kindness, humbleness of mind, meekness, longsuffering* (Col. 3:12). Dr. Steele says that all these excellencies of character are assumed at once, through the incoming of the Comforter. This represents the positive side of entire sanctification, as mortification represents the negative. (10) *And the very God of peace sanctify* [aorist] *you wholly; and*....*your whole spirit and soul and body be preserved* (initial aorist, to mark the beginning of the power which is to preserve the believer) (I Thess. 5:23). (11) *That he might sanctify* [aorist] *the people with his own blood, suffered* [aorist] *without the gate* (Heb. 13:12). (12) *If we confess* [present tense] *our sins, he is faithful and just to forgive* [aorist] *us our sins, and to cleanse* [aorist] *us from all unrighteousness* (I John 1:9). Here both the forgiveness and the cleansing are spoken of as completed acts, and there is no more reason grammatically for believing in a gradual sanctification than in a gradual justification.

HISTORICAL APPROACH TO THE SUBJECT

The doctrine of Christian perfection has come down to us from apostolic days as a sacred and uninterrupted tradition through all the Christian centuries. The different ages have been frequently characterized by a difference in terminology, which the student of history must be quick to discern, but in no age has this glorious truth suffered eclipse. "The essentials of the doctrine have been preserved, though with many minor differences, from the beginning, clearly discernible through all the ascetic, fanatical, ultra-mystical, semi-Pelagian veils which have obscured them" (POPE, *Compend. Chr. Th.*, III, p. 61). We shall trace the subject briefly through the following periods, in order to furnish a historical basis for further discussion.

1. The Apostolic Fathers are definite in their teaching upon this important subject. The last words of Ignatius before his martyrdom were "I thank Thee, Lord, that Thou hast vouchsafed to honor me with a perfect love toward Thee." Polycarp, speaking of faith, hope and charity, says, "If any man be in these, he has fulfilled the law of righteousness, for he that has love is far from every sin." Clement of Rome states that "those who have been perfected in love, through the grace of God, attain to the place of the godly in the fellowship of those who in all ages have served the glory of God in perfectness."

2. The Later Fathers bore the same testimony. We note first the words of Augustine, who at times rose to sublime heights in his conception of grace, and at others, seemed to shrink from the full truth of his positions. He declares that "no one should dare to say that God cannot destroy the original sin in the members, and make Himself so present to the soul, that the old nature being

entirely abolished, a life should be lived below as life will be lived in the eternal contemplation of Him above." Yet he believed that evil concupiscence remains throughout the natural life. Apart from this, however, he taught a full deliverance from all sin in this life. We have also the word of Cyril, bishop of Jerusalem (d. 386) who says, "But tarry ye in the city of Jerusalem, until ye be invested with power from on high. Receive it in part now; then shall ye bear it in its fullness. For he who receives often possesses the gift but in part; but he who is invested is completely enfolded by His robe." Macarius the Egyptian (c.300-391) wrote a series of homilies on Christian experience in which the idea of perfect love is given a prominent place. He says, "In like manner Christians, though outwardly they are tempted, yet inwardly they are filled with the divine nature, and so nothing injured. These degrees, if any man attain unto, he is come to the perfect love of Christ and to the fullness of the Godhead" (Homily 5). "By reason of the superabundant love and sweetness of hidden mysteries, the person arrives to such degrees of perfection as to become pure and free from sin. And one that is rich in grace at all times, by night and by day, continues in a perfect state, free and pure" (Homily 14).

3. The Mystics, notwithstanding their numerous errors and extravagances, served to preserve evangelical religion during the Middle Ages. Their contribution to this department of theology has been peculiarly rich, in that the central idea of all mysticism is entire consecration to God. It demands a separation from the creature, and perfect union with the Creator in love. Mosheim the historian, says, "If any sparks of real piety subsisted under this despotic empire of superstition they were to be found only among the mystics; for this sect, renouncing the subtlety of the schools, the vain contentions of the learned, and all the sects and ceremonies of external worship, exhorted their followers to aim at nothing but internal sanctity of heart and communion with God, the center and source of holiness and perfection (MOSHEIM, *History*, p. 390). Those forms of mys-

ticism influenced by Neo-Platonism took on pantheistic tendencies, and must be classed as more pagan than Christian.

4. The Roman Catholic doctrine was eclectic, and existed in a variety of forms, such as that of the Jansenists, the Mystics, the Ascetics and the Scholastic Fathers of the Middle Ages. It took the form of German semi-pantheism, French Quietism, and Spanish Illuminism. The Church laid a good foundation for this doctrine in its creed, but it erred greatly in building upon it a false superstructure. Thus the Tridentine Decrees in referring to the perfection of obedience, maintain that negatively there is no bar to an entire conformity to law; and that positively, a complete satisfaction of its requirements is necessary to salvation. Mohler asks the question, "How shall man be finally delivered from sin, and how shall holiness in him be restored to perfect life?" In his reply, he attacks the idea of a deliverance from sin through the death of the body, as held by some of the Protestant formularies. He attributes this error to the reformed doctrine of complete passivity in regeneration. "But the Catholic," he says, "who cannot regard man other than as a free, independent agent, must also recognize this free agency in his final purification, and repudiate such a mechanical process as inconsistent with the whole

In its purest form, mysticism proper has in every age molded an interior circle of earnest souls, seeking the innermost mysteries of the kingdom of grace by the most strenuous ethical discipline. Its methods have been from time immemorial described as, *first*, the way of PURIFICATION; *second*, the way of ILLUMINATION; *third*, the way of UNION. These may be considered as answering respectively to the evangelical doctrines of purification from sin, the consecration of the Spirit, and the estate of holiness in abstraction from self and earthly things in fellowship with God. A careful study of St. John's First Epistle will find in it laid the sure and deep foundations of this better mysticism. It gives the three principles in their order. "The blood of Jesus Christ his Son cleanseth us from all sin" (1:7); this is the mystical purgation. "Ye have an unction from the Holy One, and ye know all things" (2:20); this is the mystical illumination. "He that dwelleth in love dwelleth in God, and God in him" (4:16); this is the perfect union. A true mysticism may be traced in almost every community; and, wherever found, has taught directly or indirectly the perfection to which the Spirit of God raises the spirit of man, blending in its pursuit, contemplation and action; contemplation which is faith waiting passively for the highest energy of the Holy Ghost; and action, which works out His holy will.—POPE, *Compend. Chr. Th.*, III, p. 75.

moral government of the world. If God were to employ an economy of this nature, then Christ came in vain." He sums up his position by saying that "the Redeemer will at the day of judgment have fulfilled the claims of the law outwardly for us, but on that very account inwardly in us. The consolation, therefore, is to be found in the power of the Redeemer which effaces as well as forgives sin." But it is at this point that the doctrine of purgatory is injected. This purification is to be accomplished in a twofold way. "With some it consummates purification in this life; with others it perfects it only in the life to come. The latter are they who by faith, love, and a sincere penitence, have knit the bond of communion with the Lord, but only in a partial degree, and at the moment of their quitting life were not entirely pervaded by His Spirit; to them will be communicated the saving power, that at the day of judgment they also may be found pure in Christ." The first error in the Roman Catholic Church, as it touches this doctrine of purity, is the failure to recognize the present power of the atoning blood of Christ, for full and complete cleansing. Thus while rejecting the mechanical idea of purification by death, they very inconsistently substitute a mechanical process of cleansing after death. The second error in the doctrine of holiness is concerned with the positive aspect of divine love as the consecrating power of entire sanctification. It is held that love not only fulfills the law, but that it may more than fulfill it by keeping those counsels of perfection which are recommended though not imposed by our Lord. This position leads directly to the belief that love may achieve works of supererogation, and consequently to an undue emphasis upon good works, through an obedience which is above law.

5. The Reformers in their reaction against the erroneous position of the Roman Catholic Church concerning justification, adopted a theory of the atonement, which through a misplaced emphasis upon its substitutionary aspect, gave rise to the various theories of imputation. These have been previously discussed in the

chapters on the Atonement and Christian Righteousness, and it is sufficient here, to mention them briefly in their relation to the doctrine of Christian perfection. As there are erroneous theories of imputation concerning justification, so also the same theories are erroneously applied to sanctification. Since Christ is our substitute, the Reformers held that not only a complete justification, but also an entire sanctification was thus provided for the believer, and applied to him as a gift of covenant grace. But there is here an emphasis upon objective soteriology, or what Christ has done *for* us, to the minifying of the importance of subjective soteriology, or what He has wrought *in* us by the Spirit. Thus with their peculiar form of a substitutionary atonement, they held to a belief in the imputation to Him of our sins, and to us of His righteousness for our justification, and for our sanctification also, in so far as it applied to the cleansing from guilt. But sin itself cannot be done away by imputation; hence in the Calvinistic system it is necessary to deny that it is actually done away. It is not imputed and, therefore, not reckoned to the believer. Thus he is sanctified by imputation, that is by his "standing" in Christ, although as to his actual "state," he still has the carnal mind or inbred sin, which imputation cannot take away. This will be clearer when it is recalled that the extreme substitutionary theory of the atonement not only held, (1) that Christ's death, or passive righteousness was imputed for the remission of sins; but that (2) His active righteousness, or His life in holiness was also imputed as a substitute for the believer's imperfect obedience. Hence sin is not abolished as a principle or power, but instead, Christ's righteousness is imputed as a substitute, and inbred sin is thereby hidden under the robe of an imputed righteousness. Here is the basis of the "standing and state" theory which forms such a prominent part in some of the modern theories of sanctification. The standing of the believer is in Christ, that is by imputation; the actual state is one in which sin is repressed. and, therefore, does not reign; while sanctification is the process of bringing the principle of sin into subjection to the life of righteousness. Sanctification, therefore, according to this theory is merely progressive while the soul dwells in the body, and is completed only at death. The subtlety of a doctrine which holds that man can be instantaneously sanctified by an imputed standing, but not actually sanctified by an impartation of righteousness and true holiness, makes the error more dangerous. Anything which falls short of an actual cleansing from all sin or the death of the "old man" is anti-Wesleyan and anti-scriptural. The Reformation, however, led to other movements of a spiritual nature, which served to further the work of true holiness. Spener founded the Pietists who emphasized holiness, and organized societies in Frankfort for its promotion, much as Mr. Wesley did in London. Wesley was in some measure indebted to the Moravians for the beginning of his spiritual life, although he disagreed with Count Zinzendorf on his doctrine of imputation, and also rejected his idea that purification or sanctification took place at conversion.

6. The earlier Arminians wrote much on Christian perfection also, and their statements contain the germ of that which was later developed in Wesleyanism. Arminius defined holiness as follows: "Sanctification is a gracious act of God by which He purifies man, who is a sinner, and yet a believer, from ignorance, from indwelling sin, with its lusts and desires, and imbues him with the spirit of knowledge, righteousness and holiness..... It consists of the death of the old man, and the quickening of the new man." Episcopius says, "The commandment may be kept with what he regards as a perfect fulfillment in the supreme love which the gospel requires according to the covenant of grace, and in the utmost exertion of human strength, assisted by divine help." Limborch states that there is a "perfection in being correspondent to the provisions and terms of the divine covenant. It is not sinless or an absolutely perfect obedience, but such as consists in a sincere love of piety, absolutely excluding every habit of sin." The doc-

trine, however, was more fully developed by John and Charles Wesley and their coadjutors.

7. The Wesleyan movement which resulted in the organization of the Methodist Church, marks a revival of the doctrine and experience of entire sanctification in the eighteenth century. To the question, "What was the rise of Methodism?" Mr. Wesley replied, "In 1729 my brother Charles and I, reading the Bible, seeing we could not be saved without holiness, followed after it, and incited others to do so. In 1737 we saw that holiness comes by faith. In 1738 we saw that men are justified before they are sanctified, but still holiness was our pursuit—inward and outward holiness. God then thrust us out to raise up a holy people." Two years before his death, Mr. Wesley wrote, "This doctrine is the grand depositum which God has lodged with the people called Methodists; and for the sake of propagating this chiefly He seems to have raised us up." John Wesley was the founder of Methodism, and his Sermons and Notes, together with the Twenty-five Articles, form the standards of doctrine. Charles Wesley was the hymn writer of the movement, and John Fletcher, a member of the Anglican Church, its saint and chief apologist. The names of Dr. Coke and Bishop Asbury are prominent in the organization of American Methodism. During the nineteenth century, a fresh impetus was given to the doctrine and experience of holiness by the great national campmeetings. The Wesleyan Methodist Connection was organized in 1843, the Free Methodist Church in 1860, and the National Association for the Promotion of Holiness in 1866. In order to both promote and conserve the truth of holiness, the latter part of the century wit-

Dr. Stevens says that "The Holy Club was formed at Oxford in 1729 for the sanctification of its members. The Wesleys there sought purification, and Whitefield joined them for that purpose" (*History of Methodism*). Doubtless the ritual of the English Church assisted the Wesleys in their search after the doctrine and experience. In the ritual of the Protestant Episcopal Church, the statement is as follows: "Cleanse the thoughts of our hearts by the inspiration of the Holy Spirit, that we may perfectly love Thee, and worthily magnify Thy name, through Jesus Christ our Lord." .... "Vouchsafe to keep us this day without sin, and grant Thy people grace to withstand the temptations of the world, the flesh, and the devil, and with pure hearts and minds to follow Thee."

nessed the organization of the Church of the Nazarene by Dr. Phineas F. Bresee, the Pentecostal Association of Churches in the East, and a number of holiness movements in the South. These were later combined into one body, known as the Church of the Nazarene. This period witnessed also the combining of a number of other groups into the Pilgrim Holiness Church. These churches have sought to conserve the doctrine and experience of entire sanctification; and have persistently opposed the various fanatical groups that have obscured the pure truth, and brought into ill-repute the glorious doctrine and experience of full salvation.

8. Among the more modern developments, aside from Wesleyanism, may be mentioned the following: (1) The Oberlin Position; (2) The Theory of the Plymouth Brethren; and (3) The Keswick Theory.

(1) The Oberlin position is represented by President Asa Mahan, Charles G. Finney, and President Fairchild. According to this theory, there is a simplicity of moral action which makes sin to consist solely in an act of the will, and consequently maintains that it is impossible for sin and virtue to exist in the same heart at the same time. It accepted but one definition of sin, namely, "Sin is the transgression of the law." Several erroneous positions followed immediately—(1) It denied inbred sin as a state or condition of the soul, and held instead, to an "intermittent," "vibratory," or "alternating" theory of moral character. Of this position, Dr. A. M. Hills, himself a student at Oberlin, says, "To hold that a Christian believer in every moral act is as good or bad as he can be, and that the least sudden sin of a warm-hearted Christian plunges him to the level of the worst sinner, is too great a tax on credulity to be accepted" (HILLS, *Fundamental Chr. Th.*, II, p. 253). (2) It confused consecration with sanctification. Sanctification was made to consist in such an "establishment in consecration" as to prevent further "alternation of the will." (3) It made sanctification a matter of growth and development. Thus President Fairchild begins his chapter on sanctification with these words, "The growth and

establishment of the believer, the development in him of the graces of the gospel, is called sanctification." (FAIRCHILD, *Elements of Theology*, p. 280). President Mahan later came into the clear experience of entire sanctification, and advocated practically the Wesleyan position.

(2) The Plymouth Brethren originated in Dublin, Ireland, and almost simultaneously in Plymouth, England. In England their growth was very rapid, and hence they soon came to be known as the Plymouth Brethren. Their leading mind, if not their founder, was

> Mr. Finney denies that there is any sin or moral depravity remaining in the soul after regeneration, but this he does by denying that the states of sensibility, in which they war against the right determinations of the will, and clamor for indulgences which the will cannot allow without sin, involves sin or moral depravity. This makes the discussion turn upon the mere name by which a mental state is called, and not upon the fact of the existence of the state. That such states of sensibility exist after regeneration all must admit, but while old school men call it depravity remaining after regeneration, Mr. Finney denies that it is sin, or moral depravity, and affirms that it is physical depravity, referring to the same mental state which others call remaining sin after regeneration, allowing regeneration to take place instantaneously with justification.... He denies that any moral quality pertains to the sensibilities of the soul, and hence does not include the subjugation of the passions to the sanctified will in his idea of entire sanctification, beyond the mere fact that the will is not governed by them, and does not endorse or execute any of their irregular motions. His words are, "It is evident that sanctification in the scripture, and proper sense of the term, is not a mere feeling of any kind. It is not a desire, an appetite, a passion, a propensity, an emotion, nor indeed any kind or degree of feeling. It is not a state or phenomenon of the sensibility. The states of the sensibility are, like those of the intelligence, purely passive states of the mind, as has been repeatedly shown. They of course can have no moral character in themselves. The inspired writers evidently use the terms which are translated by the English word sanctify, to designate a phenomenon of the will, or a voluntary state of mind." (cf. FINNEY, *Syst. Th.*, II, p. 200). Luther Lee in commenting upon the above statements says, "If the above be all true, the conclusion appears undeniable, that every man is entirely sanctified the moment he wills right, and as Mr. Finney contends for the freedom of the will, that man has natural power to will right, all can sanctify themselves by an act of will in a moment ....Mr. Finney's view of sanctification, as above given, appears to be defective..... Mr. Finney's view of sanctification differs very materially from that commonly held by other schools of theology. It differs by being grounded upon a denial that moral depravity extends to the state of the intelligence and sensibility of the soul, depravity being confined wholly to the state of the will. It does differ by being made to include, according to the above view, only a right state of the will, while others hold that it includes a right state of all the powers and susceptibilities of the soul."—LUTHER LEE, *Elements of Theology*, pp. 212, 213.

John Darby, a clergyman of the Church of England, who not only withdrew from the established church, but took the position that all organization of a churchly nature was a detriment to Christianity. Their theological positions were in general, based upon the extreme imputation theories of hyper-Calvinism, which we have already treated in our discussion of the Atonement. The movement was antinomian in the extreme, and was but a revival of the principles of Moravianism against which Mr. Wesley had to contend, and those of the Anabaptists who preceded them. They said little, however, of the decrees, or of unconditional election—these being implied, rather than directly stated. Dr. Daniel Steele in his *Antinomianism Revived*, points out, that by omitting those doctrines which are peculiarly obnoxious to the Armin-

Signally useful as that beloved man of God, President Finney, was, I can but believe that he would have led many more into the experience of sanctification, had he held a different philosophy. He himself had experienced a marvelous baptism with the Holy Spirit, which made him an example to the world of "holiness and power." But when he tried to lead others into an experience similar to his own, something stood in his way. President Mahan says of him, "No one ever disciplined believers so severely, and with such intense and tireless patience as Brother Finney. Appalled at the backsliding which followed his revival, he put forth the most earnest efforts to induce among believers permanence in the divine life. He gathered his theological students together and instructed them in renunciation of sin, consecration to Christ, and purpose of obedience. They would renew their renunciations, consecrations and purpose, with all the intensity with which their natures were capable. But they were not told to exercise faith for the blessing; and all their human efforts and consecrations, ended in dismal failure, and left them in groaning bondage, under the law of sin and death."—HILLS *Fund. Chr. Th.*, II, p. 253.

When alone with God, one day, in a deep forest, I said distinctly and definitely to my heavenly Father, that there was one thing that I desired above all else—the consciousness that my heart was pure in His sight; .... In this state I came to Oberlin, as the president of that college. I had been there but a short time, when a general inquiry arose in the church after the divine secret of holy living, and a direct appeal was made to Brother Finney and myself for specific instruction upon the subject, which induced in me an intensity of desire, indescribable, after that secret. Just as my whole being became centered in that one desire, the cloud lifted, and I stood in the clear sunlight of the face of God. The secret was all plain to me me now, and I know also, how to lead inquirers into the King's highway (*Baptism of the Holy Ghost*, p. 108). His error previous to this, he states as follows, "When I thought of my guilt and need of justification, I had looked to Christ exclusively, as I ought to have done." "For sanctification, on the other hand, to overcome (the world, the flesh, and the devil!) I had depended mainly upon my own resolutions. I ought to have looked to Christ for sanctification as much as for justification, and for the same reason."—ASA MAHAN.

ians, and stressing those which appeal to the Calvinists, the errors of this movement are adapted to become widespread in both of these great branches of so-called orthodoxy.

The principal error of this system, and that upon which most if not all the others depend, is a false view of the Atonement, or the mediatorial work of Christ. The Plymouth conception of the Atonement, is that of the old commercial theory, or so much suffering as an atonement for so much sin. They regard sin as having been condemned on the cross of Christ; and consequently hold that all sin—past, present and future, has by this act been done away—not provisionally, nor actually, but by imputation of men's sins to Christ. Having been done away by imputation to Christ, men are no longer responsible either for their sinful state or sinful acts. A distinction is made between the believer's "standing" and his actual "state" or condition. Believers are accounted righteous or holy by their "standing" in Christ. God does not take account of their actual "state" for He sees them only through Christ. Sin is not actually removed from the heart and life, but only covered over with the robe of Christ's imputed righteousness. Holiness and righteousness are only imputed, never imparted. In this system, faith becomes, not the condition of personal salvation, but simply a recognition of what was done by Christ on the cross. Justification likewise is not an act in the mind of God by which the sinner is forgiven, but

An Antinomian is a professor of Christianity, who is *antinomos*, against the law of Christ, as well as against the law of Moses. He allows Christ's law to be the rule of life, but not a rule of judgment for believers, and thus he destroys that law at a stroke, as a law; it being evident that a rule by the personal observance or nonobservance of which Christ's subjects can never be acquitted or condemned, it is not a law for them. Hence he asserts that Christians shall no more be justified before God by their personal obedience to the law of Christ than by their personal obedience to the ceremonial law of Moses. Nay, he believes that the best of Christians perpetually break Christ's law; that nobody ever kept it but Christ himself; and that we shall be justified or condemned before God, in the great day, not as we shall personally be found to have kept or broken Christ's law, but as God shall be found to have, before the foundation of the world, arbitrarily laid, or not laid, to our account, the merit of Christ's keeping of His own law. Thus he hopes to stand in the great day, merely by what he calls "Christ's imputed righteousness."—JOHN FLETCHER, *Checks to Antinomianism.*

a wholesale transaction on Calvary, centuries ago, only just now recognized and accepted. Regeneration is regarded, not as an impartation of life to the soul, but as in some sense the creation of a new personality which existed alongside the old, both natures remaining un-

> The principles which underlie the antinomianism of the Plymouth Brethren are essentially those which characterized the Moravianism of Wesley's day, and of the Anabaptists which gave Luther so much concern. Mr. Wesley sums up the differences between the Moravians and the Methodists in the following statement. He says, "The difference between the Moravian doctrine and ours lies here; they believe and teach, (1) That Christ has done all which was necessary for the salvation of all mankind. (2) That, consequently, we are to do nothing, as necessary to salvation, but simply to believe in Him. (3) That there is but one duty now, but one command, namely, to believe in Christ. (4) That Christ has taken away all other commands and duties, having wholly 'abolished the law'; that a believer is therefore 'free from the law,' is not obliged to do or omit anything; it being inconsistent with his liberty to do anything as commanded. (5) That we are sanctified wholly the moment we are justified, and are neither more nor less holy to the day of our death; entire sanctification, and entire justification, being in one and the same instant. (6) That the believer is never sanctified or holy in himself, but in Christ only; he has no holiness in himself at all, all his holiness being imputed, not inherent. (7) That if a man regards prayer, or searching the Scriptures, or communicating as a matter of duty; if he judges himself obliged to do these things, or is troubled when he does them not; he is in bondage; he has no faith at all, but is seeking salvation by the works of the law."
>
> In reply to the above, Mr. Wesley gives the following of these errors in refutation. "We believe the first of these propositions is ambiguous, and all the rest utterly false. (1) 'Christ has done all which was necessary for the salvation of all mankind.' This is ambiguous. Christ has not done all which was necessary for the absolute salvation of all mankind. For, notwithstanding all that Christ has done, he that believeth not shall be damned. But He has done all which was necessary for the conditional salvation of all mankind; that is, if they believe; for through His merits all that believe to the end, with the faith that worketh by love, shall be saved.' (2-3) 'There is but one duty now, but one command, namely, to believe in Christ.' Almost every page in the New Testament proves the falsehood of this assertion. (4) 'Christ has taken away all other commands and duties, having wholly abolished the law.' How absolutely contrary is this to His own solemn declaration! "Think not that I am come to destroy the law and the prophets. I am not come to destroy but to fulfil." (5) 'We are sanctified wholly the moment we are justified, and are neither more nor less holy to the day of our death; entire sanctification and entire justification being in one and the same instant.' Just the contrary appears from both the tenor of God's Word, and the experience of His children. (6) 'A believer is never sanctified or holy in himself, but in Christ only. He has no holiness in himself at all; all his holiness being imputed, not inherent.' Scriptural holiness is the image of God; the mind which was in Christ; the love of God and man; lowliness, gentleness, temperance, patience, chastity. And do you coolly affirm that this is only imputed to a believer, and that he has none at all of this holiness in him? Is temperance imputed only to him that is a drunkard still; or chastity to her that goes on in whoredom? Nay, but a believer is really chaste and temperate. And if so, he is thus far holy in himself."—WESLEY, *Works,* Vol. VII, p. 22.

changed until death. The person, or that which in man says "I," may put itself under the direction of either the "new man" or the "old man" without any detriment to his standing in Christ, except that in the latter case, communion will be interrupted. The "standing" is eternal, and remains unchanged, regardless of the actual "state" of the professed believer. Furthermore, the doctrine of the two natures is not fully understood until it is seen, that neither of these natures is responsible for the other. Whatever may be the deeds of the "old man," the believer is not held to be accountable for them—they were condemned on the cross.

The Plymouth idea of sanctification, like that of justification, is purely Antinomian. The believer is not only made righteous in Christ, he is made holy also. The one act, viewed as righteousness, is justification; viewed as holiness, it is sanctification. One of their own writers states this position as follows: "He who is our Great High Priest before God is pure and without stain. God sees Him as such, and He stands for us who are His people, and we are accepted in Him. His holiness is ours by imputation. Standing in Him, we are in the sight of God, holy as Christ is holy, and pure as Christ is pure. God looks at our representative, and He sees us in Him. We are complete in Him who is our spotless and glorious

Mr. Wesley made an epitome of Baxter's Aphorisms on Justification, which sets forth in an admirable manner, the whole question of a believer's relation to law. "As there are two covenants, with their distinct conditions, so there is a twofold righteousness, and both of them necessary for salvation. Our righteousness of the first covenant (under the remediless, Christless, Adamic law) is not personal, or consisteth not in any actions preferred by us; for we never personally satisfied the law (of innocence), but it is wholly without us, in Christ. In this sense every Christian disclaimeth his own righteousness, or his own works. Those only shall be in Christ legally righteous who believe and obey the gospel, and so are in themselves evangelically righteous. Though Christ performed the conditions of the law (of paradisaical innocence), and made satisfaction for our nonperformance, yet we ourselves must perform the conditions of the gospel. These (last) two propositions seem to me so clear, that I wonder that able divines should deny them. Methinks they should be articles of our creed, and a part of children's catechisms. To affirm that evangelical or new-covenant righteousness is in Christ, and not in ourselves, or performed by Christ, and not by ourselves, is such a monstrous piece of Antinomian doctrine as no man, who knows the nature and difference of the covenants, can possibly entertain."—BAXTER, *Aphorisms*, Pro. 14, 15.

Head." His holiness, is purely in the "standing" which man has in Christ, that is, it is imputed only. As to the "state" or actual condition of his heart, there is no personal holiness inwrought by the Spirit. Sin continues until death, but this in nowise affects the "standing" of the believer. "We must never measure the standing by the state," says Mr. McIntosh, "but always the state by the standing. To lower the standing because of the state, is to give the death-blow to all progress in practical Christianity." Commenting upon this, Dr. Daniel Steele says, "that is to say, the fruit must always be judged by the tree; to judge the tree by the fruit, is to give the death blow to pomology."

It can easily be seen why the teachers of this doctrine have a special hostility to the Wesleyan and scriptural teaching concerning Christian perfection. The former holds to an imputed holiness; the latter to an imparted holiness. The former holds that we are merely reckoned holy; the latter that we are actually made holy. The former base everything on a logical syllogism—Christ is holy; we are in Christ; therefore we are holy. Christ is indeed holy, but the fact is overlooked, that no man is in Christ in the fullest sense of new covenant privilege, until he is cleansed from all sin by the baptism with the Holy Ghost. The intellectual assertion that a man is in Christ, does not make it so in fact; this is accomplished by an inner work of the Spirit of God. Ethically, this Antinomian doctrine breaks down all the restraints that would hinder men from sin, as set up in Arminianism and the older Calvinism. Logically, it has its issue in the doctrine of final perseverance, or what in more modern times is wrongly known as eternal security.

(3) The Keswick Movement was founded for "the promotion of scriptural holiness" as stated in the invitation to the original meeting, held in Oxford in 1874. The following year, a second convention was held at Keswick, from which the movement took its name. Here the invitation stated that the convention was for

the "promotion of practical holiness." It has been popularized by a number of nationally known evangelists and has in it many sincere and earnest Christians. They believe in the lost condition of the race, and are zealous in their efforts for the salvation of men. They insist upon the abandonment of all known sin, and a definite and complete consecration to Christ. They emphasize the necessity of an appropriation by faith, of the power of God through Christ, for both holy living and Christian service. This enduement for service is known among them as the baptism with the Holy Spirit, and is generally regarded as being subsequent to conversion. It is not, however, in the strict sense, a work of grace, for there is no cleansing from inbred sin. Their position in regard to inbred sin is essentially that of the Plymouth Brethren. It is regarded as a part of the believer's humiliation, and in a sense defiling his best deeds. It involves continuous suppression, and will continue to exist until death delivers from its defilement. The enduement of the Spirit counteracts in some measure, the carnal mind, and assists the believer in repressing its manifestations. It will be seen from these statements, that apart from other differences in theology, the power of sin is merely broken, which Wesleyanism maintains takes place in conversion. It is in no sense entire sanctification as Wesleyanism defines this term. It is rather, more closely related to the idea of positional holiness as taught by the Plymouth Brethren. The believer is holy in his "standing" but not in his "state." Holiness is thus a matter of imputation instead of impartation. Actual cleansing from all sin is rejected as being out of harmony with their general principles. The "standing" is eternal, and hence, like the former theory, logically issues in the so-called doctrine of "eternal security."

The Salvation Army, and especially its earlier leaders, have been able representatives of the doctrine of entire sanctification. General William Booth and his wife, were particularly definite in their teaching. The works of Commissioner Brengle are recognized as standard holiness literature.

The Meaning and Scope of Sanctification

We have in the two previous divisions indicated in a general way the meaning and scope of sanctification, but the subject demands a more thorough study. The term *holiness,* as it is used in this connection, refers to man's moral or religious state, and *sanctification,* to the act by which he is made holy. The idea of the divine holiness necessarily underlies our conception of human holiness—the former being absolute, the latter, relative or derived. The concept of the divine holiness was given careful attention in our study of the Moral Attributes of God (Chapter XIV); we must now study the question of human holiness in relation to our former positions. The terminology of the Greek New Testament will furnish the best approach to this subject, but must be limited solely to those words and their derivatives, which in the English translation are rendered holiness or sanctification. Other words referring to this experience will be given consideration later. In the study of these Greek words, however, we must bear in mind that the Greeks had no clear idea of holiness, such as the Christian religion demanded, and hence St. Paul was under the necessity of reading into these words, a deeper meaning, than that which they ordinarily conveyed to the Greek mind.

We shall notice, at this time, the following Greek terms. (1) *Hagios* (ἅγιος), holy. This word occurs frequently in the Scriptures, but is rarely used outside of Holy Writ. It means (a) reverent, or worthy of veneration, and is applied to God (Luke 1:49); to things on account of their connection with God (Acts 6:13; 7:33); and to persons whose services God employs

Entire sanctification is not the destruction of any faculty, affection, or passion, but the purification, sanctification, and preservation of all that is essentially human unto eternal life (I Thess. 5:23).

Dr. C. J. Fowler says that sanctification is used in the Scriptures interchangeably with justification, regeneration, adoption, conversion and the like, but not in that sense alone. The Corinthians are addressed as "sanctified in Christ Jesus," and at the same time their entire sanctification is denied, for they are addressed as "yet carnal" and exhorted to perfect "holiness in the fear of God." In Paul's epistle to the Thessalonians, prayer is offered that they may be sanctified "wholly" (cf. Fowler, *Sermon on Double Cure,* p. 103).

CHRISTIAN PERFECTION OR ENTIRE SANCTIFICATION

(Eph. 3:5). (b) To set apart to God, to be exclusively His (Mark 1:24; Luke 2:23). (c) It is used of sacrifices and offerings prepared for God with solemn rite (Rom. 11:16; 12:1; I Cor. 7:14; Eph. 1:4; 5:27; Col. 1:22). (d) In a moral sense, pure, sinless, upright and holy (Rom. 7:12; 16:16; I Cor. 7:14; 16:20; I Peter 1:16; II Peter 3:11). (2) *Hagion* (ἅγιον), neuter gender of ἅγιος and used generally to designate a holy place (Heb. 9:24, 25; 10:19). (3) *Hagiadzo* (ἁγιάζω) a verb meaning to separate, to set apart, to render or to declare holy. It means (a) to hallow (Matt. 6:9); (b) to separate from the profane and dedicate to God —things (Matt. 23:17; II Tim. 2:21); persons (John 10:36; 17:19); (c) to purify—externally (Heb. 9:13; I Tim. 4:5), by expiation (I Cor. 6:11; Eph. 5:26; Heb. 10:10, 14, 29; 13:12), internally (John 17:17, 19; Rom. 15:16; I Cor. 1:2; I Thess. 5:23; Jude 1; Rev. 22:11). (4) *Hagiasmos* (ἁγιασμὸς) is a word used only by biblical and ecclesiastical writers. It is derived from the perfect passive (ἡγίασμαι) of ἁγιάζω, and is translated sanctification or holiness. It is found in I Thess. 4:3 *this is the will of God, even your sanctification:* Heb. 12:14 *Follow peace with all men, and holiness,* (ἁγιασμὸν) (or the sanctification wrought by the Holy Spirit, αγιασμῳ Πνευματος); and again, *ye have your fruit unto holiness* (ἁγιασμὸν) (Rom. 6:19, 22). (5) *Hagiotes* (ἁγιότης), sanctity, or in the moral sense, holiness. It refers especially to the property of moral natures, and is applicable to both God and sanctified men (Heb. 12:10). (6) *Hagiosune* (ἁγιωσύνη), sanctity, sanctification, holiness. The word is generally regarded as synonymous with the preceding term, but restricted more especially in its application to men. As such it signifies emphatically, a personal purification. It is used but three times in the New Testament, (a) Rom. 1:4, where the contrast is made between Christ *according to the flesh* (κατὰ σάρκα), and *according to the spirit of holiness* (κατὰ πνεῦμα ἁγιωσύνης); (b) II Cor. 7:1, *perfecting holiness* (ἁγιωσύνην); and (c) I Thess. 3:13, *stablish your hearts unblameable in holiness* (ἁγιωσύνη).

From this brief study of *Hagios* (ἅγιος) and its derivatives, it will be clearly seen, that while the primary meaning is a setting apart, or a separation, this in the New Testament takes on the deeper significance of a cleansing from all sin. This is the dominant meaning of the terms used in the Scriptures, and from this authority there can be no appeal. The word *hagnos* (ἁγνὸς) and its derivatives, on the other hand, while implying inward purity (cf. I John 3:3), refer primarily to external or ceremonial purity, the sanctification of the body, and the general qualities of purity and chastity (John 11:55; Acts 21:24, 26; II Cor. 11:2; Phil. 4:8; Titus 2:5; James 3:17).

Definitions of Entire Sanctification. We believe that entire sanctification is that act of God, subsequent to regeneration, by which believers are made free from original sin, or depravity, and brought into a state of

We cannot pass without a definition of this word "purify." It is the very word from which we get our English derivative—cathartic. It literally means to purge, to purify, to remove dross and eliminate that which is foreign. It is identically the same word as is used in I John 1:7. It means nothing more or less than the actual cleansing of the nature of man from the virus of a sinful disposition. Let men decry the truth and resolutely clamor heresy, but the clear and unmistakable statement of Peter, whom the Holy Spirit himself directed to speak, was that the heart meaning of Pentecost then—and now—was and is the cleansing of the heart from inborn sin. To this clear witness of Peter scripture boldly attests and the lives of multitudes happily declare. This then is the privilege of every Christian.—Dr. H. V. Miller, *When He Is Come.*

Sanctified souls are inclined to name the blessing after their principal sensations, harmonizing with their emotional experiences. (1) One person realizes principally a marked increase of faith, and he calls it "the rest of faith." (2) Another is conscious of a deep, sweet resting in Christ, and calls it "resting in God." (3) Another is permeated with a sense of the divine presence, and filled with ecstatic raptures, and calls it "the fullness of God." (4) Another feels his heart subdued, melted, refined and filled with God, and calls it "holiness." (5) Another realizes principally a river of sweet, holy love flowing through the soul, and he calls it "perfect love." (6) Another is prostrated under the power of the refining and sin-killing Spirit, and calls it "the baptism with the Holy Ghost." (7) And another realizes principally a heaven of sweetness in complete submission to God, and he calls it "entire sanctification." (8) While another may feel clearly and strongly conscious of complete conformity to all the will of God, and calls it "Christian perfection." If genuine, the work wrought in each case is essentially the same.—Wood, *Perfect Love*, p. 125.

entire devotement to God, and the holy obedience of love made perfect. It is wrought by the baptism with the Holy Spirit, and comprehends in one experience the cleansing of the heart from sin and the abiding, indwelling presence of the Holy Spirit, empowering the believer for life and service. Entire sanctification is provided by the blood of Jesus, is wrought instantaneously by faith, preceded by entire consecration; and to this work and state of grace the Holy Spirit bears witness. This experience is also known by various terms representing its different phases, such as "Christian Perfection," "Perfect Love," "Heart Purity," "The Baptism with the Holy Spirit," "The Fullness of the Blessing," and "Christian Holiness" (Creed, Art. X). Mr. Wesley says that "Sanctification in the proper sense

> The literature of early Methodism on the subject of entire sanctification is peculiarly rich and prolific. We give a few of the more outstanding utterances on this subject. "From the very first years of my ministry I have held with Adam Clarke, Richard Watson, John Fletcher and John Wesley, that regeneration and sanctification are separated and distinct one from the other and therefore received at different times. They are both received by faith, and the last one is the privilege of every believer as the first is of every penitent."—BISHOP MALLALIEU. Regeneration "is a mixed moral state. Sanctification is like weeding the soil, or gathering the tares and burning them, so that nothing remains to grow there but the good seed. . . . . Entire sanctification removes them—roots them out of the heart, and leaves it a pure soil."—BISHOP HAMLINE, *Beauty of Holiness*, p. 264. "In the merely justified state we are not entirely pure. . . . . But in the work of entire sanctification, these impurities are all washed away, so that we are wholly saved from sin, from its inward pollution."—BISHOP JESSE T. PECK, *Central Idea of Christianity*, p. 52. "Regeneration removes some sin or pollution, and entire sanctification removes the corruption which remains after regeneration. This will be seen, from the authorities given, to be the Wesleyan idea of sanctification."—BISHOP FOSTER, *Christian Purity*, p. 122. "The degree of original sin which remains in some believers, though not a transgression of a known law, is nevertheless sin, and must be removed before one goes to heaven, and the removal of this evil is what we mean by full sanctification."—BISHOP HEDDING, *Sermons*. "By holiness I mean that state of the soul in which all its alienation from God, and all its aversion to a holy life are removed."—BISHOP MCCABE.
>
> From the commentators we have the following definitions: "This term (sanctify) has the Old Testament sense of setting apart to a sacred service, and the New Testament sense of spiritual purification."—JACOBUS, *Notes on John* 17:17. "Sanctification is to have soul, body and spirit, every sense, member, organ, and faculty, completely purified and devoted to the service of God."—SCOTT, *Commentary*. "True religion consists in heart purity. Those who are inwardly pure, show themselves to be under the power of pure and undefiled religion. True Christianity lies in the heart, in the purity of the heart, in the washing of that from wickedness."—MATTHEW HENRY, *Notes on Matt.* 5:8.

is an instantaneous deliverance from all sin, and includes an instantaneous power then given always to cleave to God." Mr. Watson defines entire sanctification as "a complete deliverance from all spiritual pollution, all inward depravation of heart, as well as that, which, expressing itself outwardly by the indulgence of the senses, is called filthiness of the flesh and spirit" (WATSON, *Institutes*, II, p. 450). Adam Clarke defines it as "the cleansing of the blood, that has not been cleansed; it is the washing of the soul of a true believer from the remains of sin" (CLARKE, *Christian Theology*, p. 206). Dr. Pope's definition is as follows: "Sanctification in its beginnings, process and final issues is the full eradication of the sin itself, which reigning in the unregenerate, coexists with the new life in the regenerate, is abolished in the wholly sanctified." Dr. Phineas F. Bresee in his sermon on *Divine Power* says, "It is evident that the baptism with the Holy Ghost is the conveyance into men and through men, of the 'all-power' of Jesus Christ—the revelation of Him in the soul"; and again, "The baptism with the Holy Ghost is the baptism with God. It is the burning up of the chaff, but is also the revelation in us and the manifestation to us of divine personality, filling our being" (DR. P. F. BRESEE, *Sermons*, p. 193). It will be noticed, that while Dr. Bresee never undervalued the cleansing aspect of entire sanctification, his chief emphasis was always upon the divine infilling—the unfolding of the entire being in "loyal relation to the divine." Dr. Edward F. Walker defined sanctification as a "personal cleansing from sin, in order to a holy life. Made pure in order to sustain devotion to God. A pure heart, full of holy love. Beyond this we cannot go in this world; but short of this we ought never to rest. . . . . Perfect purity plus perfect love in the heart by the efficiency of Christ and the power of the indwelling Holy Spirit equal personal sanctification" (WALKER, *Sanctify Them*, pp. 42, 49). Dr. John W. Goodwin gives us this definition: "Sanctification is a divine work of grace, purifying the believer's heart from indwelling sin. It is subsequent to regeneration, is secured in the atoning blood of Christ, is effected by the baptism with the Holy Ghost, is conditioned on full consecration to God, is received by faith, and includes instantaneous empowerment for service."

Primarily sanctification has to do with man's inner nature or condition, as justification does with his outer conduct. In a word, when a man is converted he is forgiven and restored to favor with God. The power of sin is broken, "the old man" of sin is conquered, the power of the new life within him is greater than the power of a fallen nature. This inherited bias, or "prone to wander," this inner opposition to the law of God is not destroyed, it is conquered in regeneration. It is destroyed, absolutely annihilated, in sanctification.—Dr. R. T. Williams, *Sanctification*, p. 17.

A glorious fact, however, remains for us to consider. . . . . The coming of the Holy Ghost into the heart and life in His exquisite fullness does so cleanse and empower, protect and guard that liability of spiritual failure is brought to its earthly minimum. . . . . To every soul who will yield to the Holy Ghost, He will come with loving and holy dominion driving from the heart every antagonism to all the will of God. He will then secure the entrance to the soul with His own untiring presence. Whenever the enemy attempts to come in like a flood, He himself will lift up a standard against him. He will culture the soul with skill. He will guide the life with agility. He will build fixed principles of moral living deep within the being so that the slightest insinuation of Satan will be readily recognized and repulsed. He will train the weakened propensities and appetites of a broken race till scriptural culture becomes the instinct of the soul. Thus empowered and equipped the liability of failure is brought to a conspicuous minimum.—Dr. H. V. Miller, *When He Is Come*, p. 28.

To be sanctified is nothing more or less than this one thing, the complete removal from the heart of that which is enmity to God, not subject to the law of God, neither indeed can be; and this enables the life to be fully devoted to God. Regardless of how perfect may be the consecration, no Christian is truly sanctified by Christ until the heart is made pure by His blood. This is a definite experience, a mighty work of grace, wrought by God in response to the faith of the consecrated Christian in Christ the Sanctifier. This experience marks a definite second crisis in spiritual life, it is the perfection of a spiritual relationship with God, the cleansing from all sin, when God works within us the devotedness He desires. . . . . Devotedness to God—sanctification—includes also a conscious fullness of the Holy Spirit dwelling within as the power of our love, enabling us to live in fellowship with Christ and in full obedience to Him, giving us glorious victory in the many conflicts of life. . . . . Holiness as devotedness to God involves the subordination of all other purposes to the one great purpose—the joyous acceptance and the happy doing of the will of God.—D. Shelby Corlett, *Holiness—the Central Purpose of Redemption*, pp. 22, 23.

I have called holiness the heart of Christian experience because it is by way of the full realization of what God has promised to us in the way of crises. Regeneration and entire sanctification are the two crises in which God deals with the sin problem in us and by which He takes us out of sin and then takes sin out of us. After that the Christian life is a way of process and progress, but there are no more crises until glorification comes at the return of Jesus to this world. There is all room for growth after sanctification, but there is no more place for

Justification and Sanctification. Our previous study of Christian righteousness has given us the general characteristics of justification; it remains for us now to contrast these briefly with sanctification, in order to set forth more clearly the distinctions between them. (1) Justification in a broad sense has reference to the whole work of Christ wrought *for* us; sanctification, the whole work wrought *in* us by the Holy Spirit. (2) Justification is a forensic and judicial act in the mind of God; sanctification, a spiritual change wrought in the hearts of men. (3) Justification is a relative change, that is, a change in relation from condemnation to favor; sanctification, an inward change from sin to holiness. (4) Justification secures for us the remission of actual sins; sanctification, in its complete sense, cleanses the heart from original sin or inherited depravity. (5) Justification removes the guilt of sin, sanctification, destroys its power. (6) Justification relieves the soul from exposure to the penalty of violated law; sanctification prepares it for the gracious rewards of virtue. (7) Justification makes possible adoption into the family of God; sanctification restores the image of God. (8) Justification gives a title to heaven, sanctification, a fitness for heaven. (9) Justification logically precedes sanctification, which in its lowest or initial stage,

crises. There is no state of grace beyond a pure heart filled with the Holy Spirit. But from such a heart flows forth the passive and active phases of Christian life as water flows forth from a spring. Holiness is purity—not maturity. Holiness is the goal only in that it prepares one for whatever there is of Christian life—it is the "enabling blessing" which every Christian needs.—Dr. J. B. Chapman, *Holiness the Heart of Christian Experience*, p. 10.

The Holy Spirit is vitally related to all the work of salvation. The Bible clearly presents two distinct operations or works of the Holy Spirit that are crisis works of salvation. The first of these is to be born of the Spirit (John 3:6). Birth is an act, and a crisis act. To be born is to be brought into life. In this case it is to be "born again" (verse 7), to restore a life that has been lost; it is a new spiritual birth—regeneration; it is coming to life as a babe in Christ; it is a new life forgiven and freed from the guilt of sin. The second of these is to be baptized with the Holy Ghost (Luke 3:16). Baptism is an act, and a crisis act. Baptism is something quite different from birth and cannot possibly be until after birth; one must be born before he can be baptized. These two figures that are here applied to the spiritual life necessitate two crisis experiences, the one following the other. With this baptism we have entire sanctification, cleansing from the inner state of sin.—Dr. E. P. Ellyson, *Bible Holiness*, pp. 89, 90.

is concomitant with it. (10) Justification is an instantaneous and completed act, and therefore does not take place *ad seriatim*, or by degrees; sanctification is marked by progressiveness, that is, it has stages and degrees. There is a partial sanctification which is concomitant with justification, and there is an entire sanctification which is subsequent to it. But both initial and entire sanctification are instantaneous acts, wrought in the hearts of men by the Holy Spirit.

Regeneration and Sanctification. The relation existing between regeneration and sanctification is set forth in an able and unique manner by Bishop Jesse T. Peck in his *Central Idea of Christianity.* He says, "Just as natural life and the condition of the living being are distinct, spiritual life and the moral condition of the spiritually alive are distinct. Certain invariable coincidences between these two things, in no respect interfere with their essential difference. Now, two things so entirely distinct, as the fact of spiritual life and the moral state of the spiritually alive, ought to have different names. Regeneration appropriately designates the former, sanctification the latter..... The word sanctification just as appropriately denotes certain treatment of the soul, which God has brought to life, as regeneration does the fact of bringing it to life. Sanctify is from *sanctus,* holy, and *facio,* to make. Sanctification is literally the act of making holy, and this is its essential meaning in systematic divinity. Now here are two things totally distinct from each other, as much so as a fact and a quality of a fact, a thing and an accident of a thing can be; and here are two terms, of entirely different import, completely adapted to represent these two things respectively—regeneration, the production of spiritual life; sanctification, the treatment of the soul spiritually alive—neither of which can, without vio-

Justification has reference to the disposition and mercy of God toward the repentant sinner; regeneration has respect to the offices of the Holy Spirit pursuant to the dispensation of pardon. Justification absolves from condemnation; regeneration takes away death and inspires life. Justification brings liberty; regeneration supplies power.—LOWREY, *Possibilities of Grace,* p. 185.

lence to the laws of language, perform the office of the other. We humbly submit, therefore, that they ought not to be used interchangeably, and that attempts to so use them have caused nearly all the confusion which has embarrassed these great points in theology" (PECK, *Central Idea of Christianity*, pp. 15, 16).

Generation denotes the production of natural life, regeneration the production of spiritual life. Now the force of the illustration is seen in the following particulars: (1) The soul in its natural state is "dead" —"dead" in trespasses and sins. It is so, because "to be carnally minded is death." (2) Natural life is the product of divine power alone, and spiritual life must be also. Generation expresses the operation of this power in the one instance, and regeneration in the other. A similar relation exists between the ideas represented by the words "creature" and "new creature," "born" and "born again." (3) Generation and birth produce new natural powers and functions, which demonstrate the omnipotence of their Creator; regeneration and the new birth produce spiritual powers and functions, entirely new, which demonstrate equally the divinity of their origin. (4) The result of generation is natural life with its accidents, the result of regeneration is spiritual life with its accidents; the degree of health may be mentioned as an accident of the former, the degree of sanctification or holiness as an accident of the latter.—PECK, *Central Idea of Christianity*, p. 15.

Hence the new birth, or regeneration, is the divine life of infancy. It is holiness of heart, but holiness lacking the great and chief measure consisting of salvation from all sin and the perfection of love. Regeneration bears the same relation to full redemption that infancy does to manhood, discipline to culture, feebleness to might, tuition to knowledge, and imperfection, maturity and completeness. Such being the relation of the two states, holiness can no more be separated from regeneration than the full currents of vitality in robust manhood can declare themselves unrelated to the feeble flow of blood in infant veins.— LOWREY, *Possibilities of Grace*, pp. 185, 186.

Dr. E. P. Ellyson treats the state of holiness under four different aspects, with four distinct results. (1) It is a state of moral purity. One may be far from maturity, there may be much of weakness and ignorance, the judgment may be far from perfect, but the heart may be clean; there may be nothing of moral defilement or pollution. (2) This is an experience of separation, and of being set apart. There is such devotement to God as to set one apart from the secular to the sacred. One in his consecration must thus set himself apart. In response to this consecration Christ sets him apart. (3) This is an experience of divine indwelling, of continued divine presence. With this experience, one is never alone, there are always two together; he is "filled with the Holy Ghost." (4) This is an enduement of power. The apostles were to tarry in the city of Jerusalem until they were "endued with power from on high." They had been converted and called to service as the first leaders of the church, they had been in training under the teaching of Jesus for some time; but there was a heavenly enduement with power that they needed to fit them for this place to which they were called.—DR. E. P. ELLYSON, *Bible Holiness*, pp. 104ff.

The difference between a justified soul who is not fully sanctified, and one fully sanctified, I understand to be this: The first is kept from voluntarily committing known sin, which is what is commonly meant in the New Testament by committing sin. But he yet finds in himself the

Concerning Sin in the Regenerate. It has been the uniform belief of the church, that original sin "continues to exist with the new life of the regenerate, until eradicated by the baptism with the Holy Spirit" (Creed, Art. V). As stated in the Thirty-nine Articles, "this infection of nature doth remain, yea, in them that are regenerated; whereby the lust of the flesh, called in Greek φρόνημα σαρκός, is not subject to the law of God. And although there is no condemnation for them that believe, yet this lust hath of itself the nature of sin" (Art. IX). "By sin," says Mr. Wesley, "I here understand inward sin; any sinful temper, passion, or affection; such as pride, self-will, love of the world, in any kind or degree; such as lust, anger, peevishness; any disposition contrary to the mind which was in Christ" (*Sermon: Sin in Believers*). The condition of the regenerate, therefore, previous to entire sanctification, is in a modified sense, a mixed state. There is

remains of inbred corruption or original sin; such as pride, anger, envy, a feeling of hatred to an enemy, a rejoicing at a calamity which has fallen upon an enemy. Now in all this the regenerate soul does not act voluntarily; his choice is against these evils, and resists and overcomes them as soon as the mind perceives them. Though the Christian does not feel guilty for this depravity as he would do if he had voluntarily broken the law of God, yet he is often grieved and afflicted, and reproved at a sight of this sinfulness of his nature. Though the soul in this state enjoys a degree of religion, yet it is conscious it is not what it ought to be, nor what it must be to be fit for heaven. The second, or person fully sanctified, is cleansed from all these involuntary sins. He may be tempted by Satan, by men, and by his own bodily appetites to commit sin, but his heart is free from these inward fires, which before his full sanctification, were ready to fall in with the temptation and lead him into transgression. He may be tempted to be proud, to love the world, to be revengeful or angry, to hate an enemy, to wish him evil, or to rejoice at his calamity, but he feels none of these passions in his heart; the Holy Ghost has cleansed him from all these pollutions of his nature. Thus it is that, being emptied of sin, the perfect Christian is filled with the love of God, even with that perfect love which casteth out fear.—Bishop Hedding. "This," says Dr. McDonald, "is so plain that the child may understand it, and so much in harmony with Christian experience that comment is unnecessary."—(Cf. McDonald, *Scriptural Way of Holiness*, p. 122).

Regeneration is like breaking up the fallow ground and sowing it with wheat, in the growth of which there spring up tares. It is a mixed moral state. Sanctification is like weeding the soil, or gathering the tares and burning them, so that nothing remains to grow there but good seed. In regeneration a spiritual growth is like the slow progress of the wheat, choked and made sickly by the intermingling weeds. Entire sanctification removes them, roots them out of the heart, and leaves it a pure moral soil.—Bishop Hamline.

within the heart of the believer, both grace and inbred sin, but there is not, nor can there be any commingling or blending of these antagonistic elements. They exist in the heart without admixture or composition. Otherwise we should have an adulterated holiness. Those who hold to the erroneous idea of regeneration as a making over of the old life, instead of an impartation of the new, find difficulty in accounting for a second work of grace.

Entire Sanctification as Subsequent to Regeneration. Theologians of the Wesleyan type frequently speak of the incompleteness of regeneration, and of the necessity of entire sanctification in order to complete or perfect the redemptive process. Thus Dr. Miley states that "the doctrine of an incompleteness of the work of regeneration underlies entire sanctification, particularly in its Wesleyan form" (MILEY, *Syst. Th.*, II, p. 357). There

> The Scriptures affirm that there remains in man, after conversion, what is called "the flesh," the "old man," "carnality," "wrath,"—inherited predisposition—some call this predisposition, "tendency to evil," but it is evidently more; the apostle calls it "the body of sin."—DR. P. F. BRESEE, *Sermons*, p. 46.
>
> The question is not concerning outward sin; whether a child of God commits sin or no. We all agree and earnestly maintain, "He that committeth sin is of the devil." We agree, "Whosoever is born of God doth not commit sin." Neither do we inquire whether sin will always remain in the children of God; whether sin will continue in the soul as long as it continues in the body; nor yet do we inquire whether a justified person may relapse either into inward or outward sin; but simply this, "Is a justified or regenerated man freed from all sin as soon as he is justified? . . . . But was he not then freed from all sin, so that there is no sin in his heart?" I cannot say this; I cannot believe it; because St. Paul says the contrary. He is speaking to believers in general, when he says, "The flesh lusteth against the Spirit, and the Spirit against the flesh: and these are contrary the one to the other" (Gal. 5:17). Nothing can be more expressive. The apostle here directly affirms that the flesh, evil nature, opposes the Spirit, even in believers; that even in the regenerate there are two principles, "contrary the one to the other."—WESLEY, *Sin in Believers*.
>
> Again, in his sermon on "Patience," Mr. Wesley says, "Till this universal change (purification) was wrought in his soul (the regenerate), all his holiness was mixed." In commenting on this, Rev. J. A. Wood says, "mixed, necessarily in a restricted sense. Both grace and inbred sin have existence in the same soul, though antagonistic and at war with each other. Though existing for the time in the same person in admixture, they are distinct in nature and tendency; they are 'contrary the one to the other,' and are irreconcilable enemies. Partly holy, and partly unholy, as in a sense is the case with the merely regenerate, does by no means imply a homogenous character, combining and assimilating into a common nature the elements of both holiness and sin."—J. A. WOOD, *Purity and Maturity*, p. 111.

is a sense in which this is true, but the form of the statement is unfortunate. Regeneration considered in itself is not an imperfect work. It is the bestowal of divine life, and as an operation of the Spirit, is complete in itself. But regeneration is only a part of the grace embraced in the New Covenant, and in this sense only may be said to be incomplete—incomplete as not in itself representing the totality of New Covenant blessings. Again, regeneration is frequently represented in Wesleyan theology, as the beginning of sanctification—a work which comes to its perfection in entire sanctification. Here, also, discriminating thought is necessary. Regeneration is the beginning of sanctification in this

Regeneration and sanctification both deal primarily with the sin question. That is why they are called the first and second blessings or works of grace. There are many blessings in Christian experience and Christian life, but there are two blessings that are called the first and second blessings. This is due to the fact that these two specific blessings deal with the question of sin. The one deals primarily with what we do, the other primarily with what we are. It would not be altogether correct to say that regeneration deals with the act alone. We have already stated that regeneration deals with sins committed, with spiritual death, and with acquired pollution. Neither would it be quite correct to assert that sanctification deals only with our inner state. This is true primarily, but indirectly it deals with our ethics because of the fact that our inner state makes it easier or harder for us to live right externally. . . . . Here is the great battle ground concerning holiness. The question is simply this, Is sin destroyed in the act of sanctification or not? This is the question on which turns all belief in sanctification. It is folly to try to pass as a believer in holiness and at the same time question its doctrine of eradication. There cannot be such a thing as holiness in its final analysis without the eradication of sin. Holiness and suppression are incompatible terms. "The old man" and counteraction make a pale and sickly kind of holiness doctrine. It is holiness and eradication or holiness not at all.—Dr. R. T. WILLIAMS, *Sanctification*, pp. 16, 17.

When does inward sanctification begin? In the moment a man is justified. Yet sin remains in him, yea the seed of all sin, till he is sanctified throughout.—WESLEY, *Plain Account*, p. 48.

Regeneration, also, being the same as the new birth, is the beginning of sanctification, though not the completion of it, or not entire sanctification. Regeneration is the beginning of purification; entire sanctification is the finishing of that work.—BISHOP HEDDING, *Conference Address*.

The implantation of spiritual life does not destroy the carnal mind; though its power is broken, it does not cease to exist. While the new birth is the beginning of purification, it is, perhaps, more the process of imparting or begetting spiritual life, than the process of refining or purification; which in entire sanctification is the extraction of remaining impurity from regenerated human nature.—J. A. WOOD, *Purity and Maturity*, p. 112.

That a distinction exists between a regenerate state, and a state of entire and perfect holiness, will be generally allowed.—WATSON, *Institutes*, II, chap 29.

sense only, that the life bestowed in the new birth is a holy life. This new life, being one of "holy love" may be said to be the beginning of holiness. But we are not to infer from this that the expanding of this new life by growth, or the increase and development of this love, will bring the soul to entire sanctification. Failure to discriminate here, leads inevitably to the "growth theory" of sanctification. Sanctification is an act of cleansing, and unless inbred sin be removed, there can be no fullness of life, no perfection in love. In a strict sense, regeneration is not purification. Initial sanctification accompanies regeneration, as does also justification and adoption, but regeneration is the impartation of life, and initial sanctification is the cleansing from guilt and acquired depravity. Closely related to both of the foregoing is another statement that needs to be qualified also. We refer to the expression that sanctification is not something new, but a perfecting of that which we already possess. It is indeed true that there is a *substratum* which is common to both regeneration and entire sanctification, that is, a life of moral love. But regeneration is the impartation of this life of love, and entire sanctification is such a purification of the heart as makes love sole and supreme in experience. The two works are separate and distinct, and consequently the latter is something more than the mere finishing touches of the former.

There are two questions which immediately arise in this connection, (1) Why is redemption not comprehended in a single work of grace: and (2) What length of time must elapse between regeneration and entire sanctification?

The substratum of all experimental grace, subsequent to justification is the same. It is love, perfect or imperfect. From the horizon to the zenith, from the twilight to the effulgence of day, the substance is love, love to God and to our neighbor.—LOWREY, *Possibilities of Grace*, p. 225.

That this perfect love, or entire sanctification, is specifically a new state, and not the improvement of a former state, or of regeneration, is plainly inferred from the Bible.—BISHOP HAMLINE, *Beauty of Holiness*, p. 264.

1. Concerning the first question, it is impossible to say what God may or may not do; we can form our deductions only from what He has revealed to us in His Word. We may say then that God does not justify and entirely sanctify His people by a single work of grace, (1) Because it is not so revealed in His Word. God has system and method in His works, and the work of grace is always bestowed in the same manner, although the manifestations may vary. (2) The sinner does not realize his need of sanctification. His guilt and condemnation at first occupy his attention, and only later does he come to see the need of further cleansing. (3) Life must be given in regeneration before that life can be consciously treated in entire sanctification. (4) Justification and sanctification deal with different phases of sin; the former with sins committed, or sin as an act; the latter with sin inherited, or sin as a principle or nature. It appears to be impossible to discover the latter condition without having experienced the former. Then, too, these works of the Spirit are in some sense antipodal, or directly opposite—the one being an impartation of life, the other a crucifixion or death (cf. C. W. RUTH, *Entire Sanctification*, p. 48; also LOWREY, *Possibilities of Grace*, p. 205).

2. As to the time which must elapse between the two works of grace, this depends wholly upon the experience of the individual. "This progressive work," says Luther Lee, "may be cut short and finished at any

We remark, first, entire sanctification is not usually, if ever, contemporary with regeneration. Regeneration is, in most cases of Christian experience, if not in all, initial sanctification—not completed, perfect renewal. The regenerated person is not, at the moment of his regeneration, "wholly sanctified"; he is not born into the kingdom of God a full-grown man; his new creation is not in the stature of the fullness of Christ; nor is he a child born into perfect spiritual life and health. In a good sense it may be figuratively said, as it is often said, he is a perfect child; but pleasant as the figure may be, it must not be pressed beyond the truth; though a perfect child, evincing good health, there are still in his moral nature, susceptibilities, liabilities, perhaps actualities, of disease, which may develop into speedy death, and, unless counteracted by additional grace, will certainly do so. Does anyone argumentatively ask, Does God bring into His kingdom sickly children? we must answer, He certainly does. Many such are born naturally, and there are many such among God's spiritual children—children requiring much nursing to keep them in the breath of life.—RAYMOND, *Systematic Theology*, II, p. 375.

moment. When the intelligence clearly comprehends the defects of the present state, and faith, comprehending the power and willingness of God to sanctify us wholly, and do it now, is exercised" (LEE, *Elements of Theology*, p. 214). Any delay beyond the period necessary to learn the nature and conditions of its attainment, must be charged to human weakness. God's time is the present moment. Frequently, also, there are those who enter this experience through spiritual obedience only, without any clear understanding of the theological, or even the scriptural terms in which it is expressed.

The Divinely Appointed Means and Agencies. We find it impossible to properly appreciate the nature of entire sanctification, without taking into account the means and agencies which God employs to stamp His image anew upon the hearts of men. Sanctification is said to be by blood, by the Spirit, by faith, and through the truth. (1) The originating cause is the love of God. *Herein is love, not that we loved God, but that he loved us, and sent his Son to be the propitiation for our sins* (I John 4:10). (2) The meritorious or procuring cause is the blood of Jesus Christ. *If we walk in the light, as he is in the light, we have fellowship one with another, and the blood of Jesus Christ his Son cleanseth us from all sin* (I John 1:7). (3) The efficient cause or agency is the Holy Spirit. We are saved *by the washing of regeneration, and the renewing of the Holy Ghost* (Titus 3:5); we are said to be elected *through sanctification of the Spirit* (I Peter 1:2); and again, that we are chosen to salvation *through sanctification of the Spirit and belief of the truth* (II Thess. 2:13). (4) The instrumental cause is truth. Frequently faith is regarded also as the instrumental cause, since faith is conditioned on truth. We prefer, however, to regard truth as the instrumental cause, and faith as the conditional or proximate cause. Our Lord himself, in His high priestly

---

I have been lately thinking a good deal on one point wherein, perhaps, we have all been wanting. We have not made it a rule, as soon as ever persons are justified, to remind them of "going on unto perfection." Whereas this is the very time preferable to all others.—WESLEY, (Letter to Thomas Rankin).

prayer, used the words *Sanctify them through thy truth: thy word is truth* (John 17:17). The Holy Spirit is the spirit of truth and acts through its instrumentality. Hence St. Peter says, *Ye have purified your souls in obeying the truth* (I Peter 1:22); and St. John declares that *whoso keepeth his word, in him verily is the love of God perfected: hereby know we that we are in him* (I John 2:5). (5) The conditional cause is faith. *And put no difference between us and them, purifying their hearts by faith* (Acts 15:9); *that they may receive forgiveness of sins, and inheritance among them which are sanctified by faith that is in me* (Acts 26:18). When, therefore, we speak of sanctification as being wrought by the Father, or by the Son, or by the Holy Spirit; whether we speak of it as by the blood, or through the truth, or by faith, we are referring merely to the different causes which enter in to this great experience.

Progressive Sanctification

The term progressive as used in connection with sanctification must be clearly defined. As used in the Wesleyan sense, it means simply the temporal aspect of the work of grace in the heart, as it takes place in successive stages. Each of these stages is marked by a gradual approach and an instantaneous consummation in experience, and the stages together mark the full scope of sanctifying grace. Thus "in His administration of sanctifying grace the Holy Spirit proceeds by degrees. Terms of progress are applied to each department of that work in the saint; or, in other words, the goal of entire sanctification is represented as the end of a process in which the Spirit requires the co-operation of the believer. This co-operation, however, is only the condition on which is suspended what is the work of divine

---

Dr. Edward F. Walker reduces the essentials of salvation to seven causes, as follows: (1) The first cause is the holy Father (Jude 1); (2) the procuring cause is the holy Son (Eph. 5:26); (3) the efficient cause is the Holy Spirit (I Peter 1:2); (4) the determining cause is the divine will (Heb. 10:10); (5) the meritorious cause is the sacrifice of Jesus (Heb. 13:12); (6) the instrumental cause is the truth of God (John 17:17); and (7) the conditional cause is faith in Christ.

grace alone" (POPE, *Compend. Chr. Th.*, III, p. 36). There is here a great truth which no student of theology can afford to overlook, and failure to emphasize this point, leads to confusion concerning the experience itself. But this point was not sufficiently guarded by Methodist theologians, and as a consequence, the emphasis came gradually to be placed upon the aspect of growth and development, rather than upon the crises which marked the different stages in personal experience. Later writers on this subject have more carefully guarded this point. They have emphasized the instantaneousness of sanctification as an act, and thereby preserved the truth of progressive sanctification without falling into the error of the growth theory. Three subjects must be considered in this division, as follows: (1) Sanctification as partial and entire; (2) sanctification as gradual and instantaneous; and (3) sanctification as instantaneous and continuous.

Sanctification as Partial and Entire. The concomitant blessings which make up conversion as a first work of grace, are (1) Justification as an act of forgiveness in the mind of God; (2) regeneration as the impartation of a new nature; and (3) adoption as an assurance of the privileges of heirship. To these there must be added another concomitant known as (4) "initial" sanctification. Defilement attaches to sinful acts, and so also does guilt, which is the consciousness of sin as our own. There must be, therefore, this initial cleansing, concomitant with the other blessings of the first work of grace, if this guilt and acquired depravity are to be removed from the sinner. Since that which removes pollution and makes holy is properly called "sanctification," this first or initial cleansing is "partial" sanctification. But the term is not an indefinite one, referring to the cleansing away of more or less of the sinner's defilement. It is a definite term, and is limited strictly to that guilt and acquired depravity attaching to actual sins, for which the sinner is himself responsible. It does not refer to the cleansing from original sin or inherited depravity, for which the sinner is not responsible. We may say then that initial or partial sanctification includes in its scope all that acquired pollution which attaches to the sinner's own acts; while entire sanctification includes the cleansing from original sin or inherited depravity. Since sin is twofold—an act, and a state or condition, sanctification must be twofold. There is and can be but two stages in the process of sanctification—initial and entire—the full consummation of the process being rightly known as glorification.

Sanctification as Gradual and Instantaneous. Mr. Wesley taught that there is a gradual work, both preceding and following the act of God by which we are sanctified wholly. This is true of justification as well as sanctification. To overlook the preparation of the Spirit in the hearts of men is to undervalue the prophetic work of Christ in relation to His priesthood, and to minify the importance of prevenient grace. God neither justifies a sinner, nor entirely sanctifies a believer except by grace through faith. This grace operates only on the plane of self-abnegation and godly sorrow for sin, apart from any merit in the seeker himself. And this godly sorrow for sin, or this renunciation of inbred sin, this loathing of the carnal mind with its "depths of pride, self-will and hell," is never found, either in the sinner or the child of God, apart from the illuminating, convincing power of the Holy Spirit. Thus the progressive element is seen to be fundamental to the synergistic positions of Arminian theology. This gradual,

Dr. C. J. Fowler points out that sanctification is a double term—used for the partial work of salvation, and for the complete work of salvation. This is a distinction that needs to be kept in mind in order to avoid confusion in thought. For this reason, he suggests that the qualifying word "entire" should always be used when one means complete sanctification, although it is not necessary to do so in the interest of exact statement (cf. *Double Cure*, p. 103).

Regeneration has been defined by one as an ingeneration of divine life; a sudden process by which man passes from spiritual death to a spiritual life through the quickening power of God's Holy Spirit. As has been stated, in regeneration one passes from a state of death to a state of spiritual life; from a state of guilt to a state of "forgiveness"; from a state of pollution—that is, the pollution acquired by his own acts of disobedience against the laws of God—to a state of conscious cleansing; that is, a cleansing from acquired pollution. Thus regeneration has cleansing, not from the moral corruption inherited through the fall, but cleansing from that moral pollution acquired by his own acts of disobedience.—Dr. R. T. Williams, *Sanctification*, pp. 13, 14.

preparatory work may be cut short in righteousness. When the sinner perfectly submits to the righteousness of Christ, and believes the promises of God, that moment he is justified and the Spirit imparts new life to his soul. When, also, the child of God through the Spirit, fully renounces inbred sin and trusts the blood of cleansing, that moment he may, by simple faith in Christ, be sanctified wholly.

The classic passage in support of this position is found in *The Plain Account of Christian Perfection* (p. 51). The question is asked, "Is this death to sin and renewal in love gradual or instantaneous?" The answer is, "A man may be dying for some time; yet he does not, properly speaking, die until the instant the soul is separated from the body; and in that instant he lives the life of eternity. In like manner he may be dying to sin for some time; yet he is not dead to sin until sin is separated from his soul; and in that instant he lives the full life of love." The Scriptures bear out the thought of the gradual preparation and instantaneous completion of entire sanctification so clearly stated by Mr. Wesley. Perhaps the most familiar passage is that which represents inbred sin as under the doom of death. *Our old man,* says St. Paul, *is crucified with him, that the body of sin might be destroyed, that henceforth we should not serve sin* (Rom. 6:6). Crucifixion as a

The truth seems to be this, that the conditional, preparatory work done in the soul under the guidance of the Spirit may be a process more or less lengthy, according as the seeker after sanctification is more or less receptive and yielding to the Spirit's influence. But when that preparatory work is all completed, and the soul is submissive and open to God, "suddenly the Lord whom ye seek will come to his temple"—your heart, your whole being, and fill you with Himself and reign there without a rival.—Dr. A. M. Hills, *Holiness and Power*, p. 215.

Sanctification is "distinct in opposition to the idea that it is a mere regeneration; holding it to be something more and additional; instantaneous, in opposition to the idea of growth gradually to maturity or ripeness ensuing gradual growth, but is by the direct agency of the Holy Ghost, and instantaneously wrought, however long the soul may have been progressing toward it."—Foster, *Christian Purity*, p. 46.

Those who teach that we are gradually to grow into a state of sanctification, without ever experiencing an instantaneous change from inbred sin to holiness, are to be repudiated as unsound—antiscriptural and anti-Wesleyan.—Nathan Bangs, in *Guide to Holiness*.

Though purity is gradually approached, it is instantaneously bestowed.—Bishop Hamline.

manner of death, is a gradual process, disqualifying the body from serving any master, but certainly tending to death, and having its final issue in death. The same writer in another epistle, exhorts us to *make not provision for the flesh, to fulfil the lusts thereof* (Rom. 13: 14). Here, again, the apostle speaks of the renunciation of the carnal mind, which he portrays under the strong figure of a crucifixion, or a nailing to the cross; and he commands that no provision be made for the fulfilling of the inordinate desires of the flesh. The "old man" must be kept on the cross until he dies; and when sin expires, in that moment the soul is entirely sanctified and lives the full life of perfect love.

Entire Sanctification as Instantaneous and Continuous. While there is a gradual approach to sanctification, and a gradual growth in grace following it, the sanctifying act by which we are made holy, must of necessity be instantaneous. In the words of Bishop Hamline, "It is gradually approached, but instantaneously bestowed." Dr. Adam Clarke states that "in no part of the Scriptures are we directed to seek holiness by gradation. We are to come to God for an instantaneous and complete purification from all sin, as for instantaneous pardon. Neither the seriatim pardon, nor the gradation purification, exists in the Bible" (CLARKE, *Chr. Th.,* p. 208.) But entire sanctification is not only a definite and completed act, it is also a completed and continuous

From this we may deduce two principles. First, the general bias, or character of the soul, becomes positively more and more alienated from sin and set upon good; and, proportionately, the susceptibility to temptation or the affinity with sin becomes negatively less and less evident in its consciousness. There is in the healthy progress of the Christian a constant confirmation of the will in its ultimate choice, and a constant increase of its power to do what it wills: the vanishing point of perfection in the will is to be entirely merged in the will of God. . . . . The positive side — that of consecration by the Spirit of love — is also a process, a gradual process. . . . . Hence the shedding abroad of the love of God by the Holy Ghost admits of increase. It is enough to cite the apostle's prayer: "that your love may abound yet more and more" (Phil. 1:9). This, in harmony with the uniform tenor of scripture, refers to the growth of love toward God and man. . . . . Is then the process of sanctification ended by an attainment which rewards human endeavor simply? Assuredly not; the Holy Spirit finishes the work in His own time, and in His own way, as His own act. and in the absolute supremacy if not in the absolute sovereignty of His own gracious character.— POPE, *Compend. Chr. Th.,* pp. 37, 38, 42.

act. We mean by this that we are cleansed from all sin, only as through faith, we are brought into a right relation to the atoning blood of Jesus Christ; and only as there is a continuous relation to atoning blood by faith, will there be a continuous cleansing, in the sense of a preservation in purity and holiness. In this connection we refer again to Dr. Adam Clarke, who says, "The meritorious efficacy of His passion and death has purged our conscience from dead works; and cleanseth us καθαρίζει ἡμᾶς continues to cleanse us; that is, to keep clean what He has made clean; for it requires the same merit and energy to preserve holiness in the soul of man, as to produce it" (CLARKE, *Com. I John 1: 7*). Both the instantaneous and continuous aspects of sanctification are set forth by the Apostle John as follows: *But if we walk in the light, as he is in the light, we have fellowship one with another, and the blood of Jesus Christ his Son cleanseth us from all sin* (I John 1: 7). Here there is (1) a definite and instantaneous act of sanctification by which the soul is cleansed from all sin; (2) there is a progressive sanctification, whereby those who walk in the light are the recipients of the continuous merits of the atoning blood. Viewed from the standpoint of the Spirit, those who are sanctified by His agency as an instantaneous act are through the

There is a consummation of the Christian experience which may be said to introduce perfection, when the Spirit cries, "It is finished," in the believer. The moment when sin expires, known only to God, is the divine victory over sin in the soul: this is the office of the Spirit alone. The moment when love becomes supreme in its ascendancy, a moment known only to God, is the Spirit's triumph in the soul's consecration: this also is entirely His work, and whenever that maturity of Christian experience and life is reached which the apostle prays for so often, it is solely through the operation of the same spirit. It is being filled with all the fullness of God, and that through being strengthened with might by His Spirit in the inner man (Eph. 3:16-19). POPE, *Compend. Chr. Th.*, III, p. 43.

The fact that inborn sin is a unit, an evil principle or taint infecting our nature, and cannot be removed by parts, and more than its antagonism, the principle of life in Christ, can be imparted gradually in our regeneration is evidence that sanctification is instantaneous.—J. A. WOOD, *Perfect Love*.

Salvation in all its stages is by faith and by faith alone. And this makes sanctification not only instantaneous, but creates a necessity that we should receive it as a gracious gift, bestowed in opposition to a product worked out, or resulting from development and growth.—DR. ASBURY LOWREY.

indwelling of the Spirit made the recipients of His continuously sanctifying grace. There is a remarkable degree of harmony between this text, and that found in I Peter 1:2. *Elect according to the foreknowledge of God the Father, through sanctification of the Spirit, unto obedience and sprinkling of the blood of Jesus Christ.* Here it is clear (1) that salvation is through the sanctification of the Spirit; (2) that sanctification as an instantaneous act, cleanses from all sin, and brings the believer to a place of obedience, internally and externally; (3) that walking in this obedience, the elect dwell constantly under the sprinkling of the all atoning and sanctifying blood. Sanctification as an instantaneous act cleanses us from all sin, and brings us to a place of obedience; walking in the light of obedience we are the recipients of a progressive or continuous sanctification, which renders even our obedience acceptable to God. It is important to bear in mind, therefore, that we are cleansed by the atoning blood, only as we are (1) brought into right relation to Jesus Christ; and (2) we are continuously cleansed, or kept clean, only as these right relations are continued. We are sanctified

> Observe here, (1) Sin exists in the soul after two modes or forms: in guilt, which requires forgiveness or pardon; in pollution, which requires cleansing. (2) Guilt, to be forgiven, must be confessed; and pollution, to be cleansed, must be also confessed. In order to find mercy, a man must know and feel himself to be a sinner, that he may fervently apply to God for pardon. In order to get a clean heart, a man must know and feel its depravity, acknowledge and deplore it before God, in order to be fully sanctified. (3) Few are pardoned, because they do not feel and confess their sins; and **few are sanctified or cleansed from all sin**, because they do not feel and **confess their own sore, and the plague of their hearts**. (4) As the blood of Jesus Christ, the merit of His passion and death, applied by faith, **purges the conscience from all dead works**; so the same cleanses **the heart from all unrighteousness**. (5) As all unrighteousness is sin, so he that is cleansed from all unrighteousness is cleansed from all sin. To attempt to evade this, and plead for the continuance of sin in the heart, **through life, is** ungrateful, wicked and even blasphemous: for as he who "**says he has not sinned, makes God a liar**," who has declared the contrary through every part of His revelation; so he that says the blood of Christ either cannot or will not cleanse us from all sin in this life, gives also the lie to his Maker, who has declared the contrary; and thus shows that the Word, the doctrine of God, is not in him.—Dr. ADAM CLARKE, *Com.* I John 1:7-10.

by Christ, not separate from, but in and with Himself; not only by the blood of cleansing, but under the sprinkling of that blood. Faith is the vital bond of union with Christ, and the pure in heart abide in Him only by a continuous faith. If this connection be severed, spiritual life ceases immediately. If now, we analyze this position carefully, we shall see that as in justification there was a judicial or declarative act which set the soul in right relation to God, and concomitant with it in experience, though logically following it, an inward cleansing by the Spirit from guilt and acquired depravity; so also in entire sanctification there is a *judicial* sanctification, or a declarative act which pronounces the soul holy, attended by the concomitant grace of the spirit which cleanses from all sin. This act is sometimes known as *positional,* or *imputed* holiness, in the same sense that justification is regarded as imputed righteousness. But to maintain that it is possible for a soul to be positionally holy, apart from the inner work of the Spirit which makes it actually holy is one of the errors of imputationism. All the damaging errors which underlie imputation as dissevered from impartation in regard to justification or Christian righteousness, attach likewise to entire sanctification or Christian holiness.

Dr. George Peck in his "Christian Perfection" states that sanctification implies both the death of sin, and the life of righteousness. When, therefore, we speak of sanctification, as to the former part of it, we say it may be attained at once—it is an instantaneous work. .... But in relation to the latter part, that is the life of righteousness, it is regarded as entirely progressive. The destruction of sin in the soul, and the growth of holiness are two distinct things. .... The one is instantaneous, the other gradual, hence it is that we sometimes say with propriety, that the work of entire sanctification is both gradual and instantaneous. —Dr. George Peck, *Christian Perfection.*

What is it that cleanseth the soul and destroys sin? Is it not the mighty power of the grace of God? What is it that keeps the soul clean? Is it not the same power dwelling in us? No more can an effect subsist without its cause, than a sanctified soul can abide in holiness without the indwelling Sanctifier.—Clarke, *Christian Theology,* p. 187.

To say that the doctrine of Christian perfection supersedes the need of Christ's blood is not less absurd than to assert that the perfection of navigation renders the great deep a useless reservoir of water.—Fletcher, *Last Check,* p. 574.

Entire Sanctification

Entire sanctification is a term applied to the fullness of redemption, or the cleansing of the heart from all sin. "We may open our definition of this great gift by asserting that the work of grace, of which the heart is the subject, has its inception, progress, and consummation in this life. The consummation is entire holiness" (Lowrey, *Possibilities of Grace*, p. 209). It is this consummation of the experience with which we are now concerned, "an entire conformity of heart and life to the will of God, as made known in His Word" (Wakefield, *Chr. Th.*, p. 446). We shall consider three phases of the subject as follows: (1) Entire Sanctification as a Purification from Sin; (2) Entire Sanctification as a Positive Devotement to God; and (3) The Divine and Human Elements in Entire Sanctification.

Entire Sanctification as a Purification from Sin. We have indicated that the verb *to sanctify* is from the Latin *sanctus* (holy) and *facere* (to make) and, therefore, when used in the imperative mood, signifies literally *to make holy*. In the Greek we have the same meaning from the verb *hagiadzo* (ἁγιάζω), which is derived from *hagios* (ἅγιος) holy and, therefore, signi-

"But if there be no such second change; if there be no instantaneous change after justification; if there be none but a gradual work of God (that there is a gradual work none denies), then we must be content, as well as we can, to remain full of sin till death." "As to the manner, I believe this perfection is always wrought in the soul by a simple act of faith: consequently in an instant." "Certainly sanctification (in the proper sense) is an instantaneous deliverance from all sin."—Wesley, *Sermons*.

The veil over the eyes of a man surrendered to God, is sin — not committed sins but the sin conditions which are his as a child of Adam. It blurs the vision, it hides God from the soul.—Dr. Bresee, *Sermons*, p. 135.

The attainment of perfect freedom from sin is one to which believers are called during the present life; and it is necessary to completeness of holiness and of those active and passive graces of Christianity by which they are called to glorify God in this world and to edify mankind. . . . . All the promises of God which are not expressly, or from their order, referred to future time, are objects of present trust; and their fulfillment now is made conditionally only by our faith. They cannot, therefore, be pleaded in our prayers, with an entire reliance upon the truth of God, in vain. To this faith shall the promises of entire sanctification be given, which in the nature of the case supposes an instantaneous work immediately following upon entire and unwavering faith.—Watson, *Institutes*, II, p. 455.

fies also *to make holy*. We may say, then, that the first essential element in entire sanctification is the purifying of the believer's heart from inbred sin or inherited depravity. In our discussion of this subject we shall note (1) the Twofold Aspect of Original Sin; and (2) the Extent of the Cleansing as set forth in the Scriptures.

1. Original sin must be viewed under a twofold aspect. (1) It is the common sin that infects the race regarded in a general manner; and (2) it is a portion of this general heritage individualized in the separate persons composing the race. As to the former, or sin in the generic sense, original sin will not be abolished until the time of the restoration of all things. Until that time, something of the penalty remains untaken away; and likewise something of the liability to temptation, or the susceptibility to sin, essential to a probationary state. But in the second sense, the carnal mind, or the sin that dwelleth in the me of the soul—the principle in man which has actual affinity with transgression, this is abolished by the purifying work of the Spirit of holiness, and the soul kept pure by His indwelling Presence.

2. The extent of cleansing according to the Scriptures, includes the complete removal of all sin. Sin is to be cleansed thoroughly, purged, extirpated, eradi-

Original sin, or sin as generic and belonging to the race in its federal constitution on earth is not abolished till the time of which it is said, "Behold, I make all things new" (Rev. 21:5); as something of the penalty remains untaken away, so also something of the peculiar concupiscence or liability to temptation or affinity with evil that besets the man in this world remains. The saint delivered from personal sin is still connected with sin by his own past: the one forgiveness is regarded as perpetually renewed until the final act of mercy. . . . . Hence it is not usual to speak of original sin absolutely as done away in Christ. The race hath its sin that doth so easily beset (Heb. 12:1), its εὐπερίστατον ἁμαρτίαν; and we must cease to belong to the lineage of Adam before our unsinning state become sinlessness. But original sin in its quality as the sin that dwelleth in the me of the soul, as the principle in man that has actual affinity with transgression, as the source and law of sin which is in my members, as the animating soul of the body of this death (Rom. 7:20, 23, 24), and finally, as the flesh with its affections and lusts, is abolished by the Spirit of holiness indwelling the Christian, when His purifying grace has had its perfect work.—POPE, *Compend. Chr. Th.,* III, p. 47.

cated and crucified; not repressed, suppressed, counteracted or made void, as these terms are commonly used. It is to be destroyed; and any theory which makes a place for the existence of inbred sin, whatever the provisions made for its regulation, is unscriptural. *The carnal mind is enmity against God: for it is not subject to the law of God, neither indeed can be* (Rom. 8:7). A study of the Greek terms used in this connection, will make this clear. (1) One of the most common terms is *katharidzo* (καθαρίζω), which means to make clean, or to cleanse in general, both inwardly and outwardly; to consecrate by cleansing or purifying; or to free from the defilement of sin. Some of the more prominent texts in which this word is used are the following: *And put no difference between us and them, purifying* [καθαρίσας] *their hearts by faith* (Acts 15:9); *Having therefore these promises, dearly beloved, let us cleanse* [καθαρίσωμεν] *ourselves from all filthiness of the flesh and spirit perfecting holiness in the fear of God* (II Cor. 7:1); *Who gave himself for us, that he might redeem us from all iniquity, and purify* [καθαρίσῃ] *unto himself a peculiar people, zealous of good works* (Titus 2:14); *But if we walk in the light, as he is in the light, we have fellowship one with another, and the blood of Jesus Christ his Son cleanseth* [καθαρίζει] *us from all sin* (I John 1:7). Cf. also Matt. 23:25, 26; Luke 11:39; Mark 7:19; Matt. 8:2ff; Eph. 5:26; Heb. 10:14; James 4:8. (2) Closely related to this is the word *katargeo* (κατ-αργέω) which signifies to annul, to abolish, to put an end to, to cause to cease. *That the body of sin might be destroyed* [κατ-αργηθῇ], *that henceforth we should not serve sin* (Rom. 6:6). Cf. also Luke 13:7; I Cor. 1:28; II Thess. 2:8; II Tim. 1:10; Heb. 2:14; Gal. 5:11; I Cor. 13:8; II Cor. 3:7, 11. (3) The word *ekkathairo* (ἐκ-καθαίρω) means to cleanse out thoroughly, or to purge. *Purge* [ἐκ-καθάρατε] *out therefore the old leaven, that ye may be a new lump, as ye are unleavened* (I Corinthians 5:7 cf. II Timothy 2:21). (4) Another strong term is *ekrizoo* (ἐκ-ριζόω) which means to root out, to pluck up by the roots, and, therefore, to eradicate. Thus the word *eradicate* appears in the original text but is veiled in the English translation. It is found in the word of our Lord to His disciples, *Every plant, which my heavenly Father hath not planted, shall be rooted up* [ἐκ-ριζω-θήσεται] (Matt. 15:13). This is explained by St. John to mean that our Lord came to *destroy the works of the devil* (I John 3:8) (cf. Matt. 13:29; Luke 17:6; Jude 12). (5) Perhaps the strongest term used in this connection is *stauroo* (σταυρόω), sometimes *ana-stauroo* (ἀνα-σταυρόω) or *su-stauroo* (συ-σταυρόω), which according to Thayer means "to crucify the flesh, destroy its power utterly (the nature of the figure implying that the destruction is attended with intense pain)." It is used in Galatians 5:24, *And they that are Christ's have crucified* [ἐσταύρωσαν] *the flesh with the affections and lusts.* The words ἐσταύρωμαί τινι and ἐσταύρωται μοί τι as used by St. Paul, carry with them the force of "I have been crucified to something and it has been crucified to me, so that we are dead to each other, all fellowship and intercourse between us has ceased" (cf. THAYER, *Lexicon*, Gal. 6:14; 5:24; 2:19). (6) Closely related to the previous term is the word *thanatoo* (θανατόω) signifying to subdue, mortify or kill. *Wherefore, my brethren, ye also are become dead* [ἐθανατώθητε] *to the law by the body of Christ* (Rom. 7:4 first clause); *for if ye live after the flesh, ye shall die* [ἀποθνήσκειν]: *but if ye through the Spirit do mortify* [θανατοῦτε] *the deeds of the body, ye shall live* (Rom. 8:13). Here as Thayer indicates, the word means "to make to die, that is, destroy, render extinct" (something vigorous). The Vulgate has *mortifico*, and the Authorized Version, *mortify.* (7) The word *luo*

Sanctification goes even deeper than contradiction of wrong habit or evil conduct. It strikes not only at our customs and our ideals, but it goes to the seat of wrong affections. It demands death to every wrong affection and to every wrong inner feeling and calls for the absorption of the will in the divine will. This is a glorious demand, but a costly one and, therefore, it is unpopular. Sanctification calls for the death not only of sinful acts, but sinful desires, sinful appetites and sinful affections. It goes to the center of the human character to destroy the works of the devil. Here is the great battleground of human hearts and human lives.—GENERAL SUPERINTENDENT R. T. WILLIAMS, *Sanctification*, pp. 30, 31.

(λύω) is sometimes used in this connection also. As so used it means primarily to loose or free from; but also to break up, to demolish or to destroy. *For this purpose the Son of God was manifested, that he might destroy* [λύσῃ] *the works of the devil* (I John 3:8). A careful study of these terms should convince every earnest inquirer that the Scriptures teach the complete cleansing of the heart from inbred sin—the utter destruction of the carnal mind.

Entire Sanctification as a Positive Devotement to God. The work of sanctification involves not only a separation from sin, but a separation to God. This positive devotement, however, is something more than the human consecration of the soul to God. It represents, also, the Holy Spirit's acceptance of the offering, and, therefore, a divine empowering or enduement. It is a divine possession, and the spring and energy of this spiritual devotement is holy love. The Spirit of God, as the spirit of perfect consecration is able as the Sanctifier, not only to fill the soul with love, but to awaken love in return. Hence St. Paul declares that *the love of God is shed abroad* [ἐκκέχυται, poured out] *in our hearts by the Holy Ghost which is given unto us* (Rom. 5:5); while St. Peter approaching the subject from the opposite viewpoint says, *Seeing ye have purified your souls in obeying the truth through the Spirit unto unfeigned love of the brethren, see that ye love one another with a pure heart fervently* (I Peter 1:22). The former is a positive bestowal of divine love—bestowed by the Holy Spirit, and, therefore, holy love; the latter is such a purification as removes from the heart everything that is contrary to the outflow of perfect love. We may say, then, that while entire sanctification considered from the negative point of view is a cleansing from all sin, from the positive standpoint it is the infilling of divine love. This is the first contrast.

But we have not yet reached the root of this matter. While the first contrast is between purity on the one hand, and perfect love on the other, there is a narrower contrast within the nature of holiness itself. Entire sanctification is something more than either purity or perfect love. Neither of these in the strictest sense of the term is holiness. Holiness consists in the unity of these two aspects of experience. Hence those who have been cleansed from sin, or "the veil of sin conditions" which separates between man and God; and who have been consecrated to God, thereby becoming His possession through the bestowal of the Spirit—these are the saints (ἅγιοι) or holy ones; and the state in which they live is ἁγιωσύνη or holiness. Holiness in man is the same as holiness in God as to quality, but with this difference, the former is derived, while the latter is absolute. In our discussion of the "Biblical Concepts of Holiness and Love," and the relation existing between them, (chapter 14, pp. 373ff) we indicated that the nature of God was holy love—love and holiness being equally of the nature or essence of God. But conceived in the philosophical terms of personality, holiness represents the self-grasp, and love the self-communication; hence holiness logically precedes and must be regarded as the peculiar quality of that nature out of which love flows. Now it will be seen that there is here a narrower contrast existing in holiness itself; and this is best expressed in words applied to Jesus, *Thou hast loved righteousness, and hated iniquity* (Heb. 1:9). Purity and love are thus combined in a deeper, underlying nature, which does not so much appear to indicate any particular virtue, nor all of the virtues combined, as it does the recoil of a pure soul from sin, and a love of righteousness, indicative of a nature in perfect harmony with itself.

The distinctions in holiness are ably set forth by Bishop John P. Newman in an article entitled "Scriptural Holiness" published in the *Treasury* (November, 1888). He says, "What is scriptural holiness? Can we reach its germinal idea? May we rely upon divine aid to ascertain the mind of the Spirit? .... In its radical sense it seems to be a peculiar affection wherewith a being of perfect virtue regards moral evil. In a word it is evidently the abhorrence of whatever a holy God has forbidden. *Thou art of purer eyes than to behold evil.* No severer test than this can be applied to our spiritual condition..... The Father's eulogy of His Son, and the reason He assigns for the Son's eternal kingship is, *Thou hast loved righteousness, and hated iniquity; therefore God, even thy God, hath anointed thee with the oil of gladness above thy fellows* (Heb. 1:9). In this hatred of sin and love of holiness, is the deep significance of the command, *Ye shall be holy: for I the Lord your God am holy.* If from the old dispensation we pass to the new, we find that holiness therein also implies a state of purity and an act of obedience. Christ is the only religious teacher known to man who demands of His people a moral condition antecedent to the act. He goes behind the act, behind the motive, behind the thought, and takes cognizance of that moral state out of which these spring as the effects of a persistent cause. His doctrine is, that what we think and feel and do are expressions of character which lie deeper than the will, deeper than the affections, deeper than the conscience; that this character is the sum of what a man is, in all his appetites, passions, tendencies; and that out of this character issue man's totality and finality. If God is not a respecter of persons, He is of moral character, and that He has foreordained unto eternal life. Christ's demand for a moral condition antecedent to all mental and physical action is in harmony with the order of nature. There is a passive state of our muscular force and intellectual powers upon which the active depends, and of which the active is the living expression. If the arm is strong to defend, there must be healthfulness in the muscles thereof. If the faculties of the mind respond to the will, there must be latent vigor in the intellect. Man's moral nature is both passive and active. If the affections respond only to objects of purity, if the conscience only to the voice of right, if the will only to the call of duty, there must be inherent purity and strength in all our moral powers, when quiescent; this is the glorious significance of our Lord's words, *The prince of this world cometh, and hath nothing in me*—nothing in my nature or spirit, nothing in my thoughts or motives, nothing in my words or deeds, for underlying all these is my state of purity..... In this evangelical sense, and as lying back of this hatred of sin and this state of purity, holiness is the readjustment of our whole nature, whereby the inferior appetites and propensities are subordinated, and the superior intellectual and moral powers restored to their supremacy; and Christ reigns in a completely renewed soul." Not only, therefore, in a broad sense does entire sanctification include purity and perfect love, but holiness is such that it includes both in a deeper nature—so completely renovated and adjusted by the work of the Spirit that its very expression is a love for righteousness and hatred of iniquity.

The Divine and Human Elements in Entire Sanctification. We have characterized entire sanctification in a broad sense as negatively, a purification from sin, and positively, a full devotement to God. We have seen, also, that holiness embraces both of these aspects in itself, yet nevertheless expresses in a deeper and more fundamental contrast, a nature which at once manifests itself in a love for righteousness and a hatred of iniquity. These must be regarded as fundamental aspects of the human experience, or the divine work wrought in the human heart. But now we must put this total human experience over against the divine element by which it is wrought, and set these in their proper relation to each other. The human transformation is wrought solely that the hearts of men may be prepared for the divine indwelling. There is both a saving relation from sin and the establishment of a new and holy fellowship. The efficacy of the atonement is both direct and indirect. It is direct in that it does away, not only with the veil of actual sins, which hides the face of God, but makes a new and living way through the second veil of sin conditions, purging the soul from the carnal mind, and thus bringing it into the presence of God. It is indirect in that it secures the power of the Holy Spirit which carries its virtue or efficacy into the inner man. It is the gift of the Holy Spirit. "This gift purifies the heart. That means the destruction of the body of sin, the removal of the carnal mind. It means also something far other; it is more than house-cleaning. This gift is the gift of Himself. The house is cleaned, purified, in order to receive the Guest. He makes it ready for His abode.....Neither does heavenly enduement—aside from the indwelling personality — confer upon men power, either for Christian living or service. To make a man guiltless and pure — which God has provided for—is not sufficient. If left thus he would be an easy prey for the devil and the world, and utterly unable to do the work of bringing men and women to God. We stand by faith, which is heart loyalty to God, an intense longing, trustful gazing into His face; but this would not be sufficient, only that God provides that, into such a heart, that the divine presence comes, filling it with Himself. He keeps it. He acts in and through it. It becomes His temple and His basis of operations. The Bible insists upon, and we must have holiness of heart, but we cannot trust in a holy heart; we can trust only in Him who dwells within it" (DR. BRESEE, *Sermons*, pp. 7, 8, 27). Entire sanctification as effected by the baptism with the Holy Spirit, must, therefore, be regarded as a comprehensive experience, embracing in one, both "the cleansing of the heart from sin, and the abiding, indwelling presence of the Holy Spirit, empowering the believer for life and service." Here the experience of entire sanctification is set off distinctly from that of justification and regeneration which pre-

The original teaching of Methodism was peculiar also in its remarkable blending of the divine and human elements in the process of sanctification. It invariably did justice to both the supreme divine efficiency and to the co-operation of man. The charge brought against it, sometimes malevolently, sometimes thoughtlessly, that it stimulates believers to expect this supreme and most sacred blessing at any time, irrespective of their preparatory discipline, is contradicted by the whole tenor of the authoritative standards of this doctrine. Wesley's sermon on "The Scripture Way of Salvation," contains an elaborate discussion of this point; and it must be taken as a whole by those who would understand the subject.—POPE, *Compend. Chr. Th.*, III, p. 97.

Human nature at its best, under the blessed remedial power of the blood of Jesus, is but a dwelling place from which, or an avenue through which God acts. Of course the dwelling place or avenue is glorified by His presence, as the water in the river-bed makes its banks fresh with life and beauty. There must be conditions of power, but the conditions are utterly useless without the added power.—DR. PHINEAS F. BRESEE, *Sermons*, p. 8.

cedes it; and it is equally guarded from the erroneous third blessing theory, which regards entire sanctification solely as a work of cleansing, to be followed by the baptism with the Holy Spirit as an added gift of power. The baptism with the Holy Spirit is, therefore, "the baptism with God. It is the burning up of the chaff, but it is also the revelation in us and the manifestation to us of divine personality, filling our being."

Christian Perfection

Christian perfection in the critical sense, represents the more positive aspect of the one experience, known theologically either as entire sanctification or Christian perfection. Entire sanctification, however, is a term which applies more to the aspect of a cleansing from sin, or the making holy; while Christian perfection emphasizes especially the standard of privilege secured to the believer by the atoning work of Jesus Christ. "We give the name of Christian perfection," says Mr. Fletcher, "to that maturity of grace and holiness which established adult believers attain to under the Christian dispensation; and thus we distinguish that maturity of grace, from both the ripeness of grace which belongs to the dispensation of the Jews below us, and from the ripeness of glory which belongs to departed saints above us. Hence it appears that by Christian perfection, we mean nothing but the cluster and maturity of graces which compose the Christian character in the Church militant. In other words, Christian perfection is a spirit-

In a sermon preached in Berkeley, California, May 20, 1909, from John 17, Dr. Bresee took the following positions. (1) The believer is transferred by the Father into the hands of Jesus. (2) Jesus is seeking a place for Himself—a resting place for His personality in the hearts of His people, and thus illumined by His presence, we become messengers of divine glory. (3) Entire sanctification is not the settling of the sin question only, but the incoming of the divine Personality. (4) The world is opposed to spirituality. People may live moral lives—may even become reformers without meeting much opposition, but when the Spirit of God comes, the carnal mind is stirred. It was only after the anointing of Jesus with the Spirit that His opposition began. (5) Backsliding is the open door to souls for all false teachings, but a lack of sense marvelously helps it along. (6) Unworldliness is the key to successful Christian living and Christian service. We need in spirit, a new order of Franciscans who will dare to be poor for the cause of God. (7) Pentecostal conditions, bring pentecostal results.

ual constellation, made up of these gracious stars: perfect repentance, perfect faith, perfect humility, perfect meekness, perfect self-denial, perfect resignation, perfect hope, perfect charity for our visible enemies, as well as our earthly relations; and, above all, perfect love for our invisible God, through the explicit knowledge of our Mediator, Jesus Christ. And as this last star is always accompanied by all the others, as Jupiter is by his satellites, we frequently use, as St. John, the phrase 'perfect love' instead of the word 'perfection'; understanding by it the pure love of God shed abroad in the hearts of established believers by the Holy Ghost, which is abundantly given them under the fullness of the Christian dispensation." Here the word *perfection*, used in connection with the graces of the Spirit, must be understood to refer solely to their *quality*, as being pure and unmixed, not to their *quantity*, as precluding further growth and development.

Misconceptions of Christian Perfection. There are numerous misconceptions concerning Christian perfection which must be cleared away before there can be a right understanding or a proper appreciation of this work of the Holy Spirit. The term seems to connote a standard of excellence which those who are rightly informed never claim for it. It is well, therefore, when using the word in this connection, to always accompany it with its guardian adjectives, such as *Christian* or *evangelical* perfection. Rightly understood, there can be no objection, either to the doctrine or the experience. (1) Christian perfection is not *absolute* perfection. This belongs to God only. In this sense, *there is none good but one, that is, God* (Matt. 19:17). All other goodness is derived. So, also, God alone is perfect; but His creatures are also perfect in a relative sense, according to their nature and kind. (2) It is not *angelic* perfection. The holy angels are unfallen beings, and, therefore, retain their native faculties unimpaired. They are not liable to mistake, as is man in his present state of weakness and infirmity, and, therefore, have a perfection impossible to mankind. (3) It is not *Adamic* perfection. Man was made a little lower than the angels, and doubtless in his pristine state, possessed a perfection unknown to man in his present state of existence. (4) It is not a perfection in *knowledge*. Not only was man's will perverted, and his affections alienated by the fall, but his intellect was darkened. Hence from this defective understanding may flow erroneous opinions concerning many matters, and these may in turn lead to false judgments and a wrong bias in the affections. (5) It is not immunity from temptation or the susceptibility to sin. These are essential to a probationary state. Our Lord was tempted in all points as we are, and yet He was without sin.

Perfection! why should the harmless phrase offend us? Why should that lovely word frighten us? We can speak of perfection in reference to mathematics, and all is right; we are readily understood. We speak of a right line, or a line perfectly straight; of a perfect triangle; a perfect square; a perfect circle; and in all this we offend no one—all comprehend our meaning perfectly. We speak of a perfect seed; a perfect bud; a perfect plant; a perfect tree; a perfect apple; a perfect egg; and in all such cases the meaning is clear and definite. Because a seed is perfect, no one expects it to exhibit the qualities of the plant or tree; because the plant or tree is perfect, no one looks to find in it the characteristics of the bud; nor in the bud, the beauties or fragrance of the bloom; nor in the bloom, the excellent qualities of the ripe fruit.—FLETCHER OF MADELEY.

Mr. Wesley says, "In the year 1764, upon a review of the whole subject, I wrote down the sum of what I had observed in the following short propositions:

1. There is such a thing as perfection; for it is again and again mentioned in Scripture.

2. It is not so early as justification; for justified persons are to "go on unto perfection" (Heb. 6:1).

3. It is not so late as death; for St. Paul speaks of living men that were perfect (Phil. 3:15).

4. It is not absolute. Absolute perfection belongs not to man, nor to angels, but to God alone.

5. It does not make a man infallible; none is infallible, while he remains in the body.

6. It is sinless? It is not worth while to contend for a term. It is "salvation from sin."

7. It is "perfect love," (I John 4:18). This is the essence of it; its properties, or inseparable fruits, are rejoicing evermore, praying without ceasing and in every thing give thanks (I Thess. 5:16ff).

8. It is improvable. It is so far from lying in an indivisible point, from being incapable of increase, that one perfected in love may grow in grace far swifter than he did before.

9. It is amissible, capable of being lost; of which we have numerous instances. But we were not thoroughly convinced of this, till five or six years ago.

10. It is constantly both preceded and followed by a gradual work.

11. But is it in itself instantaneous or not? In examining this, let us go step by step. An instantaneous change has been wrought in some

Implications of the Doctrine. Before considering the scriptural meaning of Christian perfection, it will be well also to give attention to some of the implications of the doctrine. (1) This perfection is *evangelical* as opposed to a legal perfection. *The law made nothing perfect, but the bringing in of a better hope did* (Heb. 7:19). Christian perfection, therefore, is of grace, in that Jesus Christ brings His people to completion or perfection under the present economy. The term "sinless perfection" was one which Wesley never used because of its ambiguity. Those who are justified are saved from their sins; those who are sanctified wholly are cleansed from all sin; but those who are thus justified and sanctified still belong to a race under the doom of original sin, and will bear the consequences of this sin to the end of the age. The term perfection, however, is a proper one, in that *the righteousness of God without the law is manifested.... Even the righteousness of God which is by faith of Jesus Christ unto all and upon all them that believe* (Rom. 3:21, 22). This righteousness is forensic, but correlative with it, sin is purged from the soul, and the perfect love of God shed abroad in the heart by the Holy Spirit. This, too, is a completed or perfected act, although the love thus imparted is capable of eternal increase. Again, perfection is a proper term, because we are conformed to the image of His Son, that is, we are made sons by a completed act, and as sons may be purged from all spiritual disease. The consequence of this is a state of gracious or evangelical perfection. (2) Christian perfection is a *relative* term. Those who use the term are frequently charged with

believers. None can deny this. Since that change, they enjoy perfect love; they feel this, and this alone; they rejoice evermore, pray without ceasing, and in everything give thanks." Now this is all that I mean by perfection; therefore, these are witnesses of the perfection which I preach. "But in some this change was not instantaneous. They did not perceive the instant when it was wrought. It is often difficult to perceive the instant when a man dies; yet there is an instant when life ceases. And if ever sin ceases, there must be a last moment of its existence, and a first moment of our deliverance from it." .... "Therefore, all our preachers should make a point of preaching perfection to believers, constantly, strongly and explicitly; and all believers should mind this one thing, and continually agonize for it."—WESLEY, *Christian Perfection*, pp. 283-285.

lowering the meaning of the word in order to make it conform to the experience of those who profess the blessing. That it is a lowering of the standard we deny, although we freely admit that it is an "accommodation" to use Dr. Pope's term, an accommodation which bears the impress of the condescension and lovingkindness of God. It is a perfection, which when viewed in relation to the absolute perfection of God, may never be reached, either in this life, or that to come; but when viewed in relation to the present economy, marks a finality, in that it is the deliverance of the spiritual nature from the defilement of sin. It is true that this redeemed and perfected spirit, dwells in a body which is a member of a sinful race, but his spirit may be lifted from darkness to light, while his body remains the same "muddy vesture of decay" that it was before his spirit was redeemed. Consequently it is still beclouded with weakness, in that the soul is under the influence of material things, and will be until the creature itself shall have put on incorruption and immortality. (3) Christian perfection is *probationary*. It is a state which is always under ethical law, and hence must be guarded by constant watchfulness, and maintained by divine grace. While we remain in this life, however deep our devotion, or fervent our religious life, there are sources of danger within us. In our nature, and as essential elements of it, there are appetites, affections and passions, without which we should be unfitted for this present state of existence. These are innocent in themselves, but must ever be kept under control by reason, conscience and divine grace. The original temptation was a skilful appeal to human elements which were not depraved, but fresh from the hand of God. The desire for pleasant food is not sinful in itself, nor is the artistic taste, which delights in beautiful form and color. Neither can we condemn the desire for intellectual development or the acquisition of knowledge. These are original and essential elements of human nature, and had they not existed before the fall, there could have been no temptation. The evil lay in the perversion of

God-given faculties to wrong ends. To argue, therefore, that Christian perfection will destroy or eradicate essential elements of human 'nature; or that a man or woman may not enjoy perfection of spirit while these elements remain, is to misapprehend entirely the nature of this experience. What Christian perfection does is to give grace to regulate these tendencies, affections and passions, and bring them into subjection to the higher laws of human nature. (4) One thing further remains —this perfection is *mediated*. It is not a triumph of human effort, but a work wrought in the heart by the Holy Spirit, in answer to simple faith in the blood of Jesus. We are kept by His abiding intercession. *I pray not that thou shouldest take them out of the world, but that thou shouldest keep them from the evil* (John 17: 15).

The Fundamental Concept of Christian Perfection. The aspect of the Christian's full privilege in Christ is estimated according to the New Testament standard of love as fulfilling the law (Matt. 22: 40; Gal. 5: 14). This can be understood only in relation to the New Covenant. Viewed from the human standpoint, wherein Christ is regarded as the "surety of the covenant," it is said, *This is the covenant that I will make with the house of Israel after those days, saith the Lord; I will put my laws into their mind, and write them in their hearts: and I will be to them a God, and they shall be to me a people* (Heb. 8: 10). Viewed from the divine standpoint in which Christ is regarded as the "minister of the sanctuary" it is said, *This is the covenant that I will make with them after those days, saith the Lord, I will put my laws into their hearts, and in their minds will I write them; and their sins and iniquities will I remember no more. Now where remission of these is, there is no more offering for sin* (Heb. 10: 16-18). Two things stand out clearly in these texts: (1) The Security

Experience shows that, together with this conviction of sin remaining in our hearts, and cleaving to all our words and actions, as well as the guilt on account thereof we should incur were we not continually sprinkled with the atoning blood, one thing more is implied in this repentance, namely, the conviction of our helplessness.—WESLEY, *Sermon: Scripture Way of Salvation.*

502   CHRISTIAN THEOLOGY

of the Covenant. The two immutable things mentioned here, in which it is impossible for God to lie, signify the minister of the sanctuary on the one hand, and the surety of the covenant on the other; and hence both the divine and human aspects center in the one theanthropic being. This gives security to the New Covenant. (2) The Nature of the Covenant. This is the full life of love, made perfect in the heart by the agency of the Holy Spirit. Pure love reigns supreme without the antagonisms of sin. Love is the spring of every activity. The believer having entered into the fullness of the New Covenant, does by nature, the things contained in the law, and hence, the law is said to be written upon his heart. *Herein is our love made perfect, that we may have boldness in the day of judgment: because as he is, so are we in this world. There is no fear in love; but perfect love casteth out fear: because fear hath torment. He that feareth is not made perfect in love* (I John 4: 17, 18).

The phrase ἄφεσιν ἁμαριτῶν, or remission of sins, means simply the taking away of sins: and this does not refer to the guilt of sin, merely; but also to its power, nature and consequences. All that is implied in pardon of sin, destruction of its tyranny, and purification from its pollution is here intended; it is wrong to restrict such operations of mercy, to pardon alone.—Dr. Adam Clarke, *Com. Acts* 10:43.

Queries, humbly proposed to those who deny perfection to be attainable in this life.

1. Has there not been a larger measure of the Holy Spirit given under the gospel, than under the Jewish dispensation? If not, in what sense was the Spirit not given before Christ was glorified? (John 7:39).

2. Was that "glory which followed the sufferings of Christ," (I Peter 1:11), an external glory, or an internal, namely, the glory of holiness?

3. Has God anywhere in Scripture commanded us more than He has promised to us?

4. Are the promises of God respecting holiness to be fulfilled in this life, or only in the next?

5. Is a Christian under any other laws than those which God promises to "write in our hearts"? (Jer. 31:31; Heb. 8:10).

6. In what sense is "the righteousness of the law fulfilled in those who walk not after the flesh, but after the Spirit"? (Rom. 8:4).

7. Is it impossible for anyone in this life to "love God with all his heart, and mind, and soul, and strength"? And is the Christian under any law which is not fulfilled in this love?

8. Does the soul's going out of the body effect its purification from indwelling sin?

9. If so, is it not something else, not "the blood of Christ, which cleanseth it from all sin"?

St. Paul uses an illustration which bears directly upon this subject. *Now I say, That the heir, as long as he is a child, differeth nothing from a servant, though he be lord of all; but is under tutors and governors, until the time appointed of the father* (Gal. 4:1, 2). We must distinguish here, between two things, (1) the growth and development of the child, by which he is brought to a relative degree of maturity; and (2) a legal enactment, declaring him to have officially entered into his inheritance. To have made this declaration without a proper period of preparation would have been to dissipate the inheritance; to have omitted the declaration would have left the legal status indefinite and uncertain. It is not the mere fact of growth that gives a youth the full rights of citizenship. A relative degree of maturity, which in the natural realm can come only through physical and mental growth, may underlie the judicial act, but he becomes of age, or ceases to be a minor and attains his majority, only at an appointed time in con-

10. If His blood cleanseth us from all sin, while the soul and body are united, is it not in this life?

11. If when that union ceases, is it not in the next? And is this not too late?

12. If in the article of death; what situation is the soul in, when it is neither in the body nor out of it?

13. Has Christ anywhere taught us to pray for what He never designs to give?

14. Has He not taught us to pray, "Thy will be done on earth, as it is in heaven"? And is it not done perfectly in heaven?

15. If so, has He not taught us to pray for perfection on earth? Does He not then design to give it?

16. Did not St. Paul pray according to the will of God, when he prayed that the Thessalonians might be "sanctified wholly, and preserved" (in this world, not in the next, unless he was praying for the dead) "blameless in body soul, and spirit, unto the coming of Jesus Christ"?

17. Do you sincerely desire to be freed from indwelling sin in this life?

18. If you do, did not God give you that desire?

19. If so, did He not give it to mock you, since it is impossible it should ever be fulfilled?

20. If you have not sincerity enough even to desire it, are you not disputing about matters too high for you?

21. Do you ever pray God to "cleanse the thoughts of your heart," that you "may perfectly love Him"?

22. If you neither desire what you ask, nor believe it attainable, pray you not as a fool prayeth?

God help thee to consider these questions calmly and impartially.—WESLEY, *Christian Perfection*, pp. 239-241.

formity to law. At that time he comes legally to manhood, with all the rights and privileges of full citizenship in the commonwealth. So also in the spiritual realm, there is a period of growth following regeneration, which precedes his coming to full age; and there will be even more rapid growth following it, but growth does not lead to Christian perfection. This is accomplished by a judicial pronouncement. It is a declarative act, wrought by the Spirit through faith. As in justification there is a judicial act in the mind of God accompanied by the work of the Spirit imparting life to the soul; so in Christian perfection there is likewise a declarative act accompanied by the purifying work of the Holy Spirit. What, then, is the appointed time of the Father—the time when the son becomes of age, when he ceases to be a minor and attains his majority? It is the hour of submission to the baptism with the Holy Spirit (Matt. 3:11, 12; Acts 1:5), which purifies the heart from sin (Acts 15:9) and fills it with divine love (Rom. 5:5). There is no need here for an extended lapse of time. It is sufficient only that the believer come to feel his need and see his privileges in Christ Jesus. Through the exercise of his senses, we

In our discussion of prevenient grace (Chapter XXVI) we pointed out the necessity of a preparatory period, wrought in the heart preceding the full state of salvation. To deny this is to deny co-operative grace, and make salvation to depend solely upon predestination and irresistible grace. This is the monergism of the Calvinistic position, against which Arminianism has always contended. To deny the preparatory period in the believer, wherein he is made conscious of the heinousness of inbred sin, and his desire for its removal stimulated, is to surrender to the idea of a mere "positional holiness" and deny the subjective work of the Spirit. Bishop Hedding says, "That faith which is the condition of this entire sanctification is exercised only by a penitent heart—a heart willing to part with all sin forever, and determined to do the will of God in all things."

The normal regenerate heart is one where the self is restricted by divine law, but yet existent. In this heart are two centers of gravity—self and Christ. Two laws are there in conflict, a horizontal earthly law and a perpendicular godly law. In such a heart the "new man created in Christ Jesus" reigns, but not without a rival — self. Thus it is that the regenerate man has a dual nature: the divine nature implanted in regeneration and the self-nature, the former being active and dominant, the latter being restricted and suppressed. Here the will must be constantly exercised and the most careful attention be given lest "a root of bitterness [self] springing up" give trouble, and the sinful nature come again into ascendancy.—DR. FLOYD W. NEASE, *Symphonies of Praise*, p. 143.

are told (Heb. 5:12-14), he comes to discern both good and evil, and thereby finds within himself the carnal mind warring against the new life in his soul. He finds, also, that God has promised a cleansing from all sin through the blood of Jesus. He lays hold of the promises of God, and in a moment, the Holy Spirit purifies his heart by faith. In that instant he lives the full life of love. In him love is made perfect, and the conditions of the New Covenant are, therefore, perfectly fulfilled in him. The law of God is written upon his heart. No longer is his spiritual status that of a child but of an adult; no longer a minor but of full age—a *teleion* (τελείων) or one of the "perfect ones." Here perfection "refers especially to the fullness of spiritual knowledge manifesting itself in the Christian profession as the antithesis of babyhood." The Greek adjective used here signifies adulthood. Hence the writer follows immediately with an exhortation: *Therefore leaving the principles of the doctrine of Christ, let us go on unto perfection* (Heb. 6:1). Here the word τελειότητα is the noun of the word used in Hebrews 5:14, and is "represented not as something realized by the lapse of time, or by unconscious growth, and least of all, attainable only at death.... For the Greek preposition 'unto' here embraces both motion to a place and rest in it, and cannot mean an unattainable ideal"

"What is Christian perfection? The loving God with all our heart, mind, soul, and strength. This implies that no wrong temper, none contrary to love, remains in the soul; and that all the thoughts, words and actions are governed by pure love." "The perfection I teach is perfect love; loving God with all the heart, receiving Christ as Prophet, Priest and King, to reign alone over all our thoughts, words and actions."—MR. WESLEY.

Whatever may be the time, whether long or short; whatever may be the manifestations of sorrow, whether groaning or tears—these things may vary; but until by an instantaneous act of the Spirit in answer to simple faith in the cleansing of Jesus sin is purged from the soul, that person does not have what we call entire sanctification. On the other hand, to expect a crucifixion of sin in the soul, without first having that sin nailed to the cross in deep and pungent conviction and self-renunciation is to develop a superficial type of experience.

Faith, in order to its exercise, presupposes a certain state of the mind and affections, and without these it cannot exist—its very existence includes them; namely in the briefest terms, it supposes the knowledge of sin, and sorrow for it; the knowledge that there is a Saviour, and a readiness to embrace Him.—BISHOP FOSTER, *Christian Purity*, p. 121.

506   CHRISTIAN THEOLOGY

(STEELE, *Half Hours with St. Paul,* p. 113). The verb *pherometha* (φερώμεθα) meaning to press on is used with *epi* (ἐπὶ), unto, as the goal to be attained; and as Delitzsch indicates, "combines the notion of an impulse from without with that of an eager and onward pressing haste." We may conclude, then, that nothing is clearer from the Scripture than that there is a perfection which may be attained in this life; that this perfection consists solely in a life of perfect love, or the loving God with all the heart, soul, mind and strength; that this perfection of love has no reference to the degree or quantity of love, but to its purity or quality; that this state of perfect love is a consequence of the purification of the heart from all sin, so that love remains in soleness and supremacy; that this purification is accomplished instantaneously by the baptism with the Holy Spirit; that the resultant state of perfect love is regarded as adulthood in grace, in that the believer enters into the fullness of privilege under the New Covenant; and last, in that love is the fulfilling of the law, this state of pure or perfect love, is known as Christian perfection.

Important Distinctions. It is necessary in this connection to emphasize a few important distinctions in order to preserve the doctrine of Christian perfection from some of the popular errors which are urged against it.

1. Purity and maturity must be carefully distinguished from each other. Failure to do this lies at the base of practically every objection to entire sanctification. Purity is the result of a cleansing from the pollution of sin; maturity is due to growth in grace. Purity is accomplished by an instantaneous act; maturity is gradual and progressive, and is always indefinite and relative. When, therefore, we speak of perfect love, we have reference solely to its quality as being unmixed with sin, never to its degree or quantity. As to the latter, the Scriptures teach that love, and all the graces of the Spirit are to increase and abound more and more. We have previously indicated that Christian perfection

is to be regarded as adulthood, in contrast with spiritual childhood; but this is true only in the sense of having been cleansed from all sin, and thereby brought into the fullness of the new covenant of love. From the standpoint of growth in grace and spiritual understanding there are "babes" and "young men" in the state of entire sanctification, as well as those of more mature experience. A clear comprehension of the difference between purity and maturity will prevent confusion, both as to the doctrine and experience of Christian perfection.

2. Infirmities must be distinguished from sins. Sin in the sense used here is a voluntary transgression of a known law. Infirmities on the other hand, are involuntary transgressions of the divine law, known or unknown, which are consequent on the ignorance and weakness of fallen men. These are inseparable from mortality. Perfect love does not bring perfection in knowledge, and hence is compatible with mistakes in both judgment and practice. There seems to be no remedy for this until the body is redeemed from the consequences of sin, and glorified. Infirmities bring humiliation and regret, but not guilt and condemnation. These latter attach to sin only. Both, however, need the blood of sprinkling. The careful student of the Levitical rites of purification will have noticed that the errors and in-

Purity and maturity! The words are similar in sound, but they are very distinct in meaning. Purity may be found in the earliest moments after the soul finds pardon and peace with God. But maturity involves time and growth and trial and development. The pure Christian may even be a weak Christian. For it is not size or strength that is emphasized, but only the absence of evil and the presence of elementary good. Purity is obtained as a crisis, maturity comes as a process. One can be made pure in the twinkling of an eye; it is doubtful that anyone in this world should be listed as really mature. Growth continues while life lasts, and for aught we know, it may continue throughout eternity. . . . . More faith, more love, more hope, and more patience incline one to think that at some undefined time we will have none of the opposites of these. But growth is not a process for purifying. Growth is addition, purifying is subtraction. And even though one may approach holiness by ever so gradual a process, there must be a last moment when sin exists and a first moment when it is all gone, and that means that in reality sanctification must be instantaneous. At this or any given moment every Christian is either free from sin or he is not free from sin. There can be no sense in which he is actually holy and at the same time still somewhat defiled.—Dr. J. B. Chapman, *Holiness the Heart of Christian Experience*, pp. 23, 24.

firmities of the individual Hebrew were put away solely by the sprinkling of blood (Heb. 9: 7); while sin always demanded a special offering. It is for this reason we maintain that there is not only a definite act of cleansing from sin, but that there is also a continuous blood of sprinkling for our involuntary transgressions. The Scriptures as well as the testimony of human experience, takes into account this distinction between sins and infirmities. St. Jude says, *Now unto him that is able to keep you from falling* [ἀπαίστους or exempt from falling. The Vulgate reads, *sine peccato,* without sin] *and*

A failure to distinguish between sin and infirmity, puts an undue emphasis upon sin, and has a tendency to discourage earnest seekers from pressing on to a full deliverance from the carnal mind. Calling that sin which is not sin, opens the door also to actual sinning. Another distinction to be kept in mind is that between humanity as such, and carnality. The latter is a perversion of the former. Entire sanctification does not remove any natural, normal, human trait, but it does purify these and bring them under subjection to the law of reason and the higher influences of divine grace.

Not only sin, properly so-called, that is, a voluntary transgression of a divine law; but sin, improperly so-called, that is, involuntary transgression of a divine law, known or unknown, needs the atoning blood. I believe there is no such perfection in this life as excludes these involuntary transgressions, which I apprehend to be naturally consequent on the ignorance and mistakes inseparable from mortality. Therefore, sinless perfection is a phrase I never use, lest I should seem to contradict myself. I believe a person filled with the love of God is still liable to involuntary transgressions.—WESLEY, *Plain Account,* p. 43.

To us the clear teaching of the Bible is, that man quits sinning when he begins to repent .... but he does need a further salvation from many other things; his ignorance—lack of skilled conformity to heavenly patterns—and from his shortcomings or limitations because of the results of old conditions. He is like a king's son who was captured and carried away to live among wild and uncivilized races, but who was at last recaptured and brought home; he is full of gladness and love, yet, in his ignorance, liable to offend in many ways against the new conditions into which he has come. Thus every Christian will always have need to say, "Forgive me my trespasses." He needs a salvation of abounding grace that will keep every element of mind and body in its normal condition as the agent and instrument of Jesus Christ. The appetites of the body are God created — right and good — and are to be held in proper poise and condition by the gracious anointings with the Holy Ghost. The attributes of the mind are, likewise, God created and must be held in balance by the same divine Spirit. Some of them will need great, direct help from the Holy Ghost, and it is necessary for our good that we realize this help and receive it in answer to prayer. ....A sanctified man is at the bottom of the ladder. He is but a child—a clean child. He is now to learn; to grow; to rise; to be divinely enlarged and transformed. The Christ in him is to make new and complete channels in and through every part of his being—pouring the stream of heaven through his thinking, living, devotement and faith.— DR. PHINEAS F. BRESEE, *Sermon: Death and Life.*

to present [στῆσαι to place in the presence of His glory] *you faultless* [ἀμώμους, without blemish, faultless, unblameable] *before the presence of his glory with exceeding joy* (Jude 24). We may be kept from sin in this life, we shall be presented faultless only in our glorified state.

3. Temptation is reconcilable with the highest degree of evangelical perfection. Jesus was holy, harmless, undefiled, and separate from sinners, but was tempted in all points as we are, yet without sin. Temptation seems to be necessarily involved in the idea of probation. No temptation or evil suggestion becomes sin, however, until it is tolerated or cherished by the mind. As long as the soul maintains its integrity, it remains unharmed, however protracted or severe the temptation may be. Several questions arise in this connection. (1) When does temptation become sin? To this most difficult question Bishop Foster replies, "Sin begins whenever the temptation begins to find inward sympathy, if known to be a solicitation to sin. So long as it is promptly, and with full and hearty concurrence of the soul, repelled, there is no indication of inward sympathy, there is no sin" (FOSTER, *Christian Purity*, p. 55). (2) What is the difference between the temptations of those who are entirely sanctified, and those who are

---

Those entirely sanctified need the atonement. "In every state we need Christ in the following respects: (1) Whatever grace we receive, it is a free gift from Him. (2) We receive it as His purchase, merely in consideration of the price He paid. (3) We have this grace, not only from Christ, but in Him. For our perfection is not like that of a tree which flourishes by the sap derived from its own root, but, as was said before, like that of a branch which, united to the vine, bears fruit; but, severed from it, is dried up and withered. (4) All our blessings, temporal, spiritual, and eternal, depend on His intercession for us, which is one branch of His priestly office, whereof therefore we have always equal need. (5) The best of men still need Christ in His priestly office, to atone for their omissions, their shortcomings (as some improperly speak), their mistakes in judgment and practice, and their defects of various kinds. For these are all deviations from the perfect law, and consequently need an atonement. Yet that they are not properly sins, we apprehend may appear from the words of St. Paul, He that loveth, hath fulfilled the law; for love is the fulfilling of the law (See Rom. 13:10). Now mistakes, and whatever infirmities necessarily flow from the corruptible state of the body, are no way contrary to love; nor, therefore, in the Scripture sense, sin."—WESLEY, *Plain Account*, pp. 42, 43.

not? The difference lies in this, that in the latter, temptation stirs up the natural corruption of the heart with its bias toward sin; while in the former, the temptation is met with uniform resistance. (3) But how may I distinguish the temptations of the enemy, from the carnal mind or corruption of my own heart? Mr. Wesley admits that sometimes "it is impossible to distinguish, without the direct witness of the Spirit." In general, however, there need be no confusion. In the sanctified soul there is a fullness of love, humility and all the graces of the spirit, so that a temptation to pride, anger, or any of the works of the flesh is met with the instant recoil of the whole being. Holiness in man, as in Christ, is found in that fundamental ethical nature which loves righteousness and hates iniquity. Temptation and trial may appear to be evils, but in reality they are God's method of establishing the believer in

Dr. George Peck says, "First, I suppose all will admit that when the temptation gains the concurrence of the will, the subject contracts guilt. There can be no doubt here. Second, it is equally clear that when the temptation begets in the mind a desire for the forbidden object, the subject enters into temptation, and so sins against God. Third, it is also clear that temptation cannot be invited or unnecessarily protracted without an indication of a sinful tendency toward the forbidden object, and consequently, such a course not only implies the absence of entire sanctification, but involves the subject in actual guilt."—Peck, *Christian Perfection,* p. 435.

Were we to discuss the problem at length we would raise the question: How could Adam and Eve ever fall, for they were complete in holiness? The answer is found in the simple recognition of the fact of the humanity of Adam. It was true, then, and now is, that the royal road of Satan to the heart of man is found through his natural appetites and desires. Temptation is ever based upon desire. It is upon this fact that he plays until he has produced an act of disobedience and again sown the seed of iniquity in the heart of man. But the questioner persists, how can sin actually get back into the heart of man after once it has been removed? The answer to this is found in a proper recognition of what sin as a principle actually is. It is here again that our human language breaks down in its efforts to describe spiritual relations. We speak of sin as a substance because of the beggary of language. It is called the old man, the body of sin. But these terms are merely figures of speech. Sin, as a principle after all, is not a substance, it is a moral quality. It is the pollution of the bloodstream of the moral nature. Were sin a substance or a thing, most assuredly it could never be placed back in the nature once it had been removed. But sin is not a substance, it is a moral condition. And just as the bloodstream of an individual, once having been cleansed by purgatives, could again become carelessly polluted by contamination, so the heart of man can again become polluted by disobedience and spiritual indolence.—Dr. H. V. Miller, *When He Is Come,* pp. 27, 28.

holiness and preparing him for the life to come. By them, God empties the appeals of the world of their urgency, and strengthens the motives of faithfulness in the kingdom of God. *Blessed is the man that endureth temptation: for when he is tried, he shall receive the crown of life, which the Lord hath promised to them that love him* (James 1:12; Heb. 12:11).

Christian Perfection a Present Experience. Christian perfection as we have shown, is nothing more and nothing less, than a heart emptied of all sin and filled with pure love to God and man. As such, it is as a state, not only attainable in this life, but is the normal experience of all those who live in the fullness of the new covenant. It is the result of a divine operation of the Holy Spirit, promised in the Old Testament, and fulfilled

St. James indicates that sin begins in lust or inordinate affection. "But every man is tempted when he is drawn away of his own lust, and enticed." Somewhere in the process legitimate desire passed over into inordinate affection, and here sin begins. "Then when lust (or inordinate affection) hath conceived, (the inward fact of sin) it bringeth forth sin (or outward manifestations of an inward sinful condition); and sin, when it is finished bringeth forth death" (James 1:14, 15).

Dr. Olin A. Curtis in his "Christian Faith" holds that character can be absolutely fixed by the free use of motives. He says, "In the motivity of every moral person there are, at the beginning of the test, two antagonistic groups of motives, the good and the bad. That is, any personal interest which can be related to conscience at all is necessarily either good or bad. By using the motive in either group, the motive so used is made stronger, and also the opposite motive, if there is one, is made weaker. Or, by rejecting a motive, it is made weaker, and also the opposite one is made stronger. That is, if you have an interest, and express it in specific volition, you will increase that interest and diminish any opposing interest; or vice versa. In this way, under the law of use, a motive can be emptied of all urgency..... The exhaustion of any one motive tends to exhaust all the motives in the same group. The moral life is so related that if you touch it anywhere you must influence the whole. For example, no man can lose all interest in honesty and not begin to lose his regard for truth. When the group entire, of good motives or of bad motives, is exhausted, then the person's moral character is fixed beyond any possibility of change."—CURTIS, *Christian Faith*, pp. 49, 50.

Temptation and trial, if rightly understood, tend to exhaust motives to sin and strengthen those which establish the character in righteousness. On the other hand, the constant rejection of the good, and the acceptance of the bad, tend to fix the character in sin and unrighteousness. When all the motives to good are exhausted, so that the Holy Spirit has no further ground of appeal to the heart, the individual is said to "cross the dead-line" or to commit the sin against the Holy Spirit. There may be and doubtless is a final act, but it is such only as the final act in a series which has hardened the heart against every appeal of the Holy Spirit.

in the New Testament by the gift of the Spirit as a Paraclete or Comforter. *And the Lord thy God will circumcise thine heart, and the heart of thy seed, to love the Lord thy God with all thine heart, and with all thy soul, that thou mayest live* (Deut. 30:6). *I indeed baptize you with water,* declared the forerunner of Jesus, but *he shall baptize you with the Holy Ghost, and with fire. Whose fan is in his hand, and he will throughly purge his floor, and gather his wheat into the garner; but he will burn up the chaff with unquenchable fire* (Matt. 3:11, 12). That these passages of scripture refer to a spiritual cleansing is confirmed by St. Peter in these words, *And put no difference between us and them, purifying their hearts by faith* (Acts 15:9). As to the manner in which this work is wrought, the Scriptures are clear—it is always wrought by a simple faith in the atoning blood of Jesus Christ; this blood of atonement being not only the ground of what Christ has purchased for us, but the occasion of that which His Spirit works within us. Nor do the Scriptures teach that a higher degree of faith is demanded for sanctification than for justification. It is not so much the strength of the faith as its purity, that is required in any operation of grace. Furthermore, there is no specific degree of conviction demanded as a prerequisite to this faith—all that is essential is a firm belief that this grace is

Among the various terms that have been used to indicate the experience of entire sanctification, this expression "the fulness of the blessing" (Rom. 15:29), has found a place. . . . . Searching into the derivation of the Greek word, we discover that it comes from a verb that has two senses, one to fill and the other to fulfill, complete, perfect, accomplish. While both meanings are present in the use of the term in our New Testament, yet the latter ones predominate at a ratio of four to one. Taking this second meaning over to the noun, which is substantiated not only by the fact that the verb more often carries this sense but also by the ending that the noun has, then the thought conveyed is that which is completed, that is, the complement, the full tale, the entire number or quantity, the plenitude, the perfection. While the term had a general sense and is used thus in the Gospels, yet in the Pauline writings it is evident that it has passed for the most part into a definite, theological and doctrinal significance. It became a word that had a very definite connotation. . . . . Among the Christians of the day it had found its way to express the thought of a complete Christian experience relative to holiness of heart as the expression "second blessing" did in Methodist circles at a much later date, and as it does now among us.—DR. OLIVE M. WINCHESTER.

needed, and that God has promised it. In every case of evangelical perfection, three things are clearly discernible: (1) A consciousness of inbred sin, and a hungering and thirsting for full conformity to the image of Christ. (2) A firm conviction in the light of the scriptural provisions, that it is not only a privilege but a duty to be cleansed from all sin. (3) There must be perfect submission of the soul to God, commonly known as consecration, followed by an act of simple faith in Christ— a sure trust in Him for the promised blessing. "The voice of God to your soul is, Believe and be saved. Faith is the condition, and the only condition, of sanctification, exactly as it is in justification. No man is sanctified till he believes; and every man when he believes is sanctified" (WESLEY, *Works*, II, p. 224). "But what is that faith whereby we are sanctified, saved from sin and perfected in love? This faith is a divine evidence or conviction (1) That God hath promised this sanctification in the Holy Scriptures. (2) It is a divine evidence or conviction that what God hath promised He is able to perform. (3) It is a divine evidence or conviction that He is able and willing to do it now. (4) To this confidence that God is able and willing to sanctify us now, there needs to be added one thing more—a

---

There can be no perfect consecration to the whole will of God until there has been a sincere repentance for the double-mindedness and wilfulness and stubbornness and love of the world, all of which are marks of an unsanctified heart. The soul's sorrow for its inward sin must be as deep and moving as was its sorrow for its outward sins. The one is just as loathsome in the sight of God as the other, and is just as effectual a bar to the perfect enjoyment of God's grace and favor. But in approaching the throne of God with this deeper need, there is a point where the seeker knows that his sorrow and repentance for his heart depravity have reached their utmost depths; where his consecration to the will of God is complete and final; possessions, time, talents, ambitions, hopes, wishes, loved ones and friends, all yielded forever to Christ; the vast unknown future placed daringly and yet confidently in God's hands, for Him to control and reveal as and when it pleases Him to do so; one's dearest Isaac bound and placed on the altar, and the knife upraised without thought of any intervening divine hand, so that it may be said of us, as of Abraham, that by faith we actually offered him up to God. One knows beyond question in such an hour that his sacrifice is complete; there is nothing he could add to it, and nothing he would take from it. And in that glorious instant the seeker has the witness of his own heart that every condition it is humanly possible to meet has been met.— DR. J. GLENN GOULD, *The Spirit's Ministry*, pp. 9, 10.

divine evidence or conviction that He doeth it" (WESLEY, *Sermons*, I, p. 390). The older theologians defined faith as the *assent* of the mind, the *consent* of the will, and *recumbency*, or a reclining with undoubting confidence in the atoning merits of Jesus Christ. Thus as we have previously indicated, faith is incomplete without the element of trust.

Evidences of Christian Perfection. It is the uniform testimony of those who believe and teach the Wesleyan doctrine of Christian perfection, that the Spirit bears witness to this work of grace in the heart, exactly as He bears witness to Christian sonship. "None, therefore, ought to believe that the work is done," says Mr. Wesley, "till there is added the testimony of the Spirit witnessing his entire sanctification as clearly as his justification." "We know it by the witness and by the fruit of the Spirit" (WESLEY, *Plain Account*, pp. 79, 118). Dr. J. Glenn Gould says that "This inner assurance is made up of three distinct phases. That is, they are logically distinct, though the sinner's experience of them may seem to be instantaneous. They are (1) the witness

>Look for it every day, every hour, every moment. Why not this hour—this moment? Certainly you may look for it now, if you believe it is by faith. And by this token you may surely know whether you seek it by faith or by works. If by works, you want something to be done first before you are sanctified. You think, I must be or do thus and thus. Then you are seeking it by works unto this day. If you seek it by faith, you expect it as you are; and if as you are, then expect it now. It is important to observe that there is an inseparable connection between these three points—expect it by faith, expect it as you are, and expect it now. To deny one is to deny them all.—WESLEY, *Sermons*, I, p. 391.
>
>As when you reckon with your creditor or with your host, and as, when you have paid all, you reckon yourselves free, so now reckon with God. Jesus has paid all; and He hath paid for thee—hath purchased thy pardon and holiness. Therefore, it is now God's command, "Reckon thyself dead unto sin"; and thou art alive unto God from this hour. Oh, begin, begin to reckon now; fear not; believe, believe, believe! and continue to believe every moment. So shalt thou continue free; for it is retained, as it is received, by faith alone.—FLETCHER OF MADELEY.
>
>The writers on this subject during the middle and last part of the 19th century were accustomed to use the term "naked faith." Rev. J. A. Wood explains the term as follows: "By simple faith is meant, taking God at His word without doubting or reasoning; and by naked faith is meant, faith independent of all feeling, and stripped of every other dependence but Christ alone. The holy Fletcher says, a naked faith, is a 'faith independent of all feelings,' in a naked promise; bringing nothing with you but a careless, distracted, tossed, hardened heart—just such a heart as you have got now."—J. A. WOOD, *Perfect Love*, p. 104.

of the seeker's own heart; (2) the witness of God's Word; and (3) the inner illumination of the Holy Spirit" (GOULD, *The Spirit's Ministry*, p. 8). The sanctified soul may know by the testimony of his own spirit, and the witness of the Holy Spirit, that the blood of Jesus Christ has cleansed him from all sin. Here we have the testimony of consciousness, which we can no more doubt than our own existence. And in addition to this, there is the direct and positive testimony of the witnessing Spirit.

To the scriptural evidences already cited, we may add also, those personal examples which confirm the doctrine of evangelical perfection. Noah *was a just man, and perfect in his generations* (Gen. 6:9). Job was *perfect and upright, and one that feared God, and eschewed evil* (Job 1:1). Zacharias and Elisabeth *were both righteous before God walking in all the commandments and ordinances of the Lord blameless* (Luke 1:6). Our Lord said of Nathanael, *Behold an Israelite indeed, in whom is no guile!* (John 1:47). St. Paul also speaks of those in the apostolic church who were evangelically perfect. *Howbeit we speak wisdom among them that are perfect* (I Cor. 2:6); and *Let us therefore, as many as be perfect, be thus minded* (Phil. 3:15). Were we to attempt to present here, the testimonies of those men and women who have enjoyed the experience of perfect love, our task would be too great. Inspiring as they are, we cannot include them. "A study of the biographies of Christian leaders," says Dr. D. Shelby Corlett, "reveals the fact that with few exceptions they all had a second crisis experience. While it is true all

---

"But does not sanctification shine by its own light?" "And does not the new birth too? Sometimes it does, and so does sanctification; at others, it does not. In the hour of temptation, Satan clouds the work of God, and injects various doubts and reasonings, especially in those who have either very weak or very strong understandings. At such times, there is absolute need of that witness, without which, the work of sanctification not only could not be discerned, but could no longer subsist. Were it not for this, the soul could not then abide in the love of God; much less could it rejoice evermore, and in everything give thanks. In these circumstances, therefore, a direct testimony that we are sanctified, is necessary in the highest degree."—WESLEY, *Plain Account*, pp. 75, 76.

would not interpret this experience in terms of Wesley's 'second blessing properly so-called'; it is also true that this second experience made a distinct change in their lives and ministry. Universally unbiased Christians long for and seek a deeper experience than that which they obtain in regeneration. Thousands have enjoyed a 'second blessing' without being instructed in the truth as taught by believers in the Wesleyan emphasis on the doctrine of entire sanctification" (DR. D. SHELBY CORLETT, *Herald of Holiness*, Vol. 27, No. 11).

We close this chapter on "Christian Perfection" or "Entire Sanctification," with what we regard as the clearest statement of the doctrine and experience ever written, aside from divine inspiration. This is the definition given by Arvid Gradin to John Wesley in 1738. On his return from America, Mr. Wesley says, "I had a long conversation with Arvid Gradin, in Germany. After he had given me an account of his experience, I desired him to give me, in writing, a definition of 'the full assurance of faith'." The definition was given in Latin, and both the Latin statement and the English translation are included in Mr. Wesley's *Plain Account of Christian Perfection*, as follows:

"*Requies in sanguine Christi; firma fiducia in Deum, et persuasio de gratia Divina; tranquillitas mentis summa, atque serenitas et pax; cum absentia omnis desiderii carnalis, et cessatione peccatorum etiam internorum.*"

Dr. Pope in emphasizing the positive phase of Christian perfection says, "It is a perfection which is no other than a perfect, self-annihilating life in Christ: a perfect union with His passion and His resurrection, and the perfect enjoyment of the value of His name Jesus, as it is salvation from sin. It is the perfection of being nothing in self, and all in Him. It is a perfection for which the elect with one consent have longed, from the apostles downward; neither more nor less than the unuttered groaning desire of the children of God in every age; the common, deep aspiration with only one note more emphatic than has always been heard, though even that has not been always wanting, the destruction of the inbred sin of our nature. He who searcheth the heart hath always known the mind of the Spirit, even when its deepest desire has not been clearly uttered. And He will yet, we dare to believe, remove the last fetter from the aspirations of His saints, and give them one heart and one voice in seeking the destruction of the body of sin as well as the mortification of its members."—POPE, *Compend. Chr. Th.*, III, p. 99.

"Repose in the blood of Christ; a firm confidence in God, and persuasion of His favor; the highest tranquillity, serenity, and peace of mind, with a deliverance from every fleshly desire, and a cessation of all, even inward sins."

"This," says Mr. Wesley, "is the first account I ever heard from any living man, of what I had before learned myself from the oracles of God, and had been praying for (with the little company of my friends), and expecting, for several years" (WESLEY, *Plain Account of Christian Perfection*, p. 8).